CONSTITUTIONS, ELECTIONS AND LEGISLATURES OF POLAND, 1493-1993

volume LXXVI

STUDIES PRESENTED TO THE INTERNATIONAL
COMMISSION FOR THE HISTORY
OF REPRESENTATIVE AND PARLIAMENTARY INSTITUTIONS

ÉTUDES PRÉSENTÉES À LA COMMISSION
INTERNATIONALE POUR L'HISTOIRE
DES ASSEMBLÉES D'ÉTATS

CONSTITUTIONS, ELECTIONS AND LEGISLATURES OF POLAND, 1493-1993

A Guide to Their History

Jacek Jędruch

Foreword by Norman Davies

EJJ BOOKS
Distributed by Hippocrene Books

For some there is satisfaction in lawmaking, but for all it is more necessary and more useful to obey the laws and to carry them out.

Krzysztof Warszewicki (1543-1603)
"De optimo statu libertatis"

This survey of the parliamentary history of Poland is dedicated to Senator F.H. Murkowski (R. Alaska) and to the Honorable D.E. Bonior (D,Mich), E.J. Derwinski (R,Ill), J.D. Dingell (D,Mich), John Fary (D,Ill), Barbara Mikulski (D,Md), R.J. Solarz (D,N.Y.), H. Nowak (D-L,N.Y.), D.D. Rostenkowski (D,Ill), and K.J. Zablocki (D,Wisc); Representatives in the 97th Congress of the United States. By reason of their descent they share in the rich parliamentary tradition of the Polish-Lithuanian Commonwealth.
The story contained here is dedicated, as well, to the people of Poland.
May they regain their basic right to have a true representation
in the national Legislature.

Jacek Jędruch
Pittsburgh, 1982

The original publication of this book was made possible through the generous support of the Joseph B. Slotkowski Publication Fund of the Kosciuszko Foundation.
Revised edition, 1998
This revised edition is distributed by Hippocrene Books, Inc.
For information, address:
Hippocrene Books, Inc.
171 Madison Ave.
New York, NY 10016
Library of Congress Cataloging-in-Publication Data
Jędruch, Jacek.

　　Constitutions, elections, and legislatures of Poland, 1493-1993 a guide to their history / Jacek Jędruch: foreword by Norman Davies

　　　p. cm.—(Studies presented to the International Commission for History of Representative and Parliamentary Institutions; v. 76 = Etudes présentées â la Commission internationale pour l'histoire des assemblées d'Etats.)

　　Includes bibliographical references and index.
　　ISBN 0-7818-0637-2

　　1. Constitutional history—Poland. 2. Election law—Poland—History. I. Title. II. Series: Etudes présentées à la Commission internationale pour l'histoire des assemblées d'Etats; 76.
KKP2101.J44　1998
342.438'029—dc21　　　　　　　　　　　　　　　　　　98-12690
Printed in the United States of America.　　　　　　　　　CIP

ACKNOWLEDGMENTS

A critical review of the manuscript for the Kościuszko Foundation by Wenceslas J. Wagner and Andrzej Kamiński is hereby gratefully acknowledged.

Numerous persons supported my efforts in the preparation of this work. Foremost among them are Bohdan Podoski, Vice-Speaker of the Seym, who reviewed and commented on the chapter dealing with the Second Republic, and Wiktor Sukiennicki who reviewed the manuscript for historical accuracy.

Thomas Steel generously contributed the translation of excerpts from Latin texts of the early charters. Lorenz Mikoletzky and Anna Bena of the Haus-, Hof- and Staatsarchiv of Vienna supplemented the data on the Speakers and Viceroys of Galicia. Karol Angerman prepared the index. The maps and diagrams in the text were prepared by Krzysztof Malczewski.

I am much indebted to Konstanty Grzybowski for the ideas on the development of the theory of representation in Poland; to Stanisław Russocki for the material on the performance of the early Seyms and other parliamentary systems, and to Józef Gidyński for the discussion of the legislative performance of the present day Seym. Work of other authors, too numerous to list here, has been of great value in preparing this study. Some attempt to give credit has been made in the Introduction and the Annotated Bibliography.

The final form of this study owes much to the helpful comments and suggestions of Emily Swan, Stanisław Wójcik, Linda Blodgett, Bernard Krasicki, Frank Thompson, Tadeusz Massalski, and William Harrison. Their willingness to give of their time and effort provided the necessary encouragement, whereas the editorial review by my wife Eva contributed much to the improvement of the literary form of the work.

Thanks are also due to Janina W. Hoskins of the Library of Congress for her help in securing some materials, to Halina Wójcicka for the permission to use quotes from the works of her father, the late Władysław Konopczyński, and to the staffs of the Widener Library of Harvard and the Hillman Library of the University of Pittsburgh for help in the use of their Polish collections.

Special thanks are due to Eleanor Iwinski for the detailed editing of the manuscript and to Yvonne Harlow for the preparation and layout of the final copy.

I wish to thank Wacław Jędrzejewicz of the Józef Piłsudski Institute of New York and Ivan Kedryn-Rudnyckyj for supplementing the list of Senators and Deputies of the Second Republic who died at the hands of the Nazis and the Soviets.For the material on Eustachy Sanguszko, the Speaker of the Seym of Lwów and the Viceroy of Galicia, the author is indebted to Roman Sanguszko of Sao Paulo, Brazil.

CONTENTS

FOREWORD by Norman Davies   9

PREFACE TO ORIGINAL EDITION   13

PREFACE TO REVISED EDITION   15

INTRODUCTION   17
  Polish Legislative Nomenclature, Geography and Chronology   20

Chapter I   HEREDITARY MONARCHY: KINGS FACE   29
  ELECTIVE LEGISLATURES
  Charters and the Early Laws: The Origins of the Constitution   30
  Seymik: The Basic Unit of Legislature   34
  General Seymiks and the Provincial Seyms   43
  The Early Seyms and the Laws They Made   50
  Seyms Demand "Execution of the Laws"   58
  Political Personalities in Seyms of the Hereditary Kingdom   67

Chapter II   MONARCHY BECOMES THE FIRST REPUBLIC: 71
  KINGS ELECTED FOR LIFE
  Seyms Claim King-Making Powers   72
  Pacta Conventa and the Rokosz, or Legalized Rebellion   83
  Cities Elect Representatives: "Civitatum Nuntii"   87
  Peripatetic Seym and the Places Where It Met   90
  Senate as "Guardians of the Law"   100
  Political Personalities in the Seyms of the Early First Republic   112

Chapter III   FIRST REPUBLIC UNDER FIRE: SEYMS   115
  AND CONFEDERATIONS
  Fire Test of the System and the Aborted Reform   116
  Procedures and Efficiency of the Seyms   124
  Confederation in Constitutional Practice in Poland   132
  The Seym and the Cossack Question   138
  State Within a State: The Jewish Representation   141
  Political Personalities in the Seyms of the First Republic   146

**Chapter IV   DECAY AND REFORM: ABSOLUTIST NEIGHBORS   151
STEP IN FOR THE KILL**

Executive vs. the Legislature: The Stalemate of the Saxon Era   152
On the Road to Constitutional Reform   157
Ink and Quill in the Service of Reform   165
The Constitution of 1791   169
The Defense of the Constitution and Its Downfall   184
Political Personalities in Seyms of the Reform Era   192

**Chapter V   PARTITIONS: POLISH LEGISLATURES UNDER   201
FOREIGN ABSOLUTISM**

The Napoleonic Touch: Seym of the Duchy of Warsaw   202
Political Personalities in the Seym of the Duchy of Warsaw   210
The Seym of Warsaw: Polish Legislature Confronts the Tsars   212
Political Personalities in Seyms of the Congress Kingdom   227
The Seym of Poznań: Polish Nationality at Bay   230
Political Personalities of the Seym of Poznań   239
Seym of the Estates in Galicia   241
The Seym of the Republic of Cracow   248
The Seym of Lwów: Peasants Enter Politics in Galicia   249
Political Personalities of the Seym of Lwów   262

**Chapter VI   SECOND REPUBLIC: THE SEYM FAILS IN   267
OPERATING THE EXECUTIVE**

Reunification of Poland and the Constitution of 1921   268
The Seym Copes with an Unworkable Constitution   277
Legislature and the Executive Separated by Force   280
The Constitution of 1935 and Its Aftermath   283
The Senate in the Second Republic   290
Provincial Seyms in the Second Republic   292
Political Personalities in the Seym of the Second Republic   300

**Chapter VII   POLISH PEOPLE'S REPUBLIC: MAKING THE BEST   307
OF STALIN'S WORST**

Make Believe Pluralism and the Pre-Screened Seym   309
Constitution of 1952: A Nation Forced in the Stalinist Mold   316
Seym Appropriates Industry to Communist Party but Snags   326
  on Agriculture

CONTENTS

Seyms of the Polish People's Republic, Second and the First Republics Compared — 330

Political Personalities in the Seym of the Polish People's Republic — 338

Chapter VIII SELECTED LEGISLATIVE PROBLEMS IN HISTORICAL PERSPECTIVE — 343

The Development of Suffrage Rights — 344

Impeachment and Judiciary Powers of the Seyms — 355

The Taxing Powers of the Seym — 360

The War and Peace-Making Powers of the Seym — 370

Seyms Legislate on the Ownership of Real Estate — 375

The Seym as a Career — 382

Chapter IX THIRD REPUBLIC: THE SEYM IN POST-COMMUNIST POLAND — 389

Compendium of the History of the Seym and Its Present Day Functions — 389

History and Chronology of Major Events—A Summary — 390

Constitutional Provisions of the Sejm and The Senate — 393

Architecture—Physical Description of Parliament Buildings—Chambers—Offices—Tours — 394

Elections—Current Party Positions—Seats—Term of Office—Membership — 398

Sessions—Annual Calendar—Dissolution—Recess — 399

How Laws are Made—Readings of Bills—Amendments—Volume of Legislation—Quorum—Private Bills — 399

Committees—Powers and Procedures—Public Hearings — 401

Budget Procedures — 403

Relations with the Executive—Monitoring Executive Performance—Ombudsman — 403

Executive Veto and Overriding Vetoes — 404

Office of the Speaker—Powers — 405

Party Caucuses and Groups—Whips and Majority and Minority Leaders—Party Discipline — 405

Debates—Interpellation—Official Record—Voting Procedures — 406

Relations Between the Sejm and the Senate — 408

Parliamentary Privileges and Immunities—Recall, Expulsion, Resignation — 409

Parliamentary Pay and Perquisites — 410

Parliamentary Ethics—Discipline ... 410
Judicial Functions of the Sejm ... 411
Parliament and Media—Broadcasting of Proceedings ... 412
Constitutionality of Laws—Emergency Powers ... 412
Statistics, Tables and Charts ... 413
Who's Who of Parliamentary Leaders ... 415
Bibliography ... 416

APPENDICES ... 417

A - Key Paragraphs in the Founding Charters of Liberties ... 417
B - Development of Seymiks as Electoral Districts ... 419
C - Chronology of Elections and Seyms Held in Poland ... 426
D - Text of Nazi-Soviet Agreements ... 432
E - Evolution of Roles of Seym & Senate ... 434

ANNOTATED BIBLIOGRAPHY ... 436

ABOUT THE AUTHOR ... 464

INDEX ... 465

CONTENTS

LIST OF SYNOPSES OF CONSTITUTIONS

Table

11	Constitutional Arrangements of the Hereditary Monarchy (1550)	64
23	Constitutional Arrangements of the Early First Republic (1609)	111
30	Cardinal Laws (Constitution) of the Late First Republic (1668)	145
33	The First Formal Constitution of Poland (1791)	181
37	The Last Constitution of the First Republic (1793)	191
38	Constitution of the Duchy of Warsaw (1807)	209
39	Constitution of the Congress Kingdom of Poland (1815)	225
42	Constitution of the Grand Duchy of Poznań (1824)	237
44	Constitution of the Galician Seym of the Estates (1817)	247
47	Constitution of Galicia and Lodomeria (1861)	259
50	First Constitution of the Second Republic (1921)	276
56	Second Constitution of the Second Republic (1935)	297
67	Constitution of the Polish People's Republic (1952)	336

LISTS OF PRINCIPAL LEGISLATIVE OFFICERS

Table

12	Hereditary Kings Confirmed by the Seym	65
35	Kings of the First Republic Elected by the Seym	190
48	Primcipal Legislative Officers of Galicia in the Era of Autonomy	260
57	Principal Legislative Officers of the Second Republic (also see Table 52)	299
68	Principal Legislative Officers of the Polish People's Republic	337

LISTS OF PRINCIPAL LEGISLATION OF THE SEYMS

Table

14	Principal Legislation of the Hereditary Monarchy	65
22	Principal Legislation of the First Republic (Part I)	110
29	Principal Legislation of the First Republic (Part II)	144
36	Principal Legislation of the First Republic (Part III)	190
49	Principal Legislation of the Seym of Lwów	262
58	Principal Legislation of the Second Republic	299
69	Principal Legislation of the Polish People's Republic	337

LIST OF TABLES

1	Changes in Designation of Legislators Through the Centuries	23
2	Seym Representation by Palatinate and Period	39
3	The Chronology of Seym Laws Relating to Seymiks	41
4	Summary of Types and Functions of Seymiks	43
5	Meeting Places of General Seymiks of the Provinces	46
6	Early Provincial Seyms Held in Masovia	48
7	Lithuanian Seyms Held Before the Union of Lublin	49
8	Early Unicameral Seyms Held in Piotrków	51
9	Membership of Legislatures of Poland	57
10	Protestant Deputies in the Seym of "the Execution of Laws" Era	60
11	Constitutional Arrangements, Hereditary Monarchy (1550)	64
12	Hereditary Kings Confirmed by the Seym	65
13	Seym Speakers in the Period of Hereditary Monarchy	65
14	Principal Legislation of Seyms of Hereditary Monarchy	65
15	Seyms of the Interregnum Periods	75
16	Candidates for the Crown Presented to the Election Seyms	79
17	Seym Attendance of Representatives of Lublin	89
18	Geography of Sessions of the Seym	95
19	Major Senatorial Families of Poland and Lithuania	102
20	Composition of Senate with Appointive Membership	103
21	Senators Serving as "King pro Tempore" (Interrex)	107
22	Principal Legislation of Seyms of the First Republic (Part I)	110
23	Constitutional Arrangements of the Early First Republic (1609), a Synopsis	111
24	Types and Functions of Seyms of the First Republic	126
25	Confederations of the Hereditary Monarchy	136
26	Confederations in the Seyms of the First Republic	137
27	Confederations Outside Seyms of the First Republic	137
28	Jewish Poll Tax in Poland	143
29	Principal Legislation of Seyms of the First Republic (Part II)	144
30	Cardinal Laws (Constitution) of the Late First Republic (1668), a Synopsis	145
31	Political Literature of the Reform Seym. 1788-1792, (Selective Titles)	170
32	Representation of Cities in the Seym After 1791	175
33	The First Formal Constitution of Poland (1791), a Synopsis	181
34	Chronology of Constitutional Movements in France, Poland and America	183
35	Kings of the First Republic Elected by the Seym	190

CONTENTS

36	Principal Legislation of Seyms of the First Republic (Part III)	190
37	Last Constitution of the First Republic (1793), a Synopsis	191
38	Constitution of the Duchy of Warsaw (1807), a Synopsis	209
39	Constitution of the Congress Kingdom of Poland (1815), A Synopsis	225
40	Nationality of Seym Deputies and of the Population of the Grand Duchy of Poznań	235
41	The Seym and the Supreme National Council of Poznań (1918)	237
42	Constitution of the Grand Duchy of Poznań (1824), a Synopsis	237
43	Attendance at the Sessions of the Galician Seym of the Estates	243
44	Constitution of the Galician Seym of the Estates (1817), a Synopsis	247
45	The Electoral Structure of the Seym of Lwów	251
46	National Composition of the Seym of Lwów	258
47	Constitution of Galicia and Lodomeria (1861), a Synopsis	259
48	Principal Legislative Officers of Galicia in the Era of Automony	260
49	Principal Legislation of the Seym of Lwów	262
50	First Constitution of the Second Republic (1921), a Synopsis	276
51	Political Distribution of Seyms of the Second Republic	289
52	Speakers of the Senate of the Second Republic	291
53	Political Distribution in the Senate of the Second Republic	292
54	Political Affiliation of Deputies in the Seym of Silesia	295
55	Legislative Activity of the Seym of Silesia	295
56	Second Constitution of the Second Republic (1935), a Synopsis	297
57	Principal Legislative Officers of the Second Republic	299
58	Principal Legislation of Seyms of the Second Republic	299
59	Results of the Referendum of 1946	311
60	Electoral Showing of PSL Candidates in 1947	312
61	Constitutional Development in Eastern Europe	316
62	Composition of Seyms of the Polish People's Republic	319
63	Election Results from Sosnowiec and Cracow in the 1976 Election	321
64	Legislative Performance of Seyms of the Polish People's Republic	324
65	Operating Statistics of the Seym of the Polish People's Republic	325
66	Comparison of Time Spent in Debating Pending Legislation	325
67	Constitution of the Polish People's Republic (1952), a Synopsis	336
68	Principal Legislative Officers of the Polish People's Republic	337
69	Principal Legislation of Seyms of the Polish People's Republic	337
70	Cities with Seym Representation in 1791	347
71	Development of Suffrage in Poland, Britain, France and the United States	350
72	Variation in Election Turnout in the Second Republic	353

CONSTITUTIONS, ELECTIONS AND LEGISLATURES OF POLAND

73 Voter Turnout in Various Provinces of Poland in 1922   353
74 Voter Turnout in Various European Countries in 1922-24   354
75 Population and Revenue in Poland   361
76 Value of Currency in Poland Relative to Gold Ducat   362
77 Percentage of Arable Land Held by the Crown and the Church
    in the Sixteenth Century   365
78 Relative Annual Tax Burden Per Head of Inhabitant (circa 1785)   365
79 Progress of Collectivization in the Polish People's Republic   382
80 The Electoral Success of Some Deputies in the 1600's   383
81 Remuneration of Speakers of the Seym   384
82 Dzieduszycki Family in the Seym of Galicia in Lwów   386
83 Victims Among the Legislators   387

FOREWORD

After conquering England in 1066, the chronicler reported that William the Conqueror "had very deep speech with his Witan." The Anglo-French word for 'speech' was *parlement*, close to the modern 'parley.' The *Witan* was the Anglo-Saxon name for the King's Council of Wise Men. Here is a classic example of the fact that the endless story of war and conquest has always had a more positive alternative in the ancient art of discussion, that is, in the ability to resolve conflict through agreed laws, chosen representatives, and recognised assemblies. For it is the parliamentary aspect of political life which has given rise to the more impressive and satisfying achievements of history, and to some of the most lasting institutions. Sir Winston Churchill was both a famous war leader and a great parliamentarian. But there is no doubt where his priorities lay. "Jaw-jaw" he said, "not war, war." In an age where an almost global ascendancy has been gained by the sort of liberal democracy for which Churchill fought so magnificently, it is absolutely natural that parliamentary traditions from all parts of the world should be highly treasured and deeply studied.

In the English-speaking world it is also absolutely natural that England's parliamentary history should hold pride of place. After all, it was the English parliamentary tradition which bred the family of democracies that now stretches across the globe not just from the United Kingdom to the USA, but also to Canada, to Australia and New Zealand, to India and to many other Commonwealth countries. One may argue that the American constitutionalists were more expert in the application of English principles than their counterparts in Britain. But John Bright's claim that 'England is the Mother of Parliaments' is hard to deny.

Nonetheless, one must equally recognise that the English-speaking world has often been unaware of parliamentary traditions other than their own. Both British and Americans tend to think that their own tradition is the only one worth knowing. Until recently, most of them would have been surprised to hear that Scotland had a separate, sovereign parliamentary history until 1707; that Ireland possessed its own parliament until 1800; or that the last independent parliament of Wales, called to Machynlleth in 1404, was crushed by those good English constitutionalists. It is not likely to strike everyone that the Scandinavian countries have democratic roots every bit as deep and strong as England's, or that in mediaeval Novgorod Russia possessed the seeds of a democratic order extinguished by Novgorod's rival, Moscow. One suspects that it will be complete news to learn that Poland of all places had established the principle of *Habeas corpus* nearly three centuries before England and had accepted the idea of 'No taxation without representation' long before England's American colonies had even been founded.

It is in this connection that Jacek Jędruch's study of Polish constitutionalism can render a signal service. It is a very thorough and systematic survey of a long, complex and interesting subject that has been sidelined all too often. It will attract readers not only among the specialists who need a reliable source of information about a hitherto inaccessible branch of history but also among all and sundry who appreciate the richness and variety of parliamentary traditions.

I would like to highlight two aspects of the work that I regard as specially commendable.

Firstly, Jędruch documents the development and evolution of his subject over five hundred years. In this way, he shows that Polish constitutionalism's period of catastrophic decline in the eighteenth century, which was ridiculed by the philosophes of the Enlightenment and which is the only piece of the story to figure in general history books, forms one short stage in a much longer process. The Liberum Veto, which was greatly abused, was not necessarily half so stupid as Voltaire and others would have us believe. Whilst recognising the failures and imperfections, one can only see the whole picture if one also takes into consideration both the 'Golden Age' of the sixteenth century and the remarkable series of adaptations to adversity and foreign rule in the nineteenth and twentieth centuries. It was Jefferson, I think, who complained about people looking on constitutions as on 'arks of the convenant, too sacred to be touched.' Jefferson knew instinctively that a constitutional tradition is a living organism, which must change and grow if it is to survive. The important thing about it is the way it develops dynamically over time. The Polish case is no exception, having developed dynamically over a very long time indeed.

Secondly, Jędruch demonstrates the extraordinary diversification of the Polish constitutional tradition in a wide variety of different places and historical situations. Unlike many Polish commentators, he does not confine his attention to the central Seym or Parliament of the old Polish-Lithuanian Commonwealth, to the famous and glorious but ineffective Constitution of 1791, or to the affairs of the inter-war republic between 1918 and 1939. In the pre-partition period, he explores the workings of the provincial assemblies, of the self-governing cities, of the so-called 'confederations' with their astonishing right of legalised rebellion, and of the far-reaching autonomy granted to Poland's large Jewish community. In the period of the Partitions,when most people might assume that Polish constitutionalism was completely abolished by the autocratic rule of Russia, Prussia and Austria, he shows how it repeatedly re-emerged in new forms and new locations in Napoleon's Duchy of Warsaw, in the Tsar's

FOREWORD

'Congress Kingdom,' in the Prussian Duchy of Poznań, and in the Austrian Kingdom of Galicia. In the twentiety century, he traces the long struggle against the authoritarian tendencies of the inter-war Sanacja Regime, against the murderous onslaught of totalitarianism, and, in the most recent phase after 1989, against the stubborn legacy of Communism.

I think it particularly welcome that Jędruch should have included a section on the Polish People's Republic as part of the overall sequence. He aptly calls it 'Making the Best of Stalin's Worst.' It is a tale well worth telling, if only as a foil for what went before and what is coming after. Of course, any competent scholar would know that the Soviet-style, Communist structures which were imposed after 1945 were incompatible with everything usually associated with terms such as 'constitution,' 'law,' 'parliament,' 'election' or 'democracy.' On the other hand, the dictatorship of the Communist Party, and of the Soviet comrades over their Polish underlings, was exercised behind a facade of state institutions which used democratic-sounding slogans and which often misled the naiver sort of western political scientist. Without a knowledge of communist usage, it was easy to be deceived. The People's Republic did possess a handsome constitution. It impressed all those who did not realise that the clause about the Communist Party's 'leading role' rendered all its other clauses inoperative. There was law of a sort, but a sort that was totally dependent on political convenience. There was a seym or parliament. It was a legislature which proposed, debated and passed laws in a framework that was completely subordinated to the organs of Party control. There were popular elections at every level. But they were elections in which there was no real element of choice since the party always pre-selected all candidates. There was widespread lip-service to democracy, 'the rule of the people.' In reality, the people were systematically excluded from power. As the Polish saying went, genuine democracy bore the same resemblance to the 'socialist democracy' of the People's Republic that a 'chair' bears to an 'electric chair.'

Of course, one had to laugh. Yet as long as the Communist dictatorship lasted, it was no joke. It was as ruinous as it was oppressive. What is more, it deliberately distorted all that was best and most valued in the nation's collective memory. Its baleful legacy will not be overcome in a day.

Like any historian, I have found many elements in Mr. Jędruch's study that I would like to query and to debate. But such questioning lies in the very nature of historical enquiry. The author has provided a fine exposé, amply supported with biographical portraits and textual appendices, which will permit his important subject to be far more widely questioned and debated than previously. We are in his debt.

Norman Davies
Oxford, 1997

11

PREFACE TO ORIGINAL EDITION

The history of elective representation in Poland starts in 1493, one year after Columbus sailed for America, and continues virtually uninterrupted until the present day. During this period Poland experienced a flowering of the early Renaissance and the Reformation in the 1500s leading to the formation of the First Republic, invasions and wars in the 1600s, decay and reform of its institutions in the 1700s, existence in partitioned form in the 1800s, and finally, a rebirth in the 1900s, including the establishment of the Second and the Third Republics. Throughout her stormy history, the institution of elective legislature survived, either in the whole or in some part of Poland, even in times when the country was without political identity. It is to show this amazing continuity and resilience of the representative institutions of Poland that the present work is written.

To do full justice to a subject with this long a history would require a multi-volume treatment. The present condensed survey is intended to fill the urgent need to bring all of the important highlights of that story under one cover and to serve as a first guide to a little known, but fascinating, subject.

In my literary efforts I was spurred on by the quizzical stares of my American friends whenever the subject of the legislative traditions of Poland came up in conversation. It soon became evident that a void exists in the English literature on the subject and a search of the Union Catalogue confirmed this suspicion. The present work is intended to fill the void by bringing together the major facts, political ideas, and main personages appearing on the parliamentary scene of Poland during the five centuries of its history. The major legislative issues highlighted here—freedom of conscience, pacifism, civil disobedience, national debt, zero-base budgeting and the nationalization of property—were all, at one time or another, the subject of legislative action in Poland. The portrait of the legislatures' handling of these issues is presented here in accordance with Cromwell's dictum to his painter: "to paint true, warts and all."

The preparation of this guide was timed to coincide with the current reconstruction of the castle of Warsaw from the ruins of the Second World War. During the last four hundred years of its history the castle served as the living quarters of the Chief Executives, whether Kings or Presidents, and housed the legislature. It is, therefore, the equivalent of the Palace of Westminster or the Capitol and the White House combined. The restoration involves all of the interiors with historical significance, including the Chambers of the Legislature. The interior of the Senate Chamber is being restored with loving care to its appearance on May 3, 1791 when, in joint session of the Seym and the Senate, the first formal Constitution of Poland was enacted. The act crowned some 300 years of past parliamentary history and ushered in the nearly 200 tumultuous years that were to follow. Thus, the restoration is a proper occasion to take a look at this record and to share the results with the English-speaking people. May it supplement the splendid efforts of the architects and conservationists of Poland, working under the guidance of Professor Stanisław Lorentz, to bring the Castle of Warsaw back to life.

While the present study was in preparation, Poland experienced the first ominous tremors of the general discontent of labor and peasants at their continuing deprivation of rights of true representation, and the resulting deterioration of their relative economic position in society. In the summer of 1980 this discontent surfaced in an eruption of mass strikes and gave birth to "Solidarity," the independent labor and peasant movement.

An understanding of the forces driving the present movement to regain the rights of true representation is impossible without learning how these rights were gained first, the price that was paid in defending them, and the circumstances of their loss. The roots of the discontent underlaying the present movement in Poland go much deeper than the effects of the immediate economic situation and have to do with the reassertion of the belief held generally by the Poles that the sovereignty of the nation rests in the people, and not in any particular class, party, ideology or administrative apparatus. The present study traces the history of this belief in the sovereignty of the people in the consciousness of the nation, and describes the institutional forms given to its expression through the centuries.

There are reasons to believe that the efforts to regain the true rights of representation in the sphere of labor, will not stop there, but will extend in the near future to the demands for the restoration of a true political representation as well.

Pittsburgh, 1981

PREFACE TO THE REVISED EDITION

"Constitutions, Elections and Legislatures of Poland, 1493-1977" was first published in 1982 and the intent of the book was, as explained by the author, to introduce to the English speaking reader the little known parliamentary history of Poland.

The book appeared at a time when Polish historians, living under the censorship of the communist regime, were not permitted to discuss the history of their country's parliamentary development. Immediately after World War II, Poland, under the Yalta agreement, was left within the Soviet sphere of influence; the constitution imposed on the country was the Stalinist model, as was the entire political system. Poland's rich, 500-year-old parliamentary tradition, was relegated to the dustbin.

It was to fill this gap in available information, in English, that my husband Jacek undertook the preparation of the guide to the parliamentary history of Poland.

Much has changed in Poland and in all of Central and Eastern Europe, since the book's first publication. The Soviet empire, which maintained its grip on most of that part of the world since the end of World War II, fell apart in 1989. Poland and the other so-called satellite countries, recovered their full sovereignty. Parliaments again became the living, representative, democratic institutions they were meant to be.

It had been Jacek's intention to come out with a second, expanded edition, which would include all the changes that had taken place. He was only waiting for Poland's parliament to pass a new constitution which had been in the works from the moment Poland regained her sovereignty. The Polish parliament passed the new constitution in May of 1997. Tragically, Jacek died in an accident in March of 1995, while travelling in Greece.

The second edition of "Constitutions, Elections and Legislatures of Poland" brings the basic text up to 1993, complemented with the most recent updates where feasible; the additional chapter, (chapter IX), is compiled from the author's notes, prepared to cover the period after 1989. Errata that he listed, and comments that he added to the original version of the book, have been accounted for in the revised version.

A few minor changes were necessary. The name "Third Republic," originally used to define the communist state after 1946, so as not to confuse the reader unfamiliar with Polish history with out-of-sequence names, has been replaced in the revised edition with its then official name of Polish People's Republic. The name, "The Third Polish Republic" is reserved for the democratic, post-communist state, reborn after 1989.

In placing this book in the hands of the reader, I hope to fulfill my husband's intention, of bringing the knowledge of Poland's parliamentary tradition and information about the functioning of her current representative institutions, to the attention of the English speaking public. At the time when Poland is preparing to rejoin Europe through NATO and the European Union, this material may prove of more than purely academic interest.

Eva Jędruch

Summit, New Jersey, 1997

INTRODUCTION

This study highlights just one aspect of the history of Poland: the development of its legislative institutions. Though often overlooked, or treated superficially, the history of that development provides, in fact, a key to the understanding of much of what took place in the last 500 years in Poland. The efforts to establish, then to expand, and finally to preserve from suppression the structure of representative government, constituted for the people of Poland an expression of their claim to full political and civil rights. This main theme is discernible to the careful observer even in the most turbulent periods of history in Poland, and the present study brings the pertinent facts, people and events into focus.

The scope of this study is limited to the history of representative bodies elected in Poland and sitting in Poland. In selecting the material to be included, a conscious effort was made to deal with the history of the legislature proper and to mention the executive and the judiciary branches of the government of Poland only in so far as they were involved in the legislative process. Furthermore, the various councils (Rada) which, from time to time, assembled in Poland and attempted to legislate were excluded if their membership was composed of nominees of political groupings, rather than elected, due to the doubtful constitutional validity of legislation produced while bypassing the voter. Similarly, the activities of Polish Deputies sitting in the parliaments of Prussia, Russia, or Austria during the period of partitions were excluded from consideration until these Deputies reappeared in the first Seym of the Second Republic in Warsaw.

The material contained in this study is arranged in three major parts. The first part describes the constitutional development in Poland during the hereditary monarchy and the First Republic, ending in 1795. The second part deals with the Period of Partitions (1795-1918) plus the Second and the Polish People's Republics (1918 until 1989), while the last part summarizes 500 years of history of major legislative issues. In the first two parts, the discussion of each significant period begins with a brief synopsis of major constitutional and political developments in the country, continues with four to six short essays on topics prominent in that period and ends in a synopsis of the constitution in force at the time, and a list of principal legislation passed in that period. [The revised edition includes an additional chapter which constitutes a compendium of the history of

17

the Seym. It covers events after 1989 which restored the democracy in Poland and led to the creation of the Third Republic.]

Since institutions are made by men, short biographical sketches of prominent legislators and political writers active in that period close each major section. These biographies were selected to highlight the achievements of outstanding individuals, noted for their leadership in the legislature or in the field of constitutional theory. The 100 or so biographies selected constitute but a tiny fraction (much less than 1%) of all the people who ever served in the legislatures of Poland, therefore the criteria for their selection had to be quite stringent. Many outstanding individuals who served as members of the judicial or the executive branch, whether kings, presidents, or chief justices, were left out unless they also had a legislative chapter in their careers. Among those included are some Deputies who achieved the distinction of being elected Speaker of the House, Senators who also served as the head of state pro tempore and Deputies or Senators who otherwise left their mark on the legislative history of Poland. Included also are the more prominent writers on constitutional issues. The range of their political views, intellectual achievements and activist stances represent well the pluralistic character of the political life in Poland. The roster ranges from a Renaissance thinker like Wawrzyniec G. Goślicki (1533-1607), who left his mark on the political thought of England, to a man who carried the political ideas of Thomas Jefferson from America to Poland, Julian Ursyn Niemcewicz (1758-1841). There are saintly figures like Mikołaj Smogulecki (1610-1656), the Deputy who became one of the early Christian missionaries in China, and knaves like Józef Ankwicz (1750-1794), the Deputy hanged for his subservience to the Russians. There are lifetimes spent in the legislature like that of Kazimierz Karwowski (1670-1746), who was elected Deputy 27 times, and lives of revolutionaries devoured by the revolution they helped create, like that of Kazimierz Pużak (1883-1953).

In addition to the biographical material, the text is supplemented by illustrations, carefully selected for their authenticity and, as far as possible, originating in the period to which they refer. There are portraits of legislators and writers, views of the places where the legislatures met, scenes from the legislative sessions, and facsimiles of title pages of laws that were passed.

The historical and legal material on which this work is based is derived for the most part from sources in Polish. For scholars with a command of Polish, a good part of this material is available in the Library of Congress. Its excellent collection of Polish Constitutional Law includes a complete edition of all the laws passed by the legislatures of the pre-partition Poland, as well as those of provincial legislatures of the Partition Period and the two Republics of the reunited state. The literature in English consists of scholarly treatments of selected periods.

The revival of interest in the history of parliamentarism in Poland dates from the turn of the century and was the work of Tadeusz Korzon, Stanisław Kutrzeba and Michał Bobrzyński. Ludwik Finkel initiated the publication of the *Bibliography of Polish History*. In the interwar period Marceli Handelsman promoted the study of constitutional history. Publication of source materials to the history of the local legislatures, initiated by Antoni Prochaska, gained momentum due to the work of Adolf Pawiński. Władysław Konopczyński not only published many of the Diaries of Debates of Seyms in the First Republic, but wrote extensively on the subject and established a chronology of all elections held between 1493 and 1793. An abstract of this chronology, extended to the present times, is included here in the Appendix. To Konopczyński goes also the credit for initiating the publication of the *Dictionary of Polish Biography*, a work still in progress.

Among historians living at the present time and devoting their attention to the history of Polish parliamentarism, there is Konstanty Grzybowski who investigated the early theory of representation in Poland, Władysław Czapliński and Henryk Olszewski who studied the Seyms of the sixteenth and seventeenth centuries, and Irena Kaniewska who studied the background of Deputies from Lesser Poland in the second half of the sixteenth century. Stefania Ochmann, Łucja Częścik and Jan Byliński studied specific Seyms, and Eugenia Triller published a bibliography of the legislation passed by the Seym in that century. Marek Borucki wrote on the legislative system and the royal elections; J. Włodarczyk and Bogdan Sobol studied the operation of Seymiks of the First Republic. The efforts of these scholars added much substance and sharpness of detail to the knowledge of this subject. Polish historians living abroad who made notable contributions include Marian Kukiel, Oskar Halecki and Piotr S. Wandycz. Jurist Wenceslas J. Wagner edited a collective work overviewing the development of Polish law through the centuries. Among Western scholars who have studied various aspects of history of Polish parliamentarism there are William F. Reddaway of Cambridge, Robert H. Lord of Harvard, Hans Roos of Göttingen, Daniel Stone of Winnipeg, and F. W. Thackeray of Indiana.

Interest in Polish legislative history has gone through several phases in Poland. Soon after the Partitions, in the first half of the nineteenth century, the feeling prevailed that the collapse of the First Republic was due to the inherent weakness of the parliamentary system of government when matched against absolutist monarchies. The "Spring of Nations" in 1848 and the subsequent introduction of parliamentary systems of government in several countries of Europe, including Prussia and Austria, led to the gradual revision of this pessimistic view. It was followed by much critical soul-searching in the Polish historiography of the time, centered around the theme: "Where have we failed in the First Republic?" The answers placed the blame mostly on the overblown powers of the Legislature (Seymocracy) for the paralysis of the executive branch of government, lame foreign policy and the neglect of the defense establishment, which preceded the collapse of the First Republic. Initially, less thought and analysis were given to external factors, and to the fact that on the continent of Europe Polish parliamentary institutions developed much ahead of their time in relation to similar developments in the neighboring countries. A lead in time of 75 years, and possibly as much as 100, is recognized by some modern political theorists. Viewed in this way and painted against the broad political background of the times when the absolutist powers of Europe were trying to contain the spread of revolutionary ideas from France, the Polish constitutional reform movement of the 1790's takes on added significance. This was brilliantly demonstrated in the study of the period: *The Age of the Democratic Revolution* by Robert R. Palmer.

Over and above the internal problems of parliamentary governments, there were the problems connected with dealings with the outside world. The representative governments, whose business is conducted in full view and with approval of the public, have a timeless security problem in relations with foreign powers whose government is conducted in secrecy and whose aims and means of achieving them are concealed from the world. This was aptly expressed by Wawrzyniec J. Rudawski (1617-1690), who wrote:

> There are no secrets with the Poles, their intentions and the method of government being known to all. I have seen copies of their laws and acts of parliament, called constitutions, sold openly in Paris, and I have heard that they can be bought in Constantinople. In these constitutions there are listed the public resources of the state, its reserves, the threatening dangers, the number of troops kept under arms. Friends and enemies are spelled out.

The statement would apply equally well to present-day America, and similar statements could be made for England, France, or any other parliamentary democracy. The problems of their dealings with the Soviet Russia bear more than a superficial resemblance to those of the seventeenth and eighteenth-century parliamentary government of Poland in its dealings with the secretive and absolutist Tsarist Russia.

POLISH LEGISLATIVE NOMENCLATURE, GEOGRAPHY AND CHRONOLOGY

It is timely to identify here at least part of the original Polish legislative terminology as a guide for interested readers, should they wish to consult the sources, and to warn them of semantic pitfalls associated with different word meanings. Otherwise, throughout the greater part of this study, English terminology will be used with only two exceptions.

INTRODUCTION

The first exception to the English usage will be made for the Polish word denoting the legislature. The Polish word for it came into use in the 1400's with the spelling "Seym" (pronounced say-m) and was used in that form well into the nineteenth century. The transition to the modern spelling "Sejm" can be pinpointed in time on the pages of the Proceedings of the Seym of Poznań, which show that it must have occurred between 1830 and 1834. The English pronunciation of the archaic form approximates quite well the Polish pronunciation of either form and, for this reason, is used here. The same applies to the word "Seymik" (pronounced say-meek), the county voters' assembly. When the word Seym came into usage as a generic term denoting the legislature, that body was still unicameral and consisted of elected Deputies and appointed members of the King's Council. When the Chamber of Deputies separated in 1493, it insisted on taking the word Seym with it and started to refer to the King's Council as the Senate. However, in the country at large, the generic meaning of Seym as legislature as a whole persisted in use. Which of the two meanings, the general or the specific, applies in the given situation is usually clear from the context. If not, the Chamber of Deputies (Izba Poselska) will be identified explicitly.

The second exception to the English usage will be made for the word "constitution." Although it has a conventional meaning now, during the period of hereditary monarchy and the First Republic the word denoted any law, except a tax law, passed by the Seym. In any given Seym as many as two hundred "constitutions" could be passed. On the other hand, if the subject matter of a law concerned the institutional arrangements of the country or the civil rights, such "constitutions" bore the name of "Cardinal Laws" (Prawa Kardynalne). This usage of the word "constitution" will be retained here in the discussion of this historical period, and the word will be spelled with a lower case 'c.' With the passage of the American, Polish and French Constitutions at the close of the eighteenth century, the present-day meaning of the word gained acceptance in Poland. When used in this sense it will be spelled here with the capital 'C' to distinguish it from the old law-constitution.

Foremost among the semantic traps involved in different word usage in Polish and English is the translation of the word *Rząd*, and the verb *rządzić*, as "government" and "to govern." The Polish meaning of the word is narrow, limited to the executive functions only. Government in the broader American sense, which includes the legislative and the judiciary branches as well, is rendered in Polish by the word *władza* with the more specific function spelled out: *władza wykonawcza* (the executive), *władza ustawodawcza* (the legislative), and *władza sądownicza* (the judiciary). It was the lack of attention to these nuances of meaning that led to the gross misunderstanding of the speech of Stanisław Car, the Speaker of the Seym, in which he introduced the Constitution of 1935 and emphasized its division of powers between the three branches of government (p. 286).

The word "Republic" makes an early appearance in Poland in legislative documents and political treatises, first in the form *Respublica* or *Reipublica* and later, when the vernacular replaced Latin in translation, as *Rzeczpospolita* often abbreviated to *Rzplita*. After the union of Poland and Lithuania (1569), it usually appeared as "the Republic of Both Nations" (Rzeczpospolita Oboyga Narodów). In that context, it is often translated into English as "the Commonwealth of Poland and Lithuania"; the historical period, however, is termed by the modern students of political history as "the First Republic" to underline the fact that it coincided with the era of elective kings co-governing with elective legislature and elective judicature. The seeming incongruity of calling a country headed by a king a republic did not perturb contemporaries, who apparently considered a king elected for life a mere chief magistrate or, with the Seym in session, a chairman of the Senate.

An institution that played a prominent, even though sporadic, role in the political life of the hereditary monarchy and the First Republic was the Confederation (Konfederacya). This was a temporary body of concerned citizens, formed spontaneously in times of national emergency for a specific political purpose. A Confederation had no legislative powers, unless it was formed within or was taken over by a Seym. As a rule, it had a formal structure, an elected executive committee, a treasurer, a publication committee which issued printed appeals to the public, etc. In present day terminology the Confederation may be thought of as an ad hoc political party, formed and operated for a fixed term to achieve a specific political objective, and then disbanded.

The title given to elected representatives in Poland in the 1400s, when Latin was the language of political discourse, was: *civitatum nuntius* or *terrarum nuntius* depending on the electorate represented, civic or county. In later times it was replaced with other designations applicable in various historical periods (Poseł, Ablegat, Plenipotencjusz, Deputowany). The relation of these designations to the historical period is summarized in Table 1. In this study, the word "Deputy" was chosen to cover all designations, with the appropriate explanation in the text.

TABLE 1—CHANGES IN DESIGNATION OF LEGISLATORS THROUGH THE CENTURIES

		Electorate	
Year	**Constitutional Period**	**Gentry**	**Town or Villages**
1493	Hereditary Monarchy	Terrarum Nuntius	Civitatum Nuntius
1580	First Republic	Poseł	Ablegat
1791	First Republic	Poseł	Plenipotent
1807	Period of Partitions	Poseł	Deputowany
1864	Period of Partitions	Poseł	
1919	Second Republic	Poseł	
1947	Polish People's Republic	Poseł	
1989	Third Republic	Poseł	

From among the Seym Deputies the Speaker (Marszałek) of the Lower House was elected. The same Polish word was also used to denote high judicial officials and court dignitaries, as well as the highest rank in the army of the Second and the Polish People's Republics. When used in the parliamentary context, Speaker of the Seym (Marszałek Seymu) was the customary form, although in the Seym of Galicia the designation was "Provincial Speaker" (Marszałek Krajowy).

Throughout the history of the hereditary monarchy and the First Republic, two appointive administrative offices and one ecclesiastic carried with them automatically a senatorial rank. These were the Castellan (Kasztelan) or the castle holder, the Palatine (Wojewoda) or the commander of territorial troops in a *levée en masse*, and the Bishop (Biskup) with the usual church responsibilities. All three titles continued in use as a designation of senatorial rank until 1831, long after the castles and the troop leader functions became antiquated. The title of Palatine was revived in the Second Republic as a designation of the top executive officer of a group of counties. Initially suppressed in the Polish People's Republic, it was again revived in the 1970s. Since the 1830s it has not, however, carried with it a seat in the Senate. Apart from titles connected with appointive offices and valid only during the life of the appointee, there were no hereditary titles recognized in Poland, except those originating in preunion Lithuania and derived from the Ruthenian title *Kniaź*. Thus the designation *baron*, which appears frequently in old Latin charters and royal decrees, in the Polish context refers to these high appointive offices and not to a hereditary order of aristocracy. It was in the nature of things that persons holding these high offices accumulated influence and property and in due time, after several generations of such appointees, elevated their families to a position where, except for the absence of titles, they were to all intents and purposes indistinguishable from aristocratic families in other European countries. All of this took place in spite of the elaborate legislative pretense which did not allow a formal recognition of titles. Ostensibly, the upper rung of the social ladder was occupied by the gentry, hereditary, but legally equal among themselves.

Throughout this study the term "gentry" (szlachta) is used to designate the social group obligated to military service, when it was based on the *levée en masse*, and rewarded for it with the vote. The continuing social stratification of gentry in Poland made the term partially misleading. As a social group the gentry constituted approximately 10% of the population, in some palatinates as high as 15%. By 1805, in the sixteen counties north of Warsaw from Płock to Grodno, the gentry constituted 34% of the population. In terms of property ownership, by the end of the First Republic, nearly half of the gentry did not own land but earned their living through service in the regular army, in the judiciary or in administrative positions. Among the landowners, the bulk of the gentry was in the yeomanry range and extended through the landed gentry into the ranks of the magnates. The yeomanry, living in the country and tilling their own land, differed little from the peasants. Thus, often the only distinction between the house of the lower gentry and the hut of a peasant was the rudimentary portico adorning the former, much in the manner in which Southerners in the United States like to make the style of their homes distinct.

The rules adopted in spelling of proper and place names in the text are as follows: Polish spelling with appropriate pronounciation marks is used throughout except for place names with a well established English form like Warsaw (Warszawa), Cracow (Kraków) or Brest Litovsk (Brześć Litewski). The first names are commonly given in their Polish form; Andrzej (Andrew) Jan (John), Łukasz (Luke), Mikołaj (Nicholas) and Krzysztof (Christopher). The names of individuals who were elected King and who thereafter signed their names on official documents in a latinized form, Casimir (Kazimierz), Ladislaus (Władysław), Stanislaus (Stanisław), are usually given in their Polish spelling in context referring to their pre-election activities, and in a latinized form thereafter. Proper names which in a modern spelling appear with a letter j, but were spelled by their bearers with a y, are left in their early form, Rey (Rej), Kołłątay (Kołłątaj), etc. The change in spelling of words derived from Latin and starting with C, to their modern spelling with K has not been followed rigorously, because of the retention of the C in English usage.

A brief note concerning the geography of the provinces represented in the Seym is also in order here. The terms describing the major provinces of Poland are a direct translation from Polish. Thus, Greater Poland and Lesser Poland are in Polish, *Wielkopolska* and *Małopolska*. The origin of the names is lost in antiquity, and the names do not refer to size or importance. In fact, during the period of interest relating to legislative history, Lesser Poland was the more politically active of the two. After the incorporation of the Kingdom of Halicz into Poland in the reign of Casimir the Great (1349), Halicia was attached to Lesser Poland as a political entity, only to be renamed Galicia in 1772 after its annexation by Austria. The northern part of the country, along the southern shore of the Baltic Sea between the outlets of the rivers Oder and Vistula, is called Pomerania, a latinized form of *Pomorze*, the–land–by–the–sea. Originally inhabited by *Kaszuby*, a Slavonic tribe speaking a Polish dialect, Pomerania emerged on the historical scene in the tenth century ruled by a local dynasty under the suzerainty of Poland.

Further along the Baltic shore, and east of the outlet of the Vistula, stretches Prussia proper. Originally inhabited by one of the Baltic peoples, possessed of their own language, pagan by religion, and warlike by inclination, it served as the cradle of modern Prussia. When the missionary efforts of Poland met with no success and the Prussian raids into Poland proved a menace, Conrad, a Masovian prince of the Polish Piast dynasty, invited in 1226 a German Order of knight-monks, the Teutonic Order of Mary, to come to Poland and help in the defense against the Prussians and, hopefully, to bring about their Christianization. The Order, unemployed after the crusading debacle in Palestine, brought its considerable resources to bear on the problem of checking the Prussians and within the next 50 years not only subdued them but also, in 1308, captured the city of Gdańsk and most of the Polish Pomerania, thus replacing the Prussians as a menace to Poland. In Prussia proper, as the original Prussians resisted to the last the German efforts to Christianize them, they were put to the sword. The resulting demographic vacuum was partially filled by Polish Masovians (Mazury) moving north to settle in rural southern Prussia and by German settlers coming to found and populate the cities, mingling with the native *Kaszuby*. In time the designation 'Prussians' was transferred from the extinct Balts to the mixed Polish-German population, and the name Prussia was extended to Pomerania as well. When the latter, together with parts of the former, threw off the yoke of the Order in 1454 and rejoined Poland, it carried the designation 'Royal Prussia' (Prusy Królewskie) with it.

Finally, the present central Poland first appears in the discussion as the province of Masovia. Originally an integral part of Poland, it had some three centuries of political independence while ruled by a cadet branch of the Polish Piast dynasty. When that branch died out, Masovia was reunited with the rest of Poland and appears on these pages as a province with its own General Seymik. Since the legislative institutions at the provincial level in Masovia, Greater Poland and Lesser Poland survived the collapse of the First Republic, the respective provincial geography is important to the story that follows.

CONSTITUTIONS, ELECTIONS AND LEGISLATURES OF POLAND

To help the readers unfamiliar with the geography of the country, several small maps have been included throughout the text. For simplicity and ease of location, only places and geographic divisions of importance to legislative history have been indicated. The places where all the Seymiks met, some 74 in the 1600s, would have been too numerous to include on these small maps. The list of these places is included in Appendix B and any good atlas will show their position.

Administratively, the First Republic was divided into 22 palatinates (województwo), and these in turn into 119 counties or lands (powiat, ziemia). The union with Lithuania added 8 palatinates, subdivided into 22 counties, and the district of Samogatia (Żmudź). Each palatinate was entitled to a Palatine-Senator appointed by the King plus a number of Castellan-Senators, one for each city or larger town; each county returned two Deputies to the Seym.

Throughout the nearly five hundred years of history of legislative institutions in Poland the Seyms met in various places, not only the capital of the country. In addition to changes in location, changes in the numerical strength of the Seym took place, reflecting changing political conditions and size of the country.

Starting with the appearance of a bicameral legislature in 1493 while the hereditary monarchy was still in existence, the Seym chronology follows the expansion of the country through the political union with Lithuania in 1569. The first true election of the chief executive followed shortly in 1573 and signalled the rise of the First Republic. The nearly two hundred years of its eventful history ended with the passage of the Constitution of 1791. The invasion of the country by the absolutist neighbors, the suppression of the Constitution, and the collapse of the First Republic ushered in the Period of Partitions which lasted until the end of the First World War. The two lower levels of the legislative structure developed during the preceding centuries, survived the collapse of the First Republic as provincial legislatures of the Duchy of Warsaw, the Congress Kingdom of Poland, the Grand Duchy of Poznań, and the Kingdom of Galicia.

The national legislative institutions were revived in 1918 with the rise of the Second Republic. The Senate, which had disappeared from the legislatures of Poznań and Galicia, was restored in the Second Republic, and its membership made elective. The twenty-year-long life of the Second Republic was terminated by the invasion of its territory by the combined forces of Hitler's Germany and Stalin's Russia, triggering the Second World War and bringing in its wake the rise of the Polish People's Republic. The Senate was again abolished but the Seym survived.

Realizing that the concept of a national state, bonded by language and common heritage, rose to its full strength only in the nineteenth century, replacing earlier bonds of dynasty, class or religion, one must view the historical Poland as a state pluralistic par excellence, whose population of many languages and religions was held together by common interest in defense and the appeal of its political institutions. Through the lands of the Commonwealth ran the boundary between the Latin and the Greek Churches, with all of the cultural influences and conflicts of loyalty that this implied. The network of those great medieval culture carriers, the abbeys of the Cistercian Order, ended on the river Vistula, and the usage of the Latin and Greek scripts in writing followed the religious affiliation of the people. The national groups which made up the state were acquired either through territorial growth or immigration, supplementing the basic core of native Poles. Encouraged by a long line of Polish princes, immigrant Germans settled primarily in towns. The annexation of Red Ruthenia by Casimir the Great (1340) brought in the first group of Ruthenians, as yet not differentiated between the Ukrainians and the Byelorussians. The Ruthenians were closely followed by the immigrant Jews and Armenians, both groups driven from their homelands by religious persecution. Finally, after the union with Lithuania (1569), the entire Lithuanian people, as well as the bulk of the Ruthenians, were added, virtually completing the establishment of the multi-national Commonwealth. What is the present day Latvia, also at one time joined the Commonwealth. Smaller national groups, mostly Scots, came in as immigrants in the 1600s.

CHAPTER I

HEREDITARY MONARCHY: KINGS FACE ELECTIVE LEGISLATURES

The death of the last male member of the native Piast dynasty in the year 1370 induced local notables to organize for political purposes into provincial legislative assemblies, the Seymiks. The Seymiks, in turn, took it upon themselves to shop around for prospective rulers. Privileges and charters issued in this period laid the foundation for later constitutional laws guaranteeing personal rights.

The period covered here (1493-1573) embraces an era during which the two-chamber legislature appeared in full bloom. It was composed of the appointive Senate and the elective Seym. The Senate was the outgrowth of the Privy Council, much expanded through the addition of castellans, palatines and bishops. The elective Seym at first worked in joint sessions with the Senate; after 1493 it started to assemble in a separate chamber. The office of the Speaker of the Seym came into existence and he was elected anew for each session by the Deputies. The king began to act as the chairman of the Senate. Laws were passed by majority vote.

During this period the Seym asserted its claim to confirm each new king in office upon the death of his predecessor. This royal confirmation was called an election, although in the true sense of the word it was not, since the candidate invariably was a member of the Jagiellon dynasty. Conflicts arose between the legislature and the administration over the coronation of sons of the king before his own death, and the legislature claimed the right to hold the election only after the death of the ruler.

Former Polish Pomeranian provinces, taken over by the Germans, revolted against their new masters and chose to rejoin Poland and to send their representatives to the national Seym. In addition, the country greatly expanded through political union with Lithuania, and its legislative institutions were extended to the new part of the Commonwealth.

Laws restricting peasantry and imposing more rigid social structure appeared.

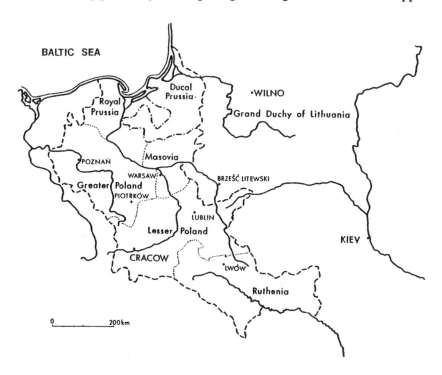

Fig. 1 - _Hereditary Kingdom of Poland after the reunion with Pomerania and Masovia in 1550s._

CHARTERS AND THE EARLY LAWS: THE ORIGINS OF THE CONSTITUTION

Constitutional development in Poland is, in a true measure, nothing else but the centuries-long growth of political awareness of an ever-larger segment of the population and the expression of its desire to control its own destiny. In the earliest times it meant the barons and other prominent people presenting their demands to the Prince which, when fulfilled, would buy their cooperation. To make such concessions of demand more legal and binding, a charter was usually requested of the Prince, describing the circumstances of the act and the details of the concession made. Thus, first constitutional documents were created.

Gatherings, originally convened to exert political pressure, later evolved into regular legislative assemblies at the county, the provincial and the national levels. In Poland they bore the name of the Seymik, the General Seymik, and the National Seym (Seym Walny). Initially unicameral and based on simple rules of operation, they succeeded in securing a number of privileges and charters in the late fourteenth and the early fifteenth centuries, which became the backbone of later Bills of Rights.

One of the earliest constitutional documents was the Charter of Koszyce, granted in 1374 by Louis of Hungary when he was briefly ruler of Poland, by which the consent of the Seymiks was acknowledged as a necessary condition before new taxes could be levied. The year 1404 saw the beginning of the movement towards the representative system of government when King Ladislaus Jagiełło, in need of funds, authorized the members of his Privy Council to travel to each district of the country and deliberate with the body of the gentry on the means of raising the money.

Among early constitutional documents one must include the privilege *nec bona recipiantur* granted by Ladislaus Jagiełło in 1422 to the barons and the knighthood gathered in preparation for war with the German Order in an army camp set up near the abbey of Czerwińsk on the banks of the river Vistula. In the privilege he promised not to allow the confiscation of privately held property without a court sentence, undertook to see to it that court sentences were based on written law, and promised not to place judgeships in the hands of administrative officials of the crown. This privilege, therefore, guaranteed the right to property, subject to existing laws which specified confiscation of property as penalty for certain offenses. One such offense was the refusal to answer a call to arms in a levée en masse during a national emergency. For example, approximately 2400 such confiscations of property took place in 1497 when part of the gentry did not answer a call to arms.

From the same period (1430-1433) dates the *neminem captivabimus* privilege of Jedlna-Cracow. The key phrase of this privilege states:

> None will be imprisoned, or ordered to be imprisoned, or afflicted with any penalty whatsoever, unless he be duly convicted by a court of law.

It is therefore the Polish equivalent of the much later English Habeas Corpus Act of 1679. Finally, the privilege of Nieszawa (1454) officially recognized the existence of the Seymik in each county and its right to approve every army call-up.

The first of the dates given in the title of this study, namely the year 1493, marks the emergence of the bicameral national parliament, composed of the Seym and the Senate. This date forms a convenient time marker, but in a true sense it does not signal the arrival of the representative system of government as we understand it today; that is a system of electing representatives to conduct the business of legislating. The reason is that the pre-1493 legislative history of Poland was the period when the presence in person of everybody concerned at the meetings of legislature was quite acceptable. The country had not yet reached its full territorial expansion, the distances were smaller, and attendance in person was possible although not always practical. The Seyms that assembled at Piotrków in 1438, 1447, 1477 and at Łęczyca in 1454 were of that type, i.e., unicameral and with open attendance.

A statement made by the legates sent by the King of Poland to the Estates of Prussia in 1480, to explain the mode of passing taxation by the Seym, throws an interesting light on how the principle of representation was understood in Poland at the time. The passage of interest runs as follows:

> It happens often that all of the Kingdom of Poland receives the Writs of Summons to the assembly, and only a third, or one-tenth arrives, but whatever is decided there, all must accept unanimously.

A later quote (1489) from the King's speech, as reported by the Prussian Ambassador, states: "Whoever is summoned to an Assembly, but does not come, consents to the decisions that were made there." The right to be present in person and to participate in the decision making on the spot survived throughout the life of the First Republic in the rules for the election of the king and the operation of the Seymiks.

The emergence of the bicameral legislature at Piotrków in 1493 was quickly followed by important developments in constitutional law. At a Seym assembled twelve years later in 1505 at Radom in Lesser Poland, a Cardinal Law was passed, known thereafter as *nihil novi* for its key words, often translated into vernacular as: "nothing new about us, without us." The key passage of this document, submitted for confirmation to King Alexander at that Seym, reads:

> Whereas common laws and public constitutions concern not one individual, but the whole nation, therefore it is ordered that hereinafter and forever nothing new will be decided by Us or our successors without the concurrence of the councillors and the deputies

Fig. 2-An illustration from the "Statutes of Łaski," showing the Seym held in 1505 in Radom at which the constitution "nihil novi" was adopted. This is the earliest known picture of a Seym in session.

The constitutional foundation established in the charters: *nihil novi, neminem captivabimus,* and *nec bona recipiantur,* was of immense practical importance to the inhabitants of Poland in the centuries that followed. The consensual requirement of law-making replaced the whim of the ruler by the rule of law, forbade postfactum legislation, and made arrest or confiscation of property permissible only in due process of law. The validity of principles embedded in them is as true today as it was when they were issued and the principles have served throughout the centuries as a point of reference, to be returned to from any temporary departure. Appendix A gives the key paragraphs of these charters in Latin.

The declaratory character of the basic charters was backed by the resolve of their beneficiaries to see to it that all actions of the executive branch of the government adhered to the principles contained in them. The real question of how to assure this adherence taxed the minds of the politically active people in Poland for nearly a hundred years until, in 1573, another important principle was formulated and put on the books as the last of the so-called "Henrician Articles."

The article stated that the executive was entitled to the loyalty and obedience of the inhabitants of the country only for as long as its own actions were in accordance with the existing law (for details see the section on Pacta Conventa).

Forming the backbone of subsequent constitutional law of Poland, the principles of the above laws were explicitly included in the Cardinal Laws of the First Republic, in the Constitution of the Congress Kingdom of Poland in the period of Partitions, and their substance was implicitly embedded in the Constitutions of the Second Republic. In the Polish People's Republic, however, a different set of principles, derived from the Soviet experience, was substituted.

SEYMIK: THE BASIC UNIT OF LEGISLATURE

The basis of legislative power in early Poland rested with the county assembly of voters, called the Seymik. Its origins, powers, and the mode of operation, greatly affected the rise of parliamentarism in Poland. Centuries of rich political life of Poland lie recorded in the acts and proceedings of the Seymiks of each territory[*].

The practice of convening Seymiks was an ancient one, predating the national Seym by at least two centuries. It emerged as one of the consequences of dynastic subdivision of the country during the Middle Ages. This territorial subdivision of Poland was quite similar to that which took place on the territories of Poland's two neighbors, Germany and Kievan Russia. The process had its roots in the structure of land ownership. In the Middle Ages the territory of the state was considered the private property of the ruler to be disposed of in any way he pleased, including the right to divide it among his heirs. In Poland, dynastic subdivision was initiated in 1138 and within a century produced a total fragmentation of the country into small principalities, each with its own court and a miniscule army. Eventually, the exigencies of defense and the gradual dying-out of the various branches of the ruling House of Piast reversed the trend towards subdivision and set in motion attempts at reunification. By 1370 the process of reunification was well set on its way. Each principality entered this era with a well-developed and politically conscious ruler's council and a numerous knighthood, which in time became the gentry. The Seymiks were born from the interaction of these elements.

---

[*] Only a small part of this material has been critically examined and published heretofore (see bibliography). The bulk, unpublished, rests with the Polish Academy of Sciences in Cracow, as "Portfolios of Adolf Pawiński." Pawiński's untimely death in 1896 stopped the planned 18 volume publication.

When the last male member of the ruling dynasty died, the Seymiks, or in the Latin usage of the times *Conventiones Terrestrae*, assumed the responsibility for negotiating with prospective rulers the conditions for ascendancy. During this period they were successful in securing a number of privileges and charters, as discussed earlier. Among them was the privilege of Nieszawa, granted in 1454, which recognized the Seymik in each county or land as a standing organization and promised that the consent of the Seymiks will be requested by the King before each call to arms is declared. Starting with the authority to deal with the army call-up, the Seymiks later extended their deliberations to tax matters, particularly in times of national emergencies. With a continuing reunification of the country, the Seymiks started to elect and send Deputies to the Provincial Seyms of Greater and Lesser Poland, and when these eventually decided to meet as one assembly for the country, the county Deputies constituted the national Seym.

The growth of the Seymik network in Greater and Lesser Poland, Masovia and Prussia was an organic process and bore, therefore, all the characteristics of a system constructed piecemeal by accretion, resulting in many irregularities quite puzzling to the present-day observer. The arrangements were more regular in Lithuania, where the full-fledged system of Seymiks was established in one swoop just before the union with Poland in 1569. As a rule, in territorially large counties such as existed in Lithuania, the Seymik of each county met separately; whereas in Greater and Lesser Poland and Prussia, where the population density was much higher and the counties, or even the palatinates, were much smaller, the Seymiks of more than one county could meet in one place and elect Deputies. Generally, even in these joint meetings the rule was observed that the Deputy elected to represent a given county should be a resident of that county. In some parts of the country even two entire palatinates met together in one place: Radziejów, for the palatinates of Innowrocław and Brześć-Kujawy; Środa, for the palatinates of Poznań and Kalisz.

The rule of two Deputies elected per county was followed closely, but not religiously. For instance, the palatinate of Sandomierz was made up of six small counties which held one joint Seymik at Opatów, and until 1736 elected six Deputies, i.e., one per county. In 1736 the number was raised to seven and the rule was introduced that each of the Deputies elected should be a resident of a different county. Similarly, the palatinate of Cracow held only one Seymik at Proszowice but elected six Deputies without distinction of county residence.

National emergencies would make it occasionally necessary to ask the cities to consent to taxation through representatives sent to the Seyms. In such cases the cities themselves served as electoral districts and sent Ablegates directly, rather than through the participation of the burghers in the Seymiks. This rule, however, was not adhered to in the palatinate of Cracow, where the city of

Cracow was represented in the Seymik held in Proszowice, nor did it apply in Prussia, where the cities were represented in the Seymiks, and the burghers sat in them together with the gentry.

Fig. 3-A Seymik,being held in the town of Środa, province of Greater Poland, in front of the parish church. In inclement weather the Seymik would be held inside.

In operation, the county Seymik resembled the Swiss Landsgemeinde, or a town meeting of a New England community. Its meetings were as a rule held either in front or inside the parish church, depending on the weather, and every adult male member of the community subject to army obligation was entitled to attend, speak up, and vote. This connection of the right to vote and the military duty is crucial for understanding the later constitutional development. For the average voter the military duty was an expensive burden and meant that the cost of a suit of armor, a charger, and the upkeep of two grooms had to be borne by the individual, severely limiting the number of people interested, or able, to undertake it. Yet, here was the gateway through which the gentry ascended to political dominance in the country, in the process converting an irksome and expensive duty into a treasured privilege. The tie between the right to vote and the military obligation, with the simultaneous absence of property or residence qualifications, held for over three centuries, in fact until 1791. It meant that those entitled to vote could vote also at other than their home Seymik, if they happened to be away from home for family or business reasons.

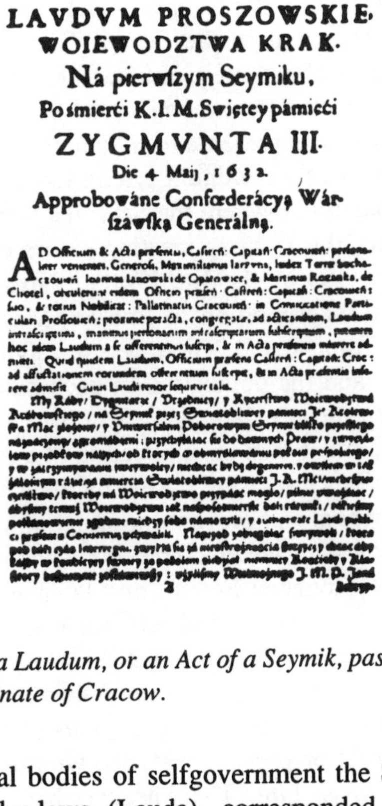
LAVDVM PROSZOWSKIE.
WOIEWODZTWA KRAK.
Ná pierwszym Seymiku.
Po śmierći K.I.M. Swiętey pámięći
ZYGMVNTA III.
Die 4. Maij, 1632.
Approbowáne Confoederácyą Wárszáwską Generálną.

Fig. 4 - Title page from a Laudum, or an Act of a Seymik, passed on May 4, 1632 at Proszowice in the Palatinate of Cracow.

In their duties as local bodies of selfgovernment the Seymiks debated, voted on, and issued local by-laws (Lauda), corresponded with the King or his Chancellor, and served as the focal point of political activity in their region. Although in this capacity the Seymik spoke for a distinct territory, the right to hold Seymiks resided with the voters, rather than the territory, so that when in the 1600s the armies of Muscovy overran and held the palatinates of Smoleńsk, Witebsk, and Połock, the voters packed up and moved to unoccupied territory where they and their descendents held the "Seymiks in Exile" (Seymiki Exultanckie) from 1659 until 1748.

Once the national legislative institutions were established, the Seymiks assumed the role of the electoral districts, in addition to their ever-expanding local functions. The system of representation embedded in the Seymik network was essentially based on the county (or land) unit, with two Deputies elected from each entity. However, the military defense system embodying the call-up of the voters was based on the next larger administrative unit, the palatinate, so that in the provincial, and later the national Seym, the Deputies were grouped and seated by palatinates, rather than by counties, while the Palatines, the appointed officials whose duty was to muster and lead the local defense units in case of war, were given a seat in the Senate. The palatinates varied in size, population and the number of counties (or lands) in their composition, and so did the number of Deputies elected from them, as can be seen from Table 2.

The size of the palatinate representations remained fairly stable over a long period of time, yet there was a continuing trend towards increasing the number of places within each palatinate where the Seymiks met to reduce the travel distance of the voters. Thus, the 16 or so meeting places of the Seymiks in the late 1400's gradually rose to 104 by the late 1700's. Part of the increase, however, was connected with the incorporation of Prussia, Masovia and the union with Lithuania, as shown in Appendix B. There was a rough proportionality between the number of counties and the population in each palatinate, and occasionally new counties and even new palatinates were formed, a result of political bargaining in the Seym, rather than an application of a rigid numerical rule.

From time to time various laws were passed by the national Seym to regularize the operation of the Seymiks and prevent intimidation of the voters. These laws are listed in Table 3. However, the electoral ordinance under which the Seymiks elected Deputies to the provincial Seyms, and later also to the national Seym, remained for a long time unwritten, and reliance was placed on custom. It was assumed that the electorate would assure that it was well represented and would police itself. The customary procedure was as follows: during the election of the Deputies by the Seymik, the voters and the candidates were required to be present in person. The election procedure started with the election of the Speaker and two Assessors to assist him. The Speaker then read the Royal Writ of Summons, and the list of the issues to be taken up at the forthcoming Seym, plus the request that Deputies be elected and authorized to deal with them. A debate followed, order on the floor being in the hands of the Speaker. The Speaker would then open the floor for nominations and record the names of candidates put up for election, after they expressed their consent. The voting itself was done by a show of hands with the assessors counting and tabulating the results in order of decreasing number of votes cast. The election would go to the candidates with the highest number of votes. The number of candidates could be quite large, for instance, the extant records of the Seymik of Proszowice in the palatinate of Cracow for April 1593 show that there were 17 candidates in the election for the six seats apportioned to that palatinate in the national Seym. The election of Deputies completed, the preparation of written instructions (Kartelusze) for the Deputies followed. On this particular occasion, the instructions on matters to be brought up at the Seym ran to 49 items. With the passage of centuries, the number of functions assigned to the Seymiks increased, and the differentiated functions were assigned to different sessions of the Seymiks by appropriate Seym constitutions, the earliest of which was passed in 1493 by a Seym sitting in Piotrków. The constitution identified 18 localities at which the Seymiks were to assemble in case of impending war, to pass an Army Tax and to fix the terms of service. Later the same functions were spread over more Seymiks. After the constitution of 1578 established the Tribunal of the Crown, that is the Supreme Court, with elective judges, the "Judicial Seymiks" started to convene once a year to elect deputy judges for that body. Seymiks for debriefing of Deputies returning from the national Seym were first called into being by a constitution of 1589. Other types of Seymiks, the Economic, the Hooded, etc. are described in Table 4. In each case the place of the meeting and the participants were the same, merely the function of the session was different as was the duration, which could vary from one day for a debriefing Seymik, several days for a pre-Seym Seymik, to longer periods for the Hooded Seymiks.

TABLE 2 - SEYM REPRESENTATION BY PALATINATE AND PERIOD

Province	Palatinate	1550	1650	1750
Greater Poland	Malborg		2*	
(12 palatinates)	Pomorze		6*	
	Chełmno		3*	
Includes	Płock	3	3	4
Masovia and	Mazowsze	20	20	20
Pomerania	Rawa	6	6	6
	Poznań	6	6	6
	Kalisz	6	6	6
	Sieradz, Wieluń	6	6	6
	Łęczyca	4	4	4
	Brześć K., Dobrzyn	4	4	4
	Innowrocław	2	2	2

TABLE 2 (CONTINUED)—SEYM REPRESENTATION BY PALITINATE AND PERIOD

Province	Palatinate	1550	1650	1750
Lesser Poland	Kraków	6	6	8**
(11 palatinates)	Sandomierz	6	6	7
	Lublin	3	3	3
Includes	Ruś, Chełm	13	14	14
Ruthenia and	Bełż	4	4	4
Ukraine	Podole	4	4	4
	Podlasie		2	6
	Wołyń		6	6
	Kiev		6	6
	Bracław		6	6
	Czernichów		4	4
Lithuania	Wilno		8	10
(10 palatinates)	Troki		8	8
	Połock		2	2
Includes	Nowogródek		6	6
Inflanty	Witebsk		4	4
	Brześć Lit.		4	4
	Mińsk		6	6
	Żmudź		2	2
	Smoleńsk		4	4
	Mścisław		2	2
	Inflanty		2	6
GRAND TOTAL		93	177	182

*Prussian representation in the early 1600s
**Includes two Deputies from Oświęcim and Zator

Fig. 5 - *A scene from a session of a Seymik held inside a church, showing the Speaker reading the Writ of Summons; from a painting by Jean Pierre Norblin (1745-1830).*

TABLE 3 - THE CHRONOLOGY OF SEYM LAWS RELATING TO SEYMIKS

Year	Subject Matter of the Law
1507	Penalties for men who came armed to Courts and Seymiks
1510	Penalties for violation of peace at the Seymiks
1520	Penalties for men who disrupted Seymiks
1565	Authorization for General Seymiks to draft Seym Bills
1578	Safety of Courts and Seymiks assured
1581	Flintlocks banned from Seymiks and Courts
1601	Flintlocks banned from Seymiks
1613	Ordinance for the Seym and the Seymiks
1638	Provision for security of the Seymiks
1647	Ordinance for Prussian Seymiks
1678	Marshal's Articles (by-laws for public safety)
1764	Safety of persons attending public meetings
1764	Active electoral rights in Poland and Lithuania defined
1768	Ordinance for the Conduct of Seymiks
1775	Members of the Army and Government banned from voting
1791	Rules for Seymik operation articulated
1793	Electoral and administrative districts redefined

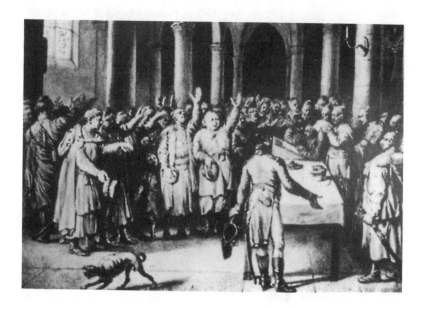

Fig. 6—*A voting scene from a Seymik showing the Speaker and one of the Assessors recording the vote; a painting by Jean Pierre Norblin (1745-1830).*

During the administration of Ladislaus Vasa (1632-1648), the local autonomy of the Seymiks reached its peak. At that time each palatinate had its own treasury, sustained by an excise tax on alcoholic beverages, and maintained its defense units. During the administration of Augustus II Wettin (1697-1733), the Seymiks were stripped of their authority over army units in their area, and in the administration of Stanislaus Augustus Poniatowski (1764-1795), the treasuries of the palatinates were abolished and taxes directed into the national treasury.

The history of the Seymiks extends well beyond the period of the hereditary monarchy and the First Republic. In fact, the lower two levels of the old three level legislative system of Poland, namely the county Seymik and the provincial General Seymik, were so durable that they survived the collapse of the national political institutions of the First Republic in 1795 and continued in existence in the period of Partitions in the Polish parts of the former Polish-Lithuanian Commonwealth. In the territory of the former Grand Duchy of Lithuania, after its incorporation into the Russian Empire, only the "Judicial Seymiks" were allowed to continue, but the deputy judges they elected were restricted to lower courts. The Court of Appeals was located in St. Petersburg; its judges were appointed by the Emperor. Otherwise, no elective representative institutions survived in Lithuania.

After the period of Partitions, in the Second and the Polish People's Republic, the true Seymik, serving as an assembly of voters debating and legislating on local issues, was not revived, although for a period local assemblies of elected representatives were given that name. Gradually, the name 'City' or 'County' Council replaced the name 'Seymik' in relation to elective local bodies.

TABLE 4—SUMMARY OF TYPES AND FUNCTIONS OF SEYMIKS (IN CHRONOLOGICAL ORDER OF APPEARANCE)

Election (Elekcyjny)—Assembled to fill a vacancy in the office of the County Judge and elected four candidates for it. The king then appointed one of them to the office. First met in the 1400s.

Pre-Seym (Przedseymowy)—Assembled to receive the Royal Writ of summons, to elect the Deputies to the National Seym and to prepare the instructions for them. Appeared with the National Seym in late 1400s.

Hooded (Kapturowy)—Called during the interregnum to maintain law and order in the absence of central administration. It was, as a rule, confederated and acted through the regular set of confederation officials, plus a temporary court. Appeared with the establishment of the First Republic in 1572.

Debriefing (Relacyjny)—Called on the return of the Deputies from a session of the National Seym to inform the electorate of the business that was transacted and of the laws that were passed. Often passed local legislation or resolutions regarding law enforcement. First met in 1589.

Judicial (Deputacki)—Assembled annually to elect deputy Judges to the Crown Tribunal, sitting alternately in Lublin and Piotrków. Of its 33 members, 27 were elected by the Seymiks from 1578 onwards. Initiated after 1581 in Lithuania.

Economic (Gospodarczy)—Assembled annually or more often, to deal with the distribution of national tax assessments, voting and collection of local taxes, approval of local expenditures. Authorized the size of county militia or local troops. From the middle of 1700s elected Commissioners of the Treasury Tribunal.

GENERAL SEYMIKS AND THE PROVINCIAL SEYMS

When the issues under consideration involved more than one county or palatinate, a provincial Seym was convened. Its composition was made up of Deputies elected by the counties and the Senators from the province. Thus, it was no longer an assembly of voters, like the Seymik, but a legislature in the present sense, i.e., an assembly of representatives.

In 1468 the provincial Seyms of Greater and Lesser Poland decided to meet together at Piotrków and thus established a national Seym. The provincial Seyms still retained their individual meetings, prior to the joint meeting, but called them General Seymiks (colloquially just 'Generals') transferring at the same time the title 'Seym' to the joint meeting. The same change in title occurred in 1528 in Masovia, when the Seym of that province became the Masovian General while its Deputies entered the national Seym, and in 1569 when the Deputies from Lithuania and Prussia decided to participate in the national Seym.

With the establishment of the national Seym, only one set of Deputies was elected by the county Seymiks, to serve at both the provincial Generals and the national Seym. In actual practice the meetings of the provincial Generals were held as stopovers for the Deputies on their way to the sessions of the national Seym. In rare instances, when war or lack of time on a pressing issue prevented the national Seym from assembling, the powers of the provincial Generals were deemed adequate to legislate on national issues. Such was the case in the years 1511, 1513, and 1577. Otherwise, the powers and the duration of sessions of the provincial General Seymiks were reduced relative to their previous status as provincial Seyms.

The area of competence of the General Seymiks was for the most part defined by practice rather than law. There is, for instance, evidence in the records that in 1468 the General Seymik of Lesser Poland decided to send to the national Seym two Deputies from each county with mandates to deal with tax matters. However, since it was apparently felt that when faced by the national Seym the Deputies might become overly compliant, the Seymik reserved to itself the right to accept or reject the taxes voted by the national Seym. A record of such acceptances, or rejections, of new taxes by the Seymik exists for the years 1467, 1468, 1470, 1472, 1474, and then annually until 1478.

The General Seymik of the province served as a meeting ground at which the provincial legislative objectives were lined up by the Deputies on their way to the national Seym, and where agreement was reached on the stand to be taken on national issues. In line with this practice, the constitution passed by the Seym of 1565 formally assigned to the General Seymiks the initial editing of first drafts of Bills, no doubt to save the very limited time allotted to this task at the six week sessions of the national Seym.

The times and places where the General Seymiks were to meet were usually specified in the Writ of Summons issued prior to the elections of Deputies to the national Seym, and were fairly standard. The General Seymik for the province of Greater Poland usually assembled at Koło, the one for Lesser Poland at Korczyn, the one for Prussia, alternately at Malbork or Grudziądz, the Masovian at Warsaw, and the Ruthenian at Wisznia. After the union of Poland and Lithuania, the Lithuanian General Seymik started to assemble at Słonim. Other places and periods of meeting of the General Seymiks are listed in Table 5. For the sake of completeness the later provincial Seyms, in fact the revived General Seymiks, are also included.

The rise of representative bodies in central Poland was followed with keen interest and imitated in the adjoining Prussia and Masovia, where the first provincial Seyms met in 1454 and 1456 respectively. In Prussia, consisting at the time of the former Polish provinces of Pomerania and Chełmno, plus the lands conquered from the pagan Prussians by the German Order, the objective of the meetings of the representatives of the knighthood, the cities and the cathedral chapters was to throw off the yoke of the German Order and to reunite with Poland. Without going into all the details of the thirteen year war (1454-1466), which the Estates of Prussia conducted jointly with Poland against the Order, let it suffice to say that at the conclusion of the war the provincial Seym of Prussia emerged as a well established body with a successful outcome of the war fully credited to it. By 1505 its composition was as follows: the upper chamber consisted of the two Bishops of Chełmno and Ermland (Warmia), the Palatines, Castellans and Chamberlains of Chełmno, Malbork and Gdańsk (Pomerania), plus two representatives each from the cities of Gdańsk, Toruń and Elbląg. Until 1662, the lower chamber consisted of representatives of the knighthood and 27 smaller towns. Thus, similarly to the provincial Seym of Masovia, this body was bicameral. Many outstanding individuals from Pomerania and Prussia participated in its activities, among them Mikołaj Kopernik (Copernicus). The Prussian General met alternately at Malbork, usually in May, and in Grudziądz in September. Its sessions dealt with law enforcement, tax matters, and after 1569, the election of Deputies to the national Seym of Poland. The vexing question of the size of that representation will be discussed elsewhere; here let it suffice to say that for a long time the size was left to the discretion of the Prussian General.

TABLE 5 - MEETING PLACES OF GENERAL SEYMIKS OF THE PROVINCES

Period	Province	Place	Years*
	Prussia	Malbork	1531-1766
	(Pomerania)	Grudziądz	1515-1767
	Greater Poland	Koło	1506-1766
		Poznań	1513
Hereditary	Lesser Poland	Korczyn	1404-1712
Kingdom and the		Pińczów	1588
First Republic		Sandomierz	1519
	Masovia	Warsaw	1530-1699
	Ruthenia	Wisznia	1522-1732
	Lithuania	Wołkowysk	1576
		Słonim	1601-1793
Partitioned	Masovia	Warsaw	1806-1831
Poland**	Greater Poland	Poznań	1827-1845+
	Lesser Poland	Lwów	1861-1918
Second	Greater Poland	Poznań	1918
Republic++	Central Lith.	Wilno	1921-1922
	Silesia	Katowice	1920-1939

*The earliest and the latest year of session held.

**Although the legislatures of the Partition Period were only provincial assemblies, and thus equivalent to a General Seymik, each of them used the name Seym in its official title, as did the Seym of Silesia in the Second Republic.

+Continued to meet beyond that date, but with a decreased proportion of Poles in its composition, and compulsory Germanization.

++In addition, in the period 1920-1939, the palatinates of Poznań and Pomerania elected their own Seymiks, thus not quite qualifying for the designation of a General Seymik.

Fig. 7 - A view of a General Seymik held in a church; a painting by Jean Pierre Norblin (1745-1830).

Fig. 8 - Mikołaj Kopernik (1475-1543) better known as Copernicus, astronomer, administrator, economist, doctor of medicine. Served as monetary expert at the General Seymik of Grudziądz in 1522.

In the formative stage of constitutional development in Poland, one must include also the rise of representative institutions in the province of Masovia. And so, in the second half of the 1400s the Duchy of Masovia was still continuing a semi-independent existence, ruled by the cadet branch of the Polish Piast dynasty. Little indicated the prominence the province was to achieve in the coming centuries, and few people expected that provincial Warsaw would eclipse Cracow, long established as the capital of Poland. In parallel to the developments in the rest of Poland, Masovia was convening provincial Seyms since the second half of the 1400s to deal with the tax matters. The Seyms were convened frequently, often two or three times a year, and the institution existed as an independent legislature for about seventy years in all. The towns of Warsaw and Zakroczym vied for hosting the Seym, to an almost complete exclusion of other towns, as is shown in Table 6.

The Masovian Seym consisted of the Duke, his Council (Senate), and the Deputies from the lands constituting the Duchy. The Senate numbered about a dozen members, and there were about fifty Deputies, the number varying somewhat from year to year. The last session of the Seym of Masovia as an independent body took place in January and February of 1529 when Sigismund I of Poland officially, and with great ceremony, reunited Masovia with Poland on the death of the last Duke of Masovia. The Seym of Masovia continued its existence between 1529 and 1540 as a Supreme Court for the province and as a Commission for the codification of its laws. The fruit of these labors is known as the Codex of W. Prażmowski and J. Goryński. During the administration of Sigismund II Augustus, the General Seymik of Masovia took over from the now defunct Masovian Seym and sent 20 Deputies to the national Seym.

TABLE 6 - EARLY PROVINCIAL SEYMS HELD IN MASOVIA

Place **Years Held**

Warsaw 1456, '70, '82, '96, '98, '99, 1500, '01, '02, '03, '05, '06, '07, '08, '10, '11, '14, '15, '16, '17, '18, '19, '20, '22, '23, '24, '25, '26, '27, '28[*]

Zakroczym 1461, '62, '64, '65, '66, '68, '70, '71, 1503, '04, '07, '08, '09, '10, '11, '12, '16, '17, '19, '20, '24, '26

---

* Last session of the Masovian Seym was held in 1528 before the province was reincorporated into Poland. At that time seven senators from the province were added to the Senate and twenty Deputies to the national Seym.

TABLE 6 (CONTINUED)- EARLY PROVINCIAL SEYMS HELD IN MASOVIA

Place	Years Held
Czerwińsk	1471, '83
Raciąż	1472, '78
Błonie	1474
Ciechanów	1485
Płońsk	1485
Płock	1490
Wizna	1518

In the preceding century the rise of the system of representation in Poland exerted a powerful influence on Lithuania which, although governed by members of the same dynasty, nevertheless continued under a straight feudal political structure. At first, the Lithuanian delegation occasionally participated in joint Seyms with Poland. Then, in the early 1500s, under the prodding of their ruler, the Lithuanians and Ruthenians started to convene their own Seyms with the participation of their princes and court dignitaries. The first such meeting took place in 1528 in Wilno. Table 7 lists these early Lithuanian Seyms, as well as the few Seyms held jointly with Poland. In the following year (1529) the Lithuanian court law was codified. Supplemented and expanded in 1566 and 1588 it formed the basis of the Lithuanian Statute, used thereafter well into the nineteenth century.

TABLE 7 - LITHUANIAN SEYMS HELD BEFORE THE UNION OF LUBLIN

Joint Polish-Lithuanian Seyms		After Inclusion of Deputies	
1448	Lublin	1566	Lithuanian Brześć
1453	Parczów	1566-7	Grodno
1564	Warsaw	1568	Grodno
1569	Lublin	1569	Lithuanian Brześć

An important step in Lithuanian constitutional development took place in 1566, when the participation of the *boyars* (Lithuanian and Ruthenian gentry) in the Seyms was assured through the stipulation that the County Seymiks should convene and elect two Deputies each to the Lithuanian Seym, much on the model of the Seym of Poland. Thus, when the Lithuanian Seym met in Brześć to debate the question of a political union with Poland, the representative character of that Seym had a much broader base. In the same year and at the same time, the Seym of Poland met in Lublin, some 75 miles away, and the negotiations between the two Seyms on the subject of the union started, and led to fruition, as described later.

The importance and the area of competence of the General Seymiks waxed and waned in reverse proportion to the importance of the national Seym. As the latter extended its field of action, the General Seymiks declined in importance, becoming towards the end of life of the First Republic mere stopping places for Deputies on their way to the national Seym. In fact, when some Deputies were late in arriving at the sessions of the General Seymiks, those present often adjourned and had the session reconvene in Warsaw, in one of the city's monasteries. Thus the sessions of the provincial General Seymiks often turned into provincial caucuses of the national Seym.

The history of Seyms continued in the period of Partitions, when the General Seymiks revived and came into their own as provincial legislatures. In fact, they revived the name Seym as soon as the electorate succeeded in gaining from the partitioning power the appropriate recognition. Usually, this took the form of a royal decree that served as a provincial Constitution. Thus, the General Seymiks, supported by the county Seymiks, continued to exist in that period as the provincial Seyms of Warsaw (1808-1812) for Greater Poland and Masovia under Napoleon's protectorate, the Seym of Warsaw (1815-1830) for Masovia and part of Lesser Poland under Russian suzerainty, the Seym of Poznań (1827-1851) for Greater Poland under Prussian suzerainty, and the Seym of Lwów (1861-1914) for Lesser Poland (Galicia) under Austrian suzerainty. The county Seymiks continued as the electoral machinery for electing the Deputies of the gentry to each of the first three of these Seyms. The Seymiks were, however, supplemented by a separate electoral machinery for election of Deputies from other segments of society.

THE EARLY SEYMS AND THE LAWS THEY MADE

Close to the border between the provinces of Greater and Lesser Poland, about half-way between the cities of Poznań and Cracow, there sits a small town called Piotrków (Peter's Town) which can truly be considered the cradle of Polish parliamentarism. At a time when both Greater Poland and Lesser Poland were vying for political leadership, and the country was in the process of reunification after earlier dynastic subdivisions, Piotrków was chosen as a compromise site for joint meetings of the delegations from the two provinces. Once selected, it served as a meeting place of the Seyms for the rest of the period of hereditary monarchy. At first, these meetings were held only between the barons and the prelates; in 1468 they were joined by Deputies elected by the counties and lands of Greater and Lesser Poland, and a unicameral parliament emerged. In 1493, during a Seym held in Piotrków, the elected Deputies decided to meet in a chamber separate from that in which the barons and the prelates sat under the King's chairmanship. This date is conventionally taken as the start of national representative institutions in Poland. It was a culmination of a long formative period during which the institution matured.

From the first appearance of elected Deputies in Piotrków in 1468 until the separation of the two chambers, 9 Seyms were held as shown in Table 8, followed by 38 Seyms of the bicameral legislature. What started as ad hoc meetings of representatives of the Seymiks of counties and lands to consider specific issues, became in time a regular, periodic meeting of the Seym for the review and legislation dealing with the current issues.

TABLE 8 - EARLY UNICAMERAL SEYMS HELD IN PIOTRKÓW

Year	Business Transacted
1468	First time elected Deputies join barons and prelates
1469	Bohemian delegation offers the crown to Prince Ladislaus
1470	Approval for tax levy requested
1472	Approval for tax levy requested
1473	Approval for tax levy requested
1474	Approval for tax levy requested, war with Mathias Corvin declared
1478	Final pacification of Prussia debated, ratification of Peace of Toruń by Pope Sixtus IV demanded
1492	John Albert declared King of Poland
1493	Deputies meet separately for the first time; the bicameral Seym emerges

In the early history of the Seyms there was no set time span prescribed between the elections to the successive Seyms, but the frequency with which they were called kept increasing during the Renaissance and the Reformation period and finally peaked at one, and occasionally two Seyms a year. Here, it is interesting to compare the frequency of parliamentary elections in Poland, England and France. In the period corresponding to the reign of Henry VIII of England (1509-1547), no less than 41 Seyms were returned in Poland but only 9 parliaments in England, with 8 sessions held by the one elected in 1529. The Estates General of France was dormant between 1484 and 1561, and thereafter met only in 1576-77, 1588-89, and 1593. In later years it did not meet at all between 1614 and 1789. By comparison, the Seym of that period was a virtual beehive of activity, with 96 Seyms returned during the 100 years that elapsed between its first session as a bicameral body in 1493 and 1593. Eventually, the frequency of Seym elections decreased and stabilized at once every two years with an occasional extraordinary Seym held out of sequence.

Although the organization and the operating procedures of the Seym developed over centuries, and as such varied somewhat with time, certain features persisted throughout its history and applied equally well to the period of hereditary monarchy and to the First Republic. The feature that did change drastically was the language of parliamentarism. Throughout the fifteenth and early sixteenth centuries extensive use was made of Latin, both as the language of debates and of the laws passed. The Renaissance and Reformation brought with them demands for use of the vernacular in transacting the business of the Seym. The introduction of Polish was gradual and Latin terminology remained in use for a long time.

The standard operating procedures were as follows: once the Deputies were gathered at the appointed time and place, the business of the Seym started with the verification of mandates of Deputies (Rugi) and the election of the Speaker from among the Deputies. The usual practice was to elect a new Speaker for each Seym, although the same person could be chosen more than once. Since much depended on the Speaker's skill in getting legislation passed by the Seym, the importance of choosing the right individual for this position cannot be overstressed. The Speaker thus elected was duly sworn in, promising to uphold the laws and enforce the rules of procedure; as a sign of his office he was given a Speaker's staff to be used in a manner of a gavel: to stomp it on the floor to call the gathering to order.

The chronology of the Seyms, given in Appendix C, includes the names of all the Speakers who could be verified, but the names of some of the earliest Speakers were not recorded. In addition, the biographic sketches of the more outstanding Speakers of the Seym of this period are given at the end of this chapter. Politicians, administrators, soldiers and even poets have at one time or another held this highly esteemed position during the 500 years of parliamentary history of Poland.

Throughout this period of legislative history of Poland, the King chaired the sessions of the Senate and acted as a mediator between the opposing factions in the Seym. Generally, a majority vote decided the choice of the Speaker and the validity of the mandates of the Deputies. In the sixteenth century the Speaker of the Seym presented to the King both the resolutions of the majority and the dissenting resolutions of the opposition, including the reasons for the dissent. The King either confirmed the resolutions of the majority and by his sanction transformed them into law, or agreed with the minority and denied his sanction on a case-by-case basis.

Considerable uncertainty surrounds the voting procedures of the early Seyms. The written rules for voting were specified only in the 1700s while prior to that, a familiarity with customary procedures was taken for granted. Apparently, at a time when the principle of representation was still evolving amidst demands from the voters for direct participation in all-country gatherings, the chief worry of the Deputies and the Executive alike was the acceptance by the electorate at large of the laws made by the Seym. Thus, the fact of the law's passage, rather than the controversy surrounding its passage were emphasized, accounting perhaps, for the scarcity of voting records. The existence of the Debriefing Seymiks*, at which the Deputies returning from the Seym had to give account of their legislative activities, encouraged the Deputies to hide behind a facade of general agreement reported from the Seym, and thus place the odium for rejecting any legislation on the home Seymik rather than assume it themselves. Because of the above considerations, the most that we know about the early laws is the fact of their passage in the absence of active opposition, as conveyed by the phrase sometimes recorded: *nemine contradicente* (none objecting). We do not know how many of the Deputies were for it, against it, or abstaining. On this basis it is impossible to state whether the law was passed unanimously or not. Unanimity implies an active decision, consent implies the absence of active opposition. This semantic distinction is important for it is known from indirect sources that many Seyms overrode opposition in passing the laws. We know, for instance, that in 1553 the propositions from the throne were opposed by 15 Deputies, yet the legislation embodying their gist was passed by the Seym.

The internal working of the Seym, the political disputes that took place there, the clashes of personalities and struggles between different interests, were for the most part recorded in the Diaries of Seym Sessions (Diariusze Seymowe). Although well into the late 1700s the debates of the Seym and the speeches on the floor were not recorded officially, private records of sessions, often in several parallel versions, exist in abundance. There were always enough Deputies anxious to retain notes on the debates for use at the subsequent debriefing sessions of the Seymiks in their home districts, foreign ambassadors who, as observers of the Seym sessions, collected notes for dispatches to their respective governments, or just plain politically motivated natives who recorded the proceedings. These chronological day-by-day records of the parliamentary transactions often incorporate copies of complete speeches, obtained by the observers from the Deputies or Senators who made them on the floor of the two chambers. The bulk of these diaries of debates survives until the present day in manuscript form, scattered in libraries throughout Poland and the neighboring countries. In fact, the late Professor Władysław Konopczyński traced the whereabouts of 900 of these Seym Diaries, covering the period 1548-1793, while Henryk Olszewski located another 630. This large mass of material, covering most of the 245 Seyms of the Hereditary Monarchy and the First Republic, still awaits the attention of future historians, since barely five percent of it, or about 60 diaries, have been published so far (see the bibliography).

---

* The debriefing sessions were similar in concept to the workshops held by the present-day U.S. Congressmen in their electoral districts but differed from them in being statutory rather than voluntary. This advanced feature of the parliamentary system of Poland was unique at the time.

As could be expected, the distribution of these diaries over the time is uneven, the most recent times being the best documented, but in this, of course, the diaries share the character of other historical records.

In the latter part of the hereditary monarchy, the royal charters began to be replaced in an ever-widening area by the constitutions passed by the Seym. These were of basically three types: permanent laws (constytucje wieczyste), the laws valid for a fixed period of time (constytucje czasowe) and, finally, the tax laws (universały poborowe). In time it became a constitutional practice to require a reconfirmation by each new King of those permanent laws which related to constitutional matters or the Bill of Rights. The reconfirmed laws were referred to as the Cardinal Laws (Prawa Kardynalne). In their totality they made up the Constitution.

Fig. 9 - A title page of a set of laws (constitutions) passed by the Seym of 1649 during the administration of John Casimir Vasa, and printed by Piotr Elert of Warsaw.

The laws were hand-written initially in Latin on parchment and published as separate acts until the second half of the sixteenth century. Thereafter, it became customary to publish all of the laws passed by a given Seym (with the exception of tax laws) as a set, issued in the name of the King with the approval of the Seym and the Senate. Starting in 1543, constitutions were written in Polish, in response to the general trend of the Reformation times, and from 1576 onwards they were printed, at first by Mikołaj Szarffenberger, then by A. Łazarz until

1606. Later printers to the Seym were Andrzej Piotrkowczyk, Sr. until 1619, and his son Andrzej Piotrkowczyk, Jr. until 1623. Their printing shop was located in Cracow. With the transfer of the capital from Cracow to Warsaw during the administration of Sigismund III Vasa, the constitutions continued to be sent to Cracow after the last session of each Seym, printed there, and returned to Warsaw. Travel time of seven days each way added to the delay, making the correction of proofs impractical. The King, therefore, transferred the title of the official printer to the Seym to Jan Rossowski of Warsaw in 1624. He was followed in this position by Piotr Elert in 1643.

Fig. 10 - *A title page of a tax law (uniwersał poborowy) passed by the Seym of 1603 in the administration of Sigismund III Vasa.*

The constitutions, after being sealed with the Great Seal of the Realm and signed by the Speaker of the Seym and the Chancellor of the Realm, were sent to each palatinate to be entered into the law books of each land. Additional copies, but without the seal and the signature, were sold to the general public. The price was 1 florin 13 gr. in 1613 and the sum was pocketed by the printers, leading to the charge that an unfair profit was being reaped, since the cost of the original printing was paid for by the Treasury. The tax resolutions were published under a separate cover. During the interregna the legislation assumed the form of resolutions of the General Confederation, but did not become law until after they were approved by the new King. In the course of time, the Debriefing Seymiks started to demand that the Deputies returning from the national Seym bring with them the printed version of the constitutions passed. This put additional pressure on the printers to speed up the publication, causing occasional printing errors and subsequent complaints. If the printed constitutions or authenticated hand-written copies were not brought back by the returning Deputies, and the legislation required new taxes, tax collection was withheld by the Seymiks until the constitutions were produced and the electorate was satisfied as to the validity of the reasons for which the taxes were imposed.

One of the perennial problems facing the Seym was the question of apportionment of seats in the House, particularly if new provinces were added to the representation through the reunification with the provinces formerly lost, or addition of new provinces through political union. Such was the case with Pomerania-Prussia, Masovia, and finally Lithuania with the Baltic provinces. Each case was treated slightly differently and so deserves a description. In the absence of good population statistics other than the data from an occasional poll tax, the rule adopted and promulgated into law in 1520 was that the Seymiks in each palatinate would elect and send to the Seym no more than six Deputies. The apportionment of representation to the three palatinates of Royal Prussia (Pomerania, Malbork and Chełmno) did not follow the usual rule at all. The Act of Incorporation of Prussia with Poland did not specify the size of the Seym representation for Prussia, but left it to the discretion of the General Seymik of Prussia. It in turn took a generous view of the situation and sent often so many Deputies as to account at times for nearly half of the Seym attendance, particularly on occasions when the General Seymiks of Greater or Lesser Poland could not agree on some legislative proposals and failed to send Deputies. The situation was completely reversed in the early 1700s. Unable to arrive at a consensus over the issue of recall of Augustus II Wettin for a second term of office, the General Seymiks of Prussia held between 1712 and 1730 disbanded without agreeing to send Deputies to the Seym, even though the Senators from Prussia continued to attend the sessions. Finally, in the 1768 activist Seym, a resolution was passed setting the Prussian representation at 40 Deputies. This high apportionment gave the three Prussian palatinates more than twice their statutory quota of 18 and took cognizance of the great economic importance of the province to the Commonwealth. The towns of Prussia formed the most prosperous part of the country. They contained the main sea ports and the commercial turnover of the city of Gdańsk at times equalled the total budget of the Commonwealth. In 1773, when most of Prussia, with the exception of Gdańsk and Toruń, were lost in the First Partition, all the Senators from the lost palatinates continued to sit in the Senate and their vacancies were reappointed by the King from among the residents of these provinces until 1793.

When Masovia was reunited with Poland in 1528 it entered the Seym as one palatinate but was given a Seym representation of 20 Deputies, which was about half the number of the Deputies formerly elected to the Masovian Seym sitting in Warsaw, but still over three times the number of Deputies normally assigned per palatinate. The dense population of this province, with a large percentage of small gentry in the yeomanry class, justified this decision.

The Act of the Union of Poland and Lithuania signed at a Seym in Lublin in 1569 provided for the formation of a joint Seym. It was decided to apportion the seats in it roughly in proportion to the population of Poland and Lithuania and to disregard the relative geographical size (Lithuania was much larger than Poland at the time). The rule adopted was that the united Commonwealth will be treated as consisting of three major parts: Greater Poland, Lesser Poland and Lithuania, a scheme in which Pomerania-Prussia and Masovia were lumped with Greater Poland, whereas Ruthenia, Volynia and Podolia with Lesser Poland. The Speaker of the Seym was to be elected in turn from among the residents of the three parts, and every third Seym was to be held in Grodno in Lithuania. The ratio of population of Poland and Lithuania generally stood at 2 to 1, and the number of Deputies in the Seym was 110 and 48, respectively (1569). The population imbalance was due primarily to the constant exposure of the North-East frontier to Muscovite incursions, and the South-East frontier to Tartar and later Turkish raids. The area ravaged by wars had difficulty in attracting and holding settled populations.

Table 9 summarizes the numerical strength of the two Houses of Legislature of Poland throughout their history.

TABLE 9—MEMBERSHIP OF LEGISLATURES OF POLAND

Body Politic	Period ++	Number of Senat.	Number of Deput.	Term* (yrs)
Hered. Monarchy (Kingdom of Poland)	1493-1504	81	54	**
	1553-1565	95	92	
First Republic (Commonwealth of Poland and Lithuania)	1598-1633	149	168+	***
	1764-1768	153	236	
	1788-1792	157	181	2
Duchy of Warsaw	1807-1809	18	100	9
	1810-1815	30	166	
Congress Kingdom of Poland	1815-1831	44	128	6
Grand Duchy of Poznań	1827-1848	—	50	6
Kingdom of Galicia, Lodomeria	1861-1907	—	150	6
	1908-1918	—	162	5

TABLE 9 (CONTINUED)—MEMBERSHIP OF LEGISLATURES OF POLAND

Body Politic	Period ++	Number of Senat.	Deput.	Term* (yrs)
Second Republic	1921-1934	111	444	5
	1935-1939	96	208	
Polish People's Republic	1947-1951	—	444	4
	1952-1963	—	425	
	1964-1989	—	460	
Third Republic	1989-	100	460	4

*Term of office of Deputies
**Three Months
***Four Months
++Details of intermediate changes were left out for clarity
+Average, dependent on the size of Prussian delegation.

SEYMS DEMAND "EXECUTION OF THE LAWS"

The rise of the Reformation in Poland coincided in time with the coming of age of the parliamentary system. The period was characterized by vigorous religious and political debates as well as by the appearance of the first printed political tracts attempting to influence the voters. Among political writers the leadership unquestionably belonged to Andrzej Frycz Modrzewski, the author of the book: *On the Improvement of the Republic*. Published in 1554, it constituted the guide book for the reform movement in the parliamentary field, whereas the writings of Jan Łaski provided the inspiration for the religious reform movement on the Protestant side of the religious issue and were ably parred on the Catholic side by those of Jakub Uchański.

The recurring political theme of many Seyms in the forty year period between 1537 and 1578 was the dissatisfaction with the way in which laws made by the Seym were enforced by the executive. The kings did not quite believe that they had to carry out each resolution of the Seym, and the Seym was still learning how to flex its muscle. Eventually, the Seym developed its own leadership and political movement. The aims of the movement were to improve the legal and administrative structure of the state, reduce the influence of the Roman Catholic Church on the conduct of secular affairs, and replace the aristocracy with the middle gentry in the political machinery of the state. The movement had a particularly large Protestant participation. Of its leaders the most prominent was Mikołaj Sienicki, a Deputy for Chełm and a member of the Arian Protestant

Church. Elected Speaker of the Seym no less than nine times, he set an all-time record. He was ably assisted by Hieronim Ossoliński and Jan Ostroróg. The membership of the Seym at the time (Table 10) was nearly one-third Protestant, and the Seym representation of some palatinates, such as that of Cracow in 1556-1557 and Sandomierz in 1565, was totally Protestant. Many of the supporters of the movement in the Seym, led by Mikołaj Rey, favored establishing a National Church of Poland, independent of the See of Rome. The movement went through several phases and left a rich legislative legacy.

Fig. 11 (Left)—Title page of the political treatise Commentariorum de Republica emendanda *written in 1554 by Andrzej Frycz Modrzewski (1503-1572), the chief thinker of the reform movement of the period.*

Fig. 12 (Right)—Mikołaj Rey (1505-1569), Deputy in the Seyms of 1543-1564 and an activist in the movement for the 'execution of laws.' Prolific writer and poet.

The first phase stemmed from a conflict of the legislative with the executive branch over the crowning of Sigismund Augustus during the life of his father, Sigismund I (the Older), without the consent of the Seym. A civil war threatened in 1537 by the gentry, mobilized as if for war. This military exercise, termed "Hen's War" (Wojna Kokosza), terminated in negotiations between the electorate and the executive. A compromise was reached at the Seym of Piotrków in 1538, and firmed up at the Seym of Cracow in 1538-9. At these Seyms Sigismund I made a commitment to enforce the laws made by the Seym, to publish no laws without the consent of the Seym, and to legalize the attendance by all gentry at every subsequent election.

TABLE 10–PROTESTANT DEPUTIES IN THE SEYM OF "THE EXECUTION OF LAWS" ERA

YEARS	1553	1556-7	1565	1569	1572
PROVINCE OF MASOVIA					
Palatinate of					
Płock	0	0	0	0	1
Masovia	0	1	1	2	1
Rawa	1	0	0	0	1
PROVINCE OF GREATER POLAND					
Palatinate of					
Poznań, Kalisz	11	8	7	9	9
Sieradz, Wieluń	1	3	3	3	3
Łęczyca	1	1	1	0	0
Brześć Kujawski	2	2	2	1	2
Inowrocław	0	2	0	2	1
Dobrzyń Land	1	1	0	1	0
PROVINCE OF LESSER POLAND					
Palatinate of					
Cracow	2	6	5	5	5
Sandomierz	5	4	6	3	4
Lublin	3	3	3	3	2
PROVINCE OF RUTHENIA					
Palatinate of					
Ruthenia, Chełm	1	4	2	2	5
Bełzec	0	1	0	1	0
Podole	1	0	0	0	0
Total Protestants*	29	36	30	32	34
Total Deputies**	92	92	92	93	93

* Mostly Lutherans, Calvinists and Arians (Polish Brethren).

** Poland only. Does not include Lithuanian Deputies added after 1569.

Note. The religious affiliation of Deputies was assigned either on the basis of Deputy's own profession or deduced from his attendance at one of the Protestant Synods.

During the second phase of the movement (1552-1575) the gentry saw the successful implementation of many of its postulates. These included the return to the state of Crown lands, put up earlier as collateral to private lenders for state debts incurred during national emergencies. The recovery of this real estate was tied to the reorganization of the Treasury and the Army, since the lands owned by the Crown supplied the revenue needed to support the Army. The Seyms of 1562-3 and 1563-4 carried out an examination of the titles of ownership of the lands in question and saw to their return to the Crown. A reform of the tax system followed. Other important achievements of this period concerned changes in the territorial structure of the country: incorporation of Duchies of Oświęcim and Zator (1564), incorporation of Courland, Livonia (Latvia) (1561), the reduction of autonomy of Royal Prussia, the transfer of Podlasia and the Ukraine from Lithuanian to Polish suzerainty, and finally the replacement of the personal union of Poland and Lithuania by a political one and the establishment of a joint Seym (1569).

The act of Union between Poland and Lithuania, concluded in 1569 at Lublin, is one of the most important constitutional documents of the era. It replaced the earlier Acts of Union of Krewo (1386), Horodło (1413), and Mielnik (1501) by which a personal union between the two countries was formed. Although sponsored by Sigismund Augustus, the King of Poland and Grand Duke of Lithuania, the Act was actually concluded between the two Seyms. As such, it bears comparison to the Union of Utrecht of 1570 by which United Netherlands were formed, the Union between England and Scotland concluded between the two respective parliaments in 1717 and, finally, the American Articles of Confederation. Compared to the American Articles of Confederation, the Union of Lublin provided for a stronger bond, but the American Constitution of 1789 bettered the Union, only to be matched again by the Polish Constitution of 1791.

The key articles of the Act of Union, concluded between the members of the Polish and the Lithuanian Seyms in Lublin in 1569 read in part as follows:

We, Lords Spiritual and Temporal, and elected Deputies of the provinces of the Polish Crown, together with the Council of Lords and elected Deputies and other estates of the Grand Duchy of Lithuania, at this General Seym of Lublin declare

That the Polish Kingdom and the Grand Duchy of Lithuania are one inseparable and united Commonwealth, which came about out of two states and nations merged into one.

That this twofold nation for eternal times is to be governed by one head, one lord and one common king, elected by common votes of the Poles and Lithuanians, the place of election being in Poland.

That agreements and covenants with foreign nations should not be planned nor concluded, nor should any ambassadors be sent to foreign countries for important matters, otherwise than with the knowledge and common counsel of both nations.

That the currency will be common both in Poland and Lithuania. That a Pole in Lithuania as well as a Lithuanian in Poland might always, on the basis of every just means, acquire property and possess it according to the law by which the property is governed.

That in all adversities, we, prelates, councils, barons and all estates, are to help one another, with all our strength and ability, when the common Council deems it in our interest and need, considering our successes and misfortunes as common, and assisting each other loyally.

That from the present time onwards His Majesty will not summon any separate Seyms of the Crown or of Lithuania, but will always summon common Seyms for this twofold nation.

And that all these matters here resolved and guaranteed are never to be shaken or changed through the ages

And for better testimony of the matters above described and for its eternal memorial, we, sworn Lords of the Council, Spiritual and Temporal, and the elected Deputies of the provinces put our seals on this document at this general and common Seym of Lublin. Written and issued at this common Seym of Lublin on the first of July in the year of the Lord 1569.

Among other problems tackled by the Seyms of the "Execution of Laws" movement was the question of the freedom of conscience, since the burning issue of the day was the rise of antagonism between the Catholics and the Protestants and the attempts to avert the outbreak of religious wars. Events in England, France, and Germany were being followed with keen interest, and a movement of reconciliation, with attempts to convoke a joint Catholic-Protestant Synod, was being sponsored by Jakub Uchański, the senior Senator and the Primate of Poland. During the interregnum, which followed the death of Sigismund Augustus in 1572, Uchański assumed the office of King-pro-tempore and oversaw the Confederation of Warsaw. The Protestant and Catholic Deputies participating in it pledged themselves to refrain from imposing on anyone religious beliefs not of his choice. The Act of this Confederation became one of the Cardinal Laws of the country and the cornerstone of religious tolerance for all denominations in Poland.

Fig. 13 - Jan Herburt (1508-1577) Deputy to the Seyms of 1553, 1556-7 and 1562-3. Appointed by the Seym to edit a compendium of laws, which subsequently was in use by the courts for over 200 years.

The final achievement of the movement for the execution of the laws was the establishment of independent Judiciary in the form of Supreme Court (Trybunał Koronny) for Poland with elective judges, instituted by a constitution of 1578, and the efforts at codification of laws. Among individuals prominent in this field were Senator Jan Łaski and Deputy Jan Herburt. The compendia of laws they produced in 1506 and 1563, respectively, were somewhat later supplemented by those prepared by Stanisław Sarnicki (1594) and Stanisław Skrzyszowski (1597). To the same period belong the final acceptance of the principle of truly elective kingship and the onset of the First Republic.

As the end of this period brought an era to a close, it is appropriate to summarize its achievements. The Seyms of this period asserted their claim to the right of passing on the choice of the ruler after the death of the incumbent; they secured the establishment of a judicature independent of the executive branch, and made progress towards the assurance that the laws they enact will be enforced.

The constitutional arrangements of the country at that time are condensed in Table 11, the last hereditary kings are listed in Table 12, the Speakers of the Seym in Table 13, and the principal legislation of the period in Table 14. The biographies of the more notable political personalitites in the Seyms of this era close this chapter.

TABLE 11—CONSTITUTIONAL ARRANGEMENTS
HEREDITARY MONARCHY

(Charters of Koszyce 1374, Czerwińsk 1422, Jedlna 1433, and the Seym constitution of Radom 1505)

The Executive Branch of Government was headed by a king chosen from the hereditary ruling house and confirmed by the Seym before receiving the kingship for life. The king appointed five ministers: the chancellor (foreign affairs), vice-chancellor, crown marshal (justice), court marshal, treasurer, as well as lower officials and the commanders of the army. He also appointed bishops from candidates selected by the cathedral chapters who were then confirmed by the Pope.

The Legislative Branch of Government consisted of the king, the Senate with appointed membership, and the Seym with elected membership. The king appointed the bishops, the palatines and the castellans to the Senate, convoked the Seym and had the legislative initiative. His approval was mandatory on all constitutions passed by the Seym and his administration enforced them. The voting in the Seym was by majority rule. Imposition of taxes over and above a statutory fixed land tax and the passage of new laws required the consent of the Seym.

Electoral Ordinance: A Writ of Summons requested all counties to elect two knights from each county and two representatives from each city summoned, to serve as Deputies. In the counties, male members of the gentry had the vote, while in the towns the property-owning burghers on city rolls could vote for the Council, which then elected the representatives.

The Judicial Branch of Government consisted of judges appointed by the king who applied laws as codified for each major province. The king had a right of pardon. In addition, common law was applicable in some areas of jurisdiction. The courts were established for each land and town or city and held sessions usually three or four times a year.

Bills of Rights were contained in a series of privileges granted by the kings to the bishops, barons*, the knighthood and the cities. The rights granted to the gentry included guarantees against arbitrary confiscation of property, arbitrary arrest, or assignment of offices to non-natives.

---

* The term "baron" appearing in Latin documents in Poland at this time refers to high administrative officials appointed by the prince, and not to a hereditary order of nobility.

TABLE 12 — HEREDITARY KINGS CONFIRMED+ BY THE SEYM

Kings of the Jagiellonian Dynasty	Term of Office
John I Albert	1492-1501
Alexander	1501-1506
Sigismund I	1506-1548
Sigismund II Augustus++	1548-1572

+These Confirmation Seyms took place in Piotrków and were formally called Election Seyms although there was only one candidate at each. The Coronation Seyms of 1502, 1507, and 1530 all took place at Cracow.

++Confirmed in succession in 1529, 18 years before actually assuming power.

TABLE 13 —SEYM SPEAKERS IN THE PERIOD OF HEREDITARY MONARCHY

Speaker+	Seym of
Jan Sierakowski	1548
Mikołaj Sienicki (first term)	1550
Rafał Leszczyński	1552
Mikołaj Sienicki (second term)	1553, '55, '56-7, '58-9
Rafał Leszczyński	1562-3
Mikołaj Sienicki (third term)	1563-4,'64,'65
Stanisław S. Czarnkowski	1569
Stanisław Szafraniec	1570
Mikołaj Grzybowski	1572

+Prior to 1548 the office of the Speaker of Seym was still in the formative stage and the names of the Deputies who presided are not known at present, possibly they were never recorded.

TABLE 14—PRINCIPAL LEGISLATION OF SEYMS OF HEREDITARY MONARCHY

1494	Incorporation of Duchy of Zator and Oświęcim ratified; Laws of Prussia confirmed
1496	Burghers barred from purchase of land outside of cities; Goods imported by gentry for home use freed of customs duty
1501	Union of Mielnik with Lithuania ratified; Election ordinance established
1504	King's dispositon of royal demesnes limited
1505	Nihil Novi—Seym's approval of new laws required; Gentry barred from engaging in city commerce; Jewish privileges confirmed
1506	Articles of War codified

TABLE 14 (CONTINUED)—PRINCIPAL LEGISLATION OF SEYMS OF HEREDITARY MONARCHY

1509	Internal tolls replaced by border customs duty
1517	Statute on Mining ratified
1520	Obligations of serfs spelled out; Electoral functions of Seymiks codified
1521	Prussian Code of Law confirmed
1524	Instructions for tax collection revised
1525	Courts established for the mining industry
1526	Incorporation of Masovia ratified
1532	Penalties for runaway serfs specified
1538	Burghers barred from purchase of lands outside of cities
1540	Electoral apportionment revised
1544	Ordinance for courts codified
1550	Gentry barred from engaging in city trade
1552	Resolutions against heresy passed
1553	Ordinance for Impeachment Tribunals of the Seym established
1556	Ecclesiastical Jurisdiction constrained
1558	Post Office established
1561	Royal demesnes' income earmarked for defense
1562	Crown property recovered from private hands
1565	Native merchants barred from foreign trade; Price control law and export limitations set
1569	Union of Lublin with Lithuania ratified; Burghers of Wilno gain Seym representation, land property rights

POLITICAL PERSONALITIES IN SEYMS OF THE HEREDITARY KINGDOM

Jan Firley (1521-74)—Elected deputy to the Seym in 1553, he was appointed Great Marshal of the Crown in 1563 and palatine of Cracow in 1572; supporter of the Calvinist Reformed Church, he opposed the new "execution of laws" movement which endangered his financial position. He supported the incorporation of Royal Prussia and the Union with Lithuania at the Seym of 1569 in Lublin, which concluded the Union. Served as the Speaker of the Seym of 1573 during which the Confederation of Warsaw was signed guaranteeing religious tolerance.

Andrzej Firley (1537-85)—Participated in the 1563-64 war with Muscovy. He was a leader of the gentry of Lesser Poland during the Royal Election of 1572 and 1575 and was the Speaker of the Seym of 1576. During the election of the king in 1575 he initially headed the anti-Senatorial faction of the gentry and supported a Polish candidate for chief executive but later switched his support to Stephen Bathory, the Hungarian candidate. In politics he represented the anti-Habsburg faction. In 1577 he took part in the expedition against the city of Gdańsk when the city persisted in supporting Maximilian II of Austria, the unsuccessful candidate for the kingship of Poland.

Jan Herburt (1508-1577)—Educated at Louvain and Bologna, in 1551 he became a secretary to King Sigismund Augustus. Elected Deputy to the Seyms of 1553, 1556-7 and 1562-3, he was entrusted with the codification of laws. The law compendium that he produced was in continuous use for two hundred years in the courts. Appointed Chamberlain of Przemyśl, and then castellan of Sanok, he took part in 1573 in the parliamentary delegation sent to France to escort the first elected King of Poland, Henri Valois. During the administration of Stephen Bathory he served as ambassador to Sweden in 1576. His publications include: *Statuta Regni Poloniae* (1563), *Locorum de fide communium latino-polonorum* (1569), *Chronica sive Historiae Polonicae compendiosa* (1571).

Łukasz Górnicki (1527-1603)—Born into a prosperous burgher family and given a liberal education which included studies at the University of Padua, he served from 1559 as the secretary and librarian to King Sigismund Augustus and was knighted in 1561. He wrote extensively, both original works and translations from Latin and Italian. The translations included Seneca's *Troas* (1589), and *Polish Courtier* (1566) which was an adaptation of B. Castiglione's *Cortegiano*. Later, he authored *A Discourse Between a Pole and an Italian* in which he severely criticized excessive political claims of the gentry. He also wrote a chronicle of the period 1538-1573, *Annals of Polish Crown* (1637), and *Writings* Vol. 1-2 (1961).

Wawrzyniec Grzymała Goślicki (1533-1607)—Educated at the Universities of Cracow and Bologna where he received a doctorate in civil and canon law. During his stay in Italy he wrote *De Optimo Senatore*, a treatise on constitutional government and the political responsibility of princes, which gained him much acclaim at home and abroad. Having served in various ecclesiastical and administrative positions in Poland under Sigismund Augustus, Stephen Bathory and Sigismund III, he headed important embassies and missions at home and abroad, later served as Senator and eventually became Chancellor of Poland.

Mikołaj Kopernik (Copernicus) (1473-1543)—Studied at the Universities of Cracow and Bologna, he obtained a doctorate in canon law at the University of Ferrara in 1503. Between 1504-10 he was secretary and physician to the bishop of Warmia. In 1516-19 he administered the property of the Cathedral Chapter of Olsztyn; in 1520-21 he commanded the defense of the town against the forces of the German Order. Having served on a legislative committee for the reform of currency (1517-19), in 1519 he submitted an outline of his monetary proposals to the Seymik in Toruń and again at the General Seymik of Prussia in Grudziądz in 1522 and expanded his monetary proposals into a treatise, *Monetae cudende ratio* (1526). From 1510 onwards he conducted astronomical observations and circulated his manuscript on heliocentric theory *Commentariolus*. His main astronomical work *De revolutionibus Orbum Coelestium* was written in the period 1515-33 and published in the year he died, 1543, opening a new era in scientific thought.

Rafał Leszczyński (1526-1592)—In the period 1545-1550 he served as Senator Palatine of Kujawy. In 1550 he resigned his Senate seat to run for Deputy in the Seym, to which he was elected in 1552 (served as Speaker), 1555, 1558, 1562 (Speaker), 1563, 1566, 1569. He became one of the political leaders of the "execution of laws" movement in the Seym, where he supported Reformation and took the stand against the aristocracy and the Roman Catholic Church. He was also connected with the Czech Brethren Movement. He was reappointed to the Senate as Castellan of Śrem in 1580.

Andrzej Frycz Modrzewski (1503-1572)—Graduated from the University of Cracow in 1522. On return from his travels in Western Europe he became associated with the humanist Protestant group. In 1536 he was responsible for transporting to Poland the library of Erasmus of Rotterdam, purchased by Jan Łaski. Appointed secretary to Sigismund II Augustus in 1547, he served on many embassies abroad. From 1550 he devoted his time to writing, espousing the cause of Reformation. He became a bailiff of Wolborz in 1554. In his writings he attacked the statutory inequality of different social strata and the prohibition of land ownership for burghers, presenting these ideas in his

Commentariorum de Republica emendanda (1554), which made him the most influential social thinker of Renaissance Poland.

Jan Ostroróg (1436-1501)—Educated at the Universities of Erfurt and Bologna, in 1459 he received the title of Doctor of Both Laws. Appointed Commissioner for the incorporation of the Duchy of Płock into Poland in 1462, he later served as ambassador to the See of Rome in 1464 and 1466. Appointed Castellan of Międzyrzec in 1465 and Grand Treasurer of the Crown 1472-74; served as Castellan of Poznań from 1474 onwards, and Prefect General of Greater Poland in the years 1493-98. His political thinking followed the Hussite ideology and favored strong central government, separation of the Church from Rome and reform of laws. Later he authored a treatise on the necessity of reform of the institutions of state, *Monumentum pro Rei Publicae Ordinatione*, which was circulated in hand-written copies.

Mikołaj Rey (1505-1569)—After a youth spent under the humanist influence of the household of A. Tęczyński, he became the chief promoter of the use of the vernacular in writing in preference to Latin. He embraced Protestantism in 1541. Elected Deputy to the Seyms held in 1543, 1556-7, 1558-9 and 1564, he wrote political tracts in Polish supporting the legislative program of "execution of laws." His moralist writings dealt with the abuses in the Church. He authored *A Short Discourse Between the Squire, the Bailiff and the Parson* (1543), *A Self Portrait of the Life of an Honest Man* (1558), *Psalms of David* (1546) and many others.

Mikołaj Sienicki (1521-1582)—A renown orator, he was a political leader of the Protestant gentry in the Seym. One of the leaders of the "execution of laws" movement, Deputy to the Seym, and then Speaker of nine Seyms between 1550 and 1575. Initially connected with the moderate Protestant faction, later he joined the Arian Sect. Having supported the proposals for the establishment of a National Church, he took part in the preparation of the Confederation of Warsaw during which tolerance of all religious faiths was formulated as a cardinal law.

Jakub Uchański (1502-1581)—Served as Secretary to Queen Bona, Canon of Cracow and Referendary of the Crown in 1538. In 1551 he became Bishop of Przemyśl, in 1557 Bishop of Włocławek, from 1562 Archbishop of Gniezno and Primate of Poland. As senior Senator he served twice as the King-pro tempore (Interrex), 1572-73 and 1575. In the Seym he cooperated closely with the leaders of the movement for "the Execution of Laws," particularly with the group led by Frycz Modrzewski, favored the formation of a National Church, and made many attempts to reconcile the Catholic and the Protestant factions through the participation in a joint synod.

CHAPTER II

MONARCHY BECOMES THE FIRST REPUBLIC: KINGS ELECTED FOR LIFE

The death of the last male member of the Jagiellonian dynasty marked the beginning of the First Republic. The better part of the period covered here, 1573-1648, was devoted to the development of a truly elective chief executive office. The kings were now kings in name only and in fact became presidents of the Senate elected for life. The candidacy for the office became open to contenders from outside the ruling dynasty, and some 'commoners' later achieved that position. The royal election Seym operated with membership open to all adult members of the gentry who cared to attend. The rules of this direct election of chief executive included some novel features such as the 'pacta conventa' or the covenant between the ruler and the ruled. It constituted in effect a Bill of Rights, including the right to civil disobedience for citizens faced with an executive acting contrary to the Cardinal Laws of the country.

In 1572 Inquisition was banned in Poland, and from 1563 onwards the state ceased to execute sentences imposed by Church courts. During the same period the principle of religious tolerance became law and placed Poland in stark contrast to other European countries torn apart by religious strife. A judiciary system was set up with elective judges, independent of the executive branch, and courts of appeal were established for Poland and Lithuania. The Seyms were elected now on a regular two-year schedule.

In this period the institutions of Jewish self-government made their appearance and developed into a unique system of representation.

Fig. 14—Meeting places of the Seyms and of the General Seymiks in the First Republic, just after the Union of Lublin in 1569.

SEYMS CLAIM KING-MAKING POWERS

The king-making power of the Seym predates the first session of the bicameral national Seym held in 1493 in Piotrków, and the General Seymik of the province of Lesser Poland should properly be credited with it. This Seymik took the initiative of offering the crown of Poland to Louis of Hungary in 1370, on the death of Casimir the Great, the last male member of the main line of the princely House of Piast. Louis was Casimir's nephew. Thus a precedent was created that the crown is the Seymik's to offer to the candidate of its choice. After Louis of Hungary died without male issue in 1382, the Seymiks of Greater and Lesser Poland offered the crown to Jagiełło, the pagan prince of Lithuania, on the condition that he marry the granddaughter of Casimir and become a Christian. The young lady in question was 24 years his junior, and totally unenchanted by the prospect. Although this marriage left no surviving issue, the Jagiellonians eventually gave Poland seven kings and the Golden Age of Renaissance. Each of the successive members of that dynasty was required to obtain the explicit consent of the national Seym, by then already well established, before being crowned King of Poland. Thus, a pseudo-election was established in which the senior heir of the preceding king was confirmed by the Seym in a procedure which began to be referred to as the royal election. This historical period is commonly called 'the hereditary monarchy with elective legislature.' It ended with Sigismund II Augustus, the last male member of the House of Jagiełło. His death without issue in 1572 marked the beginning of the era of truly elective kings and the rise of the First Republic. At the same time a political union with Lithuania replaced the former dynastic link.

Inasmuch as the royal election of 1573 was the founding date of the First Republic, it is interesting to note how the event was viewed by the electors themselves. Such insight is provided by the text of the resolution passed by the Confederation of the palatinates of Sandomierz and Cracow on December 17, 1572. The resolution reads as follows:

We, the Senators of the Crown, spiritual and temporal, and the knighthood of the palatinates of Cracow and Sandomierz, having met in Wiślica on the thirteenth day of December, for the purpose of reviewing and providing for the needs of our Commonwealth on the occasion of this interregnum, recognize that on the death of our Sovereign it is fit and proper for us to consider our freedoms and liberties, perceiving the basis for them to be in the free election of our King and Lord.

Following the example of our ancestors, and regarding ourselves as their worthy descendants, we pledge ourselves by the good and honest word of knighthood, that we do not wish to depart in any detail from our ancestral custom of electing our Sovereign, as described in our statutes and privileges, which apply to all parts of the Realm equally. Collectively, not excluding any parts of the Realm, neither those belonging to it of old, nor those belonging to it now and so confirmed, we intend to proceed freely and jointly to elect our Sovereign, and also not to allow any part of the Realm, large or small, to separate, but to elect our Sovereign we promise and pledge.

We also strongly warn that, should any part of our Commonwealth want to break away, or separate, and elect a King or a Duke for itself, without consent of all electors, we shall not accept such one as our Sovereign, but will rise against him and his followers in accordance with honour, faith and conscience and persist until they perish or return to unity with us.

To mark our knightly pledge and confirmation, we have caused our seals to be affixed to this act for our own and our descendants' sake, and we have allowed the act so sealed to be entered into the city records.

Written in Wiślica on the 17th day of December, Anno Domini 1572.

The main concerns that emerge from this act are the unity of the Polish-Lithuanian Commonwealth, established in Lublin a mere three years before and the security of the civil rights. The warning, contained in the last paragraph of the resolution, explains why on the election day all electors turned up in full armour and mounted.

The actual royal election procedure always consisted of three consecutive Seyms, held a few months apart. They were the Convocation Seym, the Election Seym and the Coronation Seym. Table 15 gives the dates and places where these Seyms were held. The Convocation Seym was invariably called by the senior Senator, the Roman Catholic Primate of Poland and Archbishop of Gniezno, who by law assumed the duties of the King-pro-tempore on the death of the reigning monarch. As the death of a king, or his abdication, was considered a national emergency, the Convocation Seym and the Election Seym were commonly confederated. As such, the decisions made by these Seyms were made by majority vote, and gained the force of law after the election of the king, when approved by him. The Convocation Seym was attended by Deputies elected by the Seymik of each county in the usual manner. It sat in Warsaw and conducted all the preliminary business of the election such as fixing its date, establishing its rules, and reviewing the candidates. The most important part of its business, however, was the preparation of the Articles of Agreement (Pacta Conventa) constituting a Bill of Rights to be sworn to by the Elect. More will be said about them under another heading. The Election Seym followed the Convocation Seym by a few months and usually met at Wola, a small village on the outskirts of Warsaw. Its operating procedures were different from those of ordinary Seyms inasmuch as this was the only occasion when every vote-carrying male could attend a Seym. In consequence, a huge *al fresco* encampment resulted, much like the Mall rallies in Washington D.C. Although many attempts were made to limit the attendance to Deputies elected by the Seymiks for that purpose, they failed, as no power could bar the electorate from attending.

TABLE 15 —SEYMS OF THE INTERREGNUM PERIODS

Convocation Seym	Election Seym	Coronation Seym	King Elected
Jan. 1573 Warsaw	Apr. 1573 Warsaw (Kamion)	Feb. 1574 Cracow	Henry Valois+
Aug. 1574 Warsaw	Nov. 1575 Warsaw (Wola)	Mar. 1576 Cracow	Stephen Bathory
Feb. 1587 Warsaw	June 1587 Warsaw (Wola)	Dec. 1588 Cracow	Sigismund III Vasa (Maximilian Habsburg)*
June 1632 Warsaw	Sept. 1632 Warsaw (Wola)	Feb. 1633 Cracow	Ladislaus IV Vasa
July 1648 Warsaw	Oct. 1648 Warsaw	Jan. 1649 Cracow	John Casimir Vasa++
Nov. 1668 Warsaw	May 1669 Warsaw (Wola)	Oct. 1669 Cracow	Michał Korybut Wiśniowiecki
Jan. 1674 Warsaw	Apr. 1674 Warsaw (Wola)	Feb. 1676 Cracow	John III Sobieski
Aug. 1696 Warsaw	May 1697 Warsaw (Wola, Kamion)	Nov. 1697 Cracow	Augustus II Wettin
Apr. 1733 Warsaw	Aug. 1733 (Wola, Kamion)	Jan. 1734 Cracow	Stanisław Leszczyński (Augustus III Wettin)**
May 1764 Warsaw	Aug. 1764 Warsaw (Wola)	Dec. 1764 Warsaw	Stanisław August Poniatowski+++

+Abdicated to become Henri III of France

++Abdicated to enter a monastery

*Outcome unsuccessfully contested by force of arms by Maximilian Habsburg

**Outcome successfully contested by force of arms by Augustus III Wettin, who finally was crowned and assumed power

+++Abdicated on the Third Partition of Poland

Fig. 15—A view of the Royal Election Field at Wola near Warsaw in 1697 when Augustus II Wettin was elected King of Poland. In the First Republic each King was elected for life. A painting by Marco Alessandri (1664-1719).

After the Speaker of the Election Seym was elected, he was entrusted with police powers and supplied with a staff adequate to maintain order. Among his duties was the layout of the election field. This was a rectangular enclosure separated by a ditch and a fence from the rest of the grounds. A wooden shed was provided at one end to keep the rain off the paperwork and the senior members of the gathering. The rest of the company had to make do as best they could out in the open. The election proceedings took place inside the rectangle, with each palatinate represented by a ten-man delegation, and the delegation voting as a block in the initial proceedings, while the rest of the electors, arranged by palatinate and province, remained outside the stockade. In the mornings, the Senate and the palatinate delegtions received in turn the representatives of the various candidates and listened to their speeches extolling the virtues of their man and the advantages of electing him. In the afternoons the palatinate delegations conveyed all of this information to the voters remaining outside the election enclosure. When all candidates were presented and the closing speeches delivered, the voting would start. In the election of 1573 voting alone took four days. All delegations received several large sheets of paper, each sheet bearing the name of one candidate. Each voter was asked to affix his seal to the sheet with the name of his choice. The sheets were then duly collected in the election shed and the total votes added up.

The result was officially proclaimed by the Interrex. The smooth operation of this vast gathering depended much on interaction between the Senators and voters from each palatinate, since it fell to the Senators to provide the assessment of the candidates and guidance in the procedures.

Fig. 16—Bird's eye view of the Royal Election Field at Wola. The voters are shown mounted both inside and outside the enclosure. The shed on the lower foreground housed the Speaker and the election staff.

Although the attendance at the Election Seyms varied greatly, and was never accurately recorded, a crowd of as little as 10,000 or as many as 100,000 could be expected. The sheer mass of people, horses and carriages must have been overwhelming, and the task of keeping reasonable order among them must have taxed the abilities of the Speaker to the limit. Dust, flies, and horse manure added to the problems. To accommodate this crowd a tent city would be erected outside the confines of the Election Field.

Candidates in the election were barred from Warsaw and its environs, but each could send a representative to the Election Seym, usually with a large retinue, and well supplied with money. Hospitality tents would be set up, and the more influential electors would be lavishly wined and dined at the end of the daily meetings, and quite often bribed on the occasion. This aspect of the election process, one strongly suspects, was what attracted such large crowds to these affairs, and often induced people to travel long distances to Warsaw. It was nice to feel like a king-maker at least once in a lifetime.

Fig. 17 - *"Hospitality Tents" set up during the Election Seym of 1733 during which Augustus III Wettin was elected King. After a French engraving.*

The Third Seym of the interregnum period was usually held in Cracow where, after having sworn to uphold all the laws on the books and the Bill of Rights contained in the *Pacta Conventa,* the elect was duly crowned King of Poland and Grand Duke of Lithuania for life. The ceremony was performed by the Interrex, who at that moment relinquished his powers. Only two kings were crowned in Warsaw instead of, as was usual, in Cracow: Stanislaus Leszczyński and Stanislaus A. Poniatowski. Both eventually abdicated. Much later, in 1829, Nicholas I of Russia was crowned King of Poland also in Warsaw, but was deposed only two years later, leading some people to remark that the choice of Warsaw for a coronation place boded ill for the incoming administration.

The list of candidates presented to the successive Election Seyms is shown in Table 16. As can be seen from it, the candidacy for the crown of Poland was open not only to the inhabitants of the country but to foreigners as well on the strength of the precedent set with Louis of Hungary and Jagiełło of Lithuania. The offer of the crown to the latter produced a very successful dynasty. Of the eleven elected kings of the First Republic seven were of foreign origin, including two born in Poland. The wisdom of allowing foreigners to be put up as candidates has been questioned at various times. The answer is not a simple one, if only for the reason that the practice seemed to offer several advantages to the electorate at the time. The concept of the 'uniform citizen,' with everyone having the same political rights as everybody else, had not yet evolved, and every politically active group in the country was competing to secure for itself the best possible set of rights and privileges from the ruler. An election of the ruler offered a perfect opportunity for bargaining with the candidates. The candidates were in a far less resistant frame of mind in the matter of making promises and commitments for the future, than a hereditary ruler would have been on ascending the throne and, furthermore, if the candidate was a foreigner, he was at a disadvantage through the lack of familiarity with people and local conditions. A native would drive a harder bargain. It is obvious that these considerations applied in other countries as well, as for instance is shown by the preference of the English Whigs for William of Orange as a replacement for the exiled native James II. Prospects for foreign alliances also played a part in the considerations. The many intermarriage links between the various ruling houses, foreign and domestic, made the practice of foreign candidature, which seems strange to us now, acceptable then. Successful kingship was an exportable profession in those days.

TABLE 16—CANDIDATES FOR THE CROWN PRESENTED TO THE ELECTION SEYMS

Year	Candidate
1573	Ernest Habsburg of Austria
	*Henri Valois, Duke of Anjou+
	Ivan IV, Tsar of Russia
	John III Vasa of Sweden
	Stephen Bathory of Hungary
1575	Jan Kostka, Palatine of Sandomierz
	Andrzej Tęczyński, palatine of Bełz
	Maximillian II, of Germany
	John III Vasa of Sweden
	Alphonso II, Duke of Ferrara
	*Stephen Bathory of Hungary
	Ivan IV, Tsar of Russia
	Wilhelm of Nuremberg
1587	Feodor, Tsar of Russia
	Andreas Bathory of Hungary
	Maximilian Habsburg of Austria
	*Sigismund Vasa of Sweden
1632	*Ladislaus Vasa of Poland
	(single candidate, unopposed)
1648	*John Casimir Vasa of Poland
	Charles Ferdinand Vasa, of Poland
	Sigismund Rakoczy of Hungary
1669	Philip Wilhelm, of Neuburg
	Charles V of Lorraine and Bar
	*Michał Korybut Wiśniowiecki
	Charles Bourbon d'Longueville

TABLE 16 (CONTINUED)—CANDIDATES FOR THE CROWN PRESENTED TO THE ELECTION SEYMS

Year	Candidate
1674	Charles V of Lorraine and Bar
	*Jan Sobieski, Army Commander
	James Stuart, Duke of York++
	François Louis d'Bourbon-Conti
	Charles Hohenzollern
	George of Denmark
1697	François Louis d'Bourbon-Conti
	James Sobieski, of Poland
	Max Emmanuel, of Bavaria
	*Frederick Augustus Wettin
	Livio Odescalchi, Duke of Ceri
	Louis, Margrave of Baden
1733	*Augustus Wettin, of Saxony
	Stanisław Leszczyński
	Emmanuel, Duke of Portugal
1764	#Frederick Christian Wettin
	*Stanisław Antoni Poniatowski
	Adam K. Czartoryski
	Jan Klemens Branicki

* Winner of the Crown
+ (later Henri III of France)
# Died of smallpox during the candidacy
++ (later James II of England)

In time the election procedure had undergone some changes. In the first election the Senators voted with and headed the delegations from their own palatinates. In the second election the gentry felt they were subject to undue influence from the Senators, and insisted on the Senate meeting and voting separately. Both groups, however, insisted on retaining the initiative of proposing candidates and taking the vote first. This led to confusion and on two occasions two different candidates were declared elected: Stephen Bathory by the Seym and Maximilian Habsburg of Austria by the Senate in 1576; similarly, Stanisław Leszczyński and Augustus III Wettin of Saxony were elected simultaneously in 1733 in separate elections held at Praga and Wola outside of Warsaw. In such cases the final verdict was often reached on the battlefield, and the support of foreign armies was helpful, but not necessarily conclusive, as was aptly pointed out by Benjamin Franklin, a contemporary to the second of these events. In *Poor Richards Almanack* for September 1748 he wrote:

> On the first of this month, Anno 1733, Stanislaus, originally a private gentleman of Poland, was chosen the second time king of that nation. The power of Charles XII of Sweden, caused his first election, that of Louis XV of France, his second. But neither of them could keep him on the throne: for PROVIDENCE, often opposite to the wills of princes, reduc'd him to the condition of a private gentleman again.

Well, not quite private. Stanislaus Leszczyński, as father-in-law of Louis XV of France, lived out his days ruling the Duchy of Lorraine.

Irregularities in the royal election procedure did occur and had lasting consequences. Such was the case of the election Seym of 1697, following the death of John Sobieski. During the Seym Senator Michał Radziejowski, serving as the Interrex, pronounced François Louis d'Bourbon Conti the winner in the heated election contest. The chief runner up in this election, Frederick Augustus Wettin, the Elector of Saxony, took advantage of Conti's delay in setting out for Poland from France, and challenged the outcome. Wettin's supporters broke into the treasury in the castle of Wawel in Cracow, secured the regalia, and succeeded in persuading Stanisław Dąbski, Bishop-Senator from Kujawy to crown the challenger, when he arrived in Poland at the head of an army. Conti, who travelled by sea from France, made only a brief landing at Oliva on the Baltic coast near Gdańsk, and hearing of the 'fait accompli' surrendered his claim and returned to France.

The irregular manner in which Augustus II Wettin attained the kingship, by contesting the outcome of the election by force of arms and by overriding the Interrex, started off his administration on the wrong foot, set the public against him, and contributed to an almost complete breakdown of cooperation between the Seym and the 'Elect'. In fact, the whole episode ushered in one of the darkest periods in the history of parliamentarism in Poland.

The forced assumption of power by Wettin could be sustained only by coercion, and unable to sustain it by means of his Saxon troops and local supporters, Augustus finally brought in the Russians. Those who voted in the royal election for Conti retained their pro-French sympathies and were in subsequent decades suitably manipulated by the Bourbon court, adding to the general confusion.

The process of electing kings produced mixed results. Of the foreigners elected, Stephen Bathory of Hungary and Ladislaus IV Vasa of Poland and Sweden were in the opinion of their contemporaries outstanding kings. The performance of Sigismund III Vasa is to this day a subject of heated controversy, but with positive reassessment of his administration coming now to the fore. The two Saxon kings, Frederick Augustus II Wettin and his son Augustus III, were unqualified disasters. Of the Poles elected only Jan Sobieski made his mark. Like Ulysses S. Grant or

Dwight D. Eisenhower, he was a successful supreme commander elected on the strength of his war record, but in later years his administration ran into political problems with the Seym. Michał K. Wiśniowiecki and Stanisław Leszczyński made too fleeting an appearance on the political stage to leave much of a mark. Concerning Stanisław A. Poniatowski, the last Pole to hold the office and the last elective king, the debate still rages. The thirty years of his administration left an imprint of a much more lasting nature than he was ever credited with during his life. Historians are slowly shifting the blame for the collapse of the First Republic to other quarters.

By the early 1700s opposition to elective kingship with a candidacy open to all gained momentum. In 1733 Interrex Theodore Potocki was able to persuade the Convocation Seym of that year to exclude all foreigners from candidacy, while "preserving all other provisions of a free election." This did not prevent Augustus III Wettin to press his claim right then. The new rule was applied after his death and favored Stanisław A. Poniatowski. By this time, however, even the principle of elective kingship came under fire as the cause of foreign meddling in Poland's internal affairs, and the Constitution of 1791 made the crown of Poland hereditary in the Saxon House of Wettin. This was a surprising twist of legislative fancy, considering the disastrous experiences with the two previous Saxon kings. Nevertheless, it was the Saxon Frederick Augustus who ascended the throne of the Duchy of Warsaw with Napoleon's blessing in 1806. He attended the two Seyms held in Warsaw in 1809 and in 1811, abdicated in 1814, and paid for the experience with the loss of half of his native Saxony to Prussia after the defeat of Napoleon.

Throughout the nineteenth century the parts of partitioned Poland remained under suzerainty of three hereditary absolutist monarchies. The Free City of Cracow, which became a Republic, constituted an exception. The Seyms of these provinces, which sat at various times in Warsaw, Poznań and Lwów, lost the constitutional power to elect the chief executives and had to accept the rulers of the partitioning powers, or their deputies. In spite of this, the Seym of the Congress Kingdom attempted the unmaking of a king. When an uprising broke out against the Russians in November of 1830, the Seym supported it and in January of 1831 proclaimed Tsar Nicholas I dethroned as King of Poland. After the collapse of the uprising, Nicholas suppressed and disbanded the Seym and the Senate of the kingdom. In another part of Poland, the Seym of Lwów in Galicia gained in 1873 from the Austrian Emperor the right to appoint the administration of Galicia, but not its chief executive. The Viceroy, usually a Pole, was still appointed by the Austrian Emperor. In the Second and the Third Republic the legislature again gained the power to elect the chief executive.

Fig. 18 - *A scene from the Election Seym of 1764 held at Wola near Warsaw during which Stanisław Poniatowski was elected King. From a painting by Bernardo Belloto called Canaletto (1721-80).*

In appraising the system of electing kings in Poland some foreign assessments point out the most important weakness of that institution. It made it impossible for the neighboring dynasties to marry into Poland's real estate, i.e., the system thwarted dynastic ambitions, just as it was intended to do. In an age of rampant dynastic ambitions, however, this simply invited foreign intervention with the intent of partitioning the country. Thus, an admirable internal political development was transformed by external factors into a great impediment to successful foreign policy and national survival, and eventually contributed to the annihilation of the First Republic.

PACTA CONVENTA AND THE ROKOSZ, OR LEGALIZED REBELLION

The formal side of the election of the chief executive developed gradually in Poland during the administrations of successive members of the Jagiełło family. The death without male issue of the last member of that family in 1572 marks the introduction of the Convocation Seym. As mentioned elsewhere, this Seym had the task of arranging for the election of the next chief executive and of drawing up the "Pacta Conventa," or the "Articles of Agreement" between the candidate and the electorate. The first Pacta Conventa were drawn up for the election eventually won by Henri Valois, and hence the articles of agreement presented to him became known as the "Henrician Articles." In essence they formed a Bill of Rights. The following obligations bound the successful candidate:

- there will be a free election of his successor

- religious tolerance will be assured in accordance with the provisions of the Confederation of Warsaw

- no additional taxes will be imposed without the consent of the Seym

- no war will be declared nor army called up without the consent of the Senate

- if, during a war, the army is used outside the borders of the Commonwealth, a per diem will be paid to each soldier

- between the sessions of the Seym a committee of 16 Senators will supervise executive actions, one quarter of the Senators to be replaced each half year

- the king will not marry without the consent of the Senate

- if any of the above articles are broken by the elect, the electorate is absolved from obedience to him.

The last of these articles became known as the *de non praestanda oboedientia* article. Together with the first article it led to a number of constitutional conflicts, while its general wording allowed various interpretations. The above articles were considered as part of the "Cardinal Laws" and were reintroduced with minor modifications at each royal election by the Convocation Seym. Usually, a list of specifics was attached to them addressing the situation at hand, such as the financial agreements, foreign treaty obligations, and so forth.

Laudable as the articles were, wiping the slate clean at each election, and writing a new contract between the ruler and the ruled on the lines later advocated by Jean Jacques Rousseau, Thomas Jefferson and Thomas Paine, they had, nevertheless, a destabilizing effect, particularly the reservation clause at the end of the Henrician Articles, which was nothing but an invitation to a legalized rebellion.

In practice, such denial of obedience took the form of a "grand remonstrance," in which the gentry would assemble armed, as if for war, and draw up demands on, or protests against, some action of the executive. If their demands were not met, a civil war started. The demonstration was given the name *rokosz* from a corruption of the name of the field of Rakos in Hungary, where a similar Hungarian demonstration took place. *Rokosz* was the supreme sanction which the gentry might invoke against the executive and was extremely damaging to the smooth functioning of the state. Its threat often paralyzed the executive into complete inaction, even in times of a national emergency.

The first *rokosz* took place in 1537, still in the period of hereditary monarchy, and lacked the constitutional sanction given to it 35 years later by the reservation clause on the refusal of obedience of the Henrician Articles. It was known as the "Hens' War." It occurred when the gentry, called to arms for war with Turkey, organized a protest against the policies of Sigismund I and the financial operations of his wife, Bona Sforza.

The gentry presented their case in 39 articles, demanding reorganization of the treasury, prohibition of purchases of real estate by the queen, codification of laws, and release from church taxes. The legislation passed during the "Executive Movement," fulfilled those demands.

The first *Rokosz* carried out under the provisions of the "Henrician Articles" took place in 1587. The Rokosz was started by the supporters of Samuel Zborowski in an effort to rehabilitate him and was directed against Chancellor Jan Zamoyski. In a rival royal election the supporters of Rokosz elected Maximilian, brother of Emperor Rudolf II, to be the King of Poland. The Rokosz ended after the defeat and capture of Maximilian by Zamoyski at Byczyna in 1588.

A bigger *rokosz* was led by Mikołaj Zebrzydowski, the Senator palatine of Cracow, in 1606, in response to the proposal of Sigismund III Vasa that the free election of his successor be abolished and his son Ladislaus be made king (he was elected later anyway). Considering it a gross breach of the first Henrician Article, the participants in the rokosz demanded that Sigismund III be dethroned. The Rokosz was supported by the Protestants demanding better protection of their places of worship. The demands of Rokosz participants, formulated in 67 articles, were rejected by the Seym of 1607; the King's army was dispatched against them, and defeated them at Guzów with a loss of 200 lives. Pacification Seym of 1609 settled the conflict and the Cardinal Laws were reaffirmed by the Seyms of 1608 and 1609.

To resolve the issue whether Zebrzydowski and his supporters were in their rights, a constitution passed by the Seym of 1607 clarified the details of the procedure and the obligations of the King in the following words:

> Should the general law, God forbid, be violated by Our conscious and willful undertaking, or should anyone be oppressed in violation of the law and general freedoms, and should this be clearly shown in cause and effect, anyone then will be free to communicate this matter to the Senator of his home constituency, and the said Senator will make the matter known to the Reverend Archbishop of Gniezno in his capacity of Primate. The latter, either by himself, or after consulting with other Senators, must admonish Us, or our successors, and We, whenever such a transgression should occur, will be obligated to correct it.

Should this not take place, the said Reverend Archbishop of Gniezno, acting in concert with other Senators, must repeat the admonition.

If without Just cause either We or our successors do not satisfactorily respond to a matter thus brought up, then all estates should act in accordance with the article *de non praestanda oboedientia.*

Another important *rokosz* was led in 1665 by Jerzy Lubomirski, the Grand Marshal of Poland and Field Commander of the Army, during the administration of the second son of Sigismund III, John Casimir Vasa. Here, again, the issue was the attempt to settle ahead of time the question of succession, in particular, the attempts of Queen Louise to promote the election 'vivente rege' of Duc d'Condé. When Lubomirski started a movement of opposition, the King countered by having Lubomirski impeached in absentia by the Seym Tribunal of 1664. When Lubomirski returned from exile and started arming his supporters, John Casimir decided to take the matter to the battlefield, a very unwise move considering the fact that Lubomirski was one of the ablest Generals of the Commonwealth. The King's army was defeated at Mątwy in 1666, but the *rokosz* was finally concluded by negotiation and the submission of Lubomirski.

As can be seen, almost all major *rokosz* cases dealt with the question of succession, indicating how important the issue of electibility of the Chief Executive appeared to the contemporaries. The person initiating the movement was invariably a high official of the Commonwealth, thus adding weight to the issue. In spite of the elaborate procedure described in the quoted constitution of 1607, this route of checking the actions of the executive tended to be settled on the battlefield. The alternative route, that of impeachment trials by the Tribunal of the Seym, was also available, and was used from time to time. This will be covered in more detail in Chapter VIII.

In retrospect, the use of the threat of civil disobedience as a constitutional safeguard had a severely adverse effect on the political tranquility of the country and at times invited abuse not only by individuals but also by groups of political malcontents. In its operation, the institution of *rokosz* took the political opposition out of the Seym, where it should have stayed and where its demands would be debated, judged, and possibly legislated on, and drove it out into the country. This encouraged political divisiveness and weakened the State by civil wars.

Legally speaking, the Kościuszko Insurrection of 1794 could qualify as a *rokosz*. In this case the citizens questioned the legality of the repeal of the Constitution of 1791 by the Seym of 1793 and the ratification by this Seym of the treaties of the Second Partition and, consequently, refused obedience to the government then in power. This subject will be covered in more detail in a later chapter.

CITIES ELECT REPRESENTATIVES "CIVITATUM NUNTII"

The representation of the towns and the cities in the early Seyms of Poland had a much more irregular history than that of the lands, i.e., the agricultural segment of the population. Its background had not been studied in detail until recent times, although the Seym attendance records of the representatives of the cities of Cracow and Lublin have been published and constitute an exception.

Lublin and Cracow fall into the category of the so-called Royal Towns, legally subject to the state rather than the land jurisdiction. The distinction arose from the origin of the founding charter of a town. Cities and towns founded by the King remained under the King's jurisdiction, were subject to separate laws, and had judges appointed by the King. Such cities generally were subject to a flat tax rate. When extra taxes or legislation involving the towns was on the agenda of the Seym, the King would send the writs of Summons to them as well as to the lands. Knowing that their delegations were invariably forced into accepting higher tax levy, the cities and towns were reluctant to respond to the summons and often would choose to accept a flat tax rate and no representation. This situation is well described by a quote from the instruction sent in 1503 to the Senate by King Alexander in connection with the forthcoming Seym in Piotrków:

> For participation in the debate on all matters, in particular the defense of the Realm, the representatives of Lublin, Lwów and other cities should be summoned. His Majesty is of the opinion that they should be summoned to the current Seym and he will consent to issuing a Writ of Summons. Prior to His Majesty's arrival, he wishes you to decide to which towns it should be addressed, and which towns should be summoned. This is to assure that whatever you decide regarding the defense, the towns will not excuse themselves and refuse to carry the burdens, which they should share together with all the lands of the Kingdom for the needs of the Realm.

The cities and the towns were accordingly invited to this Seym.

The procedure for electing the representatives of the cities differed from that of the lands. It is spelled out in the records of the Seym of Piotrków of 1565 with regard to the city of Lublin. The city councillors were directed, whenever the need arose, to send Deputies to the Seym. First, they were to call up five spokesmen from the city population at large, according to the ancient custom, then, with their consent, elect the Seym Deputies. The Deputies were to be given the postulates of both the City Council and the population at large, and were to be sent to the Seym at the expense of the City. We see, therefore, that at least in Lublin the election of the Deputies to the Seym was indirect. Table 17 summarizes the attendance record of the representation of Lublin at the Seyms of the hereditary kingdom and the First Republic. The attendance was sporadic, but not negligible. Lublin was a well-established, medium-size city, and its attendance record is probably representative of other cities as well.

The Pomeranian cities of Toruń, Elbląg and Gdańsk sent their representatives to the General Seymik of Prussia and through it participated until 1772 in the election of the Deputies to the Seym. In 1569 the city of Wilno gained the right to send Deputies to the Seym but, like other cities, used it only sporadically.

In comparison with other cities in Poland, Cracow held a position apart on the strength of a privilege given to it by Prince Leszek the Black (1279-1288), who incorporated the burghers of that city with the knighthood of the palatinate in recognition of their services in the defense of the castle of Cracow during a contest for the throne. It entitled Cracow to send its representatives to the Seymik of Proszowice, and to the General Seymik held at Korczyn. This favored position was reconfirmed in 1505 by a privilege given by Alexander I, and again by John Casimir Vasa's Coronation Act of 1649. The summons to the city were by a separate Royal Writ until the middle of the 1500s; thereafter, they were included in the standard Universal Proclamation. Although theoretically given the same rights as the Deputies from the lands, the representatives from Cracow were reluctant to use them to their full extent, and from 1565 onwards were limited to debates and votes on matters concerning the cities only.

Generally speaking, the cities had a tenuous hold on participation in the Seyms and, limited as it was, it faced a stiff opposition from the gentry, jealous of their position. The Seym of Radom of 1505 introduced an era of open challenge on the part of the gentry to the rights of the cities to send Deputies to the Seyms, and by 1518 the Deputies of the gentry demanded of the King that the Deputies from Cracow be removed from the Seym chamber. In 1537 they were forcibly ejected, and in 1539 an attempt was made to bar their entry. In 1569, during the administration of Sigismund II Augustus, Deputy M. Sienicki, leader of the liberal opposition, made a statement that he did not wish to speak in the Seym while the Deputies from Cracow were present. In spite of all these difficulties the Deputies from Cracow participated in the debates of the Seyms of 1562, 1587, 1589, and 1634. However, the general tendency of the Deputies from Cracow and other cities was to maintain a low profile. They often opted for having their proposals presented by one of the Senators. This had the adverse effect of creating the impression among other Deputies that the city Deputies had no right to speak, in spite of the repeated reassertion of this right by several kings. Sebastian Petrycy, a keen political observer, ridiculed the burghers by saying: "people from some cities attend the Seym, but sit apart, listening to the ready-made speeches." Usually the city of Cracow sent two Deputies, called Ablegates, who were commonly elected from among the members of the City Council by the Council itself, although in 1552 the population of the city elected

TABLE 17—SEYM ATTENDANCE OF REPRESENTATIVES OF LUBLIN

Year	Place	Ablegate[1]	Year	Place	Ablegate
1503	Piotrków		1693	Grodno	
1505	Radom		1695	Warsaw	
1506	Lublin		1699	Warsaw[5]	
1538	Piotrków		1703	Lublin	
1551	Piotrków		1733	Warsaw[4]	
1554	Lublin		1738	Warsaw	
1565	Piotrków		1744	Grodno	Józef Silkiewicz
1566	Lublin				Józef Wierzbicz
1569	Lublin		1746	Warsaw	
1649	Warsaw[3]		1761	Warsaw	
1659	Warsaw		1764	Warsaw	
1661	Warsaw		1764	Warsaw[2]	
1666	Warsaw		1764	Warsaw[2]	
1677	Warsaw	Stanisław Badinelli	1766	Warsaw[2]	
		Szymon Grabowiecki	1767	Warsaw	
		Jerzy Jung	1788	Warsaw	
		Tomasz Magierski	1789	Warsaw	Michał Lamprecht
1681	Warsaw	Gabriel Dobrogoszcz			Stan. Trojanowski
		Mikołaj Mołodecki	1791	Warsaw	Jakub Lewandowski[7]
1683	Warsaw	Stanisław Badinelli			Maciej Graber[7]
		Tomasz Magierski			Franciszek Reynberg
		Henryk Szulc			Michał Gautier[6]
1688	Grodno				Krzysztof Horn
1690	Warsaw	Krzysztof Cyboni	1793	Grodno	Jan Staromiejski
					Stan. Trojanowski

[1]Whose name has been preserved in the records
[2]Convocation, Election and Coronation Seyms
[3]Coronation Seym
[4]Election Seym
[5]Pacification Seym
[6]Plenipotentiary
[7]Took part in the Black Procession (see text)

two additional observers to oversee and report on the activities of the two Ablegates. The better known Ablegates of Cracow in 1575 were A. Bełza and Andrew Petricovius, Doctor of Canon and Civil Law.

The Swedish invasions (1655 and 1702) and the devastation of war contributed much to the decline of the cities in the seventeenth and eighteenth centuries. With it came the reluctance to send representation to the Seyms, and the absence from the Seyms meant further reduction in the political influence of cities. The lowest point was reached in 1765 when the Seym struck the cities from the Estates of the Commonwealth to be represented in the Seyms with a right to vote. However, only three years later in 1768, these rights were restored to Cracow, Gdańsk and Toruń, the three largest cities in the Commonwealth. By then the cities were recovering from the economic decline and were staging a political comeback. The highlight of that comeback occurred in 1789, when the representatives of 140 cities and towns assembled in Warsaw and participated in the "Black Procession" to the Seym, demanding restoration of full rights of representation. Although their demands were only partially fulfilled at the time, the movement they set in motion was unstoppable, as will be seen later.

PERIPATETIC SEYM AND THE PLACES WHERE IT MET

The process of reunification of Poland from the dynastic subdivisions of the Middle Ages, and the growth of the state through political unions, led to the gradual shift of the political center of gravity of the country. The choice of the meeting place of the national Seym followed these trends. In addition, there arose occasionally political situations which made it advisable to hold a Seym close to the scene of action. In such cases, particularly in the period of the hereditary monarchy, Seyms were held in other than customary places.

Fig. 19 - *The keep in the castle of Piotrków. Until 1567 most of the Seyms of the hereditary monarchy convened here, while their membership rose from 54 to 92 Deputies. Shown in its present-day condition, it now houses a regional museum.*

As the national Seym gained in stature and membership, it moved to more elaborate quarters. While the county and palatinate Seymiks met as a rule in parish churches, the national Seym enjoyed the hospitality of the King, and met generally in one of the royal castles, using at first such accommodations as were available. In time, however, it became a practice to set aside special quarters in each of the castles used as the meeting places of the Seym. In later years of the existence of the First Republic, when the Seym became a dominant political institution of the country, its position justified the major reconstruction of its seat to accommodate its needs. However, when the national Seym started to meet in Piotrków in 1468, all this was still in the distant future, and the first Seyms met within the confines of the castle of Piotrków in very modest surroundings indeed. Of the castle buildings, the most important still survives and is used now as a regional museum. Though originally higher and crowned by a Polish Renaissance attic, i.e., a decorative wall concealing an inverted, funnel-shaped roof, its present height is lower, as it was burned down during the Swedish invasion in 1657 and reconstructed in 1670 with a conventional roof. This is the form in which it survives until the present day. In 1578 the Tribunal of the Crown (Supreme Court of Poland) was also established at Piotrków which was, at the time, renamed Piotrków Trybunalski. The sessions of the Tribunal, lasting six months each, were held there for 214 years.

Fig. 20—The castle of Cracow, where 29 Seyms were held including 11 of the Coronation Seyms.

After Piotrków, the castle of Cracow shared the distinction as one of the seats of the early Seyms. No less than 29 Seyms were held there, and even after Warsaw became a regular seat of the Seym, Seyms continued to be convened in Cracow occasionally until 1734. The most important of these were the Coronation Seyms, conducted with much pomp and ceremony. The Coronation Seyms continued into the era of elective Kings, even though those were really Presidents elected for life rather than true monarchs. The parliamentary quarters of the castle consist of the Hall of the Deputies, also known as "the Hall under the Heads," and of the Senate Chamber. The first of these has a magnificently carved and coffered ceiling, containing 30 life-size heads of men and women dating back to the 1500s, and a wall frieze painted by Hans Dürer.* The Senate Chamber is decorated with splendid tapestries ordered by Sigismund Augustus (1520-1572) and contains a small gallery for the public. The cathedral of

---

* Brother of the celebrated Albrecht.

Cracow, also on the castle hill, was the scene of the actual coronations and contains the tombs of the Kings, both hereditary and elective. Traditionally, the crown jewels were kept in Cracow.

Fig. 21—A view of the Chamber of Deputies in the Castle of Cracow. The coffered ceiling features life-size head carvings of various personages from the 1550s. When the Seym was in session here, more elaborate seating arrangements were provided.

After the Union with Lithuania in 1569 and the rise of the First Republic, the meeting place of the Seyms was moved to Warsaw to shorten the travel distance for the Lithuanian Deputies. Except for 11 Seyms held in Grodno and an occasional Seym held elsewhere, Warsaw had become the Seym City, hosting 148 Seyms. This tradition was carried into the Duchy of Warsaw and the Congress Kingdom of Poland of the Partition period when two and four Seyms were held there, respectively, and was continued in the Second and the Third Republics, as noted in Table 18.

Fig. 22—A view of the Senate Chamber in the castle of Cracow. A gallery visible at the far wall was provided for the visitors. The Chamber is shown in its present day condition. During a session of the Senate appropriate seating arrangements were provided.

The Seyms held in Warsaw used the premises set aside for them in the Castle of Warsaw. They were constructed during the administration of Sigismund Augustus according to plans drawn up by Giovanni Battista Quadro (?-1590). The "Hall of Three Pillars" that he created for the Chamber of Deputies is in the form of a spacious hall It was divided into two aisles by a row of pillars, supporting a vaulted ceiling. On the south side the hall opened into the interior of the Town Tower. From there, a spiral staircase connected it with the Senate Chamber, located on the floor above. "The Hall of One Pillar" adjoined the Chamber of Deputies and was used for its offices. The physical placement of the Senate on the floor directly above the Seym corresponded initially to the dominating political position of the Senate at the time, and the terms the Upper and the Lower Chamber were synonymous with the Senate and the Chamber of Deputies. Both, the physical and the political position of the two chambers, were to change in due time.

TABLE 18 - GEOGRAPHY OF SESSIONS OF THE SEYM

Years	Location	Number of Seyms	Political Entity
	Warsaw*	148	
	Piotrków	38	
	Cracow	29	
	Grodno	11	Hereditary
	Lublin	5	Kingdom
1493-1793	Toruń	3	and first
	Radom	2	Republic
	Sandomierz	1	
	Bydgoszcz	1	
	Parczów	1	
1653	Brześć Litewski	1	
1807-1812	Warsaw	2	Duchy of Warsaw
1815-1831	Warsaw*	4	Kingdom of Poland
1827-1845	Poznań	7	Grand Duchy of Poznań
1861-1918	Lwów	10	Kingdom of Galicia and Lodomeria
1919-1939	Warsaw	6	Second Republic
1947-1988	Warsaw	10	Polish People's Republic
1989	Warsaw	**	Third Republic

Note: In the Hereditary Kingdom the Seym could be held in any place at the discretion of the King, providing the consent of the Senate was obtained.

*In the castle, except the Election Seyms, which were held in the open, in the suburbs of Warsaw at Wola, or at Kamion.

** Elections to the Seym held every 4 years, starting in 1989.

Fig. 23—The Castle of Warsaw, the seat of most of the Seyms of the First Republic as well as some of those of the Partition Period. The new Seym and the Senate Chambers were located to the right and the left of the tower, respectively. Shown after reconstruction from the damage of World War II.

These parliamentary premises witnessed the passage of many important constitutions, such as the Henrician Articles, the first Bill of Rights as it were, and the signing of the Act of Confederation of Warsaw, both in 1573, by which the signatories undertook to maintain the freedom of religious belief and accepted the proposal of Deputies from Sandomierz to ban the coercion of peasants in religious matters.

The cramped quarters of the Senate did not allow visitors to attend its sessions, except by special arrangement. Jan Chryzostom Pasek (1636-1701), a gentleman-soldier, left us, in his colorful diary for 1666, the following description of how one could obtain admission:

When the Deputies move to the second floor, where the sessions are held sometimes [jointly with the Senate], and the call is given:'Whoever is not a Deputy, please withdraw, one should try to make acquaintance with the Speaker, as I did and thus use the influence of important people to avoid being ousted from the chamber, by explaining: I came to drink of knowledge in this school, I'll reveal no secrets!' The Speaker would say: 'Very well, I commend your noble inclinations.' So when they chased others out of the Chamber, I simply nodded to the Speaker, while others crammed headlong through the door, some getting swatted on their backs with the Speaker's staff; then did my companions wonder: 'What luck you have! I hid myself behind the tile stove, yet was forced to leave, while you sat through the session.' They did not know I'd cajoled the Speaker into it.*

Fig. 24—Joint session of the Seym and Senate in the old Senate Chamber of the Castle of Warsaw. The empty chairs in the foreground belong to the Ministers, shown here standing at the far end on both sides of the King, as was customary, during the speech from the throne. From a seventeenth century English copperplate.

At the start of the administration of John Sobieski, in the years 1678-1681, new quarters were constructed in the west wing of the castle of Warsaw for the Chamber of Deputies. At first it consisted of a spacious one-story hall, with benches for the Deputies placed in a horse-shoe arrangement of several rows, backed by additional space on the outside for observers and visitors. Subsequently, this arrangement had to be modified as a result of a mêlée between the spectators and the Deputies which took place in 1762 and in which "swords and pistols were drawn." Enraged by this attempt at intimidation of the Deputies, the Seym stopped its activity and disbanded without passing any legislation. To prevent further threats to the Deputies, the Senate, acting in the capacity of custodian of the parliamentary quarters, decided to increase the elevation of the Chamber of Deputies to two stories and to equip it with a gallery

---

* Reprinted from "Memoirs of the Polish Baroque," Catherine S. Leach, trans., by permission of University of California Press. Copyright © 1976 by the Regents of the University of California.

for visitors on the model of the Senate Chamber. The gallery running around these walls, was entered through a staircase located along the fourth wall, and accessible from outside of the Chamber of Deputies only. The architect chosen for the design of the new chamber interior was Jakub Fontana (1710-1773); the alteration was completed by 1764, in time for the Convocation Seym of that year. The separation of the visitors proved to be quite effective and there has not been any further attempt from the gallery on the life or limb of a Deputy since. In all fairness, however, one must observe that the range and accuracy of fire arms was quite limited in those days. This feeling of security due to extra distance is no longer true in our days, as witness the events on the gallery of the U.S. Chamber of Representatives in the Capitol in 1954, when five Congressmen were shot from the visitors' gallery by Puerto Rican nationalists.

Fig. 25 (Left)—Old Chamber of Deputies in the Hall of Three Pillars in the east wing of the Castle of Warsaw. When the Seym was in session here, proper seating arrangements were provided. The Seym sat here from 1570 until 1681, when the chamber of Deputies was moved to the west wing of the Castle.

Fig. 26 (Right)—The interior of the new Senate Chamber in the Castle of Warsaw. In the First Republic the elective king served as the President of the Senate. The galleries for the public are visible on both sides.

The relocation of the Senate to the same wing followed in the administration of Augustus III Wettin, in the years 1737-1746. Now, both chambers were located on the same level, were made more roomy, and incorporated galleries for visitors. The Senate Chamber was larger and more elaborate of the two, as it was intended to accommodate the joint sessions of the Seym and the Senate, held as a rule for several days at the beginning and the end of each legislative period.

The well-known Swiss mathematician, Johann Bernoulli (1742-1807), who visited Warsaw in 1778, left us a detailed description of both Legislative Chambers. The Senate Chamber contained:

> four rows of benches covered with red cloth, arranged in an amphitheatre. Before the first row there stand 60 chairs covered with red velvet, intended for Senators. At the end of the Chamber stands the Royal throne, covered also with red velvet, with gold trim. It is an armchair placed on an elevation and under a canopy. The first two rows of benches are intended for Deputies, the next two for the more prominent visitors. The two longer walls contain galleries for gentlemen visitors. Lady visitors sit even higher, in rooms placed opposite the throne, which afford a view from above through the windows.

It was in this chamber that the joint session of the Seym and the Senate took place on May 3, 1791 during which the new Constitution of the country was adopted. For this reason the chamber has for the Poles the same emotional value as the Independence Hall in Philadelphia has for the Americans.

Bernoulli describes the Seym Chamber as:

> decorated with frescoes, and around it are placed the galleries for the visitors, equipped with benches and supported by columns in the shape of palm trees. These bear the coats-of-arms of the palatinates. Part of the gallery above the entrance is enlarged, so that it accommodates several rows of benches. In the Chamber itself, there are wooden benches painted gray, without covering.

This chamber offered much improvement, both as regards space, lighting, and provisions for visitors, over the old Chamber of Deputies in the "Hall of Three Pillars" in the east side of the castle. In the new quarters, the Seym debates on controversial issues attracted many spectators, who often spilled over from the overcrowded galleries onto the ground floor and stood in the aisles, or took up vacant seats intended for the legislators. Attempts to drive them out often proved ineffective, particulaly when directed at the ladies, who took a lively interest in the proceedings and cheered on the more popular debaters.

Besides Warsaw, some Seyms were held in Grodno, a small town in Lithuania close to the border with Poland, a site chosen following the precedent of Piotrków, located in the same relation to Greater and Lesser Poland. A constitution of 1673 specified that every third Seym should be convened in Grodno; however, the Senate which made the actual arrangements did not follow this prescription too closely, and only 11 Seyms were held there. A building of the Castle of Grodno was used on these occasions. As it happened, the last Seym of the First Republic in 1793 took place there, and two years later the

Castle of Grodno was also the witness of the last official act of the First Republic, the abdication of Stanisław August Poniatowski from the kingship of Poland.

In Warsaw, the former parliamentary quarters in the Castle of Warsaw were demolished in the late 1830s on the orders of Emperor Nicholas I as an act of vengence for the act of his dethronement passed by the Seym in 1831. At that time, the space occupied in the castle by each of the two chambers was divided by an addition of a floor and partitioned into small rooms. With the reunification of Poland in 1918 the former chambers in the castle could not be quickly restored to a useable condition. The Seym selected instead the former property of the Institute of the Gentry in Warsaw, which had been subsequently used as the Alexander and Mary Academy for Young Ladies, and ordered its adaptation to the needs of the Seym. The former chapel of the Academy became the meeting chamber of the Seym. Since the 1970s, the old chambers in the Castle of Warsaw were restored to their original form to become a historical landmark and museum.

THE SENATE AS "GUARDIANS OF THE LAW"

In the course of the fifteenth century a two-house legislative structure developed in Poland, consisting of an elective House of Deputies and an appointive Senate. The entire membership of the Senate held their seats on the strength of the office to which they were appointed outside of the legislature, either in the Church or in the administration. These offices were generally held for life, and the appointments to them were made by the King. In 1589 the Kings of Poland received from Pope Sixtus V the right to appoint bishops from a list of candidates submitted by the cathedral chapters and with the Pope's final approval. In addition to all the Roman Catholic bishops the Senate included provincial administrators, that is, palatines and castellans, with the latter subdivided into two grades: the major, and the minor. Sometimes minor castellans were not summoned to the sessions of the Senate and on these occasions they were allowed to run for Deputy to the Seym and, if elected, could also be chosen Speaker of the Seym. No minor castellans were ever appointed in Lithuania.

The members of the Senate almost invariably came from a small number of "Senatorial Families," and were aristocrats in substance, if not in title. The principal of these families are listed in Table 19. Thus, the Senate bore a close resemblance to the British House of Lords but with the membership entirely composed of "Life Peers." The number of Senators varied with the geographic extent of the country at a given period. Before the union with Lithuania in 1569, it consisted of 11 bishops and archbishops, 19 palatines and 19 castellans plus 5 ministers, 54 persons in all, each appointed by the King. Later changes in membership are shown in Table 20.

The composition of the Senate, given in this table, represents the theoretical maxima which could be achieved if none of the palatines, castellans or bishops were appointed Ministers. In practice, the Chancellor was invariably a bishop, and a sizable proportion of the ministerial chairs were filled by palatines and castellans. The number of Ministers with a seat in the Senate kept increasing with time and the early positions of Chancellor (foreign and internal affairs), Grand Marshal (Lord High Justice), Treasurer, and Vice Chancellor were later supplemented with other Ministers, as is also shown in Table 20. The step increases in the composition of the Senate took place after the reunion of Pomerania with Poland in 1466 when senatorial seats for Royal Prussia were created, and after the reunion with Masovia in 1529. The biggest increase took place in 1569 after the union with Lithuania, when the number of ministers was doubled and the Lithuanian bishops, palatines and castellans were invited to sit in the enlarged Senate as well. No minor castellans were appointed from Lithuania, possibly due to the much lower urbanization of that province as compared to Poland.

TABLE 19—MAJOR SENATORIAL FAMILIES OF POLAND AND LITHUANIA

Bieliński	+Łubieński	Sieniawski
Branicki	Małachowski	Siemieński
Chreptowicz	Massalski	^^Sobieski
Chodkiewicz	Miączyński	Sołtyk
Chomentowski	Mniszech	Sułkowski
Czapski	Morsztyn	Szembek
Czarnecki	Myszkowski	Szołdrski
+Czartoryski	Naruszewicz	Szydłowiecki
Dąbski	Ogiński	Tarło
Działyński	Opaliński	Tarnowski
Dzieduszycki	Ossoliński	Tęczyński
Firley	Ostrogski	Tyszkiewicz
Fredro	Ostroróg	+Uchański
Gałecki	Pac	Ustrzycki
Gembicki	Pociej	+Wężyk
Jabłonowski	Podoski	Wielopolski
*Karnkowski	^^Poniatowski	^^Wiśniowiecki
Konarski	*+Potocki	Wyżycki
Konopacki	Prażmowski	Załuski
Koniecpolski	Przebendowski	Zamoyski
Kos	Pstrokoński	Zborowski
Krasicki	Raczyński	Zebrzydowski
Krasiński	Radomicki	Żółkiewski
Lanckoroński	+Radziejowski	
Ledóchowski	*Radziwiłł	
^^Leszczyński	Rudziński	
Lipski	Rzewuski	
Lubomirski	*Sanguszko	
Łaski	Sapieha	

^^ Families from which a King of Poland was elected
+Families whose members had served as an Interrex
*Families from which a Viceroy of Galicia or the Grand Duchy of Poznań was appointed

TABLE 20—COMPOSITION OF SENATE WITH APPOINTIVE MEMBERSHIP

Ministers	Kingdom of Poland		Commonwealth Poland & Lithuania			Kingdom of Poland
	1493[1]	1564[2]	1633[3]	1768	1791	1830
Grand Chancellor	1	1	2	2	2	-
Vice-Chancellor	1	1	2	2	2	-
Grand Marshal	1	1	2	2	2	-
Court Marshal	-	1	2	2	2	-
Grand Treasurer	1	1	2	2	2	-
Court Treasurer	-	-	-	-	2	-
Grand Commander[7]	-	-	2	2		-
Field Commander[7]	-	-	2	2		-
Bishops[4]	8	9	16	17	18	9
Palatines	13	15	33	37	38	18
Major Castellans	16	17	40	35	34	37
Minor Castellans[6]	39	49	49	49	50	--
Prefect of Żmudż	--	--	1	1	1	--
Total[5]	81	95	149	153	157	64

Notes:
[1]After reunion with Pomerania and incorporation of Prussia
[2]After reunion with Masovia
[3]After union with Lithuania
[4]Includes Archbishops
[5]Theoretical. In practice some castellans and palatines held ministerial appointments reducing the total
[6]Minor castellans were not summoned to all sessions of the Senate and if not summoned could run for Deputy to the Seym
[7]One each for Poland and Lithuania

Fig. 27—Stanisław Krasiński (1585-1649). Elected Speaker of the General Seymik of Masovia in 1633, 1635, Chief Justice of Crown Tribunal in 1633, Deputy of the Seyms of 1634, 1635 and 1638. Appointed Senator in 1641. A portrait by Daniel Schultz (1615-1683).

A legislative career in the Senate usually started in the lower chamber. The first step was to run for Deputy to the Seym. If then a successful Deputy was elected Speaker of the House, his further career in the administration was assured and an appointment to a senatorial position frequently followed. The senatorial positions, in turn, had a definite graduation, starting from a minor castellan in a provincial town and ending in a ministerial position of the national government. Talented individuals usually passed through a sequence of these positions. Although each appointment was for life, resignation and reappointment were the rule. This selection process brought many outstanding individuals into public life. Scholars, administrators, soldiers, and occasionally a major political thinker, graced the Senate roster. One such outstanding thinker, whose influence left an imprint both at home and abroad, was Senator Wawrzyniec Goślicki (1530-1607) better known abroad under a latinized form of his name, Laurentius Grimaldus Goslicius. William Shakespeare, a contemporary of Goślicki, modeled on him the figure of Polonius, Lord Chamberlain of Denmark in Hamlet, creating a figure of garrulous disposition but worldly wisdom. Goślicki's distinguished career in politics and diplomacy was supplemented by original writing, the best known work being a treatise on political theory *De optimo senatore libri duo*, originally printed in Venice in 1568, and reprinted in Basel in 1593. It has as its main theme the idea that "in the private happiness of the subjects consists the general and publick happiness of the commonwealth," and the principle that laws must be greater than any individual, including the King. The book intensely opposes the "divine rights of Kings," and this probably accounts for its popularity in England. Three English translations of *De optimo senatore* were published: *The Councellor exactly protraited in two books* (1598), *A Commonwealth of good Counsaile* (1607) published with the section on the rights of kings deleted, and finally, *The Accomplished Senator* in two books (1733). The ideas contained in the book were considered dangerous enough to cause the suppression of each successive translation in England. Nevertheless, to judge by quotations from it appearing in several English political pamphlets in the 1600s, enough copies survived to fuel the agitation against the arbitrary rule by the Stuarts. The book's influence surfaced again in the American Declaration of Independence, where some phrases and ideas bore a striking resemblance to Goślicki's formulations.

During an interregnum following the death in 1572 of Sigismund Augustus, the last hereditary King of Poland and Lithuania, the necessity of establishing an interim central administration became evident, primarily to set in motion a single electoral machinery for the state, and thus to prevent regional separatist movements from gaining momentum. Because this was the first election open to foreign as well as native candidates, the ambassadors, arriving in the country to introduce and promote their candidates, had to be received and dealt with. In these circumstances, Senator Jakub Uchański, the Archbishop of Gniezno and the Primate of Poland, took the initiative and claimed the powers of the king-pro-tempore (Interrex) on the strength of the tradition which assigned to the Primate the function of crowning the next king. The powers of the Interrex developed to include the right to summon the three Seyms in the royal election sequence: the Convocation Seym, the Election Seym, and the Coronation Seym, to receive and dismiss foreign ambassadors, and to make any other executive decisions that the situation demanded. This precedent was respected until the end of the First Republic, and 10 Interrexes served (see Table 21).

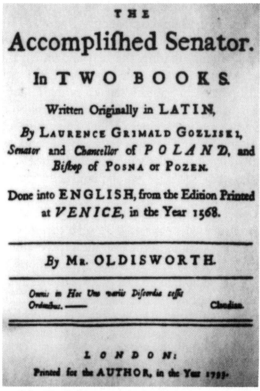

THE
Accomplifhed Senator.

In TWO BOOKS.

Written Originally in LATIN,

By LAURENCE GRIMALD GOZLISKI,
Senator and Chancellor of POLAND, and
Bifhop of POSNA or POZEN.

Done into ENGLISH, from the Edition Printed
at VENICE, in the Year 1568.

By MR. OLDISWORTH.

*Omnis in Hoc Uno variis Difcordia teffit
Ordinibus.* ——   *Claudian.*

LONDON:
Printed for the AUTHOR, in the Year 1733.

Fig. 28—Title page of the English version of De optimo senatore *by Senator Wawrzyniec G. Goślicki. This handbook on representative government was popular with the English public for over a hundred years. Of the three translations, produced in 1598, 1607 and 1733, this is the last one, done by William Oldisworth.*

The Senator-Primate assumed the duties of an Interrex automatically when he issued an official announcement of the last king's death and relinquished them on the day he crowned the Elect. An exception to this procedure occurred in 1674, during the interregnum following the death of Michał K. Wiśniowiecki, when the country was at war with Turkey. Senator Florian K. Czartoryski assumed the duties of an Interrex, as expected, but died while in office. Andrzej Trzebicki stepped in as the next senior Senator-Bishop. The election went to John Sobieski, in command of the army fighting the Turks. He assumed office at once, but the coronation had to be postponed until the end of the war in 1676.

TABLE 21 —SENATORS SERVING AS "KING-PRO-TEMPORE" (INTERREX)*

Interregnum	Senator	Term of Office
1572-1574	Jakub Uchański (first term)	18 months
1575	Jakub Uchański (second term)	8 months
1586-1587	Stanisław Karnkowski+	11 months
1632-1633	Jan Wężyk	9 months
1648-1649	Maciej Łubieński	8 months
1668-1669	Mikołaj Prażmowski	13 months
1673-1674	Florian K. Czartoryski**	6 months
	Andrzej Trzebicki++	1 month
1696-1697	Michał Radziejowski	12 months
	Stanisław Dąbski^	3 months
1733-1734	Teodor Potocki+++	11 months
1763-1764	Władysław Łubieński	13 months

*Senator who at the time of the King's death served as the Archbishop of Gniezno assumed the office of Interrex

+Crowned Stephen Bathory in 1576 thus pre-empting the duties of Jakub Uchański, as well as Sigismund III Vasa during his own term of office

**Died in office, while the Election Seym was in progress

++The actual crowning of Jan Sobieski was performed in 1676 by Jędrzej Olszowski, the two year delay being due to the intervening war with Turkey.

^Supported the successful challenger of the outcome of the election, Frederick Augustus Wettin, and preempted the duties of Radziejowski.

+++Imprisoned in Toruń by Russian troops, actual coronation performed by Jan Lipski.

Fig. 29—A view of the legislature of Poland in session, taken from the compendium of laws published by Jan Herburt in 1570. The Senators are shown seated, while the Deputies are standing in the rear, indicating the dominating position of the Senate at the time. In the following centuries, the importance of the Senate declined.

In addition to their legislative functions carried out while the Seym was in session, the Senators were looked upon as "Guardians of the Laws," i.e., the persons entrusted with the duty to see that the laws were in fact executed as written. This duty was formalized by a constitution passed by the Convocation Seym of 1573 and incorporated in the first *Pacta Conventa* written in that year. The constitution specified that 16 Senators were to reside with the King and oversee the exercise of his duties. The constitution of 1641 increased their number to 28 and provided for rotation. In the actual execution of its duties, the senatorial committee would meet between the regular sessions of the Seym whenever executive action was required and would be available for consultation at other times. The resolutions of this senatorial committee (senatus consulta) were recorded and reported to the Seym when it was in session. The legislative duties of the Senate between the periodic sessions of the Seym also included availability for consultation by the King immediately preceding the issue of the Writ of Summons of the Seym itself. With the Senate consenting, the date, place, and major legislative matters to be brought up at the Seym were chosen. This consultation could be carried out by mail if most Senators were away in the provinces at the time.

During the administration of Sigismund III Vasa, the electorate began to question the constitutionality of some of his actions, and when the gentry gathered in Cracow for the Assizes on January 11, 1607, an admonition was prepared and sent to the King to refresh in his mind the major principles of Poland's government. This interesting memorandum shows how the voters viewed their government at the time and, in addition, describes the Senate as "guardians of the law."

These are, Your Majesty, our major and basic privileges:

- The first is that we freely elect our rulers, and nobody inherits the right to rule over us, but we all participate in this election, even though it vexes us all.

- Our second privilege, Your Majesty, is that our rulers, elected freely by us, do not rule over us except with the consent of all Estates, as the Commonwealth reserves unto itself the right of rule and heredity, provides for its rulers an office for life only, and even that it constrains by laws.

- Our third privilege, Your Majesty, is that the rulers, elected freely by us, may not burden anybody's rights with favours and hatreds. The laws were so enacted that kings should not pass judgement on us in private, but only in the presence of the Senate, our elder brothers, during the session of the national Seym when the Chamber of Deputies, our younger brothers, also meets; they will see to it that our laws are not tampered with by our rulers, and that nobody is oppressed in contradiction to the law. They offer a refuge in danger; from them should everyone draw help and succor; and Your Majesty should, on their intercession, moderate and amend your actions.

- Our fourth privilege is, Your Majesty, that the sword which was placed by the Polish Republic in your hand for the defense of her borders and the punishment of crimes, shall not be used as an extraordinary power. The law was enacted that your Majesty should not wage war against foreign enemies until the Seymiks and the Seym warn us by a general resolution. You cannot smite anyone with this sword until he be convicted by laws which we have freely enacted: *de nemine vindictam sumemus, nemini bona adimemus, neminem captivabimus, nisi iure victum per barones nostros praesentes.* In these freedoms, Your Majesty, our glorious state grew up.

The constitution of 1773 enlarged the executive participation of the Senate by creating the Permanent Council (Rada Nieustająca) composed of 18 Senators and 18 Deputies. The Council controlled five committees: foreign affairs, the army, police, justice, and the treasury. The King sat as the president of the Council and the Council's resolutions were binding on him.

The creation of the Permanent Council had the effect of strengthening the administrative apparatus of the state and limiting the freedom of action of the King and the magnates who occupied the positions of commanders of the Army. The economic effects of the operation of the Treasury Committee of the Permanent Council were also positive for the development of the country, but the directives of semi-legislative character issued by the Council, ostensibly in clarification of points of law, were resented in the country as transgressing on the prerogatives of the Seym. In consequence, this dissatisfaction led to the abolition of the Permanent Council by the constitution of 1788, and its replacement by the "Guard of the Laws" composed of the King, the Primate (Archbishop of Gniezno), and five Ministers, as provided for in the Constitution of 1791. The Permanent Council was reestablished by the last Seym of the First Republic sitting in Grodno, in 1793, but this change did not progress beyond the paper stage.

Throughout most of the life of the First Republic the Grand and the Field Commanders of the Army (Hetman) had no seat in the Senate, unless they were, at the same time, appointed to an office which held a senatorial rank. This, however, was usually the case. The elevation of the offices of the Grand and the Field Commanders to senatorial rank took place in the administration of Stanisław A. Poniatowski (1768). The last appointees to that office (Piotr Ożarowski, Szymon Kossakowski and Józef Zabiełło) played a questionable role in the Second Partition of Poland by failing to provide military protection for the Seym of 1793 held in Grodno and were among the six Senators who were tried and hanged for treason during the Revolution of 1794.

Taking into consideration the fact that the membership of the Senate of the First Republic was composed of local administrators, lay and ecclesiastic, it is not

---

* "We shall not condemn anyone arbitrarily, we shall not confiscate anyone's property, we shall not imprison anyone, unless he be overcome by law in the presence of our barons."

surprising that it became involved in the executive side of the central government through the Permanent Council. The administrative functions of selected Senators were also provided for in the government of the Congress Kingdom of Poland, established in 1815, but were discontinued in the governments of other provinces of Poland during the Partitions period.

Following the First Partition in 1772, Austria put an end to the pretense that Poland had no aristocracy at all, and gave aristocratic titles to the heads of all senatorial families resident in parts of Lesser Poland which she annexed. The title of count was given to former palatines and castellans, and that of a baron to elected county officials. The Lithuanian and Ruthenian dukedoms were recognized as well, thus bringing the magnates of Galicia in line with the aristocratic arrangements in the rest of the Austrian Empire.

In the Second Republic, established in Poland after the First World War, all aristocratic titles were again abolished, the membership of the Senate this time became elective, and its functions purely legislative. The emergency function of President-pro-tempore was transferred from the senior Senator to the Speaker of the Seym by the Constitution of 1921, but it was transferred back to the Speaker of the Senate by the Constitution of 1935. The latter Constitution also made part of the membership of the Senate appointive again, with the appointive power vested in the President of the Republic.

TABLE 22—PRINCIPAL LEGISLATION OF SEYMS OF THE FIRST REPUBLIC (PART I)

1573	Agreement on Religious Tolerance ratified
	Ordinance for Royal Elections formulated
	Royal candidates' Articles of Agreement set
	Resident senatorial committee established
1576	Proclamation in defense of the Jews issued
1578	Supreme Court established for Poland
	Commission for the mines established
	Granting of Knighthood reserved for the Seym
1581	Supreme Court established for Lithuania
1590	Treasury divided into state and privy parts
1598	Prussian Code of Law revised
1607	Refusal of obedience to the King specified
1611	Refusal of obedience to the King clarified
	Burghers banned from buying landed estates
1613	Tax Court for the Treasury established
1619	Agreement with the Cossacks authorized

TABLE 22 (CONTINUED)—PRINCIPAL LEGISLATION OF SEYMS OF THE FIRST REPUBLIC (PART I)

1621	Gentry's military duties reiterated
1623	Ordinance for commerce promulgated
1629	Instructions for customs service approved
1632	Law on Taxation passed
1633	Mint put under Seym control Serfs' labor rent for land increased Penalties for runaway serfs specified
1637	Agreement with the Cossacks ratified
1638	Use of Titles, other than knighthood, banned
1641	Resident Senatorial committee enlarged Issue of coinage regulated
1643	Maximum rates of interest on loans specified

TABLE 23 —CONSTITUTIONAL ARRANGEMENTS OF THE EARLY FIRST REPUBLIC—A SYNOPSIS

Seym constitutions of 1572, 1578, 1607, 1609,

The Executive Branch of Government was headed by a king elected for life by the Seym. Native and foreign candidates were accepted. The successful candidate signed the Articles of Agreement (Pacta Conventa) reaffirming the Bill of Rights. The king appointed five ministers for Poland and five for Lithuania: chancellor (foreign and home affairs), vice-chancellor, grand marshal (justice), court marshal (household affairs), treasurer, also grand and field commanders of the army as well as lesser members of the administration. An explicit consent of the Seym was required before the King could travel outside the boundaries of the country. After the King's death the senior Senator, the Archbishop of Gniezno, acted as the king-pro-tempore (Interrex) until a new King was elected, and inaugurated.

The Legislative Branch of the Government consisted of the King, presiding in the Senate, the Senate and the Chamber of Deputies. All Senators (bishops, palatines and castellans) were appointed for life by the King. The King convoked the Seym with the advice and consent of the Senate and had the legislative initiative and veto power. The Senate had the right to review all laws made by the Seym. It also appointed 16 resident Senators to rotate in groups of four (a bishop, a palatine, and two castellans) to oversee the King's actions. The Seym passed all the laws, voted taxes, ratified treaties, received and sent embassies in conjunction with the King. Majority rule applied in voting in the Seym.

TABLE 23 (CONTINUED)—CONSTITUTIONAL ARRANGEMENTS OF THE EARLY FIRST REPUBLIC—A SYNOPSIS

Electoral Ordinance provided for the election of two Deputies from each county by male members of the gentry. The right to vote carried with it the obligation of military service in a levée en masse. The Seyms were summoned at regular two year intervals for a session of six weeks. Extraordinary Seyms were summoned occasionally for a two-week session. Representatives of the towns other than Cracow and the towns of Prussia, were elected by the city councils and were summoned infrequently.

The Judicial Branch of the Government comprised of judges appointed by the King in royal towns and elected judges in courts for the gentry. The Appellate Courts consisted of two tribunals, one for Poland and one for Lithuania operating with elective judges. The King had the right of pardon in cases of burghers in royal towns, which remained under the King's jurisdiction.

Bills of Rights were contained in articles of pacta conventa, and in earlier charters. They included the guarantees of personal freedom, ownership of property, religious tolerance, and the right to renounce obedience to the King when the latter broke the law. These laws extended to that part of the population which was obligated to military service, i.e., the gentry. The rights of the burghers were specified either in the Nuremberg Code or the Polish City Code, depending on the type of founding charter issued by the King. A separate charter covered the rights of the Jewish population.

POLITICAL PERSONALITIES IN THE SEYMS OF THE EARLY FIRST REPUBLIC

Stanisław S. Czarnkowski (1526-1602)—Referendary of the Crown 1567-76, secretary to Sigismund I the Elder and to Sigismund II Augustus, became a supporter of the pro-Habsburg orientation. Elected Deputy to the Seyms of 1569 and 1574, he served as Speaker of the 1569 Seym. In 1576 he was deprived of the position of Referendary for his participation in political moves against Stephen Bathory. During the royal election of 1587 he supported the candidacy of Maximilian Habsburg and opposed Sigismund III Vasa and Chancellor Jan Zamoyski.

Stanisław Krasiński (1585-1649)—Parliamentarian and jurist, he was appointed in 1627 the Judge of the Land of Ciechanów and served in judicial capacity during the interregnum Confederation of 1632. Elected twice deputy judge of the Treasury Tribunal of Radom, and a Commissioner for the 1633 Commission for settlement of boundry disputes between the Crown and private properties in Masovia, he was elected in the same year Chief Justice of the Crown Tribunal (Supreme Court) of Piotrków. Elected Deputy for Ciechanów to the

Seyms of 1634, 1635, 1638, he served also as the Speaker of the General Seymik of Masovia in 1633 and 1635. He participated in the Coronation Seyms of 1633 and 1649. He was appointed Senator in 1641.

Jerzy Ossoliński (1595-1650)—Politician and diplomat, he served twice as the Speaker of the Seym in 1631 and 1635. In 1643 he was appointed Chancellor of the Crown and later became a close adviser to Ladislaus IV Vasa. With the support of the aristocracy he favored the strengthening of the executive. After the death of Ladislaus IV, he was responsible for the candidature of John Casimir Vasa and his success in the election. During the Cossack uprising of Bohdan Chmielnicki, he was credited with the conclusion of the Agreement of Zborów in 1649. He was known as an excellent public speaker, and he authored the diary of the embassy to Germany (1877) and to Rome (1883), as well as *Memoirs, 1595-1621* (1952).

Krzysztof Radziwiłł (1585-1640)—Politician and army general. He served in 1632 as the Speaker of the Seym. Appointed palatine of Wilno in 1633, and the Commander-in-Chief of the Lithuanian army in 1635, he took part in the campaign against the Swedes in Baltic countries in 1621-22 and concluded a truce without the permission of the Chief Executive. He also took part in the 1633 campaign against Muscovy. He commanded the troops at Smoleńsk and was instrumental in obtaining the capitulation of the Russian army. He was in political opposition to Sigismund III Vasa and after Sigismund's death he supported the candidacy of Ladislaus Vasa in the election of the Chief Executive. On his lands in Kiejdany he set up a Calvinist cultural and religious center.

Lew Sapieha (1557-1633)—He served as the Speaker of the Seym of 1582. Adviser to Sigismund III Vasa and one of the planners of the Union with Muscovy in 1600, he master-minded and participated in the expeditions against Moscow in 1609-18. He was appointed Commander in Chief of the Lithuanian Army in 1625.

Jakub Sobieski (1588-1646)—Father of King John III, he served at the court of Ladislaus IV and took part in the war with Muscovy and in the negotiations at Deulin in 1619. He participated in the Chocim campaign in 1621. Elected Deputy to seven Seyms between 1623 and 1632, he served as the Speaker in 1623, 1626, 1628, and 1632. He took part in the negotiations at Szumska Wola between Poland and Sweden in 1635. Appointed Cup Bearer in 1636, palatine of Bielsko in 1638, palatine of Ruthenia in 1641, he was made castellan of Cracow in 1646. He authored: *Commentariorum Chotinensis belli libri tres* (1646) and instructions written for the journey of his sons to Cracow (1640) and France (1645) which contain the principles of best liberal education of the times.

Krzysztof Warszewicki (1543-1603)—Studied in the years 1556-1559 at the Universities of Leipzig, Württenberg, and Bologna. He supported Henri Valois in the first royal election. In subsequent years he belonged to the proHabsburg party. He served on several diplomatic missions and, in 1598, was appointed a canon of Cracow. In his political writings he criticized the abuses in parliamentary practice, advocated the strengthening of the executive branch of government and in the religious sphere outlined a program for counter-Reformation. He authored *De optimo statu libertatis* (1598); *Turcicae quatrodecim* (1595), the latter advocating a crusade against Turkey; in *Rerum polonicarum libri tres* he described the interregnum after the death of Sigismund Augustus (1589); wrote a treatise on diplomacy, *De legato legationque liber* (1595), and made a first attempt at bibliographic registry of works of 29 Polish writers in *Reges, sancti, bellatores, scriptores Poloni* (1601).

Jan Wężyk (1575-1638)—Appointed Bishop of Przemyśl in 1619 and Bishop of Cracow in 1624, he became the Primate of Poland in 1626. As a senior Senator he assumed the office of King-pro tempore (Interrex) in 1632 on the death of Sigismund III Vasa. While exercising this office he was very active in promoting the cause of improving the procedures of the royal elections. He relinquished this office at the coronation of the next elected King, Ladislaus IV Vasa in February 1633. He authored *Synodus provincialis Gnesnensis A.D. 1628 die 22 mai celebrata* (1629), *Synodus provincialis Gnesensis* (1634), and *Constitutiones Synodorum Metropolitanae Ecclesiae Gnesnensis Provincialium* (1630).

CHAPTER III

FIRST REPUBLIC UNDER FIRE: SEYMS AND CONFEDERATIONS

In this historical period (1648-1696) the work of the Seyms was completely dominated by the questions of defense. Religious wars in Northwestern Europe spilled over into Poland in the guise of dynastic intervention by the Protestant Swedes. Combined with the Cossack rebellion and the Russian incursion, they laid waste to the country. The war, and the plague that followed, reduced the population of the country by some 40%. The end of this period coincided with the highwater mark of the territorial expansion of the Mohammedan Turkey in Europe and involved Poland in wars on the South-East frontier, in which some territory was lost to Turkey.

Devastated cities declined in political importance and reduced their participation in Seyms. The Seyms coped with the defense and the economic problems as best they could, but in the superposition of the external and internal problems the viability of political institutions became impaired. The political activity became increasingly extra-parliamentary and moved from the Seym to Confederations formed outside of it by activist factions.

The Seym witnessed a gradual change in its rules of voting on bills put before it. Deputies now insisted that unanimous consent be obtained for each bill. Later, the rule was extended to cover all bills in any given session. This greatly hampered the legislative process, particularly since the Seym adopted at the same time the zero budgeting and taxing principle. Specific authorization was now required for each tax collection and expenditure. Attempts were made by the executive and some members of the legislature to promote constitutional reform, but they did not meet with success. Some Seyms closed their sessions with no legislation passed at all.

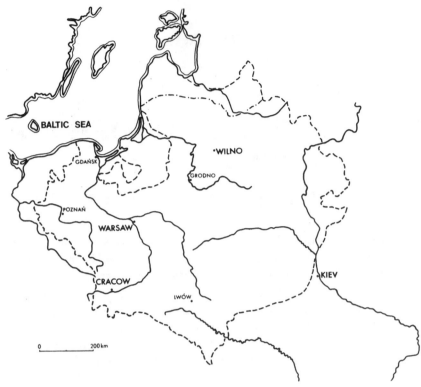

Fig. 30—Polish-Lithuanian Commonwealth in the late 1600s

FIRE-TEST OF THE SYSTEM AND THE ABORTED REFORM

In the mid 1600s Poland followed with keen interest the political developments in the other major parliamentary system of Europe, that of England: the conflict between the Parliament and Charles I, the fortunes of the Cromwellian Protectorate, and of the Stuart Restoration. The trial and execution of Charles I coincided in time with the election of John Casimir Vasa to the kingship of Poland in 1648 and cast a shadow of suspicion over any attempt on his part aimed at increasing royal powers.

The constitutional structure of the First Republic was subjected to its most severe test during the twenty year long administration of John Casimir Vasa (1648-1668). His election brought a most unlikely person to the office of chief executive at the most challenging of times and furnishes one more proof that character does grow to match the office. John Casimir was the youngest son of Sigismund III Vasa. He chose a religious vocation, renounced the world and became a novice of the Jesuit Order. The untimely death of his brother thrust him into the political arena and made him a candidate in the royal election. Released by the Pope from his religious vows of celibacy and obedience, he was put up for election and won the kingship. He married his brother's widow and assumed office at the time of extreme crisis in the country.

Without going into the details of the history of this most chaotic and turbulent period, let it suffice to say that John Casimir's administration weathered in succession the Cossack Rebellion of 1648-55, the Russian War of 1654-67, the Swedish invasion of 1655-60, and the Hungarian invasion of 1655. In the war-devastated country major famines broke out in 1656-59 and 1662-63, and the pestilence ravaged the land in 1659-63. Two revolts by the unpaid army broke out in 1661-63 and 1666-67. Understandably, this period in the history of Poland is called "the Deluge." Such a sequence of calamities would have cowed the strongest of characters, yet, both John Casimir and the political system survived; the latter, however, was severely damaged in its fabric. Remarkably, war or not, elections were held, and Seyms returned to cope as best they could with the situation at hand. Nevertheless, the overload imposed on the legislative system by the adverse political circumstances caused the Seyms to grow belligerent and suspicious. Increasingly signs of friction between the Seym and the Executive made their appearance and grew in intensity. The Seyms were becoming less flexible in responding to the executive, suspecting the latter of having precipitated the series of disasters through inept foreign policy.

A significant factor in the preceding Swedish war was the question of succession to the throne. As all signs indicated the likelihood of another foreign intervention in the event of John Casimir's death, the need for reform of royal election became evident to some politically active people. Others, however, saw in the appeal for reform a desire to tamper with the constitutional arrangements of the country, in particular, with the elective kingship. Casting around for a method to stop this tampering, the conservatives in the Seym chose to introduce the requirement of unanimity of vote on constitutional matters as their preferred method.

The application of the unanimity principle, or, conversely, the recognition of the power of a single Deputy's veto, was initially tested on a trivial constitutional matter. The first Seym terminated by a unitary veto, or *liberum veto* as it was called, occurred in 1652 when Władysław Siciński, Deputy for the County of Upita in Lithuania, objected to the session being extended beyond the statutory six weeks, in spite of the fact that none of the bills put before the Seym had been voted on. Siciński's objection was sustained by Andrzej Maximilian

Fredro, the Speaker of the Seym, and the Seym broke up without approving any legislation. Fredro saw in the legalization of a single Deputy's objection a chance to make the resulting requirement of unanimity into an instrument capable of preventing the introduction of undesirable constitutional changes. It took about 20 years before Fredro's ruling on the right of a single Deputy to stop the action of the Seym hardened into law, and this outcome was by no means certain. In the intervening period, some Seyms upheld the validity of this new procedure, such as the Seym of 1654, which sustained the veto of Deputy P. Białobłocki, while other Seyms overruled it, as was the case with the veto cast by Deputy Tobiasz Wiszowaty in 1658, during the passage of the constitution banning the Arian Sect (Polish Brethern) from Poland. Although intended to eliminate tampering with the major constitutional laws passed in the preceding decades, in actual practice, the acceptance of unitary vetoes was gradually extended to tax and other matters.

Fig. 31—Andrzej M. Fredro (1629-1679), Speaker of the Seym of 1652, who set a precedent by accepting the objection of a single Deputy as a valid cause for termination of a Seym session.

The changes in practice and interpretation of the rules of voting in the Seym were opposed by the executive branch all along. The King summoned extraordinary Seyms after each Seym which disbanded without passing legislation, and when this strategem proved of little value, an attempt was made to suspend, rather than disband, Seyms threatened with a veto. Neither practice brought a permanent cure to this evident aberration of parliamentary development. In its essence, right to require the unanimity of Deputies was tantamount to the transfer of sovereignty from the chamber as a whole to the individual members of the Seym. In critical situations, the rule of unanimous consent could be circumvented by organizing the Deputies elected to a given Seym into a Confederation. Should this move gain acceptance, the resulting Confederated Seym would vote by a majority rule. The problem was to get the Confederation started within the Seym rather than outside of it.

The program of reform, presented to the Seym by the King in 1658 half-way through his administration, contained the following points: voting rules in the Seym should be changed to require two-thirds majority for the passage of bills, the unitary veto (liberum veto) should be banned, permanent taxes should be instituted, and a Permanent Council should be formed as an executive committee of the Seym with membership made up of Deputies and Senators. The Seym was unreceptive to this first reform proposal and rejected the program.

One aftermath of the Seym of 1658 was the passage (over the veto by Wiszowaty) of the law expelling the Arian Sect from Poland. The Arians were an anti-Trinitarian Protestant sect, pacifist in their beliefs and opposed to military service on grounds of conscience. Their pacifist stance in times of foreign invasions and of desperate struggle to drive out the invaders aroused great resentment in the public and led to their expulsion. One suspects, however, that the real reason why in the passage of the Act of Expulsion the Lutherans and Calvinists voted in the Seym together with the Catholics, was grounded in their common disapproval of the Arian denial of the Divinity of Christ. Formally, the expulsion law was in contradiction to the resolutions of the Confederation of Warsaw of 1573, guaranteeing the freedom of religious belief. On the other hand, the right to vote was in that period tied to a military service obligation and the refusal to bear arms in the defense of the country ran afoul of the law of 1510 which prescribed banishment and the loss of civil rights for refusal to answer the call to arms. The expulsion law was a decision in conformance with the earlier of the two laws. The expelled Arians settled in Holland, Germany and England, where their religious beliefs contributed to the rise of Socynianism, and eventually the Unitarian Church.

To the period of the Swedish wars belongs also the involvement of the Seym in the revision of the legal status of Ducal Prussia, the predominently German and Protestant part of Prussia, which remained since 1563 under the feudal rule of the Prussian branch of Hohenzollerns as a fief of Poland. Apart from the duty to do homage to each new ruler of Poland, to pay a nominal fealty fee, and to supply troops in case of war, the link between the Ducal Prussia and Poland remained loose. The Hohenzollerns refused to assume their seat in the Polish Senate, Ducal Prussia did not send Deputies to the Seym, and showed

119

questionable loyalty in various wars of Poland. In 1611 the East Prussian line of Hohenzollerns found itself without male heir, and succeeded in securing from Poland the transfer of the Prussian fief to the Hohenzollern Elector of Brandenburg. During the Swedish invasion of Poland in 1655, the Brandenburg Hohenzollerns sided with the Swedes, showing that the value of the feudal link to Poland was minimal. Pressed by the exigencies of the "Deluge" and being in principle opposed to forced political marriages, the Seym decided to sever the connection. This was accomplished by means of two treaties: of Welawa, concluded on September 19, 1657, which released the Hohenzollern Elector of Brandenburg from his Prussian fealty to Poland, and the treaty of Bydgoszcz of November 6, 1657, by which an alliance with him was concluded against the Swedes. Both treaties were in due time ratified by the Seym, but not without a good deal of opposition from those Deputies who questioned the value of that alliance and the wisdom of putting the territory on both sides of Royal Prussia in the same foreign hands. Although the treaties provided the much needed relief to the hard pressed country, the future was to show the critics right. In the long run, however, the seemingly least important last article in the treaty of Welawa was going to take hold. The Article provided for the return of Ducal Prussia to Polish sovereignty in the event it be no longer ruled by the Hohenzollerns. It is this last article which provides the legal basis for the present-day annexation of East Prussia to Poland (in force since 1945).

Fig. 32—Title page of "Merkuryusz Polski Extraordynaryiny," the first political news-paper printed in Poland. An issue for May 4, 1662.

The question of parliamentary reform came up again in 1661. In that year the reform-minded faction, supported by the King, made a conscious effort to mold public opinion in favor of reform. In the Spring of that year a political weekly was launched in Cracow entitled "Merkuryusz Polski Extraordynaryiny." It was sponsored by Łukasz Opaliński, the one-time Speaker of the Seym of 1638, and appeared with H. Pinocci as the editor, and J. Gorczyn as the publisher. It was the first political paper in Poland. Altogether twenty-seven issues of the paper were published between January 3 and May 4, 1661 in Cracow, and fourteen issues between May 14 and July 22 in Warsaw while the Seym was in session. With the help of the paper the reform program revived, and the campaign preceding its introduction at this Seym made it a test of strength between the reform and the conservative factions. The reformist and the conservative stances were advocated through books and pamphlets. The conservatives were led by the eloquent and popular Andrzej Maximilian Fredro, the Speaker of the Seym of 1652, who first established a precedent for the veto procedure. Fredro favored the idea of retaining the *liberum veto* as a means of preventing the constitutional change unwanted by the conservatives. His stance was summed up in a two-liner:

Things are just right, I confess
Since we got by on even less
(Dobrze jest jak jest
Tak nie było i też było)

which voiced a conservative mood prevalent in the country, combined with the fear of change.

The administration was pushing in the Seym for a reconsideration of the ban on the election of the next chief executive while the present one was still in office, i.e., it favored the so-called election *vivente rege*, which would provide for a smoother transition between successive administrations. Speaking in favor of reform, John Casimir Vasa made an historic address to the Seym on June 6, 1661, predicting that in the absence of reform the presently practiced form of royal election will be the cause of the ultimate undoing of the country:

One must fear that without such election (vivente rege) the Commonwealth will fall prey to the neighbouring nations. Russia will appeal to the people of the same language and will set Lithuania aside for herself. The borders of Greater Poland stand open to the Brandenburgian and one can assume that he will wish to contend for the whole of Prussia, with the House of Habsburg coveting Cracow, it will not pass up a good opportunity of dismembering the state, and will not abstain from a partition.

The speech fell on deaf ears, for few suspected at the time how prophetic it was. The conservatives won out, and the reform program was defeated.

R O Z M O W A

PLEBANA Z ZIEMIANINEM

ALBO

DYSZKVRS

O POSTANOWIENIV

TERAZNIEYSZYM

RZECZY POSPOLITEY.

r

O S P O S O B I E

Z A W I E R A N I A

S E Y M O W.

◄(S)►

Roku Pańskiego DC. XXXXI.

Fig. 33 (Left)–Łukasz Opaliński (1612-1662) Speaker of the Seym of 1638 and the Grand Marshal of the Court. A portrait by S. Kostecki shows him holding the Staff which served as an emblem of his office.

Fig. 34 (Right)—Title page of a political tract written in 1641 by Łukasz Opaliński: "A Discussion Between the vicar and the Squire, or a Discourse on the Present State of the Republic and on the ways of Convening Seyms."

Agitation in favor of royal election vivente rege turned out to be politically a most divisive issue. It involved Jerzy Lubomirski in an impeachment trial at the Seym of 1664 and led to the subsequent Rokosz. The details of this event are discussed elsewhere. The repercussions, however, were felt in all the remaining Seyms of John Casimir's administration. By combining the attempt to firm up the rules of voting in the Seym with the proposal to introduce also the royal election vivente rege, John Casimir made a tactical mistake which was going to have far reaching consequences for further constitutional development of the First Republic. Coming, as it did, at a time when England was going through the Cromwellian experience, and France was seeing the consolidation of absolutist power of the Bourbons, the second part of the program aroused deep hostility in the electorate and caused an overreaction in the form of acceptance by the

Seyms of the validity of the requirement of unanimity of votes on the bills before it. This acceptance was by no means general in the country at large, and in fact was considered illegal by the more articulate part of the society. That this was so is attested to by the instructions prepared by the Seymik of Rawa, meeting in 1667 under Jan Chryzostom Pasek as its Speaker. The instructions (Kartelusze) were prepared for Adam Nowomiejski and Anzelm Piekarski, the two Deputies elected on February 7 to represent the Rawa district at the forthcoming Seym in Warsaw. Responding to a sequence of four Seyms disbanding without legislation through a veto applied and recognized by the successive Speakers (Seyms of 1664-5, 1665, 1666), the first point of these instructions reads:

> As it is through frequent, unfounded, and illegal vetoes that the Seyms are dissolved and, being to the greatest damage of the Commonwealth, we commend their honorable lordships, our Deputies, above all to find a way of concluding the Seyms, of limiting such vetoes by firm law so that we might once again bring a session to a successful end.[*]

In this administration, however, except for the Seym of 1667, all legislation was vetoed. The extraordinary Seyms called in 1665 and 1668 were not able to solve the problem and John Casimir, despondent over his inability to get out of the impasse, gave up the fight at the Seym of 1668 and announced his abdication. The Seym voted him a separation pay of 150,000 zł, to be paid by his successor. Having been widowed in the meantime, John Casimir returned to religious life, went to France and was appointed the Abbot of the Benedictine abbey of St. Germain-des-Prés, then just outside Paris. There he lived out the rest of his days.[**]

The conservatives won the battle in the long run and succeeded in making the recognition of the veto procedure statutory during the coronation Seym of 1669 in Cracow. The action was subsequently confirmed by another constitution passed in 1673. The solidification into law of the seemingly illogical development of liberum veto at these two Seyms touches on a deeper constitutional issue. The recognition of the rule of unanimous consent, and its corollary, the unitary veto (liberum veto), was in all sincerity viewed as a

---

[*] Reprinted from: *Memoirs of the Polish Baroque*, Catherine S. Leach, trans., by permission of University of California Press. Copyright (c) 1976 by the Regents of the University of California.

[**] The abbey church still survives in reasonably good repair. Boulevard St. Germain passes in front of it and a street separates it from Café Deux Maggots, so popular with American expatriate writers in the period between the two world wars. The abbey church contains John Casimir's tomb monument, bearing his life-size likeness dressed in monk's garb and handing his crown away. The tomb stands empty now, for the remains of John Casimir were transferred from Paris to Poland in 1676 for reinterment in the royal tombs in Cracow.

foolproof method of stopping all attempts at interference with the existing procedures of royal elections. Its victory furnished an instrument for arresting in Poland the feared progress toward absolutist monarchy.

In this respect the move was successful, even though, at the same time, the victory of the concept crippled the operation of the system in the forthcoming decades. Embedded even deeper in this problem was the delay in the realization on the part of the electorate, that the source of the civil and political rights rests in the electorate itself, and that the electorate does not really need the king to grant, or confirm rights and privileges, for the Seym could vote them itself. Thus, the retention of the opportunity offered by each royal election of bargaining with the candidates for those rights and privileges was in reality a moot question. The realization of this point came to the electorate eventually one hundred years later, in 1764, during the Convocation Seym preceding the election of Stanisław A. Poniatowski to the kingship.

Looking back at much of the parliamentary obstructionism of this period, which caused John Casimir's withdrawal from politics, it becomes evident that, in addition to domestic causes, it contained a large element of response to the developments abroad. This was the period of the rise of absolutist monarchies when Bourbon, Stuart, Hohenzollern, Romanov and Habsburg dynasties were enhancing their power through the creation of centralized and efficient administrations, taxation systems geared to the support of large standing armies, and the use of these armies in territorial expansion. There were good reasons for opposing the introduction of these trends in Poland, for the enhancement of powers of central government was in almost every case accompanied by a corresponding decrease in the political rights of the populations. It took the Cromwellian Revolution, or the Seym's obstructionism, to stop the trend.

PROCEDURES AND EFFICIENCY OF THE SEYMS

The duration of the Seym session was intially undefined, but on the death of Sigismund Augustus in 1572, and the establishment of the First Republic with elective Kings, a statutory requirement concerning the length of Seym sessions was written into the Pacta Conventa, or the Articles of Agreement presented to the candidates in the Royal Election. The law specified that the regular Seyms will last six weeks, and will be called into session every two years. Extraordinary Seyms could be called in an emergency out of sequence, for a session of two weeks' duration. The Convocation and the Coronation Seyms were included in the two week category, whereas the Election Seym, requiring more time, was allotted six weeks. The duration of a Seym could be extended if all Deputies attending consented. This consent was not easily obtained, since the Deputies were reimbursed for their expenses by the Seymiks with a lump sum covering only the Seym session proper. In connection with this it is worth observing that the Deputy's term of office spanned approximately four months, set by the statutory requirement of his participation in four distinct functions. The first of them was his physical presence at the Seymik which elected him, to receive the oral and the written instructions on matters to be brought up at the National Seym on behalf of his constituency. The second was the required attendance at the pre-Seym meeting of the General Seymik of his province. Travel to Koło, Korczyn, Malbork, Warsaw, Słonim or Wisznia was required, depending on the province in which the Deputy's constituency was located. Alternately, attendance at a provincial caucus in Warsaw, just before the Seym assembled, could be required. The third, and the most important function, was the attendance at the six week session of the Seym, usually in Warsaw or Grodno. Finally, the fourth required function was the Deputy's appearance at the debriefing Seymik in his home constituency. The four months between the election and the debriefing constituted the actual term of office. While it lasted, the Deputy was covered by parliamentary immunity: he could not be imprisoned, subpoenaed, and all outstanding litigation in which he was possibly involved had to be suspended for the duration. Furthermore, any attempt against the Deputy's life, limb or property was classified as an act of lèse majesté, since in responding to the royal Writ of Summons he became the King's agent for the duration of his term of office.

Throughout the early history of the Seyms, most of them were called in the late fall or early winter after the harvest was in, so as not to take the Deputies away from farming, on which most of them depended for a living. In addition to the Ordinary, the Extraordinary, the Convocation, the Election and the Coronation Seyms, each of which was of a statutory variety, there were two other types of Seyms called from time to time. These were the Pacification and the Inquest Seyms. The first of these was called after an election of the King, if such an election had led to a great difference of opinion and internal turmoil. Its purpose was to bring the opposing sides to the conference table and pacify the opponents through political concessions. Five such Seyms were held: in 1598, 1673, 1698, 1699 and 1735. The Inquest Seyms dealt with royal impeachments and were ordinary Seyms, but with their business entirely devoted to investigating the non-constitutionality of the Chief Executive's actions. Two such Seyms were held, in 1592 and 1646. Except for these two types of special Seyms, the characteristics of the regular Seyms are summarized in Table 24. Regardless of the type of Seym held, the procedures and the mode of voting were the same, with two exceptions: the Confederated and the Election Seyms operated under modified rules of procedure.

Throughout the 1500s and the first half of 1600s the political minorities in the Seym would concede to the majority in the acceptance of bills before the Seym, and would allow them to be passed. There is ample evidence to indicate that important constitutional laws passed by the Seyms in the years 1548, 1553, 1563, and 1565 were passed by majority vote.

TABLE 24—TYPES AND FUNCTIONS OF SEYMS IN THE FIRST REPUBLIC

Ordinary (Walny)—Convoked by the King on the advice of Senate, originally as often as needed, after 1573 every two years. Duration: six weeks. Attended by the King, the Senate and the Deputies. Voting initially by majority rule. After 1652, the individual veto (liberum veto) was allowed.

Extraordinary (Ekstraordynaryjny)—Convoked by the King on the advice of the Senate in an emergency. Duration: two weeks. Composition and rules of voting as above. First appeared in 1613.

Confederated (Konfederacyjny)—Convoked either by the King, or the Interrex under an a priori agreement between the Deputies to vote on legislation by majority rule. Composition as above. First appeared in 1573.

Convocation (Konwokacyjny)—Convoked by the Interrex on the death of the King, to set the political conditions for the candidates to the kingship. As a rule confederated. Duration: two weeks. Composition: Interrex, the Senate and Deputies. First appeared in 1573.

Election (Elekcyjny)—Convoked by the Interrex to elect a new King. No set duration. Composition: Interrex, Senate and anyone with the right to vote who could attend. After 1573, as a rule, confederated. Voting by palatinate under majority rule. First appeared in 1501.

Coronation (Koronacyjny)—Convoked by the Interrex to swear in the new King. Composition: the Interrex, the Elect, the Senate and the Deputies. First appeared in 1502.

General Council (Rada Walna)—Convoked by the Archbishop of Gniezno when the King could not attend; without legislative powers. Attended by the Senate and the Deputies from the previous Seym. Only three were ever held; 1576, 1710, and 1734.

In the normal course of events, the laws made by the national Seym were sent to the Seymiks to be implemented. The Seymik of each county or palatinate could, and on occasion did, refuse to implement the law in its own territory. To avoid post factum rejections, in the 1600s the Seymiks started to equip their Deputies to the Seym with a set of instructions as to which laws will be rejected if passed by the Seym. Thus the vetoing of legislation was transferred from the local to the national scene.

Fig. 35—A scene from a session of the Seym held in Warsaw in 1623. From an engraving by G. Lauro.

After considering in detail the mode of operation of the Seyms it is illuminating to take a brief look at the number of Seyms and their legislative record. The voluminous legislative output of the first 300 years of the operation of the Seyms of Poland is contained in the "Volumina Legum," a compendium of legislation described in more detail in the Bibliography. Lists of major laws are shown in Tables 14, 22, 29, and 36. A summary of the Seym's meeting record is also presented here for the 245 Seyms of the hereditary kingdom and the First Republic, in the form of a bar graph in Figure 36. The graph shows the number of Seyms which completed their business and passed legislation, Seyms which were incomplete for some reason, either through a lack of quorum, or because they were suspended and later recalled, or disbanded through the king's inability to attend, and finally, the Seyms which had their legislation vetoed. The bars are drawn for each decade between 1490 and 1800. With the statutory frequency of one Seym elected every two years, as specified by the pacta conventa of 1573, there should have been at least five Seyms per each decade. The excess over five represents extraordinary Seyms called in war time, on the death of a king, for pacification after political unrest, or in an attempt to revive legislation killed at the preceding Seym by a legislative veto. In all, the record shows a total of 192 completed Seyms spanning the 300 years (1493-1793). This can be compared with the 95 Congresses of the United States returned every two years during the past 200 years in America. The 192 fruitful Seyms represent a solid legislative record for the years during which the Seyms were returned, made laws, declared wars and made peace, and in general conducted the business of the state in the hereditary monarchy and the First Republic.

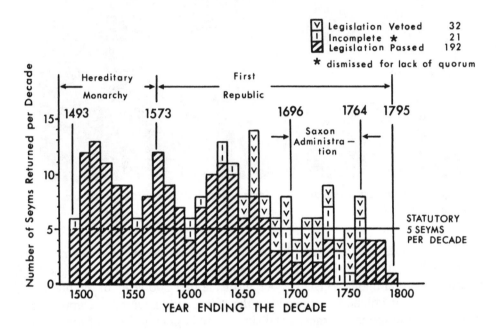

Fig. 36—Frequency of Elections and the Outcome of Seyms of the Hereditary Monarchy and the First Republic

A concise description of the mode of operation of the Seym and the Seymiks was published in England in 1678 by Moses Pitt of London. Although inaccurate as to the number of Deputies returned by the Seymiks in the General Elections, it does give a contemporary English view, interesting enough to quote it at length:

The Councils, or Parliaments of Poland, are of two sorts: 1. Civil, to which Councellors come in their Gowns. 2. Military, to which they come in Military habit. The latter are only held in the time of an Interregnum. The former are frequently called: and are 1. Ordinary; which by the Laws are summoned once in two years. 2. Extraordinary; which are assembled as the necessity of affairs requires. When either Ordinary or Extraordinary Councils are to be convened, the King by his Letters summons the lesser Councils or Conventions, in the several Palatinates, larger Provinces, and certain

Districts. These Conventions precede the general Assemblies of the Kingdom six weeks, unless some extraordinary accident; and are held in the proper Cities of the Palatinates and Provinces, appointed for that purpose.

Here, after they have chosen a Marshal (who seems to be much like our Speaker, as being the Director of the Convention) they first consider such things as are propounded to them by the Kings Deputies, dispatched away to every Convention, and what other business is to be motioned at the General Session. After that they choose the Land Deputies, or provincial Delegates, for the General Assembly. Every Province sends so many (almost in the same manner as our Shires, save only that they are not chosen by the people) till the whole number amounts to about 300. These Deputies are generally elected out of such Magistrates as are not of the Senatorian order; excluding all Judges and their Assistants, Collectors, and all Officers of the Exchequer, unless they have exact and full acquittances from the Treasurer. The Delegates, like our Burgesses, have a certain allowance from their respective Provinces, during the sitting of the general assembly.

The particular Conventions being broken up (which by the Law are not to sit above four days) three weeks before the Senators and Delegates repair to the Grand Session, they meet at the general Committees for the several Provinces; where they again read over the Kings commands, the instructions given to the Delegates, and what was thought needful to be propounded for the publick good.

The grand Assembly being met, the Deputies repair to their Chamber and choose their Marshal or Director; which done, they are all conducted to kiss the Kings hand: and after that ceremony perform'd, the Chancellours of the Kingdom and the Dukedome, in order, declare to them the substance of those affairs which are to be the subject of their Debates. Before they depart, they put the King in mind of supplying such employments as are vacant with deserving persons; and desire an account of such Laws or Ordinances as have been made by the resident Senators since the sitting of the last grand Convention. Having so done they return to their Chamber.

The power of these Nuncii, or Deputies, is very great: for when they send any of their number to the King, they are presently admitted, let the King be never so busy, and have an immediate dispatch. If they clash in their debates, the King is careful to send some of the Senators to reconcile them; who then give them the Title of 'Mości Panowie Bracia' or Gracious Lords Brothers. They have also power to impeach any great Officer of Misdemeanours, and to put the King himself in mind of his promises touching the Laws and privileges of the Kingdom; neither is any constitution valid, that has not its Original from the Chamber of the Deputies. And, which is yet more, if any one of the whole number of the Nuntii dissent, nothing can be legally concluded. So that upon the protestation and departure of one Deputy, the whole Convention is ipso facto dissolv'd.

Whilst the Deputies are thus consulting, the King and the Senators have little to do, but to hear certain criminal cases appointed before hand for the first week, and certain civil controversies the second; till the return of the Deputies embodies the whole Senate together. Then every man has liberty to deliver his mind, with the leave and direction of the Marshal. The King suspends his own opinion, till the Senators and Deputies, or the major part of them agree. Then he endeavours to reconcile their different votes; or if he cannot prevail, concurs with that party which has voted most conformably to the Laws and privileges of the Realm. These consultations by the Law, ought not to be continued above fifteen days after the joining of both Houses: though sometimes urgency of affairs causes further prolongation.

When the session breaks up, the Deputies returning home give notice of their return to the Captains with Jurisdiction, and the Palatines or Vice-Palatines give the same notice of the return of the Deputies to the Nobility, inviting them withal to the Post-Comitial Assemblies or Conventions of Relation: the meeting whereof the King appoints. In these Conventions, the Deputies produce the constitutions made in the last general Assembly of the Estates, delivered to them under seal by the Chancellours, and take care that they be fairly transcribed into the Land and military Registers; not omitting, after this, to give a full account of what they have acted in discharge of their Trusts.

The terminology used by Moses Pitt in the passage quoted above is based on the Latin equivalents of the corresponding Polish words. Thus, the Seymiks, the General Seymiks and the National Seym are referred to by him as the particular Conventions, the general Committees for the provinces, and the Grand Session, respectively. The Debriefing Seymiks are termed by him the Conventions of Relation.

In the administration of Jan Sobieski the much publicized impeachment of Jan Andrzej Morsztyn, the Minister of the Treasury, took place, followed by a break in diplomatic relations with France lasting some ten years. The impeachment was precipitated by Morsztyn's inability to resist Louis XIV's bribery practices. Thus, while the rest of central Europe was toeing Louis XIV's line by allowing him to buy his way into their internal affairs, only the Seym of Poland chose to stop his interference and twitched his nose. More will be said about this in Chapter VIII.

In the 100 years separating the administration of John Casimir Vasa and Stanisław August Poniatowski, the administrations of Michał Korybut Wiśniowiecki (1668-1674) and Jan Sobieski (1674–1696) limped along, hamstrung by the requirement of unanimity, while in the following two Saxon administrations, aggravated by the habits of political thought brought by the Saxons, the system ground down to a complete standstill.

In spite of the tremendous impediment of the rule of unanimity, when it became accepted as a constitutional principle in the second half of the 1600s almost all of the earlier, and a fair though ever decreasing fraction of the later Seyms were completed successfully. In all, the legislation of 32 out of 245 Seyms of the hereditary monarchy and the First Republic was vetoed. The high proportion of success could be taken as a high measure of civic responsibility, which was certainly not lacking in the earlier history of the Seyms.

Fig. 37—Jan Andrzej Morsztyn (1621-1693) elected a Deputy to six Seyms between 1648 and 1659 for the county of Opatów, served on numerous Seym commissions and diplomatic missions. Impeached by the Seym of 1683 for his involvement in promoting Louis XIV's interests in Poland while holding a position of a Minister. A portrait by Jeremiasz Falck (1619-1677).

It is worth observing that the acceptance of the requirement of unanimity reached its peak in the period of intense conflict between the legislative and the executive branches of the government which characterized the administrations of the two Saxon Kings (1696-1764).

Some penetrating remarks on the operation of the majority rule were put forward by a modern historian of Polish parliamentarism, and one time himself a Seym Deputy, the late Władysław Konopczyński. They are quoted here in a synopsis made by R. R. Palmer, to bring out the assumptions implicit in the majority rule.

The acceptance of majority rule... is in fact a difficult, artificial, and acquired habit of mind. It depends on several prerequisites: first, that votes be counted, not evaluated in importance according to the identity of the voter; that is, all votes must be considered equal. In the order of business, discussion must distinctly be followed by voting, lest nothing emerge but a vague sense of the meeting, or apparent unanimity in which responsibilities are indefinite, and differences of opinion are temporarily covered up, only to break out later. There must be a party of some kind, personal, political, religious, or economic, willing to work for years to carry out a decision, and to resist its reversal. It is well to have a settled and fixed population, for if dissidents can simply go away, or retire so far into the depths of the country as to be forgotten, they never learn to submit to majority wishes, nor does the majority learn to govern. A strong executive is useful, for there can be no majority rule unless minorities are obliged to accept the decisions once made.

The bad will and political manipulation, which characterized the two Saxon administrations, made the unworkability of the existing constitutional arrangements apparent, and calls for reform produced some legislation. Thus, a constitution passed in 1764 exempted from the rule of unanimity the economic and tax matters.*

CONFEDERATION IN CONSTITUTIONAL PRACTICE IN POLAND

One of the oldest constitutional devices through which the population of Poland participated in the affairs of state in an emergency was the Confederation. This was a voluntary association of individuals, towns, or gentry governing the entire state or a part of it in a national emergency when a regular governmental machinery was incapacitated or needed additional assistance. As the inspection of the attached list of major Confederations will reveal, the institution was older than the national Seym, and developed at about the same time as the Seymik. The practice of forming Confederations was an expression of an activist spirit and was perfectly legal for centuries until a ban was placed on it in the Constitution of 1791. It was a well established constitutional liberty, though poorly defined by legislation, and the King could not legally oppose it. In concept, the institution was similar to "covenanting" in seventeenth century Scotland.

In essence, the Confederation was an organization of "concerned citizens." A typical Confederation would start with a group of people that would elect their Speaker, a Treasurer and, if military, a commander, plus other lower officials. The group would formulate its aims, publish them in a form of a proclamation, and issue an invitation for others to join. Confederations were formed as a rule during an interregnum, during a foreign invasion, or in a grave constitutional

---

* R. R. Palmer,*The Age of the Democratic Revolution: A Political History of Europe and America, 1760-1800*, Vol. I. Copyright (c) 1959 by Princeton University Press, excerpt from p. 417. Reprinted by permission of Princeton University Press.

crisis. When formed within the Seym, among the Deputies, the Seym thus constituted voted by majority rule, the instructions given by the Seymiks to the Deputies did not apply, and the rule of unanimity (liberum veto) could be overridden. The Confederation device could be, and often was, abused as when civil war or a rebellion of unpaid armies took the form of a Confederation to appear legal.

One of the most famous Confederations was organized in 1440 by the towns and gentry of Prussia against their German rulers. This was the territory of Polish Pomerania and of Prussia, overrun some 200 years before by the Teutonic Knights of the German Order of Mary, a crusader organization seeking new territory after the loss of the Holy Land to the Saracens. In 1446 the towns revolted against the rule of the Order, and the Confederation (Związek Pruski) became a military one. In 1454 it dispatched a delegation to the King of Poland to ask for reincorporation into Poland. A war with the German Order ensued, lasting thirteen years (1454-1466), and the area was reunited with Poland.*

Fig. 38—_The text of the agreement between Catholics and Protestants to support religious tolerance in Poland. The Agreement was contained in the Act of Confederation of Warsaw of 1573 and was included in the_ pacta conventa _drawn up for a royal election._

---

* Five centuries later this was destined to be the "Polish Corridor" to the Baltic Sea and the bone of contention between the Second Republic and the Third Reich. Polish refusal to yield it to Germany was the formal cause of the Second World War.

Confederations could and often did prepare legislative measures for enactment by the Seym. One of the principal pieces of legislation dealing with the question of religious freedom and aimed at the prevention of civil wars over differences of religious preference, is contained in the Act of the Confederation of Warsaw of 1573. This Confederation was organized within the Convocation Seym held upon the death of Sigismund II Augustus, the last male member of the Jagiellonian dynasty; its purpose was to draw up the conditions to be accepted by the successful candidate in the forthcoming royal election. The conditions formed a part of the Articles of Agreement (pacta conventa) presented to candidates in all subsequent royal elections. The key passage in the Act of Confederation reads as follows:

> As in our Commonwealth there exists great dissidence in the cause of Christian reli-
> gion, to prevent the growth of any harmful sedition, such as can be clearly seen in other
> realms, we promise in our names, and in the name of our successors in perpetuity and
> bound by oath on our faith, honor and conscience, that we who differ in religion will
> keep peace among ourselves and for reason of different faith and religious practice will
> not shed blood, nor penalize by confiscation of wealth or good name, prison or exile,
> and we will not help any authority or office in such undertakings: instead, should
> anyone try to shed blood claiming an exalted cause, we shall all be responsible for
> preventing it, even if it were attempted under the pretext of a decree, or a court
> decision.

The Act was successful in barring from Poland the application of the rule cuius regio eius religio, i.e., the imposition by force of the religion of the ruler on the subjects. As practice would show in the following centuries, it was also successful in preventing civil wars over religious issues, but it did not prevent the Protestant Swedes, intoxicated by their successes in the religious wars in Germany, from invading Poland in 1655. This invasion put the Act to its most severe test when the members of the pacifist Arian Sect (Polish Brethern) refused to bear arms in the defense of the country, claiming conscientious objection. As the country had no natural boundaries, and its existence as an independent state stood at all times entirely on its ability to defend itself, this led to the decision by the Seym of 1658 to expel the Arians from the country. All other religious denominations were left undisturbed. The same Swedish invasion offered the opportunity for one of the most effective uses of a Confederation when, in the administration of John Casimir Vasa the country was overrun by the Swedes and the King was exiled in Silesia. A revival of national resistance took the form of a General Confederation, a wide-spread partisan movement was organized, the army was reassembled and the Swedes defeated and driven out. Later Confederations, however, were used mostly in periods of civil upheavals and added greatly to the confusion and the general disorientation of the body politic.

Confederated Seyms held during the interregna offered a fertile ground for initiating constitutional changes (such as took place at the Seyms of 1573, 1649, and 1764) and set a stage for the appearance of outstanding personalities. One such was Mikołaj Smogulecki, Deputy to the Convocation Seym of 1632, who in his later years became a Jesuit, joined one of the two pioneer missions maintained by Jesuits in Japan and China, and won recognition as a scientist and astronomer from the Emperor of China.

In the closing decades of the First Republic, the form of a Confederation was given to both the Seym of 1788-1792 and to its opposition united at Targowica. The confederated form of the former allowed it to overcome the liberum veto and pass the Constitution of 1791. The new Constitution abolished the liberum veto and made further Confederations illegal. The Confederation of Targowica, organized in 1792, was therefore formally illegal. Its success in overturning the Constitution of 1791 cost the country its independence. The last significant Confederation ever activated was that of Warsaw in 1812 during the Napoleonic Wars.

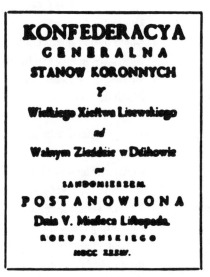

Fig. 39—Title page of the Act of the General Confederation of Dzików, organized in 1734 to support Stanisław Leszczyński in his claim to the crown of Poland.

In retrospect, the Confederations of the period of hereditary monarchy and the First Republic may be thought of as incipient political parties formed ad hoc to deal with a pressing issue, and limited in existence to a definite period which could vary from several months up to several years. A summary of major Confederations held in this period, both in and out of the Seym, is given in Tables 25, 26, and 27.

Finally, one may observe that the 1980 "Solidarity" movement in Poland bears a remarkable likeness to the Confederations of old. The public organized spontaneously in the face of a grave crisis and a government unable to cope with it, to formulate and offer alternatives.

TABLE 25—CONFEDERATIONS OF THE HEREDITARY MONARCHY

Year	Place	Organizer/Cause
1298		Clergy, to promote their interests
1302		Towns, for safety from highway robbers
1311		Towns, supported by the King
1349-50		Towns, supported by the King, to promote public safety
1352	Gr. Poland	Maćko Borkowic, gentry, against excesses of the prefect
1382	Radom	On death of King Louis, for safety during interregnum
1384	Radom	Magnates, gentry and towns, to support Queen Jadwiga
1406	Piotrków	North of Poland, against clergy's right to tithe
1407		Clergy in defense of its right to tithe
1423-24	Wieluń	In defense against Hussite invasion, supporting the King
1438	Korczyn	Twenty gentry families, supporting the King
1438	Sieradz	Ruthenian gentry, during minority of the King
1439	Nowy Korczyn	Spytko of Melsztyn, supporting Hussites
1440	Kwidzyn	Towns of Prussia, against the German Order
1464	Lwów	Gentry and the City, aganist excesses of the prefect

TABLE 26—CONFEDERATIONS IN THE SEYMS OF THE FIRST REPUBLIC

Year	Place	Type of Seym	Occasion Election of:
1573	Warsaw	C, E*	Henri Valois
1575	Warsaw	C, E	Stephen Bathory
1586-87	Warsaw	C, E	Sigismund III Vasa
1632	Warsaw	C, E	Ladislaus IV Vasa
1648	Warsaw	C, E	John Casimir Vasa
1668	Warsaw	C, E	Michał Korybut Wiśniowiecki
1674-76	Warsaw	C, E	John III Sobieski
1696	Warsaw	C, E	Augustus II Wettin
1733	Warsaw	C, E	Augustus III Wettin
1764	Warsaw	C, E	Stanisław A. Poniatowski
1717	Warsaw	Mute Seym	Wind up Confederation of Tarnogród
1735	Warsaw	Pacification	To reconcile opposing parties
1768	Warsaw	Extraordinary	Wind up Confederation of Radom
1773-75	Warsaw	Extraordinary	Ratify the First Partition
1776	Warsaw	Ordinary	Reform the government
1788-92	Warsaw	Ordinary	Enact a new Constitution
1793	Grodno	Extraordinary	Repeal the Constitution, ratify Second Partition

* C,E—Convocation and Election Seyms of the royal election sequence

TABLE 27—CONFEDERATIONS OUTSIDE SEYMS OF THE FIRST REPUBLIC

Year	Place	Organizer/Cause
1615-23		Cities of Gdańsk, Toruń and Elbląg for mutual support
1655	Tyszowce	Army, gentry opposing the Swedes
1672	Szczebrzeszyn	Pro-French Party, against Michał Korybut Wiśniowiecki
1673	Gołąb	Pro-Austrian Party, in support of Wiśniowiecki
1698		Lithuania opposing K.J. Sapieha
1703	Środa	Greater Poland, against Augustus II, Saxon Army
1704	Sandomierz	Augustus II, to gain support
1704	Opatów	Army supporting Augustus II, against Lubomirski

TABLE 27 (CONTINUED)—CONFEDERATIONS OUTSIDE SEYMS OF THE FIRST REPUBLIC

Year	Place	Organizer/Cause
1704	Warsaw	Radziejowski Party, to depose Augustus II
1715	Gorzyce	Polish Army, against Saxon Army
1715	Tarnogród	Against the Saxon Army and Augustus II
1733	Kolbuszowa	In support of S. Leszczyński, against German influences
1734	Dzików (Tarnobrzeg)	In support of Stanisław Leszczyński
1764	Wilno	Czartoryski, opposing K.S. Radziwiłł
1767	Toruń	Protestants, demanding restoration of rights
1767	Słuck	Greek Orthodox, demanding restoration of rights
1767	Radom	Religious Dissidents, supporting K.S. Radziwiłł
1768	Bar	Gentry, against Poniatowski, dissidents and the Russians
1769	Dowspuda	Lithuanians, in defense of independence
1792	Targowica	Conservatives, against constitutional reforms
1812	Warsaw	In support of Napoleon, against the Russians

THE SEYM AND THE COSSACK QUESTION

Among the vexing problems occupying a succession of Seyms in the 1660s was the Cossack question. It emerged as one of the side issues of the union between Poland and Lithuania, concluded at Lublin in 1569. The state of Lithuania had reached the zenith of its territorial expansion shortly before its union with Poland as a result of a series of successful wars against the Mongols. Three hundred years earlier, the Mongols had invaded, beaten and conquered Kievan Russia and even made some incursions into Poland. Formed as a result of dynastic subdivisions in the later Middle Ages, the Kievan principalities were no match for the Mongols and were subjugated by them one by one. The Lithuanian reconquest encompassed not only the Kievan Russia but also the virtually uninhabited borderlands, stretching southwards on both sides of the river Dnieper between Kiev and the Black Sea and adjoining the last remnant of the Mongol empire in Europe, the Tartar Khanate of Crimea. This was the "Savage Steppe" (Dzikie Pola), an area where border clashes between the Lithuanians and the Tartars were frequent, and where any dare-devil could make his fortune by raiding the Tartar coastal towns grown rich on the Black Sea trade.

After the union with Poland, the area along the river Dnieper became a catchment basin for all the adventurers, fugitive serfs, and other outlaws, who banded together to form a community on an island just above the rapids on the river. The community became known as the Sich, and its inhabitants as the Kazaks or Cossacks, a Tartar word meaning "Freebooters." There was a striking parallel between this Polish-Lithuanian "Wild East" of the 1600s and the American "Wild West" of the 1800s. Both lured farmers away from settled parts of the country to the unsettled borderlands, and both produced unruly, selfreliant communities where the gun was often the wage-earner. The Cossack raids on the Crimea led in turn to reprisal raids by the Tartars on the lands of the Polish-Lithuanian Commonwealth.

The Seym tried to deal with the chaotic border situation in the south-east by a series of acts which would give some coherence to the problem. At first, attempts were made to enlist the Cossacks into the Army of the Commonwealth, and in 1590 a Registry of Cossacks was established, a pay scale for the registered Cossacks was fixed, and a Commander of Cossacks was appointed. The chief difficulty turned out to be keeping the Registry down to a fairly reasonable size, initially set at 6,000 as a peace-time complement. The assurance of pay and the quasi-legal character given to the Cossack establishment led to a rapid increase in their number. They fought on the Polish side in the 1579-82 war with Muscovy at a strength of 12,000. In later wars with Muscovy, 1619-21, their number increased to 30,000. Difficulties arose over providing pay for this mass of soldiers and over the reduction of their number to the statutory 6,000. The commonwealth could rarely utilize that many mercenaries in times of peace. An armed intervention by the Regular Army against the Cossacks was required in 1625.

The Seym Act of 1635 enlarged the Cossack Registry to 20,000, but even that fell short of their expectations and did not prevent their eventual revolt. After the First Cossack War of 1648, an Act of Seym of 1649 abolished the Cossack Registry, since the Commonwealth had found itself in the unpleasant situation of financing every outlaw in the country and provoking the Tartar and later Turkish wars as well. The Second Cossack War in 1651 (the Chmielnicki Rebellion) left large areas of south-east Poland devastated. In 1658 at Hadziacz the Seym delegation made an offer to the Cossacks to create an autonomous "Ruthenian Duchy" out of the palatinates of Kiev, Czernichów and Bracław, to serve as their home. The agreement ran into ratification delays in the Seym and the lack of consensus between the Cossacks themselves, eventually causing part of the Cossacks to transfer their allegiance to Muscovy.

Fig. 40—*A scene from the joint session of the Seym and the Senate held in 1611 showing Stanisław Żółkiewski presenting Tsar Vasyl Shuyski, taken prisoner during the Russian campaign. The scene took place in the Old Senate Chamber in the Castle of Warsaw. A painting by Thomas Dolabella (1570-1650).*

A rare opportunity was missed here to recreate a nucleus of Ruthenian statehood, for while the offer of Hadziacz included the recognition of the status of Cossacks as freemen, and would have given their internal assemblies the status of Seymiks with their powerful long range effect of awakening national political consciousness of the region, the Russian tutelage resulted in just the opposite: the submission to central absolutist government and the indefinite postponement of their political aspirations. Subsequently, Muscovy ran into the same problems with the Cossacks as Poland did, and solved them in the 1700s by uprooting the Sich Cossacks from their settlements along the river Dnieper and resettling them farther east on the river Don. There, the Cossacks continued their semi-independent existence, supplying the Russian Army with cavalry regiments for use in foreign wars, conquest of Siberia, and for suppression of national and revolutionary movements. They were used by the Russians, in that capacity in Poland to suppress the National Uprising of 1864.

The modern sequel to this story took place in this century after the 1917 revolution in Russia. The Cossacks declared themselves independent of Russia and were beaten into submission by the Bolsheviks only with great difficulty at the end of the Civil War. The story was movingly told by M. Sholohov in *Quiet Flows the Don*.

The last act of the Cossack drama unfolded during the Second World War and involved also the British and the Americans. During the German invasion of the Ukraine, the Cossacks switched their allegiance to the Germans when the latter reached the Don area in their drive towards Stalingrad. Subsequently, a Cossack division fought on the German side until Germany's collapse. Finding itself at the end of the war at Lienz, in Austria, the division surrendered to the Western Allies and was turned over by them to the Soviets who proceeded to ship it off to concentration camps for destruction.

STATE WITHIN A STATE: THE JEWISH REPRESENTATION

A discussion of Polish legislative institutions would be incomplete without the mention of the legislative system of the Polish Jewry in prePartition Poland. That system existed as a separate representative entity for some two hundred years, overlapping the latter part of the Hereditary Monarchy and most of the life of the First Republic. A large Jewish community grew over the centuries in Poland, encouraged by royal grants permitting the settlement of Jews who sought refuge from persecution in other countries. The royal grants were followed by laws made by the Seyms, establishing the legal status of Jews. Relative to other social strata in the Commonwealth the status was that of freemen, somewhere between the gentry and the burghers, both as regards the personal rights and the structure of representation.

In 1551 Sigismund Augustus issued a charter which was to become a Magna Carta for Jewish selfgovernment in Greater Poland. The charter specified that the Jewish communities elect their own rabbis and judges to conduct their religious and administrative affairs. The elected officials were authorized to elucidate all questions of religious ritual, to perform marriages and grant divorces, legalize transfers of property, and settle disputes between the Jews. The charter provided a legal basis for the organization of the Jewish self-governing community at the local level, the Kahal. The executive functions of the Kahal were carried out by its board. It varied in size from ten persons in smaller towns to forty in the larger ones, with its membership elected annually. The Kahals became particularly important in the second half of the sixteenth century. It was during this period that further development of Jewish representation took place with striking similarities to that of the gentry. Thus, analogous to the surrounding Polish community, the administrative functions of the Kahal corresponded to the committees elected annually by the gentry assembled in the county Seymiks. The Kahal, like the Seymik, collected and turned over to the Exchequer the state taxes, arranged the assessment of imposts, and provided funds for the support of the local Jewish institutions and schools. In addition, it executed real-estate deeds. The jurisdiction of the Kahal of each city extended over the Jews settled in the countryside, who did not have an autonomous organization of their own.

In time, provincial conferences of the representives from the local Kahals developed, much along the lines of the General Seymiks of the provinces. These periodic conferences were called "Vaads" and were attended by rabbis and Kahal leaders. The first of these provincial assemblies are known to have taken place in the middle of the sixteenth century and met at the time and place of great fairs. Litigation between disputing parties could be brought to the Vaad, which would then act as an appellate court. The city of Lublin, in the province of Lesser Poland, was the chief meeting place of the Vaads. In the second half of the sixteenth century the Vaad meetings became more frequent and regular and were also attended by the representatives of Jewish communities in other provinces. Their deliberations were extended to cover administrative as well as legal matters. The Vaad took it upon itself to determine the order of Kahal elections and the area of competence of rabbis and judges, and issued permits to publish Jewish books.

A separate and important area of Vaad competence developed when it started to make proposals for laws relating to Jewish affairs to be considered by the Seym. It then appointed delegates and sent them to the meeting places of the Seym to lobby for their passage. Should the laws be passed by the Seym, the Vaad took it upon itself to endorse them and to see to their enforcement in the Jewish community. As an example, the Vaad which sat in Lublin in 1580 endorsed a law which barred the Jews of Poland from farming state revenues and collecting taxes from the gentiles since it was felt that the people involved might, through greed and desire of profit, harm the good name of the Jewish community and endanger it.

In its mature form, the Vaad was attended by Jewish representatives from the provinces of Greater Poland (Poznań), Lesser Poland (Cracow and Lublin), Ruthenia (Lwów), and Wołyń (Ostróg and Kamieniec). Because of this it became known as the "Council of the Four Lands" (Vaad Arba Aratzoth). At one time the delegates from Lithuania also participated, making it the "Council of the Five Lands." In 1623 the Kahals of Lithuania withdrew and formed their own representation. It was attended by delegates from Brześć, Grodno and

Pińsk. In 1653 the Kahal of Wilno was added, and in 1691 the Kahal of Słuck joined.

The Council of the Four Lands met once or twice a year, alternately in Lublin in the spring and Jarosław at the end of summer. Organizationally, it was made up of one delegate of each principal Kahal, selected from among its elders, and several leading Rabbis of Poland, the equivalent of Bishop-Senators in the Senate. In the middle of the sixteenth century there were six Rabbis. Altogether, the lay and religious members numbered about thirty. After the Council of the Four Lands became an established institution, the individual Kahals in each province started to hold their own provincial Vaads, which stood to the Vaad Arba Aratzoth in the same relation, as the General Seymiks to the national Seym. In its totality, this was the legislative and administrative system of the Jewish community, which paralleled the Polish national legislative system, and formed a state-within-a-state.

In its function as the guardian and administrator of Jewish interests in Poland, the Council of the Four Lands acted as the central tax-imposing and collecting authority of the Jewish community. Table 28 shows the taxes collected as they followed the growth of the community in numbers over nearly two centuries.

TABLE 28—JEWISH POLL TAX IN POLAND

Year	Amount (zł)
1591	20,000
1634	80,000
1656*	70,000
1661	105,000
1673	105,000
1714	210,000
1726	220,000
1756	220,000

*Loss of population due to wars and pestilence

The separate tax system for the Jewish community came to an end in 1764, when the reform of the tax system was carried out by the Seym. At that time both the Seymiks and the Vaad were stripped of their tax collecting powers, and a national tax service replaced them in this function. The Council of the Four Lands and the Lithuanian Council did not survive the collapse of the First Republic and the imposition by the Partitioning Powers of more restrictive constitutional and civil rights arrangements.

In retrospect, it is worth observing that the Jewish legislative institutions in Poland were unique in Jewish history in the entire period between the Sanhedrin of antiquity and the Knesset of the State of Israel. They contributed substantially to the survival of the Jewish traditions in an otherwise hostile world and the preservation of their national consciousness.

The history of this period provides an explanation of why it was Poland, among all the countries of Europe, that became a home of a large, thriving and vigorous Jewish community.

To bring the description of this period to a close, the major facts relating to the national legislative and constitutional developments are tabulated. The major legislation of the period 1573-1699 is listed in Table 29. The constitutional arrangements of the First Republic are summarized in Table 30. Biographical notes on more prominent parliamentarians of this period close this chapter.

TABLE 29—PRINCIPAL LEGISLATION OF SEYMS OF THE FIRST REPUBLIC (PART II)

1648	Register of taxation for Prussia established
1649	Mining laws confirmed
1650	Mint commission established
1654	Devaluation of coinage authorized
1657	Excise tax law passed
	Treaty of Bydgoszcz-Welawa,
	Prussian fief relinquished
1658	Burghers of Lwów given Seym representation
	Arian Sect expelled from Poland
1659	Copper coinage authorized
	Agreement of Hadziacz with Cossacks ratified
1662	Royal Election 'vivente rege' prohibited
1667	Andruszów truce with Russia ratified
1668	Abdication of John Casimir Vasa ratified
1670	Burghers of Kamieniec Podolski given vote
1676	Treasury operations revised
1677	Rates of Church tax contribution set
1687	Grzymułtowski Peace Treaty with Moscow concluded (ratified in 1710)
1699	Karłowice Peace Treaty with Turkey ratified

TABLE 30—CARDINAL LAWS (CONSTITUTION) OF THE LATE FIRST REPUBLIC—A SYNOPSIS

Specified in the Seym constitutions of 1669, 1673, 1768, 1773, 1775

The Executive Branch of Government was headed by a king elected for life by the Seym. Native and foreign candidates were accepted. The successful candidate signed the Articles of Agreement (Pacta Conventa) reaffirming the Bill of Rights. All Senators (bishops, palatines, castellans) and ministers, were appointed for life by the King; each from a list of three candidates presented by the Permanent Council. The executive power was vested in the Permanent Council. It consisted of 18 Senators and 18 Deputies of the Seym elected every two years by a majority of secret votes in the Seym. It was presided over by the king and operated five departments: Army, Foreign Affairs, Treasury, Police, and Justice. All internal regulations had to be submitted to the Permanent Council for approval before they were proposed to the Seym. Questions concerning foreign affairs were decided in the Permanent Council by a majority vote. The King required an explicit consent of the Seym before he could travel outside the boundaries of the country. After the King's death the senior Senator, the Archbishop of Gniezno, acted as the king-pro-tempore (Interrex) until a new King was elected, and inaugurated.

The Legislative Branch of the Government consisted of the King, presiding in the Senate, the Senate and the Chamber of Deputies. The King convoked the Seym with the advice and consent of the Permanent Council. The Seym passed all the laws, voted taxes, ratified treaties, received and sent embassies in conjunction with the King. Rules of voting on the laws required unanimity, later limited to constitutional matters only.

Electoral Ordinance provided for the election of two Deputies from each county by male members of the gentry. The right to vote carried with it the obligation of military service in a levée en masse. The Seyms were summoned at regular two year intervals for a session of six weeks. Extraordinary Seyms were summoned occasionally for a two week session. Representatives of the towns other than Cracow and the towns of Prussia were elected by the city councils and were summoned infrequently.

The Judicial Branch of the Government comprised of judges appointed by the King in royal towns and elected judges in courts for the gentry. The Appellate Courts consisted of two tribunals, one for Poland and one for Lithuania, operating with elective judges. The right of pardon passed from the King to the Seym, except in cases of burghers in royal towns, who still remained under the King's jurisdiction.

Bills of Rights were contained in articles of pacta conventa, and earlier charters. They included guarantees of personal freedom, ownership of property, religious tolerance, and the right to renounce obedience to the King when the latter broke the law. These laws extended to that part of the population which was obligated to military service, i.e., the gentry. The rights of the burghers were specified either in the Nuremberg Code or the Polish City Code, depending on the type of founding charter issued by the King. A separate charter spelled out the civil rights of the Jews.

POLITICAL PERSONALITIES IN SEYMS OF THE FIRST REPUBLIC

Andrzej Maksymilian Fredro (1620-1679)—Political and military writer. First elected Deputy to the Seym in 1643, he was active in many subsequent Seyms, serving on various Seym committees. In his political life he supported the maximalistic claims of parliamentary privilege, and as Speaker of the Seym of 1652 he recognized the validity of cancelling the legislative work of that Seym through the veto of a single Deputy. In 1654 he was appointed castellan of Lwów. From 1660 onwards he opposed the proposals for royal election vivente rege and remained in contact with Jerzy Lubomirski. He authored several works on politics, history, and military craft, as well as *Sayings from Current Speech* (1658). His major work, outlining maximalistic claims of privileges of the gentry, was titled *Monita politico-moralia* (1667); *History of the Polish Nation under Henri Valois, King of Poland, Later King of France* (1652).

Jan Gniński (?-1685)—Politician, priest, diplomat, he participated in the wars between Poland and Sweden. He served as Speaker of the Seym of 1659, and in 1660 participated in the conclusion of the Treaty of Oliva with Sweden and served as envoy to Sweden and Denmark. He was appointed palatine of Chełmno in 1668, and Vice-chancellor of the Crown in 1681. Active in the administration of John III Sobieski, he worked for the realization of the alliance with Austria. He participated in the expedition for the relief of Vienna besieged by the Turks in 1683. After 1679 he relinquished the office of Palatine and was ordained a priest.

Krzysztof Grzymułtowski (1620-1687)—Politician and diplomat. He was elected Speaker of the 1654 Seym and in 1655 participated in the Confederation of Tyszowce organized by the army and the gentry to repel the Swedish invasion. In 1660 he took part in the ratification of the Treaty of Oliva. In 1665 he headed the opposition party of the gentry in the province of Greater Poland and participated in the rokosz of Lubomirski. In 1672 he was appointed palatine of Poznań. He supported the election of John Sobieski to the Kingship of Poland, but in 1683 opposed the war with Turkey. Appointed a commissioner in the peace negotiations with Muscovy, he was instrumental in the conclusion of a peace treaty of Moscow in 1686, which made permanent the conditions of the truce of Andruszów.

Rafał Leszczyński (1650-1703)—The father of Stanisław Leszczyński, the Swedish sponsored King for three years, he served as the Speaker of the Seym of 1683. He was appointed first palatine of Kalisz in 1685, then palatine of Poznań in 1687. He participated in the rescue of Vienna from the Turks in 1683. In 1685 he was made palatine of Łęczyca, and in 1702 the Treasurer of the Crown. He was the leader of the pro-Swedish party in Poland. He wrote the *Diary of the Mission to Turkey Accomplished in 1699.*

Hieronim A. Lubomirski (1648-1706)—Politician, administrator, soldier, he was appointed Standard Bearer of the Crown in 1676 and served as Speaker of the Seym of 1681. In 1683 he was appointed Marshal of Court, and made Treasurer of the Crown in 1692. He served in succession as the palatine of Cracow, castellan of Cracow, then Commander-in-Chief of the army. He participated in the expedition to lift the siege of Vienna by the Turks in 1683. In 1696 he supported the candidacy of the Duke of Conti in the election of the Chief Executive. He took part in the Confederation of Warsaw of 1704 and was in favor of dethroning Augustus II Wettin.

Stanisław H. Lubomirski (1642-1702)—Politician, writer, poet. He was educated in France, Spain and Italy. Elected Deputy to the Seym of 1670 he served as its Speaker. He was appointed Marshal of the Court in 1673 and Marshal of the Crown in 1676. In recognition of his services the Seym of 1683 granted him the estates of Ujazdów and Czerniaków just outside of Warsaw. On their territory, with cooperation of the architect Tylman van Gameren, he laid out a large complex of parks and pleasure pavillions, which to this day form the most attractive part of Warsaw. He translated from Italian *Don Alvarex, Comedy of Lopez,* dramatic idyl *Ermida* (1664), and wrote works on political and moralistic subjects, *Conversations of Artaxes and Ewandr* (1683).

Jan Andrzej Morsztyn (1621-1693)—Parliamentarian, diplomat, financier, of Protestant background. Educated at the University of Leyden, he was elected Deputy for Opatów to the Seyms of 1648, 1650, 1653, 1658, and 1659. He served on numerous Seym Committees for legal, diplomatic and fiscal matters. He took part in the campaigns against the Cossacks and the Swedes and served on diplomatic missions to Hungary 1653, Sweden 1655, Austria 1656, Paris 1667. Appointed Referendary of the Crown in 1658 and Treasurer of the Crown in 1668, he amassed a large fortune. He promoted the French candidate in the royal election of 1668, becoming the chief instrument of French influence during the next decade; eventually he accepted a pension and French citizenship from Louis XIV. When these facts became known, he was impeached by the Seym of 1686, stripped of his offices, and banned from the country. He settled in France and lived out his days there. He coauthored a proposal for the reform of Seym procedures *Points Ordering the Proper Manner of Seym Operation* (1660), produced a large body of poetry, and the first translation into Polish of Corneille's Cid (1660).

Łukasz Opaliński (1612-1662)—Politician, writer, publisher. Served in 1638 as Speaker of the Seym. He was made Marshal of the Court in 1650, and chairman of the Seym Tribunal of 1652 which banished H. Radziejowski for collaboration with the enemy during the Swedish invasion. In 1661 he was a coinitiator of the first Polish political weekly Merkuriusz Polski Ordynaryjny, which appeared once a week in Cracow between January and May 1661 and in Warsaw from May to July of that year. In his writings he criticized the shortcomings of the political system of the First Republic and the lack of political spirit among the gentry and the aristocracy. He authored *Conversation of a Parson with a Country Squire* (1641), and his *New Poet* (1661) was the first work in Polish on the principles of poetry. Recent re-editions of his works include *Polish Writings* (1938) and *Selected Works* (1959).

Mikołaj Ostroróg (?-1651)—Politician and army general, he served as the Speaker of the 1633 Seym. Appointed Cup Bearer of the Crown in 1638, he was one of the three regimentaries of the Crown army defeated by the Cossacks at Piławice in 1648. He served in the defense of Zbaraż against the Cossacks in 1649. In Seym debates he defended the policies of the administration and was known for his erudition in Polish and Latin.

Hieronim Radziejowski (1622-1667)—Politician and diplomat. He served as Speaker in the Seym of 1645, and as Vice-Chancellor of the Crown in 1651 he conspired against the administration of John Casimir Vasa. He was tried and sentenced to infamy and banishment from the country by a Seym Tribunal in 1652, and went to Sweden. In 1655 he accompanied the Swedish army in its invasion of Poland and was instrumental in persuading the mobilized gentry to lay down their arms at Ujście. After the expulsion of the Swedes from the country, the Seym of 1662 restored his rights. In 1667 he was sent as envoy to Turkey.

Mikołaj Smogulecki (1610-1656)—Deputy, theologian, astronomer. He received his university education at Freiburg and Rome in the years 1626-29 in philosophy and law. On his return to Poland he was appointed Prefect of Nakło and shortly afterwards elected Deputy to the Convocation Seym of 1632. Two years later he decided to enter religious life, joined the Jesuit Order and started on his theological studies. In 1640 he went to Rome for further theological studies, and in 1645 traveled from Portugal through India to China. In 1646 he arrived in Nanking and assumed the Chinese name Mu Ni-co. In the years 1647-51 he conducted missionary work in the province of Fukien and taught astronomy and mathematics, applying logarithms to astronomical calculations for the first time in China. His scientific fame secured him recognition from Emperor Szi-Tsu. He worked also in Manchuria and in 1655 in Kuang-tung. His student Lie Fong-tsu published under his name two astronomical works: Tien-pu- tsheng-iuen and Tienshio-hue-tong.

Jan Sobieski (1629-1696)—Parliamentarian, general, King. He studied philosophy at the University of Cracow 1643-46 and took the grand tour of Europe during which he met Charles II of England and Wilhelm II of Orange. In 1654 he took part in the embassy to Turkey. In 1659 he was appointed colonel in the Army, and in the same year elected Deputy to the Seym where he served on the Seym committee preparing the Agreement of Hadziacz with the Cossacks. Elected Deputy for Wisznia to the Seym of 1664-5, he was appointed Grand Marshal of Poland in 1665, after supporting the King in the impeachment proceedings against Jerzy Lubomirski. He was defeated by Lubomirski in the battle at Mątwy. In 1666 he was made Field Hetman of Poland. He commanded the Army in the wars against the Cossacks and the Turks, defeating them at Chocim and Podhajce. He was made Grand Commander of the Army of Poland in 1668 and was elected King of Poland in 1674. He formed an alliance with Austria in 1683 and led the Polish Army in an expedition to relieve the Turkish siege of Vienna. In 1686 he concluded perpetual peace with Russia. He was the author of *Letters to Marietta* first published in 1962.

CHAPTER IV

DECAY AND REFORM: ABSOLUTIST NEIGHBORS STEP IN FOR THE KILL

During this period (1696-1795) the constitutional crisis deepened and eventually led to reform. The conflict between the poorly chosen chief executive and the legislature slowed the legislative machinery to an almost complete standstill through the refusal of a long series of Seyms to legislate at all. The requirement of unanimous consent was used by foreign influences and native obstructionists to wreck the legislature.

Decentralization of government and the transfer of taxing powers and the control of the Army to the lower tier of the legislative structure at the provincial level were the devices used by the legislature to keep the power out of the hands of an unsatisfactory Chief Executive.

Pacifism and financial mismanagement combined and led to a serious underfunding of the defense establishment. Much of the political initiative of the period became extra-parliamentary, was centered in Confederations and added to the political disorientation of the public. The weakening of the central government led the country into deblitating civil wars and invited foreign invasions. Politically, the country became a satellite of Russia.

Eventually, a movement towards constitutional reform was started and resulted in a slow but steady progress in the improvement of the legislative structure and rules of operation. The reform culminated in a new Constitution voted in 1791. The reform movement was opposed by local conservatives and was eventually stopped by foreign intervention. The response led to a revolution, which in turn was quenched by the concerted military action of neighboring powers. The state collapsed and was partitioned.

Fig. 41—First Republic in Decay.

EXECUTIVE VS. THE LEGISLATURE: THE STALEMATE OF THE SAXON ERA

The irregular manner of election of Augustus Wettin of Saxony to the kingship of Poland by the Seym of 1697 (see Chapter II, the section on royal election) ushered in an era of conflict between the executive and the legislature. The conflict escalated in time to the point of bringing the legislative machinery of the state to a complete standstill and brought the political life of the country into total disarray. The era extended into the next Wettin administration as well.

Fig. 42—Stanisław A. Szczuka (1654-1710). Speaker of the Pacification Seym of 1699, held to mollify the public outcry over the irregular manner of election of Augustus Wettin to the Kingship of Poland.

The Wettin administration started with the Pacification Seym of 1699 during which the supporters of the Bourbon candidate who felt they had been cheated in the royal election, were to some extent mollified by distribution of offices and preferments. Next, the administration had to tackle some conflicts left over from its predecessor. Such was the question of impeachment of Kazimierz J. Sapieha, the Grand Commander of the Army of Lithuania and Senator-Palatine of Wilno, for the abuse of his office. The Seym of Lublin in 1703 disposed of this matter. For details see Chapter VIII.

The Wettins brought with them a tradition of absolutism and an expectation of unquestioning obedience from their subjects, as well as complete ignorance of parliamentary procedure. Unlike the Catholic branch of the Vasa dynasty, they had a reliable home army and a treasury at their disposal to give them a feeling of confidence in attempting to resolve by force any conflicts arising with the legislature of their newly acquired domain. Thus, they had no incentive for compromise or accommodation which are indispensable to the smooth operation of the parliamentary machinery. Initially they hoped to change the constitutional arrangements more to their liking; when this proved impractical through persuasion or patronage, they attempted to intimidate the Seyms or to have them disrupted and to administer the country without recourse to legislature.

The country responded with extra-parliamentary Confederations which, in their effect, amounted to the setting up of rival political centers. Without going into the complex history of that period involving, as it did, the operations of Saxon, Russian and Swedish armies, Seyms, Confederations, a pseudo-election of Stanisław Leszczyński as a counter-king (1705), abdication (1706) and reaccession (1709) of Augustus II Wettin, let it suffice to say that the Seyms of that period ceased to legislate. They were elected, they assembled, the protests and counter-protests were recorded, and they disbanded without any action. The idea formed in the mind of the body politic that the march of events could be stopped, and the constitutional change arrested by the denial of legislative sanction, even though that denial meant that taxes were not voted, the Army was left unsupported, and laws were not made. Associated with the loss of political direction and the lack of success of various political initiatives was the visible introversion of interests of many people. Fortune-making, enjoyment of social life and the pleasures of the table became the order of the day. The prevailing attitudes were aptly summed up in a two-liner:

In Saxon King's time we all felt:
Eat, drink, and let out the belt

(A za Króla Sasa:
Jedz, pij i popuszczaj pasa)

Yet the interest in politics did not die out completely, and some individuals were as active as Kazimierz Karwowski. Jurist by education and parliamentarian by choice, he ran for the Seym and was elected Deputy no less than 26 times in his long and active life, achieving an all-time record in the 500 years of Polish parliamentarism. An accomplished public speaker and a keen political observer, he lobbied for parliamentary reform, but the public mind was still unreceptive and his efforts went unrewarded. His efforts were seconded by Stanistaw Dunin-Karwicki, a seasoned Deputy of Calvinist religious persuasion. In particular, Karwicki proposed that the Seym remain in permanent session, have the power to prorogue itself, and reopen its debates any time between successive elections. He also proposed that voting should be by provinces in the royal elections.

Another parliamentarian lobbying for reform in that period, but in the area of state finances, was Stanisław A. Szczuka, Vice Chancellor of Lithuania, and a former Speaker of the Seym. To increase the profitability of royal demesnes, he proposed in 1709 the transfer of leases on them out of the hands of major magnates; demanded that the size of the regular army be increased to 36000 men and that it be supported by standing taxes levied on the property of the gentry and the church. In the area of education he proposed public schools, to be supported by the national treasury. Parts of this program were realized in 1717, when standing taxes for the support of the army, but at half that size, were passed and in 1773 when the Commission for National Education was formed.

Unfortunately, events would not stand still, and the balance of forces outside the country shifted towards those who took an active stand and were able to influence events through an expenditure of money and use of armies, or political intrigue. When Augustus II was not able to subdue the country with his armies, and the Swedes were not able to eliminate him, the Russians decided to intervene. The country responded with the Confederation of Tarnogród (1715). In these circumstances the Seym of 1717 was convened to put an end to the impasse between the Confederation and Augustus, with the Russians acting as arbitrators. The Seym was under constant threat of disruption, and to avoid it, the Confederation was extended into the Seym. It was agreed beforehand that no one except the Speaker, Stanisław Ledóchowski, and the Deputy reading the compromise resolutions would be allowed to have the floor; that is, no debate of any kind would be allowed. For this reason this Seym is known, in the legislative history of the First Republic, as the "Mute Seym" (Seym Niemy). It sat for one day only, to vote acceptance of compromise resolutions which included the reaffirmation of all Cardinal Laws in force, the limitation of the Saxon troop complement stationed in Poland, the removal of Saxon officials, the establishment of a constant tax levy for the support of a regular army, and the reduction of its size to 24,000 men for Poland, 6,000 for Lithuania. In addition, Russia was recognized as a guarantor of these conditions. These last two points, the statutory limitation on the size of the Army and the recognition, by statute, of the Russian right to see to its enforcement, formalized the reduction of the country to the status of a protectorate of Russia.*

The little legislation that was passed during the Saxon administration reduced the rights of religious dissidents. Thus, a law of 1717 forbade holding Protestant religious services in public, and the law passed at the confederated Election Seym of 1733 took away from the Protestants and the Greek Orthodox members of the electorate their passive electoral rights, i.e., the right to be elected a Deputy to the Seym or a Judge of the Crown Tribunal (the Supreme Court), but left the right to vote undisturbed. These restrictions were modeled on the Corporation Act and the Test Act passed in 1673 in England to restrict the access of Catholics and non-conformists to office, but in Poland were applied to Protestants and Orthodox instead. This regressive legislation came at a time when the weakness of the country, torn by constitutional conflict, gave both Russia and Prussia encouragement and an excuse to champion the political rights of their co-religionists.

A notable sequence of Seym disruptions occurred in the administration of Augustus II Wettin in connection with the domestic issue of the appointment to the Supreme Command of the Army (Hetman). To be legal, such appointments had to

---

* Curiously enough a similar step will be taken 260 years later, by the Seym of 1976, with an amendment to the Constitution which again recognized "the Russian Connection."

be made by the King during a valid session of the Seym. The King chose Stanisław Poniatowski (father of a later King) for this position. The Potocki family, who grew to consider the Army Command their due in the previous administrations, discovered the plan prior to the Seym, and resolved to prevent the legal opening of the Seym until the King yielded to their demands. By exerting their influence over the Deputies from their home counties, they managed to disrupt every Seym from 1729 on, even before the Speaker was elected. This obstructionism continued until 1735, when a Potocki was appointed to the High Command by Augustus III Wettin, the son of the obstinate Augustus II. In the process great harm was done to the political machinery of the state. On other occasions, the unitary veto was used by individual Deputies to prevent, by witholding consent, the enactment of legislation to which they were strongly opposed. A mild modern equivalent of this strategem can be seen in the practice of filibuster in the U.S. Congress. Both have the same cause, and both are difficult to remedy.

The device of withholding consent from the administration by vetoing the total legislative output of a Seym on the last day of its session was soon perverted and bent to the use of outside powers. All that was needed to bring the national politics to a standstill was to bribe one Deputy. More Seyms were disrupted this way by foreign influence than by native politics. Particularly bad in that respect were the two administrations of the Saxon kings. Out of 28 Seyms held in that period, 23 were disrupted by a veto. Prussia and France were credited with having caused seven disruptions each, Russia was involved in eleven disruptions. Only six Seyms were disrupted due to native politics.

The bribery practices of foreign powers were brought out into the open at the Seym held in Grodno in 1744, when Deputy Franciszek Wilczewski pretended to take a bribe and subsequently, after an impassioned speech on the floor of the Seym condemning the corrupting practices of foreign powers, dramatically tossed on the floor the 300 ducat bribe he had just received. The sobering effect this produced did not last long enough to make much difference, until the rules of voting in the Seym started to be amended in response to pressure from the constitutional reform movement in the later 1700s. These developments will be given fuller treatment under another heading.

In this politically dangerous situation a strange inertia prevailed for many decades before the reform movement was born. Yet, the damaging effects of the disruptions of the Seyms which deprived the country of much needed legislation, were understood by the contemporary politicians, certainly the more thoughtful ones. Even in the darkest period voices condemning the disruptions were raised, as witnessed by the speech of Speaker of the Seym, Józef Massalski, on October 26, 1752, delivered in the flowery style of High Baroque to the Seym which was disbanding without legislation.

Displaced from firm foundation of good government, stripped of her adornments, deprived of her old glory, pressed by poverty, fallen in justice through which alone states are upheld, the Republic sought in this Seym the advice and succor from her sons; she showed all her needs, bared her mortal wounds, a sight which would move the most cruel of hearts, but found herself rejected, abandoned, neglected and made a laughing stock of the world.

I shall not list the damage the Republic suffers without recompense through the willful disruption of the present Seym, but let it be noted, that when she expected help in what seemed like more favourable circumstances, she saw, instead, all her hopes dashed.

I dare not utter this pitiful farewell which should have been instead one of thanksgiving and praise for your splendid efforts, for favours rendered to me, and affections shown on all occasions, for errors overlooked, for shortcomings rectified, and for honest and diligent contribution which should have caused the Speaker's Staff, which you have placed so graciously in my hands, to flower and to bring forth the fruit of universal happiness. Instead, it has withered now into a barren and dried out stick.

ON THE ROAD TO CONSTITUTIONAL REFORM

The paralysis of the legislative activity caused by the conflict between the legislature and the Saxon kings came to an end with the death of Augustus III, and the election in 1764 to the kingship of Stanisław Antoni Poniatowski, a native candidate supported by the Russians. In the years preceding this election, Poniatowski ran for the Seym and was elected Deputy in 1750, 1758, 1760, 1761, 1762, and 1764. Thus among the Chief Executives of the First Republic he had the most parliamentary experience and appreciation of how the system worked. This became evident in his skillful dealings with the Seyms of his thirty-year long administration. The Seym came back to life, in stark contrast to the dismal Saxon times. On assuming office Poniatowski changed his middle name to Augustus.

The year 1764 marks another milestone in the constitutional development in Poland, since it was recognized for the first time in that year that the constitutions passed by the Convocation and the Election Seyms have validity in themselves and do not require a separate sanction by the newly elected King after his coronation. The future King was among the Deputies formulating this change and possibly thought it unnecessary to reapprove the laws he already had voted for as Deputy. The Convocation Seym of 1764, with Adam Czartoryski serving as the Speaker and Poniatowski as one of the Deputies, also clarified the voting rules in the Seym. It was decided to divide the legislative matters formally into "matters of State," primarily constitutional questions, and "economic matters," primarily taxation. On matters of state the veto of a single Deputy was still allowed to stand, whereas in economic questions decision making by majority rule was to apply, even in non-confederated Seyms.

This was the beginning of a long and hard struggle towards deeper reform, aiming at the improvement of the rules of operation of the Seym, and the permanent removal, rather than through the temporary device of a Confederation, of the impediment of the rule of unanimous consent. Some idea of how set the things were at the time is provided by the text of an oath prescribed by the Seym of 1768 for each newly elected Speaker of the Chamber of Deputies.

The oath reads as follows:

> I swear to Almighty God, One in Holy Trinity, that I shall not accept as valid, shall not sign and pass for inclusion in the Register of Laws, any constitution dealing with a matter of state which was not passed unanimously, without contradiction, ascertained by me through a triple query, and in matters subject to majority approval, when majority vote was not obtained. In the case of contradiction in the matters of state, with even one Deputy halting the action of the Seym, I shall not accept any further bills for consideration, nor shall I accept directives from any person, except from the whole Republic asembled in the Seym. I shall truly note economic matters passed by majority vote, and will not bar anyone from obtaining a copy of the constitutions approved, but will issue a copy with my signature. After a completed Seym, on leaving the Senate Chamber, I shall enter the constitutions passed in the record books of the city. In the performance of all duties, required of me by the office of the Speaker, I shall conduct myself in accordance with God, Law, and Conscience.

This oath was in use from 1768 until 1791, when the new Constitution abolished the rule of unanimity, and subjected all voting in the Seym to majority rule, with a two-thirds majority required for removal of ministers. More will be said about this in a later section.

The operation of these new voting rules was tested at the first ordinary Seym in the administration of Poniatowski, held in 1766. The Seym was neither vetoed nor disrupted, instead, it was the scene of resistance to demands pressed by Russia and Prussia for the restoration of passive electoral rights, i.e., the ability to run for office, to the Protestants and the Greek Orthodox members of the gentry. These rights were withdrawn from them by the constitution of 1733. Nothing was done about these demands at this time, but matters came to a head at the Seym of 1767-8. Called as an extraordinary Seym and an extension of the Confederation of Radom, it was completely dominated by the Russian Ambassador Nikita W. Repnin. Repnin demanded that the Seym select a Committee (Delegacja) to prepare bills for approval by the plenary session. Such a committee, if its membership were carefully selected, could be more easily browbeaten into submission than the plenum of the Seym, and the debate on the bills would also be shortened correspondingly. Interestingly enough, this Russian preference for preparation of all legislation by a select small committee, followed by its briefest appearance before the plenum, will surface again two hundred years later, together with the unanimous votes on the legislation, in the Russian-dominated Seym of the Polish People's Republic.

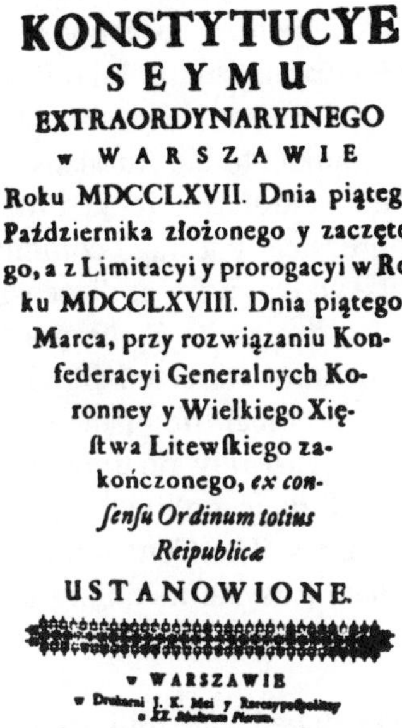

KONSTYTUCYE
S E Y M U
EXTRAORDYNARYINEGO
w   W A R S Z A W I E

Roku MDCCLXVII. Dnia piątego
Paźdiernika złożonego y zaczęte-
go, a z Limitacyi y prorogacyi w Roku MDCCLXVIII. Dnia piątego
Marca, przy rozwiązaniu Konfederacyi Generalnych Ko-
ronney y Wielkiego Xię-
ſtwa Litewſkiego za-
końozonego, *ex con-*
ſenſu Ordinum totius
Reipublicæ
U S T A N O W I O N E.

w   W A R S Z A W I E
w Drukarni J. K. Mci y Rzeczypospolitey
o XX. Scholarum Piarum

Fig. 43—Title page of the constitutions passed by the extraordinary Seym of 1768.

Repnin's demands in 1767 were vehemently opposed by a group of participants in the recent Confederation of Radom. The group was headed by Senator-Bishop Kajetan Sołtyk. To stifle the opposition to the enfranchisement of the Greek Orthodox, Repnin arranged for the abduction from Warsaw of Senators Kajetan Sołtyk, Józef A. Załuski, Wacław Rzewuski and Deputy Seweryn Rzewuski. They were carried off to Russia, and imprisoned there until 1773 at Kaluga. The Seym, now suitably intimidated, went into session on October 4, 1767, selected a committee of 71 members, and adjourned until February 1768. The committee prepared bills for the restoration of full political rights to the Protestants and the Greek Orthodox and restated all the Cardinal Laws in force. The bills were approved at the plenary session held in February of 1768; they were then submitted to Catherine of Russia for a guarantee. This started a chain of events which ended in a major disaster for the country.

The crass breach of the sovereign rights of the legislature by the "protective power," through the abduction of the members of the legislature, and the restoration of rights to the minorities under Russian guarantee, triggered a wide-spread revulsion against the spineless stance of the government, rallied many people to the otherwise unattractive cause of Sołtyk and company, and directly gave rise to the formation of the Confederation of Bar in 1768. It was to go down in history as the last mass movement of the gentry, and it bore all of their characteristics at the time. A mixture of nationalism, religious bigotry, revulsion against foreign interference, and a desire to restore things to their former state activated the movement. Superimposed on this was the general feeling that politically active citizens should take it upon themselves to set the ship of state back on the right course, in a situation in which the executive appeared to be excessively compliant to the Russians.

The organizers of the Confederation overlooked the obvious, namely the fact that the Confederation, being basically a huge committee, lacked the command and administrative apparatus which were indispensible for success. Formed outside the government, it also denied itself the use and loyalty of the regular army. The aims of the Confederation, directed simultaneously against the King, the Russian interference in the political life of the country, and against that part of the population which seemed to rely on foreign help for support of their demands for the restoration of their political rights, were indicative of the political disorientation of the times. The Confederation of Bar was undoubtedly patriotic in wanting to eliminate Russian meddling in Polish religious and civil rights questions, however, its own stand on these issues was regressive and narrowly Catholic.

The Confederation soon developed into military operations of partisan units against the Russian troops stationed in the country. It made an aborted attempt to seize the King and after much marching, counter-marching, and scattered battles throughout the country was finally defeated by the Russians. Reprisals of the Confederate troops against the suspected Russian adherents and the counter-reprisals of the Russians against the adherents of the Confederation were usually carried out by burning and looting the villages and estates. In its wake the Confederation left suppression, devastation of the economy, and worst of all, through a demonstration of the internal division of the country, it encouraged the neighboring states to take advantage of its exhausted condition and force on it an acceptance of a limited partition. The best intentions and occasional heroism of the participants were, in the final analysis, totally counter-productive. One of the confused patriots participating in the Confederation was Kazimierz Pułaski, who distinguished himself as a military commander. After the defeat of the Confederation by the Russians in 1772, he left the country, went to America and served with distinction as a commander of a cavalry brigade in the American Revolutionary Army in the years 1777-79. He died of wounds received in the battle of Savannah.

Fig. 44 (Left)—Kajetan Sołtyk (1715-1788), Senator-bishop abducted to Russia with three other legislators from the Seym of 1767. The country responded to this outrage with the Confederation of Bar. The suppression of the Confederation led in turn to the First Partition of Poland. A copperplate of a portrait by Giovanni Battista Lampi (1751-1830).

Fig. 45 (Right)—Tadeusz Reytan (1746-1780] Deputy to the Seym (1773) from Nowogródek. He led the opposition to the ratification of the Treaty of the First Partition.

While some political activists were attempting to rally public opinion through their writings and to revive parliamentary action to the point where it would influence the chain of events brought on by the suppression of the Confederation of Bar, others became resigned to the situation and attempted an accommodation. In these dismal circumstances the Seym of 1773 was called to ratify the First Partition of Poland. The complete inability of the country to exert any resistance at this time became painfully obvious. The reduction of the executive powers of the government by the Seym, the reduction of taxes and the underfunding of defense, the frequent transfers of control from the government to the extra-parliamentary Confederations and the dissipation of power in internal fighting, all finally exacted their price.

The willingness of the public to accept the consequences of the situation foisted upon the country by the concerted action of Russia, Prussia and Austria was minimal, and great difficulties were experienced during the election of Deputies to the Seym which was called to swallow the bitter pill and formalize the partition.

No less than thirty-two Seymiks were disrupted and only 108 Deputies were returned to the Seym, the lowest number ever in the history of the First Republic. They were joined by some 36 Senators and Ministers. It was a dispirited and seemingly compliant group that assembled in Warsaw.

The neighboring powers, intent on partitioning the country, cast about for a man to aid their design, and found him in the person of Adam Poniński. He was ambitious, unscrupulous and intent on making a fortune in the quickest possible way. The foreign powers proposed that the Seym be confederated, to eliminate the possibility of any one Deputy vetoing the treaties by which parts of the country were to be ceded to the foreign powers. Poniński was nominated for the Speaker of the Confederation in the Seym, and a generous reward was offered to him in the event he succeeded in the ratification of the partition treaties.

When the legislators assembled in Warsaw, the task of forming a Confederation among the Deputies and the Senators proved more difficult than expected, for even in that cowed group of individuals there were a few unwilling to lend their name to the odious deed. The opposition group was led by Tadeusz Reytan and Samuel Korsak, the Deputies for Nowogródek, Stanisław Bohuszewicz, Deputy for Mińsk, and Senator Gabriel Wodziński, the Bishop of Smoleńsk and included six other Senators and seventeen Deputies. Led by Reytan* , three of these Deputies decided to barricade themselves in the Senate Chamber in the castle of Warsaw, and thereby prevent the Confederation from forming during the opening joint session of the Seym and the Senate. The protest occupation lasted for 38 hours, but even this delay failed to gain a majority for the opposition in the Seym. Discouraged by the lack of response, Reytan withdrew from the Seym and left Warsaw, but the other members of the group continued to voice their opposition.

To handle the unpleasant duties, the assembly decided to operate as a Committee Seym (Seym Deputacyjny), and after the membership of the committees was set, the Seym adjourned. The committees took two years to complete their tasks, which included the transfer of 36,300 sq.km of the territory of the Commonwealth to Prussia, 81,900 sq.km to Austria and 93,000 sq.km to Russia. The full Seym reassembled on September 30, 1773 and ratified the Partition Treaties. It then proceeded to make some constitutional changes, the most important of which was the creation of the "Permanent Council," composed of eighteen Seym Deputies and the same number of Senators, selected by the respective Houses. The Permanent Council normally operated through five committees: Foreign Affairs, Treasury, Defense, Justice, and the Interior (Police). It could also meet in a body chaired by the King, and then it made decisions by majority vote. These decisions were in the area of administrative interpretation of existing laws. In practice, the

---

* The gesture of Deputy Reytan barring the Senate door served as an inspiration 93 years later to Jan Matejko who represented the event in a celebrated painting.

interpretation often stretched the intent of the law. The Council was, therefore, a mini-Seym, always in session and in which the unitary veto did not apply. It combined, through its committees, the function of ministries. The Council operated continuously between the sessions of the Seym held two years apart, and it made for a tighter and smoother functioning of the government. However, the ability of the Permanent Council to override the decisions of constitutional Ministers engendered their enmity.

The Seym of 1773-5 also passed a law allowing members of the gentry to engage in commerce without losing their electoral rights, thereby repealing the restrictive constitution of 1505. In addition, the same Seym again restricted the passive electoral rights of the Protestants and the Greek Orthodox by allowing only three non-Roman Catholic Deputies to be elected, one each from the provinces of Greater Poland, Lesser Poland, and Lithuania.

The disestablishment of the Jesuit Order by the Pope in 1773 left the country with much property used formerly to support an extensive educational establishment run by the Order for the benefit of the gentry. Part of this property was designated by the Seym of 1773-5 for funding the activities of the "Commission for National Education," whose establishment was authorized at the same time by an appropriate constitution. In effect, a national ministry of education was thereby formed and endowed. The Commission for National Education was, according to the constitution passed on October 14, 1773, one of the "Grand Commissions" set up by the Seym to act as a central state institution of ministerial rank but collegiate structure. The other Grand Commissions were established earlier, in 1764, for the Treasury and the Army, separately for Poland and Lithuania.

The chief promoters of the Commission for National Education were Ignacy Potocki, Hugo Kołłątay and Adam K. Czartoryski. The Commission took over the schools of the former Jesuit Order and supplemented them with schools sponsored directly by the Commission. These consisted of: two universities, Cracow, founded in 1364, and Wilno, founded in 1579; 74 secondary schools operated in the palatinates, and approximately 1600 parish schools. The third university of Poland, that of Lwów, founded in 1661, was lost to Austria in the First Partition. In addition the Commission established the Society for Elementary School Books with the aim of publishing textbooks for the new school system. Grzegorz Piramowicz served as its secretary from 1775 until 1787 and conducted competitions for the best text book in each subject with prizes awarded to the authors of books adopted for use.

Fig. 46—Adam Kazimierz Czartoryski (1734-1823 Deputy to several Seyms of the First Republic, candidate in the royal election of 1764, who withdrew in favor of Stanisław A. Poniatowski and served as the Speaker of the Confederated Seym of 1812. A portrait by Thomas Gainsborough (1727-1788) painted when Czartoryski visited England during the grand tour of Europe he took in his youth.

Under the directive of Stanisław August Poniatowski, invitations were extended to foreign experts and consultants to participate in the development of the national school system. One such expert brought in to work under the sponsorship of Adam Czartoryski was Pierre Samuel du Pont de Nemours. He arrived in Poland in July 1774 with his wife and two sons, and spent several months working on the plans for the national educational system. This appointment put him in the limelight and subsequently brought him an appointment in the French Government. After the French Revolution he went to America with his son Irenée and established there the gun powder mills and the company which in time grew into the Du Pont chemical empire.

In the following years a revised codification of the Law of the Land was requested by the Seym. When it was presented to the Seym of 1780, it became apparent that the Codification Committee, headed by Andrzej Zamoyski, chose the codification as a convenient vehicle for introducing constitutional changes, much needed, but also much opposed by conservatives in the Seym and throughout the country. The Seym, therefore, rejected it as a back-door attempt to amend the Cardinal Laws.

The Seym of 1782, sitting under Kazimierz Krasiński as the Speaker, was much preoccupied with the fate of Kajetan Sołtyk, the Senator-Bishop from Cracow, back home after his release from Russian captivity. He returned to Poland broken in spirit and with indications of mental disease. His attempts to regain control of his bishopric from the Chapter which administered it in his absence were accompanied by some extravagant behavior and in the end failed. The case attracted much attention and in 1781 a special commission was appointed by the Permanent Council to investigate it. The commission reported Sołtyk to be in a state of mental confusion which would not allow him to carry out his duties as a Senator and placed him in the custody of four guardians drawn from among his family and neighbors. In spite of the above-board action of the Commission, it was alleged that the decision was politically motivated and that Sołtyk was being denied the rights of personal freedom due him under the Cardinal Law *neminem captivabimus*. The law had no provisions in it for restraint of mentally ill persons. Several bills to remedy this deficiency were submitted in the Seym but ran into filibuster, blocking the passage of other legislation as well.

INK AND QUILL IN THE SERVICE OF REFORM

A description of the tumultuous period preceding the rise of the Constitution of 1791 would be incomplete without mentioning the contribution of the principal political writers of that period. While the need for constitutional reform was becoming obvious to the thinking part of the public, the consensus regarding the nature and specifics of the needed changes was lacking. Indeed, many people with a vested interest in maintaining the status quo, were questioning even the need for reform. In this situation the task of forming and influencing public opinion traditionally fell to the political writers, who were often active parliamentarians as well, and were always present in the public life of Poland. In the past, such writers as Andrzej Frycz Modrzewski, Mikołaj Rey, Wawrzyniec Goślicki, or the unsuccessful royal candidate Stanisław Leszczyński, left their imprint on the political thinking of their times. Much of their political writing was reformist rather than innovative, reflecting the fact that the rise of elective representation and the formation of the constitutional framework of the First Republic were an organic process and not a product of political upheaval. Reform is often more difficult to initiate and carry through than innovation or adoption of foreign ideas introduced from above, and requires persuasive skills more than fervor. This lent a special flavor to the writings of this period. In times when newspapers were just beginning to become influential and books were the only means of reaching wider public, the assimilation of ideas contained in them was slow and the writers had to reckon in decades, rather than years or months, before their influence was felt by a sufficient number of people to make an impact on political life.

Interest in constitutional reform led at first to attempts at securing foreign expertise. The Americans were still ripening for their own revolution and most of the European philosophical interest in political matters emanated from France. It is therefore no coincidence that in 1771 Michał Wielhorski, a representative of the Confederation of Bar residing in Paris, commissioned Jean-Jacques Rousseau to commit to paper his thoughts on the best direction to take in constitutional reform in Poland. The author of *The Social Contract* put his mind to work on this more specific and complex problem and in six months' time produced an analysis of the ills and a rather conservative prescription for the cure. The work appeared under the title *The Government of Poland*, was promptly translated into Polish and received with interest. Rousseau favored a federal regime and showed concern for the rights of the Seymiks, and in fact advocated the retention of the *liberum veto*, fortified with the provision, however, that its frivolous use be punishable by death. Interesting comparisons have been made between the federal ideas of Publius (Alexander Hamilton, James Madison, John Jay) put forward in *The Federalist Papers* for the United States and those proposed for Poland some twenty years earlier by Rousseau. Rousseau seems to be starting from a more homogeneous national basis with less competition between the different religious and social groups than that seen by Publius. Both models place supreme authority in the legislature, but the Publian model envisages the legislature operating free from local instructions, whereas Rousseau sees usefulness in the binding instruction of the Seymiks and their reportorial function as well. When viewed as an attempt by political theorists to apply the principles of democratic theory to evolving political regimes, both *The Government of Poland* and *The Federalist Papers* complement each other.

Rising interest in political reform stimulated the publishing business, with a demand for books of domestic authors, and foreign authors in translation. Book imports, particularly from France, were on the rise and book printers in Dresden, Saxony, developed a thriving business printing books specifically for export to Poland.

Of great influence at this juncture of Polish constitutional history were the writings of Stanisław Konarski, who wrote and published between 1761 and 1763 a three-volume political treatise titled *On the Effective Conduct of Debates in Ordinary Seyms*. The influence of this book can be measured by the fact that after the third volume appeared in 1763 no Seym had its legislation vetoed or saw its proceedings disrupted again. Konarski's influence extended beyond the ranks of the readers of his political works. An educator by profession, he established in 1740 in Warsaw the *Collegium Nobilium,* a college for the sons of the gentry, using its program of studies in civics to imbue the students with his ideas on the much needed constitutional reform. Several people active in the constitutional reform movement at the end of the century were among its graduates, including Stanisław Kostka Potocki, the leader of the Patriotic Party in the Reform Seym of 1788-1792, Ludwik Osiński, and others.

Another influential political writer of the period was Józef Wybicki. His *Political Thoughts on Civil Liberties* published in 1775 had a great impact on political life. He served on the Seym committee, headed by Andrzej Zamoyski, for the revision of the general code of law for Poland. As the author of *Patriotic Letters* published in two volumes in 1777-78, he attempted to gain public acceptance for the reform of the Code of Law when it was presented to the Seym of 1780. He participated in the coming decades in all constitutional reform movements.

Possibly the greatest writer of this period in terms of progressive political ideas was Hugo Kołłątay. He was the organizer and the mainspring of a political club in Warsaw in which the political ideas underlying the attempted reform were hammered out and the text of the proposed new Constitution was formulated. For this reason the club gained the appelation "Kołłątay's Forge."

In the years 1788-89 he published *Anonymous Letters to Stanisław Małachowski,* the Speaker of the Seym of 1788, in which he proposed egalitarian constitutional ideas. In 1790 Kołłątay published another book, *The Political Law of the Polish Nation.*

Konarski, Wybicki and Kołłątay occupy in Polish political writing of this era the same place as their contemporaries, Hamilton, Madison and Jay, hold in the political thought of America.

In 1787 Stanisław Staszic published a book: *Remarks on the Life of Jan Zamoyski,* the one-time Chancellor of the Realm in the administration of Stephen Bathory and the ancestor of Andrzej Zamoyski. Staszic used this biography as a vehicle for presenting his own ideas on needed constitutional reform. The book is credited with winning considerable support in favor of the liberal cause. In the same period Senator-bishop Józef Załuski, aided by Stanisław Konarski, decided to republish all of the legislation passed by the Seyms. The set was to be financed by an advance subscription. The first volume contained laws still written in Latin; the later volumes were in Polish. The first six volumes of the set appeared between the years 1732 and 1739. The edition was a best seller with approximately 1500 persons participating in the advance subscription, witness to the lively interest in constitutional matters at the time. In 1786 volumes seven and eight appeared, since the work was intended as a continuing publication of the Seym. The whole work is known under the title *Volumina Legum.*

Fig. 47—Stanisław Konarski (1700-1773) Educator and influential political writer. Right, the title page of his three volume treatise, On The Effective Conduct of Debates in Ordinary Seyms *published in the years 1760-1763.*

Fig. 48—Józef Wybicki (1747-1822), parliamentarian and one of the mainsprings of the reform movement in the Seym of 1788. Right, the title page of Political Thoughts on Civil Liberties *he authored in 1775. He also composed the Polish National Anthem.*

Fig. 49—*Hugo Kołłątay (1750-1812) Writer, political activist, philosopher. Organizer of a political club for promotion of constitutional reform and one of the authors of the Constitution of 1791. A portrait by L. Marteau (1715-1804).*

Once the Reform Seym of 1788-1792 was set on a firm course, a flood of political literature on constitutional matters followed. Deputies, Senators, and people outside the legislature participated in the creation of a rich political literature of this period. Table 31 shows a selection of titles. The effect of this literature lasted beyond the duration of the Reform Seym and it provided a guiding light in the dark days ahead.

THE CONSTITUTION OF 1791

Efforts directed at constitutional reform were now coming to fruition as the body politic started to respond to the prodding from the political clubs and the reform-minded members of the administration. The movement was by no means countrywide but rather represented bright islands in a sea of apathy or downright conservatism.

The Seym elected in 1788 was to be known as the four-year Seym of Reform. While the reform minded majority among its membership seemed able to accomplish its objectives, unanimity among the Deputies was not to be expected, for too many people extolled the shortcomings of the existing constitutional arrangements as virtues. For this reason some involved political maneuvering was needed to convene the Seym as a Confederation of its Deputies; this arrangement gave the reform faction the benefit of voting by majority rule. How important this consideration was can be judged by the fact that the reform group aimed at no less than the abolition of the unitary veto (liberum veto), thus preventing any Deputy from using his veto to kill the reform legislation. In forming the Confederation the major part of the proposed reform program had to be concealed from the Conservatives, lest they refuse to participate in forming the Confederation. Stanisław Małachowski was elected Speaker of the Seym, a choice well made, for he combined a sympathy for reform with willingness to give consideration to the opinions of the Conservatives. He steered the legislative ship skillfully through these dangerous waters and saw the successful passage of the desired legislation. Because of the strong legislative momentum achieved in preparing and passing the reform program, when the term of the 1788 Seym expired it was decided to retain the 181 Deputies of this Seym and combine them with a new complement elected in 1790, both groups charted to work together under the same Confederation. By this novel strategy the reform faction hoped to avoid opposition to the forming of a new Confederation from the Conservatives, who were becoming alarmed at the legislative pace. Unless a Confederation was sustained, the voting by majority rule would cease.

Unable to prevent the continuation of the Confederation, the Conservatives went into the election determined to see that the country would return a conservative majority in the second complement of Deputies. In this they very nearly succeeded, so that the double Seym sitting in the years 1790-92 was almost evenly matched between the liberal and the conservative factions. The Conservatives also insisted that a second Speaker be elected and succeeded in putting Kazimierz N. Sapieha in that post. The two Speakers were to preside in turn over the sessions of the Seym and it was hoped that the influence of the liberal Małachowski would be counter-balanced by that of the conservative Sapieha.

TABLE 31—POLITICAL LITERATURE OF THE REFORM SEYM, 1788-1792 (SELECTED TITLES)

J. Ankwicz	Protection of the National Government (1790)
T. Czacki	Political Law of the Polish Nation (1790)
F.K. Dmochowski	On Taxation (1791)
F. Jezierski	In Praise of Useful Citizen (1789)
F. Karpiński	On Succession and Election of Kings (1790)
H. Kołłątay	Political Law of the Polish Nation (1787)
I. Potocki	Principles for the Reform of Government (1789)
J. Krzywkowski	On Royal Succession and the Rule of Estates (1791)

TABLE 31 (CONTINUED)—POLITICAL LITERATURE OF THE REFORM SEYM, 1788-1792 (SELECTED TITLES)

K. Kwiatkowski	Brief Advice on Writing a Good Constitution (1790)
M. Ogiński	Thoughts on State of Legislation in Poland (1789)
O.L. Włóczkiewicz	Thoughts on Military Matters (1789)
M. Piaskowski	Notes for the Committee on Form of Government (1790)
K. Plater	A Cosmopolitan to the Polish Nation (1789)
S. K. Potocki	Thoughts on a General Reform of Government (1790)
A. W. Rzewuski	On the Republican Form of Government (1790)
S. Rzewuski	On Law Which Would Strip Gentry of Seymik Vote (1790)
J. Spławski	For and Against the Succession to the Throne (1789)
S. Staszic	Warnings for Poland (1790)
J. Suchorzewski	Principles of Municipal Laws (1789)
W. Turski	Thoughts on Kings, Succession and Government (1790)
A. Mędrzecki	Laws of Polish Towns (1789,1790)

Fig. 50 (Left)—Stanisław Małachowski (1736-1809) Speaker of the Reform Seym of 1788-1792 and the coauthor of the Constitution of 1791. A portrait by Marcello Bacciarelli (1731-1818).

Fig. 51 (Right)—Title page of the Journal of Debates of the Reform Seym of 1790. The Phrygian cap hoisted aloft, symbolized liberation.

The decision to operate with a double complement of Deputies made for very crowded conditions in the Seym Chamber. The situation became so bad that a Deputy wishing to have a seat at all had to get in early and stay for the length of the session. The great interest of the public in the proceedings of the Seym did not help either, since the public galleries became overcrowded and the observers spilled over onto the ground floor. Impromptu sketches made at the time by the French painter Jean Pierre Norblin give some idea of the conditions prevailing in the Chambers.

In November of 1789 the urban government of Warsaw took it upon itself, with urgings from Hugo Kołłątay and under the leadership of Jan Dekert, the Mayor of Warsaw, to organize a convention of representatives of 141 cities and towns for political purposes. A program was worked out, including among its major points the demand for equality before the law for all burghers, broadening of self-government in Royal Cities, and the creation in the Seym of a separate chamber for the Deputies from the Cities. A delegation was elected to present the petition formally to the Seym. The City of Cracow sent a separate representative.

Fig. 52—A scene in the new Seym Chamber in the Castle of Warsaw recorded during the 1790-92 session showing the crowded conditions, when the Seym sat with the doubled complement of Deputies. A sketch made by Jean Pierre Norblin (1745-1830).

The presentation of the petition took place on December 2, 1789; this date was recorded in history as the "Black Procession." The Delegation, all dressed in black and led by Jan Dekert, rode in coaches from the City Hall of Warsaw to the Castle where the Seym sat and then to the residences of the two Speakers of the Seym: Stanisław Małachowski and Kazimierz Nestor Sapieha.

Fig. 53—Jan Dekert (1738-1790)—The Mayor of Warsaw and the organizer of the "Black Procession" of 1789 during which representatives of 141 cities and towns presented their demands to the Seym. Painted by R. Kaniewski.

The demonstrative manner of presentation of the petition and the demands it contained filled the conservative faction in the Seym with indignation, while the similarity to the Black Procession earlier the same year in France generated fears of radicalism at work. The reform faction in the Seym, however, was fully aware of the importance of the initiative taken by Dekert, and indeed, was appraised of the moves that were afoot by the more active of their members. These members participated in gatherings held in private homes in the city, under the auspices of Hugo Kołłątay's political club. A political process which was to bear fruit in a year's time was set in motion and gradually gathered momentum as political consciousness of the burghers emerged from its previous lethargy, awakened by events at home and abroad.

Before the Seym returned to domestic issues, a treaty of alliance was signed with Prussia in March of 1790, giving the Seym a false sense of security on the northwest border. On March 24, 1791 the Seym tackled the long-overdue question of electoral reform by passing a law setting new rules for operating the Seymiks. To remove the influence of the magnates at election time over the landless gentry who were employed in the administration of their estates, this gentry was stripped of active electoral rights. It is estimated that about 300,000 persons out of a total electorate of 700,000 were thus disfranchised. As could be expected the law met with cries of opposition. Under the new rules of voting established for the Seymiks, persons entitled to attend and vote were limited to tax-paying landowners, their brothers and sons, or persons holding land in lease but paying at least 100 zł of tax per annum. On the other hand, landowners in military service had their voting rights restored to them, thereby repealing the law of 1775. The same law of 1791 explicitly stripped active electoral rights from gentry holding property granted to them by the magnates or the king, since it was felt that they thereby incurred an obligation to vote in a way that pleased the grantor. As for the voters at large their lower age limit was set at 18, whereas the lower age for candidacy to any office, or a seat in the Seym, was set at 23. Eligible voters could declare themselves as candidates in writing beforehand but had to be present at the election in person.

Fig. 54—A view of the new Senate Chamber in the Castle of Warsaw during the debates on constitutional reform in 1791. An ink drawing made at the time by Józef Peszka (1767-1831).

In general, throughout the years there occurred a gradual tightening of rules governing the operation of the Seymiks and the law of 1791 was the most specific and detailed legislation in this matter. These rules survived the collapse of the First Republic and continued in use by the Seymiks in the various provinces of the country for at least another fifty years to be gradually replaced by electoral districts separated from the function of local government.

Meanwhile, in the city outside the Seym, the news from France, particularly the part played by the burghers in the events in Paris, stirred up the townsmen of

Warsaw into voicing their demands for a share in the decision making of the government. The rumblings coming from the city reached the Chambers of the Seym and the Senate and set them thinking that unless they compromised and conceded to the demands of the cities, as presented by Dekert, they might find themselves in the same hot water as the supporters of the *ancien régime* in France. On April 18, 1791, in response to the demands from the cities, the Seym passed a reform law on the status of the cities and the rights of the burghers. The draft of the bill was prepared by Deputy Jan Suchorzewski and was passed virtually unchanged by the Seym. By it the cities gained the right to elect and send to the Seym 21 representatives (see Table 32) to sit on government benches as *Plenipotentiaries,* with the right to take the floor on matters concerning the cities, industry, and commerce. Both seats and votes were given to them on the executive commissions of the Seym for the Treasury, the Police, and the Judiciary, each commission to consist of 15 Deputies and 6 Plenipotentiaries. Thus the Plenipotentiaries' position was identical to that held today in the United States Congress by the Delegates of Washington, D.C., Puerto Rico, the Virgin Islands, and Guam. The law also extended the application of the *neminem captivabimus* privilege to burghers. Furthermore, they gained the right to purchase landed estates, thereby repealing the provisions of the law of 1505. In addition, easier access was provided for them to the lower administrative and judicial offices of the state and to the rank of officer in the army, with the exception of cavalry. Easier access to gentry status was also provided with about 200 burghers, mostly delegates to the convention, given titles of gentry status on the spot.

TABLE 32—REPRESENTATION OF CITIES IN THE SEYM AFTER 1791

Province and City	Plenipotentiary	Committee Assignment
Greater Poland		
Gniezno	Wojciech Chęciński	Judiciary
Warsaw	Antoni Chevalier	Police
Łęczyca	Aleksy S. Dembowski	Treasury
Kalisz	Paweł Grochalski	Judiciary
Wieluń	Walenty Kochelski	Judiciary
Płock	Maciej Łyszkiewicz	Treasury
Poznań	Józef Wybicki	Police
Wschowa	Hiacynt W. Zakrzewski	Judiciary

TABLE 32 (CONTINUED)—REPRESENTATION OF CITIES IN THE SEYM AFTER 1791

Province and City	Plenipotentiary	Committee Assignment
Lesser Poland		
Kamieniec	Grzegorz K. Czajkowski	Judiciary
Lublin	Michał Gautier	Treasury
Sandomierz	Szymon Sapalski	Judiciary
Cracow	Józef Jagielski	Police
Winnica	Kajetan Jedlecki	Treasury
Żytomierz	Jan Lewandowski	Judiciary
Łuck	Iwo Stecki	Police
Drohiczyn	Paweł Szumowicz	Judiciary
Lithuania		
Kowno	Józef Fergis	Police
Brześć	Jan Romanowski	Judiciary
Wilno	Daniel T. Paszkiewicz	Treasury
Mińsk	Ignacy Tarankiewicz	Judiciary
Pińsk	Jan Teodorowicz	Judiciary
Grodno	Józef Żyliński	Police
Nowogródek	?. Henzel	Treasury

It may be noted at this point that the population of Poland in the 1780s numbered about ten million of which about 500,000 were burghers, 700,000 gentry, 900,000 Jews and the rest made up of the peasantry. The disfranchisement of almost half of the gentry and the enfranchisement of the burghers went far towards a more equitable distribution of political influence between the most literate and politically conscious groups.

In the years 1787-92 Russia found herself at war with Turkey and was forced to withdraw her troops from Poland to reinforce the army in the war theatre. This gave Poland a temporary respite from Russian interference and opposition to constitutional reform. The Seym took advantage of the situation and worked feverishly at its reform tasks. The mood of the Seym of 1788-92 was recalled eight years later by Deputy Julian Ursyn Niemcewicz, on the occasion of his visit to the United States Congress sitting at Philadelphia in 1798. Observing the contrast between its orderly and unharried mode of operation and the feverish activity of the Seym in 1791 he wrote:

> It was necessary to create an army, establish taxes, etc., etc., and that in the middle of foreign faction, in the middle of prejudices rooted in centuries; always in haste, seizing

the favourable moment which seemed so precarious and which lasted only so long as the troubles of our neighbours;*

The passage by the Seym on March 24, 1791 of the Law on the Seymiks, and on April 21, of the Law on the Cities, cleared the way.

Fig. 55—The new Senate Chamber of the Castle of Warsaw shown during the joint session of the two Houses on May 3, 1791, in the course of which the new Constitution was passed by acclamation. A painting after a sketch by Jean Pierre Norblin (1745-1830).

In May of 1791 a new Constitution, or as it was called "the Law on the Government" (Ustawa Rządowa), was adopted by the Seym through a coup d'état. Advantage was taken of the absence from Warsaw for Easter recess of many conservative Deputies and Senators who opposed constitutional changes. The Seym was called back into session by the King with recall notices sent only to those legislators who were not clearly identified as strong opponents of the proposed new Constitution. On May 3 the Seym assembled with 182 Senators and Deputies present; that was just over one half of the regular complement of Senators and Deputies, or over one third of the legislature expanded by the addition of the second complement of Deputies. The opposition on the floor was led by Deputy Jan Suchorzewski, the author of the just adopted "Law on the

---

* Reprinted from: *Under Their Vine and Fig Tree, Travels Through America in 1797-1799, 1805*, by Julian Ursyn Niemcewicz. Transl. by Metchie J.E. Budka. Copyright,© 1965 by Metchie J.E. Budka. By permission of the New Jersey Historical Society.

Cities," and supported by Ksawery Branicki and Józef Kossakowski. In addition to pointing out the doubtful validity of attempting to pass a new Constitution with so many legislators absent from the chamber, they brought up all of the other objections to the constitutional change which for so many decades hampered the attempts at reform. In spite of these objections those in favor of the passage of the new Constitution had an overwhelming majority among those present and the Constitution was passed. The act was followed by a public swearing in at the Cathedral of Warsaw. Table 33 gives a synopsis of the new Constitution.

In the same year (1791) the Prussian General Code of Law was introduced, Britain issued the Canada Act and the French National Assembly formalized the fruits of the French Revolution in the articles of the French Constitution. This was the year of Basic Laws. The comparative chronology of the French, the Polish and the American constitutional movements is shown in Table 34 together with the part played in the events by Thaddeus Kościuszko.

In the liberality of its provisions the Polish Constitution of 1791 fell somewhere below the French, above the Canadian, and left the Prussian far behind. It was, however, no match for the American Constitution.

In its specific provisions the Constitution of 1791 abolished elective kingship and designated the Saxon House of Wettin as hereditary, constitutional rulers. In the Seym a simple majority vote was specified for law-making and a 2/3 majority for vote of non-confidence in the Ministers, who were now to be appointed by the King for two years only. All Confederations in the Seym or out of it were banned. The possibility and the procedure for the revision of the Constitution were going to be provided for by an extraordinary Seym to be called every 25 years. The law on the Seymiks and the Law on the Cities became part of the Constitution. The duality of institutions for the Crown (of Poland) and Lithuania was abolished and replaced with a single Treasury, Judiciary, etc. It is interesting to note that this political act, coming so close to the end of life of the First Republic, attempted to strengthen the bond between Poland and Lithuania. It came at a time when Russia was offering herself as the alternate partner in the union to the unwilling and, in fact, unconsulted Lithuanians, about the intended substitution.

A most significant novelty in this Constitution was the change in the electoral basis of the Seym. It abandoned the rule that the active electoral rights were a personal, inheritable privilege tied to military obligation but independent of the financial status of the voter, and replaced it by a property qualification. This was the first time that such electoral basis was used in Poland, although similar property qualifications were at the time in force in England and America.

To put the hereditary monarchy clause into operation, a delegation headed by Adam Czartoryski was dispatched to Dresden to urge Frederick Augustus of Saxony to accept the Polish offer to succeed Stanisław August Poniatowski. The

Saxon, however, declined; ten years later Napoleon persuaded him to change his mind.

The Constitution presented to the Seym for approval on May 3, 1791 was authored mainly by the King, Ignacy Potocki and Hugo Kołłątay, with the first one mostly credited for the general provisions, the last for the editorship of the final form. Kołłątay favored a "gentle revolution," the King aimed at strengthening the hand of the Chief Executive, Potocki wanted to retain the key role for the Chamber of Deputies.

USTAWA RZĄDOWA.

PRAWO UCHWALONE.
Dnia 3. Maia, Roku 1791.

w WARSZAWIE,
w Drukarni Uprzywileiowaney M. Grolla,
Księgarza Nadwornego J. K. Mci.

MIASTA NASZE KROLEWSKIE

WOLNE w PAŃSTWACH
RZECZTPOSPOLITEY.

P R A W O

UCHWALONE

Dnia 18. Kwietnia, Roku 1791.

Fig. 56—Law on the Cities and the Law on the Government from the Constitution of 1791. Their liberal content incited the neighboring countries to partition Poland in 1793 and 1795.

Among the people prominent in giving the Constitution their moral and political support through writings and public declarations was Senator Ignacy Krasicki. Krasicki's sharp pen was particularly effective in devastating satires on the conservative viewpoint, written under an assumed name and featuring various rural characters in situations with a political message. In May 1791 an "Assembly of Friends of the Constitution" was formed with 150 founding members and 63 joining later. Its roster included 125 Deputies and 14 Senators, all working to advance the Constitution just passed. This political party obtained its initial impulse and direction from "Kołłątay's Forge."

Foreign reaction to the passage of the new Constitution varied from outright hostility in the courts of Poland's immediate neighbors to reserved praise in England. Edmund Burke, who had just published in London the English translation of the text of that Constitution in the Annual Register, recorded his views of it in a letter to Stanisław August Poniatowski, dated February 28, 1792. The letter reads in part:

> Much, Sir, has been already done in Poland: and it seems to me to be perfect from this Circumstance - That it facilitates any good that may be attempted hereafter. There is room for a long succession of acts of Politick beneficience. Nothing is forced, or crude, or before its time. The circumstances which make the improvement gradual, will make it more sure, and will not make it less rapid. The reformation your Majesty has made, by submitting the power of the Diet and your own, to the sovereign Nature of things will engage the Nature of things to a reciprocity. She, in her turn, will aid your Majesty, and the coadjutors who are worthy to cooperate with you in all your future Labours, as she has done in all your past. This, Sir, is a great and sure Alliance. It is worth purchasing by subjecting our Enthusiasm to her Laws. An arbitrary and despotick spirit may be shewn even in plans which have Liberty for their Object.
>
> But there is no mixture of weakness or rushness in your beneficient designs. You neither force, nor are forced. You proceed under the array of Justice, and you put it under the orders of its natural Guide, and cause it to be attended with its well assorted companions. What, in the Event, you may suffer from Men and accidents, as the humors of men, and the turns of Fortune are out of all calculation I cannot divine - But your Glory is safe. *

As it turned out, Burke's prediction of stormy waters ahead proved more than true, whereas Poniatowski's part in the reform movement still awaits full recognition.

It is worth noting here that the Constitution of 1791 marked the formal end of the First Republic, inasmuch as it transferred the powers of the Chief Executive from the hands of an elective chief magistrate to a hereditary monarch. The constitutional monarchy, thus established, aimed at removing the process of royal election from under foreign influence by abolishing it.

---

* Reprinted from: *The Correspondence of Edmund Burke*, P.J. Marshall, J.A. Woods, edit., Vol VII, January 1792 - August 1794, by permission of the University of Chicago Press. Published by the University of Chicago Press, 1968. All rights reserved.

Fig. 57—Stanisław Kostka Potocki (1755-1821) Deputy to the Seyms of 1778 and the following. One of the leaders of the Patriotic Party in the Reform Seym. Prime Minister of the Duchy of Warsaw. A portrait by Anton Graff (1736-1813).

TABLE 33—THE FIRST FORMAL CONSTITUTION OF POLAND: A SYNOPSIS

Voted in 1791 by the Seym as: the Law on the Seymiks, March 24; the Law on the Cities, April 18; and the Law on the Government, May 3.

The Executive Branch of the Government was headed by an hereditary king from the House of Wettin, the office to be held "by the grace of God and the will of the Nation." The king appointed five ministers, possibly from among the Senators, for a two-year term of office. Together with him and the Primate of Poland, they constituted the cabinet, termed "The Guard of Laws." The ministries were those of Chancellory, Foreign Affairs, Treasury, Defense and Police. The ministers were responsible to the Seym and could be removed from office by a two-thirds vote of non-confidence, and in cases of gross breaches of law, they could be impeached by a Tribunal of the Seym. The king presided over the Senate and had one vote in it, to be used in case of a tie. He had legislative initiative and was not responsible for the actions of ministers.

The Legislative Branch of the Government was made up of appointive Senate and elective Seym. The Senators were appointed for life by the king and numbered 130: bishops, palatines and castellans. The ministers sat in without the right to vote. The Senate had suspensive veto over the laws passed by the Seym, valid until

TABLE 33 (CONTINUED)—THE FIRST FORMAL CONSTITUTION OF POLAND—A SYNOPSIS

the next election. The Seym consisted of 204 Deputies and 21 Plenipotentiaries of the cities. The Deputies had the right of legislative initiative. Simple majority vote was required to pass peace and commercial treaties, budget, war taxes, currency issue, education, police and treasury organization, requests of regional administration. Treaties of alliance, declaration of war, Army complement; increases in the national debt required two-thirds majority for approval, while permanent taxes needed three-fourths majority vote. The Constitution could be amended by an extraordinary Seym every twenty-five years.

The Electoral Ordinance was based on property requirements. Only tax-paying male landowners 18 years of age and above had the right to vote in the County Seymiks electing 204 Deputies; 2 from each county, 68 each from the provinces of Greater Poland, Lesser Poland and Lithuania. The property-owning burghers elected 21 Plenipotentiaries of the cities, 7 each from the three provinces. The elections were held every two years and the Seym was in readiness to be called into session at any time throughout that period.

The Judiciary Branch of the Government was separated from the executive and the legislative branches of government and was carried on by elective judges. Courts of first instance were established for each palatinate and ordered to be continuously in session. Apellate Tribunals were established for each province with elective judges. The Seym elected from among its Deputies the judges for Tribunal of State to handle major cases as Supreme Court.

Bill of Rights was extended by applying the law *neminem captivabimus* to burghers and by taking the serfs under the protection of the referendary courts of each province. Confederations in or out of the Seym were banned henceforth.

TABLE 34—CHRONOLOGY OF CONSTITUTIONAL MOVEMENTS IN FRANCE, POLAND, AMERICA

Year	France	Poland	USA
1782		*Seym Elected*	
1783			War of Independence ends; T. Kościuszko made Brig. General by the Continental Congress
1784		*Seym Elected*; Kościuszko returns from America	
1785			
1786		*Seym Elected*	Virginia and Maryland call for Annapolis Convention
1787	Assembly of notables meets	Kołłątay organizes "Constitutional Forge"	Constitutional Convention meets in Philadelphia
1788	*Estates General Elected*	*Seym Elected*, Confederated, Kołłątay publishes *Anonymous Letters*	CONSTITUTION RATIFIED, Hamilton, Madison, Jay publish the *Federalist*
1789	*Constituent Assembly*; "Black Procession"; National Assembly Meets	"Black Procession" in Warsaw, 141 towns demand representation	*Congress Elected*: Washington elected President
1790		*Seym elected*; Confederation extended	Rhode Island last to ratify Constitution
1791	Legislative Assembly; CONSTITUTION PASSED; Rights of Man voted	Law on the Cities Voted, Law on the Seymiks Voted, CONSTITUTION PASSED	Bill of Rights ratified
1792	*National Convention, Revolutionary Wars*, Republic Proclaimed	War in Defense of the Constitution; Kościuszko made Major General	*Congress Elected,* Washington re-elected President
1793	Louis XVI executed	*Seym Elected*; forced to repeal the Constitution ratifying Second Partition	United States declared neutral

TABLE 34 (CONTINUED)—CHRONOLOGY OF CONSTITUTIONAL
MOVEMENTS IN FRANCE, POLAND, AMERICA

1794	Robespierre executed	Revolution in Warsaw; six senators executed; General Insurrection; Kościuszko in command	*Congress Elected*
1795	*Five Hundred Elected;* CONSTITUTION ; PASSED; Directory set up	Russia, Austria, and Prussia invade Poland; Kościuszko captured	Senate ratifies Jay treaty with Britain
1796		First Republic collapses	J. Adams elected President

THE DEFENSE OF THE CONSTITUTION AND ITS DOWNFALL

The passage of the new Constitution was received with much enthusiasm in Warsaw and much opposition in the provinces. It seemed that the brilliant preparatory work of "Kołłątay's Forge" did not reach far enough into the country. Outright propagandist efforts were, of course, difficult in a country dominated, and most of the time occupied, by Russia. Catherine of Russia opposed any changes in the Constitution which would strengthen the country she wanted to control.

When the dust settled, the opposition organized itself into the Confederation of Targowica and asked for Russian intervention on the strength of the guarantee given by Russia to the old Cardinal Laws under the treaty of 1775. The principal figures in the Confederation were Seweryn Rzewuski, Stanisław Szczęsny Potocki, Franciszek K. Branicki, Szymon and Józef Kossakowski.

To defend the Constitution the Seym voted an increase in the Army complement to 100,000; however, due to the shortage of time, money, and arms this target figure was never reached. One of the field commanders of the Army was Major General Thaddeus Kościuszko, who recently returned from America where he participated in the War of Independence and where, in 1787, the United States Congress conferred on him the rank of Brigadier General. The War in defense of the Constitution was fought in 1792; although the battles at Zieleńce and Dubienka ended in a draw, it was not possible to rout the Russian Army. The King lost heart and decided to abandon the fruit of his labors. He entered into negotiations with

Empress Catherine II, joined the Confederation of Targowica, and ordered the Army to cease fighting.

It was during the war in defense of the Constitution that King Stanislaus Augustus established the *Order of Virtuti Militari,* to be awarded to those who distinguished themselves on the field of battle. To this day it continues in Poland to be the highest award for valor. One of the first to receive it was General Thaddeus Kościuszko, who commanded in the battle of Dubienka, as well as other officers and men who distinguished themselves in this battle and at Zieleńce. When the Army was ordered to stand down the men just recently decorated were forbidden to display their decorations on pain of dismissal from the Army. In response, General Kościuszko wrote to Stanisław Szczęsny Potocki, inspirator of the prohibition, protesting its injustice. Potocki's reply is worth quoting, in part, for it demonstrates the depth of political disorientation of those opposing the reform, who saw the strengthening of the executive as a menace to the country, while failing to recognize the true danger posed by Russia. After affirming that Poland is a Republic, where the King has no power to legislate decorations, Potocki went on to say:

> We do not therefore take away from our warriors the decorations they could have received, but we say that they did not receive them at all, since what the King established is null and void. This kind of war for the support of the Warsaw conspiracy and the monarchical power established by this conspiracy, was in fact a war against the Republic, therefore the Republic cannot reward the deeds of the misled Army, and should not sustain decorations illegally established by the King. Although the Army of the Republic fought against foreign forces, it acted against the Republic, since the foreign power was allied to Poland and intended to restore, rather than conquer, the Republic.

Obviously, the author had no inkling of the price Russia would exact from Poland less than a year later for the assistance rendered. For the time being she merely insisted on having the Constitution formally repealed by a Seym. That Seym was to meet in Grodno, Lithuania in 1793.

Simultaneously an agreement was made between Russia and Prussia to partition the country again and to force the Seym to ratify the act. Great difficulty was experienced in convening the Seym. Intimidation of each Seymik by Russian troops was needed, plus a considerable injection of money for bribes, before enough Deputies were elected to make the Seym legal.

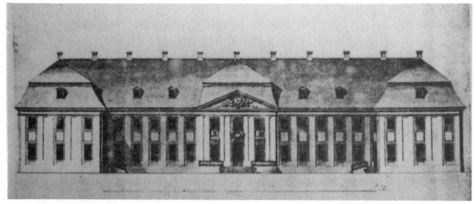

Fig. 58—The Castle of Grodno in Lithuania where 11 Seyms of the First Republic were held. Here, in 1793, with the Russian cannon trained at the building, the last Seym of the First Republic was forced to repeal the Constitution of 1791 and to ratify the treaties of the Second Partition. Two years later the captive Stanisław August Poniatowski was brought here to sign his abdication.

The last Seym of the First Republic assembled on June 17, 1793 in Grodno with Stanisław Bieliński as the Speaker. Most Senators refused to attend. When the demand for the ratificaton of the Partition Treaties was presented to the Seym, it refused to concur. On the night of July 2 Russian troops were brought in and surrounded the town. The Deputies Szymon Szydłowski, Dionizy Mikorski, Antoni Karski, and Szymon Skarzyński were arrested at their quarters and removed from the town. The following morning the Seym was pressed to select a committee which would sign the treaties and repeal the Constitution. On the night of September 25 the Partition Treaty with Prussia was presented for debate. The Seym refused to debate and sat throughout the night in silence, whereupon the silence was declared to be a sign of approval. On October 5 a similar approval for the Treaty with Russia was pronounced valid. By these Treaties the country lost 57,100 square kilometers to Prussia and 250,200 square kilometers to Russia. Austria abstained.

In this charade of acceptance Deputy Józef Ankwicz was the first to recognize the utter helplessness of the Seym, deprived of the protection of its country's troops, and urged cooperation. In recognition of his services he received a pension at this time from Empress Catherine of Russia.

After the ratification of the Partition Treaties the Seym prepared a new Constitution and established a new administrative division of what remained of the country. The Constitution of 1793 provided for an elective kingship, unicameral legislature, and restored the unitary veto in constitutional matters. The Seym was to meet every four years for an eight week session. A Russian guarantee of this Constitution was accepted and sanctions for its nonobservance were specified.

The country responded to this Second Partition with the Uprising of 1794. A revolution broke out in Warsaw, Cracow, and Wilno in late April and early May of 1794. The Russian troops were driven out of Warsaw; barricades were put up and defenses were organized. At the same time Revolutionary Tribunals were set up to try and mete out summary justice to those members of the Legislature whose activities at the Seym of 1793 of Grodno were deemed treasonable. Six Senators and Deputy Józef Ankwicz were found guilty of treason and were sentenced to death by hanging. The gallows were set up in city squares and the executions took place in public on April 25 in Wilno, and in Warsaw on April 28 and May 9 of 1794.

Fig. 59—A scene from the revolution of 1794, showing the execution in Warsaw of Deputy Józef Ankwicz and Senators Piotr Ożarowski and Józef Zabiełło condemned for their part in the Seym of 1793. A sketch made on the spot by Jean Pierre Norblin (1745-1830).

In the military arena the troops were mobilized again and the Supreme Command was given to General Thaddeus Kościuszko in recognition of his experience gained in the American Revolutionary War. The country was being invaded by the Russians, Prussians and Austrians. In the ensuing campaign the army was overwhelmed, and the country collapsed. Kościuszko was severely wounded by a lance driven into his hip joint and was taken prisoner by the Russians at the battle of Maciejowice on October 10, 1794. In 1795 the Third Partition of the remaining territory of Poland took place, with Austria, Russia and Prussia participating. Stanisław August Poniatowski abdicated.

In Polish historiography this difficult period of miscarried constitutional reform and the resulting collapse of the institutions of state are given much space and provoke frequent moralizing. While the Constitution of 1791 itself is seen as evidence of moral regeneration of the country from the visible decay of the Saxon times, its practical effect is considered negligible, as it was in force for just over a year. Its successor, the Constitution of 1793, had even less impact due to its rejection by the country and the collapse of the state under foreign intervention. However, two provisions of the Constitution of 1791 survived in the Constitution of the Duchy of Warsaw of 1807: 1) the choice of the House of Wettin as a hereditary ruling dynasty, and 2) the function of the Seymiks in electing the Deputies to the Seym. Perhaps the most significant effect of the Constitution of 1791 was not tangible but inspirational, for it led to the reawakening among its citizens of interest in, and the feeling of responsibility for the political well-being of the country.

Looking back at the political history of the First Republic, it is appropriate to ask how well did the electorates of the Prussian, Lithuanian and Ruthenian provinces adjust to the workings of the joint parliamentary system of the Commonwealth, and how did their contribution affect it in turn. Three measures of this adjustment suggest themselves: 1) the regularity of returning Deputies to the Seym, 2) the frequency of vetoes cast by the Deputies from the given province in the period when the unitary veto was considered constitutionally binding, and finally 3) the number of times when significant separatist movements or revolts were started in the province. In each province the details of adjustment were different; nevertheless, a distinct general trend is discernible.

Of the three provinces, Royal Prussia was very irregular as regards the number or frequency of return of Deputies. It participated through large delegations in the royal elections, sent between ten and twelve Deputies in the early 1600s, and absented itself altogether in the mid 1700s. The palatinates of Lithuania and Ruthenia were reasonably regular in returning Deputies throughout the 1600s and 1700s, except, of course, in times of war or invasion. The differences in the number of vetoes cast by Deputies from different provinces are even more striking. Bearing in mind that some vetoes involved more than one Deputy, even though a unitary veto was sufficient to block the entire legislative output of a Seym, the following statistics can be considered. Of the 70 Deputies participating in vetoes only 10 were returned from the provinces of Greater Poland, 8 were returned from Masovia, 24 from Ruthenia (Ukraine) and 28 from Lithuania. The differences are related to variations in political tradition and social structure. In both Lithuania and

Ruthenia the various princely families of the province retained their influence over the voters and the Deputies they elected after the Union of 1569, and supplied many Senators. The Union merely replaced the former prince-subject relation with a patron-client one. Existing disparities in wealth and position afforded means of enforcing it. Furthermore, there is solid evidence to support the contention that many a veto was engineered outside the Seym by a provincial magnate but actually cast in the Seym by a client Deputy. In Poland proper, where the princely Piast family died out centuries earlier, a more democratic tradition was established and the rising senatorial families provided a much weaker version of the patron-client relationship. Obedience was not expected and pressure was more difficult to apply. This difference in mental attitudes was aptly caught in a contemporary two-liner:

> In Ruthenia you must obey
> But in Poland, have it your way
> (Musi na Rusi,
> a w Polsce, jak kto chce)

In this connection, the almost total absence of Prussian vetoes in the Seym is worth noting, although it is difficult to ascertain whether this was due to the higher civic responsibility of the Prussian Deputies or their poorer attendance record. The last measure of adjustment, the presence of separatist movements, was most pronounced in Ruthenia (Ukraine), where several armed revolts of the Cossacks took place in 1630-1638 and again in 1702-1704, and in 1658 an agreement was even signed with the Cossacks setting up a "Ruthenian Duchy" in the palatinates of Kiev, Czernichów and Bracław; however, the agreement was not put into operation. The separatist movements were less pronounced in Lithuania, but even there, in 1655 during the Swedish invasion, Janusz and Bogusław Radziwiłł contracted with the Swedes for a union between Lithuania and Sweden, a plan that fell through when the Swedes were driven out. In the Prussian province the separatist movements were least evident, and, in fact, even after the first Partition in 1772, both the Cities of Gdańsk and Toruń refused to yield to Frederick of Prussia and continued their association with Poland until the Second Partition in 1792. On the basis of these indicators one may conclude that the extension of the parliamentary institutions and sovereignty of Poland to the Ukraine was a failure; in Lithuania it was a partial success; and in Prussia it produced an even break.

The Kings elected by the Seyms in that period are listed in Table 35, while the principal legislation of the Seyms in the years 1703-1793 is summarized in Table 36. A synopsis of the Constitution of 1793 is given in Table 37. Biographical notes on prominent parliamentarians of that period follow.

TABLE 35—KINGS OF THE FIRST REPUBLIC ELECTED BY THE SEYM

KING	TERM OF OFFICE
Henri Valois	1573-1575*
Stephen Bathory	1576-1586
Sigismund III Vasa	1587-1632
Ladislaus IV Vasa	1632-1648
John II Casimir Vasa	1648-1668*
Michael Korybut Wiśniowiecki	1669-1673
John III Sobieski	1674-1696
Augustus II Wettin	1697-1733**
Augustus III Wettin	1733-1763
Stanislaus Augustus Poniatowski	1764-1795*

*Abdicated
**Served two terms 1697-1706 and 1709-1733. Forced to abdicate after the first term by the Swedes, who imposed on the country the three-year administration of Stanisław Leszczyński.

SPEAKERS OF THE SEYM IN THE FIRST REPUBLIC

Over 160 Deputies served as the Speaker of the Seym during the First Republic. The list is too long to quote here but their names are listed in Appendix C under the Seym in which they served.

TABLE 36—PRINCIPAL LEGISLATION OF SEYMS OF THE FIRST REPUBLIC (PART III)

1703	Burghers of Lublin gain Seym representation, land purchase right
1717	Seymiks' tax and the Army rights restricted
	Tax to support an Army of 24,000 voted
	Russian guarantee of status quo accepted
	First budget formulated and accepted
1726	Procedures of Supreme Court improved
1732	Mandate for issue of currency issued
1733	Non-Catholics banned from Seym candidacy
1734	Ordinance for the Post Office passed
1736	Ordinance of Kurland (Latvia) passed
1761	Universal proclamation on coinage issued

TABLE 36 (CONTINUED)—PRINCIPAL LEGISLATION OF SEYMS OF THE FIRST REPUBLIC (PART III)

1764	Seymiks'and Vaads' tax duties abolished
	Royal elections closed to foreign candidates
	Self-government restored to the cities
	Ordinance for the Courts revised
1764	Mint transferred to Executive control
	National Treasury Commissions established
1766	Reform of coinage voted, tax law revised
1768	Candidacy rights restored to Non-Catholics
	Cardinal Laws restated
	Voting rules in the Seym modified
1773-75	Hearth tax, customs duty equalized
1775	Army complement set at 30,000; 24,000 for Poland, 6,000 for Lithuania
	Treaties of First Partition ratified
	Permanent Council established
	Army, Education commissions established
	Lithuanian Burghers get land buying rights
1782	Treasury Commission reorganized
1785	Permanent Council reformed
1788	Army complement of 100,000 authorized
1789	10% tax rate for gentry, 20% for the clergy
1790	Treaty of Alliance with Prussia ratified
	City Commissions of Good Order set up
1791	Electoral Ordinance for the Seymiks revised
	Seym representation voted for burghers
	New Constitution (of May 3) voted
1793	Constitution of 1791 repealed
	Treaties of Second Partition ratified
	Conservative constitution voted

TABLE 37—LAST CONSTITUTION OF THE FIRST REPUBLIC—A SYNOPSIS (VOTED BY THE SEYM ON NOVEMBER 23, 1793)

The Executive Branch of the Government was headed by the king elected for life by a Seym composed of three times the regular number of Deputies. The candidacy for kingship was open to all contenders. The successful candidate was required to sign the Articles of Agreement in which his prerogatives and duties were detailed. In the execution of his duties the king was assisted by the Permanent Council, composed of ten Senators and fourteen Deputies. The Permanent Council operated through six departments.

191

TABLE 37 (CONTINUED)—LAST CONSTITUTION OF THE FIRST REPUBLIC—A SYNOPSIS

The Legislative Branch of the Government was composed of 54 Senators and 108 Deputies sitting in joint session. Among the Senators there were 10 bishops, including the Greek Catholic Archbishop, 18 palatines, 18 castellans and 8 ministers. The sessions of the Seym were to be held in Camera and were to last eight weeks. Voting was by majority rule with the first vote by voice and the next by colored balls. Unitary veto was valid in constitutional matters. The competence of the Seym included taxing powers, army call-up, initiation and ratification of treaties with foreign powers, and the appointment of ambassadors and administration officials. In the event of the king's death or abdication, the senior Senator, Senator-Archbishop of Gniezno, acted as the king pro-tempore (Interrex) until the new King was elected and inaugurated.

The Election Ordinance gave the voting rights to members of the gentry only. The Seym Deputies were to be elected once every four years for a single ordinary session of eight weeks. The same Deputies could be summoned to an extraordinary session. Six Deputies per palatinate were to be elected from each of the eighteen palatinates. The towns were unrepresented. Drafts of bills and the proposed order of debates were to be submitted to the Seymiks before the elections.

The Judiciary Branch of Government was composed of judges to be elected every two years by the Seymiks of each land. Each palatinate was divided into three such lands, instead of as formerly into counties.

The Bill of Rights included the guarantees of property and personal freedom as well as freedom of speech for the gentry and the burghers, with the exception of persons who agitated against religion or the Constitution. Religious tolerance was guaranteed for all denominations.

POLITICAL PERSONALITIES IN SEYMS OF THE REFORM ERA

Józef Ankwicz (1750-1794)—Parliamentarian, diplomat; he was appointed minor castellan of Nowy Sącz in 1782 and took part in the Seyms of 1782-90, supporting the political line taken by the King. In 1791-92 he served as Ambassador to Denmark. After the passage of the Constitution of 1791 by the Seym he joined the oppositon organized in the Confederation of Targowica. Elected Deputy from Cracow to the 1793 Seym of Grodno, he accepted a Russian pension and moved during that Seym that the Treaty of the Second Partition be accepted unconditionally. On Russian direction he was appointed the Speaker of the Permanent Council revived by the Seym of 1793. During the Revolution of 1794 he was arrested in Warsaw, tried by the Revolutionary Tribunal and sentenced to death for his complicity in the Second Partition. He died in a public execution. He authored *Protection of the National Government* (1790).

Franciszek K. Chomiński (?-1809)—Politician, writer; he was elected Deputy of the Seym held at Grodno in 1784 and served as its Speaker. Appointed palatine of Mścisław in 1788, he supported the Constitution of 1791. After the partitions of Poland he followed the political orientation of A. Czartoryski, who was active in exile in Paris. As part of his literary endeavors he wrote poetry and epigrams, and translated Racine's *Fedra* into Polish.

Celestyn Czaplic (1723-1804)—Politician, poet; he was elected Speaker of the Seym of 1766 and appointed Chief Huntsman to the Crown in 1773. During the four year Reform Seym of 1788-1792 he served as a member of the Military Commission. He was author of fairy tales, idyls, and other light poetry; *To Solec* (1774), *History, or the Strange Adventures of Olind with Amarylla* (1774).

Adam K. Czartoryski (1734-1823)—Politician, writer, patron of the arts; he became Prefect General of Podole in 1758; was elected a Deputy to several Seyms of the First Republic; a candidate for the kingship of Poland, he withdrew in favor of Stanisław Poniatowski and served as the Speaker of the Convocation Seym of 1764 which preceded this election. He reorganized the Army of Lithuania in 1766. Later he joined the Confederation of Radom opposing the King. He was appointed Commander of the Royal Military Academy in 1768. Elected to the Reform Seym of 1788 as Deputy for Lublin, he became reconciled with the King and helped create the Commission for National Education. In 1791 he was sent on an unsuccessful embassy to Dresden to persuade Frederick Augustus to accept the crown. He was elected Speaker of the extraordinary Seym of the Duchy of Warsaw in 1812. He authored *Thoughts on Polish Writing* (1810) and many comedies and stage plays.

Jan Dekert (1738-1790)—Merchant, administrator, politician. He was initially a cloth merchant in Warsaw, cofounded the Company of Woolen Manufacture in 1766. In 1766 he leased from the Treasury the Tobacco Monopoly and in 1786 the Theatre in Warsaw. He became Alderman of the City of Warsaw in 1769 and served as Alderman of the Confraternity of Merchants between 1771 and 1785. He was elected Delegate to the Seyms of 1784 and 1786 from the City of Warsaw and Deputy from the City of Warsaw to the Reform Seym of 1788. Elected Mayor of Warsaw in 1789, he organized the Confederation of 141 cities and led the presentation of their demands for fuller representation in the Seym in the Black Procession on December 2, 1789. He was reelected Mayor in 1790.

Stanisław E. Denhoff (1675-1728)—Politician, army general, he was a coorganizer of the Confederation of Sandomierz in 1704 which supported Augustus II Wettin. In 1709 he was appointed Field Commander-in-Chief of the Army of Lithuania. He headed the General Council of Warsaw in 1710 ratifying the return of Augustus II as Chief Executive. He served as the Speaker of the Seym of 1710. Made palatine of Połock in 1717, he joined the opposition against Augustus II.

Kazimierz Karwowski (1670-1746)—Jurist and parliamentarian, carefully educated in law, history and languages, an effective speaker and debator, he was elected Deputy no less than 27 times, an all-time record in 500 years of Polish parliamentarism. He participated in the General Council of Warsaw in 1710. In 1714 he was elected Deputy Judge to the Crown Tribunal, and in 1715 Municipal Judge in Brańsk. During his Seym career he took part in the initiatives to establish permanent salaries for Deputies, to reform the tax structure and army finances, to settle affairs of Kurland (1727-28), and to modify the procedures of the Crown Tribunal. During the Potocki obstructionism at the Seyms of 1729, 1730, and 1732 he urged the King to convene a Confederated Seym. Elected Speaker of the Seym in 1740 he was not able to prevent its disruption. He repeatedly urged reform of Seym procedures.

Stanisław Dunin-Karwicki (1640-1724)—Parliamentarian and writer, he served as treasurer of the palatinate of Sandomierz. Elected Deputy to the Seym of 1674 and several subsequent ones, he served as a harbinger of the reform movement of the eighteenth century in the political sphere with his treatise *De ordinanda Republica seu de corrigendis defectibus in statu Reipublicae Poloniae.*

Hugo Kołłątay (1750-1812)—Priest, philosopher, writer, politician; he was active in the Commission for National Education 1777-1786; Chancellor and reformer of the University of Cracow. During the Reform Seym, in 1788-89 he published a series of anonymous letters addressed to S. Małachowski, the Speaker of the Seym, outlining a program of constitutional reform in the republican spirit. In 1789 he formed a radical club "Constitutional Forge." He was one of the coauthors of the Constitution of 1791. Appointed Vice-Chancellor of the Crown in 1791, he favored compromise during the war in defense of the Constitution. In 1794, during the Kościuszko Insurrection, he served as a member of the Supreme Council. He was imprisoned by the Austrians (1794-1802). During the years 1809-1810 he reformed the germanized University of Cracow. He authored: *Anonymous Letters to Stanisław Mała- chowski* (parts 1-3, 1788-89); *Political Law of the Polish Nation* (1790); *On the Introduction and Collapse of the Constitution of May 3* (1793); *Remarks on the Present Situation of Those Parts of Polish Territory which after the Peace of Tilsit Started to be Called the Duchy of Warsaw* (1809); *Physico-Moral Order* (1811); *Condition of Education in the Last Years of the Reign of Augustus III* (1841).

Stanisław Małachowski (1736-1809)—Politician, parliamentary leader; he was Grand Referendary of the Crown 1780-1792; served as the Speaker of the four year Reform Seym 1788-1792, and took part in the writing of the

Constitution of 1791. A member of the Patriotic Party, he supported the demands of the burghers for the extension of their political rights. On his estates he replaced the work levy with rent for his peasants. He opposed the Confederation of Targowica. After the partitions he was made Chairman of the Governing Commission and then of the Council of Ministers of the Duchy of Warsaw in 1807, and finally of the Senate.

Jacek Małachowski (1737-1821)—Politician, administrator; in 1764 he was appointed Chief Referendary of the Crown and in the same year was elected Speaker of the Seym. In 1780 he was appointed Vice-Chancellor of the Crown and Chancellor in 1786. He was a supporter of the pro-Russian orientation. During the four year Reform Seym he supported the strengthening of the executive and enlargement of the army with Russian support. He opposed the Constitution of 1791 and joined the Confederation of Targowica to overthrow it.

Józef A. Massalski (1726-1765)—Parliamentarian, politician; elected Deputy to the Seym of 1744 for the county of Grodno; he was made Prefect of Grodno in 1748, as well as President of the Tribunal (Supreme Court) of Lithuania. He was Deputy to the Seym of Warsaw of 1750 and 1752 where he was elected Speaker. After the legislation of that Seym was vetoed, he made an impassioned farewell speech to the House stressing that time is running out for saving the Commonwealth from collapse and placing the responsibility on the Seym. He also presided over the Seyms of 1754 and 1756, of which the first was disrupted by a veto and the second could not convene legally in the absence of the king who remained in Saxony. He served as Deputy to the Seym of 1758 and only then was able to pass the Speaker's staff on to his successor. In 1765 he was made a member of the Lithuanian Treasury Committee.

Stanisław August (Antoni) Poniatowski (1732-1798)—Parliamentarian, king; graduate of Teatine College in Warsaw; he was elected Deputy for Zakroczym to the Seym of 1750; and appointed colonel of militia and Commissioner of the Treasury Tribunal. He made a Grand Tour of central and western Europe. In 1755 he was appointed Steward of Lithuania and under the sponsorship of the Czartoryski family went to St. Petersburg where he assumed the duties of secretary to the British Ambassador Ch. H. Williams, developing at the same time a liaison with the Grand Duchess Catherine, the future Empress of Russia. His second term in St. Petersburg as envoy of the Elector of Saxony (1757-58) was terminated when the affair with Catherine became public knowledge. In 1758 he was elected Deputy to the Seym for Inflanty, again elected to the Seym of 1760 for Przemyśl and in 1761 for Bielsko when he contributed to the veto against the legislation. Elected Deputy again for Mielnik in 1762 and to the Convocation Seym of 1764 for Warsaw, he was put up as a candidate in the royal election by the Czartoryski family with the support of Empress Catherine. Elected King, he attempted some work on constitutional reform but was checked in 1768 by the Confederation of Bar, which tried to dethrone him and to abduct him from Warsaw. In 1772 he was forced to accept some reforms, becoming in the process president of the Permanent Council, a government elected every two years by the Seym. He became the mainspring of a cultural and artistic revival and participated actively in the Four Year Seym 1788-1792, coauthoring the Constitution of 1791. During the war in its defense he lost heart and ordered the army to stand down. He then participated in the captive Seym of 1793 in Grodno where the Russians forced him to accept the Second Partition. He lost effective control of the government during the Kościuszko Insurrection and, after its collapse, was held captive at Grodno abdicating there in 1795. He died in semi-captivity in St. Petersburg in 1798. He authored the *Memoirs*, two volumes (1914-24) and a voluminous correspondence.

Adam Poniński (1732-1798)—Politician; appointed Chief Treasurer of the Crown in 1773; was one of the leaders of the Confederation of Radom; served as the Speaker of the 1773-1775 Seym which ratified the first partition of Poland; remained in pay of foreign powers and usurped for private use funds from former Jesuit properties intended for the Commission for National Education. He was impeached by the Seym Tribunal of 1788, stripped of his office and banished from the country. The sentence was annuled by the Seym of 1793 under Russian pressure.

Stanisław Szczęsny Potocki (1751-1805)—Army general, parliamentarian; appointed Senator-palatine of Ruthenia he served from 1782 until 1788 when he resigned his seat in the Senate to run in the elections for Deputy to the Seym. In the period 1788-1792 he served as a general of artillery in the army of Poland. As Deputy in the Reform Seym of 1788-92, he led the opposition to the reform movement and supported the retention of the elective kingship. After the passage of the Constitution of 1791 he was one of the mainsprings of the Confederation of Targowica, aimed at having the Constitution overthrown with Russian help. During 1794 he was tried for treason in absentia and sentenced to death. After the Third Partition in 1797 he was appointed a general in the Russian Army. Coauthored with S. Rzewuski *Protestation Against the Succession to the Throne in Poland* (1790).

Stanisław Kostka Potocki (1755-1821)—Parliamentarian, army general; elected Deputy to the Seym of 1778 and the following Seyms; in 1782 he became a member of the Permanent Council. During the Reform Seym of 1788-92 he was one of the leading activists of the Patriotic Party. Served as Major General of Artillery during the war for the defense of the Constitution in 1792. Senator for the Duchy of Warsaw he became in 1809 the Prime Minister and Chairman of the Council of State. In the Congress Kingdom of Poland he served as the President of the Council of State and from 1818 on as the President of the Senate. As Director of the Department of Education and Religious

Denominations, he steered an anticlerical course. He was an active Mason and a member of the Association of Friends of Science of Warsaw. He authored *Commendations, Speeches and Discussions*, two volumes (1816); *Journey to the Land of Ignorance*, four volumes (1820), and many studies on architecture and art.

Karol S. Radziwiłł (1743-1790)—Politician; Sword Bearer of Lithuania in 1752; appointed palatine of Wilno in 1762-1764. In 1767 he became the marshal of the Confederation of Radom and the Speaker of the Seym of 1768. Acted in opposition to the Czartoryski Party and the king and became a willing tool of the Russian ambassador, N. W. Repnin. He joined the Confederation of Bar as one of its leaders. After its collapse in 1777 he went into exile but later became reconciled with the king through the intercession of Empress Catherine of Russia. During the four year Reform Seym he opposed the constitutional reform, relying for support on his popularity among small gentry.

Tadeusz Reytan (1746-1780)—Parliamentarian; elected Deputy to the Seym of 1773 for Nowogródek where he led the opposition to the ratification of the Treaty of the First Partition. In particular, he objected to the formation of the Confederation in the Seym and the election of Adam Poniński as its Speaker. To stop the Deputies from entering the Seym Chamber, which would be tantamount with the Seym recognizing the Confederation, he barricaded himself with a few fellow Deputies in the Seym Chamber. All this was to no avail. He became despondent over the subsequent turn of political events and eventually committed suicide.

Wacław Rzewuski (1706-1779)—Politician, army general, writer, poet; he was Deputy to the Seym of 1736 and served as its Speaker; he was appointed Field Commander-in-Chief of the Army of Poland in 1752. Initially in favor of moderate political reforms he engaged, in 1764, in polemics with S. Konarski in support of liberum veto rule of the Seym. During the Seym of 1767 he opposed the restoration of political rights to religious dissidents and was kidnapped on orders of the Russian ambassador, N. W. Repnin, and carried off to captivity in Russia. On his release in 1773 he was made Commander-in-Chief of the Army of Poland and in 1778 the palatine of Cracow. In his residence at Podhorce he maintained a private theatre for which he wrote plays *Żółkiewski* (1758), work on poetry *On the Art of Writing Poetry* (1762), *Play with Words and Verses* (1762).

Kazimierz Nestor Sapieha (1754-1798)—Between 1767-71 he attended the Warsaw Military Academy, which counted among its graduates also Thaddeus Kościuszko and Julian U. Niemcewicz. On his return home from further studies in Italy he was appointed, in 1773, General of Artillery in the Army of Lithuania. Elected as Deputy to the Seym for Lithuanian Brześć, he served there 1778-1788, and in 1786 he was instrumental in the defeat of King Poniatowski's proposal for the reform of the Army. During the Four Year Reform Seym, he was elected in 1790 as the Speaker of the Confederation in the Seym of the Second complement of Deputies. During this Seym he initially espoused the conservative course and supported the opposition to reform centered around his uncle, F. K. Branicki. Later, under the influence of his co-Speaker Stanisław Małachowski, he joined the supporters of the Constitution of May 3, 1791. Following the overthrow of the Constitution he left the country for Dresden, but returned to Poland in 1794 and participated in the Insurrection of Kościuszko. After the last partition he went into exile in Vienna and died there three years later.

Kajetan Sołtyk (1715-1788)—Churchman, parliamentarian; appointed Bishop of Kiev in 1756 he entered the Senate as an opponent of the restoration of passive electoral right to the Greek Orthodox; appointed Bishop of Cracow in 1759. During the administration of Stanisław August Poniatowski, he opposed the reform program fostered by the King and the Czartoryski family. His leadership of the opposition to the demands of the Russian Ambassador, N. W. Repnin, during the Seym of 1767 prompted Repnin to engineer his abduction to Russia together with two other Senators. This breach of legislative immunity became one of the causes of the formation of the Confederation of Bar. Released from captivity after five years, he returned to Cracow in an unbalanced state of mind and was not able to resume his duties.

Jan Suchorzewski (?-1809)—Parliamentarian, politician; was appointed chamberlain to King Stanisław August Poniatowski in 1788; elected Deputy to the Seym of 1788 from the county of Kalisz, he became noted for his oratorical talent. In 1791 he submitted a bill to the Seym on municipal self-government. In May of the same year he led the opposition to the passage of the new Constitution in a dramatic scene on the floor of the Senate Chamber during the joint session on May 3, 1791, when the Constitution was passed with barely one-third of the Senators and Deputies present. In the Summer of 1791 he participated in a conspiracy organized by Jakov I. Bulhakov and Franciszek K. Branicki to abduct the King from Warsaw. In 1792 he joined the Confederation of Targowica, organized to overthrow the Constitution of 1791, and was appointed commander of the Bracław brigade of cavalry. He authored: *Priciples of Municipal Law* (1789) and *Remarks on the Polish Constitution of 1791* (1791).

Stanisław A. Szczuka (1654-1710)—Parliamentarian, writer. He started his political career on the staff of the Supreme Court of Poland (Trybunał Koronny); subsequently he was appointed a secretary to the King and a Referendary of the Crown. Elected Deputy to the Seym of 1688, he served as its Speaker. During the Royal Election of 1699 he supported Augustus Wettin, and attempted to mollify the public outcry over the irregular manner of that election, serving as the Speaker of the Pacification Seym of 1699. In the same year he was appointed

Vice-Chancellor of Lithuania. Continuing acrimony connected with Augustus' administration prompted him to switch in 1706 his political support to Stanisław Leszczyński, the puppet king sponsored by the Swedes. He authored a program of reform of the Treasury and proposed that the regular army be increased to 36,000 and supported by property taxes. Authored: *Eclipsis Poloniae orbi publico demonstrate* (1709).

CHAPTER V

PARTITIONS: POLISH LEGISLATURES UNDER FOREIGN ABSOLUTISM

During the period of Partitions (1795-1918), the national legislature was suppressed following the collapse of central government. The Provinces of Greater Poland and Masovia, Lesser Poland (Galicia), and Lithuania, became parts of the three neighboring empires. These empires were absolutist monarchies. Governing without elective representation, their rulers relied on the 'divine rights of kings' for justification of their edicts. Yet, in spite of these adverse conditions, the Seymiks and the provincial General Seymik, i.e., the lower two tiers of the representative system of the First Republic, survived and operated in each of the provinces of Poland in turn, while in Lithuania the legislative institutions died out.

The torch of the elective representation was kept burning in Warsaw in the years 1809-1812, first under Napoleon then in the years 1815-1831 under Alexander I and Nicholas I of Russia. It moved to Poznań under Prussian rule in the years 1827-1848, then on to Lwów in Galicia under Austrian rule in the years 1864-1918. In each of these three zones the age-old Polish tradition of elective representation clashed with the absolutist tradition of the partitioning powers, showing the innate incompatibility of these two approaches to government. Armed revolts against arbitrary rule took place whenever the consent of the governed was disregarded.

Revolts against the Russians in 1830 and the Prussians in 1848 resulted in the suppression or crippling of Seyms in these provinces; however, as soon as legislative institutions in one zone were suppressed, or made unrepresentative through interference with its electoral ordinance, another province succeeded in having its legislature recognized.

All the while progress was being made in extending the suffrage rights to ever broader strata of society, first by bringing in the burghers to participate in the Seyms of Warsaw and Poznań, then the peasants in the Seyms of Poznań and Lwów. Legislative methods and procedures improved steadily. At the end of this period Poland witnessed the adoption of the elective system of representation by each of the partitioning powers in their home lands.

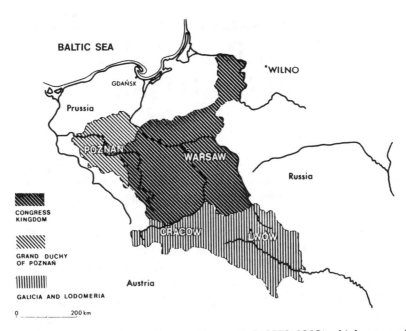

Fig. 60—Parts of Poland during the partition period (1772-1918) which returned provincial Seyms.

THE NAPOLEONIC TOUCH: SEYM OF THE DUCHY OF WARSAW

The revival of legislative institutions in Poland took place sixteen years after the last partition and led to the establishment of provincial Seyms. These Seyms operated at various periods, overlapping at times, in three provinces of the Polish section of what had been the Polish-Lithuanian Commonwealth. With the exception of the short-lived Seym of Central Lithuania (1922), no Polish Seyms were ever reestablished in the Lithuanian part of the former Commonwealth.

In terms of the centuries-old legislative traditions of Poland, the provincial Seyms of the partition period corresponded to the middle tier of the former three-tier legislative system, i.e., to the General Seymik of the province. Nevertheless, each of the provincial legislatures used the word 'Seym' in its title, reverting to the usage of the fifteenth century, from before the formation of the National Seym.

The first of the provincial legislatures to revive owed its existence to the military exploits of Napoleon. In the course of his campaigns against Prussia he reached the former Polish provinces of Pomerania and Greater Poland, and was able to stir up considerable national enthusiasm in his favor. People started to enlist into army units under his command, augmenting the number of Poles already serving in the French Army. The new army units thus formed took part in the rest of Napoleon's Prussian campaign of 1807 and participated in the siege of Gdańsk. In consequence, Napoleon resolved to form, out of the lands taken from Poland by Prussia in the Second and Third Partitions, a Duchy of Warsaw with its own government and legislature. Another campaign against Austria added to the Duchy the lands taken by Austria in the Third Partition, thus incorporating in the Duchy all of the province of Masovia, Greater Poland and parts of Lesser Poland.

In the rump state thus formed hopes ran high that the Constitution of May 3, 1791 would again be put into operation with perhaps minor modifications. In fact, that Constitution was already much outdated and no longer completely aligned with the revolutionary spirit of the times.

A parliamentary delegation, headed by Stanisław Małachowski, the distinguished Speaker of the four-year Reform Seym of 1788-92, Stanisław Kostka Potocki and Józef Wybicki, was dispatched in 1807 to Dresden, to present the Polish constitutional proposals to Napoleon. The delegation was flabbergasted when Napoleon produced in one short dictation a Constitution of his own for the Duchy of Warsaw and insisted that it be adopted without major changes. In these circumstances the delegation was in no position to refuse.

The Constitution given to the Duchy of Warsaw conformed in major points to the model adopted by Napoleon for his satellite states. Altogether there were to be several such Constitutions:

1807	Duchy of Warsaw
1807	Kingdom of Westphalia
1808	Kingdom of Naples
1812	Grand Duchy of Berg

Fig. 61—Napoleon handing the Constitution of the Duchy of Warsaw to the Seym delegation. Stanisław Małachowski is about to receive the document. Józef Wybicki stands at the extreme right. A painting by Marcello Bacciarelli (1731-1818). Also shown are: Walenty Sobolewski, Franciszek Działyński, Piotr Bieliński, Ludwik Gutakowski, Jan Luszewski, Stanisław Potocki.

which held some characteristics in common, the principal of them being the strong central executive, the limitation of the legislature to budgetary and judicial matters, introduction of equality of all citizens before the law, and the abolition of privileged classes. Access to positions in the administration and the army was open to all citizens, and the Code Napoléon was made the basis of civil law. The legislatures were, as a rule, appointive. The Constitution of the Duchy of Warsaw differed from the above model in several important aspects, reflecting the previous constitutional experience of the country. In particular, a bicameral legislature with an elective lower chamber was provided. In the new constitutional arrangements the Seymiks were retained as electoral assemblies for the gentry. In addition, communal assemblies for the villages and towns were provided for electing Deputies by the townsmen and the peasants. The chief executive office was assigned to the Saxon house of Wettin rather than to a close relative of Napoleon or a deserving French Marshal. The complete separation of the executive from the legislative functions and placement of the constitutional matters in the hands of the executive differed so much from the previous constitutional experience of the Poles, that a considerable mental adjustment was needed to accept the Napoleonic concept.

In the Seym, the function of the Deputies was reduced to voting on bills presented to them by the three committees of the Seym: the treasury, the criminal law and the civil law. Each committee was composed of five members and only the members of the committees were allowed to debate the bills on the floor of the chamber. The members of the committees were elected by the chamber in a secret ballot.

The executive was nominally headed by the King of Saxony, acting as the Duke of Warsaw. The choice of the ruling House and the retention of the Seymiks were carried over from the Constitution of 1791. In practice, the executive function was placed in the hands of Prime Minister Stanisław K. Potocki in the absence of Frederick Augustus Wettin, who for the most part resided in Dresden and made only four visits to the Duchy. In the absence of Frederick Augustus, the Senate sat under Tomasz A. Ostrowski.

Fig. 62—Tomasz A. Ostrowski (1735-1817) Senator and Minister of the First Republic, Chairman of the Senate in the Duchy of Warsaw.

Under the new Constitution only two legislatures were returned during the life of the Duchy. Those were the Seyms of 1809 and 1811. Much of their business was taken up with financial matters: how to raise taxes on a sufficiently high scale to support an army of 30,000 with a population base of 2.6 million and how to cover a debt of 20 million francs assumed by the Duchy from the Prussian government. For that matter, the whole period of the Duchy's existence might be viewed as a rude awakening of the legislature to the financial and budgetary burdens of the modern state. On the whole, the Seym was not equal to the task, nor could the devastated country, after the wars in defense of the Constitution of 1791, the Kościuszko insurrection of 1794, and the recent Napoleonic campaigns of 1806 and 1809, carry the burden.

The Seym spent a great deal of time on reestablishing and reorganizing the administration of the country. The Napoleonic Constitution brought some drastic changes in this area. Napoleon insisted on the creation of a state-paid administration and ministries; he argued that with pay better performance could be demanded. At the same time positions would be opened to talented individuals who would have been unable to accept them under the old system of honorific officialdom which required private financial resources. Thus, in 1808, the ranks of full-time bureaucrats were staffed with 4700 public officials; their number rose to 9000 after the annexation of a part of Lesser Poland to the Duchy of Warsaw in 1809. The cost of the paid administration much increased the already heavy financial burden of the state. This ran contrary to the habitual thinking, carrried over from the days of the First Republic, which demanded that taxes be kept low for the maximum benefit of the public. The financial matters included the reactivation of the Mint, and the replacement of the Prussian coinage, then commonly in circulation, with coinage of the Duchy.

The last legislative action of the Seym before the collapse of Napoleon's plans in the East, was the proclamation of a General Confederation in 1812, on the eve of the invasion of Russia, in the hope of rallying public support for reviving the old Polish-Lithuanian Commonwealth. This was the last Confederation ever called. The Act of the Confederation contained 18 articles. The first six are relevant to constitutional matters, and are worth quoting; the rest deal with administrative matters.

The Act of Confederation, dated June 28, 1812, in Warsaw, reads in part:

Article 1.   The Seym constitutes itself into a General Confederation of Poland.

Article 2.   The General Confederation of Poland, exercising to the full extent the powers serving the universal National bond, declares: that the Kingdom of Poland is restored, and the Polish Nation is in one body reunited.

Article 3.   Throughout the Duchy Seymiks will be convened with the objective of joining the Confederation. The Acts of Access of each Seymik will be transmitted to the Council of the General Confederation.

Article 4.   All Poles are summoned and authorized to accede to the present Confederation, either individually or as groups, and to send as soon as possible their Acts of Access to the General Council.

Article 5.   All parts of Poland are summoned to accede to the Confederation as soon as the withdrawal of the enemy offers an opportunity. They are summoned to convene the Seymiks and to send Delegates to the General Council for the purpose of transmitting the Acts of Access. These Delegates will become Deputies to the Confederated Seym.

Article 6.   All officers, soldiers, civil and military officials, Poles by birth and residing in Poland, unjustly held back by Moscow, are summoned to leave the service of that power.

Thus, the Act of Confederation can be seen as an attempt to undo the Acts of Partition. In the event, the Moscow campaign of Napoleon was too short for the effects of the Confederation to show; besides, many people were disillusioned with the institution of Confederations and approved of the ban placed on them in 1791.

During the existence of the Duchy of Warsaw, the Royal Society of Friends of Science in Warsaw resumed its activity with the Seym's help and encouragement. Formed in 1800 on the initiative of Stanisław Sołtyk to create a forum for scientific exchanges as well as to further the advances of practical arts, it included among its membership Julian Ursyn Niemcewicz, the Secretary of the Senate, and Thomas Jefferson. The latter took an interest in its activities, in spite of the distance separating the two countries, and reported in a letter of December 15, 1813 to Niemcewicz the latest American advances in practical arts:

I addressed my answer to you without delay, acknowledging my obligation to the Royal Society of Friends of Science in Warsaw for their nomination of me as one of their members, expressing my sense of honor of being associated with their body, and tending any services which at this distance, I could render them.

I take the same occasion of recalling myself to your recollection, and expressing the satisfaction I feel in reviewing the agreeable moments I have passed with you in Paris and Philadelphia

(after reviewing the recent American victories in the war of 1812, Jefferson concludes)

Latrobe has been till lately engaged at Washington in the business of civil engineering, but is now gone to Pittsburg to take part in the enterprise of furnishing steamboats for the Ohio and Mississipi. These boats, of invention of Mr. Fulton, have obtained the most perfect success, and are now extending to all our rivers.

This notice of some of your friends here, I have thought might not be unacceptable, and among them I pray you count none as entertaining sentiments of higher esteem and respect for you than myself.

Th.Jefferson

Jefferson refers above to their first association in Paris in 1787 when he served there as American Ambassador and to the meetings in Philadelphia at the sessions of the American Philosophical Society, of which Jefferson was President and Niemcewicz a member since 1798, when he was elected during his first stay in America (1797-1802).

As a matter of interest, the first steam engine was used in Poland in a mine in 1817, and the first steam boat appeared on the River Vistula in 1828.

Fig. 63—*Julian U. Niemcewicz (1758-1841) Deputy to the Reform Seym of 1788-92. In exile after the collapse of the First Republic, he settled in New Jersey and was a member of the Philosophical Society of Philadelphia. Minister of the National Government in Warsaw 1830-31. A portrait by Jean Antoine Gros (1771-1835).*

With the collapse of the Napoleonic system in the wake of the unsuccessful invasion of Russia, most of the constitutional arrangements imposed by Napoleon on the vassal states did not survive. An exception was the preservation of the extended civil liberties and the application of the Code of Civil Law, the Code Napoléon. The code had many advantages which accounted for its durability in central Europe. In Poland it continued in use until the First World War.

It is interesting to note that the area of acceptance and application of Code Napoléon extended from its east-most outpost in Poland, through Germany, France, and Spain, all the way to America. Here, in Quebec and Louisiana it became the basis of provincial and state law, respectively. East of Poland, in the lands of the former Grand Duchy of Lithuania, the Lithuanian Statute of 1566 continued in use.

The political thought in the Duchy of Warsaw was dominated in this period by the writings of Hugo Kołłątay, Stanisław Staszic, and Wawrzyniec Surowiecki. Julian Ursyn Niemcewicz, newly arrived from his sojourn in the United States, brought with him the appreciation of American constitutional developments and contributed significantly to the formation of political opinion in Poland at the time. Kołłątay, generally regarded as a Jacobin, was not given a position in the administration; nevertheless, he exerted a powerful influence on the minds of the body politic. In 1808 he wrote a work titled, *Remarks on the Present Condition of That Part of Polish Territory Which After the Peace of Tilsit Started to be Called the Duchy of Warsaw*. In it he had foreseen the breakdown of the peace just concluded between France and Russia, and a possibility of a different solution for the Polish question. He viewed the Duchy as a nucleus of the reconstructed state.

The constitutional arrangements of the Duchy of Warsaw are summarized in Table 38 and are followed by the biographical notes on the more prominent parliamentarians of that province.

TABLE 38—CONSTITUTION OF THE DUCHY OF WARSAW—A SYNOPSIS

(Granted by Napoleon Bonaparte on July 22, 1807, amended February 24, 1810)

The Executive Branch of the Government consisted of the hereditary duke from the Saxon House of Wettin, assisted by the Council of State composed of six ministers plus a Prime Minister. Later the number of ministers was increased to thirteen. All ministers were appointed from among the Deputies to the Seym. The duke and the Council of State had the legislative initiative. The duke appointed the Chairman of the Senate and the Speaker of the Seym, had the right of legislative initative and the right of veto.

The Legislative Branch of the Government consisted of an appointive Senate and an elective Seym. The Senators were appointed by the duke and included: six bishops, six palatines, and six castellans; the 1810 amendment increased their number to ten each. The Seym Deputies were elected; there were initially 100 of them; after 1810 their number was increased to 166. By simple majority vote the Seym could accept or reject bills submitted by the duke or the Council of State, but it did not have legislative initiative. Its area of competence was limited to tax laws, budgetary matters, changes in civil and penal law, and matters relating to the monetary system. The constitutional and administrative decrees were issued directly by the duke. The Seym was called for a fifteen day duration every two years.

TABLE 38 (CONTINUED)—CONSTITUTION OF THE DUCHY OF WARSAW— A SYNOPSIS

The Electoral Ordinance provided for the election of 60 of the Deputies by the gentry assembled in Seymiks and of 40 by the communal assemblies for non-gentry electors. The country was divided into 40 communes, 8 of which were allotted to Warsaw. The candidates had to be at least 24 years of age and could not be government officials, priests, or officers in active service. They were elected for a nine year term with one-third of the Deputies elected every three years.

The Judiciary Branch of the Government consisted of Justices of Peace in each county, a civil tribunal in each palatinate, and an appellate court in Warsaw. The justices were appointed by the duke from lists of candidates prepared by the Seymiks. The Council of State acted as the Supreme Court. The duke had the right of pardon.

Bill of Rights prescribed that all citizens are equal before the law and thereby abolished serfdom. However, the peasants were not given ownership of the land they tilled. The equal rights provision was suspended temporarily with regard to Jews by the decree of the duke.

POLITICAL PERSONALITIES IN THE SEYM OF THE DUCHY OF WARSAW

Józef Godlewski (1773-1867)—Politician in the Duchy of Warsaw; he was elected to the Seyms of 1809, 1811 as Deputy for Mariampol; led the opposition to the financial policies of Treasury Minister F. Łubieński, proposing the replacement of paid judges and bureaucrats by voluntary workers. He spoke for the Jacobin faction in the Seym and demanded tax reform. Elected Deputy to the Seym of Congress Kingdom, 1818-1820, where he cooperated with the Deputies from Kalisz in demanding from the Emperor adherence to the Constitution.

Tomasz A. Ostrowski (1735-1817)—Father of Władysław T., administrator and politician. From 1765 he supported the policies of Stanisław August Poniatowski. Appointed castellan of Czersk in 1777, he then served as member of the Permanent Council. In 1791 he was made Grand Treasurer of the Crown and a member of the "Guard of the Laws." He opposed the Confederation of Targowica. Later he served as the Chairman of the Senate in the Duchy of Warsaw and opposed the introduction of Code Napoléon.

Stanisław Sołtyk (1753-1831)—Politician who served as the Grand Steward of the Crown in 1784-89 and supported the constitutional reform in the Seym of 1788-92; he was a cofounder of the Society of Friends of the Constitution. After the collapse of the First Republic he initiated various organizations aiming at the recovery of independence of Poland; served as the Speaker of the 1811 Seym of the Duchy of Warsaw. In the Congress Kingdom he was active in the Society of Patriots. Arrested and tried in connection with the Decabrist plot in Russia he was sentenced to two years imprisonment in 1825.

Stanisław Staszic (1755-1826)—Scientist, priest, politician; he was one of the leading members of the reform group during the Seym of 1788-92. After the partitions he became active in education, arts, and sciences. In 1808 he became the President of the Society of Friends of Sciences of Warsaw for which he erected the headquarters. He was a member of the Chamber of Education 1807-12 and cofounder of the University of Warsaw in 1816. He was also a member of the Commission on Education and Religious Denominations 1815-24. He was appointed Secretary of State in 1824 and served also as Director General of the Department of Industry and Crafts and contributed to the initiation of coal mining in the Dąbrowa District. He authored: *Observations on the Life of Jan Zamoyski* (1787); *Warnings for Poland* (1790); *Thoughts on the Balance of Power in Europe* (1815); *Philosophical and Social Writings* (1952); *Pedagogical Writings and Statements* (1956); *On the Statistics of Poland* (1807).

Wawrzyniec Surowiecki (1769-1827)—Economist, politician; wrote extensively on economics. A member of Warsaw Society of Friends of Sciences from 1807. He was appointed General Secretary of the Ministry of Education in 1812, professor of the School of Law and Administration in Warsaw 1812-13. One of the first proponents of classical economics in Poland, devoting his attention to the problems of land ownership and development of industry and commerce, he wrote *Remarks Regarding Serfs in Poland and Proposal for Their Emancipation* (1807); *On the Decay of Industry and Towns in Poland* (1810); *Investigation of the Origins of Slavonic Nations* (1824).

Józef Wybicki (1747-1822)—Parliamentarian, writer, jurist. Elected Deputy to the Seym of 1767, 1784 and 1790. One of the leading activists in the constitutional reform movement. 1776-80 secretary to the judicial committee preparing revisions of civil law (Zamoyski code proposal). Served on the commission of National Education, carried out reforms at Academy of Wilno, 1778. Participated in Kościuszko uprising. After 1785 in exile, in Paris, then in Italy, promoted formation of Legion of Dąbrowski. Served on Temporary Governing Council of Duchy of Warsaw in 1807, and Chairman of the Supreme Court of the Kingdom of Poland, 1817-1820. Authored the Polish National Anthem, "Patriotic Letters" vol. 1-2, 1777-78, "My Life" (1840) and numerous poems, stage plays, etc.

THE SEYM OF WARSAW:
POLISH LEGISLATURE CONFRONTS THE TSARS

The settlement of European affairs after the defeat of Napoleon, carried out at the Congress of Vienna, abolished the Duchy of Warsaw and led to another stage in the constitutional history of Poland. The Congress resurrected a rump Polish State with a parliamentary system, a government, and an army left over from the Napoleonic adventure. The whole was placed under Russian rule with Tsar Alexander I serving as King of Poland.

The arrangement turned out to be an experiment in compatibility of an elective legislative system and an autocratic empire. Alexander was one of the most liberal rulers Russia ever had and, in addition, he had had considerable exposure to Western ideas and influences in the course of the various anti-Napoleonic campaigns in Western Europe. Furthermore, he had developed a personal friendship with Adam Czartoryski, a member of one of the senatorial families of Poland with a long tradition of political reform activity behind it.

Influenced by Czartoryski, Alexander decided to use the remnants of Napoleon's arrangements in Poland as an experiment of his own, whereby the Polish part of his empire would be allowed to operate as a constitutional monarchy with an elective legislature and an autonomous government, a treasury, and an army of its own. In Poland he would leave behind his autocratic self and appear in Warsaw as a constitutional monarch. In that respect the experiment would be mutual, inasmuch as the Seym would have to learn to deal with a ruler used to autocratic thinking and an unquestioning acceptance of all his wishes and commands as law. Good will and the best of intentions were required on both sides for the experiment to succeed.

Not everybody viewed the chances of this experiment as high. General Thaddeus Kościuszko, who commanded the army in the war in defense of the Constitution of 1791, reported his thoughts on the matter in a letter to Thomas Jefferson, dated April 1, 1816. Commenting on Emperor Alexander's announcement at the Congress of Vienna that he intends to establish the Kingdom of Poland, Kościuszko wrote:

> Undoubtedly, even [the use of] the name "Poland" already means something, and we are grateful forever to Emperor Alexander. However, nothing has as much significance for a country as its extent and the size of its population. Emperor Alexander promised me to extend the borders of the Duchy of Warsaw up to the rivers Dźwina and Dniepr, our old borders, but his executive cabinet did not comply with the Emperor's generous and magnanimous intentions, and as it happens, unfortunately, the Kingdom of Poland is now smaller than the Duchy of Warsaw by a third.
>
> I went to Vienna for the purpose of learning all details, as I did not wish to return to Poland in response to the Emperor's invitation, until I became convinced of his real

intentions, not having received a satisfactory reassurance from his Minister. I wrote to the Emperor, imploring him to confirm in writing the promises he made to me verbally, and I assured him I shall keep this confidential, until the arrangements are in effect. I did not have the good fortune to receive an answer, and so I returned to Switzerland, not wishing to abuse the trust my countrymen placed in me.

Aye, my dear Friend, I remembered about good laws; Emperor Alexander promised me a constitutional government, liberal, independent, plus the liberation of, and a grant of land to our wretched peasants. Just this act alone would have made him immortal— all this, however, disappeared like smoke.

Kościuszko lived out his days in Switzerland, observing from afar the political developments, in which only a part of his maximalistic political program saw realization.

The constitutional experiment in Poland unfolded slowly with participation on the Polish side of many personalities which had been involved in the constitutional reform movement in the last decade of the 1700s. Among them was a former Adjutant to Kościuszko and a Seym Deputy, Julian Ursyn Niemcewicz, who brought from his lengthy stay in America an appreciation of the constitutional developments there.

It was widely believed at the time that the success of the constitutional arrangement in Poland might lead to a similar accommodation in Russia and produce the liberalization of an otherwise autocratic regime.

The preliminaries to the drafting of the Constitution took place in a series of meetings in Warsaw in the house of Tomasz A. Ostrowski, the Speaker of the last Seym of the Duchy. A group of Senators prepared a document titled: *Principles of the Constitution of the Kingdom of Poland*, which listed Polish postulates. The document went through several revisions, each one longer and more elaborate than the one before it. On the basis of these principles Czartoryski prepared a draft of the Constitution.

Czartoryski's draft was reworked in turn by Emperor Alexander during his stay in Warsaw in November of 1815 with the participation of N. N. Novosiltsov, the Russian Commissioner in Warsaw. Novosiltsov was known as an opponent of the autonomy of the Kingdom and he is credited with having made a number of seemingly minor but, in fact, very significant changes in the Constitution, which were to lead to great difficulties in practice.

Fig. 64—Aerial view of the Castle of Warsaw. Seyms of the First Republic, the Duchy of Warsaw, and the Congress Kingdom of Poland sat within its walls. Shown before the damage of World War II.

The first of these alterations was the omission from the Constitution of the phrase that the Constitution forms the bond uniting the Kingdom with the Russian Empire, thus reducing the stature of the document.

Second, in the reaffirmation of the old habeas corpus law of the First Republic, the key phrase: "neminem captivabimus nisi iure victum" (we shall imprison no one, except in due process of the law), was changed to: "neminem captivare permittemus" (we shall permit no one). The implication of the change clearly was that now arrest was at the pleasure of the ruler, contrary to the law's intent, since the law was instituted in the first place to remove the power of arbitrary arrest from the discretion of the ruler and to lodge it with the judiciary, working on the basis of written law.

DZIENNIK

POSIEDZEŃ

IZBY POSELSKIÉY

w CZASIE SEYMU

KRÓLESTWA POLSKIEGO

w Roku 1820.

ODBYTEGO.

w WARSZAWIE

w Drukarni Xięży Piarów.

Fig. 65—A scene in 1815 in Warsaw showing the public reading of the Constitution of Congress Kingdom of Poland.

Fig. 66—Title page of the Journal of Debates of the Seym of the Congress Kingdom of Poland, held in Warsaw for the 1820 session.

The last modification made at the suggestion of Novosiltsov, was the removal from Article 162 of the Constitution of the provision that the first budget drawn up by Alexander will remain in force only until the first session of the Seym. This alteration was used later to strip the Seym of control over the budget.

The Constitution was signed by Alexander on November 27, 1815 and went into effect after the election of the first Seym. By this Constitution, out of the province of Masovia and parts of Lesser Poland a political entity was created in the form of a hereditary monarchy, vested in the House of Romanov. The government was based on an appointive executive, and an elective legislature, supplemented by a Senate composed of members sitting ex-officio, on the model of the First Republic.

The voting rights were given to approximately 100,000 people out of a population of 2.7 million, thus making this Constitution one of the most liberal in Europe. The liberality of the law was not, however, matched by practice in the exercise of Deputies' prerogatives.

The constitutional experiment lasted for fifteen years, long enough for four Seyms to be returned. The first three were duly opened in 1818, 1820, and 1825 by Alexander, who suffered some discomfort during the Seym of 1820, unused as he was to having any of his pronouncements questioned, by being asked to explain his reasons for the various executive actions taken. The last Seym of 1827 was returned during the administration of his successor, Nicholas I, and had to deal with a monarch totally unreceptive to any constitutional restraints on his prerogatives. Both Alexander I and Nicholas I relied on their brother, the Grand Duke Constantine, assisted by Novosiltsov and other Russian residents, to provide local supervision of the government of the kingdom.

Right from the beginning of the life of the Congress Kingdom, as this creation of the Congress of Vienna was named by the natives, difficulties arose over budgetary control. Novosiltsov's influence prevented any discussion of the budget by the Seym. Without the Seym's supervision the Minister of the Treasury ran up a huge deficit, while the Seym was powerless to intervene. The matter was finally brought to the attention of Alexander and the Minister of Treasury, J. Węgleński, was replaced by Xavier Drucki-Lubecki, a very able administrator of finances, who was able to restore the Treasury to order and was instrumental in stimulating the economic development of the country. Much progress was achieved in rebuilding the economy from the ravages of the past wars, in improving the administration, and in placing the educational system on a firm footing.

Among the principal legislation passed by the Seym of the Congress Kingdom one must include the Law on Mortgages (1817), the Penal Code (1818), and the Civil Code (1825) replacing the part of Book I of the Napoleonic Code dealing with the persons and the family.

The Russian supervised administration of the kingdom lived under constant pressure to muzzle any expressions of public opinion critical of the Russians. Only four years after the Constitution was granted to the Kingdom, one of the explicit provisions of its bill of rights, namely the guarantee of the freedom of the press, was broken by Alexander in 1819 by the imposition of the censorship of the press. This left only the Seym, at one of its infrequent sessions, to serve as the forum for the expressions of public opinion.

The next issue to cause constitutional conflict arose over the freedom of speech in the Seym. This was the arena in which the political ideas of the time could be aired, and the general public took great interest in the Seym debates. Of particular interest were the opinions voiced by the two brothers Niemojowski, both Seym Deputies sitting for the palatinate of Kalisz.

Fig. 67 (Left)—Rajmund Rembieliński (1775-1841) Speaker of the 1820 Seym of Congress Kingdom in Warsaw. He had decisive influence on the expansion of the textile industry in the area of Łódź.

Fig. 68 (Right)—Bonaventura Niemojowski (1787-1835) Politician and writer, Deputy in the Seyms of Congress Kingdom, Minister in the Revolutionary Government, 1830. A portrait by Ch. Bazin.

Vincent and Bonaventura Niemojowski were great admirers of Benjamin Constant, the ideologist of French liberalism. Furthermore, they both pleaded eloquently during the 1818 and the 1820 sessions of the Seym for the preservation of the spirit of the Constitution. Their constituents took pride in their patriotic spirit and returned them to the Seym in the elections of 1822, however, Alexander was so much put off by the criticism he was subjected to during the Seym of 1820, that he never called the Seym elected in 1822 into session. When it was finally decided in 1824 to call for the elections of a new slate of Deputies for the 1825 Seym, special efforts had been made, mostly successful, to elect a more pliable Seym. To block the opposition headed by the Niemojowski brothers, Bonaventura was involved in trumped up criminal indictment, and a special royal decree was issued by Alexander, on Novosiltsov's suggestion, which banished Vincent from the Emperor's presence, thus making it impossible for him to attend any Seym sessions at which Alexander was present. Suffice it to say, all this chicanery further inflamed the public opinion against the Russian interference in the operations of the legislature.

Fig. 69—Vincent Niemojowski (1784-1834) Brother of Bonaventura, Deputy in the Seyms of the Congress Kingdom. Author of The Voice of Deputy for Kalisz at the Seym of the Kingdom of Poland of 1818. *Died in a Russian prison. A portrait by Dilliard.*

Fig. 70—Constantine Romanov (1779-1831), brother of Alexander I and Deputy in the 1818-1830 Seyms of Warsaw.

The resident Russians found the Seym speeches of the Niemojowski brothers to have an inflammatory effect on the public and prevailed on Alexander to have the Seym debates held 'in camera.'

This muzzling of the Seym was achieved by amending the Constitution in February of 1825, prior to the Seym session. The extra article added to the Constitution by Alexander I in that year closed the debates of the Seym to the public, with the preamble stating:

> taking into consideration, that the open debates in both chambers of the legislature provoke the members of the legislature to be guided in their speeches not by considerations of public good, but by popularity with the public, and to make their speeches empty declarations, ...we decided to alter by the additional Article one of the rules of procedure, which experience has shown to be inconvenient to Us.

But then, open debates of public issues are the backbone of parliamentary systems and anathema to the autocratic ones.

The muzzling of open expression of opinion in the Seym and its suppression outside of it led to the formation of various conspiracies among the politically minded. These in turn were used by the Russian residents as a justification for stepping up the activities of the secret police agents in the Congress Kingdom. Alexander felt these police activities indispensible for the administration of Russia as well as Poland, whereas the Seym felt they were incompatible with a constitutional government. This question more than anything else put the Emperor and the Seym on a collision course.

The army allowed to the Congress Kingdom was formed around a nucleus of officers and non-commissioned officers with a long record of service under Napoleon. Its military worth was considered excellent and it became the object of pride of the Grand Duke Constantine Romanov, Alexander's brother, who was made its commander. Nevertheless the harsh treatment he meted out to its officers and men, put their loyalty to a severe test and led to numerous suicides among its officer corps. To mollify his behavior, and to involve him more deeply in the operation of the parliamentary system, Constantine was put up as a candidate from the eighth electoral district of Warsaw and was elected Deputy to all Seyms between 1818 and 1830.

Constantine was the middle of the three brothers Romanov and, after Alexander I, next in line of succession to the imperial throne of Russia. Following his marriage to Joanna Grudzińska, a Polish commoner, he was forced by the Russian aristocracy to renounce his right of succession in favor of his younger brother Nicholas. In spite of this impediment, Constantine was the preferred choice of the Russian liberals for the next ruler of Russia, primarily on account of his involvement in the parliamentary life in Poland.

After the death of the liberal Alexander in December of 1825, the accession to the throne of the autocratic Nicholas I was met by the Decembrist conspiracy in Russia, formed by the liberal elements within the Russian Army with previous exposure to Western ideas received during the many campaigns conducted against Napoleon. The conspiracy aimed for a Constitution to replace autocracy and used for its rallying call: "Constantine and Constitution." A military plot developed in which some Poles were implicated. The movement was abortive and its Russian participants were either executed or given stiff prison sentences in Siberia. The Poles implicated in the conspiracy were to be tried in Poland by a Tribunal appointed by the Seym, on the insistence of Nicholas.

During the trial the conflict between the autocracy of Russia and the liberal constitutional tradition of Poland came into full focus. The Seym Tribunal could find nothing subversive in the attempts of the Russians pressing for constitutional government. In fact, the Tribunal represented such a government and in spite of great pressure from the Russians, found the defendants guilty only of a misdemeanor, and not treason; in 1828 those implicated were sentenced to three years imprisonment.

Fig. 71—A scene from the opening session of the Seym of 1818 in Warsaw. The Emperor of Russia, Alexander I Romanov, presides as the King of Poland over the joint session of the Seym and the Senate, held in the Senate Chamber of the Castle of Warsaw.

Two years later, in the Fall of 1830, the collision point was reached when Nicholas ordered the Russian and the Polish Armies to mobilize with the intent of intervening against revolutionary movements then rising in Western Europe. This ran contrary to the political sentiment in Poland at the time. Finally, on the night of November 29, 1830, the young hot-heads in the officer cadet school mutinied, captured the main arsenal of Warsaw, and attacked the Belvedere palace in which the Grand Duke Constantine Romanov resided. The revolt spread to other army units, and this action precipitated a general uprising. A war between the Congress Kingdom and Russia broke out. The Seym appointed a new government and regained control over the budget. New taxes were raised and the Army was expanded.

In the course of the revolution, the insurgents ransacked the government archives and found in them a copy of the draft Constitution of the Russian Empire, prepared on Alexander's order in 1819, but subsequently put aside. Capitalizing on this discovery, the Seym ordered 2000 copies of the document printed and disseminated, as evidence of a desirable alternative to autocracy in Russia. The document followed closely its Polish model, except for the provision that only half of the Deputies to the Russian Parliament be elected, the other half appointed by the emperor. To the autocratic Nicholas, the document was political dynamite, and he ordered every effort to be made to recover and destroy all existent copies of this document. In the course of the ensuing Polish-Russian war 1578 copies of the proposed Russian Constitution were captured and destroyed by Russian officials.

In ransacking the police archives the insurgents found lists of spies and informers used by Nicholas, Constantine and Novosiltsov in Poland. When these lists became public knowledge, the mob hunted down and lynched the compromised individuals who did not manage to escape in time from Warsaw. Among the victims was General Maurycy Hauke*, whose fine past military record, dating to the service in the war of Defense of the Constitution in 1792, and service in the Polish Legion during all of Napoleonic campaigns up to the defense of Zamość against the Russians in 1812, was marred by his later subservience to Nicholas.

At the time of the November revolution, the Speaker's chair in the Seym was occupied by Józef G. Lubowidzki, the vice-president of the Bank of Poland. An able financier and a lawyer, he was appointed to this position in May 1830 sponsored by Xavier Drucki-Lubecki, the minister of the Treasury. It was hoped that the appointment will establish a better linkage between the Seym and the Treasury. At the outbreak of the uprising, during that fateful November night, the cadets attacking the Belvedere Palace surprised there and wounded the Speaker's brother Michał E. Lubowidzki, the Chief of Warsaw Police. Arrested on charges of warning the Grand Duke Constantine of the impending attack, Michał was transferred under guard to a military hospital, from which he subsequently escaped, apparently with connivance of his brother. In view of these developments, the Seym suspended the Speaker and placed him under house arrest pending an investigation. It then appointed Władysław T. Ostrowski to the Chair. Lubowidzki was released from house arrest in March 1831, but never resumed his seat in the Seym.

Early in 1831 the Seym debated all the breaches of the Constitution that had taken place. During the debate on January 25, 1831, Deputy Roman Sołtyk moved that Tsar Nicholas be dethroned and succeeded, after an all-night debate, in having the motion passed. The task of drafting the Act of Dethronement was entrusted to Julian Ursyn Niemcewicz. A former Deputy to the Reform Seym of 1788-92, an adjutant to Kościuszko, and his companion in exile after the collapse of the First Republic, Niemcewicz became, during his residence in America, an admirer of Thomas Jefferson. It is no surprise, therefore, that Niemcewicz made the Act of Dethronement into a Declaration of Independence:

---

* The daughter of the luckless Hauke, Julia, was made the Princess of Battenberg in 1858 as a result of her liaison with Alexander, the younger son of Louis II, of Hesse-Darmstadt. This started a new line of Battenbergs who settled in England. In 1917 they anglicized their name to Mountbatten.

Fig. 72—Roman Sołtyk (1791-1843), Deputy to the Seym of 1825, member of the Patriotic Society, in exile after its suppression, and Deputy of the Seym during the uprising of 1830-31.

The most sacred and solemn agreements hold only as long as they are faithfully adhered to by both parties. Our long sufferings, known to the entire world, our freedoms, guaranteed by two monarchs but many times violated, in turn release the Polish Nation from its allegiance to the present ruler. The words uttered by Emperor Nicholas himself, saying that the first shot from our side will be a signal to annihilate Poland forever, deny us all hope for redress of our grievances, and leave us nought but noble despair.

Therefore, the Polish Nation in Seym assembled, declares itself an independent people, and proclaims its right to entrust the crown of Poland to one worthy of its trust, one who can be expected to keep faith, and to safeguard unimpaired, the freedoms he swore to uphold.

In these few sentences, with more than a hint of Jeffersonian influence, Niemcewicz invoked the last clause of the Henrician Articles: the right of citizens to rebel against the Chief Executive who violates the law of the land. This was a return to the idea of Social Contract, hailed by Jean Jacques Rousseau and deeply embedded in Polish constitutional thought.

The Act of Dethronement was a gauntlet thrown in the face of the Emperor, certain to require a bloody war to enforce it. Not all of the Deputies and Senators present at the session of January 25 were confident of its outcome; in fact, some were turned back at the gate when they tried to slip away in the night without signing the Act.

Fig. 73—A scene from the night session of the Seym of Warsaw, held on January 25, 1831, during which Nicholas I was declared dethroned. A drawing by N. Thomas.

Under the pressure of the more radical faction in the Seym, led by Joachim Lelewel, some attempt was made to examine the question of land ownership by the peasants and the ways to improve their lot, but legislative proposals for land reform that were submitted had to be tabled under the press of war-related business.

On January 29, 1831 the Constitution was amended to give the Seym the power to appoint the Executive committee, the commander-in-chief of the Army, and the Senators, to pass the budget, and to ratify treaties.

Both Niemojowski brothers became active again in politics and rose to high positions in the government. However, liberal and pro-war sentiment was by no means universal among the Deputies of the Seym, and since some of the Deputies were pacifist, at times it became difficult to keep a quorum in the Seym. Elections for vacant seats were authorized by the law of February 12, 1831, and in addition, a written permit from the Speaker was required before a Deputy could leave town. On February 19, 1831 a law was passed declaring the Seym in continuous session. To prevent the repetition of events in Grodno in 1793, when the Seym sat surrounded by the Russian Army and legislated at bayonet point, the sessions of the Seym held in Russian-controlled territory were declared illegal. A quorum requiring 11 Senators and 33 Deputies was established, or a joint session of both Chambers with at least 33 members present was declared sufficient to pass laws.

Fig. 74—Joachim Lelewel (1786-1861), Historian and political activist. Deputy to the 1830 Seym of Warsaw and member of the Patriotic Society. Deputy Chairman of the International Democratic Society in 1847, a position he shared with Karl Marx.

The fortunes of war swayed several times; each was accompanied by a change in command. Eventually a siege was laid to Warsaw. The Russians offered amnesty and retention of constitutional form of governnment on the condition that the Seym dissolve itself and the Army capitulate. Both demands were turned down. In early September the Army withdrew from Warsaw and took the Seym with it.

The last session of the Seym was held in Płock in September of 1831 when a decision was made to go into exile rather than submit to the Emperor. Many of the Deputies, several thousand officers and men of the Army, as well as almost all members of previous governments, left the country for exile. They included the presiding officer of the government, Bonaventura Niemojowski. His brother, Wincenty, fell into Russian hands and died in prison. The war between the very unequal contestants lasted until the first days of October and ended in the defeat of the forces of the Kingdom. Nicholas suppressed the legislature and replaced the constitutional government of the Congress Kingdom with an administration based on Russian autocratic principles. He also ordered the Chambers of Deputies and Senate in the Castle of Warsaw to be demolished as an act of revenge for the dethronement. The Polish-Russian constitutional experiment failed completely, showing the basic incompatibility of the elective and the autocratic forms of government within one political entity.

Fig. 75—Władysław T. Ostrowski (1790-1869), Speaker of the 1830-31 Seym which directed the uprising of 1830. Shown holding the Speaker's Staff, a badge of his office.

Going into exile the Seym took with it a record of its proceedings and enactments. Regarded as symbols of the demand for representative government, they were saved from destruction at the hands of the Russians, and were eventually published in Galicia some 80 years later, when the Seym of Lwów succeeded in establishing a much freer political climate.

The constitutional arrangements of the Congress Kingdom of Poland are summarized in Table 39 and are followed by short biographies of more prominent parliamentarians of this period.

TABLE 39—CONSTITUTION OF THE CONGRESS KINGDOM OF POLAND—A SYNOPSIS

(Granted by Alexander I of Russia, November 27, 1815, amended February 13, 1825, and January 29, 1831)

The Executive Branch of the Government was headed by a hereditary king from the House of Romanov. He appointed Ministers, Senators and other high officials. He had the right to initiate legislation and the right to veto it. The executive proper was called the Administrative Council and consisted of five

TABLE 39 (CONTINUED)—CONSTITUTION OF THE CONGRESS KINGDOM OF POLAND—A SYNOPSIS

Ministers: Education and Religious Denominations, Justice, Interior and Police, Defense, Treasury and Revenue. Each operated a corresponding commission, made up of the minister and several councillors. These five Ministers and twelve Councillors formed the Council of State. A Viceroy replaced the King in his absence.

The Legislative Branch of the Government consisted of appointive Senate and elective Seym. The Senate was made up of 9 bishops, 18 palatines and 37 castellans. The Seym consisted of 128 elected Deputies. One of them was appointed Speaker by the King. The Seym was called by the King into a 30 day session every two years. It legislated in civil, penal and administrative matters, minting of currency and the size of the army draft. Taxation and the budget were also within its competence. The Seym selected three commissions: treasury, civil and penal matters, and administrative matters. Each commission had five members. The Senate selected corresponding commissions of three members each. To pass the laws a simple majority in each House was required. The Senate served as impeachment tribunal in cases involving Senators, Ministers, Councillors of State and Referendaries. Parliamentary immunity was granted to all Deputies.

The Electoral Ordinance provided that gentry assembled in county Seymiks will elect 77 Deputies, and the communal assemblies will elect 51, the term of office to last six years with one third of the Deputies to be elected every two years. The candidacy was limited to literate males, thirty years of age or over, and paying at least 100 zł of tax annually. The voting rights were restricted to property owners, lease-holders, teachers. Peasant lease holders on national land were included, but the exclusion of Jews from the electorate was carried over from the Duchy of Warsaw. The candidates for Senators had to be thirty-five years of age and pay at least 2000 zł of tax annually. The Senators were appointed for life by the King from among two candidates submitted to him by the Senate.

The Judiciary Branch of the Government consisted of lower courts in each commune and town, handling civil and police cases not exceeding 500 zł in value. For larger offenses, or litigation in excess of 500 zł, palatinate and city courts were established. Two Appellate Courts for the country as a whole were established and a Supreme Tribunal of Warsaw to handle all cases except those reserved for the Tribunal of State. Judges were appointed by the King but could be removed by a decision of a higher court. The Tribunal of State consisted of all Senators sitting to judge cases of treason and impeachment of members of the administration.

The Bill of Rights included guarantees of due process of law. Personal liberty, ownership of property, freedom of the press and the exercise of religion were protected by law.

POLITICAL PERSONALITIES IN SEYMS OF THE CONGRESS KINGDOM

Wincenty Krasiński (1782-1858)—Father of the poet Zygmunt, general, Senator of Congress Kingdom, political activist. In 1803 he formed in Warsaw a secret Society of Friends of the Fatherland. From 1804 he was a member of the Association of Friends of Knowledge; from 1806 he worked in the service of Napoleon; in 1813 he was appointed general of the army. He was Speaker of the 1818 Seym of the Congress Kingdom. In 1826 he was appointed general of cavalry. He served in 1827 as deputy chairman of the Seym Tribunal during the trial of Poles implicated in the Decabrist conspiracy. In a minority opinion he voted for the death sentence for the accused. In consequence he was barely saved from being lynched by the crowd during the 1830 Uprising against Russia. After the collapse of the Uprising he served as deputy Viceroy of Poland in 1855-56.

Joachim Lelewel (1786-1861)—Historian, parliamentarian, professor of history at the University of Wilno in 1815-24 and at the University of Warsaw in 1824-30. He was a member of the Patriotic Society, elected Deputy to the Seym of 1830; he was Minister of the Revolutionary Government during the 1830-31 Uprising. After the collapse of the government he went into exile in Belgium. In 1837 he organized the Union of Polish Exiles. He joined the Polish Democratic Society in 1846 and became the deputy chairman of the International Democratic Society in 1847, a position he shared with Karl Marx. In his historical works he created the first synthesis of the national and social history of Poland. He authored: *History of Poland Told in Everyday Language* (1829); *Three Polish Constitutions* (1831); *Numismatique du moyen age* (1835); *Poland Regenerating Itself* (1837); *Remarks on the History of Poland and Its People* (1844); *Lost Citizenship of the Peasants* (1846); and *The Fall of Bolesław Śmiały* (1853).

Józef Lubowidzki (1788-1869)—Jurist, financier, parliamentarian. Educated at the Universities of Königsberg and Warsaw, he devoted his early career to law and finance, becoming the president of criminal court of Płock and Augustów in 1825, and a Justice of the Supreme Court shortly thereafter. He participated in the creation of Land Credit Society of Warsaw and in 1828 he was appointed vice-president of the Bank of Poland. In the same year he was elected Deputy of the Seym, and in May 1830 he was appointed its Speaker. He lost this position in the November 1830 uprising, accused by the patriots of assisting in the escape from Warsaw of his brother Michał, the Chief of Police. In 1831-43 he served as the President of the Bank of Poland. He participated in ventures financing the textile industry, grain wholesaling, and the construction of the Warsaw-Vienna railroad. In 1843 he was accused of financial mismanagement of the Bank, and after a five year investigation sentenced to four years imprisonment.

Tadeusz A. Mostowski (1766-1842)—Publicist, literary critic, political activist. As a supporter of Hugo Kołłątay he coedited the "National and Foreign Gazette," during the Uprising of 1794 he was a member of the Supreme National Council. From 1802 he printed in his publishing business outstanding works of Polish literature. He was Minister of the Interior of the Duchy of Warsaw (1812) and of the Congress Kingdom. He served as Senator Palatine of the Congress Kingdom from 1825. After the 1831 uprising he lived in exile.

Julian Ursyn Niemcewicz (1758-1841)—Writer, politician, publisher, graduate of the Military Academy of Warsaw, appointed adjutant to A. K. Czartoryski in 1777. He was elected a Deputy to the Reform Seym of 1788-1792, became a member of the Patriotic Party, and served as coeditor of the "National and Foreign Gazette." During the Kościuszko Insurrection he was adjutant to General Kościuszko and stayed with him when Kościuszko was severely wounded and taken prisoner by the Russians in the battle of Maciejowice. After release from Russian captivity he migrated to America where he settled and lived in New Jersey (1789-1807). He was befriended by Thomas Jefferson and in 1798 was elected a member of the Philosophical Society of Philadelphia. After the Duchy of Warsaw was established he returned to Poland and served as the secretary of the Council of State and the Senate. In the Congress Kingdom he continued in these positions. In 1822, after setbacks of the liberal opposition in the Seym, he withdrew from political life. Although opposed to the uprising of 1830, he became a member of the National Government and Senator-Castellan. He wrote the Act of Dethronement of Nicholas I in 1831 and was sent as envoy to England in an effort to secure help for the Uprising. After its collapse he settled in France. Authored a large body of writings: *Works* Vol. 1-5 (1883-86); *Under Their Vine and Fig Tree*, New Jersey Historical Society, (1965).

Bonaventura Niemojowski (1787-1835)—Parliamentarian, noted political activist and writer. Elected Deputy to the Seyms of Congress Kingdom, he became the leader of the liberal opposition group consisting of Deputies from the palatinate of Kalisz. His outspoken stand in the Seym led the Russian authorities to bar him from attending the sessions of the Seym. During the November Uprising he served as the Minister of Interior in the Revolutionary Government and was deputy Prime Minister from August 15, 1831 and then finally Prime Minister. He undertook to defend Warsaw on the barricades against the Russians. After the collapse of the Uprising he went into exile where he wrote: *On the Last Events of the Polish Revolution* (1833).

Wincenty Niemojowski (1784-1834)—Brother of Bonaventura. Like his brother, a political activist, writer and a Deputy to the Seyms of Congress Kingdom. He became the principal leader and ideologue of the liberal opposition group from Kalisz. Persecuted by Grand Duke Constantine, the brother of the

Russian Emperor, he was barred from the Seym, though repeatedly elected by his constituents. During the November Uprising he was a member of the government. He was captured after the collapse of the Uprising and died in prison while on the way to imprisonment in Siberia. Author of *Voice of the Deputy for Kalisz at the Seym of the Kingdom of Poland of 1818* (1818), *On Public Authorities in a Constitutional Monarchy* (1820), *On Constitutional Monarchy and the Guarantees of Public Authorities* (1831).

Antoni J. Ostrowski (1782-1845)—Parliamentarian, businessman, son of Tomasz A., brother of Władysław T. Graduated in 1800 from the University of Leipzig; appointed Director of the Department of Defense in the Supreme Chamber of Defense Administration in the Duchy of Warsaw in 1806; elected Deputy to the Seym of 1809, he took part in the Napoleonic campaigns of 1812-1814. In the Kingdom of Poland established by the Congress of Vienna, he was appointed a Senator Castellan. In 1828 he was appointed to the Seym Tribunal set up to try the members of the Patriotic Society. He represented the liberal faction of the gentry in the Seym. In the economic sphere he participated in efforts to promote industrialization. He founded the town of Tomaszów Mazowiecki and a company of wool producers. In the Uprising of 1830 he served as a commander of the National Guard and after the collapse of the Uprising went into exile in France. He authored: *Biographies of Poles of XVIII and XIXc* (1839); *Memoirs of the Time of November Uprising* (1861).

Władysław T. Ostrowski (1790-1896)—Son of Tomasz A., parliamentary politician; served as Deputy in the Seyms of the Congress Kingdom of Poland. Initially he was a supporter of the liberal wing headed by the Deputies from Kalisz, Bonaventura and Wincenty Niemojowski. Elected Speaker of the 1830-31 Seym during the anti-Russian Uprisings, he later joined the conservative faction. After the collapse of the Uprising he went into exile in France.

Rajmund Rembieliński (1775-1841)—Political and economic activist, graduated from the Military Academy of Warsaw. He became a lawyer and a member of the Association of Polish Republicans. In 1809 he was appointed President of the Administrative Chamber of the Department of Łomża. Speaker of the 1820 Seym of the Congress Kingdom. In the Seym he was much criticized by the Niemojowski brothers. As Chairman of the Commission for the palatinate of Masovia, he was credited with decisive influence on the expansion of textile industry in the Łódź area. He was the author of many publications on economy.

Roman Sołtyk (1791-1843)—Parliamentarian, army officer and historian; he was a graduate of École Polytechnique in Paris (1805-07); afterwards he served with distinction in the Army of the Duchy of Warsaw and in Napoleon's Russian campaign. In 1822 he was elected member of Council of the palatinate of Sandomierz and in 1825 a Deputy to the Seym of the Congress Kingdom in Warsaw where he was a member of the opposition. He participated in the activities of the Patriotic Society and when the latter was suppressed he fled to Germany, was extradited, but shortly thereafter he was released. Elected Deputy again to the Seym of 1830 for Końskie, he gained fame by his proposal to spend the money, appropriated by the Seym for a statue of Alexander I, for the purchase of land for landless peasants. During the November 1830 Uprising he served in the Army in the rank of colonel. In the Seym on January 20, 1831 he moved that Nicholas Romanov be dethroned. After the collapse of the Uprising he went into exile in France and England. He was the author of *Napoleon en 1812* (1836).

THE SEYM OF POZNAŃ: POLISH NATIONALITY AT BAY

The province of Greater Poland was reunited with Masovia and parts of Lesser Poland for a few years (1807-15) during the Napoleonic era. In that time it elected and sent Deputies to the two Seyms that were held by the Duchy of Warsaw in 1809 and 1811. Citizens from the province were appointed Senators of the Duchy as well. After the defeat of Napoleon in 1815 the Congress of Vienna detached the province from the then created Congress Kingdom and annexed it to Prussia. Under the Prussian rule the province was named the Duchy of Poznań. Initially, with a population of 776,000 which grew to 1.1 million by 1830, it was the smallest of the zones of partition.

The Seym of Poznań was established in 1823 by a decree of the King of Prussia which called into being the provincial legislatures in various parts of Prussia. The specific decree for the province of Greater Poland was issued in 1826 and the first Seym assembled on December 24, 1827 with Antoni Sułkowski as the Speaker. It was composed of 46 elected Deputies and 4 aristocrats sitting by virtue of their social position. In the first Seym there were 22 Poles and 26 Germans. This national composition was the result of an electoral law designed to favor Germans and in no way represented the national makeup of the province which was 65% Polish.

In the autocratic structure of government at the time, the Seym of Poznań, like the other Landtag Assemblies, was a purely advisory body with no right to legislate on its own except in strictly local matters, and its main function was to draw up petitions to the Prussian King. The King did not come down to Poznań for the sessions of the Seym but had the petitions brought up to Potsdam by the Viceroy. He then either graciously consented to, or more often rejected, the Seym's proposals for legislation.

Fig. 76—Paweł Antoni Sułkowski (1785-1836), First Speaker of the Seym of the Grand Duchy of Poznań in 1827. A lithograph by J. Sonntag.

During the years of its existence most of the Seym's business dealt with the questions arising from the abolition of serfdom, then being phased out throughout Prussia, and with the political rights of the Polish majority in the province, increasingly excluded from the administration and the judiciary by the Prussian government.

In 1827 the Seym petitioned the Prussian King for the establishment of a "Euphorate," an office to supervise the schools and to assure that Polish language and culture will be equally represented with the German. It was to submit periodic reports to the Seym. The petition was refused by the King Frederick Wilhelm III. The Prussian government in turn requested the opinion of the Seym on the subject of the extension of civil rights of the Jewish population, held still under the old law of the Duchy of Warsaw promulgated by the Saxon King. The Prussian law of 1812, removing all civil distinctions due to religion, was not extended by the Prussians to the province when it was created. The Seym proposed in this matter a transition period in extending political rights and obligations to the Jews in combination with access to non-denominational schools. The intent was to remove gradually cultural barriers, unwittingly created by the structure of Jewish autonomy inherited from the First Republic. This proposal was accepted by the King.

Fig. 77—*The building on the left served as the seat of the Seym of Poznań between 1827 and 1874. It was originally constructed in 1733 to the designs of Pompeo Ferrari (1660-1736) to house a Jesuit College. It now houses the City Council of Poznań.*

Der

erſte Landtag

des

Großherzogthums Poſen

im Jahr 1827.

PIERWSZY SEYM

WIELKIEGO XIĘSTWA POZNAŃSKIEGO

W ROKU 1827.

Poſen,
gedruckt und zu haben bei B. Decker und Compagnie.
1828.

Der

ſiebente Landtag

des

Großherzogthums Poſen

im Jahr 1845.

SIÓDMY SEJM

WIELKIEGO XIĘSTWA POZNAŃSKIEGO

w roku 1845.

Poſen,
gedruckt bei B. Decker & Comp. Königl. Hofbuchdr.
1846.

Fig. 78—*Title pages of the Proceedings of the first (1827) and the seventh (1845) Seym of Poznań showing the change in spelling from 'Seym' to 'Sejm' which took place in the early 1840s.*

The second Seym assembled on January 10, 1830. Deputy Kossecki demanded that the political organization given by Frederick Wilhelm to the Duchy be replaced by the formerly used Constitution of the Duchy of Warsaw. Deputy A. Niegolewski protested against the germanization of the Judiciary and the administration. The Seym calculated that in the district of Poznań only 4 out of 23 administrative officers were Poles, and in that of Bydgoszcz there were no Poles at all among its 14 officers. In the 7 courts for the gentry there were 12 Poles and 48 Germans sitting as judges.

During the 1830 uprising in the Congress Kingdom against the Russians, many Poles from the Grand Duchy of Poznań participated in the hostilities on the Polish side, and 1400 of them were imprisoned by the Prussians upon returning home.

In the dark period following the suppression of the Seym of Warsaw in 1831 by Nicholas I of Russia, the Seym of Poznań was the only elected representative body operating on Polish soil. In spite of its modest role it carried on the traditions of the General Seymik of Greater Poland, and in full awareness of its unique position it insisted on using the word 'Seym' in its title.

In 1833 the county Seymiks in the Grand Duchy were stripped of the right to elect the officials heading the local administration (landrats). Thus, apart from the right to elect the Deputies to the Seym, the Seymiks lost their biggest prerogative and retained only the duty to distribute service obligations to the state, the responsibility to organize local help in case of natural calamities, and the right to dispose of a small local tax income. In the same year the privileges and duties of village headmen were taken away from the large landowners and entrusted to paid officials of the State.

In 1837 the Roman Catholic Archbishop Dunin of Poznań was imprisoned by the Prussian government over the issue of mixed marriages. This caused great public commotion, spilling into the Seym debates, with the division of opinion following national and religious lines, the Germans being mostly Protestant and the Poles Catholic. The Archbishop was eventually released but the polarization of opinion persisted long after his release. The arbitrary actions of the government came increasingly under questioning and passive acceptance of these actions became a thing of the past.

In the early eighteen-forties it became evident to the people of Central Europe that the absolutist form of government had outlived its time. For Poles, in particular, absolutism was a return to the political forms of three hundred years ago. The nations no longer believed in allknowing, benevolent autocrats. The chained diets in various European countries were no longer satisfied with submitting petitions to the King for legislation needed and humbly waiting for his condescension. They wanted to legislate for themselves. The last petition was submitted by the Seym of Poznań in 1841. It demanded equal rights for the Poles constituting the majority of the population in the province and the elimination of the germanization policies of the government. The petition found a sympathetic ear in Frederick Wilhelm IV and some relief was provided.

In the Seym itself, the political sentiment was divided between the liberal faction, ready to join the German liberals in the all-Prussian constitutional movement and to support the demands for political rights in the German provinces of Prussia, and the conservative faction, led by Edward Raczyński, opposed to joint action and expecting correctly that the outcome would be the abolition of the separate institutions of the Duchy and amalgamation within the German Reich.

Fig. 79—Edward Raczyński (1786-1845), Deputy to the Seym of Poznań in 1841, founder of the Raczyński Library of Poznań, a prominent civic leader. Portrait by Jan Gładysz (1762-1830).

In many instances the response of the King to the petitions received from the Seym was minimal, as the King was in no manner obligated to take them into consideration and thus the situation was getting ripe for a revolution. The explosion in Poznań occurred in 1848 as part of a larger chain of similar revolutions spreading throughout Germany, Austria, France, Italy, and Hungary, as well as all zones of partitioned Poland. A spirit of self-determination was in the air and the "Spring of Nations" was about to begin.

In Poznań a Polish administration was installed in the Town Hall and irregular Polish units under the leadership of L. Mierosławski fought the regular Prussian Army in several battles. Similar events occurred in other parts of Prussia. Eventually, the King was forced to allow the provincial parliaments, the Seym of Poznań included, to send Deputies to an all-Prussian parliament.

The Prussian parliament that met in Berlin in 1851 gained real legislative powers, thus preempting the significance of the provincial parliaments, which had petitioning powers only. The Seym of Poznań continued to operate after the uprising of 1848; however, it was given a new electoral law which further reduced Polish representation in it, even though the percentage of Poles in the province remained basically unchanged, as shown in Table 40 below.

TABLE 40—NATIONALITY OF SEYM DEPUTIES AND OF THE POPULATION OF THE GRAND DUCHY OF POZNAŃ

Election Year	Nationality of Deputies			% of Poles in the
	Poles	Germans	Year	Population
1827	22	26	1830	65.0
1845	25	25	1870	56.0*
1854	17	33	1900	62.0
1918	8	40		

*Large German garrison was included in the population statistics of that year.

In all, 49 Seyms were returned by 1918 but only the first 7 Seyms, when the language of debates and the Speakers of the Seyms were Polish, can be considered as part of the Polish legislative tradition. After 1877, even the Proceedings of the Seym were published in German only. In these years the attention of the Polish part of the population of the Duchy turned towards the effort of assuring Polish representation in Berlin.

Numerous Polish Deputies were elected to the Prussian Parliament in Berlin, thereafter, forming there a Polish Parliamentary Circle, some 22 Deputies strong. They sat in the Prussian Parliament amongst an overwhelming majority of German Deputies elected from other parts of Prussia. The electoral law under which they were elected was, however, more fair than that given by the King of Prussia to the Seym of the province of Greater Poland. Activities of these Polish Deputies in the Prussian Parliament are outside the scope of this survey, which is limited to representative bodies with largely Polish composition and sitting in any of the Polish provinces. It may be mentioned, however, that the minority Polish group in Berlin was not able to prevent the passage of legislation detrimental to Polish interests. The pessimistic predictions of the Poznań conservatives came true. Such was the case in Bismarck's administration when a law was passed by the Prussian Parliament forbidding Poles in Greater Poland to construct farm buildings on their own land. Then, in 1908, a law was passed giving the Prussian government the right to expropriate lands of Polish owners for sale to Germans, and in 1913 a law was instituted which abolished the Grand Duchy of Poznań and incorporated the province into the German Reich.

Fig. 80—Building of the Polish Land Credit Society in Poznań purchased for the seat of the Seym of Poznań in 1873, after the Society was suppressed by the Prussian Government. At the same time the Seym was forced to germanize completely, even its proceedings were printed in German only. The building now houses the palatinate offices.

To keep the narrative continuous it may be pertinent to mention here events which belong to the history of the Second and the Polish People's Republics. In the long run all efforts to suppress Polish interests and to germanize the Duchy were of no avail. In 1918, at the end of the First World War, the province revolted against the Germans and was reunited with Poland in 1919, not by force but by its own choosing.

The forced reduction of Polish representation in the Seym of Poznań, imposed by the Prussian government after the revolution of 1848, was swept away by the revolution of 1918 in Germany at the close of the First World War. By the end of November, 1918, mass meetings were held in the former provinces of Poland taken over by Prussia in the Partitions: the Grand Duchy of Poznań, Silesia, Pomerania, Ermland (Warmia) and Mazury, and among natives of these provinces scattered throughout Germany in units of the German Army, and in the coal mines of Westphalia. In all these places elections of Deputies to the Seym of Poznań were held. Altogether 1403 Deputies were elected, as shown in Table 41.

TABLE 41—THE SEYM AND THE SUPREME NATIONAL COUNCIL OF POZNAŃ, 1918

Province Represented	Number of Deputies	Supreme National Council
Grand Duchy of Poznań	521	29
Silesia	431	27
Pomerania, Ermland, Mazury	262	12
Emigrants in Germany	142	—

The Seym met in Poznań from the third to the fifth of December, 1918. It set up as its executive organ the Supreme National Council, which took over the administrative functions of the province. Army units were organized and independence from Prussia was declared. In the ensuing fighting against the German units the province was able to maintain its independence; in the course of 1919 the provinces of Greater Poland, Pomerania, and part of Silesia and Mazury were reunited with Poland. Ermland remained under German control until the end of the Second World War. Thus, the will of the population to restore a legislative and administrative structure responsive to its needs reasserted itself again.

Ironically, the Prussian efforts to keep the Polish representation in the Seym of Poznań low after 1848 were paralleled by the Ukrainian underrepresentation in the Seym of Lwów, condoned for so long by the Poles of Galicia. Both led to explosive situations in 1918: the Polish uprising in Greater Poland and the Ukrainian attempt at military take-over of Eastern Galicia.

The later history of the Province of Greater Poland was even stormier. Forced incorporation of the province into the Third Reich during the Second World War, followed by attempted genocide of the Polish population in the German-occupied territory, had far reaching repercussions for the Germans. At the end of the Second World War the German part of the population was expelled not only from the provinces of Greater Poland and Pomerania, but also from Silesia and part of East Prussia, while the State of Prussia was disestablished. It grew over centuries mostly on lands taken away one by one from Poland, either directly, or by taking them second hand from Austria (Silesia). This rapacity of Prussia eventually brought on its own extinction.

The constitutional arrangements of the Grand Duchy of Poznań are given in Table 42, followed by the biographical notes on its parliamentarians.

TABLE 42—CONSTITUTION OF THE GRAND DUCHY OF POZNAŃ—A SYNOPSIS

(Granted by Fredrick Wilhelm III of Prussia, March 27, 1824)

The Executive Branch of the Government was headed by a hereditary King, represented in the Duchy by a Viceroy, whose duty it was to call county Seymiks and the Seym into session. The Viceroy supervised the elections of Deputies to the

TABLE 42 (CONTINUED)—CONSTITUTION OF THE GRAND DUCHY OF POZNAŃ—A SYNOPSIS

Seym and submitted, for discussion and comment, the legislative proposals drafted by the King. The administration of the Duchy was in the hands of a Provincial President, assisted by County Prefects, who were initially elected by the Seymiks, later appointed.

The Legislative Branch of the Government of the province consisted of a unicameral Seym with 46 elective Deputies and two to four heads of magnate families domiciled in the Duchy. The area of competence of the Seym was limited to provincial matters. In its deliberations it responded to the Royal Writ, presented by the Seym Commissioner appointed by the King, and expressed its opinion, or submitted to the King petitions with requests for legislative action. The laws were issued by the King directly so that the Seym had only an advisory role. It could legislate in matters of communal self-government and could distribute and spend some taxes, but it did not have the power to impose new taxes. The votes on proposals to and from the King required a two-thirds majority, while in other matters a simple majority sufficed. A session of two months' duration was held every two to three years.

The Electoral Ordinance gave the active electoral rights to Christian males of at least twenty-four years of age and in possession of some real estate. The passive electoral rights were limited to persons above the age of thirty and satisfying a high property qualification. In larger towns, the property requirement for candidates was 36,000 zł, decreasing to 12,000 zł in smaller towns. The Deputies to the Seym were elected by the Seymiks of the gentry, where twenty-four Deputies were elected; the town assemblies elected sixteen Deputies and the village communes elected eight. Several small towns together elected one Deputy. For villages, one Deputy was elected by three to four counties, and the candidate was required to own land worth at least 1800 zł*. The Deputies were elected for six years. Every three years one-half of the seats were up for reelection.

The Judiciary Branch of the Government of the province, originally enforcing the Code Napoléon through a system of local and appellate courts, was subjected later to the Prussian legal system. Appointed judges enforced laws decreed by the King. The King held a right of pardon.

Bill of Rights was embedded in the Prussian General Code. The code recognized the right to demand protection of person and property.

---

* Using the relation: 6 zł per thaler.

POLITICAL PERSONALITIES OF THE SEYM OF POZNAŃ

Dezydery A. Chłapowski (1788-1879)—General, cultural and economic activist, participated in the Napoleonic campaigns. In 1818-19 he studied the agricultural methods in England; he promoted economic development in Greater Poland. He served as Deputy to the Seym of Poznań in 1827 and in 1830 was Deputy Speaker in that Seym. In 1830-31 he participated in the November uprising in the Congress Kingdom. In 1831 he was named Commanding Officer of the Lithuanian Army. After the collapse of the uprising he crossed into Greater Poland and was imprisoned by the Prussians. After his release he cooperated with K. Marcinkowski in "organic work." He authored *On Agriculture* (1875) and *Memoirs* (1899).

Tytus A. Działyński (1796-1861)—Politician, patron of the arts, participated in the uprisings of 1830-31 and of 1848. He served as Deputy to the Seym of Poznań of 1830 and Deputy to the Prussian Parliament in 1858-61. He was one of the cofounders of the Poznań Association of Friends of Learning and its President from 1858. He was the publisher of historical source materials: *Statutes of Lithuania* (1841); *Sources to the History of the Union of Poland and Lithuania* (1856-61), and *Acta Tomiciana*, vol. 1-8 (1858-60). He also founded the Library of Kórnik.

Józef I. Grabowski (1791-1881)—Parliamentarian and writer; educated in Warsaw, Wrocław and Poznań as well as at the University of Dresden. In the years 1810-11 he served in the administration of the National Forestry in Poznań. Councilor for the county of Obornik in 1812, in the same year he joined the army of the Duchy of Warsaw and participated in the campaign of 1812, '13, and '14 and was decorated and demobilized in the rank of major in 1816. In 1816 he joined the management of the Land Credit Society of Poznań and became its local manager in 1828. In 1829-30 he served as a substitute Deputy in the Seym of Poznań to which he was then elected in his own right in 1834 and 1837 from the county of Buków and Obornik. He was General Director of the Land Credit Society in 1839-44. He was a member of the management and a shareholder in the Central Department Store (Bazar). Speaker of the Seym of Poznań in 1845 and in 1852 he was elected from the counties of Buków and Obornik to the Prussian Higher Chamber. In 1859 he sold his interests in the Grand Duchy of Poznań and settled in the Congress Kingdom. He authored: *Memoirs of Staff Officer in Napoleon's Army*, 1812-14 (1905), and *Observations on the Causes of Failure of Estates in the Grand Duchy of Poznań* (1852).

Wojciech Lipski (1805-1855)—Liberal politician in Greater Poland; he was a social activist; participated in the 1830 uprising in the Congress Kingdom; served on the board of directors of the Association of Friends of Learning in 1841. In the same year he was elected Deputy to the Seym of Poznań. He participated in the uprising of 1848 in Greater Poland. In the years 1848-49 he served as Deputy to the Prussian Parliament and was a member of the Polish League.

Maciej Mielżyński (1790-1870)—Politician of the Grand Duchy of Poznań, active in the Masonic Movement, and in the paramilitary Association of Spikemen. Imprisoned by the Prussians in 1825. Elected Deputy to the Seym of Poznań in 1827. Participated in the Uprising of 1830 in Congress Kingdom. After its collapse reoriented his interests to economic sphere and became a member of management of Central Department Store (Bazar Poznański) in Poznań. Supported the demands for autonomy of the Grand Duchy of Poznań. After the collapse of the uprising of 1848 in Greater Poland, was elected Deputy to the Prussian Parliament.

Andrzej Niegolewski (1786-1857)—Father of Władysław M., political activist in the Grand Duchy of Poznań; Colonel in the army, he participated in the Napoleonic Spanish campaigns as an officer in the cavalry regiment, and was wounded in the charge at Samosierra that opened the road to Madrid. He served as Deputy to the Provincial Seym of Poznań where he represented the liberal gentry opposition.

Władysław M. Niegolewski (1819-1885)—Son of Andrzej, liberal gentry politician in the Province of Greater Poland. He participated in the uprisings of 1846 and 1848 and was imprisoned by the Prussian authorities but was found innocent in the Trial of Moabit. He was Deputy to the Prussian Parliament in 1849-52 and again in 1859-81. During the February 1863 uprising he was a member of the "Whites" Party. He was a cofounder in 1872 of the Association for Education of Peasants and also a Deputy Director of the Poznań Association of Friends of Learning.

Gustaw Potworowski (1800-1860)—Politician of Greater Poland; participated in the uprising of 1830 in the Congress Kingdom; he was an associate of Karol Marcinkowski and one of the initiators of the movement towards the economic improvement of the country. He supported financially the foundations of various establishments for social work. He was elected Deputy to the Seym of Poznań in 1843. During the 1848 uprising in Greater Poland he served as a member of the National Committee. Elected to the Prussian Parliament in 1848, he served as Chairman of the Polish Circle in that parliament in the years 1848-50.

Edward Raczyński (1786-1845)—Conservative politician in the province of Greater Poland; patron of the arts; he participated in Napoleonic campaigns of

1806-09 and 1812. He served as Deputy to the Seym of the Duchy of Warsaw and as Deputy to the Seym of Poznań. He supported conciliatory attitude toward the Hohenzollerns. He collected works of art and his private library formed the foundation for the Raczyński Library of Poznań.

Paweł A. Sułkowski (1785-1836)—General of infantry; from 1807 he served as colonel in the infantry of the Duchy of Warsaw. In 1808 he equipped, at his own expense, a regiment of the army and served at its head in Spain, becoming brigadier general in 1810. He took part in Napoleon's Russian campaign in 1812. After the death of Józef Poniatowski he was made supreme commander of the army of the Duchy of Warsaw. He was a member of the Military Commission of the Congress Kingdom and served as General Adjutant of Alexander I. In 1818 he retired to private life but in 1827 he returned to public life and became the first Speaker of the Seym of Poznań.

SEYM OF THE ESTATES IN GALICIA

The province of Lesser Poland was taken over almost in its entirety by the Austrian Empire in two steps, in the First (1772) and in the Third (1795) Partitions and annexed under the name of Galicia and Lodomeria, a corruption of the latinized names of the Kingdom of Halicz and Włodzimierz (Halicia and Vlodimeria). However, the lands gained by Austria in the Third Partition were soon lost to the Duchy of Warsaw when the latter waged a war on Austria in 1806.

Three years after the First Partition, to neutralize a possible opposition to Austrian rule, the Austrian Court allowed a representation of the gentry to assemble in the so called "Postulate Seym," i.e., a body whose function was to present petitions and to serve in an advisory capacity to the Austrian government. The Seym assembled in 1782, '84, '86, and '88 in Lwów for sessions of a few days' duration, with Emperor Joseph II attending one of the sessions in person. After the session of 1788 the Seym was allowed to lapse until the end of Napoleonic wars, and revived in 1817 by a decree of Francis I of Austria. Now called the "Seym of the Estates" it was meeting again in Lwów. The Estates in question were: the Clergy, represented by the archbishops, bishops and the delegates of the cathedral chapters, sitting ex-officio; the Aristocracy with the dukes, counts and barons for the most part recently created by the Emperor, sitting in person; the Gentry above certain income level, and finally, the Burghers, represented by two Deputies from the City of Lwów. The Chancellor of the University of Lwów was later added to the roster. The total number of members was not fixed and each represented only himself, rather than a constituency. A special uniform was prescribed by the Emperor for the members of the Seym, to be worn at the opening session of the Seym.

Fig. 81—The uniform prescribed by the court of Vienna to be worn on gala occasions by the members of the Galician Seym of the Estates. This was the only deliberative body in Poland that ever required a specific attire.

The Seym of the Estates met once a year for a few days and attempted to exercise its limited prerogatives which included hearing the Emperor's postulates, preparing petitions in the interest of the community and appeals for redress of grievances, and distributing tax assessments. The setting of tax rates was reserved for Vienna. The Seym could also grant Galician titles of nobility to persons who already held such titles in Austria. Indeed, it was a sad remnant of the prerogatives held by the Seyms of the First Republic.

The high income bracket required for membership in the Seym and the nonelective character of this body, denied representation to the numerous yeomanry, to say nothing of the peasants and the burghers from towns other than Lwów. This was a far cry from the representation given by the Constitutions of the First Republic and the Duchy of Warsaw, and accounted for the conservative character of the Seym. Because of its nonelective membership, the Seym of the Estates of Galicia is not included in the chronology of all the elections to Seyms in Poland given in Appendix C. Instead, the chronology of its meetings and the attendance at its sessions are listed in Table 43. The constitutional arrangements of Galicia at that time are shown in Table 44.

TABLE 43—ATTENDANCE AT THE SESSIONS OF THE GALICIAN SEYM OF THE ESTATES

Year	Attendees	Year	Attendees	Year	Attendees
1782	289	1823	75	1835	54
1784	62	1824	64	1836	60
1786	93	1825	62	1837	53
1788	78	1826	85	1838	49
——	*	1827	83	1839	100
1817	213	1828	51	1840	46
1818	126	1829	64	1841	96
1819	73	1830	70	1842	124
1820	69	——	**	1843	128
1821	76	1833	106	1844	104
1822	83	1834	41	1845	145***

* Not convened during the Napoleonic Wars
** Not convened during the Uprising in Congress Kingdom
*** Disbanded during the miscarried insurrection and revolt in Galicia

In the early years of its existence the Seym concentrated on maintaining the status quo. This was evident in such actions as the attempts to retain for the landowners the alcohol retail rights; the opposition to the revision of illegally imposed labor duties; and the proposals to replace the number of days of labor, required of serfs for the use of land they tilled, by a fixed piece of work.

Among the progressive actions of the Galician Seym of the Estates credit must be given for its support of the establishment of the Ossoliński Foundation. Started in 1817 by Józef Maximilian Ossoliński (1748-1826) as a public library and expanded through a large legacy left by him in 1827, the Foundation has ever since supported historical research, publication of source materials, and financed the serial edition of classics of Polish literature, under the imprint of "Ossolineum" of Lwów, now, of Wrocław.

The conservative attitudes of the Seym were modified by the influx of new members in the later 1830s and the early 1840s. Among them was Leon Sapieha, who at the end of 1830s changed his domicile from the Congress Kingdom to Galicia, bringing with him the administrative experience gained as collaborator of Xavier Drucki-Lubecki, the Minister of Treasury of the Congress Kingdom. Under his influence the Seym assumed a more active and representative role. In time, Sapieha was joined in the Seym by such able individuals as Władysław Badeni and Agenor Gołuchowski who subsequently left his mark on Galician and Austrian politics.

Fig. 82—Leon Sapieha (1803-1878), First Speaker of the Seym of Galicia in Lwów. Promoter of many financial institutions and of the first railroad in Galicia. Painting by H. Rodakowski (1823-1894).

The more activist stance assumed by the Seym after the injection of new blood led it to take up the question of the abolition of serfdom. Outright abolition was, of course, outside the limited range of powers allowed the Seym by the Austrian Emperor and, furthermore, was resisted by the more conservative members. The matter could only be introduced through petitions. In 1842 Kazimierz Krasicki introduced a memorandum on the need to abolish serfdom and to grant land to the peasants. A toned-down petition for a commission to examine the improvement of relations between the landed gentry and the peasants was submitted to the Emperor by the Seym of 1843. Vice-Speaker Tadeusz Wasilewski sponsored the petition. In response, the Court of Vienna requested a clarification of the issues involved. The Seym of 1844 elucidated its stand by explaining that the intention was to guarantee the peasants the use of the land they tilled and a share in the use of commons without, however, abolishing serfdom. The opinion of the Seym on this matter was divided between the conservative faction headed by Władysław Sanguszko, favoring the status quo, and the liberal faction headed by Alfred Potocki, favoring the grant of land to the peasantry.

The last Seym of the Estates, held in 1845, voted for the broadening of the powers of the commission to investigate the replacement of peasant labor duties by a fixed share in the grain harvested, or its cash equivalent, as well as the substitution of a grant of pasture land for the use of the common. Deputy Maurice Kraiński sponsored this resolution. In spite of its cautious wording the resolution contained nothing less than the proposal to abolish serfdom, and give full property rights of the land to the peasantry in exchange for extended cash payments. The vote in favor of the abolition was 116, 10 voted against it. Through procrastination and lack of decision from Vienna the commission to implement this resolution was never appointed. The matter was of great urgency because parallel to these ineffectual parliamentary activities, extra-parliamentary action was being planned by the Democratic Society. This Society had been formed in exile by some political emigrés from the 1830 uprising in the Congress Kingdom. Directed from Paris, and revolutionary in character, the Society had many adherents in Galicia, Congress Kingdom and the Grand Duchy of Poznań. Hot-heads in Galicia, influenced by democratic ideas then sweeping through Europe, prepared for an uprising under the guidance of the Society. It was hoped that direct action would force the hand of the Austrian government, gain for the province more national and political freedom, and advance the cause of agrarian reform.

Fig. 83—Agenor Gołuchowski (1812-1875), Deputy to the Galician Seym of the Estates in 1843. Served three times as Viceroy of Galicia: 1849-58, 1866-68, 1871-75. Sponsored founding of the Academy of Learning in Cracow and the Technical University of Lwów.

The attempt at revolt misfired. It was skillfully turned by the Austrians into a peasant rebellion by convincing the peasants that the insurrection was intended to harm them rather than help them. In the peasant rebellion of 1846 some 2000 persons suspected by the peasants of favoring the insurrection were killed and some 4700 manors were looted or burned. In the wake of the rebellion the sessions of the Seym of the Estates were suspended, and with them the plans for the land reform commission. However, only two years later, the revolution of 1848 spreading over all lands of the Austrian Empire, forced the Emperor to accept the abolition of serfdom and to grant, by an imperial decree, some land to the peasants. At that crucial moment Galicia had no representation whatsoever, since the attempt by the Emperor to convene the Seym in the revolutionary turmoil of 1848, was met with a demand from its membership that the Seym be converted to an elective body, be made more representative and given more powers. In this demand the Seym was backed by the National Council formed by the inhabitants of Lwów. The Emperor initially turned down this demand. Thus, there was no Seym in which all parties interested in abolishing serfdom could present their case. Without the machinery for airing the issues, debating different courses of action, and adjusting the solutions accordingly, a rare chance was missed for reforming the land ownership structure. As it was, the Emperor's land grant was inadequate to assure the viability of peasants' holdings, nor was there an adequate financial credit structure provided to assure a smooth transition. Consequently, Galicia was saddled with a mass of small peasant holdings unable to support former serfs. When combined with a high birth rate in the province, the resulting demographic pressure could only be relieved by large-scale emigration from Galicia to America, primarily the United States and Brazil. The emigration lasted throughout the second half of the nineteenth and the first decade of the twentieth century. Thus, to a degree, the existence of a large group of Polish-Americans in the United States today is the outcome of the powerlessness of the Seym of the Estates of Galicia to solve the agrarian question.

Following the demise of the Seym of the Estates, an interval of sixteen years elapsed before the legislative institutions of Galicia were revived in 1861, and the first Galician Seym of Lwów was elected. In this Seym the peasants were given representation, but the question of further land reform was not taken up again until the first Seym of the Second Republic assembled in Warsaw in 1919.

The Seym of the Estates had no permanent home. While in operation, it held its meetings in the building of the former Order of the Holy Trinity. Originating in France, the Order operated between 1688 and 1783 in Poland on a charter from King Jan III Sobieski, collecting funds for ransom of hostages and prisoners of war held by Turkey. With the end of wars with Turkey, the order became defunct, and in 1784 its buildings were transferred to the University of Lwów. The former church of the Order was converted into a university auditorium, and when the Seym of the Estates started to operate, the University extended its hospitality at the time of each annual session.

To bypass the limitation imposed on the Seym of the Estates by the Emperor, regarding the range of subjects allowed for debate, the members of the Seym held as a rule presession meetings at another location. It was during such a presession meeting held on the premises of the Ossoliński Institute in 1848 that it was decided to meet the Emperor's Writ of Summons with a demand for an elective Seym. As mentioned above, the Galicians had to wait until 1861 for the realization of their demands. The provincial Seym that was reestablished then, had eventually a building erected for its seat in 1880, and occupied it until 1918. When the national Seym reassembled in Warsaw in the following year, the Seym of Lwów terminated its activities and on that occasion repaid the University for its hospitality of a hundred years earlier (1817) with a gift of its building to the University. The meeting chamber of the Seym became in turn the auditorium of the University of Lwów.

TABLE 44—CONSTITUTION OF THE GALICIAN SEYM OF THE ESTATES—A SYNOPSIS

(Given by Francis I of Austria January 13, 1817)

The Executive Branch of the Government of the province was headed by the Emperor who was represented in the province by a Governor, who in turn appointed county Prefects. The administration was run centrally from Vienna and enforced the laws made by the Emperor directly. The limited executive functions of the Seym were exercised by the Home Department consisting of two assessors from each Estate.

The Legislative Branch of the Government in the province was shared between the Emperor and the Seym of the Estates consisting of: the Clergy, the Magnates, the Knighthood and the Cities. The Seym met annually and sat for a few days in the city of Lwów. The area of competence of the Seym included all matters concerning the province on which the opinion of the Seym was requested by the Emperor. This encompassed the preparation of petitions to be submitted to the Throne, the upkeep of the tax registry, distribution of taxes, grants of patents of Galician nobility and the upkeep of the registry of the gentry. The Seym could not impose new taxes or make new laws. These legislative functions were reserved for the Emperor. The Seym could send Deputations with petitions to the Emperor only with the latter's permission.

The Electoral Ordinance of the Seym was nonexistent: all its members were nonelective. The right to sit in the Seym was given to residents of the province who paid 75 florins annually in tax and belonged to one of the four Estates. These were: the Clergy, represented by the archbishops, bishops, abbots, and the representatives of cathedral chapters; the Estate of the Magnates, which included dukes, counts and barons; the Estate of Knighthood which encompassed all gentry immatriculated in the General Register; and finally the Cities, which initially were limited to Lwów only, and represented by two Delegates.

The Judiciary Branch of the Government of the province consisted of judges appointed by the Emperor or by the minister of Justice, and distributed in a multi-level court organization. The courts enforced imperial decrees.

The Bill of Rights was not defined other than by the laws made for the empire as a whole, and these were subject to change at any time in accordance with the Emperor's wish.

THE SEYM OF THE REPUBLIC OF CRACOW

Parallel to the developments in Galicia there existed, in the years 1815-46, the Republic of Cracow, established as a Free City by the Congress of Vienna. Its territory was just over one thousand square kilometers, and the total population was over 100,000 in the 1830s. It was under the supervision of three Commissioners appointed by the partitioning powers and was provided with a Constitution prepared by Adam Czartoryski.

The Constitution provided for a Senate of 12 Senators and a Chairman. Nine Senators were to be elected by the House of Representatives, two were appointed by the University of Cracow and two by the Cracow Cathedral Chapter. The Senate was to act as the executive committee of the Free City. The House of Representatives (the Seym) was given a membership of 41, of which the communal assemblies elected 26, the Senate, the Cathedral Chapter and the University elected 3 each, and 6 justices of the peace were given a seat in it ex-officio. Thus, there existed an incestuous relation between the Senate and the House of Representatives, each electing members of the other body. In the territory surrounding the city, each village with more than 10 households was entitled to send a representative to a communal assembly, which elected the Deputies to the Seym. For nonrural citizens the property qualification for exercising active and passive electoral rights was set very low in order to allow for wide participation.

The boundaries of the City Republic encompassed 224 villages, of which approximately 100 belonged to the State or the Church. Starting with these properties, the Seym of Cracow carried out the parcelling of 91 of these estates to create 5500 individual peasant farms. The reform was completed in 1846.

The reform converted the labor duties of peasants into rent on the individual farms thus created, but it did not give the land outright to the peasants. In the course of time, however, the new farmers bought out their holdings, converting the long-term leases into freeholds.

In the political field the small size of the City Republic belied its importance. Its territory served as a refuge for political exiles from other provinces of Poland who ran afoul of the partitioning powers. Furthermore, the Republic's solution of its agrarian problem gave an indication of what that solution could have been in the rest of the country had the First Republic succeeded in defending its Constitution of 1791 and its own survival.

The seat of the Chairman of the Senate was occupied for the first ten years by Stanisław Wodzicki, who increasingly relied on political assistance from the three Commissioners of the Partitioning Powers in the exercise of his duties. When he failed to win the elections of 1828, the Commissioners took over, deposed Józef Nikorowicz, who was duly elected to that position and temporarily suspended the operation of the Seym. Several subsequent changes in the Constitution reduced the membership in the House of Representatives to twenty.

When the uprising against Russia took place in the Congress Kingdom in 1830, Cracow was occupied by the Russian Army for two months in the autumn of 1831. Political freedom was severely restricted. In 1836 incidents which occurred in connection with house searches for political refugees, served as an excuse for Austria to occupy the Republic and remain there until 1842. In 1848 an uprising took place in Cracow, and a National Government was formed. Austria suppressed this uprising and incorporated the territory of the Republic into Galicia.

THE SEYM OF LWÓW: PEASANTS ENTER POLITICS IN GALICIA

At the time when the Seym of Poznań was made unrepresentative through the distorted structure of its electoral ordinance and both the Galician Seym of the Estates and the Seym and Senate of the Free City of Cracow were in eclipse, there came into being the Seym of Lwów. Established as a result of the upheaval of 1848 and its persistent after-effects, it soon came into its own and provided an important forum and an instrument for political action. Called "the Seym of the Land" (Sejm Krajowy), the Seym of Lwów had limited but well-defined legislative powers and had an elective membership for all but a few Deputies sitting ex-officio.

In terms of the Polish legislative tradition, the Seym of Lwów was a provincial legislature which combined and resumed the operation of the General Seymiks of

Lesser Poland and Ruthenia. These Seymiks met formerly at Korczyn and Wisznia. Although it represented only the middle tier in the three-tier legislative structure of the First Republic, it assumed the title of Seym, rather than General Seymik, to increase its stature and notify thereby that it intended to carry on the tradition of the National Seym.

Fig. 84—The building of the Seym of Galicia in Lwów, constructed in the years 1877-81 to the plans of Juliusz Hochberger (1840-1905); The Seym sat here between 1881 and 1918. The building now houses the University of Lwów.

The electoral area of the Seym encompassed Galicia and Lodomeria, to use the official Austrian designation, that is parts of the province of Lesser Poland with parts of Red Ruthenia attached to it, as well as the former Free City of Cracow now incorporated into Galicia. The capital of the province was Lwów, which by then was well on the way to surpassing Cracow, the former capital of Lesser Poland, in importance and size. The rivalry between the two cities persisted right up to World War I in the area of cultural and political leadership and many influential political newspapers were published in Cracow rather than Lwów.

The Constitution of the province, contained in the Emperor's patent of 1861, placed the administration in the hands of the Viceroy and the Department of the Interior (Wydział Krajowy) with the heads of the different sections appointed from among the Deputies of the Seym and reporting periodically on their activities to the Seym. The structure of the Seym was unicameral, with 141 Deputies elected through the "curia system," in which each social group of the province was given a different weight for electing Deputies. In addition, nine Deputies, such as chancellors of Universities, archbishops and bishops, sat ex-officio. Table 45 gives the relative weight of each curia, used in 1861.

TABLE 45—ELECTORAL STRUCTURE OF THE SEYM OF LWÓW

Curia #*	Composition of Curia	Deputies per Curia	Electors per Deputy
1	Great Landowners	44	52
2	Chambers of Commerce of Lwów, Cracow, Brody	3	39
3	Townsmen with Property Requirements	20	2264
4	Rural Communes	74	8764
	Sitting ex-officio	9	—

*Later reforms added a fifth curia. The number of Deputies went up to 161.

Fig. 85—*The interior of the Chamber of Deputies of the Seym of Galicia in Lwów, as seen from the visitors' gallery. Shown with the Seym in session.*

The elections to the Seym were called at the Emperor's pleasure, as a rule every five to six years, but the sessions of the Seym were held annually. The Speaker of the Seym and the Viceroy were appointed by the Emperor (see Table 48). During the 54 years of its existence the elections to the Seym took place ten times, the last in 1913. In that time the Seym had produced a considerable body of legislation, particularly in matters relating to education, local self-government, and administration, as well as in the regulation of commerce, industry, and finance, as shown in Table 49.

Between 1861 and 1873 the Seym of Lwów reverted to the function of a General Seymik of the province, in that it selected and sent to the parliament of Vienna 38 of its Deputies to serve as Deputies in that body. After 1872 the administration of the province was completely transferred to the Poles, and the Polish and Ukrainian languages (the latter in Eastern Galicia) were reintroduced as official languages. Polish was restored as the language of instruction at the Universities of Cracow and Lwów and used in the newly established Polytechnic Institute of Lwów. An Academy of Learning was established in Cracow in 1872.

Although initially the Seym was dominated for several decades by conservatives, gradually other parties emerged and asserted themselves.

The modest structure and limited field of action of the Seym of Lwów, as well as its far from democratic suffrage, arbitrarily set by the Emperor, gave no indication of its future influence on legislative developments in Poland as a whole. This influence arose from three facets of its activity. They were: the entry of peasants into politics, the formation of a Polish administration supervised by the Seym, and finally, the emergence of the Ukrainian national movement in the Seym of Lwów.

The emergence of the peasants on the political scene found its expression in the formation of the Peasant Party. This party was first formed in Galicia; however, it was going to play a key role in the national politics of the Second Republic and be the chief obstacle to the Communist takeover in the Polish People's Republic. In addition to the Peasant Party, Galicia was the scene of activity of all major political parties which survive to this day, even though the leadership of some of them had to reside in exile abroad [until the fall of communism in 1989]. At the time of the rise of Galician autonomy, the other political parties were being organized in several provinces of Partitioned Poland as well; however, only in Galicia did they have a free political environment. They were: the Peasant Party, representing the populist ideology; the National Democrats, grouping the burghers and larger farmers; the Socialist Party, grouping the industrial working people; the Christian Democratic Party, drawing most of its support from Western Galicia and the Silesian industrial region; and finally the conservatives, who not only dominated the Galician administration but also supplied the Austrian Imperial Government with a series of capable ministers. With the exception of the conservatives, these groups were to dominate the political life of the Second Republic and were to form the backbone of the resistance movement to the German occupation in the Second World War.

Fig. 86—Alfred Potocki (1817-1889), Speaker of the Seym of Lwów (1875-77) and the Viceroy of Galicia (1877-83); he is shown holding the badge of his office. A portrait by Jan Matejko (1838-1893).

As a result of the social structure of Galicia and the curia system of elections, the bulk of the Deputies in the Seym represented a conservative view and favored the interests of the gentry. This conservatism was visible even in the dress of the Deputies. As late as the first decade of this century, some of the gentry among the Deputies could be seen wearing to the opening sessions of the Seym the traditional Polish dress and sword, which in other parts of the country went out of use some 75 years earlier.

The dominance by the gentry of the Polish representation in the Seym much hampered the political emergence of the representatives of Polish peasantry. In rural districts, the tendency of the Ukrainians was to elect Ukrainian peasants, whereas the Poles, at first, elected members of the gentry to represent them. Although in the first three elections there were 35, 34, and 23 peasant Deputies returned respectively, there followed a gap until 1889, when Polish peasant Deputies were returned again. Eventually, the Polish peasant representation started to grow, particularly after the Peasant Party (SL) was formed in 1895. Nine peasant

Deputies were returned to the Seym in that year and, in time, the Peasant Party became an effective instrument for presenting and advancing the peasant interests in the Seym of Lwów.

Fig. 87—Closeup of the Speaker's dais in the Seym of Lwów. The Deputies are shown wearing the traditional costume of Polish gentry. After a drawing by A. Fiedler.

The first peasant political leaders to emerge in the Seym were Jakub Bojko, Stanisław Stojałowski, Jan Stapiński, and Wincenty Witos. Even though few, they effectively presented the peasant cause in the Seym and eventually gained great popularity with the public. Witos was elected Deputy of the Seym of Lwów in 1908. In 1913 he was chosen by the electorate to represent it in the Austrian Parliament in Vienna as well, and in the Second Republic he became the undisputed leader of the peasant movement, serving three times as the Prime Minister of the Republic.

The liberal faction in the Galician Seym was represented by Franciszek Smolka. His broad political outlook and identification with the cause of independence gained him much respect as well as recognition. Throughout his life he advocated the conversion of the Austrian Empire into a confederation of five autonomous states: Austria, Hungary, Bohemia, Galicia and Croatia, modelled on the early United States. When, in the mid-1800s, the citizens of Galicia decided to commemorate the 300th anniversary of the Union of Lublin (1569) between Poland and Lithuania, by erecting a high mound of earth on the outskirts of Lwów,

Deputy Smolka, with his sleeves rolled up, was among the crowd of people pushing wheelbarrows full of earth up the ramp leading to the top of the mound. His handle-bar moustache and a stately beard caught the eye of a visiting high Austrian dignitary:

"What do you do in your spare time, my good man?" asked the visitor. "I preside over the Austrian Parliament" was the reply.

He served as the speaker of the Austrian Parliament in 1848-49 and 1881-93, attaining in Vienna a position of influence. On his return to Galicia he served with distinction as the mayor of the City of Cracow, the ancient capital of Poland.

Fig. 88 (Right)—Franciszek Smolka (1810-1899), liberal politician and Deputy to the Seym of Lwów in 1861.

Fig. 89 (Left) - Eustachy Sanguszko (1842-1903), Deputy to the Seym of Galicia in Lwów (1873-1903), Speaker of the Seym of Lwów (1890-95), Viceroy of Galicia (1895-1898). Promoter of economic development of the province.

For the same 300 year anniversary, the Seym of Lwów commissioned Jan Matejko to paint a large canvas for its meeting chamber depicting the final swearing in of the Union of Poland and Lithuania at the Seym of Lublin. Both of these memorials, the mound and the painting, show how alive the memory of the Union was. Many of those who refused to accept the validity of the Partitions insisted that the Act of the Union was still in force as well. Later history was to show that the concepts of Independence and the Union were in fact separated by the rise of nationalism in Lithuania and the Ukraine.

The National Democratic Party became active in Galicia and gained much popular support at the turn of the century, with Roman Dmowski as its main ideologue and spokesman. Gaining support in the province of Greater Poland as well and sending Deputies from the Congress Kingdom to the Russian Duma after 1905, this party became the chief exponent of the anti-German orientation during the First World War.

The rise of autonomy of Galicia and the flowering of political movements coincided in time with the surge in the socialist activities. Among the leaders of the Socialist Party in Galicia, Ignacy Daszyński and Józef Piłsudski rose to prominence. The leaders of political opinion in Galicia, who were also Austrian subjects (Dmowski and Piłsudski were not), as a rule commenced their political career in the Galician Seym and continued it in the Austrian Parliament in Vienna. At the end of the First World War these Deputies were coopted outright to the Seym of the Second Republic in Warsaw and served there until the elections could be held in the war-torn Galicia. Piłsudski was chosen by the Seym of Warsaw to serve as the first Head of State of the Second Republic, a position he held with distinction right through the crucial period of the Polish-Soviet war, while Dmowski very effectively represented the reborn Republic at Versailles during the Peace Conference in 1919.

In the Seym of Lwów the Ukrainian national movement made its first appearance. In the first Seym of 1861 the Ukrainians returned 49 Deputies, i.e., just under a third of the total number of Deputies. Since the Ukrainian population of Galicia constituted about 43% of the total (census of 1880) and was almost entirely composed of peasants, the curia electoral system, with its under-representation of the peasantry, left the Ukrainian part of the population continually under-represented. Superimposed on this were the fluctuations in the Ukrainian electoral performance, as shown in Table 46. This situation was exacerbated by the political moves of the Polish majority aimed at retaining the advantage offered by the Constitution of Galicia.

Fig. 90 (Left)—Mikołaj Zyblikiewicz (1823-1887), Speaker of the Seym of Lwów from 1881 to 1886.

Fig. 91 (Right)—Jan Tarnowski (1835-1894), Speaker of the Seym of Galicia (1886-90); shown with the Speaker's staff, the badge of his office. A portrait by H. Rodakowski (1823-1894).

Among the ex-officio members of the Seym, the three Greek-Catholic bishops were invariably Ukrainian. After 1867 one of the two Vice-Speakers of the Seym was Ukrainian.

The years 1901-1912 were marked by rising antagonism of the Ukrainian population. Between 1901 and 1903 the Ukrainian Deputies disrupted the operations of the Seym by unruly behavior in the meeting chamber. The year 1908 saw the assassination of Viceroy Andrzej Potocki by a Ukrainian extremist and during the second period of noncooperation, 1909-12, Ukrainians prevented the Seym from passing the budget by provoking riots in the chamber.

TABLE 46—NATIONAL COMPOSITION OF THE SEYM OF LWÓW

Election Year	Number of Ukrainians	Deputies Total
1861	49	150
1867	37	150
1870	34	150
1877	16	150
1883	13	150
1889	20	150
1895	17	152
1901	16	161
1908	23	161
1913	35	161

On the eve of the First World War, on the initiative of the Polish leadership in the Seym, a modus vivendi was arrived at and produced a more equitable electoral law. However, the outbreak of the war prevented its implementation.

Eventually, the conflict with the Ukrainians escalated from the legislative arena of the Galician Seym into a civil war in and around the City of Lwów in 1918-19 when the Ukrainians made an abortive attempt to capture the city. The conflict returned to the parliamentry arena in the Seym of the Second Republic, and in 1930 it produced unrest in the eastern parts of Galicia and was accompanied by a wave of terrorist acts. Army units had to be moved into the area to intimidate the population in the manner of the dragonnades of Louis XIV, and keep the situation under control. During the Second World War armed conflict broke out again, resulting in much bloodshed and internecine fighting between rival partisan units composed of Poles and Ukrainians.

With the Communist take-over after the Second World War, Polish and Soviet army units went into coordinated action along the south-east part of the border to supress the Ukrainian insurgency. The Polish part of the operation was commanded by Karol Świerczewski, a Polish born operative in the Soviet NKVD (Political Police) and an expert on military pacification. Previously he had won his laurels operating in the same capacity on behalf of the Communists in the Spanish Civil War, where he conducted pacifications in the territory controlled by the Republican Government. While there, he was immortalized in that role as General Groza (in Polish: Dread) in Ernest Hemingway's novel, *For Whom the Bell Tolls*. In Poland, he met his premature end at the hands of the Ukrainian partisans in 1947 and joined the pantheon of officially approved Communist saints.

Fig. 92—Włodzimierz Dzieduszycki (1825-1899), Speaker of the Seym of Galicia in 1876, an office he held for one year as a compromise candidate to break a deadlock between the Poles and the Ukrainians in the Seym. A portrait by H. Rodakowski.

The constitutional arrangements of the kingdom of Galicia and Lodomeria are summarized in Table 47, the chief legislative officers are listed in Table 48, and the principal legislation of the Seym of Lwów is given in Table 49. Biographical sketches of prominent parliamentarians of that province follow.

TABLE 47—CONSTITUTION OF GALICIA AND LODOMERIA—A SYNOPSIS

(Granted by Franz Joseph of Austria, February 26, 1861)

The Executive Branch of the Government of the province was headed by the Emperor who appointed a Viceroy to act in his place in Galicia. He was assisted in the execution of his duties by county prefects and city presidents. A minister for Galicia was later included in the Austrian government in Vienna. As an executive organ of the Seym operating between the sessions of the Seym, the Executive Committee was appointed consisting of six Deputies and the Speaker of the Seym serving as its chairman.

The Legislative Branch of the Government of the province consisted of a unicameral Seym in which all but nine of its 150 Deputies were elective. Later, the membership was increased to 161, with ten members sitting ex-officio. The Seym debated and passed laws in matters dealing with education, cultural institutions, public welfare and assistance, by-laws in civil, criminal and police matters,

TABLE 47 (CONTINUED)—CONSTITUTION OF GALICIA AND LODOMERIA—A SYNOPSIS

communal self-government, public works, and some church and army matters. It could also impose supplementary taxes, not to exceed 10% of the direct tax.

The legislative initiative was given to the Emperor, the Seym executive committee and the individual Deputies. A majority vote in the presence of at least half the Deputies was required to pass a law. Amendments to the Constitution required the presence of at least three-fourths of all Deputies and a vote of two-thirds of those present. The Emperor's signature was required on all laws.

The Electoral Ordinance was based on the curia system. Under this system large landowners elected 44 Deputies, small landowners elected 74, the towns elected 20, and the chambers of commerce elected 3. In addition, 7 archbishops and bishops, plus 2 presidents of universities sat ex-officio. The Deputies were granted legislative immunity from arrest and were elected for six years. All taxpayers participated in communal elections in which they were divided into three curiae.

In the period 1861-73 the Seym of Lwów selected and sent to the Austrian Parliament in Vienna 38 of its Deputies to sit there as Representatives for Galicia.

The Judiciary Branch of the Government of the province consisted of judges appointed either by the Emperor or by the Minister of Justice. A multitier system of appellate courts was in existence. The Emperor held the right of pardon.

The Bill of Rights did not exist as a separate document, but the rights of the citizens were contained in the provisions of many imperial decrees and patents, as a rule different for each class and nationality. Protection of life and property, as well as free exercise of religion was provided. Secrecy of private mail was guaranteed.

TABLE 48—PRINCIPAL LEGISLATIVE OFFICERS OF GALICIA IN THE ERA OF AUTONOMY

Viceroy of Galicia	Period in Office
Wacław Zaleski	1848-1849
Agenor Gołuchowski, first term	1849-1859
Karl Mosch	1859-1861
Alexander Mensdorf-Pouilly	1861-1864
Franz Paumgartten	1864-1866
Agenor Gołuchowski, second term	1866-1868
Ludwik Possinger-Choborski	1868-1871
Agenor Gołuchowski, third term	1871-1875
Alfred Potocki	1877-1883

TABLE 48 (CONTINUED)—CHIEF LEGISLATIVE OFFICERS OF GALICIA IN THE ERA OF AUTONOMY

Viceroy of Galicia	Period in Office
Filip Zaleski	1883-1888
Kazimierz Badeni	1888-1895
Eustachy Sanguszko	1895-1898
Leon Piniński	1898-1903
Andrzej Potocki*	1903-1908
Michał Bobrzyński	1908-1913
Witold Korytowski	1913-1915
Hermann Colard**	1915-1916
Erich Diller**	1916-1917
Karl Huyn**	1917-1918

*Assassinated in office by a Ukrainian nationalist
**Austrian generals appointed while Galicia became the combat zone during the First World War

Speaker of the Seym of Galicia	Period in Office
Leon Sapieha	1861-1875
Alfred Potocki	1875
Włodzimierz Dzieduszycki	1876
Ludwik Wodzicki	1877-1880
Mikołaj Zyblikiewicz	1881-1886
Jan Tarnowski	1886-1890
Eustachy Sanguszko	1890-1895
Stanisław Badeni, first term	1895-1901
Andrzej Potocki	1901-1903
Stanisław Badeni, second term	1903-1912
Adam Gołuchowski	1912-1914
Stanisław Niezabitowski*	1914-1918

*Deported to Soviet Union during WWII, died there in 1941 in captivity.

TABLE 49—PRINCIPAL LEGISLATION OF THE SEYM OF LWÓW

1866	Administration of City of Cracow Reorganized
	Administration of Large Estates Regulated
	Self-Government of Communities Defined
1867	Language of Instruction in Schools Defined
1868	Restrictions on Sales of Landed Property Abolished
1873	Compulsory Church Tithes and other Duties Abolished
1875	Landowners' Monopoly on Alcohol Sales Abolished
1882	Building Code for Cities Established
1884	Regulation of Oil Industry Established
1885	Operation of Village Schools Improved
1889	Administration of Larger Cities Reorganized
	Building Code for Large Cities Established
1900	Provincial Statute Amended
1905	Land Use Rent Regulated
1907	Language of Business in Village Self Government Defined
1908	Provincial Statute Amended
1914	Provincial Statute Amended
	Voting Rules Changed

POLITICAL PERSONALITIES OF THE SEYM OF LWÓW

Stanisław M. Badeni (1850-1912)—Conservative politician of Galicia, member of the Provincial School Council and Deputy to the Seym of Galicia in Lwów; he was appointed member of the Austrian House of Peers in Vienna in 1891. From 1895 he served as the Speaker of the Seym of Galicia where he cosponsored the School Law of 1894, which equalized the financial burden of the support of schools and distributed it between the peasantry and the gentry. He was instrumental in the return of the Wawel Castle of Cracow to public use and initiated its restoration so that in time it became a national shrine.

Michał Bobrzyński (1849-1935)—Historian, parliamentarian, administrator; appointed professor of history of law at the University of Cracow in 1877 and elected a member of the Academy of Learning of Cracow in 1878. He entered politics of Galicia and became the leader of the Conservative Party in the Seym of Lwów, to which he was elected a Deputy in 1885. In the same year he became a member of the Austrian Council of State. In the years 1891-1901 he served as the president of the Education Council of Galicia and contributed to the expansion of the school system at all levels. Appointed Viceroy of Galicia, he served until 1913, and was responsible for the reform of the electoral system. He authored: *Polish Seyms in Jan Olbracht's and Alexander's Era* (1876); *History of Poland in Outline* (1879); *Rebirth of the Polish State in Outline* (1920-1925); and *From My Memoirs* (1957).

Jakub Bojko (1857-1943)—Peasant Party politician, one of the organizers of the peasants of Galicia; he was elected Deputy to the Seym of Lwów in 1895 and to the Austrian Parliament in 1897. Vice-chairman of the Peasant Party (SL) in 1895 and Chairman of the Polish Peasant Party (PSL) "Piast" in 1913, he served as Deputy Speaker of the 1919-1922 Seym of the Second Republic, and as Deputy Speaker of the Senate in 1922-27. Elected to the 1928 Seym on the government list, and to the Senate in 1930-35, he withdrew from politics in 1935. For many years he served as editor of *Friend of the People, Piast*, and wrote *Two Souls* (1904) and *Writings and Speeches* (1911).

Julian A. Dunajewski (1824-1907)—Conservative politician of Galicia; he was educated as an economist and statistician; he was made professor of the Law School of Bratislava in 1855, of the University of Lwów in 1860, and of the University of Cracow in 1861 and became a member of the Cracow Academy of Learning in 1871. Politically, he was an opponent of the 1863 uprising against Russia. Elected Deputy to the Galician Seym in Lwów in 1870 and to the Austrian parliament in 1873. He served as Minister of Treasury of Austria in 1880-1891 and supported the pro-Austrian orientation in Polish politics. He authored: *A Course in Political Economy* (1935).

Alexander Fredro (1793-1876)—Parliamentarian, playwright and poet; served in the army of the Duchy of Warsaw in 1809-15 and took part in Napoleon's expedition to Moscow in 1812. Between 1833 and 1842 he served as Deputy in the Galician Seym of the Estates. In 1848 he was nominated a member of the National Council of Lwów and in 1861 he was elected Deputy to the Seym of Lwów. He was a member of The Society of Friends of Learning from 1829 onwards and of the Cracow Academy of Learning from 1873. He was a prolific writer of comedies which enjoy unflagging popularity on the stage to the present day. His collected works were reissued in thirteen volumes (1955-71).

Agenor Gołuchowski (1812-1875)—Politician of Galicia and an Austrian statesman who from 1843 became active in the Galician Seym of the Estates and cooperated in the preparation of the statute abolishing serfdom in the province. Between 1859 and 1861 he served as Minister of the Interior in the Austrian government and introduced the use of Polish in schools and public offices in

Galicia. He served three times as Viceroy of Galicia, 1849-59, 1866-68, and 1871-75. In 1860 he was the author of the *October Diploma* outlining the plan for decentralization of the Austrian administration. During his second term he made first steps towards polonizing the administration of the province, and in his third term he promoted the foundation of the Academy of Learning of Cracow and the Lwów Polytechnic Institute.

Adam Gołuchowski (1855-1914)—Son of Viceroy Agenor Gołuchowski, graduate of the University of Lwów; was elected in 1885 as Deputy to the Austrian Council of State in which he served until 1897. Elected Deputy to the Seym of Lwów in 1895, he served until his death in 1914. As its Speaker between 1912 and 1914 he saw to the passage of the reformed electoral law.

Kazimierz Grocholski (1815-1888)—Politician of Galicia; he was one of the leaders of the conservative Deputies in the Seym of Lwów in which he served from 1861. Member of the Council of State in Vienna and for many years chairman of the Polish Circle of Galician Deputies to the parliament of Vienna. Politically he represented the group demanding autonomy for Galicia. As a minister for Galicia in the Austrian government he was credited with helping to establish the Academy of Learning of Cracow in 1871.

Eustachy Sanguszko (1842-1903)—Parliamentarian of Galicia; following service on the Tarnów County Council he was elected in 1873 a Deputy to both the Seym of Galicia in Lwów and the Austrian Council of State in Vienna. In 1879 he took a seat in the Austrian House of Peers. During his thirty years of service in the Seym of Galicia, he served as its Speaker in the years 1890-1895 and thereafter was appointed Viceroy of Galicia in 1895-98. Throughout the long years of public service he was instrumental in placing the finances of the province on a firm footing, and was credited with the passage of legislation setting up the Fund for the construction of railroads, regulation of rivers, expansion of the school system and assistance to small farmers. In 1890 the Cracow Agricultural Society elected him its president.

Leon Sapieha (1803-1878)—Political activist of Galicia; participated in the 1830 Uprising in the Congress Kingdom and after its collapse moved to Galicia where he became active in the Seym of the Estates. He demanded abolition of serfdom in Galicia and the introduction of Polish as the language of instruction in schools. When the Seym of Lwów was established he served as its first Speaker from 1861 until 1875. He served as chairman of the board of directors of numerous financial institutions, among them the Land Credit Society and the Galician Savings Bank. He founded the Agricultural School of Dublany. In 1856 he organized a corporation for the construction of the first railroad in Galicia from Cracow to Lwów, and himself financed the construction of its section between Dębica and Lwów.

Franciszek Smolka (1810-1899)—Liberal politician of Galicia, a lawyer by education; in the 1830s he participated in conspiratorial movements working for the independence of Poland. He was arrested in 1841 and sentenced to death in 1848 but was amnestied. In 1848 he assumed the leadership of the Polish national movement in Galicia. From 1861 he served as Deputy in the Seym of Lwów and from 1862 in the Parliament of Vienna. He favored the transformation of Austria into a federation of five autonomous states. He was Speaker of the Lower House of the Viennese Parliament twice: 1848-9 and 1881-93. He authored: *Peoples of Austria* (1848).

Jan Stapiński (1867-1946)—Activist in the peasant movement, coorganizer in 1895 of the Peasant Party in Galicia he became its leader. He served as Deputy to the Austrian Parliament in 1897-1900 and to the Seym of Galicia in 1901-18. He was the Chairman of the Polish Peasant Party in 1908-13 and the editor of peasant periodicals, among them *Friend of the People*. He was elected again to the Austrian Parliament in 1907-18; served as Deputy to the Seym of the Second Republic in 1919-22; was Chairman of the Peasant Union in 1924-26; Deputy in the Seym again in 1928-30; and after the coup d'état of 1926 he supported the Piłsudski group. He withdrew from political life in 1934.

Ludwik Wodzicki (1834-1894)—Parliamentarian and publisher, conservative political activist; one of the leaders of "Stańczyk, a political group, and coauthor of *Stańczyk's Portfolio*, published in 1869 as an ideological declaration of the conservatives of Galicia. He was elected Deputy to the Seym of Galicia in 1865 and also served as a Deputy to the Austrian Council of State in 1867. He was one of the founders and the editor of *Polish Review*, a cultural monthly published in Cracow in 1866-1914. He served as the Speaker of the Seym of Galicia in 1877-81.

Mikołaj Zyblikiewicz (1823-1887)—Galician politician and lawyer; elected Deputy to the Seym of Lwów in 1861 he demanded the use of Polish language in schools and in the administration. He became Deputy to the Council of State in Vienna and was a member of the Polish Circle there. In 1872 he became a member of the Academy of Learning of Cracow. He was mayor of the City of Cracow from 1874 to 1880. From 1881-86 he was Speaker of the Seym of Lwów and Chairman of its executive committee. He initiated new economic policy.

Stanisław Niezabitowski (1860-1941)—Parliamentarian and administrator. Elected deputy to the Seym of Lwów in 1895, served in that capacity until 1913. In 1914 was appointed Speaker of the last Seym of Lwów, holding that office until the Seym disbanded itself upon the creation of the national Seym in Warsaw in 1919. During Second World War was arrested by the Russians and deported to Kazakhstan for slave labor. Died in captivity.

CHAPTER VI

SECOND REPUBLIC: THE SEYM FAILS IN OPERATING THE EXECUTIVE

The close of the First World War saw the reemergence of Poland as an independent state. Between the years 1918-1945 the reunited state encompassed most of the ethnically Polish lands plus those parts of the former Grand Duchy of Lithuania which had large Polish settlements. The reconstituted state reverted to the republican form of government. Provincial legislatures were replaced by a national Seym in all provinces except Silesia and a Constitution modeled on that of the French Third Republic was adopted with an electoral law based on proportional representation. Suffrage became universal and women gained voting rights.

Most of the legislative efforts in this period were directed at developing a uniform system of laws out of diverse legislation passed in the period of partitions, at gaining formal recognition abroad for the reunited state, and at defending it against Russia. Extensive social legislation was passed by the Seym, land reform was set well on its way, and an appropriate financial structure was created to supply funds for its realization. There was a marked government investment in industry, intended to remedy the shortage of private investment capital.

In the political sphere much grief was caused by the unstabilizing effects of the proportional system of representation through its encouragement of fragmentation of parties. Constitutional domination of the executive branch by the legislature, in which no combination of parties was able to form a stable majority, led to a rapid turnover of cabinets. Peaceful constitutional reform proved impossible and a coup d'état took place, leading to a change in the Constitution aimed at separation and strengthening of the executive branch.

Fig. 93—Second Republic in the period 1923-1939

The extreme left in the Seym was dominated by the Soviet Union and, when the latter became unsure of its control of the Polish CP, the leading parliamentarians of the left were invited to Moscow and executed. An agreement between Hitler and Stalin to invade and partition Poland brought an end to the Second Republic and initiated the Second World War, when the Second Republic decided to resist, rather than yield, to Hitler's demands.

REUNIFICATION OF POLAND AND THE CONSTITUTION OF 1921

The process of restitution of legislative bodies in the Kingdom of Poland started on December 6, 1916 when the Regency Council appointed the Temporary Council of State with the objective of organizing and holding elections to the

Council of State. With Wacław Niemojewski as the Speaker, the Temporary Council sent on January 27, 1917, a message to President Wilson thanking him for his declaration of January 22 in which he supported the restoration of a united and independent Poland. President Wilson's declaration was eventually formalized as the thirteenth point in his statement of aims for the Versailles Peace Conference.

The Temporary Council of State took over a year to prepare the elections that were held on April 6, 1918. The first session of the Council of State took place in Warsaw on June 22, 1918 with 110 Deputies present. Franciszek Pułaski was elected Speaker. The period of legislation of the Council eventually lasted six weeks, but its legislative achievements were meager, reflecting perhaps its unrepresentative character. Of the 110 Deputies, 55 were elected by the local councils, 12 held their seats "ex officio," and 43 were nominated by the Regency Council. Politically, 41 were members of the Inter-Party Club and 48 represented the views of the Center, i.e., bourgeois interests. No representatives of the Socialists were present, as the Left boycotted the elections.

The Council of State is credited with initiating the organization of the Polish civil administration to replace the Russians who evacuated Warsaw, and with raising two regiments of the Army before the collapse of the Central Powers in November of that year. The nascent Polish administration proved invaluable to the formation of the Second Republic in the chaotic conditions of the collapse. Starting from nil, and later supplemented by administrators from Galicia, the civil service had an empty treasury at its disposal and a multitude of problems with which to deal, not the least of which was a severe food shortage in the country, caused by the demands of the occupying German and Austrian armies. On October 7, 1918 the Council of State was dissolved and the independence of Poland was declared by the Regency Council.

This crucial period offered an opportunity for the country to regain independence after the long and difficult period of Partitions. The circumstances of the moment, i.e., the collapse of Russia and the Central Powers, were insufficient in themselves to accomplish this, as the examples of Byelorussia and the Ukraine were to show. No less than a concerted effort was needed on the part of all politically active segments of society, and a degree of political maturity which would override the normal divisions of political viewpoint. The various political movements, described earlier, that arose independently in the course of the nineteenth century in the three zones of partitions, each contributed in its own way towards promoting the badly needed political maturity, in spite of the deep ideological differences that divided them on the issues of social policy. The only group that stood apart at this turning point in history of Poland was the left wing of the Social Democratic Party of Poland and Lithuania, led by Julian Marchlewski and Rosa Luxemburg, which vehemently opposed the independence movement and supported Lenin's internationalism. This stand isolated it from the mainstream of aspirations of the

Poles at the time and made it the instrument of future Soviet efforts to gain control of Poland.

Fig. 94—Seym building in Warsaw. The part shown was originally constructed as the Institute of the Gentry. It was used from 1919 as the meeting place of the Seym and the Senate of the Second Republic.

Over and above the political considerations, a focus for the independence efforts was needed in a person unequivocally identified in the public mind with an uncompromising pro-independence stance, who would provide leadership impartial enough to political divisions. Such focus was found in the person of Józef Ginet Piłsudski. What became known in other countries as the Armistice Day, November 11, 1918, in Poland became the Independence Day, and the start of a long struggle to defend that independence against enemies foreign and domestic. On that day the Regency Council yielded the reigns of government to Józef Piłsudski, on his release from internment in Germany. Piłsudski was the Commander of the Polish Legion organized in the early days of the First World War under Austrian auspices. Former antitsarist revolutionary and a charismatic personality, he achieved wide recognition for his pro-independence stand. As head of the government he immediately proceeded to organize the elections to the first national Seym since 1793. The country had as yet no fixed boundaries; the province of Greater Poland was still in German hands but had succeeded in convoking in December 1918 a Seym in Poznań; civil war raged between the Poles and the Ukrainians in the eastern part of Lesser Poland.

The elections to the first Seym of the Second Republic took place on January 26, 1919 in 31 electoral districts in the former Congress Kingdom and the district of Podlasie from which 230 Deputies were returned, and in 11 electoral districts in the western part of Lesser Poland which returned 72 Deputies. To represent the province of Greater Poland the 20 Deputies elected from that province to the German Parliament were coopted by the Seym. The same procedure was applied to the 26 Deputies elected earlier to the Austrian Parliament from the eastern part of Lesser Poland. From the Silesian district of Cieszyn, where the elections were prevented by the Czech invasion, the persons appearing on the joint candidate list were coopted by the Seym as Deputies. As the various territories came under Polish suzerainty elections were held: on April 25, 1919 in Greater Poland; June 15, 1919 in the district of Białystok and Podlasie, May 2, 1920 in Pomerania; and the Deputies formerly coopted yielded place to the new arrivals unless, of course, they themselves were reelected. Finally, on March 24, 1922 the 20 Deputies elected by the Seym of Wilno to represent Central Lithuania joined the Seym in Warsaw. Thus the Seym grew from 348 to 432 members. Once constituted, it proceeded to elect Wojciech Trąmpczyński, a former Deputy from Poznań to the German Parliament, as the Speaker of the Seym. The results of these elections are included in Table 51; the voter turnout in Poland is compared with other countries in Table 74, whereas its variation with time and region is given in Tables 72 and 73 in Chapter VIII.

Fig. 95—One of the early Seyms of the Second Republic shown in session. After 1929 the chamber shown above was used by the Senate and the Seym was moved to new quarters nearby.

The tasks faced by the Seym were monumental. Foremost was the necessity to consolidate the country and to assure its survival in the face of the belligerent forces of the Russian Revolution. There was a pressing need for a modern Constitution and an effective land reform to repair the social fabric damaged by earlier inadequate land grants to the peasants, decreed by the Austrian and the Russian governments at the abolition of serfdom. Economic recovery was aided by American food relief, organized by Herbert Hoover.

The political atmosphere in the country at large in the first decade of the Second Republic was that of a besieged state surrounded on all sides by enemies, the successor states of the Partitioning Powers. The borders on all sides were being contested, the loyalty of large national minorities was questionable, and a heated controversy over the political course to be taken by the resurrected state raged between political groups from different provinces. Poles who fought in the First World War on different sides often subconsciously carried the affiliations forced on them by earlier history into the political arena of the Second Republic. The fear for the safety of the newly restored state was combined with the fear of foreign interference and subversion.

Fig. 96 (Below, Left)—Wojciech Trąmpczyński (1860-1953), Speaker of the first Seym of the Second Republic.

Fig. 97 (Below, Right)—Edward Dubanowicz (1881-1943), Jurist and Parliamentarian. Principal editor of the Constitution of 1921.

Added to all these difficulties was the lack of parliamentary experience of the majority of Deputies in the first Seym. The only group with experience as a majority party, carrying the responsibility for an affirmative legislative program, were the former Deputies of the Seym of Lwów. They were now a minority in the Seym of the Second Republic. The second group in the Seym with parliamentary experience were the Poles who, before 1918, had been elected Deputies from the various provinces of Poland to the parliaments of the Partitioning Powers, where they constituted a minority, generally in opposition to the government. As a rule they carried this opposition attitude with them into the Seym of the Second Republic. Thus, in these early Seyms it was easy to find critics and difficult to find supporters for whatever policy was in need of implementation. In less stressful times the passage of time itself would have brought with it the rise in political responsibility. As it was, the Seym was in deep waters before it could swim properly.

The most urgent of its tasks, the question of defense, was tackled by the Seym by declaring a general draft into the army of five yearly contingents, and by placing the organization of that army in the hands of Józef Piłsudski. The officer and noncommissioned officer corps of his former Legion became the backbone of the armed forces of the Second Republic. Strengthened by trained Polish military personnel inherited from the armies of the former partitioning powers, the new army was able, in the course of the next two years of bloody war, to defend the country from a Russian take-over.

The problem of land reform was addressed in two laws passed by the Seym in 1919 and 1920, amended in 1925. The passage of the first of these laws at the height of the Polish-Soviet war, helped to remove the agrarian question from the list of issues which could have been used by the Soviets to gain favor with the landless peasants. The details of the land reform and its degree of success, as well as some unforeseen tragic consequences during the Second World War, are discussed under a separate heading.

The third of the major issues facing the Seym of 1919 was the development of the Constitution. From the start it became obvious that neither the Constitution of 1791 nor the Napoleonic Constitution of 1807, could be adapted to modern conditions. The Alexandrine Constitution of 1815 was too restrictive, as was the Constitution under which the Seym of the province of Greater Poland functioned. Until the First World War the Seym of Lwów operated on the basis of explicit recognition of the class structure, and this too was unacceptable to the egalitarian spirit of the times. Other models, or a blend of traditional Polish principles, had to be considered in the creation of a new Constitution. The urgency of the situation inveighed against the latter. In consequence, the Seym looked further afield for a model and its two main constitutional experts, Kazimierz Lutosławski and Edward Dubanowicz, came up in 1921 with a Constitution closely resembling that of the

French Third Republic. As practice was to show, it was an unfortunate choice, for this Constitution had built-in organic faults which produced unstable governments in France as well as in Poland. It gave the Seym complete control over the executive, while making the Seym practically immune to dissolution during one of its frequent deadlocks over executive policy issues. The deadlocks, in turn, were a result of a great diversity of political parties represented in the Seym, none of which had a clear majority. The process of consolidation of the major political streams was hampered rather than aided by the faulty Electoral Ordinanace introduced by the Constitution of 1921. The all-nation electoral districts combined with the principle of proportionality encouraged splinter groups in the Seym. The institutional arrangements based on the Constitution of 1921 are summarized in Table 50.

In spite of these shortcomings much useful legislation was passed, particularly in the area of reunification of the diverse legal and administrative systems inherited from the Partitioning Powers. Among the main items of business were the efforts to gain a formal recognition for the reunited State, its new borders, and the ratification of the resulting international treaties. Foremost among these was the negotiation of a Peace Treaty of Riga of 1921 with the Soviet Union, formalizing the reassertion of Poland's claim to independence and the end of the Polish-Soviet war of 1919-1920. In that war the Army commanded by Józef Piłsudski took the initiative and, by first launching an offensive into the Ukraine and then by checking the Soviet counter-offensive, thwarted the Soviet plans to bring the revolution to Central Europe and, in the process, to impose a Soviet sponsored government on Poland. The resulting military draw led to peace negotiations conducted on the Polish side by a multi-party Peace Commission made up of Deputies of the Seym. The border settlement followed in the main the border line between Poland and Russia ratified by the Seym of Grodno in 1793 after the Second Partition with minor modifications in the region of Pripet marshes in favor of Poland, to put the border at least thirty miles east of the only North-South railroad crossing the marshes. The treaty provided also for the repatriation of Poles evacuated to Russia during the First World War and the return of cultural and historical collections removed from Poland to Russia at various times.

Other important legislation of this period included the establishment of the state-sponsored health insurance scheme of 1920 and 1921 with contributory provisions, as well as the Unemployment Insurance Act of 1924. These two Acts, and the various additions and amendments to them voted in later years, went a long way towards satisfying some of the major political demands included in the election platforms of the parties of the left.

One of the many difficulties besetting the Second Republic in its early years was the chaotic situation in the North-East provinces. With a large proportion of Byelorussians in its population the area was selected as a target for subversion

274

directed from the Soviet Union. Armed raiding parties were being sent across the border to sow terror and to disorganize the administration in the hope of encouraging the inhabitants to revolt.

To cope with this situation the Seym authorized, in 1924, the replacement of border guards, working on foot and equipped only with side-arms, with the "Borderland Protection Corps" (KOP), with army-type command structure, equipped with machine guns, and including some mounted units. These units were able to challenge and give chase to the raiding parties crossing the border and did not hesitate to cross it in pursuit. This had a sobering effect on the Soviet government and the over-the-border raids ceased.

Coupled with the Soviet-organized raiding parties was a political effort to infiltrate Communists into the Byelorussian political parties and their Seym representation. Funding and direction from the Soviet Union were provided and a sizable political organization was developed which, though ostensibly independent, strictly followed Soviet direction. Counter-intelligence services eventually traced the route of the funds and contacts from Soviet agents to some of the Deputies of the Hromada Byelorussian Party in the Seym. The judicature requested the Speaker of the Seym to have their parliamentary immunity lifted and the Deputies in question placed at the disposal of the courts. This was done and the Deputies Bronisław Taraszkiewicz, Szymon Rak-Michajłowski, Paweł Wołoszyn, Piotr Miotła, as well as Feliks Hołowicz from the Independent Peasant Party were brought to trial in 1928; they were convicted and imprisoned. Subsequently, the Soviet Union offered to exchange some Catholic priests and Polish intelligence agents in its custody for these Deputies. The exchange took place, but the exchangees who accepted Stalin's invitation perished in the wave of terror that Stalin imposed on Russia in the Thirties.

The great diversity of political parties which appeared on the political scene at the inception of the Second Republic should not obscure the fact that there were basically only four main political streams of any consequence. These were the Polish Socialist Party, with Ignacy Daszyński, Mieczysław Niedziałkowski and Norbert Barlicki in the lead; the Peasant Party, with Wincenty Witos and Stanisław Thugutt leading its two wings; the National Democratic Party, with Roman Dmowski as its chief ideologue, Stanisław Stroński and Marian Seyda as its main activists; finally, the Christian Democratic Party led by Wojciech Korfanty. In addition, there were parties representing the Ukrainians, Byelorussians, Germans and Jews, the national minorities which constituted 31.1% of the population of the state.

In terms of electoral showing prior to the passage of the Constitution of 1935, the National Democratic Party was in the lead, winning 101 seats in the Seym of 1922 and 63 seats in 1930, by which time its name had been shortened to the National Party. It formed or participated in several governments of that period and its parliamentary representation included such able men as Stanisław Grabski and his brother Władysław. The latter, serving in the period 1923-25 as both Prime Minister and Minister of Treasury, contributed significantly to the economic stabilization of the newly reconstructed state. At other times the National Party served as the major opposition Party in the Seym.

The Peasant Party, although often split into competing groups, contributed significantly to the vigorous parliamentary life and had a major influence on legislation dealing with land reform and other economic matters. Its leading parliamentarian, Wincenty Witos, served several times as Prime Minister, including the crucial period of the Polish-Soviet War, when his parliamentary leadership was decisive in the formation of a united national effort opposing Russian take over.

The Communist Party (CP) emerged in its Polish, Ukrainian and Byelorussian branches and voted in the Seym as a block. At the height of its strength in the 1920's it could muster, together with various front organizations, 14 votes in a Seym of 444 Deputies. Racked by internal dissentions and under suspicion of not following the Moscow line closely enough, the CP of Poland was dissolved by Stalin in 1938. Its leaders were invited to Moscow and shot there. Among those executed were the following former Deputies: Jerzy Czeszejko-Sochacki, Adolf Warszawski, Tadeusz Dąbal, Stefan Królikowski, plus sixteen members of the Central Committee and over 200 members of the Polish Section of the Communist International (Comintern). One Bolesław Bierut served at this time as investigative judge in the special section of NKVD and carried out Stalin's directives. After the Second World War he was rewarded for his services by Stalin with the post of the President of Poland in the Soviet-sponsored Polish People's Republic.

TABLE 50—FIRST CONSTITUTION OF THE SECOND REPUBLIC—A SYNOPSIS

(Voted by the Seym, March 21, 1921, Amended August 2, 1926)

The Executive Branch of the Government was headed by a President, elected for a term of seven years by the National Assembly (Seym and Senate in joint session). He was not responsible to the Seym for his legal actions, except for high treason, violation of Constitution or penal offenses. Each of the above formed grounds for impeachment. Impeachment of the President required the vote of a three-fifth majority of Deputies with at least one-half of their total number voting.

The President appointed and dismissed the Prime Minister and the ministers, but the cabinet and each of the ministers was obliged to resign on a simple vote of non-confidence from the Seym. The President could not dissolve the Seym or the Senate except with a two-thirds consent of at least half the Deputies or three-fifths of the total number of Senators. The amendment of 1926 added to the powers of the President the right to dissolve the Seym and call for new elections.

TABLE 50 (CONTINUED)—FIRST CONSTITUTION OF THE SECOND
REPUBLIC—A SYNOPSIS

The Legislative Branch of the Government consisted of a Seym of 444
Deputies and a Senate of 111 Senators, both elected for a term of five years. The
Seym's area of competence included the budget and imposition of taxes and
customs duties, extension of state loans, authorizations for sale of state real estate
property, creation of monopolies, control over the issue of currency, ratification of
treaties, decisions on the size of the army complement. The Deputies could
question the ministers about their conduct and that of their subordinates in
execution of their duties and could force their dismissal by a simple nonconfidence
vote. The legislative initiative was in the hands of Deputies and members of the
cabinet. In the event of the President's death or resignation, the Speaker of the
Seym acted as President pro tempore.

The Electoral Ordinance provided voting rights for both sexes in an electoral
system based on the d'Hondt method. Minimum age for candidacy to the Seym
was twenty-five years and for electing Deputies twenty-one. For the Senate the two
ages were forty and thirty, respectively. The voting was by an equal, secret,
universal, direct and proportional ballot. The Deputies were given immunity from
arrest during their term of office.

The Judiciary Branch of the Government was composed of judges appointed
by the President of the Republic, except for Justices of Peace who were elected.
They were not recallable or subject to arrest or prosecution except by competent
courts. Their sentences could not be overridden by either an executive or a
legislative decision.

The examination of validity of laws passed by the Seym was not in the area of
competence of the courts but was left to the Seym itself.

Trial by jury was required in cases involving severe penalties and in political cases.

The Bill of Rights and Duties of the citizens was included in thirty-eight
Articles of Section V of the Constitution. Protection of life, personal freedom and
property was guaranteed; freedom of speech, secrecy of correspondence and
unhindered exercise of religion were also guaranteed.

THE SEYM COPES WITH AN UNWORKABLE CONSTITUTION

The presence of a large number of parties in the Seym with frequent splits and
maneuvering for office made Seym control over the executive highly erratic. This
resulted in frequent changes of government, which in turn brought in ministers
who had little chance to familiarize themselves with the job before being turned
out of office by the Seym. The Seym, concentrating on the supervision of the

government, fell behind in legislative work and had continuous trouble with passing the budget on time. The resulting delay in payments of salaries and government bills added to the confusion. Eventually, the continuing paralysis of the executive branch reached the proportions of a constitutional crisis.

The failings of the Constitution and the election ordinance magnified each other. Specifically, the electoral ordinance was based on the so-called "five-adjective" principle. In accordance with it the election of Deputies to the Seyms was to be: 1) universal—all adults, regardless of sex or national origin, would have the right to vote; 2) secret—the voter's choice registered on the ballot card would not be revealed until the vote counting time; 3) equal—one vote per citizen; 4) direct—no electoral college would be interposed between the elector and the elected, at least in voting for Deputies; the President would be elected indirectly; and 5) proportional—the total number of seats in the Seym would be apportioned between the contending parties in proportion to the number of votes cast for them. To apply this last principle the electoral wards were made large and multi-seat, to allow for the election of an assortment of Deputies from each ward that would be representative of the spectrum of political opinion in that ward. That is, instead of candidates from the various parties contending for one seat in each ward, as in England or the United States, the parties contended for several seats and then apportioned them to candidates of each party in accordance with the percentage of the votes received. If the ward was large enough even the smallest party could elect a Seym Deputy. To account for fractional Deputies falling to a ward, national catch-all lists were created, for party-designated Deputies. It was this last pro-vision, the proportionality rule, that contributed more than anything else to the downfall of the Constitution of 1921.

One consequence of this system was to encourage, rather than inhibit, the formation of numerous political parties. These, in fact, numbered as many as 31, and none was able to capture an absolute majority in the Seym. To make matters worse, the Constitution did not separate the executive from the legislative branch but, instead, gave the legislature the right to dismiss any minister by a simple majority vote. No consequences for such dismissal were attached to the Deputies themselves, such as precipitating an election which would have given the electorate a chance to pass judgement on the antics of the Seym. The majority needed for a minister's removal could be obtained through a fleeting combination of Deputies from various parties, and a rapid turnover of governments resulted; 14 governments fell between November 1918 and May 1926. Since ministers were usually appointed from among the Deputies, it seemed as if it were the ambition of each Deputy to become a minister at least once. Should the Seym be unable to form a government, the President of the Republic had no effective power to dissolve the Seym and put the matter in the hands of the electorate. The total effect of this constitutional arrangement was an almost complete crippling of the executive branch.

The unworkability of this arrangement became evident to Piłsudski, even before it was put into operation, and he refused to run for the Presidency in 1922, saying that he was not interested in an office with purely ceremonial duties. Thereupon, the National Assembly (Seym and Senate in joint session) elected Gabriel Narutowicz, a friend and associate of Piłsudski to the Presidency. A few days later, Narutowicz was assassinated by a political extremist. Maciej Rataj, the Speaker of the Seym became President-pro-tempore. A week later the National Assembly elected Stanisław Wojciechowski President of the Republic.

Fig. 98—Maciej Rataj (1884-1940), Speaker of the Seym of the Second Republic. Served twice as a pro-tempore head of State. Executed by the Germans during the Second World War.

The political events of the following five years fully confirmed Piłsudski's worst fears. The relations between the Seym and the executive branch of the government, under the provisions of the Constitution of 1921, were such that it was possible, and indeed practiced all the time, for the party leaders in the Seym to use the threat of removal of ministers from office to force on them the appointment of political favorites, not only to positions in the administration, but also in the companies under control of a given Ministry. As increased government participation in the management of finance, industry and communications was forced on the Republic by the economic crisis and the undercapitalization of the private sector of the economy, the abuses of politization of these sectors grew in importance. It was evident that under this arrangement the hapless body of the Republic was viewed as a big cake to be constantly redivided in accordance with the fleeting combination of political forces in the Seym. The spectacle had a highly demoralizing effect on the public who grew cynical about the ways and means of politics.

There were two ways to stop this: either remove the Ministries from under the direct control of the Seym, or to remove the various state-controlled enterprises from the control of the Ministries by creating independent agencies on the present-day American model. Eventually, the first of these courses of action was taken. It required a change in the Constitution, however, and the Seym was deadlocked and unable to support any initiative of constitutional reform.

LEGISLATURE AND THE EXECUTIVE SEPARATED BY FORCE

During Wojciechowski's presidency the unworkability of the Constitution became increasingly apparent, and demands for its reform started to gain strength. Of immediate concern was the difficulty for the Seym to handle the day-to-day business and its inability to reform its rules. Long range interest pointed to the need to separate the legislative and the executive branches of government. It fell to Józef Piłsudski to cut the Gordian knot.

After the election of Wojciechowski, Piłsudski retired from the army and active political life and devoted his time to writing, but the rise in political acrimony and the wallowing of the ship of state in stormy waters without effective executive guidance, plus the demands of his former army comrades that he supply the leadership for reform, finally goaded him into staging a coup d'état in May 1926. After several days of fighting in Warsaw, the government and President Wojcie-chowski resigned. The National Assembly elected Ignacy Mościcki President, and a new government was installed, at a price of 371 lives lost in street fighting.

The coup had a sobering effect on the Seym and an amendment to the Constitution of 1921 was proposed and passed on July 22, 1926 by a vote of 246 to 95; the remaining Deputies abstained. The amendment gave the President the right to dissolve the Seym when it was deadlocked and call for new elections. The maximum interval allowed between the dissolution of the Seym and the next elections was set at nine months. A maximum of five months was allowed for the debate on the budget; should it fail to pass in that time, the preceding budget was made automatically valid.

Following the coup d'etat, the country was governed by a close-knit group of followers of Piłsudski. Their past credit included the organization of the army that resisted the attempted Soviet takeover in 1920. Their aims after the coup included a more substantial reform of the unworkable Constitution, and the elimination of corruption among some of the Deputies who used the legislative immunity for their private gain.

In the Seym the governing reform group had the largest following among the Deputies of the Socialist Party. Many of its senior leaders shared with Piłsudski a common revolutionary past and were willing to overlook the nonconstitutionality of some of his moves. But the Socialists were in a minority, and further constitutional reform required a much broader base to overcome the parliamentary deadlocks. The governing group, however, was unable to organize either a political party with the reform program as its main platform or to rally the existing parties to its cause. Instead, in 1927, a Non-Party Block of Cooperation (BBWR) was formed in the hope of attracting individual Deputies to the reform program advocated by the government. This was a sort of ideological predecessor to the French RFP movement organized by Charles de Gaulle after the Second World War.

The first elections after the coup d'état were held in 1928 and Ignacy Daszyński was elected Speaker of the Seym. He had become a socialist in the 1880s and had entered politics via the parties of Galicia. With the emergence of an independent Poland he was elected Deputy to the Seym in 1919.

From 1926 until 1930, when poor health forced his withdrawal from politics, he was an effective supporter in the Seym of the changes brought about by the coup d'état of 1926.

In 1930 the Seym went into one of its traditional deadlocks and the President, using his newly approved powers, dissolved it.

Fig. 99—*Ignacy Daszyński (1866-1936), Socialist politician from Galicia, Speaker of the 1928-30 Seym of the Second Republic.*

Fig. 100—*A view of the interior of the new Seym Chamber showing the Seym in session. The semi-circular chamber was constructed in the years 1925-29 to the designs of Kazimierz Skórewicz (1866-1950). When the Seym moved here, its old chamber was taken over by the Senate.*

Had the constitutional reform stopped at the amendment of 1926 and had this been supplemented by the abolition of the proportionality feature of the electoral law, the political parties would probably have accepted the situation, for the need for reform of political institutions was widely felt. As it was, the attempts to woo away individual Deputies to BBWR and the fear of losing the political leverage given to the parties by the patronage structure, set off a violent reaction. A wave of protest strikes, mass meetings, and violent demonstrations was staged by Center-Left opposition, the chief losers in the reform.

At this point the leaders of the demonstrations were arrested by the government, while they were not covered by parliamentary immunity in the period between the dissolution of the Seym and the election of the next one. They were imprisoned at Brześć and brought to trial in Warsaw charged with an attempt to stage a coup d'état (sic!). The trials lasted from October 1931 to January 1932. Among the defendants were the former Deputies Kazimierz Bagiński, Norbert Barlicki, Adam Ciołkosz, Stanisław Dubois, Władysław Kiernik, Herman Liberman, Mieczysław Mastek, Adam Pragier, Józef Putek, Adolf Sawicki, and Wincenty Witos.

All but one of the defendants were found guilty and given prison sentences varying in length from one and a half to three years. After the trial most of them fled the country rather than serve the sentence. Wincenty Witos, the leader of the Peasant Party, settled in Czechoslovakia. On the eve of the Second World War most of them returned to Poland and were pardoned after a few symbolic days in prison.

The election held after the arrests, in November of 1930, gave the coalition of the Conservatives and the Non-Party Block of cooperation a slight edge (247 out of 444 Deputies) in the Seym.

Kazimierz Świtalski was elected Speaker and served in that capacity until 1935.

With this slim majority the government faced the depth of the Depression, then sweeping Europe, and the rise of Hitlerism in Germany. Tightly sandwiched between militant Communism and Hitlerism, both more than willing to invest money and people in subversion, the government of Poland attempted the difficult task of steering a middle course. When the Ukrainian nationalists in East Galicia, financed and supplied with weapons by Germany, staged a wave of terrorist actions in 1934, including the assassination of the Minister of the Interior, Bronisław Pieracki, the government responded by establishing a detention camp for them at Bereza-Kartuska. During its existence, between 1934 and 1939, its population varied between 300 and 400 inmates and consisted of Ukrainian extremists, an assortment of Communist propagandists, and members of the pro-nazi Falanga group. The period of detention was normally three months, but there were cases of extension. Since the detentions were carried out on the orders of an investigative judge and were outside the regular court procedures, a wave of protests was set off by political parties.

Fig. 101—Wincenty Witos (1874-1945), son of an ex-serf, Deputy to the Seym of Galicia 1908-14, Deputy to the Seym of the Second Republic and three times Prime Minister.

THE CONSTITUTION OF 1935 AND ITS AFTERMATH

Although the amendment of 1926 improved somewhat the operation of the Seym, the political spoils system still remained and the faulty electoral system continued to fragment Seym representation. Proposals for constitutional reform were brought before the Seym but were usually debated to death. The situation dragged on for seven years and it was becoming evident that the benefactors of the political spoils system in the Seym would not yield them, nor provide the executive branch with more powers to handle the difficult problems dominating the political scene in the late 1920s and the mid-1930s. Even though there were four proposals submitted to the Constitutional Committee by the Center, Left and Right groupings in the Seym, none of them commanded the majority of votes needed to pass the amendments satisfying their respective political line and the deadlock prevented compromise proposals reaching the floor. The situation changed after the elections in 1930 and the reactivation of the Constitutional Committee, which now included Stanisław Car, Walery Sławek, Bohdan Podoski, Stefan Mękarski, and S. Mackiewicz. The Non-Party Block of Cooperation submitted to the Seym a constitutional proposal on March 3, 1931. The opposition rejected it and the Block did not have the qualified majority needed to vote it. The operations of the Constitutional Committee of the Seym were boycotted by the opposition, and its Deputies walked out whenever another proposal came up in the Chamber. To vote a new Constitution 296 votes were required, if all Deputies were present. The Constitution could be amended by a two-thirds vote with at least half the Deputies present. The reform faction (BBWR) had 246 Deputies in its ranks at the time. The amendment route offered an opening. The Reform Group decided to turn this to their advantage. On January 26, 1934 Stanisław Car submitted to the Seym a progress report on the work so far accomplished by the Constitutional Committee in the form of 63 "theses." The Opposition declared disinterest in further constitutional reform and all but one of the Opposition Deputies left the Chamber of the Seym, missing the fact that in their entirety the 63 articles formed a complete draft of the reformed Constitution. Whereupon, Deputy Stanisław Car moved that the Deputies present, who happened to constitute a quorum, approve the 63 theses as a constitutional amendment. Stanisław Stroński, the sole opposition Deputy present, placed an objection pointing out that Car's motion is unconstitutional since the debate on the constitutional proposal was not entered in the Calendar of Debates at least fifteen days in advance and requested by at least one quarter of the Deputies, as specified in the Rules of Procedure. In response, a counterproposal was made for modifying the Rules of Procedure. It was put to a vote and approved. Next, the Draft Constitution was given second and third readings, passed with the statutory two-thirds majority, with more than half of the Deputies present, and sent to the Senate for approval.

This was a small coup d'état, strongly reminiscent of 1791, when the Reform faction took advantage of the absence of the Opposition during the Easter recess and held an emergency session. At this point it is perhaps instructive to review the issue at hand. The two contending factions in the Seym both claimed to be motivated in the constitutional controversy by patriotism and to have the best interest of the citizens at heart. The situation was more than superficially similar to the one that faced the Reform Seym of 1788-92, when the retention of maximum powers of the Seym to block legislation (liberum veto) was favored by one faction, whereas limited powers, combined with strengthening the executive branch, were favored by the reform group. Prior to 1791, the Constitution required detailed legislative approval of each action of the Executive and allowed the Seym to paralyze the executive by the refusal to pass laws. The Seyms under the Constitution of 1921 achieved the same ends by day-to-day questioning and frequent dismissal of Ministers.

Fig. 102—Stanisław Car (1882-1938), coauthor of the Constitution of 1935, Seym Deputy 1930-35, Speaker of the Seym 1935-38.

On the constitutional plane the positions were as follows: the Opposition (Center-Left coalition) was in favor of retaining maximum powers for the Seym and a parliamentary type of Executive on the English model, whereby the Seym could make or break the Government. It stopped short of making the Deputies responsible to the electorate for these actions through an immediate election after the fall of each government; the Reform faction (the Non-Party Block of Cooperation) favored the presidential type of Executive on the American model with the Government, including the Prime Minister, appointed by the President and the Ministers responsible to him. It stopped short of the American model in that the President was to be elected by the Seym and the Senate combined. This left the Presidency without the popular mandate derived from direct election.

With the constitutional proposal in the Senate, the Opposition marshalled its forces. The proposal was debated thoroughly in the Senate for a year by the government and the opposition Senators; amendments were made to it; and after an approval by 74 to 24 votes it was returned to the Seym.

The supporters of the new Constitution worked with a sense of urgency forced on them by the failing health of Piłsudski, hoping to achieve its passage before a terminal illness took him away.

The Seym debate on the Senate's amendments took place on March 23, 1935, 260 Deputies voting for their acceptance, 139 voting against. Although within the 11/20 majority needed to approve the Senate amendments, the adequacy of this rule in this particular context has been questioned ever since.

On May 12, 1935 Piłsudski died and the Constitution so strongly influenced by his thinking was put to the test of life.

According to the new Constitution, the Seym membership was reduced to 208 Deputies elected from 104 electoral districts under a four-adjective method of a free, equal, direct, and secret ballot. The new electoral ordinance, specified by the law of July 8, 1935, removed the proportionality feature of the Constitution of 1921, and also disposed of nationwide election quotas. Originally added to the Constitution of 1921 to assure the election of known political figures who were unsure of obtaining enough votes in any one electoral district, the feature was the source of many abuses. With nationwide quotas about 208 of the seats in the Seym were made available for distribution by each party to its trusted people, the absolute number being proportional to the vote received by the given party. These favored individuals could not be voted out of the Seym, for the voter did not vote for them directly but through the party list. This feature in a short time provided the Seym with a standard set of party stalwarts, immune to election defeat, save in a total party disaster, and whose only worry was to remain in good graces with the party of their choice. The new law eliminated this patronage, and restored to the electorate the right to elect all Deputies by name, instead of just part of them.

The introduction of two-mandate electoral districts and the reduction of seats in the Seym from 444 to 208 was intended to rid the Seym of all the deadwood. Two-mandate electoral districts in regions with nationally mixed population, say Polish and Ukrainian, gave the electorate a chance to elect one Deputy of each nationality. Though much criticized by the parties, the new electoral ordinance gave them the chance to shed some of the odium attached to their previous mode of operation.

The first Seym elected on the basis of the Constitution of 1935 met for its opening session on November 5, 1935. Stanisław Car, one of the authors of this Constitution, was elected Speaker of the Chamber of Deputies. A quote from his opening speech deserves attention, for it summarizes the rationale behind some of the provisions of the new Constitution:

> The Seym is a prime legislative body and is equipped with broad powers for the exercise of checks over the activities of the Executive, but its competence is bound within these limits. The executive functions of the government of the State do not belong to it.
>
> Our own and foreign experience indicates that attempts of the legislature to exercise the executive functions have ruinous consequences for the course of affairs of the State, and may even weigh on its fate, bringing no credit or glory to the Seym, since a numerous and multi-headed body does not possess the characteristics required for the exercise of the executive functions, and cannot be the center of decisions made quickly, efficiently and firmly.

For this reason, the Seyms from the period of Seymocracy, in spite of their great ambitions, did not command respect. In his *Remarks on the Government of Poland*, Rousseau expressed this point forcefully by observing with regard to the old Seyms, that although nobody controlled them, nobody obeyed their decisions either.

It is obvious from these remarks that the history of the earlier failures of the legislative machinery of the state was very much on the minds of the framers of the new Constitution. Nevertheless, they chose to go back to the Seym of the First Republic and borrow some of its features. Such was, for instance, the partial return to the appointive Senate, and the specification of two-mandate electoral districts. On the other hand, by introducing the separation of powers and removing the principle of proportional representation and the all-state electoral lists, the Constitution went a good way towards reestablishing a working government structure.

The weakest link in the new Constitution turned out to be the modified electoral ordinance, which took away from the traditional parties the power of selecting the candidates. Under the new electoral law the candidates were selected by district electoral assemblies which were dominated by representatives of the government, the communal or territorial institutions, and professional organizations. The number of sponsors required now to put forward a candidate was increased from 50 to 500. This system gave the government an opportunity to manipulate in its favor the selection of candidates.

In the second half of the last decade in the life of the Second Republic and after the adoption of the Constitution of 1935, the major political parties felt they had lost their main instrument of affecting the day-to-day operations of the government due to the principle of separation of powers of the executive and the legislative branches of the government.

All of these moves combined with the Brześć trial of the political leaders of the Center-Left coalition, completely antagonized the major political parties and they countered the government moves by ordering their supporters to boycott the elections of 1935 and 1938.

The boycott was not entirely successful, but it was sufficient to distort the composition of the Seym to the point where it did not reflect the political profile of the country. In the country as a whole 46.5% of the electorate voted, compared to 67.9% in 1922 and 78.3% in 1928. However, by the time the elections of 1938 were held, the turnout rose again to 67% of the electorate. By then the supporters of the government ran under a different banner, for in 1937 the BBWR was replaced by the Camp of National Unity (OZN). In November 1938 it won 161 out of the 208 seats in the Seym and all elective seats in the Senate.

The major political parties, having removed themselves from the Seym through boycott, retained their organization and strength intact throughout the country, and they were able to propagandize, win local elections, and organize strikes and demonstrations.

Fig. 103—Walery Sławek (1879-1939), Deputy to the Seyms of 1928-38, Prime Minister in 1930, 31, 35. Coauthor of the Constitution of 1935, Speaker of the Seym of 1938.

The municipal elections of December 1938 showed the Socialists (PPS and the Jewish Bund) to be the leader with 55% of the vote in the city of Łódź, 43% in Warsaw, and 35% in Cracow. OZN received between 13 and 39% of the vote in the cities of Warsaw, Cracow, Łódź, and Poznań, a proportion reflecting its actual strength. The National Party won 74% of the vote in Poznań, its stronghold. Even though these municipal results give no indication of the strength of the Peasant Party, which did not run in the municipal elections, it was obvious that the political opinion of the country was dominated by the Peasant and the Socialist Parties, both outside the pro-government camp.

Within the government camp the Hamlet-like figure of Walery Sławek stands out. An associate of Piłsudski from his earliest revolutionary days, and an activist in the secret organization working for rebuilding of the State, he served as a Seym Deputy from 1928 to 1938, and was one of the principal authors of the Constitution of 1935. Though one of the founders of BBWR, he became increasingly critical of it, eventually dissolving it. Under his guidance, a liberal election ordinance for municipal self-government was passed and gained acceptance of the opposition parties. When OZN was formed, he and his supporters in the Seym worked against it, attempting to reverse the drift towards an authoritarian government. After the death of Stanisław Car, Sławek was elected Speaker of the House on June 22, 1938 by 114 votes to 62. His political following outside the Seym was strongest among the left-wing opposition, and he took it upon himself to act as its spokesman in the Seym. Sławek's activities in the Seym alarmed the President sufficiently to disolve it on September 22, 1938 and call for new elections. In the last elections of the Second Republic held on November 6, 1938, Sławek was not reelected and four months later committed suicide. He was succeeded as Speaker of the Seym by Wacław Makowski, who served from the November 1938 elections until the German-Soviet invasion of the country in September of 1939.

TABLE 51—POLITICAL DISTRIBUTION OF SEYMS OF THE SECOND REPUBLIC

	Number of Deputies Returned in the Election of					
Party	1/26 1919	11/5 1922	3/4 1928	11/16 1930	9/8 1935	11/6 1938
Piłsudski Block	...	...	135	247	153	
Conservative	44	19				166
National Democrats	72	101	37	63	... (a)	
Christian Democrats	31	41	61	30	... (a)	
National Labor	25	18				
Middle Class	63	5	...	...	...	...
Peasant Piast		53				
Peasants' Total	90		41	41	... (a)	
Peasants' Union		33				
Peasant Wyzwolenie	24	26				
Socialist	34	41	64	21	... (a)	
Communist (b)	2	17	7	...	...	
Minority						
Jewish (c)	16	35	13	7	6	5
Ukrainian	...	21	43	20	19	19
Byelorussian	...	7	6	1	...	
German	2	17	19	5	...	
Small Parties,						
Independents	29	19	18	9	30	18
Total Deputies						
Elected	432	444	444	444	208(d)	208
Total Votes Cast(M)	5.0	8.8	11.3	11.8	7.6	11.8
Electorate (Million)	..(e)	13.0	15.0	15.8	16.3	17.6

a) Boycotted the elections.

b) Polish, Ukrainian and Byelorussian. Polish CP was disbanded by Stalin in 1938, its leaders invited to Russia and shot.

c) Minority Parties only. Other Jewish Deputies ran on various party tickets.

d) Constitution of 1935 reduced the number of Deputies to 208.

e) Held during Polish-Soviet war, eastern boundary not yet defined.

In retrospect, it is interesting to note that many of the constitutional problems connected with the unworkability of the Constitution of 1921 can be traced back to the unworkability of its model, the Constitution of the Third French Republic. That Constitution was revived after the Second World War in the Fourth French Republic and found again to be unworkable. Charles de Gaulle, who overthrew that Constitution and succeeded in replacing it with one strengthening the executive branch, spent the years 1920-21 in Poland teaching at the Staff Officers' College in Warsaw. There, he was exposed to Piłsudski's criticism of the French Constitution and may have been influenced to change it on the model of the Polish Constitution of 1935.

THE SENATE IN THE SECOND REPUBLIC

The Constitution of the Second Republic passed on March 17, 1921 revived the institution of the Senate but made it a fully elective body, thus breaking with the tradition of the First Republic, the Duchy of Warsaw, and the Congress Kingdom of Poland where the Senate was fully appointive. The 111 Senators were to be elected by a universal, equal, secret, and proportional suffrage and elections to the Senate were to be held one week after the elections to the Seym. The Senate would then elect its own Speaker. The dissolution of the Seym and the Senate required the assent of three-fifths of the total of 111 Senators in the presence of at least half of the 444 Deputies. In practice, such majority could never be obtained. Together with the Seym, the Senate made up the National Assembly which elected the President of the Republic. In addition, an affirmative vote of the Senate was required on all bills submitted by the Seym before they could become law.

The amendments to the Constitution voted on August 2, 1926 left the powers of the Senate virtually unchanged, except for the power to dissolve both chambers before term which was now vested in the President. Lack of action within five months on the part of the Seym or the Senate on the budget submitted by the government would give the budget proposal the force of law. As it turned out the Senate played an important role in the 1935 constitutional debate when the Seym sidestepped the issue. After the passage of that Constitution the character of the Senate changed more significantly. The number of Senators was reduced from 111 to 96, of which 64 were to be elected by an electorate limited to members of local legislative councils, university graduates and holders of high decorations. The President was given the power to appoint the remaining 32 Senators. Furthermore, in case of death of the President of the Republic, the Speaker of the Senate became President-pro-tempore, thus reverting to the practice of the First Republic, when the senior Senator became King-pro-tempore in the event of royal death. These changes in the way in which the Senate was constituted made it look more like the Senate of the First Republic, a place to collect men of distinction, and a refuge for "elder statesmen." The partly-appointive feature gave the President a chance to give better representation to national minorities and other groups in the state deemed underrepresented. Table 53 lists the composition of the Senate in the Second Republic. During this period the seat of the Speaker of the Senate was held by five men, most with previous service in the Seym (see Table 52).

Fig. 104—Aleksander Prystor (1874-1941), A socialist revolutionary in Tsarist times. Deputy to the Seym of the Second Republic, Senator, and the Speaker of the Senate, 1935-38. Died of dysentery in a Soviet prison in Oriel, Russia.

TABLE 52—SPEAKERS OF THE SENATE OF THE SECOND REPUBLIC

Wojciech Trąmpczyński	1922-1928
Julian Szymański	1928-1930
Władysław Raczkiewicz*	1930-1935
Aleksander Prystor**	1935-1938
Bogusław Miedziński	1938-1939

*Served as the President of Poland in exile in England during the Second World War.
**Deported to Russia during the Second World War, he died in a Russian prison in Oriel in 1941.

When the Polish People's Republic was established at the close of the Second World War, a referendum was held on June 30, 1946, and one of the questions asked of the electorate was, "Are you in favor of abolishing the Senate?" The majority voted in favor and the Senate was abolished. There were allegations, however, that gross falsification of results on this and other questions asked in the referendum took place. This topic is discussed elsewhere in the text.

TABLE 53—POLITICAL DISTRIBUTION IN THE SENATE OF THE SECOND REPUBLIC

	Senators Returned in the Election of				
	11/12	3/11	11/23	9/15	11/13
Party	1922	1928	1930	1935	1938
Piłsudski Block*	...	49	75	61	59
Right	49	16	12	...	
Center	...		17	...	...
Left and Communist	36	20	...	...	
National Minorities	26	24	7	12	10
Independents	...	...	...	23	27
Total Senators	111	111	111	96**	96
Total Voters (Mil.)	5.6	6.4	6.8	0.2+	0.2+
Electorate (Million)	9.0	9.5	10.9	0.3	0.3

+Membership of county Seymiks and social organizations, choosing 2577 and 3032 electors, respectively,

*BBWR, OZN after 1938

**Reduced to 96 by the Constitution of 1935

PROVINCIAL SEYMS IN THE SECOND REPUBLIC

During the life of the Second Republic two provincial Seyms were in existence. Because of the limited area they represented they should properly be classified as General Seymiks, even though the word 'Seym' appeared in their title.

The first of these Seyms was the short-lived Seym of Central Lithuania, formed in 1921 at the close of the Polish-Soviet War when Wilno was reoccupied by the Polish troops under General L. Żeligowski. The troops were native to the region, strongly favored the restoration of the union with Poland, and were in opposition to the Lithuanian government of Kovno. Żeligowski claimed to be acting without orders and proceeded to set up an independent state under the name of Central

Lithuania with the capital in the city of Wilno. This he was able to do in spite of military resistance on the part of the troops of the Kovno government.

On November 30, 1921 the Żeligowski government issued a call for elections on the territory under its control, which encompassed an area of approximatey 15,000 square miles and a population of about one million. The elections were held on January 8, 1922 with the participation of 64.4% of the electorate; ethnic Lithuanians and, in some sectors Byelorussians and Jews, abstained. The Seym thus elected sat in Wilno from January to March of 1922 under Speaker Antoni Łokuciewski. In the Seym, the faction favoring the continuation of the union with Poland numbered 69 out of the total of 101 Deputies. On February 20, 1922 the Wilno Seym voted for the union and then proceeded to elect twenty Deputies to represent the province in the National Seym in Warsaw. They took their seats there on March 2, 1922 and the Wilno Seym disbanded.

The other provincial Seym of the Second Republic was longer lived. It was formed in 1920 when the National Assembly (Seym and Senate combined) passed on July 15, 1920 the Organic Statute for Silesia. Formerly, the only parts of Silesia to send Deputies to the Seym of the First Republic were the Duchies of Oświęcim[*] and Zator. The part of Silesia which was returned under Polish suzerainty after 600 years' absence had just emerged from two uprisings against German rule, in 1919 and 1920. It had a mixed Polish-German population and was hotly contested by both countries on account of its rich coal deposits and its highly developed industrial district.

To decide the fate of the disputed area a plebiscite was held there under the auspices of the League of Nations on March 20, 1920. The irregularities in the plebiscite and the small award to Poland set off another uprising in 1921, after which the territory awarded to Poland was enlarged. This area became the palatinate of Silesia.

To satisfy the demands of the German minority living within its borders, the palatinate of Silesia was guaranteed autonomy within Poland and was given a provincial Seym, which sat at Katowice throughout the years 1920-39. In the first elections, held on September 3, 1920, 48 Deputies were elected and the Seym met with Konstanty Wolny of the Christian Democratic Party as the Speaker. After the elections of 1935, he was replaced in the Speaker's chair by Karol Grzesik.

In the elections of October 24, 1922 the electorate numbered 527,228 of which 388,769 or 73.7% voted. The votes were divided between Germans and Poles as follows: 70.1% Poles, 26.8% Germans.

---

[*] Oświęcim became notorious during the Second World War, when the Germans built on its territory the Auschwitz extermination camp. About four million people were gassed to death in this camp.

Fig. 105—Konstanty Wolny (1877-1940), First Speaker of the Silesian Seym.

The next Silesian Seym, elected on May 11, 1930, was short-lived; it was dissolved after only one session by the President of the Republic together with the National Seym, and new elections to it were held on November 23, 1930. Table 54 shows the political distribution in the Seym of Silesia in the two elections of 1930.

The last elections to the Seym of Silesia were held on September 24, 1935. The German Soviet invasion of Poland in 1939 put an end to its session. After the Second World War the Silesian Seym was abolished.

The area of legislative prerogatives of the Silesian Seym was quite broad. It included the control over police forces in Silesia, the local budget and taxation, welfare matters, the provincial education system. The Seym operated through ten committees: budgetary, rules, legal, social affairs, schools, housing, agriculture, refugees and veterans of Silesian Uprisings, food, and petitions. The legislative record of the Seym peaked in 1924 and then settled at a steady level, as shown in Table 55.

As one of the prerogatives of their office, the Deputies of the Silesian Seym enjoyed parliamentary immunity from arrest. This immunity was invoked in 1930 when Wojciech Korfanty, the leader of the last Silesian anti-German uprising and the Deputy of the Silesian Seym, was arrested in connection with the Brześć Trial. He was released at the request of the Silesian Seym and continued as its Deputy until 1935. The history of the Seym was otherwise uneventful.

TABLE 54—POLITICAL AFFILIATION OF DEPUTIES IN THE SEYM OF SILESIA

Party Affiliation of Deputies	May 11 1930	Nov. 23 1930
Non-Party Block of Cooperation	10	19
Christian Democrats	16	19
German Minority Party	15	7
National Workers' Party	5	3
Communist Party	2	—
	48	48

TABLE 55—LEGISLATIVE ACTIVITY OF THE SEYM OF SILESIA

Year	Number of Laws Passed	Year	Number of Laws Passed
1922	40	1926	27
1923	121	1927	23
1924	47	1928	23
1925	29	1929	3

Originally, the Constitution of 1921 provided for the formation of Seymiks in each palatinate. In practice, in addition to the Seymik of Silesia, upgraded to the status of a Seym within the framework of Silesian autonomy, only two other General Seymiks were formed. They were the Seymiks of Greater Poland and Pomerania. Their membership was elected by the cities and the counties in the two palatinates.

The Seymik of Greater Poland sat in Poznań and consisted of 85 Deputies. It was the continuation of the Seym of Poznań of the Partition period but on a much reduced scale. The Seymik of Pomerania sat at Tczew and consisted of 55 Deputies. Here again a connection to the General Seymik of Prussia could be seen on the historical plane. Both of the above Seymiks, however, were now organs of local self-government and did not participate in the election of Deputies to the National Seym nor in the implementation of the laws passed by that Seym.

The county Seymiks in the Second Republic were also reduced to the function of territorial self-government. Their legal status was established by a law of March 23, 1933. According to that law the Seymik represented village communes and towns of less than 25,000 inhabitants. The Seymik was no longer a community meeting with everyone allowed to attend and vote, but it became instead a local legislature composed of elected Deputies. In addition to local legislative powers, the Seymiks were given supervisory powers over county and village administration. Elections to the Seymiks were held every four years with each village commune electing two Deputies; each town elected up to five Deputies in proportion to its size. The number of Seymiks corresponded to the number of counties and was 264 in 1939.

Fig. 106—Building of the Seym of Silesia in Katowice. The Seym and the provincial executive offices were housed here in the years 1921-39.

Fig. 107—Wojciech Korfanty (1873-1939), Leader of the Silesian Uprising against Germany. Deputy to the Seym of the Second Republic 1919-1930, and to the Silesian Seym 1922-1935. Vice Prime Minister of Poland, 1923.

The executive arm of each Seymik consisted of a Chairman and six members. The chair was held ex-officio by the county Prefect appointed by the Minister of the Interior. The six members were elected by the Seymik. This appointive feature of the chairmanship led to the subordination of the county self-government to the state administration. Formally the Seymiks were under the jurisdiction of the palatine, who was given the power to dissolve the executive committees of the Seymiks and to suspend their decisions. This amounted to the veto power in the hands of the Minister of the Interior since he appointed all palatines.

The electoral law appended to the Constitution of 1935 granted to the Seymiks of all the counties throughout the country and of the palatinates of Silesia, Greater Poland and Pomerania a role in the election of Senators by including their Deputies in the restricted senatorial electorate. In a manner, this was a throw back to the arrangements of the First Republic, except that it now applied to the Senate rather than to the Seym. As will be recalled, the entire membership of the Senate of the First Republic was appointed by the Chief Executive. Since the Constitution of 1935 gave the President of the Republic a right to appoint one-third of the membership of the Senate, there was more than a hint of a return to the historical precedent embodied in that Constitution.

For the elective two-thirds of the Senate the electorate was limited to graduates of senior high schools, universities and military academies, grade and high school teachers, bearers of military and civil decorations, Deputies of the Seymiks, members of the chambers of commerce, presidents of technical societies, and so forth. Only two elections were held while this electoral law was in force, on September 15, 1935 and on November 13, 1938, before the Second Republic was overrun by the armies of the unholy alliance of its Nazi and Communist neighbors.

The constitutional arrangements of the Second Republic after the passage of the Constitution of 1935 are summarized in Table 56, the principal legislative officers and the legislation of the Republic are given in Tables 57 and 58 and are followed by the biographical notes on the principal parliamentary figures of that period.

TABLE 56—SECOND CONSTITUTION OF THE SECOND REPUBLIC—A SYNOPSIS

(Voted by the Seym on April 23, 1935)

The Executive Branch of the Government was headed by a President elected for a seven year term by 50 electors designated by the Seym, 25 designated by the Senate, and 5 electors sitting ex-officio as the Speakers of the Seym and the Senate, Chief Justice, Prime Minister and the Chief Inspector of the Armed Forces. The powers of the President included the appointment of Prime Minister,

TABLE 56 (CONTINUED)—SECOND CONSTITUTION OF THE SECOND
REPUBLIC—A SYNOPSIS

Chief Justice, Inspector General of the Army, Chief Comptroller and one-third
of the Senators. He could appoint his successor in case of war and was not
subject to impeachment.

In case of a nonconfidence vote in the Seym for a cabinet or a minister, the
President could dismiss either one, or dissolve the Seym and the Senate and call
for a new election. The President had legislative initiative for constitutional
amendments and the right of pardon in judiciary cases.

The Legislative Branch of the Government consisted of an elective Seym of 208
Deputies, and a Senate in which 64 Senators were elected and 32 were appointed by
the President. The term of office of both Senators and Deputies was five years. The
area of competence of the Seym included control over the activities of the executive,
imposition of taxes and approval of the budget. The Seym could demand the
resignation of a minister or a cabinet, question any minister on the conduct of his
office, approve each year final state accounts, keep control of state debts. The
Deputies held legislative immunity for their official activities but were subject to
prosecution in criminal cases with the approval of the Seym. Voting in the Seym was
by a simple majority with at least one-third of all Deputies present. A resolution of
the Senate, rejecting or amending a bill accepted by the Seym, could be overriden by
a three-fifths vote of the Seym.

The Seym continued in session for at least four months each year unless the
budget was approved sooner. In the event of a President's death or resignation,
the Speaker of the Senate acted as the President-pro-tempore.

The Electoral Ordinance based the election of Deputies on universal, secret,
equal and direct suffrage. The voting age was set at twenty-four years. Candidacy
required the age of thirty and a nomination of an electoral assembly composed of
representatives of territorial, professional and economic governing bodies. The
electoral rights for Senatorial elections were limited to persons who held university
degrees, were bearers of certain decorations, or were officers in the Armed Forces
or had been elected to offices in economic, professional or technical societies.
Deputies of county Seymiks were included in the Senate electorate.

The Judiciary Branch of the Government was composed of judges appointed
by the President; they were not recallable or subject to arrest or prosecution except
by competent courts. Their sentences could not be overridden by either an executive or a legislative decision.

A Supreme Court for criminal and civil suits was established, together with a network
of district and municipal courts. The validity of laws could not be tested in the courts.

To try impeachment cases of Ministers, Deputies and Senators, a Tribunal of
State was established, composed of the President of the Supreme Court and six
judges selected by the Seym and the Senate from the judiciary.

298

TABLE 56 (CONTINUED)—SECOND CONSTITUTION OF THE SECOND REPUBLIC—A SYNOPSIS

The Bill of Rights was carried over in its entirety from the first Constitution of the Second Republic.

TABLE 57—PRINCIPAL LEGISLATIVE OFFICERS OF THE SECOND REPUBLIC

Chief Executive	Term of Office
Józef Piłsudski	1918-1922
Gabriel Narutowicz*	1922
Stanisław Wojciechowski**	1922-1926
Ignacy Mościcki***	1926-1939

*Assassinated after one week in office by a Polish extremist
**Resigned after coup d'état
***Resigned after German-Soviet invasion of Poland

Speaker of Seym	Term of Office
Franciszek Pułaski*	1918
Wojciech Trąmpczyński	1919-1922
Maciej Rataj**	1922-1927
Ignacy Daszyński	1928-1930
Kazimierz Świtalski	1930-1935
Stanisław Car	1935-1938
Walery Sławek	1938***
Wacław Makowski	1938-1939

*Speaker of Council of State, the interim legislature
**Served twice as pro-tempore head of state, executed by the Germans during the Second World War
***June to November. Lost the 1938 election

TABLE 58—PRINCIPAL LEGISLATION OF SEYMS OF THE SECOND REPUBLIC

1919   Peace Treaty of Versailles ratified, Objectives of Land Reform defined, Bank of Agriculture chartered

1920   Covenant of the League of Nations ratified, Health Insurance scheme for industrial workers established, Compulsory land purchase for Land Reform authorized, Organic Statute for Silesia passed

1921   Compensation scheme for work-related accidents established, Health insurance for office workers established, State Bank of Agriculture chartered to finance land reform, New Constitution of Second Republic passed, Peace Treaty of Riga with Soviet Union ratified

1924   Compensation scheme for work-related accidents extended, Unemployment Insurance Scheme established

TABLE 58 (CONTINUED)—PRINCIPAL LEGISLATION OF SEYMS OF THE SECOND REPUBLIC

1925	Arbitration Pact with Germany ratified, Compensation for work-related accidents extended, 200,000 hectares/year set aside for Land Reform
1926	Unemployment Insurance scheme extended
1928	United Code of Penal Procedure passed, Kellog-Briand Pact ratified
1932	Polish-Soviet nonaggression Treaty ratified
1933	General Health, Unemployment and Accident Insurance passed, Code of Civil Procedure and General Penal Code passed, Convention for the Definition of Aggression ratified
1934	Polish-German nonaggression Treaty ratified, Code of Legal Obligations and Commercial Code passed
1935	New Constitution for the Republic passed
1939	Polish-British Mutual Aid Agreement ratified

POLITICAL PERSONALITIES IN THE SEYM OF THE SECOND REPUBLIC

Dawid Abrahamowicz (1839-1926) member of an old Armenian-Polish family; he was first elected Deputy to the Seym of Galicia in 1867 and then to every Seym of Galicia until 1918. In the Seym he led the Podole group of conservative Deputies. He served as Deputy in the Austrian Parliament in the period 1875-1918 and was elected chairman of the "Polish Faction" in the Austrian Council of State. In the years 1907-09 he was the Minister for Galicia in Vienna. He served again as Deputy in the Seym of the Second Republic in Warsaw in the years 1919-22, thus bringing to a conclusion one of the longest (55 years) careers in the history of Polish parliamentarism. He funded in Lwów a foundation for the education of youth.

Stanisław Car (1882-1938)—Lawyer, politician, parliamentarian, he served as Minister of Justice from 1928 to 1930. In 1930 he was elected to the Seym on the BBWR ticket. He became Vice-Speaker of the Seym and a member of the commission working on the reform of the Constitution of which he became the primary legal architect. After the new Constitution was passed in 1935, he was elected Speaker of the Seym and served until his death in 1938.

Ignacy Daszyński (1866-1936)—Political activist in the workers' movement, political writer; he was one of the cofounders of the Polish Social Democratic Party of Galicia and Silesia; he was editor of *Naprzód*, 1897-1918 and Deputy to the Austrian Parliament. He was a supporter of J. Piłsudski and Deputy to the

Seym since 1919, elected Speaker of Seym in 1928; he served until 1930. In the Second Republic he was a leading figure in the Polish Socialist Party (PPS), and actively supported Piłsudski's coup d'état in 1926. In 1922 he was a cofounder of the Polish Workers' University (TUR) in an attempt to raise the cultural and intellectual level of working people. He wrote *A Short History of the Development of the Socialist Parties of Galicia* (1894); *On Forms of Government* (1902); *Memoirs* (1925-26), *Seym, Government, King, Dictator* (1926).

Jan Dębski (1880-1931)—Parliamentarian, peasant movement leader; he was one of the organizers and General Secretary of the Polish Peasant Party (PSL), the "Piast" branch. Elected Deputy to the Seym of 1919, he was the chairman of the Seym delegation which conducted the peace negotiations with the Soviet Union at the close of the Polish-Soviet War 1919-1921, first at Mińsk, then at Riga. In the same period he served as Vice-minister for Foreign Affairs. Dissatisfied over matters of policy, he left PSL Piast in 1923 and formed PSL "Peasant Unity," which then joined PSL "Liberation." He became a cofounder of the Peasant Party and subsequently of the Center-Left parliamentary coalition. He served as Vice-Speaker of the Seym 1928-1930. Authored *Peace Treaty at Riga* (1931).

Roman Dmowski (1864-1939)—Political writer and activist in the National Democratic Party. From 1895 he published in Lwów the *All Poland Review*. After 1905 he became active politically in Warsaw; elected Deputy to the Russian II and III Duma in 1907. During World War I he represented the pro-Russian and pro-Entente orientation. At the close of World War I he represented Poland at the negotiations leading to the Treaty of Versailles. Politically he was opposed to the federalist schemes advanced by J. Piłsudski as a solution to the minorities problem. Elected Seym Deputy in 1919, he did not take an active part in political life, but devoted himself to political writing. Betwen 1919-23 he participated in the government of W. Witos, and served briefly as Foreign Minister. He wrote: *Thoughts of a Modern Pole* (1903); *Problems of Central and Eastern Europe* (1917); *The Decline of Conservative Thought in Poland* (1914); *Polish Politics and the Reconstruction of the State* (1925); *Post-War World and Poland* (1931), and *Coup d'état* (1934).

Edward Dubanowicz (1881-1943)—Parliamentarian, jurist, educator, professor of state law at the University of Lwów, member of the National Democratic Party 1904-08, he was elected Deputy to the Seyms of 1919-22 and 1922-27 as a member of the Christian Union of National Unity. Principal co-author of the Constitution of 1921. From 1922 he was active as a leader of the right wing National People's Union. After 1927 he withdrew from politics. Authored: *Revision of the Constitution* (1926); *Towards a Stable Constitution of the Polish State* (1936); and *Civic Instruction* (1943).

Jan S. Jankowski (1882-1953)—Politician, agricultural expert, active in the National Worker's Party from 1920 onwards. Minister of Labor and Social Welfare in 1924 and 1926, he was elected Deputy to the Seym, in which be served during 1928-35. Active in the Labor Party from 1937 onwards, during the Second World War he served on the council of the Social Assistance Board and at the same time became one of the leaders of the anti-German Resistance movement in Poland. In 1944 he was appointed Vice-Prime Minister of the Polish Government in exile and its Plenipotentiary in Poland. He took part in the uprising against the Germans in Warsaw, August-September 1944, and evaded imprisonment after its collapse. In 1945 he headed a sixteen man parliamentary delegation invited by the Soviets to Moscow to discuss the formation of the first postwar government in Poland. Instead, together with the entire group, he was put on trial for alleged anti-Soviet activities and sentenced to eight and a half years imprisonment in Russia, a sentence he did not survive.

Władysław Konopczyński (1880-1952)—Historian, appointed professor of University of Cracow in 1917, he was a member of the Polish Academy of Learning since 1922. He served as Deputy to the Seym 1922-27. He edited numerous historical source materials and initiated the publication of the *Polish Biographical Dictionary* and served as its editor 1935-49. Foremost historian of Polish parliamentarism. Authored: *Poland in the Era of the Seven-Year War* (1909-1911); *Genesis and Establishment of the Permanent Council* (1917); *Confederation of Bar* (1936-38); and *Le Liberum Veto* (Paris, 1930).

Wojciech Korfanty (1873-1939)—Silesian politician and parliamentarian, he joined the National League in 1901. He was the editor of *Upper Silesian*, Deputy to Prussian Parliament 1904-1918, member of the Supreme National Council in 1918 and the leader of the Silesian uprisings against Germany. In the Second Republic, Deputy to the Seym of 1919-1930 for the Christian Democratic Party and Deputy to the Seym of Silesia 1922-35. He served as Vice-Prime Minister in 1923 and from 1924 he was the editor of *Rzeczpospolita and Polonia*. He opposed the policies of Piłsudski, was arrested in connection with the Trial of Brześć, and released claiming immunity as Deputy to the Silesian Seym. In exile from 1934 he returned to Poland in 1939.

Wacław Makowski (1880-1942)—Lawyer and politician; professor of political and criminal law from 1920, he was a member of the Codification Commission of the Republic. He represented the sociological school of criminal law. Three times Minister of Justice, he was also Seym Deputy elected on the BBWR ticket 1928-1935, Senator 1935-38 and Speaker of Seym 1938-39. Wrote *Criminal Law* (1920-24).

Mieczysław Niedziałkowski (1893-1940)—Parliamentarian, writer; joined the Polish Socialist Party in 1914 and became a member of its central committee in 1916 and secretary of its executive committee 1921-24. He was elected

Deputy to the Seym of 1919 and reelected until 1935. Vice-Chairman of the Central Executive Committee of the Polish Socialist Party 1924-31, he became a member of the executive committee of the Second International in 1932. He served as editor of *Workers' Unity* 1917-18, and *The Worker* 1927-39. During the German-Soviet invasion of Poland in 1939 he served as member of the Defense Council of Warsaw and as one of the organizers of the Workers Defense Battalions. He was executed by the Germans in the Palmiry Forest in 1940. Authored: *Upper Chambers in Contemporary Parliaments* (1918); *Theory and Practice of Socialism Confronting New Problems* (1926); and *Parliamentary Democracy in Poland* (1930).

Bohdan Podoski (1894-1984)—Lawyer, politician, parliamentarian; Deputy to the Seym 1928-35; parliamentary Secretary of BBWR 1930-35; coauthor of the Constitution of 1935; Vice-Speaker of the Seym 1935-38; Judge of the Court of Appeals in Warsaw 1938-39. Soviet political prisoner 1940-41. Served in the Polish Armed Forces under the command of General W. Anders 1942-46. In exile from 1948 in Great Britain.

Aleksander Prystor (1874-1951)—Revolutionary, politician, parliamentarian. In his youth one of the leaders of the paramilitary branch of the Polish Socialist Party carrying out terrorist actions against the tsarist government, he was in a Russian prison from 1912-17. In the Second Republic Vice-Minister of Labour 1918-19, then active in the administration of his native district of Wilno and its reunion with Poland, 1919-20. Minister of Labor 1929-30; elected Deputy to the Seym of 1930-35; Minister of Industry and Commerce 1930-31; Prime Minister of Poland 1931-33; Senator from 1935-38, he served as the Speaker of the Senate. During the Second World War he was deported to Russia, and died of dysentery in a Soviet prison in Oriel.

Maciej Rataj (1884-1940)—Political activist in the Peasant Party, writer, teacher; Deputy to the Seym of 1919, he was elected its Speaker in 1922 and served in that capacity until 1927. Throughout 1920-21 was Minister of Education and Religious Denominations. Twice he acted as the head of State: after the assassination of President G. Narutowicz, and after the resignation of President S. Wojciechowski. One of the organizers of the Center-Left Coalition after the 1926 coup d'état, in 1931 he was the cofounder of the Peasant Party and a member of its executive council. During the Second World War he was active in the resistance movement, captured by the Germans and executed at Palmiry. Wrote *Memoirs 1918-1927* (1966).

Walery Sławek (1879-1939)—Revolutionary, politician, parliamentarian; a member of the Polish Socialist Party (PPS) from 1900; between 1902-05 he was a member of the Workers' Central Committee. He cooperated with J. Piłsudski in terrorist activities against the tsarist government. A bomb which he was assembling exploded in his face and severely wounded him. From 1914 he served in the Legion organized by J. Piłsudski under Austrian auspices. One of the cofounders and the chairman of BBWR, he was elected Seym Deputy in 1928. He served as Prime Minister of the Republic 1930-31 and 1935. One of the co-authors of the Constitution of 1935. He was elected Speaker of the Seym in 1938. Despondent over political setbacks, he committed suicide in 1939.

Stanisław Stroński (1882-1955)—Parliamentarian, philologist; until 1908 he was active in the National Democratic Party in Galicia and served as Deputy to the Seym of Galicia 1913–1914. Interned by the Austrians 1914-17, then active in the Polish National Committee in Paris 1918-19. He was appointed professor of the University of Cracow 1919. Elected Deputy to the Seym of 1922-27 for the Christian National Party. Member of the National Party and Deputy of the Seym 1928-35, where he opposed the policies of the Piłsudski group. 1927-39 he was professor of the Catholic University of Lublin. 1939-43 he was Vice-Prime Minister of the Polish Government in exile in England. Authored: *First Ten Years, 1918-1928* (1928); *Polish Foreign Policy, 1934-1935* (1935); plus numerous works on Provensal literature.

Kazimierz Świtalski (1886-1962)—Politician. During the First World War he served in Piłsudski's Legion and later was one of his closest associates. He served as Prime Minister of the Second Republic in 1929, as Seym Deputy in 1930-1935, as palatine of Cracow in 1935-36, as Speaker of the Seym in 1933-35, and Deputy Speaker of the Senate in 1935-39. During World War II he was in a German prisoner-of-war camp in Dobiegniew. He returned to Poland at the end of the Second World War and was imprisoned by the government of the Polish People's Republic, 1948-1956. 1953 Mokotów Prison. Author of prison songs.

Stanisław Thugutt (1873-1941)—Parliamentarian, writer; member of Polish Military Organization (POW) and the Polish Legion organized by J. Piłsudski during the First World War. He was a member of the Polish Peasant Party (PSL) "Liberation" branch since 1917. He was imprisoned by the Germans in Modlin. Minister of Internal Affairs 1918-19 and chairman of PSL "Liberation" 1921-24, he was elected Deputy to the Seym of 1922-27 and was one of the organizers of the Center-Left coalition. He joined the Peasant Party (SL) in 1931, became the chairman of its Governing Council and held this position throughout 1935-38. Chairman of the Institute for Problems of Nationalities from 1925 onwards, and Vice-President of the League for the Defense of Rights of Man and Citizen, from 1928 he was active in the rural cooperatives for retail and produce marketing. Authored: *From the History of Underground Press in Warsaw*, 1914-1918 (1935).

Wojciech Trąmpczyński (1860-1935)—Politician, lawyer, writer; he practiced law in Poznań from 1886. In the period 1890-94 he organized private teaching of Polish in the schools of Poznań. He became associated with the National Democratic Party. In the years 1900-11 he was a member of the City

Council of Poznań. Between 1912 and 1918 he served as Deputy in the German Parliament. In 1918-19 he served as Chairman of the Regency Council of Poznań and between 1919 and 1922 as the Speaker of the Seym of the Second Republic. In 1922 he became the Speaker of the Senate and held the post until 1927.

Wincenty Witos (1874-1945)—Politician in the Peasant Party; son of a former peasant serf. He entered politics through the Seym of Galicia to which he was elected as Deputy in 1908-14. He was a Deputy to the Vienna Reichsrat (1911-18). He was elected Deputy to the first Seym of the Second Republic in 1919 and remained there until 1930 when he became one of the defendants in the Trial of Brześć. He served three times as Prime Minister of the Republic: 1920-21, 1923, and 1926. Although he was in exile in Czechoslovakia in 1930-39 he remained throughout the life of the Second Republic the undisputed leader of the Peasant Movement. He wrote: *My Reminiscences*, three volumes (1965).

Konstanty Wolny (1877-1940)—Silesian politician and lawmaker, educated at the University of Breslau. In 1907 he became the first Polish lawyer to practice in the Silesian town of Gliwice. In 1911 he defended in a German court the participants of secret courses in Polish language, which were conducted in the local high schools. During the First World War he was imprisoned by the Germans in Nysa. In 1918 he became a member of the Supreme National Council of Silesia and served on the Plebiscite Commission set up to partition Silesia along national lines between Poland and Germany. He was elected dean of the Bar Association and a member of its executive committee. Under the auspices of the Christian Democratic Party he was elected Deputy to the Silesian Seym and served as its Speaker in the period 1922-34. Authored numerous publications on legal problems of Silesia.

CHAPTER VII

POLISH PEOPLE'S REPUBLIC: MAKING THE BEST OF STALIN'S WORST

The rise of the Polish People's Republic at the close of the Second World War covers the period (1945-1988). The borders of the country were shifted West by a takeover of former German territory at the end of World War II and the area populated with Poles moved from Eastern Poland. A Communist administration was imposed on the country by the Soviets, accompanied by gross reverses in the development of representative government. A referendum abolished the Senate. Approximately one million people suspected of opposition to the Communist takeover were deprived of their right to vote. Civil war broke out between the members of the former anti-German underground and the administration imposed and aided by the Soviets.

The first elections (1947) were marked by a level of violence unprecedented in the whole of Polish electoral history. Non-Communist candidates were imprisoned or disqualified in such numbers that by election day only a handful remained on the electoral lists. Leaders of the Polish Peasant Party elected to the Seym were forced to flee the country in fear for their lives and the remnants of the Socialist and the Peasant Parties, as well as the Christian Democratic Party, were forced to amalgamate with 'licensed' parties organized by the Communists. Parties which refused to endorse the Communist ideology were suppressed.

Fig. 108—Polish People's Republic in 1945 after the westward shift of the borders.

Soviet-style Constitution was adopted in 1952; the sessions of the Seym were made as brief as possible; open debate was reduced to a minimum; and the laws were passed by unanimous votes. Successive legislatures were now composed of hand-picked candidates limited to a government approved list, although an illusion of a pluralistic system was maintained by retention of two licensed parties besides the CP. Voting was made compulsory.

In the early part of this period legislation was enacted nationalizing the ownership of industry, commerce, and the communication media. The new Constitution of 1952 gave the CP an effective control of the nationalized properties equivalent to their collective ownership by the party. However, all attempts to collectivize agriculture led to severe food shortages, riots and economic collapse, which in turn forced changes in the CP leadership and policies. This set the pattern for subsequent changes of government. Amendments to the Constitution enacted in 1976 made the CP control of the government and submission to the Soviet Union statutory.

MAKE-BELIEVE PLURALISM AND THE PRE-SCREENED SEYM

In the decade folowing the collapse of the Second Republic some of the problems besetting it through minority conflicts, industrial underinvestment and an unworkable representation in the Seym, were reduced by circumstance; some by enemy action during the Second World War. Thus, the Ribbentrop-Molotov Treaty brought with it the loss of over 40% of the territory to Russia and with it almost all of the Ukrainian and Byelorussian minority, as well as 5.3 million Poles, some of whom, however, were subsequently resettled in central Poland and in the territories taken over from Germany. The death toll due to the invasion and to the mass extermination of large groups of population by the combined efforts of Germans and Russians, amounted to over six million lives out of a population of 33 million. This tragic total was almost equally split between Christians and Jews, with the Germans responsible for the death of most of the Jewish and about half of the Christian victims, and the Russians bearing the guilt for the death of about 1.5 million, mostly Christians.

The easily noticeable disparities in the social structure were levelled out during the war by the disproportionately high losses among the well educated, the well to do, and the prominent in every walk of life, since they, in particular, were the object of attention of the Gestapo and the NKVD, the German and the Soviet secret police. The industrial under-investment was partially remedied by the westward shift of the boundaries of Poland by some 250 km, as a result of the Yalta and the Potsdam Agreements, to include within the new borders the entire province of Silesia with its large industrial base.

The outcome of the Second World War left Poland in the Soviet sphere of influence and occupied by Soviet troops. The establishment of the Polish People's Republic in 1945 under Soviet sponsorship marked a forced transition from political institutions based on free associaton and consensual legislation to one based on cooptive association and coercive legislation. Uniformity was now the order of the day. This required no less than a complete abandonment of the political heritage of Poland in which the Seym traditionally served as the central political forum and where legislation was adopted only after extensive debate involving the different viewpoints represented in the Seym. An undertaking of this magnitude required the elimination of all political associations and parties not meeting the following criteria:

1) Friendly to the Soviet Union and willing to endorse every Soviet move without reservation or criticism;

2) Willing to support the program and all political actions of the newly reconstituted Polish Communist Party (CP);

3) Willing to have the CP handle all of their publicity, through the state–controlled public communication media, and all other contacts with organizational membership and with the public.

As could be expected, none of the genuinely Polish political parties could satisfy all three of these conditions simultaneously. Those that did not were slated for elimination in a two-step process: first, the forcible removal of the party leadership and second, the amalgamation of the leaderless membership with small, licensed groups of the same name as the traditional party but operated by politically reliable personnel delegated by the CP. The first step was initiated in January 1945, when fifteen leading members of the major non-Communist Polish political parties were invited to a conference in Moscow, ostensibly to discuss the formation of the first post-war government in Poland. The group included: Aleksander Zwierzyński, the former Vice-Speaker of the Seym, Kazimierz Pużak, Jan Stanisław Jankowski, Zbigniew Stypułkowski, Kazimierz Bagiński, Franciszek Urbański and Stanisław Michałowski, all former Deputies of the Seym; Adam Bień and Stanisław Jasiukowicz, who together with Jankowski were the only members of the Polish government operating under cover in German-occupied Poland; Józef S. Dąbski, Eugeniusz Żarnowski, Józef Chaciński, Kazimierz Kobylański, Antoni Pajdak, Stanisław Mierzwa. The sixteenth man was General Leopold Okulicki, the last Commander of the Polish Underground Army, the equivalent of the French Resistance, which throughout the war fought the German occupant. Okulicki succeeded in command General Bór-Komorowski, taken prisoner in Warsaw after the collapse of the two-month long uprising in August–September 1944 against the Germans. Prior to his parachute drop into Poland, Okulicki served in the Polish units under British command in Africa.

In Moscow, the sixteen invitees were taken to the Lubianka prison instead of the conference table. In June, 1945, after six months of intense brain-washing, the group was put on trial in Moscow accused of collaborating with the Germans and of anti-Soviet acts. The start of the trial was carefully orchestrated to coincide with the opening of the organizing conference in San Francisco for the formation of the United Nations. Poland was one of the founding members. The timing of the trial had a dual purpose: to checkmate the Western Allies over the issue of the United Nations, the primary interest of the Allies, and to test their willingness to pay for Soviet participation in the organization by the surrender of the eastern half of Europe to Soviet control. No mean prize was at stake, for Eastern Europe contained about 100 million people and two of the four large industrial areas in Europe: the Silesian and the Czech. Its placement under Soviet control would almost double the industrial resources available to the Soviets and immensely enhance their relative economic standing in the world, while correspondingly weakening Europe as a whole.

The Moscow trials lasted three days. General Okulicki was sentenced to ten years imprisonment but apparently was executed within a year. Jankowski received a sentence of eight and one-half years, which he did not survive, while the Ministers Bień and Jasiukowicz received five years each. A similar sentence was given to Pajdak. Other verdicts varied from a few months to acquittal.

Kazimierz Pużak received a sentence of one and one-half years. There was bitter irony in this verdict, for Pużak was one of the leading revolutionary figures in pre-World War One Poland and for his socialist revolutionary activities he was imprisoned by the Tsarist government from 1911 to 1917 in the Schlüsselburg fortress in Russia. A Deputy in the Seym of the Second Republic and the revered chairman of the Polish Socialist Party, he was back in prison in Russia. Here it appeared that the Soviet government neatly stepped into the Tsarist shoes. After completing his sentence he returned to Poland and, fearing further arrest, feverishly wrote his memoirs to record for posterity in bitter prose what had happened in Moscow. Just as he expected, the arrest ordered by the CP took place in 1948, followed by a trial and another five year prison sentence, which he did not survive. His memoirs were later smuggled out of Poland and published in Paris, a monument to an unbroken though greatly embittered spirit.

The two legislative acts which initiated the Polish People's Republic [PRL] were the Referendum, held on June 20, 1946 and the passage of the "Small Constitution." The questions put to the electorate in the Referendum, and the answers obtained are summarized in Table 59.

In counting the votes cast in the Referendum, the results reported from electoral districts where the vote-counting was done by the CP personnel only, were at great variance with the results from those districts where the Peasant Party managed to retain its participation in the electoral committees, leading to suspicion of fraud on the part of the CP.

TABLE 59—RESULTS OF THE REFERENDUM OF 1946

Question Asked	Number of People Answering (in Millions)	
	Yes	No
Should the Senate be abolished	7.8	3.7
Should the industry be nationalized and remaining estates broken up	8.9	2.6
Should the western frontier be moved to the Oder-Niesse Rivers	10.5	1.0

The major objects of property, whether real estate or industrial, were seized immediately, but their formal transfer to the control of the CP started with the first election, held in January 1947. In view of the fact that this was the last election in which any non-CP sponsored or controlled parties were allowed to run, namely the Polish Peasant Party (PSL), the Polish Socialist Party (PPS), and the Labor Party (Christian Democratic) (SP), it is worthwhile to review this election in some detail, particularly since it was claimed that this was the election in which Poland chose socialism for its system and the CP for its "leading role."

The pertinent facts were summarized recently by Stanisław Wójcik, the then First Secretary of PSL. The election ordinance of 1921 was used, i.e., multi-mandate electoral districts were formed, 52 in number. The contesting parties were allowed to put up more candidates than the seats in the Seym, and PSL entered the election with more than 1000 candidates for the 444 seats in the Seym. The fate of these candidates is summarized in Table 60. In addition, 128 local PSL party workers and organizers were murdered during the election campaign by the Communists. These figures show a level of lawlessness unmatched by anything in the 500 years of electoral history of Poland.

TABLE 60—ELECTORAL SHOWING OF PSL CANDIDATES IN 1947

Number	Electoral Outcome
28	were elected
98	were deprived of the right to vote in the election*
76	were in the ten districts where the PSL lists were banned*
14	on the national lists were arrested
135	on the district lists were arrested

*thereby becoming "disqualified"- as candidates

While it is difficult to say with certainty how many of the PSL candidates "withdrawn" from the election by the Communist-controlled police and electoral commissions would have won if given a chance, the chance must have been estimated high by the Russians and their Communist protegés, to judge by the lengths to which they went to intimidate the electorate and falsify the results. The bulk of the vote-counting was done by the Communists themselves, while the representatives of the PSL were banned from the premises. Table 62 shows the final results.

The "Small Constitution," passed shortly after the elections, on February 19, 1947, abolished the Senate and established a Council of State, composed of the President of the Republic, the Speaker and the Vice-Speaker of the Seym, the Comptroller General, plus three other members, with powers to issue decrees with the force of law, to be later approved by the Seym.

Fig. 109—Map of the Polish People's Republic on the eve of the 1947 elections showing the electoral districts into which the country was divided. The shaded areas are the ten electoral districts in which the candidate lists of the Polish Peasant Party were "disqualified" from running. The districts contained 5.3 million out of the 24 million population of the country and were in the areas of the greatest strength of the Peasant Party.

Reprinted from The Rape of Poland *by Stanisław Mikołajczyk, copyright 1948 by Stanisław Mikołajczyk; used with permission of McGraw-Hill Book Company.*

The results of the 1947 election were hailed as an overwhelming victory for the Communists. The few PSL and SP Deputies elected were subjected to further threats, with the result that the leadership of the party were forced to flee the country in fear for their lives: first Stanisław Mikołajczyk, then Stanisław Wójcik, followed by Stanisław Bańczyk and Stefan Korboński, as well as Tomasz Kołakowski of the SP. They were subsequently deprived of their seats in the Seym and stripped of their citizenship. Some of the remaining Deputies of the PSL were

313

deprived of their seats under various pretexts and imprisoned, so that by November of 1947, a mere ten months after the election, the PSL Seym representation was down to fourteen Deputies. The now headless remainder was forced to amalgamate in 1949 with the Communist-sponsored Peasant Party (SL) to form the United Peasant Party (ZSL). The Polish Socialist Party, decapitated already in the Moscow trial, came in the election with two more seats than the Communists, but was nevertheless also forced to amalgamate with the CP (PPR) in 1948. The Labor Party (Christian Democratic) (SP) amalgamated with the CP-sponsored Democratic Party (SD) in 1950. In each case the purge of the ranks followed, to assure CP control of each body, and the era of make-believe pluralism began.

Fig. 110—Stanisław Mikołajczyk (1901-1966), Deputy to the 1930 Seym of the Second Republic and the 1947 Seym of the Polish People's Republic where he led the opposition to the Communist takeover until forced to flee the country.

Concurrently with the formal changes of the political parties, their mode of operation was changed drastically. In place of free association, where anyone could join a party of his choice, the association by co-optation was introduced with an oddity called "the candidature to the party membership," requiring the performance of various deeds demonstrating political reliability before admission to full membership. This co-optive feature is, of course, the hallmark of every entrenched class system.

The Communist Party itself was reconstituted from the debacle of 1938, when its entire leadership was invited to Russia and shot. The post-war party was restaffed with personnel more pliant in the hands of Moscow and, after the amalgamation with the Polish Socialist Party, was supplied with a new name: "The Polish United Workers Party" (PZPR). From then on its political apparatus started the long term operation of transferring all significant individual property and political rights of the citizens to the collective ownership of the Communist Party, the transfer to be accomplished and made to appear legal through the manipulation of the legislature. The details of this process are given in the next section.

The philosophy of the takeover process was clearly recognized by Milovan Djilas, a disillusioned and thoughtful Yugoslav Marxist in a high party position. He observed that if the control of management and income, plus the power to dispose of real property are attributes of ownership, then in the Communist-controlled countries they rest exclusively in the hands of the CP and the CP, and not the people, is the de facto owner of most of the state. Poland had at that time, therefore, a new self-perpetuating and closed ownership class governing the country. It renewed its membership by co-optation and held by force its privileged position, based on its self-professed knowledge of the processes by which history, helped along by the Soviet Union, marched inexorably on.

It is interesting to note the curious dichotomy apparent in the Communists' writings about this period. In an attempt to justify their control of Poland there was a discernible yearning for proofs of legitimacy, hence the claims of having been duly elected. Closer examination of the crucial election of 1947 was, however, forbidden lest the truth come out. On the other hand, the Leninist ideology of the CP required that it come to power by force, hence making its own legitimacy questionable in the light of the centuries-old constitutional traditions of Poland requiring a fair election. The above question is of more than purely philosophical importance, since the concommitant tradition of Poland is that the citizens owe loyalty and support to legitimate governments only and are released from this obligation to governments that do not abide by the law. This principle was embedded in the Cardinal Laws for some 200 years in the form of the explicit "release from obedience" clause of the Henrician Articles, and its implicit validity was reasserted by the Seym of 1831 when it dethroned Nicholas I. Measured in these terms, all the Communist governments since 1947 were legitimate only to the extent to which the election results of that year were true.

CONSTITUTION OF 1952:
A NATION FORCED IN THE STALINIST MOLD

In the years 1944-47 the countries of Eastern Europe occupied by the Soviet Armies were forced to accept restrictions on their pre-war Constitutions; then in the period 1947-48 some were given intermediate Constitutions; and finally, in the years following 1952, new Constitutions modelled on the Stalinist Soviet Constitution of 1935 were imposed. The circumstances under which these new constitutional arrangements were made, formalizing the vassal status of the occupied countries, bore more than a fleeting resemblance to the imposition of Constitutions based on the standard Napoleonic model in the early 1800s. Now, as then, several countries of Europe were involved, but only Poland was party to both events.

In the period following World War II, the constitutional change involved for some countries an intermediate step in which Upper Chambers were abolished, electoral ordinances were distorted by a ban on the participation of some parties in the elections, etc. In the final step all pretense of popular support was abandoned in favor of outright recognition of the virtual dictatorship by the Central Committee of the CP; the state apparatus was made a mere appendage to it. The final stage usually also involved the abolition of the Presidency and the substitution of a multi-body Council of State. At the time it was felt to mean that Stalin was the formal head of the conglomerate of the Soviet Union and the satellite Republics. Following his death some back-tracking occurred in the constitutional sphere and the Presidencies were restored, while in the USSR the Party chairmanship was merged with the Presidency in the later 1970s after Brezhniev, visiting France as a mere Chairman of the Soviet CP, was piqued by the denial of a 21-gun salute due only to the visiting heads of state.

The time-table of the Constitutional changes in Eastern Europe is summarized in Table 61.

TABLE 61—CONSTITUTIONAL DEVELOPMENT IN EASTERN EUROPE

	Constitution		
Country	Modified Pre-War	Intermediate	Stalinist
Bulgaria	1944(1897)	1947	---
Hungary	1946	---	1949
Rumania	1944(1923)	1948	1952
Poland	1947(1921)	---	1952
Czechoslovakia	1945(1920)	1948	1960

In each country elections were held under conditions similar to those which occurred in Poland in 1947, with similar results.

The operation of the legislative systems, established as a result and on the strength of these elections, is a phenomenon of its own and well worth studying, for it was by no means limited to Poland only, but rather embodied all the characteristics common to the system imposed by the Soviets on all their Satellites. Its unique feature in Poland concerned the make-believe pluralistic political party structure. In addition to the Communist Party (United Workers Party), two more parties were licensed to operate on the condition that they accept without reservation the Communist program and abstain from presenting to the electorate the least variation in political choices. These were the United Peasant Party and the Democratic Party.

The system was engineered to provide the appearances of legality while retaining for the Communist Party full control over the results. It assured the security of ownership position for the Party and eliminated electoral surprises. The process of manipulating the electorate started long before the ballot box was reached, with the selection of candidates for election as Deputies to the Seym. The only body entitled to put up candidates was the Electoral Commission of the so called Front of National Unity (FJN). The district personnel directors of the Party and its affiliates who served on it, selected candidates for screening by the Political Police. The candidates were then displayed to the electorate, usually a week before the elections, at "meet the electorate" meetings.

The participation in the elections was in fact compulsory, and the police came to the homes of the laggards, who had not voted by a certain hour of the day, and escorted them to the ballot box. In the elections of 1952, taking place after the amalgamations of the parties were completed, a single list of candidates was presented to the electorate and every candidate was elected.

The choice offered to the electorate in the subsequent elections is described in an official publication of the Polish People's Republic:

> The elections to the Seym held in January 1957 were organized on the basis of the new voting regulations (Law of October 24, 1956) which introduced substantial modifications. The most important change consisted of the fact that the number of candidates on the ballot was higher than the number of mandates allotted to a given constituency. The new regulations make it possible to choose from among persons representing the programme of a list, while the principle of putting forward uniform lists of the National Unity Front was maintained.

As can be seen, the choice offered to the electors is similar to that once facetiously given by Henry Ford to buyers of his Model T cars: "You can have it in any color you want, as long as it's black."

With this type of a choice, it is no wonder that the public went through the motions of the election without paying the least attention to the results.

In October of 1956, during a plenary meeting of the CP, Władysław Gomułka made a speech outlining the reforms proposed by his new administration, brought on by the wide-spread rioting of the industrial labor force against the preceding administration. The speech contained the following startling statement with reference to the forthcoming elections: "the new electoral law will allow the people to elect, instead of merely voting." Alas, it did not, for the government still retained its apparatus for vetting all candidates in conjunction with the CP and allowed only the hand-picked set to appear on the candidate lists.

Gomułka's real views on the subject were recorded by his Polish-German interpreter and made public when the latter left Poland for the West. During the July 1968 summit meeting of the Communist Chieftains in Warsaw, questions were raised by the East German delegates on the apparent availability of choice between the candidates offered to the voters of Poland following the reforms mentioned above. Gomułka had the following to say through the interpreter:

> If we are in a position to vet four hundred and fifty people before the elections, we can just as easily vet six hundred. The people are pleased that they have a choice, and even the Western press is full of praise for us. As you see, we can achieve positive results without taking the slightest risk.[*]

Fig. 111—Jan Dembowski (1899-1963), Zoopsychologist and politician, Speaker of the 1952-56 Seym of the Stalinist period.

How little risk was taken, and how well things were controlled is apparent from the examination of Table 62, showing the election results in the Polish People's Republic. After 1961 the party distribution of seats became cast in concrete. It

---

[*] From: *At The Red Summit* by Erwin Weit, transl. by Mary Schofield, copyright by MacMillan Publishing Co. (1973). Reproduced with permission of MacMillan Co.

was referred to, in government announcements of election results, as "customary."

Somehow, it takes all the excitement out of the elections, but tells more about the [communist] system than a lengthy discourse.

It is worth while to examine the details of the election procedure in Polish People's Republic and compare election results from the two most different regions. First, Article 80 of the 1952 Constitution stated:

Elections to the Seym and to the People's Councils are universal, equal, direct and carried out by secret ballot.

Second, Article 57 of the Electoral Law of 1976 stated:

The elector votes for as many candidates as are to be elected in the given electoral district. The names of the candidates, for which he votes, should not be crossed out on the ballot. By leaving more names of the candidates not crossed out than the number of seats falling to the given electoral district, the elector votes for these candidates not crossed out, whose names appear at the top of the list.

TABLE 62—COMPOSITION OF SEYMS OF THE POLISH PEOPLE'S REPUBLIC

Year	1947		1952	1957	1961	1965	1969	1972
Number of Deputies	444		425	459	460	460	460	460
Party:								
PPR*	114							
		PZPR*	273	239	256	255	255	255
PPS	116							
SL*	109							
		ZSL**	90	118	117	117	117	117
PSL	27							
SD**	41							
		SD**	25	39	39	39	39	39
SP	15							
Non-Party	---	***		37	63	48	49	49	49

*Polish CP

**Licensed Peasant and Democratic parties, allowed a different name, but not a different program

***Independent Catholic groups

This means that unmarked ballots were counted as valid, and since the candidates particularly favored by the CP were always placed at the top of the list, the election results could be adjusted in their favor by the simple addition of blank ballots.

In the actual voting procedure the voter could either pick up the ballot and drop it unmarked in the ballot box and be checked off the voters list immediately, or take the ballot to the balloting booth, cross off some names, and then put the ballot in the ballot box. Making this choice, the voter was checked off the voters list twice, once for the ballot, once for the use of the booth. The second step put him on the suspect list. Voters knew it and were intimidated by it, in spite of the fact that the above Article 57 of the Electoral Ordinance was clearly in violation of Article 80 of the Constitution, which presumably guaranteed the secrecy of voter's choice and freedom from intimidation on this account. What the elections showed in reality was not the popularity of a given candidate but the degree of intimidation of voters in a given electoral district. Table 63 shows the two extreme results reported for the 1976 election.

The voting results in all 71 electoral districts of the country looked alike except that the percentage of non-intimidated people, those who actually marked the ballots, varied from district to district within the range of the extremes shown in Table 63, i.e., between 5.32% shown for Cracow and 0.18% shown for Sosnowiec. These results could be viewed with amusement, if they did not conceal an important message: the percentage of voters that would not be intimidated into casting unmarked ballots was markedly higher in all districts where in the past there have been mass demonstrations of workers against the exploitation by the CP, suppression of freedom of conscience and the like. Thus, higher percentages showed up for Warsaw (3.04%), Nowy Sącz (4.30%), Poznań (3.12%), Radom (3.00%), Szczecin (2.75%), Tarnów (3.81%), Wrocław (4.37%), and the two electoral districts of Cracow with 3.68% and 5.32%, respectively. The stiffest electoral stance of Cracow stemmed from the decade-long campaign conducted by the Catholic laymen of the district, led by Cardinal Karol Wojtyła (elected Pope John Paul II in 1978), to assert their demand for freedom of conscience of the inhabitants of the suburb of Cracow called Nowa Huta. The suburb, constructed after the Second World War to house the labor force of the new steel works nearby, was to be the first Marxist model town in Poland not permitted to have a church. Since the government had a monopoly on production and sale of building materials and on the issue of building permits, the ban seemed easy to enforce. However, the population of the town, now numbering in excess of 100,000, thought otherwise. Through a series of mass demonstrations repeated over many years, and gradually increasing in intensity, it forced the government to reverse the ban. As a result a fine modern church now graces the center of the town and offers Sunday masses on a round-the-clock basis.

TABLE 63—ELECTION RESULTS FROM SOSNOWIEC AND CRACOW IN THE 1976 ELECTION

	District 24 Sosnowiec	District 32 Cracow
No. of Seats	7	9
Electors	377,834	485,756
Voters in 1976	377,330	479,217
Percent Voting	99.87	98.65

Candidate	% Votes	Candidate	% Votes
Gierek Edward	99.99	Jabłoński Henryk	97.22
Seta Antoni	99.87	Kuran Kazimierz	94.52
Lokkaj Jadwiga	99.67	Trębaczkiewicz K.	96.57
Konieczny Mar.	99.67	Cabaj Władysł.	95.92
Skorupa Zdzis.	99.67	Brazda Stefania	95.90
Maszczyk Dan.	99.92	Janowski Jan	97.07
Odrzywolski F.	99.94	Hołuj Tadeusz	95.65
Lizurek Jan	0.18*	Mięsowicz Marian	96.66
Pietraszek Edw.	0.11*	Śliwa Gustaw	96.74
Szarawarski A.	0.05*	Nowakowska Jad.	5.32*
		Baron Rajmund	4.45*
		Radecki Janusz	3.21*

*Percentage of people who actually voted for a Deputy, rather than just deposited unmarked ballots

Note: from the above it may seem that Gierek is more popular than Jabłoński, yet in the topsyturvy world of Communist-supervised voters the reverse was true. It was to Jabłoński that the farmers addressed nearly 400,000 letters of protest in 1978, hoping for a sympathetic ear in demands for a more equitable distribution of social insurance taxes and the prevention of the forced surrender to the government of their farms.

The press and other communication media passed over the question of who ran for office and who got elected, or what the election issues were, and concentrated instead on the percentage of the electorate that "have done their duty" and voted. The 96-98% turnout was then duly reported and broadcast as evidence of solid support for the government. Under these conditions the question arises as to the purpose of the elections. One suspects here the return in modern form to the medieval procedure of doing homage to the ruler; those not complying were singled out as disloyal.

Fig. 112—Seym of the Polish People's Republic in Warsaw, shown in one of its infrequent and brief plenary sessions open to the public.

The Seym thus elected was characterized by the uniformity of political views; decoupling of its decisions from the wishes of the electorate; by the lack of discussion of policy issues underlying the legislation submitted for its approval by the government, and by the speed with which the bills were processed. As a rule, the Seym assembled twice a year for a two-week session. The Deputies were allowed to hold government jobs on a full time basis, and no pretense was made of any independence of judgement in legislative matters. This made for a compliant and trouble-free body. Its legislative efficiency was remarkable as can be seen from Tables 64 and 65. It is not an exaggeration to say that the Seym approved any bill put before it, and did so with remarkable compliance. During the years 1965-1977, the record speed was reached in 1972 when in a five-day period, divided into four sittings, the Seym passed twenty-one laws. The activity on government bills peaked, however, in 1950. During a sixteen day period, divided into thirteen sittings, the Seym passed one hundred laws and approved thirty-three decrees with the force of law, thus averaging six laws and three decrees per day. This feat, no doubt, set a world record for legislative rubber-stamping. The time spent in session by legislatures of other countries is shown in Table 66 for comparison.

Such legislative performance stemmed in some measure from the feeling of insecurity surrounding the Seym, and the part played in it by the political police.

For instance, on the eve of the first elections under the Polish People's Republic in 1947, some candidates for Deputy to the Seym were requested to sign in advance a public declaration by which they resigned their seats in the Seym "for reasons of health." Thus any disappearance from the political scene could be plausibly explained while, barring that, legislative discipline could be much improved. To make the Deputies, once elected, feel even more insecure the concept of "Substitute Deputies" was introduced in 1952. Placed lower on the ballot, these surrogates would automatically take the seat in the Seym should the incumbent resign for any reason.

Forced withdrawals from the political scene of higher members of the Executive Branch were more difficult to arrange and often involved a ceremonial state funeral. For instance, when the former Chief Executive of the Polish People's Republic and Seym Deputy Bolesław Bierut was summoned to Moscow in 1956 to attend a meeting of the Communist Chieftains, he developed severe health problems there. His body was returned to Poland for burial. Since similar circumstances surrounded the homecoming in 1949 of the Bulgarian Chief of State Georgi Dimitriev and Czechoslovakia's Klement Gottwald in 1953, the following ditty was coined in Poland to describe the change of attire to be expected on these trips:

Pojechał w futerku,
Powrócił w kuferku.

Went up in his togs,
Came back in a box.

It was obvious that quiet disappearances, such as occurred to some former Polish Seym Deputies invited to Russia in the 1930s, were no longer practicable.

The oath administered to each newly elected Deputy of the Seym of the Polish People's Republic put in question his political freedom of thought, or choice of opinion, for it forced each Deputy to undertake the support of one political ideology, regardless of the nominal political affiliation under which he or she was elected. The oath read as follows:

I solemnly swear as a Deputy to the Seym of the Polish People's Republic to work for the good of the Polish Nation and to deepen its unity, to contribute to the strengthening of the bond between the state authority and the working people of towns and villages, to do everything for consolidation of independence and sovereignty, and for successful socialist development of the Polish People's Republic.

The underlined word was added in 1961 to the text of the oath, amid claims that the addition will not restrict the Deputies' action. In fact, it pre-empted their freedom of choice. The simple truth, that the best bond between the government and the electorate is formed through an honest, unfettered election, seemed to have escaped the authors.

This change signalled further moves toward integrating the constitutional framework of the state with that of the Soviet Union. The biggest step in that direction was the amendment to the Constitution, passed on February 10, 1976. In it the following phrase was added to Article 3a of the Constitution:

> Polish People's Republic in its policies is guided... by the interests of the Polish Nation, its sovereignty, independence and security... it strengthens the friendship and cooperation with the Union of the Soviet Socialist Republics and other socialist states.

There is a precedent for writing Russia into the constitution in the history of the First Republic. It took place in 1717, when the Russian guarantee was accepted for the constitution of the country. The long-term consequences of that guarantee were disastrous. In both cases, 1717 and 1976, the ruling group hoped to reconcile the Russian guarantee for their privileged position with retaining the sovereign position of the country. Instead, they merely formalized its subservient status.

TABLE 64—LEGISLATIVE PERFORMANCE OF SEYMS OF THE POLISH PEOPLE'S REPUBLIC

Election Year	1947	1952	1957	1961	1965	1969	1972
Number of:							
Deputies	444	425	459	460	460	460	460
Committees	20	11	19	19	19	20	22
Sessions	12	19	8	9	9	5	2
Sittings	108	39	59	32	23	18	8
Days in Session	108	39	71	44	40	22	11
Laws	394	42	174	93	60	36	
Decrees	349	161	13	1	1		
Questions*	65	69	140	13	15	37	

*Number of written questions put to Ministers by the Deputies during a given session

TABLE 65—OPERATING STATISTICS OF THE SEYM OF THE POLISH PEOPLE'S REPUBLIC

Year	No.	Duration(hr)	Year	No.	Duration(hr)
1952**	3	6	1962	9	73.5
1953	5	24	1963	8	59.5
1954	4	22	1964	6	54
1955	5	22.5	1965	6	51
1956	16	89	1966	6	51.5
1957	12	101.5	1967	6	
1958	17	127.5	1968	4	53
1959	14	93.5	1969	7	33.5
1960	9	67.5	1970	5	15
1961	14	80	1971	8	58

*Total number of hours per year spent in plenary sessions where debate and voting take place.
**New Constitution was prepared in this year, debated and voted in.

TABLE 66—COMPARISON OF TIME SPENT IN DEBATING PENDING LEGISLATION

Country	Hours Per Year Spent in Session*
Great Britain (Commons)	1528
United States (Senate)	1146
Canada	942
India	729
Italy	606
France	510
Austria	356
West Germany	313
Belgium	307
Switzerland	263
Japan	82
Poland (Polish People's Republic)	42**

*Data for 1968-1973, five year average
**Data for 1967-1971, five year average

SEYM APPROPRIATES INDUSTRY TO COMMUNIST PARTY BUT SNAGS ON AGRICULTURE

The second question of the Referendum held in June 1946 dealt with the ownership of industry and land. In the course of World War II all industry and large farms were confiscated by the occupying powers, by the Soviets east of the Ribbentrop–Molotov line and by the Germans in Silesia, Greater Poland and Pomerania, with both occupying powers following almost identical policies in this respect. In Central Poland the Germans either confiscated major industries, or placed them under the administration of Nazi appointed *Treuhanders*. These confiscations remained in force when the CP took over under Russian supervision.

In the territories acquired from Germany after World War II in the country's shift westwards, all property, large and small, with the exception of that owned by Poles resident in those territories before the war, became government property to be disposed of as the government saw fit.

The Communist take-over of the industry was the first step in the process astutely identified by Milovan Djilas as the "transfer of property from individual ownership by members of the public to the collective ownership by the Communist Party." Significantly, the Referendum aimed at obtaining a post factum approval of the takeover and was supplemented by a number of laws passed later by the Seym. The process was finally completed as late as 1976 when the "Leading role of the Party" was made an article of the amended Constitution. The first part of the process, that is the nationalization, was made easier by the war-time confiscations described above and by the fact that under the Second Republic about twenty percent of all industry, as well as railroads, telephone and telegraph lines, airlines, and major banks were already government-owned. Thus, when the CP took over and monopolized the government, the ownership of the bulk of the economy passed to the Communist Party. The hasty nature of the take-over of industry and the lack of proper debate in the Seym or gradual adjustment to the new social order, greatly added to the hardships experienced by the population badly in need of respite after the Second World War. If former owners of confiscated property were Polish citizens they were not compensated for their loss. Foreign investors, other than Germans, were able to use leverage, such as the refusal of their respective governments to conclude commercial agreements with Poland, until the CP made suitable arrangements for compensation.

The immediate benefit of the new ownership structure accrued to the CP itself, for it provided the state support for its apparatus through salaries, pay bonuses, pensions, state operated vacation resorts for the CP membership, etc. To the individual party members it often meant a doubling of their salaries, as compared to non-CP citizens. Thus, a privileged New Class has been established at taxpayer's expense. The cost to the nation was estimated for 1972 to be seven billion złotys and equalled in magnitude the total cost of support of medical personnel and hospital facilities in the country. That the population was well aware of the new property relationships was attested by the name commonly applied to the CP apparatus: "Proprietors of the People's Poland" (Właściciele Polski Ludowej). The CP wished to foster a passive acceptance of this state of affairs by the rest of the population and the people, in turn, summed up this wish in a two-liner:

> Nic nie gadaj, nie podskakuj,
> Siedź na tyłku i przytakuj

> Don't jump up, don't digress,
> Just sit tight, and nod: yes

The period following the Second World War was marked by a tremendous effort on the part of the entire society to rebuild the country from the ravages of war. The legislation passed by the Seym in this period had a mixed effect. On the positive side one must mark the decision to expand the educational facilities and provide them with sufficient funding to overcome the war losses in the educated segment of society. The ostensibly free higher education was, however, tied to obligatory, government-designated employment at low salary, or full repayment of costs. This last provision did much to deflate the government claim of providing free education.

Socialization of medicine and attempts by the government to provide badly needed new housing were similarly a mixed success. The housing shortage remained acute, and eventually the CP was forced to retreat from its ownership position and allow private housing construction in an attempt to reduce the usual six to twelve year waiting period required by a new family to get accommodations from the state.

In the economic sphere, the question of investment and adequate labor motivation dominated the scene. The rejection of the American offer of aid under the Marshall Plan and the forced nationalization of industry hampered the effort of reconstruction by further disrupting the war ravaged social and industrial structure, so that recovery and expansion were slow in the years 1952-1956. Moreover, it took almost until the 1970's to replace the nearly total economic dependence on the Soviet Union by closer ties to the West, particularly through the decision to inject imported capital into the industry. This was a Marshall Plan with a thirty years' delay and a repayment scheme attached.

By far the most troublesome aspect of the take-over of industry, commerce, and services by the CP had been its inability to exercise the rights of ownership to the satisfaction of the labor force. The slogans to the effect that the industry was now owned by the workers simply did not ring true in a country which had a CP of 2.2

million, of which only 51.8% were admittedly workers (1972 figures), while the labor force numbered some 10 million, thus at best only one-tenth of the labor force shared in the privileges of ownership. To the other nine-tenths, the CP-controlled state represented just another employer with whom the relations were formalized through the new labor legislation. The new Labor Code, passed as law on January 1, 1975, dealt with the rights and obligations of labor in every aspect of employment and labor discipline, barring one position that of the striking worker.

Fig 113—The Seym building in Warsaw, reconstructed in 1948 from the damage of the Second World War to the designs of Bohdan Pniewski (1897).

The assumption of the prerogatives of ownership of the bulk of the economy by the CP was accompanied by a proclamation of full employment. To make this proclamation more convincing, the chief feature of the social legislation of the Second Republic, namely the unemployment insurance scheme, was abolished forthwith. This hasty step produced unexpected results, totally unintended by the legislators. The difficulties started in the early 1950's when labor unrest, brought about by low wages and food shortages, led to an eruption of strikes. The Seym stood idly by while the CP-controlled government attempted to restore labor discipline by sending the offenders to forced labor camps, some located in the Silesian coal-mining region. To enforce the so-called "socialist discipline" a network of these camps was created with legislative approval of the compliant

Seym, willing and ready to grant all budgetary requests of the Ministry of Internal Security. The most notorious of these camps were those located at Mielęcin near the city of Włocławek and at Jaworzno, between Katowice and Cracow. The population of each of these camps was between 10,000 and 30,000 unfortunates who in one way or another had displeased the CP establishment. The presence of camps in turn, generated further resentment among the free labor in the mines; the miners were forced to compete on unfair terms with convict labor. The situation became explosive and contributed much to the upheaval of 1956 which led to a change of administration. The decision to abandon these oppressive measures is credited to the post-1956 administration. A milder course adopted in managing the industry did not, however, quell the dissatisfaction with the new owners, and the strikes kept recurring over the same issues of low wages, poor food supplies, and housing shortages. If anything, the strikes became a regular feature after each hike in food prices announced by the government, gaining in intensity and becoming more wide-spread.

When labor dissatisfaction erupted in strikes the strike leaders, such as could be identified by the CP, were, as a rule, dismissed from work and heavily fined. The new Labor Code offered no protection and the dismissed and their families became destitute. Their plight precipitated in the years 1976-77 a spontaneous movement throughout Poland for organizing the Committees for the Defense of the Workers (KOR). The committees collected funds from private donors for the support of dismissed strikers and payment of their fines and attempted to find them other employment. This became, in effect, a private unemployment insurance and labor exchange, both previously abolished by the misguided legislation passed by the Seym.

The key to the vicious circle of rising prices, food shortages, and the ever larger strikes triggered by them, lay in the faulty legislation enacted in the agricutural sphere and in the lack of true representation of peasant interests in the Seym. This, in turn, stemmed from the fraudulent motives underlying the land reform carried out in the early days of the Polish People's Republic.

The suspicion of fraud arose already at the time of the 1946 Referendum with the seizure of the remaining large estates for parcelling. The plots of land given out then to landless peasants were, as a rule, about four hectares in size, whereas eight hectares were considered a minimum for a viable one-family farm under the earlier Land Reform of 1920. The new farms were not intended to be viable.

Strengthening the suspicion that the Land Reform was just a temporary political move, was the fact that the payment demanded from the new farm-owners for the land was nominal: an equivalent of the price of 1,000 to 1,500 kilograms of rye per hectare as compared to the equivalent of 15,000 kilograms of rye grain per hectare used under the Second Republic, which more approximated the value of the land.

All evidence pointed to an attempt to perpetrate on the Polish peasant the "Lenin Swindle:" give the peasants land to hold until the CP is firmly in the saddle, then collectivize. Awareness of what happened in the 1930's in Russia was wide-spread in Poland and probably accounted for the fact that in the Civil War, fought in Poland in 1945-47 against the Communist take-over, most of the opponents of the Communists were peasants.

The suspicions of fraud proved true when an intensive drive to collectivize agriculture was launched in 1952. Its prime targets were the weak new farms. At the same time a discriminatory policy was established against the larger, more efficient older farms with respect to sales of fertilizer and farm machinery to cripple them as well. Police measures were used to deprive individual farmers of control over their farms and to place it in the hands of CP appointed collective farm managers. Though formally successful at first, the collectivization campaign was intensely unpopular with the farmers, and by the end of 1956 farm production collapsed and caused the bloody food riots in the cities and industrial areas of Poznań, Gdańsk and Warsaw that eventually toppled the government.

A spontaneous movement among the farmers led to the breakup of most of the collective farms in east-central Poland. The remaining collective farms were mostly located in the territories taken over from Germany after the Second World War and did not involve land taken from the Polish peasants. One can conclude, therefore, that here the ghost of Lenin ran into a snag.

SEYMS OF THE POLISH PEOPLE'S REPUBLIC, SECOND AND THE FIRST REPUBLICS COMPARED

In the Polish People's Republic all the unsavory features of the political life of the closing years of the Second Republic became magnified. In place of a close-knit group of people governing the country on the strength of their record of resistance to Russian domination, the country was saddled with a close-knit governing group imposed and maintained in power by the presence of Russian troops in the country. Instead of opposition parties outside of the legislature, no opposition parties were allowed to operate in the country at all, and anybody attempting to organize one was either imprisoned or assassinated. In the Seym, instead of the "Camp of National Unity" (OZN) hand-picking candidates for Deputies acceptable to the governing group, the country had the "Front of National Unity" (FJN) which not only hand-picked the candidates but also had a law passed which made any effort at boycotting the elections punishable by a fine or imprisonment. Thus, the option of not voting for unacceptable candidates was eliminated as a means of expressing disapproval of the government's actions. In lieu of the "Trial of Brześć" during the Second Republic in which the defendants were given sentences of up to three years imprisonment, which none of them served, the Polish People's Republic had the "Trial of Cracow" for Peasant Party leaders in which eight persons were given death sentences, three of which were carried out. Other defendants were given sentences varying in severity up to life. These were eventually commuted in 1956 when the government fell after severe rioting and demonstrations throughout the country, and the persons concerned were rehabilitated.

During the last five years of the Second Republic the country had a detention camp where, at various times, about 400 persons were held by administrative order for periods of up to half a year, but without loss of life. In the Polish People's Republic, up to the death of Stalin, the government managed to accummulate in prisons and detention camps some 100,000 political prisoners. The camps were concentrated in the industrial region of Silesia, where convict labor was used in the coal mines. The death toll in prisons, camps and coal mines has never been fully documented. The number of deaths which occurred for political reasons outside prison camps in the period preceding the first election, and officially acknowledged, was 16,000. It was truly a government at war with its own citizenry.

In the elections of 1947 the Peasant Party was a torch-bearer for the opposition to the Communist take-over and 128 of its regional workers and organizers were murdered by the Communists in an effort to intimidate the electorate. Thus, all the faults of the pre-1939 political system of the Second Republic were magnified and made more destructive under the Polish People's Republic. After Stalin's death, during the years 1955-56, some 100,000 political prisoners were released and their civil rights restored. However, the people responsible for initiating and carrying out these previous excesses were generally shielded from justice and not made answerable for their actions, particularly if they belonged to the political leadership of the CP.

The role of the Seym during that period was limited to full acquiescence, whereas in the Second Republic the Deputies protested and questioned the Ministers in each case of unconstitutional behavior by members of the administration. The timidity of the Deputies or the outright condonation of the oppressive policies of the administration of the Polish People's Republic can only be interpreted as reflecting their belief that in the Seym they represented the administration and not their constituents.

Comparison of the Seym of the Polish People's Republic with that of the First shows the apparent return to the requirements of unanimity in voting on bills submitted to the Seym. This procedure had been the rule since the independent parties were eliminated from the Seym, and the Constitution of 1952 had been enacted and placed in operation. It was, of course, nothing else but the return to the discredited practices of the Saxon era, when liberum veto ruled, except that now the direction of the unanimity rule has been reversed: it was used to pass all bills, rather than reject them. The public was denied the benefit of having its views known through appeals to its Deputies and the resulting variations in the outcome of the Seym votes. Conflicting points of view and diverse interests present in any society did not get an airing, and were not taken into consideration in preparing legislation.

Exceptions to the unanimity of vote were so rare in the Seyms of the Polish People's Republic that they can be listed individually. The first occurred in 1964 when Deputy Stefan Kisielewski abstained from voting on the budget as a protest against the government directive to schools ordering the removal of crucifixes from the classrooms. The second was on June 14, 1967 when Deputy Konstanty Łubieński abstained from voting on the CP-sponsored condemnation of Israel in the wake of the Arab-Israeli war. A more recent case occurred in 1976 when Deputy Stanisław Stomma abstained from voting on the amendments to the Constitution which affirmed "the leading role of the CP" in the government and made "friendship with the Soviet Union" a statutory requirement. Both amendments were highly unpopular in the country and precipitated a letter-writing campaign addressed to the Speaker of the Seym, protests from the Roman Catholic Episcopate, plus a round robin from the leading intellectuals. Stomma, like Kisielewski, was dropped from the candidate lists put up by the CP-controlled Front of National Unity in subsequent elections. These rare responses of Deputies to the demands of the electorate all came from a handful of independents representing Catholic interests in the Seym.

Fig. 114 (left)—Stanisław Gucwa (1919-), activist in the licensed Peasant Party and Speaker of the 1972 Seym of the Polish People's Republic.

Fig. 115 (right)—Aerial view of the Seym building in Warsaw after the reconstruction and expansion following the Second World War. The building on the right is the Seym Hotel, provided for the convenience of the Deputies.

The virtual elimination of debate from the proceedings of the Seyms of the Polish People's Republic and the transfer of all work on pending bills, save the final vote, to the committees working in camera made the Seym of the Polish People's Republic resemble the Seym of the Congress Kingdom after the amendment of 1825 banned public debates. It is characteristic that whenever Russian influence dominates the Seym it is forced to operate through small committees, easier to control than the full assembly, and the time allowed for debate on the floor is reduced to a mere token or altogether eliminated. This was true of the "Mute Seym" of 1717, the "Delegation Seym" of 1772-73, of the last two Seyms before the Revolution of 1830, and again of the Seyms of the Polish People's Republic.

One can also measure the performance of the political institutions of the Second and the Polish People's Republic against the standard of the three basic principles on which the 500 years of Polish constitutional development were built, namely the constitutions *neminem captivabimus, nihil novi,* and *nec bona recipiantur.*

The Second Repubic failed in its last decade to live up to the constitutional standard of *neminem captivabimus* by denying to several hundred of its citizens incarcerated in the Bereza detention camp the benefits of a due process of law. It performed reasonaby well, however, when judged against the *nihil novi,* since much of the legislation enacted in that period conformed to the popular aspirations of the time. As regards the assurance of the right to property or the enforcement of laws derived from the constitutional principle *nec bona recipiantur,* the only confiscations of property witnessed by the Second Republic were those in which the property, taken over by the former partitioning powers from Polish citizens after the various uprisings and awarded to members of their administrations, was recovered, in some cases from the descendants of the original awardees. Restoration to the original Polish owners was not always possible, particularly in what had been the Congress Kingdom since there, as a rule, the post-uprising confiscations were accompanied by deportations of the owners to Siberia, where many of them perished.

The other large transfers of property rights in the Second Republic were those connected with the land reform. Here the rule of compensating owners of large estates which were being parcelled out was strictly followed with long term payments.

The reluctance of the Seyms of the Second Republic to depart from the principle of "no confiscation except through the due process of law," embedded in the rule *nec bona recipiantur,* accounted for the acceptance of the border settlement in the peace treaty with the Soviet Union in 1921 which left large Ukrainian and Byelorussian minorities within Polish borders. The sorting out of the populations from the ethnically mixed regions would have demanded large–scale confiscations of property with little hope of providing equitable compensation, to say nothing of the hardships and suffering resulting from such dislocations of a large number of people.

When judged against the standard of *nihil novi*, the legislative record of the Polish People's Republic is for the most part a dismal failure. Legislation was enacted against the interests of large groups within the society: laws promoting the initial collectivization of agriculture, expropriation of large and small businesses without compensation, oppressive and arbitrary tax laws designed to destroy private commerce, legislation denying workers the protection of the right to strike and to have true representation in wage disputes, and many others.

The performance of the institutions of the Polish People's Republic, when measured against the principle of "no arrest without due process of law," as formulated in *neminem captivabimus*, is even more dismal as attested by some 100,000 people who went through the forced labor camps in the period 1947-56. In later years the tendency has been to have the Seym pass legislation which allowed certain oppressive measures to be applied legalistically, thus formally satisfying the letter but not the spirit of *neminem captivabimus*. The legislation so passed still failed in the test of *nihil novi*, since one can reasonably expect that the popular will, when expressed freely, would not have approved of the passage of laws destined to oppress the people. In this matter, the chief offender was the new Code of Criminal Procedure, passed in 1969. With its vaguely defined reasons for which arrests could be made and convictions imposed, it gave plenty of leeway for arbitrary arrests and rash sentences.

In the area of assuring the citizens of their right to property and safety from arbitrary confiscation, that is the application of the principle of *nec bona recipiantur*, the departure of the practices of the Polish People's Republic from the mainstream of Poland's constitutional tradition and philosophy was equally drastic. Large scale confiscations of houses, land and businesses were carried out with owners not guilty of breaking any law, nor convicted of any crime, other than that implied in the "guilt by ownership" as defined by the CP.

When the legislative efforts of the three Republics in the economic sphere are compared, there is a visible trend towards increased participation in steering of the economy, not always with the best results. Starting with the early efforts of the Seyms of the First Republic to regulate the issue of coinage, in which the mint was first taken away from under the control of the Executive, then returned to it when the Seym's control proved ineffective, it blossomed into attempts to control prices and regulate interest rates on loans. In many cases the policies set fast in legislation were counter-productive or too rigid to follow the ever-changing demands of economic life.

In the Second Republic, the economic effects of Seym activity were felt mainly through the rather extensive legislation dealing with the social services and the land reform. The Seyms authorized government participation in industrial investment through the creation of the Central Industrial Region (COP), the coal railroad from Silesia to the Baltic, and the erection of the port of Gdynia, this last project authorized post factum. We will return to the Gdynia project in connection with the Czechowicz affair, in the section on the impeachment powers of the Seym. Most of the economic interventions were beneficial, though unable to override the effects of the Great Depression.

In the Polish People's Republic the Seym plunged heavily into economic matters, first legislating the various confiscation schemes in the industry, services, commercial housing and commerce, and then giving a stamp of approval to the various five year economic plans developed by the now greatly expanded Executive Branch. In this latter role the Seym bore the responsibility, and part of the blame, for the gross misdirection of some of the efforts in the national investment area, where attempts to satisfy all directives from Moscow did not coincide with the best interests of the country. The effects of the misdirection did show up in chronic shortages of certain commodities, violent labor unrest, and erratic progress of investment policies.

Finally, it would not be out of place to remark here on the role of political parties in the scheme of things. In a democracy they should serve as the vehicle for crystallizing the will of the people, and for converting it into legislative and executive action. But when political parties assume the role of a sovereign, as they attempted to do in the first decade of the Second Republic, and as the Communist Party succeeded in doing in the Polish People's Republic, the well-being of the nation suffers greatly.

The system operating under the Polish People's Republic, whereby the processes of selection of government and the review of its performance was decoupled from the elections, and in which the wishes of the Central Committee of the CP were substituted for those of the electorate, had in effect produced a system in which the successive governments had to be forced out of office instead of being voted out. The electorate still asserted its wishes but did so outside the constitutional framework through riots, strikes, and demonstrations pointing to the pressing need for the revision of that framework.

A new political consensus emerged among the industrial workers of Poland which identified the CP as the chief exploiter, as evidenced by the first move the striking and revolting workers usually made: to set fire to the district headquarters of the CP, as had occurred in 1956 in Poznań, again in 1970 in Gdańsk, and in 1976 in Radom. The governing philosophy, marketed in Marxist packaging, but based on the traditional Russian autocratic principle, that the ruler knows best and the citizenry must be coerced into unquestioning obedience, was again questioned: a return to government with the consent of the governed was the end sought.

The constitutional arrangements in force in the Polish People's Republic are summarized in Table 67, its chief legislative officers are listed in Table 68, and the principal legislation in Table 69.

TABLE 67—CONSTITUTION OF THE POLISH PEOPLE'S REPUBLIC—A SYNOPSIS

(Voted July 22, 1952; amended 1954, '57, '60, '61, '63, '72, and '76)

The Executive Branch of the Government was vested in the Council of State, composed of a President, four deputy presidents, a secretary and eleven other members. It had the power to issue decrees with the force of law, to ratify or denounce international treaties and had the right of pardon. It could lift parliamentary immunity from the Deputies of the Seym.

The Council of State appointed 22 ministers, who then formed the Council of Ministers. It also nominated members of the Supreme Court for a term of five years.

The Legislative Branch of the Government consisted of a unicameral Seym of 460 Deputies elected for a term of four years. The Seym passed laws, approved the budget and the economic plans. It had the power to exercise control over the administration of the State. The legislative initiative was vested in the Council of State, the Ministers and the Deputies.

An extension of the Council of State was provided at the palatinate and county levels in the form of National Councils. These Councils acted as supervisory bodies for the administration and were in turn supervised by the Council of State. Their membership was elective, with a four year term of office and candidacy limited to persons selected by the Front of National Unity.

The Electoral Law was based on universal, secret, direct, and equal suffrage of citizens of 18 years of age or over. Secrecy of the ballot was not compulsory and unmarked ballots were valid. Deputies had to be at least 21 years of age. The candidates could be nominated only by the Front of National Unity. The Deputies, once elected, could be recalled by the electorate.

The Judiciary Branch of the Government was composed of Judges and public prosecutors appointed and recalled by the Council of State. The courts were organized on three levels: District and Palatinate Courts and the Supreme Court.

Bill of Rights guaranteed the freedom of speech, personal movement and possession of property, with the upper limit for each specified by law. Access to printing presses, radio, and other mass media were ostensibly guaranteed to working people.

TABLE 68—PRINCIPAL LEGISLATIVE OFFICERS OF THE POLISH PEOPLE'S REPUBLIC

Chief Executive	Term of Office
Bolesław Bierut	1947-1952*
Aleksander Zawadzki	1952-1964
Edward Ochab	1964-1968
Marian Spychalski	1968-1970
Józef Cyrankiewicz	1970-1972
Henryk Jabłoński	1972-1989
Wojciech Jaruzelski**	1989-1991

Speaker of the Seym	Term of Office
Władysław Kowalski	1947-1952
Jan Dembowski	1952-1956
Czesław Wycech	1957-1971
Dyzma Gałaj	1971-1972
Stanisław Gucwa	1972-1985
Roman Malinowski	1985-1989

*Died while on a trip to Moscow
** Assumed the presidency as a compromise candidate.

TABLE 69—PRINCIPAL LEGISLATION OF SEYMS OF THE POLISH PEOPLE'S REPUBLIC

1947	Small Constitution approved
	Former members of Resistance amnestied
	Three-year plan for post-war reconstruction
1950	Local Administration reorganized
	Six-Year Plan for economic development voted
	Border Treaty with East Germany ratified
1952	Constitution passed
1955	Jurisdiction over civilians transferred from military to civil courts
1956	General Amnesty Law passed
	Factory/state-farm workers' councils formed
	Four-Year Plan 1956-60 approved
1957	Constitution amended by addition of a Supreme Control Chamber
1960	Number of Seym Deputies increased to 460
	Code of administrative procedure passed

TABLE 69 (CONTINUED)—PRINCIPAL LEGISLATION OF SEYMS OF THE POLISH PEOPLE'S REPUBLIC

1961	Four-Year Plan 1961-65 approved
1963	Subdivision of farms limited
1964	Code of Civil Law and Family Code passed
1965	Insurance Plan for Craftsmen created
1966	Air-pollution control law passed
	Office of Weights and Measures reorganized
	Four-Year Plan 1966-70 approved
1967	Office of the Public Prosecutor reorganized
1968	Reform of Old Age Pension Plan approved
	Unjustified absenteeism from work condemned
	Consolidation of fragmented farm property
	Expropriation of farm property of low productivity authorized
	Pensions for farmers in exchange for their farms voted
1969	Code of Criminal Procedure passed
1969	General Amnesty proclaimed
1970	Polish Academy of Sciences reorganized
1971	Churches in Western Poland turned over to the Episcopate
	Compulsory sales of farm produce abolished
	Four-Year Plan 1971-75 approved
1972	Ministry of Ex-combatants formed
	One-family housing and co-ops decontrolled
1973	Office of Atomic Energy established
	Law on academic degrees changed

POLITICAL PERSONALITIES IN THE SEYM OF THE POLISH PEOPLE'S REPUBLIC

Jan Dembowski (1889-1963)—Biologist, zoopsychologist, and politician; he was a member of the staff and later the director of the Institute of Experimental Biology in Warsaw (1919-1934); Associate Professor of the University of Warsaw (1929-34). During 1944-47 he served as scientific attaché to Polish Embassy in Moscow. Chairman of the Polish Academy of Sciences (1948-1952). He was elected to the Seym and served as its Speaker in 1952-56 and was appointed Deputy Chairman of the Council of State. Author of *The Natural*

History of Simple Organisms (1924), *Animal Psychology* (1946), and *Psychology of Apes* (1946).

Dyzma Gałaj (1915-)—Sociologist and political activist; member of the peasant underground during World War II. In 1957–63 he edited *Contemporary Village*. In 1970 he became professor at the Central School of Agriculture. From 1972 he served as director of the Institute for the Development of Agriculture of the Polish Academy of Sciences. He became deputy chairman of the Executive Committee of the United Peasant Party (ZSL) in 1971. Elected Seym Deputy in 1956, he served as its Speaker in 1971-1972. In 1972 he became a member of the Council of State. He is author of *Social Economic Activity of Peasants* (1961) and *Peasant Political Movement in Poland* (1969).

Stanisław Gucwa (1919-)—Activist in the peasant movement who was a member of the peasant underground during World War II. After the war he became a member of the Communist–sponsored Peasant Party (SL), and after 1949 a member of the United Peasant Party (ZSL), becoming a member of its Executive Committee in 1959. Elected to the Seym in 1961, he served as its Speaker 1972–1985. Between 1957 and 1968 he served as Under Secretary in the Ministry of Agriculture and between 1968-71 as Minister of Food Industry. Member of the Executive Committee of the Front of National Unity (FJN) since 1971.

Stefan Kisielewski (1911- 1996)—Composer, music critic, writer. A graduate of the Warsaw conservatory of Music (1934), he divided his time between teaching and work for the periodical "Polish Music." During the Second World War he participated in the resistance movement against the Germans and took part in the Warsaw Uprising in 1944. Appointed Professor of Higher School of Music in Cracow (1945-49), editor of the *Musical Movement* in 1945-46 and again in 1957-59, he was a regular contributor to the *Universal Weekly*, a Catholic periodical. He was one of the few Catholics allowed to run for a seat in the Seym, to which he was elected as Deputy and served during 1957-65. He was the author of numerous musical works, including several symphonies and concertos and he published a selection of essays *Politics and Art* (1949), *Stories and Travels* (1959), *With Music Through the Years* (1957), and others.

Władysław Kowalski (1894-1958)—Activist in the peasant movement, writer, member of the Communist Party of Poland (KPP) in 1918-24. He became a member of "Wyzwolenie" Peasant Party, between 1924-27 he was a member of the National Peasant Party (NPCH), and between 1928-33 he was editor of "Peasant Self-help." In 1944 he joined the Russian sponsored Lublin Committee (KRN) and served as Minister of Culture and Arts between 1945 and 1947. Elected to the Seym, he served as the Speaker of the First Seym of the Polish People's Republic. He was a member of the Council of State in 1952-56 and a member of the Executive Committee of the Communist-sponsored Peasant Party

(SL), and after amalgamation with the Polish Peasant Party (PSL), served as the chairman of the United Peasant Party (ZSL). He authored novels: *In Grzmiąca* (1936) and *Far and Near* (1948).

Stanisław Mikołajczyk (1901-1966)—Political activist in the Polish Peasant Party. In 1918 he participated in the uprising against German rule in the province of Greater Poland. He was a cofounder of the Association of Village Youth (ZMW) and its chairman in 1928. He served as Deputy to the Seym of the Second Republic from 1930 to 1935. From 1931 he was a member of the executive committee of the Peasant Party and its deputy chairman from 1935. In 1936 he was elected chairman of the Agricultural Circle Association and was one of the organizers of the strike of agricultural workers in 1937. During World War II, in exile, he was the Prime Minister of the Polish Government in England in 1943-44. After the war he was the chairman of the Polish Peasant Party (PSL) and deputy Prime Minister of Poland 1945-47. Elected Deputy to the Seym of the Polish People's Republic in 1947, after an election campaign marked by political terror against candidates of PSL, he went into exile under threat of death and settled in the United States of America. He authored *The Rape of Poland* (New York, 1948).

Kazimerz Pużak (1883-1950)—Revolutionary, politician, parliamentarian; active in socialist underground operating against the Tsar, was arrested in 1911 and sentenced to eight years imprisonment to be followed by exile for life in Siberia. Released by the Russian revolution, he served as the chairman of the Polish Socialist Party in the Second Republic from 1921 onwards. Deputy in the Seyms of 1919-1935. During the Second World War he was one of the organizers and leaders of the anti-Nazi underground in Poland and the last Chairman of the Council of National Unity, the political directorate with representation of the Peasant, Socialist, Christian Democratic, and National Democratic Parties. Invited in 1945 with fifteen other parliamentarians and leaders of the underground to Moscow to participate in the formation of the first post-war Polish government, he was instead put on trial, accused of pro-German and anti-Soviet activities. After two years in prison he returned to Poland, wrote his memoirs, and was imprisoned again by the Polish Communist Party. He died in Rawicz prison in 1950. He wrote: *Memoirs 1939-1945* (Paris 1977).

Stanisław Stomma (1908-)—Writer and social activist, associate professor of criminal law at the University of Cracow. Active in Catholic social organizations and one of the few Catholics allowed to run for a seat in the Seym, he was elected a Deputy in 1957. He was the Chairman of the Catholic group in the Seym and the sole Deputy to abstain from the 1976 vote on amending the Constitution with the clause making the friendship with Russia a constitutional duty, and thus formally turning the clock back to 1717.

Czesław Wycech (1899-1977)—Teacher, politician, activist in the peasant movement; from 1919 he was active in the Association of Polish Teachers (ZNP), and from 1938 served as its deputy chairman. He became minister of Education (1945-47) and member of the Executive Committee of the Polish Peasant Party. In 1949 he was instrumental in the elimination of the Polish Peasant Party (PSL) by accepting the amalgamation with the Communist-controlled Peasant Party (SL) and endorsement of its program, including the collectivization of agriculture. Seym Deputy from 1947, he served as Speaker of the Seym from 1957 to 1971, he was also deputy Chairman of the Council of State in 1956-57.

CHAPTER VIII

SELECTED LEGISLATIVE PROBLEMS IN HISTORICAL PERSPECTIVE

In this section a historical perspective is given to selected legislative problems. The areas covered are the development of suffrage rights during the last five centuries in Poland and their progressive extension to an ever-widening segment of the population. Comparisons of suffrage rights in Poland and other countries are made on a historical time scale. Next, the handling of several important areas of responsibility by the Seyms is considered in separate treatments, each extending in time over the whole period covered in this study. Among the areas selected for highlighting are: the impeachment and judiciary powers of the Seyms, the problems of taxation and other state revenue, war- and peace-making activities, as well as legislation relating to the ownership of real estate. Finally, the Seym as a career is given a brief examination.

Appendices contain the Latin texts of the key paragraphs in the founding charters of civil liberties, the historical development of the Seymik network, the chronological tables of all elections held since 1493, listing the places where the Seyms were convened. Also included are the texts of the secret protocols in which parts of the old Polish-Lithuanian Commonwealth were traded between Germany and the Soviet Union, the collusion initiating the Second World War.

The bibliography contains a guide to all publications of the legislation produced by the Seyms during the 500 years of their existence, the Journals of Debates, Directories of Deputies and Senators, as well as the literature both in Polish and in English dealing with the activities and history of the Seyms.

THE DEVELOPMENT OF SUFFRAGE RIGHTS

Throughout the first part of this study numerous references were made to the suffrage rights at various periods in the history of the legislature in Poland. Here they are brought together and supplemented with a discussion of the technicalities involved in making the voting rights work. In addition, comparisons are drawn with suffrage rights in other contemporary legislative systems. Three aspects of suffrage rights are of interest here, namely: the legal, who is entitled to vote; the socio-political, who is capable of voting by reason of literacy, access to political life, etc.; and finally, the civic, who is willing to vote, i.e., the question of voter turnout.

In comparing suffrage statistics over several centuries, basic demographic facts need to be kept in mind to make these comparisons meaningful. Of particular importance is the size of the base used. If the adult population is chosen as a base of comparison, corrections must be made for the fact that the age distribution of populations differed in the past from what is common today. This is illustrated in Figure 116 by means of two life-trees of the population of Poland drawn from data taken some seventy years apart. They show the distribution of the population in 1900 and 1972 by age and sex group. The life-tree for 1900 is based on the population census taken in that year in Galicia. This life-tree is representative of the population of any country in the days before modern medicine made its impact. It is characterized by a broad base at infancy and a narrow peak at old age, reflecting short life expectancy. In that year median age was about 20. The life-tree for 1972 is characteristic of modern societies with a more even distribution of age groups between infancy and adulthood. In the case of Poland, it shows additional perturbations due to the severe loss of life in the Second World War. Of particular interest here is the fact, that adults (over 20) constituted 47% of the population in 1900 but the percentage increased to 64.4% in 1972. Since prior to about 1920 in all countries with electoral systems only adult men had a right to vote, the above percentages must be reduced by a half, assuming an approximately equal distribution of sexes in the population. Thus, the percentage of potential voters was about 23.5% of the total population in the past. This basic figure was then subject to further reduction through restrictions based on class, property, or religion.

With these technical points in mind one can follow the historical development of suffrage rights in Poland during the last 500 years, using total population as a base of comparison of the size of electorate between different periods and countries. It marks a steady progress towards an ever-broadening participation of the population in the law-making process, though not without setbacks and difficulties at various times.

Life Trees of Population of POLAND in 1900 and 1972

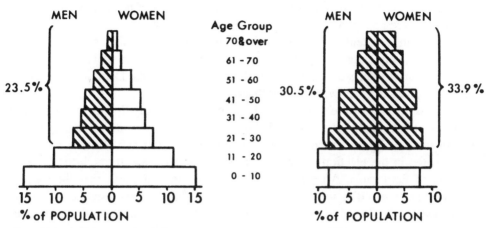

Fig. 116—Life Trees of Population of Poland in 1900 and 1972.

A detailed discussion of the population and its political representation in the earlier period is much hampered by the absence of good population statistics. For most of the life of the hereditary monarchy and the First Republic, population figures are based on estimates derived from the tax rolls which were inaccurate at the best of times. In the fourteenth century, when Peter's Pence was converted from household tax to a poll tax, a valuable source of population statistics was added; when the state attempted to impose the poll tax, however, the move was so unpopular that in 1662 the Seym ordered the destruction of the tax rolls; however, this did not occur until after the taxes had been collected. Then, as now, indirect taxes were favored over the poll tax. The first partial census made specifically for tax purposes was not conducted until 1764. In spite of these difficulties, enough data is available for estimates of total population. Estimates of the number of gentry are more difficult to make since the gentry repeatedly refused to have themselves tabulated, fearing the creation of a permanent tax roll. Using data based on land ownership records, the proportion of gentry is put at 10% of total population, increasing to 15% for the central palatinates of Kujawy, Masovia, and Podlasia.

If we define suffrage as an opportunity to express a binding opinion on a political issue, then in the earliest times this right would have been limited to the Prince alone. Gradually, it was expanded to include the Prince's council. When the bicameral Seym made its appearance on the political scene of Poland in 1493, the Deputies to the Seym entered the picture. They were elected by the Seymik of each county with the participation of all the gentry and the local Senators. The right to vote was bound to the obligation of military service in the levée en masse and was hereditary. It was not, however, tied to the ownership of land. In fact, in the final years of the First Republic most of the voters were members of the yeomanry, or altogether landless. Initially, the Senators, i.e., Palatines and Castellans resident in the area, had the right to appoint half the Deputies. The gentry eventually came to oppose this practice and at the Seym of 1520 demanded an extension of their suffrage rights to the election of all the Deputies. The Seym of 1538-9, held in Cracow, conceded this demand.

At the time, cities were few and far between, but the early Seyms included their representatives regularly. After 1505 the representation of cities became sporadic, except for the City of Cracow. The Prussian cities of Gdańsk, Toruń and Elbląg participated in the election of deputies to the national Seym through the General Seymik of Pomerania. After the union with Lithuania in 1569, first the City of Wilno then other cities were confirmed in the right to be represented: Lwów in 1658, Kamieniec Podolski in 1670, and Lublin in 1703. The city representatives carried the title of Ablegate and voted on city matters only.

The Constitution of 1791 placed the matter of town representation on a more equitable basis by requiring that all towns in which the appellate courts sat, elect and send to the Seym one Plenipotentiary. In the twenty-one towns and cities listed below only property owners had the right to vote in the election of Plenipotentiaries. The candidates for this office were required to have held an elective municipal office beforehand. Twenty-one such Plenipotentiaries were to sit on the Treasury, Police and Judiciary Committees of the Seym, with the right to vote on matters relating to towns and commerce. In other matters they had a consultative voice only. Thus, the Plenipotentiaries had a position similar to the Delegates of Washington, D.C. and Puerto Rico in the present-day Congress of the United States. Constitutional and tax matters were outside their competence. The following towns and cities were electing Plenipotentiaries under the law of 1791 (the population of the major ones at the time is given in parentheses):

TABLE 70—CITIES WITH SEYM REPRESENTATION IN 1791

Lesser Poland	Greater Poland	Lithuania
Cracow (20,000)	Poznań (20,000)	Wilno (24,000)
Lublin (12,200)	Kalisz	Grodno (5,000)
Łuck	Gniezno	Kowno (4,500)
Żytomierz	Łęczyca	Nowogródek
Winnica	Warsaw (96,100)	Mińsk
Kamieniec (6,000)	Sieradz	Brześć
Drohiczyn	Płock	Pińsk (4,500)

The Pomeranian towns of Gdańsk (36,700) and Toruń (9,000), cut off from mainland Poland by the First Partition, were allowed to send special delegations to the Seym at their own discretion.

The later 1600s and early 1700s mark the introduction of restrictive changes in the laws dealing with passive electoral rights, i.e., the right to run for office. As a result of two major invasions by the Protestant Swedes during which the loyalty of some of the Polish Protestants came into question, a militant Counter-Reformation movement gained wide acceptance. The law of 1658 denied political rights to Arians and banned them from the country for refusing to bear arms even in defensive wars. In 1717 the Seym excluded one of the seven Protestant Deputies, and the law of 1733 revoked passive electoral rights of all non–Catholics altogether, as well as the right to be elected deputy Judge in the Tribunal of the Crown. These restrictions were similar to the provisions of the Test Act of 1673 in England aimed against non-Anglicans. In 1733 the Protestants in Poland numbered approximately 200,000 among the townsmen, plus about 1,000 gentry families. The other large non-Catholic group in the country were the Greek Orthodox, who also fell under the provisions of the 1733 Act. The restrictions on passive rights did not affect the electoral rights of the religious minorities, i.e., the right to vote. It is reasonable to assume, however, that without coreligionaries sitting as Deputies in the Seym, the interests of minority religious groups would not be well represented.

Laws limiting passive electoral rights on purely religious grounds went through several turns. The law of 1733 was repealed in 1768. The Seym of 1773-5 again restricted the passive electoral rights of the Protestants and the Orthodox by limiting to three the number of Deputies representing non-Catholics in the Seym, one from each major province. The Constitution of 1791 repealed these restrictions once more.

An equally significant change in the rights of representation occurred also in 1791. The new Constitution passed in that year divorced active voting rights from the personal obligation of military service in the 'levée en masse' and replaced it with property qualification. Land ownership or the payment of taxes in excess of 100 złotys a year became the qualification for the gentry. This removed some 500,000 of the landless gentry from political participation (men, women and children), that is, approximately one-fourth of that number (adult males) from the electoral rolls. At the same time the Law on the Cities, mentioned above, gave to the cities and towns with an aggregate population of approximately 500,000, a representation in the Seym through the Plenipotentiaries. Thus, on the face of it, the total size of the electorate remained approximately the same, while a better social balance was achieved. Nevertheless, the change was regressive since the size of the electorate did not increase, while that part of the gentry which was stripped of the right to vote joined the ranks of the opponents of the Constitution, confirming the view that every disfranchisement constitutes political dynamite.

The Constitution of 1791, or specifically, the new operating ordinance for the Seymiks incorporated in this Constitution, set the voting age at 18 and the age of eligibility to run for Deputy at 23. The Constitution of 1793, passed by the last Seym of the First Republic sitting at Grodno, did not restore voting rights to the landless gentry, but only to those members of the gentry who held their possessions by the grace of the magnates. This was clearly a political bribe. The right of representation of the cities in the Seym through the Plenipotentiaries was repealed at that time, reducing the size of the electorate. This Constitution, however, was rejected by the country.

To gain a better perspective of the development of representation in Poland, it is instructive to compare the size of the electorate relative to the size of the population of the country in England, Poland and America in the late 1700s. It is estimated that the entire electorate in England in 1769 numbered approximately 250,000 out of a population of 12.2 million, or 2%. The electorate was very unevenly distributed both geographically and socially. It was determined that 5,723 persons chose half the Members of the House of Commons through the system of "rotten boroughs." In the United States at the close of the Revolutionary War the population consisted of 2.0 million of free Americans of all ages plus 0.6 million Negro slaves and 0.3 million indentured servants, giving a total population of 2.9 million. The number of people qualified to vote through property requirements was 120,000, or 4%. In Poland, before the First Partition in 1773, the electorate of all ages and both sexes numbered between 0.85 and 0.9 million out of a population of 14.0 million. Assuming 25% of that number to be adult males, this gives 1.5% of eligible electors. In 1791, before the passage of the Constitution of that year, the total population of Poland was 8.7 million, while the electorate and its families numbered 725,000 and with the adult males at 25% of that number, the eligible electors constituted about 2% of the total population. By imposing property requirements, the Constitution of 1791 shifted the social distribution of the representation, but it left the size of the eleccorate basically unchanged. The significance of these comparisons is that in each of the three countries the size of the electorate as a percentage of the total population fell within the narrow range of 2-4%, mostly determined by property requirements (see Table 71 and Figure 117).

Fig. 117 —Growth of the Electorate in Poland, Great Britain, France and USA:

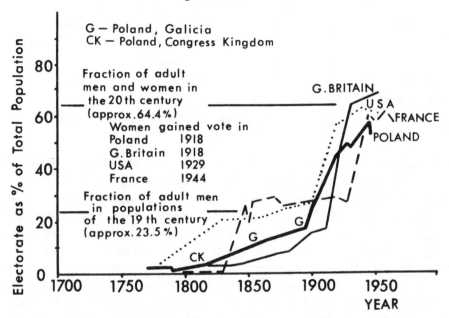

The suffrage rights given by the Napoleonic Constitution of 1807 vested the election of the Deputies to the Seym in the Seymiks of the gentry, and in the communal assemblies of the non-gentry where voting rights were extended to non-gentry landowners, craftsmen, tradesmen, army veterans and army officers of all grades while away from their garrisons. The gentry elected 60, the communal assemblies 40 Deputies, who were equal in every respect in their legislative powers but had different titles, a feature which would be carried over to the next Constitution. While this latest arrangement still left all the landless peasantry without a vote, it greatly increased the representation of the townspeople and the artisans and, in a typically Napoleonic fashion, gave recognition for military service. A setback occurred, however, in the position of the Jewish population.

TABLE 71—DEVELOPMENT OF SUFFRAGE IN POLAND, BRITAIN, FRANCE AND THE UNITED STATES

Electorate as Percentage of Total Population

Poland		Britain*		France		United States	
Year	%	Year	%	Year	%	Year	%
1790	2.0	1769	2.0	1799	0.3	1790	4.1
1815	3.0			1815	0.3		
1830		1835	3.3	1830	0.5	1830	20.9
1860	12.5	1846	3.9	1850	19.1	1860	21.8
1896	17.8	1892	16.2	1889	27.1	1900	26.8
				1919	29.4		
1922	46.9	1922	47.2			1920	57.3
1947	52.9	1951	69.5	1951	58.0	1940	63.4

*United Kingdom: England, Wales, Scotland and the applicable part of Ireland.

—Figures below this line include women's suffrage introduced in Poland and Britain in 1918 in the United States in 1920, and in France in 1944.

With their own representative system in abeyance since shortly before the collapse of the First Republic, the extension of their civil rights in the Duchy was suspended for ten years by decree of the Saxon King Frederick Augustus, who, with Napoleon's blessing, had assumed the executive powers in the Duchy. The reason given in this document was "insufficient assimilation" with the rest of the citizenry. At the time Jews constituted 7% of the total population and 28% of the townspeople, and lack of assimilation was, of course, the other side of the coin to the centuries-old autonomy which the Jewish population had enjoyed in Poland. The autonomy was highly valued by the Jews at the time, for it allowed the Jewish community to preserve its language, customs and religion in an otherwise hostile world. It accentuated differences, rather than similarities. This, however, did not justify the discriminatory character of the decree.

The next change in suffrage rights occurred with the introduction of the Constitution of the Congress Kingdom of Poland in 1815, a constitution considered one of the most liberal in Europe at the time. It gave voting rights to approximately 100,000 people in a country with a population of 3.3 million. The electorate included property owners and people of intellectual achievements, as well as the gentry. The property requirement associated with non-gentry franchise was given to those who paid the land tax, or had a minimum capital of 10,000 złotys. The right to vote was given also to ministers of religion and school teachers. These additional voter categories swelled the ranks of the voters to the point where the gentry were just about matched in numbers by the non-gentry. To be more specific, by 1827 there were in the Congress Kingdom 301,971 persons of gentry status (men, women and children) of which 62,593 were heads of families, this in a total population of 4,137,634 (1830 census). Thus, the gentry as a whole constituted 7.3% of the total, while the heads of families, who all had the right to vote, made up 1.5% of the total. The total percentage of voters, including nongentry, was about 3% in 1815, and probably slightly higher in 1830. The gentry elected its 77 Deputies in the Seymiks, while the 55 non-gentry Deputies were elected in communal assemblies. The system was weighted in favor of the gentry, and as a further concession to their tradition-bound sensitivities, the gentry and the non-gentry Deputies were given different titles, namely, *Poseł* and *Deputowany*, but the same legislative powers.

The province of Greater Poland constituted a part of the Duchy of Warsaw during the years 1806-15 and shared in its suffrage rights, electing Deputies to the Seym in Warsaw. With the separation of the province in 1815 by decision of the Congress of Vienna, the population of the newly created Grand Duchy of Poznań lost its suffrage rights altogether until 1827, when the Seym of Poznań began to assemble. The first elections to it were carried out under the old electoral ordinance of the Duchy of Warsaw i.e., the county Seymiks elected Deputies with the weighted representation of the gentry while the communal assemblies elected Deputies for the towns and the village communities. For the second Seym of Poznań, Frederick Wilhelm of Prussia gave his own electoral law which did not, however, greatly depart from that of the Duchy of Warsaw. The ownership qualifications were retained and the suspension of political rights of Jews continued, although the King requested the Seym's opinion on this last point. It was debated by the Seyms of 1827 and 1830 and the Seym recommended a gradual integration of Jews into the obligations of citizenship through the removal of their army draft exemption and the introduction of Polish and German languages into Jewish schools; electoral rights were to be granted at the end of the transition period. The population of the Grand Duchy of Poznań was multilingual and the 1830 census listed 680,000 Poles, 300,000 Germans and 70,000 Jews in a population of 1,100,000. The Seym operated under this electoral law for some 20 years between 1827 and 1848; in that period seven Seyms were returned.

The weighted representation used by the Seym of Poznań meant that: the four princely families domiciled in the Duchy were each represented by the head of the family himself; the gentry, which constituted about 10% of the total population, elected 22 Deputies; the towns with 12% of the total population elected 16 Deputies; and the peasants, who constituted the remaining 78%, elected only 6 Deputies through the village communal assemblies.

Significant changes towards a more equitable distribution of rights of representation occurred in Poland and in England in the second half of the nineteenth century. In England they took the form of several Suffrage Reform Acts, while in Poland they were connected with the development of the suffrage rights in Galicia. The Galician electoral law enacted in 1861 for elections to the Seym of Lwów was based on a weighted representation, formally given the name of the Curia System. Under this system the number of electors varied from 52 per Deputy elected by the great landowners, through 2,264 electors per Deputy elected by the towns, to 8,764 electors per Deputy in the rural communes. Thus, an electorate of 0.6 million existed in a population of 4.8 million in 1860, or 12% of the population. This electoral ordinance was significantly modified in 1896 when the electoral law reform was put into effect in Galicia. It provided for the formation of the fifth electoral curia, the so-called universal one, with about 70,000 electors apportioned per Deputy. The voting age population increased at that time from 1.7 million to about 5.0 million, that is about 1.25 million adult males with a right to vote in a population of 7.0 million. The electorate, therefore, formed 17.8% of the total population. This reform was due to the efforts of Kazimierz Badeni, who to the last days of his life served as Deputy in the Seym of Lwów. Although the electoral law reform increased the total representation in Galicia, the problem of more equitable representation of the Ukrainians in the Seym was still unsolved and caused much friction. The last reform, increasing the Ukrainian representation, was voted in 1914 by the Seym, but the outbreak of World War I prevented its implementation.

The restoration of independence to the country and the formation of the Second Republic on November 11, 1918, brought with it major changes in suffrage rights in Poland. Suffrage rights were made equal, direct and universal, and they were extended to women as well as men. The voting age was set at 21. Seymiks were made organs of local government and were no longer a part of the national electoral machinery. An exception to this rule was made in 1922 when the provincial Seym of Wilno was allowed to elect Deputies to represent Central Lithuania in the Seym of Warsaw until the next general election. The practical effect of these sweeping changes in suffrage rights, i.e., the extent of voter participation in elections, varied greatly from province to province, and was related to the degree of literacy of the population (see Table 73). Literacy was highest in the Grand Duchy of Poznań and Pomerania, intermediate in the Congress Kingdom and lowest in Galicia and the lands of the former Grand Duchy of Lithuania, which included one of the most backward areas of Europe, the Pripet marshes. The situation in the former Russian zone of partitions was particularly bad. Imposition of Russian as the language of instruction in schools after the uprising of 1863 was greatly resented and in rural districts illiteracy was often chosen by parents for their children in preference to the Russian schools. The Second Republic attempted to overcome this handicap where possible. When it was discovered that many of the illiterates were in fact number-literate, e.g., could tell the value of money when shown the numerals, parties participating in the elections were designated on the ballots numerically rather than by name.

A proportional system of representation was adopted, based on the Belgian d'Hondt method. The system allowed candidates to appear on either local or national lists. However, it created problems of governmental instability, since on occasion the numbers designating parties went as high as 30 due to the large number of parties which hoped to return at least a few Deputies on a country-wide electoral district possible with a national list.

In spite of various inducements, voter participation never approached the size of the eligible electorate. Nevertheless, it was still comparable to that in other European countries, as can be seen from Table 74. The lower participation in regions of higher illiteracy indicates, however, that in spite of the voting by number, the system could have been still too complicated, or the ability to follow political developments without reading about them too difficult. The problems of illiteracy faded to insignificance with the passage of time and with improvements in the national educational system. The legal barriers to voter participation were removed to the maximum extent, raising election turnout in 1928 to 78% of the eligible electorate.

TABLE 72—VARIATION IN ELECTION TURNOUT IN THE SECOND REPUBLIC

Year	% of Electorate Voting
1919	64
1922	68
1928	78
1930	75
1935	46*
1938	67

*Election boycotted by major parties

TABLE 73—VOTER TURNOUT IN VARIOUS PROVINCES OF POLAND IN 1922

Region	% of Electorate Voting
Greater Poland and Pomerania	86.5
Masovia, Podlasia, Lublin	77.0
North-East (Central Lithuania)	57.0
Lesser Poland, Galicia	54.0

TABLE 74—VOTER TURNOUT IN VARIOUS EUROPEAN COUNTRIES IN 1922-1924

Country	% of Electorate Voting
Belgium	82
Germany	77
Switzerland	75
Norway	68
Poland	68
Italy	55
Sweden	54

The establishment of the Polish People's Republic in 1945 brought with it a retreat from the position of maximum access to the ballot box. Political limitations were imposed, ostensibly under the provisions of the Potsdam Agreements, which provided for "participation in the free and unfettered elections of all democratic and anti-Nazi Parties." The electoral law of September 22, 1946 left the interpretation of who was democratic to the National Councils (Soviets), set up by the Communists under Russian protection. The councils, as a rule, decided that any former member of the anti-Nazi resistance movement was a Fascist, unless he was a Communist, which would have made him a democrat. Similarly, anyone opposed to the Communist takeover, or suspected of opposition, was declared a Fascist and deprived of his electoral rights. Some one million people in an electorate of thirteen million were thus disfranchised. This preparatory operation took place between the referendum held on June 20, 1946 and the elections held on January 17, 1947, although the government would not admit that anything was amiss. The Chief Electoral Commissioner, M. Bzowski, attributed this decrease in the size of the electorate during one year to the change of address. In this and successive elections, suffrage rights were denied to people deemed "socially unqualified," particularly those who had been deprived of their property through confiscations. On the other hand, the remaining electorate was forced to participate in the elections and to cast ballots containing a single list of candidates. A gradual departure from these practices could be observed after the death of Stalin and particularly after the riots of 1956 forced a change in the CP leadership. However, the ritualistic nature of voting, devoid of political meaning, remained [until the fall of Communism, in 1989.] The age for participation in these forced displays of loyalty was set at eighteen.

IMPEACHMENT AND JUDICIARY POWERS OF THE SEYMS

The normal investigative and judiciary functions of the state developed in Poland in the course of centuries and came to rest on the basis of codified law, administered by a system of courts, generally outside the legislative bodies. The major codifications were those carried out under Casimir the Great in 1347, known as Statutes of Wiślica and Piotrków, for Lesser and Greater Poland respectively, the Lithuanian Statute of 1529, prepared during the administration of Sigismund I, the Masovian Statute of 1576, and the Prussian Statute of 1598. Each of these statutes had undergone later modifications. A complete description of the system of the judiciary branch of government falls outside the scope of this study, and deserves a separate treatment. Here attention will be limited to those parts of the system in which the legislature was involved directly.

Court cases of major importance usually wound up in one of the two Appellate Tribunals, established in 1578 for Poland, during the administration of Stephen Bathory. These Tribunals were located in Piotrków for the province of Greater Poland, and at Lublin for Lesser Poland, and were staffed with deputy judges elected annually by the county Seymiks. The Supreme Right of Appeal was vested in the National Seym, or more specifically in the Seym Tribunal.

Impeachment is usually defined as a formal accusation of a high official of the State, rendered by the lower house of legislature, which commits him for trial in the upper house for abuse of his office or unconstitutional acts. In Poland the power of accusation rested with the Chamber of Deputies, and the power to try these cases rested with the Tribunal of the Seym, later called Tribunal of State.

The judicial functions of the Seym Tribunal of the First Republic grew out of the functions of the Senate as the Supreme Appellate court of the hereditary monarchy. Originally it consisted of the King and the Senate. In 1588 a decision was made to add to the Tribunal eight Deputies, and exclude the King from it in trial of cases of impeachment and *lèse majesté*. In 1670 the number of Deputies in the Tribunal was increased to twelve. More detailed rules of procedure for the Tribunal were spelled out in a constitution passed in 1641. In 1775 the number of Deputies in the Tribunal was increased again to 54, but was reduced to 30 only a year later.

The cases judged by the Seym Tribunal fell into four categories:

1. Matters in which legislation was lacking, or doubt existed as to which of the existing laws were applicable. These were commonly cases of appeal from the Tribunals of Lublin and Piotrków.

2. Cases against corrupt judges. In this capacity the Seym Tribunal acted as a Board of Judicial Review.

3. Cases of *lèse majesté*. These involved attempts on the life or limb of the King, the ministers, judges, Senators, or Deputies. The Deputies held the privilege of legislative immunity from the moment of their election (commonly six weeks before the Seym convened), until after the Debriefing Seymiks were held (commonly up to four weeks after the end of session of the Seym).

4. Impeachment cases against the King or any of the Ministers of Poland or Lithuania, when the individual concerned acted in breach of the Constitution. Major cases are described below.

The first such case arose in 1590, when it came to the attention of the Seym that Sigismund III Vasa made an agreement with the Habsburgs to surrender the throne of Poland to Archduke Ernest in return for the transfer of Estonia to Sweden and the payment by the Austrians of 400,000 zł. Apparently, Sigismund hoped that these two morsels would enhance his standing in the eyes of the Swedes and enable him to regain his father's throne in Sweden. The secret agreement was leaked to the public as a result of internal rivalries at the court of Vienna, and the public opinion in Poland was one of rage. In consequence, an "Inquest Seym" was held in Warsaw in 1592, and Sigismund was impeached. He was told by the Seym that the office to which he was elected for life was not his to dispose of, or pass on as an inheritance. He was censured and forced to swear again to abide by the *Pacta Conventa*, and to issue a declaration that any dealings with the Habsburgs concerning the succession to the throne of Poland were illegal and harmful to the country.

The second "Inquest Seym" was held in the administration of Ladislaus IV Vasa in 1646. It was precipitated by the administration's decision to start, at the urgings of the Pope and the Venetian ambassador, an army draft in anticipation of an intended war with Turkey. In this instance, the fears of an expensive foreign war added fuel to the existing indignation at the unconstitutional actions involved in initiating an army draft before the Seym's authorization was obtained. Under pressure from the resident Senators, the King realized that a Seym will have to be summoned and did so in the autumn of 1646. When it assembled, instead of debating the advisability of joining in a coalition against Turkey, the Seym undertook to investigate the unconstitutional actions of the Chief Executive and threatened to invoke the constitutional right of disobedience. In consequence, the King was forced to disband the unauthorized army, to reduce the size of his personal guard, and to dismiss his foreign advisers who had urged him to disregard constitutional limitations. In the following year the Seym dealt with the merits of the political situation at hand, and eventually authorized an increase in the army complement.

Another such weighty case occurred in 1664, when a Seym Tribunal was convened to try *in absentia* the case of Jerzy Lubomirski, Grand Marshal of the Crown and Field Commander of the Army, accused of inciting rebellion in the

Army, thus taking a page out of Cromwell's book. King John Casimir presided at the Tribunal, in contradiction to the constitution of 1588. Lubomirski's action stemmed from opposition to the political moves of Queen Marie Louise, who hoped to assure the election *vivente rege* of the French Duc de Condé to the throne of Poland. On December 29, 1664 a verdict was reached finding the accused guilty, depriving him of all his offices, placing him under infamy, confiscating his property, and sentencing him to death. Lubomirski was not present at his trial and escaped abroad. He returned in 1666, organized an army and defeated the King's army at Częstochowa and Mątwy. The conflict was settled on July 31, 1666 when the King proclaimed a general anmesty and promised to give up plans for the election of de Condé. Lubomirski arranged for a personal reconciliation with the King and asked for his forgiveness. As a result, his death sentence was lifted, but his offices and property were not restored. He left the country and died of apoplexy one year later at Breslau. The whole episode paralyzed the legislative process and led to the disruption of the Seyms of 1664-5, 1665 and the two Seyms of 1666. The Seym of 1667 reconfirmed the principle of free royal election to be held after the death of each incumbent, and restored a semblance of equilibrium to the country. John Casimir became so discouraged with the resulting acrimony that he abdicated in 1668.

In the administration of Jan Sobieski, there took place an impeachment of Jan Andrzej Morsztyn, a distinguished diplomat and the Deputy to the Seym of 1653. Appointed Grand Treasurer of Poland, he used his position to enrich himself and to further French interests in his native country. Having received the French citizenship, a pension and the position of secretary to Louis XIV in 1678 without the consent of the Polish King and the Seym, he was severely criticized by the Seym of 1681. Formal impeachment proceedings against him were started by the Seym of 1683 after correspondence of a highly compromising nature between him and Louis XIV was intercepted and submitted in evidence. During the proceedings he pleaded for a recess to give him time to prepare his defense and, subsequently, used this opportunity to flee to France. The Seym tried and condemned him in absentia, stripped him of his offices and demanded a return of misappropriated funds. These involved part of the Crown Jewels and a one and one-half year's income from the Crown Mint. Although Morsztyn returned the jewels, he never returned to Poland but lived out his days in self-imposed exile in France.

Exactly twenty years later another impeachment action took place in the Seym. The person involved was Kazimierz J. Sapieha, the Grand Commander of the Army of Lithuania and Senator-Palatine of Wilno. An active leader of the opposition in the administration of Jan Sobieski, he was accused of abusing his official position by billeting the troops under his command on the property of the people he wished to intimidate and of unduly interfering with the free operation of Seymiks in his palatinate. Attempts made to have Sapieha impeached by the

Seyms of 1693 and 1695 came to nought through vetoes cast by his supporters. When the abuses of his position did not stop with the death of Sobieski in 1698, the gentry of Lithuania, driven to desperation, organized a military Confederation in 1698, and defeated Sapieha and his supporters in the battle of Olkieniki in 1700. Subsequently, his command was reduced to a token force and then, at a Seym held in 1703 in Lublin, in formal impeachment proceedings, he was stripped of all his offices and banished from Lithuania. Sapieha staged a temporary comeback during the occupation of Poland by the Swedish troops under Charles XII during the Northern War, when Augustus Wettin was forced to abdicate and Sapieha cooperated with the puppet administration set up by the Swedes under Stanisław Leszczyński. With the collapse of the Swedish plans in Poland, and the recall of Augustus by the General Council of Warsaw in 1710 for a second term of office, Sapieha's public career came definitely to an end. Among the casualties of the case were the defendant's son Michał Sapieha who died at Olkieniki, and his brother Benedykt Sapieha, the Grand Treasurer of Lithuania, who was forced to resign his office.

The next case of impeachment involved Adam Poniński, the Grand Treasurer of Poland and the former Speaker of the Seym of 1773-5, which ratified the first Partition of Poland. He was brought before the Tribunal of the Seym in 1789 and accused of diverting for private use funds derived from the disposal of Jesuit property after the dissolution of that order. The funds were earmarked by the Seym for use by the Commission for National Education to finance the operation of the school system. In addition, Poniński was accused of accepting bribes from foreign powers and acting against the best interests of the country. The proceedings dragged out for nearly a year, with Poniński held in custody. Eventually, he was found guilty as charged; his property was confiscated and he was banished into exile. He went to Russia, in whose pay he had been before, and there joined the group opposed to the program of constitutional reform. That group proceeded to organize the Confederation of Targowica in 1793 and overthrew the Constitution of 1791. The repeal of the Constitution was formalized by the legislation passed by the last Seym of the First Republic, sitting under Russian guns in Grodno in 1793. Among the legislation passed by that Seym was an act repealing the verdict against Poniński.

After the collapse of the First Republic, the next case in which the Seym acted as a tribunal took place in the Congress Kingdom of Poland, in 1827. The Tribunal of the Seym was convened under the chairmanship of Senator P. Bieliński to consider the case of eight Poles implicated in the Russian conspiracy of 1825 against Nicholas I, Emperor of Russia and King of Poland. Among the accused was Senator Stanisław Sołtyk, the aged Senator castellan of Warsaw. He served as the Speaker of the Seym of 1811, and earlier he was a member of the reform group preparing the Constitution of 1791. The accused were charged with "helping remotely in a treasonous act." The Tribunal deliberated from January to May, did not find the accused guilty of treason but of a lesser offense and issued sentences varying from three years imprisonment to acquittal. Sołtyk was given a two year sentence of house arrest.

During the life of the Second Republic a notable case of impeachment involved Gabriel Czechowicz, the Finance Minister of the Republic. During the fiscal year of April 1, 1927 through March 31, 1928 he permitted various government agencies to spend 565 million zł in excess of the budget authorized by the Seym. The money came from surplus revenue and amounted to about 28% of the budget. It was spent on the development of the port of Gdynia on the Baltic coast and other similar projects. In March 1929 the Seym Budget Committee initiated legal steps against Czechowicz. Czechowicz resigned from his post and submitted a memorandum in which he acknowledged the violation of the law, but pointed out that it was ironic to see impeachment proceedings instituted against the first finance minister who managed to balance the budget and produce a surplus. The case was tried by a Tribunal of State consisting of the president of the Supreme Court, eight members selected by the Seym and four by the Senate. The Tribunal ruled that a breach of law took place, but ordered the Seym to make a separate evaluation of the expenditures incurred on their own merits. Following the next elections the expenditures were authorized retroactively and Czechowicz was acquitted.

In the Polish People's Republic, the Seym left its impeachment powers in abeyance and, instead, concentrated on policing its own membership, particularly of those members suspected of a critical position towards the government. Such was the case when on February 19, 1949, a communiqué of the Minister of Public Security, Stanisław Radkiewicz, was used as a starting point in the proceedings to deprive Seym Deputies Stanisław Wójcik, Stanisław Bańczyk and Tomasz Kołakowski of their Polish citizenship and Seym seats. The Deputies fled the country in fear for their lives; the threat stemmed from the attentions of members of the Political Police, operating under the command of the same Radkiewicz. The charges were upheld and the deprivation voted by the Seym. After the fall of the government in 1956, revelations of the terror tactics used by the Political Police led to the removal of Minister Radkiewicz; the Seym, however, chose to let the matter rest rather than impeach him for his criminal activities.

Another instance of the abdication by the Seym of its impeachment powers occurred in the Spring of 1968 when financial irregularities were discovered in the Supreme Board of Control (Comptroller's General Office). The Deputy President of the Board and several of his subordinates were accused of improper conduct and of deriving personal gain from their positions. The individuals involved were dismissed without, however, the initiation by the Seym of the regular impeachment procedure. The Deputy President of the Board was a member of the Politburo, and for this reason the scandal was hushed up. It certainly was a suitable occasion to ask the classical question:-"Who controls the controllers?" The answer obviously was: "Nobody" - certainly not the Seym, nor the courts. Gone were the days when, in the words of the 1607 letter to Sigismund Vasa, the electorate could "draw help and succor" from the Seym.

THE TAXING POWERS OF THE SEYM

The tax structure of Poland had undergone great changes throughout the history of the three Republics, reflecting not only the variations in demand placed on revenue in times of peace and war, but also the alterations in the tax base and the fiscal philosophy, as well as changes in population and area. Some idea of the size of the revenue can be gained from Table 75. Although all figures in the revenue table are expressed in the same units, namely the *złoty*, care must be taken in comparing its magnitude in different periods, since the value of the złoty changed as well. To help with this problem, Table 76 expresses the value of the złoty in terms of the ducat, often called the florin, a coin with approximately 3.5 grams of gold content, serving for a long time as a standard of exchange throughout Europe. Also shown in the table is the złoty valuation of the thaler, another popular unit of coinage in continental Europe. This last unit was the precursor of the American dollar, the name derived from the corruption of the word "thaler."

The right to tax was a highly valued legislative prerogative, conceded to the Seym by early rulers and reaffirmed in each new *pacta conventa* in the era of elective kings. The tax authorizations and the tax laws were not included in the constitutions passed by each Seym, but were issued under a separate cover as the "Universal Tax Proclamations" (uniwersał poborowy).

During the period of hereditary monarchy and the First Republic, the general land tax (tanowe) was in use. Its rate was standardized in 1578, set at one złoty per tan (17 hectars) and imposed either at this basic rate (simpla), its double (dupla), triple (trypla) or a higher multiple.

TABLE 75— POPULATION AND REVENUE IN POLAND

Year	Area (1000 km2)	Population (million)	Revenue (million zł)	Revenue by Source (%) Tax	Other*
1500	1,140	7.5	-		
1650	990	11.0	2.6		
1768	773	--	10.0		
1776	512	8.8	12.0		
1791	512	10.3	30.0		
1820 **	231	K 3.5	42.7		
		G 3.9	40.0		
		P 0.9			
1924	389	28.7	1,453		
1939	390	35.1	2,458	67	33
1951	312	25.0	63,600	36	64
1970	312	32.6	389,600	19	81

*Income from state lands, forests, mines, monopolies and state-operated enterprises, including commerce in the Polish People's Republic.

**K—Congress Kingdom   G—Galicia   P—Grand Duchy of Poznań

+During the period 1500-1791 area includes the Grand Duchy of Lithuania

TABLE 76—VALUE OF CURRENCY IN POLAND RELATIVE TO GOLD DUCAT

When minted in Poland the gold ducat, or florin, was called the "red złoty" to distinguish it from the unit of account denoting 30 grosz, and called "white złoty, later simply "złoty." The first 1 złoty (30 grosz) coins were minted in 1564. In 1924 złoty was decimalized and set equal to 100 grosz.

| | Złoty Equivalent of one: | | Silver Contents of | |
| | Gold Ducat (or 3.5 gms | Silver Thaler (variable silver | One Thaler | One Złoty |
Year	of gold)	content)	(gms)	(gms)
1528[1]	1.50	1.00	31.19	31.19
1578	1.80	1.17	30.32	25.98
1611	2.33	1.33	26.73	20.04
1635	5.50	2.50	21.26	8.50
1650	6.00	3.00	23.38	8.12
1676	12.00	6.00	23.38	4.06
1766	16.75	8.10	23.38	2.93
1787[2]	18.00	8.10	22.40	2.80
1794	18.00	6.00	16.60	2.76
1810	16.25	6.00	16.50	2.68
1830[4]	19.52	6.00	--	2.71
1842	--	--	--	2.67
1925[3]	12.05[5]	--	--	2.15
1934	20.72[6]	--	--	1.65
1978	3353.37[7]	--	--	--
1981	-- --	--	--	0.103
1990	--	--	--	0.000311

Coinage minted at:
[1]Cracow, Elbląg, Gdańsk, Toruń, Wilno
[2]Warsaw
[3]Warsaw, Paris, London, Philadelphia
[4]Last ducats were minted in Warsaw in 1831
[5]At 3.44 zł/gm of gold, or 5.18 zł/$
[6]At 5.92 zł/gm of gold after devaluation
[7]At 958.11 zł/gm of gold, or 29,800 zł/Krugerrand

During the life of the First Republic additional taxes were gradually introduced. They were the excise tax on alcohol (czopowe), voted in 1511, and the hearth tax (dymowe), voted in 1629. These taxes, voted when the need arose, were all temporary, for the Seym made it a policy to use an early form of the "zero base budgeting" principle: each tax collection required a specific authorization which was valid for a limited period only.

War-time demands of the defense establishment, requiring quick injections of ready cash, were usually satisfied by floating loans with crown property used as a collateral. Two laws passed by the Seym in 1504, specified that such arrangements required specific authorization from the Seym. From 1562 on, the defense establishment was supported by a 25% tax on the income derived from leases of state-owned land (kwarta). Because of various adjustments, in reality it netted only 20% for the treasury. This tax base was subject to a slow but continuous erosion from the effects of using the same state lands as collateral on emergency loans, since it often happened that the next emergency arose before the last collateral was redeemed, and the lands in question remained in private hands, subject to a much lower general tax level.

The transfers of the state-owned land into private hands, the resulting reduction in the revenue available from it for the maintenance of the defense establishment, and the pressure from the Executive Branch on the Seym to make compensatory increases in the general tax level, prompted the Seym to engage in numerous attempts to recover the Crown property. This task was among the objectives of the "Execution Movement" dominating so many Seym sessions in the 1500s.

With each decade that passed the total fiscal commitment required for the redemption of the Crown lands grew, reaching the point where, finally, all attempts at redemption were given up. In reviewing this fragment of history one cannot but notice the striking parallel between those problems of the First Republic and the present-day management of the national debt in the United States. Situations are similar, but the collateral is missing.

The transfer of Crown lands into private hands created, of course, a tax base in the private domain. Unfortunately, the taxpayers became accustomed to thinking that defense was to be financed by the 25% tax on the income from the Crown lands and all attempts to impose a direct tax on individual income invariably met with strong opposition in the Seym. What complicated the issue even more was the statutory requirement, that each able, enfranchised male respond to a call to arms in a national emergency on pain of forfeiting his property and the right to vote. The right to declare a state of emergency was reserved for the Seym, which considered the Reserve Army formed from a levée en masse sufficiently strong to handle any crisis. In fact, its military value was small and decreased even further after the introduction of cannon into the professional armies of the neighboring states. For this reason the Reserve Army was called only four times in the 1600s. Assurance of adequate financial support for the regular Army, through the imposition of a poll tax on the entire population, was resisted by the gentry, who feared .the establishment of a precedent for regular taxation. Nevertheless, in times of national emergency the gentry were forced to yield, and a poll tax was voted in 1520 by the

Seym sitting in Bydgoszcz, to provide for the defense against Tartar raids. It was imposed again by the Seym in 1590 in anticipation of the war with Turkey, but was cancelled when the danger of war disappeared. During the administration of John Casimir Vasa, a poll tax was imposed in 1662 to pay off the Army which formed a Confederation to demand the settlement of arrears in pay. The impost was a one-time affair, and the authorization specified that printed instructions for collecting this tax be issued only in as many copies as there were towns, and all be destroyed after the tax was collected.* In spite of all of this, it was necessary to levy a general poll tax, using the 1662 instructions, in 1673, during the administration of Michael Korybut Wiśniowiecki, to pay off the Army in the war with Turkey. It was imposed again by the Seym in 1674 and 1676. The tax rates established in 1676 and the corresponding tax regulations were used for the poll tax levies of 1677 and 1683, and again annually for 58 years between 1717 and 1775. The proceeds from this tax were used to support the Army.

The Constitution of 1677 dealt extensively with the details of the population census and the manner of tax collection, as well as with the rules for the *subsidium charitativum*, i.e., the voluntary contribution to the Treasury from the otherwise tax-exempt Church properties. The tax exemption of the Church came under heavy fire during the Reformation, but the Protestant Deputies in the Seym were never able to get it abolished. The argument in favor of keeping it was, that, in addition to pastoral work, hospitals and orphanages were all Church supported and therefore warranted the exemption. Table 77 shows the size of Church land holdings relative to those of the Crown in the 1500s.

The state machinery set up to handle the fiscal affairs of the Commonwealth eventually became unequal to the task. After the Seym of 1613 reached the end of its session without settling the treasury accounts with the tax collectors or passing the Army support bills, two Treasury Committees, were formed, one for Poland, and one for Lithuania, to provide help to the Treasurer. Six Senators and one Deputy from each palatinate made up the membership of these committees which were officially titled "Treasury Tribunals" and were located in Radom for Poland and in Wilno for Lithuania. Starting in 1667, the palatinates replaced their Deputy members on these Committees by Commissioners, elected by the Seymiks specifically for that purpose, with a two year tour of duty. The army was represented at the sessions by its own Commissioners. The matters dealt with by the Tribunals included all business pertaining to the support of the army, including civil cases brought against it, as well as all other tax matters; the army was obliged to submit a full account of its financial status, the number of men in the ranks, etc. The sessions of the Tribunals lasted six weeks each year.

---

* This was carried out so thoroughly that the instruction books for that year are now a rarity in the old print trade.

TABLE 77—PERCENTAGE OF ARABLE LAND HELD BY THE CROWN AND THE CHURCH IN XVI CENTURY

Province	Church*	Crown
Greater Poland	10.3%	9.08
Lesser Poland	15.5	7.5
Masovia	25.0	4.6
Podlasia	4.7	19.4
Red Ruthenia	3.0	22.0

*Tax exempt

TABLE 78—RELATIVE ANNUAL TAX BURDEN PER HEAD OF INHABITANT* (ABOUT 1785)

Country	Tax Burden
United Provinces (Holland)	35
Great Britain	34
France	21
United States (Massachusetts)	18
Austrian Monarchy	12
Spain	10
Russia	6
Prussia	6
Poland	1

*Abstracted from: R. R. Palmer, *The Age of the Democratic Revolution*, Princeton University Press, Princeton, NJ, Vol. I, p. 155 (1974).

In 1764 the Treasury Committees were replaced by the newly organized Treasury Commissions, which operated continuously. They were located in Warsaw for Poland and in Grodno for Lithuania, and the membership of each consisted of three Senators and six Seym Deputies. Their area of competence extended over all state revenue and included the supervision of commerce and inland transport. Thus, effectively, they acted as the Ministry of the Treasury, Interior and Commerce combined. The operation of the Treasury was thereby much improved and the effects were soon felt throughout the country.

Supervision of royal demesnes came also under the Seym's authority. The efforts of the Seyms to assure adequate return from the royal demesnes date back to the sessions of 1562-63 and 1563-64, when the rule was established that 60% of the income from the demesnes will accrue to the King, 20% will go towards the support of the army and 20% will constitute the remuneration of the administration of each demesne. The assessments were to be made periodically by a special commission appointed by the Seym. Inspections for the purpose, however, became very irregular: 1564-65, 1569-70, 1616-20, 1658-68 and 1764-65. The tardiness of the Seyms in appointing the inspection commissions at the turn of the seventeenth century reflects the impasse in relations between the Seym and the executives of that period, and the inability of the Seyms to take any effective action in the face of the paralyzing effects of frequent legislative vetoes.

In the nearly 100 years between the last two inspections of the royal demesnes, their income kept rising, while payments to the treasury were still pegged to the 1668 assessment, the differential enriching their holders and impoverishing the Treasury. Specifically, just before the 1764-65 inspection, payments from that source to the Treasury totalled 256,780 zł per annum, but after the reassessment of that year they rose to 2,311,310 zł per annum. Even at that figure they were still considered much too low by king Poniatowski. As the holdings were awarded to various office holders in lieu of salaries by the king, and the awards did not require the Seym's approval, the Seym's tardiness created a regular pork barrel, and many private fortunes were made in this way.

Generally, the authorization for new tax collections was granted reluctantly by the Seym and the tax rates were set very low compared to other countries in Europe (see Table 78), reflecting a pure agricultural type of economy. In turn, the low revenue received by the treasury dictated a small standing army and an administrative apparatus run mostly by unpaid volunteers. This reliance on the honorific workers in the administration required that there be a sufficient number of people able to devote their time free of charge to the service of the State. In practice, only the well-to-do could afford to be public-spirited on a continuing basis.

Reliance on land taxes and on the revenue from Crown property was becoming outdated, in view of the changes taking place in the economic structure of the country during the second half of the eighteenth century. On the one hand, the Crown property dropped to a small fraction of the total, such that in Galicia for instance, it constituted only 6% of the total arable land. On the other hand, the population of the cities was rising, and the economy was gradually shifting from low-intensity agriculture to more intensive trade and commerce in the cities. The change was reflected in the rise of tax yield from the cities just before the Partitions.

During the same period it became customary for the Treasury to present to the Seym estimates of revenue for the coming year. Such estimates were presented to the Seyms of 1766, 1767-8 and 1773-5; in 1776 the income and the disbursement were balanced for a time. These were, in effect, the first attempts at formulating the state budget for legislative approval.

After the First Partition in 1773, Poland lost control of the lower Vistula to Brandenburg-Prussia, although she retained the possession of the two major towns located on it, Toruń and Gdańsk. As the bulk of Poland's foreign export trade in grain and timber was fed by inland traffic on the Vistula, this gave the Prussians an

366

opportunity to levy a 12% transit tax on the goods passing down the river. This economic blockade in the years 1773-1792 was aimed at forcing the submission of Gdańsk and Toruń to Prussian demands for annexation. The transit tax supplied approximately 15% of the Prussian revenue. To make matters worse, the silver content of Prussian coinage was lower than that of Polish coins at the time. Taking advantage of this fact, Frederic of Prussia ordered the Polish coinage obtained from the transit tax to be melted down and reminted with a lower silver content, but the same face value. It is estimated that this operation alone cost Poland some 40 million zł in lost silver. Finally, in 1786, the Seym was prodded into authorizing the issue of a new design of coinage, with the silver content of the thaler reduced from 23.8 to 22.4 grams, bringing the Polish coinage closer to the Prussian standard, thus cutting the Prussians off from this source of revenue.

The economic effects of the First Partition were not limited to the sea trade. The loss of Galicia to Austria at that time also meant the loss of the mines in Wieliczka and Bochnia, which supplied the bulk of common salt for the country. Control of the mines gave Austria a source of revenue which amounted to some 12 million zł annually. These two revenue losses, the Prussian and the Austrian, impeded the economic progress and reduced the tax base of the national treasury. The above figures have to be compared to the total size of the revenue of Poland, which at the time of the Reform Seym of 1788-1792 amounted to some 30 million zł.

It must be observed that the fiscal reforms described earlier were being carried out at a time of great political turmoil, when the country was in the grip of a constitutional reform movement, and revolutionary ideas from France were firing the imagination of the public. It is in the nature of the economic life that effects of any changes in this sphere take much longer to be felt than those of political arrangements of the country, so that the reform of the tax structure is a more formidable task than, say, that of the voting procedure in the Seymiks or the legal position of the cities.

Although the machinery for tax collection was improved, the level of the tax rates still remained dismally low, while the narrowness of the tax base aggravated the problem of raising adequate revenue for the support of the defense establishment. This predicament became painfully obvious in 1792, when a large army was required to defend the new Constitution passed by the Seym in the preceding year. The tax base turned out to be insufficient to support an army of 100,000 authorized by the Seym, and the 60,000 that were eventually raised were unequal to the task of defending the country and preventing its partition. It is interesting to note that at the time the size of the standing armies of the neighboring countries, which succeeded in overrunning and partitioning Poland, was almost in direct proportion to the per capita tax rate imposed on their subjects. Their tax revenues were earmarked almost entirely for the support of their respective armies. In terms of the loot plundered in Poland, the financial investment in their armies paid off handsomely, whereas the skinflint policies of the Commonwealth merely encouraged the would-be aggressors to take advantage of the situation.

During the Partition Period, the rise in the tax rates was particularly steep in the Duchy of Warsaw at the time of the Napoleonic Wars, when the small Duchy was required to support a large army. In the Congress Kingdom of Poland the Seym lost control over the budget through the systematic sabotaging of the Constitution by the Russian Court. It regained the control only during the years of the Uprising of 1830-31. The budgetary control of the Seym of Galicia in Lwów was limited to only a small fraction of the revenue during its first decades in operation. In 1875, when the law was passed granting the provincial government monopoly on the sales of alcohol, the Seym gained its first sizable and totally controlled source of revenue, which enabled it to start funding some credit institutions for financing agriculture and industry. On the whole, these were modest efforts indeed.

With the rise of the Second Republic at the close of the First World War, the Seym obtained full control over taxation and over the budget. By that time the government either inherited from the Partitioning Powers or gained by direct investment a share in various profit making enterprises. These included the railroads, the telephone and telegraph lines, shipping and the airlines, plus several state monopolies such as the sale of alcohol, tobacco, etc. In the aggregate, the revenue from these sources reached about 30% of the total state revenue, the rest being raised by taxes. Some total figures are shown in Table 75. Generally, the tax rates were commesurate with the ability of the business taxed to bear them; i.e., they were non-confiscatory in character and not intended to be a tool of social engineering. Such changes in social structure as were undertaken through the land reform laws involved transfers of property with compensation.

In the Polish People's Republic, instituted under Soviet sponsorship after the Second World War, the Communist Party first gained control of the Seym by eliminating all other independent parties, and then used the Seym to pass legislation transferring to the government the ownership of all industry, and a good part of all other real estate, with the exception of farmland owned by small farmers. The government, in turn, was completely placed in the hands of the CP. The above legal operation radically changed the revenue structure. Instead of the former 30% of revenue derived from the monopolies and the state-owned enterprises, their share was 75%, the rest coming from taxes and social insurance premiums. Even more significant from the economic view point was the government control over prices of food and consumer goods. The power to regulate food prices was used to make up any shortfalls in revenue. The changes in food prices could be drastic. On January 3, 1956, for instance, retail prices in government controlled commerce were increased by 35% overnight. In response the workers rioted. Throughout the years all major price rises were met with similar response, as the labor force grew to believe that it is being forced to pay for the economic inefficiencies and ineptitudes of the system. Such was the case with the so-called "bread riots" of 1956, 1970, and 1976.

In the first decade of the Polish People's Republic the taxing power of the state was also used in a confiscatory mode to transfer control of all rental buildings to the government. This was accomplished by first freezing the rents and then increasing the property taxes, to the point where the tax exceeded the income to such an extent that within a period of a few years the property had to be handed over to the government in lieu of tax arrears. This policy was eventually reversed after the government found that the maintenance costs on the properties thus acquired were showing up as a large item in its budget.

The elimination of small private businesses in the area of services and retail sales was carried out in the early 1950s through another taxing device, the so-called "additional measure" (Domiar). In essence, it consisted of authorizing the tax collectors to reimpose the business tax in the same year in which it had already been paid, and to repeat the procedure until the business went bankrupt and its owners went to work for wages in one of the state enterprises. The objective was to eliminate the self-supporting middle class and turn it into urban proletariat. The operation was so successful that the bulk of the services provided by repairmen, plumbers, private garages and service shops, as well as the corner grocery store and the haberdashery, were eliminated. This, in turn, made each attempt to secure everyday repairs and services a major effort, thus adding greatly to the sum total of the annoyances and inconveniences of the already regimented life. In fact, the conditions in the service area became so bad that [in the last years of the regime of the Polish People's Republic] a decision was made to reverse these policies and again allow some people to set up small businesses, particularly if combined to form a cooperative.

Under the heading of the taxing powers of the Seym one must include the authorizations issued to the treasury to replace the entire currency in circulation by another issue rated relative to the previous one at 100:1; while, at the same time, the pay rates, retail prices, social insurance contribution rates, and tax rates were reset at the ratio 100:3. This operation was authorized by the Seym in October 1950, ostensibly with the intent of "preventing speculation," but in reality wiping out the cash assets of the population by reducing the purchasing power of the money in circulation to one third of its previous value.

THE WAR AND PEACE-MAKING POWERS OF THE SEYM

The appointment of peace commissions and the ratification of the resulting peace treaties was claimed by the Seym of the First Republic as one of its prerogatives and was explicitly stated as a such in Article IV, *Materie Status* in Cardinal Laws of 1768, in the Constitution of 1791 and in the Constitutions of the Second and the Polish People's Republics. These powers came into play during the various wars the hereditary kingdom and the First Republic conducted with the neighboring countries in the course of the first 300 years of existence of the elective legislature in Poland.

Chronologically, the earliest of these conflicts involved attempts to recover the province of Pomerania from the Teutonic Order. The province was lost to the Order in 1308 with the capture of Gdańsk. The Order was, however, unable to assimilate it and the province revolted, its cities forming the Prussian Confederation (Związek Pruski). A series of wars and peace treaties followed, the last war taking place in 1519-1521 with a peace treaty of 1525 ratified by the Seym. By the terms of this treaty, Albrecht Hohenzollern of Prussia became a vassal of Poland, and Pomerania returned to Poland.

Two wars with Sweden, 1626-1629 and 1655-1660, were concluded with the peace of Oliva in 1660, duly ratified by the Seym. The second of these wars coincided with the Cossack rebellion, Russian invasion, and general devastation of the country by the fighting armies. It is estimated that approximately forty percent of the population perished as a result of the Swedish and Cossack invasions and of the bubonic plague that followed closely thereafter.

In the wars with Muscovy the conflict extended over nearly 200 years, with a truce after each war and two major peace treaties negotiated. The first four wars: 1492-1537, 1560-1582, 1609-1617, and 1632-1634, were concluded with the Peace of Polanów, in which Russia gave up claims to the Baltic states and paid Poland 200,000 rubles indemnity, while Poland gave up the claim to the throne of Muscovy. The next two wars: 1654-1656 and 1658-1667, ended with the Treaty of Moscow in 1686, with negotiations conducted by a Seym Commission headed by K. Grzymułtowski and ratified by the Seym.

The wars with Turkey were also punctuated by two peace treaties. The wars of 1497-1498, 1620, and 1672, when the Turks besieged the city of Lwów, led to the signing of the Treaty of Buczacz under the terms of which Poland lost to Turkey some territory and was obliged to pay an annual tribute of 22,000 zł. This treaty was so disadvantageous that the Seym refused to ratify it and instead authorized a bigger army and declared war on Turkey again in 1673. The last stage of this conflict involved the relief of the siege of Vienna by John Sobieski and several less successful campaigns in Moldavia. The Peace Treaty of Karłowice in 1699 brought the conflict to an end and was duly ratified by the Seym.

The next two ratification actions occurred seventy and ninety-five years later, when the First Republic was crumbling. The Seym of 1773–1775 had a bitter pill to swallow, when it was forced to ratify the First Partition of the country between Prussia, Austria and Russia with a loss of almost 30% of its territory. The sobering effect of this action contributed much to the birth of the constitutional reform movement. However, time had run out before the impact of the reform could be felt in the strengthening of the country, and in 1793 the Seym was forced to ratify the treaties of the Second Partition. These treaties were rejected by the country at large, and the Insurrection, led by Thaddeus Kościuszko, attempted unsuccessfully to prevent the partition.

In the Partition period, the Seym of the Congress Kingdom in effect declared war on Russia, when on January 25, 1831 it dethroned Emperor Nicholas I as King of Poland. The war, however, was lost, after about one year of fighting.

The next war between Poland and Russia was fought against the background of the Russian, German and Austrian empires disintegrating at the end of the First World War. It lasted two years, 1919, 1920, and was accompanied by the revival of the national spirit and the restoration of the institutions of State in Poland.

At the same time, Byelorussia remained by and large passive politically, with the exception of the Polish minority which succeeded, on the collapse of the Russian Imperial Army, to organize an army corps under the command of General Dowbór-Muśnicki, from the Polish personnel drifting into Byelorussian Mińsk. The corps held the area as an independent entity until disarmed by the German Army advancing east, after the conclusion of the Brest-Litovsk Treaty. In the Ukraine, various political factions contended for leadership, but none was successful in establishing its authority over the entire territory inhabited by ethnic Ukrainians, long enough to let the state and the army organization jell. The most politically conscious Ukrainian group, with any political or military organizing experience, were the Ukrainians from the eastern part of Galicia. They failed to become the backbone of the incipient Ukrainian state and, instead, dissipated all their energies in contesting, in a bloody military campaign, the control of the ethnically mixed areas in the eastern part of Lesser Poland. Only a small part of the politically active Ukrainians joined, under the leadership of S. Petlura, in the Polish campaign in the Ukraine. They were unable, however, to rally to their cause any significant following from the amorphous mass of the Ukrainian peasantry. As a result, the independence of the Ukraine was short lived.

The 1918 revolution in Germany deposed the Hohenzollern dynasty, and automatically activated the provisions of the last article of the Treaties of

Welawa-Bydgoszcz[*], ratified by the Seym of 1657. Under this article, the sovereignty over East (Ducal) Prussia was vested in the Hohenzollerns, and was to revert to Poland in the event East Prussia ceased to be ruled by them. Rather than invoke this treaty, the 1920 Seym of Poland chose to fall on the principle of national self-determination, as formulated by President Woodrow Wilson, and requested a plebiscite in those parts of East Prussia which sent Deputies to the 1918 Seym of Poznań and which had a sizable fraction of Polish-speaking populations. By an unfortunate stroke of fate, the time set for the plebiscites, the summer of 1920, coincided with the peak of the 1921 Soviet offensive in Poland and the battle of Warsaw, during which the Soviet army commanded by General Tuhachevski attempted to outflank the defenses of Warsaw and overran the area between the southern border of East Prussia and the northern bank of the Vistula, reaching as far as Bydgoszcz. The Soviet offensive was defeated by a Polish counter offensive directed from the south towards the East Prussian border. To avoid capture, a good part of the defeated Soviet troops crossed into East Prussia and were allowed by the German Government to make their way to safety over the disputed territory. This adversely affected the results of the plebiscite, as many of those voting for German sovereignty, hoped to stay out of Soviet reach. As a result, Germany retained sovereignty over East Prussia for another 25 years, and even pressed claims to the Polish Pomerania (the so called 'corridor').

At the close of the Polish-Soviet war of 1919-1920, the Seym selected a peace delegation for negotiating the peace terms with Russia again. This was an all-party group, headed by Deputy Jan Dąbski and Władysław Kiernik of the Peasant Party, with Stanisław Grabski of the National Democratic Party as the deputy chairman and Norbert Barlicki of the Polish Socialist Party rounding out the group. Leon Wasilewski[**] was one of the principal plenipotentiaries of the Polish delegation. The delegation met with the Soviets initially at Mińsk in Byelorussia, then at Riga in Latvia, where the peace treaty was finally signed on March 18, 1921. The border settlement of 1921, reached at Riga, incorporated enough of the Byelorussian and Ukrainian population into Poland to create a serious national minority problem without weakening the Soviet Union sufficiently to prevent it from trying to partition Poland again. The several months which elapsed between the start of the

---

[*] The last article of the Welawa-Bydgoszcz Treaties (see p. 133) of 1657 finally took effect in 1945 when, under Soviet sponsorship Poland annexed a better part of former Ducal Prussia, with the Soviets getting their pound of flesh in the form of the north-east corner of this unhappy territory, including Königsberg, its capital.

[**] It is interesting to note that twenty-five years after the first border treaty with the Soviets, Wanda Wasilewska, daughter of Leon Wasilewski, was instrumental in forcing on Poland the Soviet solution to the border question, along the lines of the secret protocol to the Molotov-Ribbentrop Treaty signed by Germany and the Soviet Union in preparation for the invasion of Poland in 1939.

conference and the signing of the treaty, were spent in acrimonious debate in the Seym on the adequacy of the peace terms. The eastern border set by the treaty followed roughly the line of the Second Partition, as ratified by the Seym of Grodno in 1793. It retained for Poland territories from the Lithuanian part of the First Republic, which had sizable Polish districts within it, but left the bulk of Byelorussia and the Ukraine on the Soviet side. The wisdom of incorporating territories with mixed populations has been much questioned ever since, but seemed an equitable solution at a time when mass uprootings of populations, practiced later by the Germans and the Soviets, were still unthinkable.

Various assessments have been made of the border settlement reached with the Soviet Union at Riga by the Seym Peace Commission. Its implications reached far beyond the mere determination of the frontier line and were to have tragic consequences in the following decades for millions of people inhabiting the borderlands. In territorial terms, the outcome was advantageous to Poland, for it assured the inclusion within Polish borders of all areas with large Polish settlements. It represented, however, a failure of the attempt to revive the multi-national, federalistic character of the First Republic. Of its former constituent parts, only Lithuania was able to form a viable goternment during the upheaval of the Russian Revolution, and even this government was set on going it alone, as a small, nationally-based state, rather than trying to revive the old union with Poland. The small Lithuanian state was not able, however, to resist Russian annexation in 1940.

It has been argued that a less ambitious border settlement in 1921 could have been achieved at the price of mass resettlement of mixed populations to make the state boundaries coincide with language boundaries. This, however, went against the generally accepted principle in Poland that each person has a right to his home and property. The Russian Revolution brought with it a new era of mass deportations, confiscation of property, and physical destruction of entire populations in forced labor camps. High death toll and great hardship were inflicted by militant Marxists on hapless populations with complete disregard for human dignity, in the name of "immutable laws of history." The revived, two-year old Second Republic was just strong enough to assure its survival for the next twenty years, but was not strong enough to revive the multinational Commonwealth. Had it succeeded, the populations of Byelorussia and the Ukraine would have been spared the horrors of collectivisation, and the Polish population from the contested areas would have been spared deportation to Siberia in 1940-41. The 1921 border settlement represented, therefore, the maximum that could be achieved at the time by force of arms.

Prior to the invasion of Poland by Germany and the Soviet Union in 1939, a secret protocol attached to the ostensibly peaceful non-aggression treaty between the two countries (Molotov-Ribbentrop Pact), spelled out the details of how the loot was to be split. The original version of the protocol (see Appendix C) provided for the partition of Poland along the river Vistula and for the incorporation of all Baltic States, with the exception of Lithuania, into the Soviet Union. An amendment to the agreement was made in the course of the hostilities in Poland, and in it Russia traded central Poland to Germany in exchange for Lithuania. Thus, long after the Union of Poland and Lithuania became inoperative, the fate of the two countries was still inextricably linked. Both of these secret agreements came to light during the search of the archives of the German Foreign Office, when evidence was collected to be used in the Nuremberg Trials against the German leaders on charges of starting the war. Curiously enough, one of the two aggressors managed to gain and retain a position on the judges' bench in spite of the revelations from the German archives.

When the Polish People's Republic was set up under Soviet sponsorship at the end of the Second World War, the question of border between the two countries was settled long before the first post-war Seym had a chance to debate the matter. On August 16, 1945 an agreement between the Lublin committee set up by the Soviets and the Soviet Union was signed, following strictly the lines of the second secret Molotov-Ribbentrop protocol as far as the delineation of the border was concerned. Some modifications were made to it in later years when new oil deposits were found in one border area. The area was ceded to the Soviet Union and the change was ratified by the Seym.

The Seym's role in the settlement of the western border of Poland was even more curious.

In the early years of the Second World War, one of the coalition parties in the political leadership of the anti-German underground advanced, as a major point of its political program, a demand that Poland seek a post-war compensation from Germany for the damage inflicted on Poland, in the form of transfer of territory in the area of Silesia and Western Pomerania. These areas had been part of Poland up to the twelfth and thirteenth centuries and Silesia still had sizable Polish settlements. The program of compensation was proposed by the Polish National Party through its participants in both the underground and in the Polish government in exile in London. It gained the support of other parties and was taken up by Roosevelt and Churchill at the conferences of Teheran and Yalta as a scheme to compensate Poland for the loss of the eastern half of the country to Russia, and to serve as war reparation from Germany. The proposal was taken up and, indeed taken over by the Polish Communist Party which, however, proceeded to accuse the National Party of being pro-German collaborationists (sic!) and eventually banned it from participating in the elections and in the Seym. In the event, the western border was moved to the Oder-Niesse rivers, giving Poland control of the remainder of the industrial region of Silesia plus all of Pomerania and part of East Prussia. The change of border was formalized by a treaty with East Germany concluded in 1950 and ratified by the Seym.

SEYMS LEGISLATE ON THE OWNERSHIP OF REAL ESTATE

The laws relating to the ownership of property form a large block of legislation enacted by the Seyms during almost 500 years of their existence. Included here are the establishment and the abolition of serfdom, the rights of ownership of real estate in towns, the endowment of former serfs with land, the restoration of property confiscated by the partitioning powers, and finally the land reforms of the Second and the Polish People's Republics. These laws are of particular interest when viewed in the light of the social engineering applied through the legislation of the Polish People's Republic.

The telescopic view of the legislation dealing with private property presented in this section, will show how the ownership of land was transferred first from the prince to the numerous gentry, and then from the gentry to the even more numerous peasantry. Also, centuries of development of parliamentary institutions in Poland saw the parallel transfer of political power from the prince to the gentry, and then to the population at large with an ever increasing part of the population sharing in both. In contrast, much of the legislation passed by the Seym of the Polish People's Republic aims at setting the clock back by some 500 years and returning to the social and property arrangements of the paternalistic age in which the government, personified by the Prince, owned all property, possessed all political power, and demanded unquestioned obedience to the laws it made.

At the time when the first legislative institutions appeared in Poland, the rights of property ownership, primarily land, fell into two major categories: allodial ownership (dominium directum), and the usufruct ownership (dominium utile). The former applied primarily to gentry, who were completely released from feudal obligations to the prince due to the extinction of the ruling House of Piast. It implied hereditary, unlimited ownership. The second category applied to a limited ownership by a tenant, commonly a peasant, in temporary possession and with right of usufructs of the landlord's land, on the condition of fulfillment of some services which took the form of labor on the landlord's estate and were treated as rent in kind.

In line with the contemporary view, which considered the population of the state as consisting of distinct classes, or "estates," some of the earliest legislation in the area of proprietary rights aimed to fix the type of property (as well as occupation) allowed each group. The statutory intervention of the Seym in proprietary rights started as early as 1496, with the passage of a constitution banning, the burghers from the purchase of land outside the city walls. The ban did not apply to the cities themselves, and since the cities possessed a legal identity, it was possible for the city as a whole to buy land to expand the area encompassed within its walls. Along the same lines, but directed at the gentry, was the constitution of 1505, by which the Seym banned the gentry from acquiring property in the cities and from engaging in trade or commerce.

Into a separate category fell the rights of the state, or *regalia*, under which various monopolies were operated. Carried over from the days before ownership was individualized, they constituted a legal basis for the levy of tolls and various excise duties. The regalia included originally the rights to underground mineral deposits. With passage of time various of these rights were granted to the gentry or were abolished by legislation. Thus, a constitution passed by the Seym in 1573 and reconfirmed in 1776, abolished the mining rights regalia and transferred the ownership of minerals under the surface to the owners of the land. The waterways were declared public by constitutions passed in 1496 and 1511. The laws on expropriation of property with compensation appeared in 1591, when the National Treasury Commission took over the jurisdiction for expropriations relating to road and canal building. At the same time, drainage of water from navigable canals was prohibited. Liens on movables and on real estate were set and the method of obtaining mortgages was initiated, by prescribing in a constitution passed by the Seym in 1588 how they are to be entered in the judicial records: the entries had to be detailed and public, with priority granted to the entries in accordance with their date.

In terms of magnitude, by far the largest property problem was the relation of peasants and gentry to land ownership and legislation concerning serfdom. Concurrent with the various property laws, the legal position of the serf was tightly circumscribed. What started as an obligation to pay rent in labor became in 1532 a coercion to labor when the Seym passed a constitution prescribing penalties for runaway serfs. The freedom to leave the land for other occupations was first limited to one son per family, then to one person per year, per village. These restrictions were introduced gradually in constitutions passed in 1496, 1501, 1503, 1510, 1511. Similar or even more restrictive laws, were in force in the neighboring countries. Generally, the enforcement of these restrictions was difficult, and the existence of the Cossack settlements in the Wild East provided a safe haven for runaway serfs. Eventually, the system of rents paid in labor became uneconomical, and in the second half of the eighteenth century, the conversion to cash rents appeared. The problem, however, was not tackled in earnest until the nineteenth century during the partition period.

The Napoleonic Constitution of 1807 affected peasant right to land tenure. This Constitution was a drastic departure from previous practice, inasmuch as it gave the peasants their first political rights. The abolition of serfdom contained in it was a purely legalistic measure and left the ownership of land still in the hands of the gentry, and its use by the peasants had to be paid for in labor or in cash. The situation had a parallel in the abolition of slavery in the United States in 1864; the slaves were set free but left without means of support. Various political writers in

Poland argued at the time in favor of securing for the peasant the right to the land he cultivated and for the regulation of rents. Among these writers were Stanisław Staszic, who in his *Remarks on the Statistics of Poland*, showed that the growth of the economy is dependent on universal land ownership by the peasants, and Wawrzyniec Surowiecki who counseled the introduction of long-term land leases for peasants, with the right of eventual purchase.

The interpretation of the 1807 constitutional provisions, with regard to peasant rights, was contained in a decree issued by the Minister of Justice of the Duchy of Warsaw on December 21, 1807. The decree advised the use of contracts to regulate the mutual obligations of the former serfs and the landowners without, however, making them obligatory. The peasant was no longer tied to the land, but he had no property either: his shackles were taken off together with his boots, as was said at the time. A later view held that this interpretation was inconsistent with the spirit of the Constitution, and that the grant of land to the peasant was not specifically spelled out due to Napoleon's unfamiliarity with the actual ownership rights, these being different from the French. The issue at stake was how to convert the *dominium utile*, i.e., the right of use of land and buildings on peasant lots, with rent on them paid in compulsory labor for the manor, to a non-obligatory relation. The conservatives argued that, with the cessation of rents in labor, the right to the peasant lots ceased as well. The progressive view held that cash rents should be substituted for labor rents, with rates set low enough to allow the peasants to buy out the land they cultivated within a reasonable time. A further complication arose out of the fact that most farm draft animals and farming tools were peasant-owned, and a dissolution of the mutual obligations left the manors high and dry. After the brief life of the Duchy of Warsaw ended, all the problems of land ownership were inherited by the Congress Kingdom of Poland.

The conservative character of the Russian Empire, which embraced the Congress Kingdom, left little scope for social reform. Furthermore, the Seym found itself at loggerheads with the Emperor and was continually hobbled in its actions. The land ownership questions did not show up on its agenda in a significant manner until the revolution against Russian interference broke out in 1830, and the Seym regained freedom of debate and action. A proposal was submitted in the Seym for the grant of land to peasants living on state property, but the more sweeping proposals made by Deputy Olrych Szaniecki for a general grant, including private properties, did not receive support from a Seym occupied with questions of defense. The collapse of the uprising put an end to these proposals for another thirty years.

An interesting illustration of how far, but not further, a peasant serf could advance in his life by his own efforts within the legal framework existing in the Congress Kingdom in the second half of the nineteenth century, can be found in the Annals of the Agricultural Society of the Kingdom of Poland for the year 1858. In that year the Society sponsored a country-wide competition for the best small farmer. The competition was open to farmers who tilled land not exceeding fifty hectares in area, regardless of their legal status, whether a perpetual lease holder, temporary tenant, a serf, or gentry part owner of a village (yeoman). In addition to a cash prize and a certificate of achievement, the publication in the Annals of the Society of the farming methods and the biography of the winner were assured. In 1858 the prize went to one Jan Jędruch, a peasant serf in the village of Lelowice, county of Miechów. His biography, submitted by the lord of the manor, lists him at the start of his farming career in 1830 as supporting a family of six by farming 1.12 hectares, allotted to him by the manor as a "one-day serf." The term refers to the obligation to work for one day each week for the manor in return for the use of this land. Twenty-eight years of hard work later (1858) found him farming 3.4 hectares as a four-day serf and owning livestock of three horses and seven cows. He was supporting a household of eight and he also served as a bailiff for the village. With four days a week labor obligation to the manor, he had only two days a week left to farm his land allotment and had about reached the upper limit of his life's possibilities. Furthermore, he did not own the land he tilled, for it belonged to the manor. This example of a success story shows the severe limitations imposed by the system of serfdom. The need for its abolition was keenly felt in Poland at the time.

In the 1860s, out of a total 325,000 peasant farms in the Congress Kingdom, 182,000 were already converted from serf labor to cash rent status. The need to convert the rest was subject to much political agitation. Unfortunately, since the suppression of the Seym by the Emperor of Russia in 1831, the law-making power was totally in his hands, and he chose not to use it.

In 1863 an uprising against the Russians broke out. A Revolutionary Government was formed in Poland and extensive partisan warfare developed, but the conditions did not allow for holding elections. Instead, the Revolutionary Government issued a decree granting land ownership in perpetuity to the peasant serfs. After a year of bloody fighting, the uprising was crushed by the Russian Army and the members of the Revolutionary Government were captured and hanged in the citadel of Warsaw. The land decree, however, forced the hand of the Emperor and he felt obligated to issue a similar decree of his own in 1864. Thus, only six years after he won his competition, Jan Jędruch became the owner of the land he tilled. There was still a long road to be travelled to full enjoyment of political rights, denied at the time to all inhabitants of the Russian Empire.

With the rise of the Second Republic after the First World War, the legislation dealing with the problems of land ownership once again surfaced on the agenda of the Seyms and was dealt with. A difference in approach to the problem of land ownership at the time in Poland and in the Soviet Union had tragic consequences for peasants in Eastern Poland, who benefited from the land reform in the period between the two World Wars. Laws regulating the land reform were passed by the

Seym on July 10, 1919; July 15, 1920; and July 20, 1925. The first of these acts was declaratory in nature, stating that the upper limit on the size of land holdings subject to land reform was to be between 60 and 400 hectares, depending on the type of land: cultivated, pasture, forest, or fisheries. The second law provided for the compulsory buying out of large estates by the Land Reform Commission at half the market price and resale to the landless peasants with the help of long-term credit. The third law supplemented these provisions and specified that at least 200,000 hectares per year of State, Church, and private property was to be subject to land reform. A very important section of the same law provided for consolidation of the much subdivided peasant holdings into unified farmsteads, supplemented by land from the breakup of the large estates, until a viable size farm was reached. Land drainage was provided in wet areas where needed. The minimum farm size was set at fourteen hectares in the provinces of Greater Poland and Pomerania to match the size of the holdings established a hundred years earlier for liberated serfs. In central and eastern provinces, the minimum size farmstead was set at eight hectares after an extensive study to determine the size of a viable one-family farm.

In parallel to the land reform, the Bank of Agriculture was created by the law of 1921 and charged with providing credit to finance the erection of farm buildings and the purchase of livestock and farm implements by the new farm owners.

During the period between the two World Wars, 2,655,000 hectares of farmland were parcelled out, together with an additional 281,000 hectares transferred from large estates to the small one–family farmsteads, in return for the release from the obligation to supply pasture. The total land transfer to new ownership was therefore 2,936,000 hectares, and as a result 734,000 farmsteads were either formed or enlarged. At the same time the consolidation of farm holdings fragmented through inheritance partitioning affected 5,423,000 hectares.

At the outbreak of World War II the land reform was not yet completed with 3,733,000 hectares still remaining in holdings in excess of 50 hectares, amounting to 14.6% of the arable land out of a total area of approximately 25,600,000 in agricultural use. The pace of the land reform was set by the ability of the economy to adjust to these changes without adversely affecting agricultural production. This aim was achieved, inasmuch as the production of foodstuffs had increased by 31%, in the period 1934-38 relative to that of 1922-26.

The tragic consequences of this land reform emerged from the conclusion of the Ribbentrop-Molotov Treaty, signed in August 1939 between the Soviet Union and Hitler's Germany and amended in September of the same year, as has already been mentioned in the preceding chapter. On the part of the signatories, the pact was a repudiation of the non-aggression treaties, concluded by both parties with Poland only a few years before. The agreements were contained in the secret protocols to the Molotov-Ribbentrop Treaty, and their practical consequences are of interest here. As a result of this accord some 50% of the territory and 37% of the population of Poland were annexed to the Soviet Union, and in what concerns land ownership, Soviet rules were applied to the newly acquired population. The Soviet Union had just completed the "dekulakization" and collectivization of its vast territory. In the first of these steps, any farmer owning more than four hectares of arable land was classified as a "kulak," a Russian word meaning "the clenched fist." The kulaks, in turn, were declared the enemies of the people. An extensive network of concentration camps was erected to receive them and a large armed force of the Ministry of Internal Affairs (NKVD) was organized and trained to carry out the deportations. The frightened remains of the Soviet farm population were then asked to opt for the collectivization of farms. By the late 1930s the process was basically completed and the camps were processing this huge mass of unfortunates to oblivion, through over-work and malnutrition. This human tragedy was movingly described by Alexander Solzhenitsyn in his *Gulag Archipelago*.

When Eastern Poland was annexed to the Soviet Union, both the NKVD apparatus and the camps became available for processing the population of the newly annexed territories. The autumn of 1939 and the early winter of 1939-40 were spent in converting the railroad network in Eastern Poland from the standard European gauge to the wide Russian gauge. At the same time, name lists of the people to be deported were prepared, no mean task in itself considering the vast number to be affected. Similar preparations were carried out in Lithuania, Latvia and Estonia, but with one year delay in timing relative to Poland, since there the charade of asking for Soviet protection, and then for incorporation into the Soviet Union, had to be carried out first.

In Poland, a total of four major deportations were carried out, not only of peasants but also of other categories of people deemed undesirable. The first deportation took place on February 10, 1940 in unusually cold weather with temperatures falling as low as -40°F. Settlers on the land and their families as well as staff from the public services, such as road maintenance and forest guards, were included. The deportees were loaded into freight cars, with some cars holding as many as sixty persons. Altogether, 110 trains, with an estimated load of 220,000 people were moved from Poland to the region of Archangielsk in Northern Russia. Loss of life en route was very high due to freezing, particularly among the children and the elderly. The second deportation took place on April 13, 1940 when 320,000 persons were carried away in some 160 trains. The deportees were farmers who benefitted from the Land Reform Act and now fell victim to the difference of four hectares between Stalin's definition of a kulak and the Seym's definition of what constituted a viable size farmstead. This deportation included also the families of members of the armed forces and of the police, plus the previously arrested public servants and social workers. The destination for the deportees was Kazakhstan in Central Asia. The third deportation took place at the end of June and the beginning of July of 1940, involving some 240,000 persons, mostly refugees, who fled Western Poland in the face of the advancing German armies. The fourth deportation included members of the professions, qualified craftsmen, railway men, and the like. Some 200,000 people were involved.

These four deportations, added to the prisoners of war taken in Poland, accounted for the approximately 1.5 million persons carried off to Russia. The bulk of the deportees perished in the camps or at forced labor. When the Soviet-German war broke out some 130,000 of the emaciated survivors were discharged from the camps and allowed to leave the Soviet Union under the auspices of the Polish Army. Their depositions and discharge papers constitute the best documented support for Solzhenitsyn's story and are available for study by interested scholars at the Hoover Institute at Stanford University.

The land reform, partially carried out in the interwar period, was completed after the Second World War under the Polish People's Republic. The remaining large estates were confiscated and the local Communists were instructed to parcel out the land under the watchful eye of the Soviet occupying force. It was hoped that this move would generate public support for the sovietization of the country about to begin. As it was, it generated little enthusiasm chiefly because the size of the parcelled plots was mostly in the four hectare range, and the new owners were discouraged from building on the lots in anticipation of the forthcoming collectivization. Parts of the large estates were retained in direct government control, as State Farms, on the model of the Soviet Sovhoz. Significantly, the peasants participated in large numbers in the partisan resistance movement and in the civil war waged against the Communist take-over that lasted from 1945 until 1947.

Suspicions regarding the nature of the Communist-sponsored land reform were soon confirmed. In 1952 a move was initiated to collectivize small farms and police terror, administrative chicanery, and an intensive propaganda drive characterized the program. By 1954 some 10,000 collective farms were formed, while at the same time agricultural production dropped to an all time low and total economic collapse was imminent. Wide-spread food riots in 1956 brought about the fall of the government. The farmers started a mass movement to break up the collectives. Over 808 were broken up and such as remained located mostly on land taken from expelled Germans were based on voluntary associations with minimal CP control.

The role of the Seym, during the period 1952-56, and in particular of the licensed Peasant Party Deputies, is the subject of continuing embarrassment to everybody concerned. Far from taking a cue from the unceasing hostility of the peasants towards the social experiments sponsored by the Communists, the Seym representation of the United Peasant Party went along and fully approved all legislation in support of collectivization, only to see the effort blow up in their faces in 1956 (see Table 79).

Other legislation involving property rights included the Referendum held on June 20, 1946 in which one of the questions asked for approval to nationalize industry. This question turned out to be less controversial than one might have thought, for two reasons. First, under the Second Republic a sizable component of the industry was already owned by the government as a result of direct government investment in undercapitalized industries. Secondly, there was sizable investment of foreign capital in private industry. Part of that capital was German and was confiscated outright in compensation for the war damages inflicted by the Germans. Later legislation dealt with the compensation of French, English and American investors, and secured extended terms for payment of this compensation. Thanks to the favorable conclusion of this phase of nationalization, Poland was able to obtain further foreign credits for industrialization in the 1970s.

TABLE 79—PROGRESS OF COLLECTIVIZATION IN THE POLISH PEOPLE'S REPUBLIC

Year	Collective Farms Operating	Arable Land Covered (Thousand Hectares)
1950	2,100	190
1952	4,478	757
1954	9,322	1,713
1956	1,510	260
1958	1,838	201
1960	2,072	267

Nationalization of industry placed it entirely under the control of the CP, giving the Party an opportunity to exercise all powers of ownership. In 1976 this ownership by the CP was formalized through an amendment to the Constitution acknowledging the "leading role of the Party," a euphemism for denoting ownership.

THE SEYM AS A CAREER

The constitutional arrangements of the First Republic recognized the election of the King and the appointment to the Senate to be valid for the life of the individual. The Ministers had senatorial rank and were in the same category. This arrangement not only assured a continuity of policies but made it virtually impossible to change or reverse them, for even the death of a King and the election of his successor did not lead to a complete change of government other than by the regular process of

382

attrition. In terms of financial reward, during most of the life of the Republic, the ministerial and senatorial positions carried no salary, but the use of lucrative property and the allotment of fees for the execution of various duties more than compensated for this shortcoming.

In the Seym the situation was quite different. Deputies were elected anew to each Seym, although no rule barred the same person from being elected repeatedly. In fact, some Deputies had phenomenal electoral records, as the examples given in Table 80 indicate. The data was compiled from the records of the Seymiks of the Palatinate of Kujawy for the period 1650-1700. An all-time high record of electoral success in the whole history of Polish parliamentarism was achieved by Kazimierz Karwowski, who was elected Deputy no less than 27 times and, finally, in 1740, became the Speaker of the Seym.

TABLE 80—THE ELECTORAL SUCCESS OF SOME DEPUTIES IN THE 1600'S

Deputy's Name	Years in which Elected*
Sebastian Jarnowski	1668, 69, 70, 71, 72, 73, 74, 75, 76, 83, 90, 93
Spytek Pstrokoński	1654, 59, 61, 62, 67, 68, 69, 70, 71, 72, 75, 76
Maciej Gąsiorowski	1683, 90, 93, 95, 99, 1703, 1710**
Andrzej Gąsiorowski	1662, 66, 70, 71, 72, 75, 76
Andrzej Niemojewski	1669, 72, 73, 74, 85

*Elections were often held in December for the Seym of the following year.
**General Council, rather than a Seym, was held in

In the period 1569-1775 the office of Minor Castellan occupied an unusual position, for although it was appointment for life to a senatorial position, Minor Castellans were not summoned to each Seym, and when not summoned they could, and often did, run for a seat in the Seym.

The arrangements for reimbursing Deputies for their expenses had a checkered history. In the period of hereditary monarchy it became customary for the King to cover the per diem expenses of the Deputies. In fact, records of the disbursements made by the Treasury constitute some of the earliest existing lists of Deputies. That such disbursement was made at the pleasure of the King is obvious from the Diary of Debates of the Seym of 1556-57, which records Sigismund Augustus' reply to the demands of the Deputies for payment of the cost of their meals. Annoyed at their tardiness in voting the taxes, he replied in part:

> We have no obligation to take care of your expenses, for there is no law to this effect, and disbursements granted by Our grace, cannot be demanded. Whatever had been given in the past, was later reimbursed to the Treasury from the taxes then voted.

There was a lesson here still to be learned: he who holds the purse strings must bear the odium for reimbursing himself. In the First Republic, the Deputies could at best hope to be reimbursed by the Seymiks which elected them. These reimbursements were often erratic, particularly in times of war, foreign invasion, or natural disaster. The records for the palatinate of Kujawy list a lump sum of 1,000 zł as the usual reimbursements for a six-week session of the Seym. The two-week extraordinary sessions carried a smaller stipend. In addition, lodgings in Warsaw were provided free of charge. Expenses of Ablegates of the cities fell roughly into the same category. Records of the treasury of the City of Lublin show reimbursements between 2,000 and 4,000 zł per Seym attended, covering the two Ablegates sent. These amounts seem to remain constant throughout the years for which records survive, in spite of the gradual devaluation of the currency. Service as Deputy in the Seym of the First Republic was not a road to enrichment, particularly since the sessions of the Seym were scheduled only every other year. On the other hand, the remuneration of the Speaker of the Seym was quite substantial, as is shown in Table 81.

TABLE 81—REMUNERATION OF SPEAKERS OF THE SEYM

Speaker	Remuneration (zł)	Seym of
Stefan Czarniecki	100,000	1673
Tomasz Działyński	40,000	1690
Krzysztof Zawisza	80,000	1697
Stanisław Denhof	10,000	1710
Stanisław Ledóchowski*	300,000	1717+
Franciszek M. Ossoliński	40,000	1722
Stefan Potocki	60,000	1724
Leon Sapieha	16,800**	1861
Stanisław Badeni+	40,000***	1901
Stanisław Gucwa	68,000	1985
Wiesław Chrzanowski	11,312,000^	1993

*Served as Speaker of the Confederation of Tarnogród and the one-day "Mute Seym."
**Using the relation: 8 zł per 1 thaler.
***24,000 zł stipend + 16,000 zł expense account.
+Speakers of the Galician Seym of Lwów.
^Monthly remuneration. At the time exchange rate was 22,000 old zł to US$1.

In the Second Republic the Deputy's salary was 1,000 zł per month. The sessions, however, were much longer and were held at least twice a year, every year, making the function of a Deputy a full-time job. In addition to the salary, the Deputies were given free rail passes on state railways in lieu of a travel allowance.

SELECTED LEGISLATIVE PROBLEMS IN HISTORICAL PERSPECTIVE

In the Polish People's Republic, in 1947, the Deputy's stipend rose to 4,000 zł per month, plus travel allowance. In addition, pensions were provided for the Speaker and the Vice-Speakers of the House on their retirement.

Service in the Seym of the First Republic had, however, other rewards; in particular, the election to the Chair of the Speaker of the Seym was often a first step on the path to a political career on a national scale. As can be seen from the biographical notes included at the end of each major section of this overview, many of the people who rose later on in their lives to ministerial or senatorial rank started as Speakers of the Seym. Some were elected repeatedly to the Chair, like Mikołaj Sienicki (eight times), or Jakub Sobieski (four times). Such popularity attested to their parliamentary skills and these families supplied several Speakers over the years; such was the Małachowski family (four Speakers), Radziwiłł (five Speakers), and the Sapieha family with a record of six Speakers spanning the 300 years from 1582 to 1861. The longest parliamentary career of a single individual was that of Adam Czartoryski, who chaired the Election Seym of 1764 and the Confederated Seym of 1811, and about whom Napoleon said facetiously: "through him speak the ages."

The Lubomirski family supplied four Speakers in the 100 years between 1643 and 1746, while the Massalski, Potocki and Ogiński families supplied two Speakers each.

The men elected to the office of the Speaker covered a broad spectrum of ability and patriotic attitude. Among the exceptionally effective Speakers was Jakub Sobieski (Seyms of 1623,'26, '28,'32) who became known for his knack to focus the deliberations of the Seym on the most pressing issues. Active as a political writer as well, he had given much thought to the education of his sons and the development of their political aptitudes. One of them, John, was eventually elected King of Poland in 1674. Among the most ill-chosen Speakers was Adam Poniński, who used his position for personal enrichment and was eventually impeached by the Seym of 1788, stripped of his offices and exiled.

The practice of using the Speaker's Chair as a stepping stone to the Senate was occasionally reversed as the ascendency of the Seym over the Senate increased. The first case involved Senator Rafał Leszczyński, who resigned his palatinate in 1550 to assume the leadership of the Protestant faction in the Seym. He ran successfully for Deputy seven times and was elected Speaker of the Chamber in 1552 and 1562. In 1580 he was appointed to the Senate again as the Castellan of Śrem. Two later Senators who attempted this maneuver were Wacław Rzewuski, who resigned from the Senate in 1750 and Szczęsny Potocki, who did the same in 1788. Subsequently, both ran in the elections for the Seym, hoping that once in they would then be elected to the Speaker's Chair. Although elected to the Seym, their stratagems were resented by the House and their bid for the chair failed. Rzewuski managed to have his Senate seat restored to him later by the King.

After the collapse of the First Republic, the interest of the politically active families in legislative careers found an outlet in the provincial Seyms. For instance, the Niemojowski family had two of its members serving as Deputies in the Seym of the Congress Kingdom in Warsaw. Both actively opposed the Russian breaches of Constitution, and both participated in the Revolutionary Government during the Uprising of 1830-31. On the collapse of the Uprising, Wincenty Niemojowski was taken prisoner by the Russians and died in prison on the way to Siberia. In the Seym of Galicia in Lwów various members of the Dzieduszycki family sat in the House throughout most of the years of its existence, as shown in Table 82. One of the members of the Dzieduszycki family who served in the Seym, Włodzimierz, was elected to serve as the Speaker of the Seym in 1876 as a compromise candidate of both the Poles and the Ukrainians, who otherwise could not agree on anyone else in that year. Another one, Karol Dzieduszycki, participated in the ill-fated expedition to Mexico of Archduke Maximilian, sent by Emperor Franz Joseph in 1864, and witnessed the execution of the Archduke by the Mexicans.

TABLE 82—DZIEDUSZYCKI FAMILY IN THE SEYM OF GALICIA IN LWÓW

Deputy	Term
Dzieduszycki, Alexander	1861
Dzieduszycki, Kazimierz	1861-1863
Dzieduszycki, Władysław	1861
Dzieduszycki, Włodzimierz (Speaker)	1861-1876
Dzieduszycki, Wojciech	1876-1888
Dzieduszycki, Tadeusz	1880-1892
Dzieduszycki, Karol	1885-1902

In our times a legislative career became a hazardous occupation. During the interwar period several Communist leaders, who served as Deputies in the Seym of the Second Republic, were invited by Stalin to the Soviet Union after the Polish CP was disbanded by him in 1938, and were subsequently executed. During the Second World War Maciej Rataj, the Speaker of the Seym, was arrested by the Gestapo and executed in 1940 in the forest of Palmiry on the outskirts of Warsaw, while the Speaker of the Senate, Alexander Prystor, was deported to Russia by the NKVD and died in prison in Oriel in 1941. Numerous other Deputies and Senators of the Second Republic perished at the hands of either the Russians or the Germans. They died by execution in prisons, concentration camps, or from malnutrition, overwork and diseases to which they were exposed in forced labor. They are listed in Table 83. Just before the conclusion of the Second World War, during the Communist takeover, Deputy Kazimierz Pużak, then Chairman of the Polish Socialist Party, was invited with a group of other political leaders and

Deputies to Moscow for talks, but was imprisoned instead. Eventually released, he returned to Poland where he was jailed again by the Communists and died in prison. On the eve of the elections in 1947, even the candidacy for Deputy to the Seym became a hazard; wholesale imprisonments of candidates of the Polish Peasant Party took place, and of those elected some had to leave the country in fear for their lives.

TABLE 83—VICTIMS AMONG THE LEGISLATORS

OF THE NAZIS

Maciej Rataj (Seym Sp.)

Norbert Barlicki

Kazimierz Bartel

Józef Biniszkiewicz

Adolf Bniński

Feliks Bolt

Kazimierz Czapiński

Seweryn S.Czetwertyński

Włodzimierz Dąbrowski#

Aleksander Dębski

Jerzy B. Dominirski

Stanisław Dubois

Hipolit Gliwic

Ignacy Kalaga

Stefan Kapuściński #

Kazimierz Kierzkowski

Jan Kornacki

Irena Kosmowska

Mikołaj Kwaśniewski

Jan Lewandowski

Kazimierz S. Mirski

Stanisław Mróz

Mieczysław Niedziałkowski

Marceli Nowakowski

Bolesław Pochmarski

Józef Prądzyński

Jan Rudowski

Roman Rybarski

Stefan Sacha

Zygmunt Sioda

Antoni Snopczyński

Stefan Sołtyk

Stefan Starzyński

BłAżej Stolarski

Tadeusz Styczyński

Tadeusz Święcicki

Piotr Szturmowski

Michał Szulczewski

Marian Wadowski

Stanisław Wańkowicz

Józef Wieczorek #

Dominik Zbierski

Bronisław Ziemięcki

OF THE SOVIETS

Aleks. Prystor (Sen.Sp.)

Władysław Baczyński

Stefan Bilak

Henryk Bitner

Stanisław Burzyński

Maksym Czuczmaj

Włodzimierz Celewicz

Jerzy Czeszejko -Sochacki

Tomasz Dąbal

Włodzimierz Decykiewicz

Tadeusz Dworakowski

Damian Gersztański

Zygmunt Glücksmann #

Stanisław Głabiński

Jan S. Jankowski

Stanisław Jasiukowicz

Paweł Komander #

Borys Kozubski

Stefan Królikowski

Włodzimierz Kuzmowycz

Stanisław Łańcucki

Olena Lewczaniwska

Dmytro Lewicki

Symon Lubarski

Ostap Łucki

Władysław Małski

Zygmunt Piotrowski

Kazimierz Pużak

Jan Śląski

Konstanty Stypuła

Bronisław Taraszkiewicz

Hrynko Terszkowec

Ferdynand Tkaczow

Adolf Warszawski

Antoni Wasynczuk

Paweł Wasynczuk

Dmytro Welykanowicz

Sylwester Wojewódzki

Jan Załuska

Tadeusz Żarski

Władysław Daniecki

Wacław Budzyński

Janusz Wielowiejski

Deputies of the Silesian Seym

CHAPTER IX

THIRD REPUBLIC: THE SEYM IN POST-COMMUNIST POLAND

COMPENDIUM OF THE HISTORY OF THE SEYM AND ITS PRESENT DAY FUNCTIONS

The swift desintegration of the Soviet empire, following Poland's successful attempt to break out of the Soviet bloc in 1989, set once more in motion the democratic institutions in Central Europe. All those countries which had been forced into the bloc as Russian satellites in 1945 through the Treaty of Yalta, with their imposed Soviet-style, rubber-stamp parliaments, now found themselves free to revert to truly representative parliamentarv systems.

The changes with which the Polish society was faced were both sudden and earthshaking, for a people who had been denied their right to a democratically chosen representation for almost half a century by a repressive regime. Yet the truly parliamentary system was embraced immediately. Surely, the speed with which the change occurred can be credited in a large measure to the 500 year old parliamentary tradition of Poland.

Thus, it is fitting at this point to recapitulate the major events in the history of the parliamentary system of Poland underpinning the rise, development, suppression and eventual rebirth of the Seym. It is also appropriate to describe the day to day functioning of an institution, which once again has become a living expression of a free and democratic society.

HISTORY AND CHRONOLOGY OF MAJOR EVENTS— A SUMMARY

In the 1400's the legislature of Poland is referred to in legal Latin documents as "Consilium Generale," which when the vernacular came into use in the 1500's, was replaced by the Polish word "Seym." It has a generic meaning, denoting the Polish legislature. Eventually, "Seym" came to denote only the Chamber of Deputies. Four centuries later, in the early 1800's, the spelling, although not the pronunciation, changed to "Sejm," and so it remains to this day.

Three basic constitutional charters ultimately laid the foundation for all later Polish constitutions. These charters were conceded by the king to his subjects to secure their cooperation and thus, in effect, constituted a contract between the ruler and the ruled. The first charter: "nec bona recipiantur" (no confiscation of property without court verdict), granted by Ladislaus Jagiełło in 1422, states in part:

> Likewise, in order that we might please them by more abundant favors, and also that they might honor us with loyalty and better services, we promise that, from this day forward, we will neither possess nor confiscate, nor cause to be possessed or confiscated, the hereditary property of any royal subject, of whatever rank, position, or prominence he may be, or rank he may have been; nor, through us, our officials, or any others, will we visit the penalty of this confiscation, for any illegal or blameworthy act, unless, first, our judges, which we have assigned to the case, together with our bishops and barons, have conducted a full legal inquiry, and second, a sentence has been handed down.

The "neminem captivabimus" act (no imprisonment without due process of law), granted by Ladislaus Jagiełło in 1433, states:

> Moreover, we promise and pledge that: for some impropriety, we will neither seize at once, nor order the seizure of, any propertied native individual; nor shall the same be punished, unless justly convicted through a criminal proceeding. As for jurisdiction and judges, an accused will be tried in the locale of his name, by judges of that same place. Exceptions to the foregoing: the above does not apply in the case of a man caught in the act of stealing or of public crime (viz, arson, voluntary manslaughter, rape of maidens and matrons, pillaging and despoiling of villages), nor in the case of those, who should be unwilling to honor or pay an outstanding debt, bordering on an excessive or criminal amount.

The "nihil novi" act (no new laws without the consent of the governed) granted by Alexander Jagiellonian in 1505, states:

> Because common laws and public ordinances affect not one, but all people in common, therefore, at this Seym of Radom, with all the judges, councillors, barons, and territorial deputies assembled together, we have reasonably moved and, further,

adopted, the following equitable resolution: that, because such might become a detriment and injury to the State, an injury and misfortune of whatever sort to the private individual, and make for change in regard to public right and liberty, hence-forth, and in future times in perpetuity, no new laws shall be made by us or our successors, without the consent of the councillors and territorial deputies.

The rise of the Sejm and the Senate of Poland dates from the same period, thus Polish parliament has 500 years of history. Summoned by the king, the assemblies of the gentry and high state dignitaries from the provinces of Greater and Lesser Poland started to assemble annually in Piotrków, a small town on the border between these two provinces. The Deputies to the Sejm were elected by the county assemblies of the gentry, the Senators were appointed by the King. Initially meeting as a unicameral body, the Chamber of Deputies separated in 1493. Both chambers deliberated on legal matters, the treasury, the defense and were asked to consent to the decrees issued by the king as laws.

The word Seym (pronounced: "saym") appears already at this early period and replaces the Latin "Consilium Generale".

Incorporation of Prussia (1466), and Masovia (1529) and union with Lithuania (1569) made it necessary to move the meeting place of the joint Sejm to Warsaw, the capital of Masovia, closer to Prussia and Lithuania. Occasionally the Sejm met in other towns such as Cracow, Grodno, Radom, Lublin. In 1569 a political Union of Poland and Lithuania was formed and from 1572 onwards the kings ceased to be hereditary and became elected for life. The newly created political entity of Poland and Lithuania begun to be referred to as a Commonwealth of Both Nations. In modern terminology it is called the First Republic.

The two hundred year period from 1572 to 1772 was characterized by a gradual modification of the Sejm's role. From a body introducing political and constitutional initiatives, the Sejm begun to see itself as being the principal defender against the encroachment of absolutism. It became entrenched in the defence of the status quo, and as its most effective instrument adopted the requirement of unanimity of vote in the passage of all laws (liberum veto). This requirement was overruled only when the Deputies agreed beforehand to vote by majority rule in what was called a Sejm Confederation. It was thought safe to organize such confederations during the Interregna, i.e. in the period between the death of one king and the election of the next. Major political changes and important laws were introduced during such periods, and their acceptance by the candidates for the crown was made a condition for their election. During the remainder of a given administration the system froze, until the next royal election. Although effective in preventing the rise of absolutist government in Poland at a time when all the surrounding countries were ruled by absolutist monarchs, in practice it made the day to day process of governing the country very ineffective. Reform of the constitutional arrangement was needed.

A landmark of the constitutional history of the First Republic was the passage by the Sejm and the Senate of the Constitution of 1791. It reformed the creaky machinery of the state laying the foundation of a modern political structure. The reform was crushed by the neighboring absolutist powers. Russia, Prussia and Austria invaded Poland, defeated her army and partitioned the territory of the country between themselves. During the pre-partition period 251 Sejms were elected.

Although the national Sejm and Senate disappeared as a result of the dismemberment, each of the partitioned zones succeeded in turn to elect provincial Sejms, albeit of much reduced powers. The 23 Sejms of that period (1795-1918) sat in turn in Warsaw, Poznań and Lwów in the territories annexed by Russia, Prussia and Austria.

Following the First World War, the country was reunified as the Second Republic. Its constitution of 1921 adopted the French cabinet model and the proportional system of representation for both the Sejm (Chamber of Deputies) and the Senate. The period was characterized by Party fragmentation which impeded the creation of stable parliamentarv majorities to support the cabinet in office. A coup d'état in 1926 eventually led to the replacement of this constitution in 1935 with one based on the presidential model and a majority system of representation, but this did not eliminate party strife and electoral boycotts. Seven Sejms sat between the two World Wars in Warsaw: a provincial Sejm of Silesia sat in Katowice.

Following the Second World War, the Yalta Agreement left Poland in the USSR's sphere of influence. Political terror and intimidation by Communists supported by the Soviets prevented a return to democracy. A referendum abolished the Senate in 1946 and a Sejm elected in 1947 passed the so called "Small Constitution," followed in 1952 by a "Stalinist" constitution establishing a Soviet style "Polish People's Republic". The presidency was replaced with a collegial Council of State. Centrally planned economy became the rule. Ten Sejms of that period were elected from a list of candidates restricted to those accepting beforehand the communist ideology, and once elected, willing to condone wholesale confiscations of property, loss of civil liberties and imposition of one official ideology. These were presented as necessary to assure full employment, free schools and medical services for everybody.

Eventually, the centrally planned economy, additionally burdened with the expansion of the armaments industry dictated by the Warsaw Pact, proved unequal to the ambitious task. In the 1970's, the Polish government, under the First Secretary of the Communist Party. Edward Gierek, embarked on a massive industrial expansion, financed by huge loans from Western banks and governments, burdening the country with a 30 billion dollar foreign debt. The emphasis was on heavy industry, with total disregard for the needs of the consumer market. Endemic shortages of housing, food supplies and consumer goods fueled labor unrest that culminated in the rise of the "Solidarity" labor movement in 1981, while similar economic difficulties in the Soviet Union created a climate favorable to reform. In Poland, this led in 1989 to the collapse of the one party rule, return to market economy, political pluralism and restoration of the Presidency and the Senate, culminating in the first free elections to the Senate in June of that same year.

The country reverted to its pre-World War II name of the Republic of Poland, assuming the name of the Third Republic as of 1989.

CONSTITUTIONAL PROVISIONS OF THE SEJM AND THE SENATE

In the present day Poland the position of the Sejm as the highest organ of government of the Republic of Poland is defined by Article 95 of the constitution of April 2, 1997. The President of the Republic summons the voters to elect the Sejm and the Senate, and dissolves the two bodies when they are no longer able to support a government or pass laws.

The Sejm consists of 460 deputies, the Senate of 100 senators. Both groups are elected by universal, equal, direct and secret ballot for a 4-year term of office.

The main constitutional powers of the Sejm include the passage of laws, undertaking of resolutions determining the basic directives for the policies of the Republic, and control over other organs of government and state administration. Sejm deputies have the right of legislative initiative.

Among exclusive competencies of the Sejm are: the passage of the budget of the Republic, the overall control of the finances of the state, and the control of balance of foreign as well as domestic income and expenditure of the population. Major changes in the allotment of budgetary expenditures can only be realized with the approval of the appropriate Sejm commission. The Minister of Finance has the duty to present periodically to the Sejm budget commission information on the realization of the budget.

An amendment to the constitution of 1952, passed in 1989, provided for the restoration of the Senate, defines its composition and powers. The latter include the right of legislative initiative in all matters except the budget, which is reserved to the Sejm.

The constitutional position of the Sejm and the Senate relative to the executive and the judicial branches evolved over centuries from a subordinate to a dominating role in the government. The table in Appendix E summarizes the evolution.

ARCHITECTURE—PHYSICAL DESCRIPTION OF PARLIAMENT BUILDINGS —CHAMBERS—OFFICES—TOURS

Between 1556 and 1831 the Sejm and the Senate sat in separate chambers in the royal castle of Warsaw. The chambers survived until the reign of Tsar Nicholas I, who served uncomfortably as a constitutional monarch of Poland. They were demolished and divided into small offices on his orders, following the uprising of 1831, when the Sejm dethroned him for breaches of constitution. The castle itself was burnt by the Germans in the siege of Warsaw 1939 and the remaining walls were dynamited by them in 1944 after the Warsaw Uprising. The building and the Senate chamber were reconstructed in the 1980's as a museum.

The modern buildings of the Sejm in Warsaw are located on a high scarp overlooking the Vistula River at 4/6 Wiejska Street. The district adjoins the Ujazdów Avenue, along which are located the American and French Embassies. Originally housing an academy for young ladies, after the First World War the buildings underwent extensive modifications and additions to house the parliament of the Second Republic. The Chamber of Deputies was built in 1925-29 to the designs of Kazimierz Skorewicz (1866-1950) to replace the then non-existent Chamber of Deputies of the First Republic in the royal castle. The Senate Chamber, the offices and the 200 room Sejm Hotel were added in the following years as different wings of a complex structure. The building was severely damaged in the Second World War.

The present buildings were reconstructed in 1948 to the designs of Bohdan Pniewski (1897-1965). The semicircular Chamber of Deputies (Sejm) seats 460 deputies, plus members of the executive. A gallery for the public is provided and may be visited while the Sejm is in session. Tickets for the visit are available from the Sejm office.

The Senate was abolished in 1947, and thus its chamber was not rebuilt after the Second World War. Eventually, in 1989, the ruling Communist-dominated coalition agreed in the "Round Table Talks" with the "Solidarity" labor union to restore the Senate. Consequently, a new Senate Chamber was built to the designs of Andrzej Kaliszewski in 1990-91, to seat 100 senators. It has been in use since 1992. A new Deputies' Hotel was added in the spring of 1989 to supplement the old Sejm Hotel.

The Museum of the History of the Sejm is part of the Sejm and Senate complex and is open to the public.

394

Aerial View of Seym Complex.

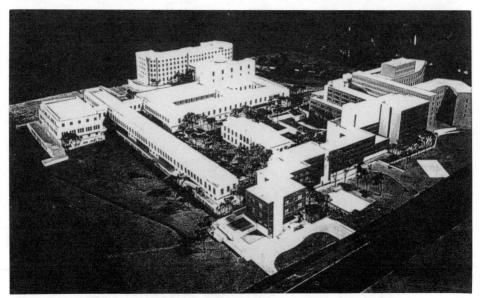

The overview of the Parliamentary buildings.

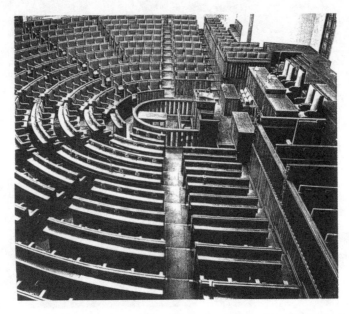

Above: Chamber of the Seym (Deputies). Below: Chamber of the Senate.

Above: Inside the Seym building. Below: Entrance to the Senate Chamber.

ELECTIONS—CURRENT PARTY POSITIONS—SEATS—TERM OF OFFICE—MEMBERSHIP

The electoral ordinance now in force for the Senate was passed on May 10, 1991 and is based on the majority principle. One hundred Senators are elected, two from each voivodeship, except for Warsaw and Katowice where three Senators are elected.

The electoral ordinance for the Sejm was passed on May 28, 1993 and is based on proportional principle. Of the total four hundred and sixty Deputies, 391 are elected from multi-mandate districts returning from 3 to 17 deputies, and 69 Deputies from all-country lists of candidates. There are two thresholds for election: 5% of the vote cast entitles a party, and 8% of the vote cast entitles a coalition of two or more parties to be seated in the Sejm and share in the distribution of seats.

To be elected Deputy or Senator the candidate must be a Polish citizen, be 21 years of age, and have resided in the country for a minimum of 5 years preceding the election. Minimum voting age of constituents is 18 years.

The cost of elections and of the broadcast of election programs of all election committees by the Polish Television is paid for from the national budget.

Party positions in the II Sejm and the III Senate elected on September 19, 1993* were as follows:

		Sejm	Senate
SLD	Democratic Left Alliance	171	37
PSL	Polish Peasant Alliance	132	36
UD	Democratic Union	74	4
UP	Labor Union	41	2
KPN	Confederation for an Independent Poland	22	-
BBWR	Non-Party Block to Support Reform	16	2
MN	German Minority	4	0
	"Solidarity" Independent Labor Union	-	9
	Independent (unaffiliated)	-	10
		460	100

*1997 Elections returned a majority from the "Solidarity" movement to the Sejm: a coalition of AWS (Akcja Wyborcza Solidarność) gained a majority and coalesced with UW (Unia Wolności) party of Solidarity liberals, thus gaining about 50% of seats.

The term of office of both Senators and Deputies runs concurrently and is for 4 years, unless the President of the Republic dissolves both chambers before the end of their term.

SESSIONS—ANNUAL CALENDAR
—DISSOLUTION—RECESS

The restoration of the Presidency in the Round Table Talks of 1989 also gave the President the power to issue decrees with the force of law between the sessions of the Sejm. Subsequently, General Wojciech Jaruzelski was elected to that office by the National Assembly of Sejm and Senate combined. The next election, held on popular basis, returned Lech Wałęsa to the presidency.

The Constitutional Act of October 17, 1992 provides that the Sejm may dissolve itself through a resolution taken by two thirds majority, with at least half of all deputies present at the vote. Alternately, it can be dissolved by the President after consultation with the Speakers of the Sejm and the Senate, if it fails to select a cabinet within three months of its election, fails to pass the budget within three months, passes an act or adopts a resolution making it impossible for the President of the Republic to exercise his powers. Such dissolution was ordered by President Wałęsa in 1993 when the government of Hanna Suchocka failed to secure the vote of confidence from the Sejm.

In the event of dissolution of the Sejm, the President of the Republic sets the date of elections to the Sejm and the Senate, not sooner than three months and not later than four months from the date of dissolution.

[The new Constitution passed in April of 1997 provides the same basis for the dissolution of the Sejm and Senate.]

HOW LAWS ARE MADE—READINGS OF
BILLS—AMENDMENTS—VOLUME OF LEGISLA-
TION—QUORUM—PRIVATE BILLS

Legislative initiative is accorded by the constitution to the President, the Cabinet, the Senate, the Sejm committees or a group of at least 15 Deputies. No private bills are recognized. A bill may propose to amend existing legislation or to create a new law. Attached to the bill must be a review of the existing legislation on the subject, or a justification why new legislation is needed, financial consequences of its enforcement, and sources of funding, if expenses are to be incurred by the Treasury, all this supported by expert opinion.

A Deputy, a Senator, a member of the Cabinet, or a representative of the President presents the Bill to the full Sejm in the first reading if the bill concerns changes in the constitution, civil rights and freedoms, the electoral law, codes of law, taxes or finances. After an opening debate the bill is sent to an appropriate committee for detailed analysis.

In the case of Bills dealing with matters outside those listed above, a Bill can be presented for first reading directly to the appropriate committee of the Sejm, rather than to the Sejm as a whole.

After completing the analysis of a Bill, the committee presents its agreed upon position to the Sejm in a plenary meeting for a second reading. At this stage Deputies are given a chance to submit their own proposals or amendments. If there are no changes or amendments, the Sejm may vote on the Bill.

If there are changes, the Bill returns to the committee for an evaluation of changes and amendments, and Deputies who submit amendments participate in the work of the committee. The resulting additional report is tabled at a plenary session of the Sejm for a third reading and the vote. If the Bill is passed, it goes to the Senate for consideration.

The appropriate Senate committee examines the Bill and presents its recommendations to the full Senate, which either votes to accept the Bill and sends it to the President of the Republic for signature, or proposes amendments and sends it back to the Sejm; alternately, the Senate may recommend the rejection of the Bill, sending the vetoed Bill back to the Sejm.

If the Sejm does not reject the Senate's amendments, they are automatically adopted and the law goes to the President for signature. When signed by him and published in the Journal of Laws (Dziennik Ustaw) the law comes into force. The Sejm may reject the Senate's amendments or veto the entire law by an absolute majority, thus terminating its legislative path.

The President may refuse to sign a law and return it to the Sejm within 30 days for reconsideration. However, this presidential veto may be overruled by a 2/3 majority of the Sejm, forcing him to sign it and publish it as a law.

The process of making a law may be speeded up through the use of the quick legislative path for urgent bills, or through issue of decrees with the force of law. In the first case, the Senate and the President must table their reservations within seven days. In the second case, the Cabinet may be empowered by the Sejm to pass decrees with force of law, except on certain issues defined by the Constitution. The decrees must also be signed by the President.

Half the membership of the Sejm and the Senate constitute a quorum. Assuming there are no vacancies due to death, resignation or expulsion, this means 230 deputies in the Sejm and 50 senators in the Senate.

The second Senate of the Republic (1991-1993) met 40 times: in four 3-day sittings, twenty one two-day sittings and fifteen 1-day sittings, for a total of 69 days.

During this period the Senate submitted nine legislative initiatives, four of which were accepted by the Sejm. It also made 47 amendments to 102 acts passed by the Sejm. Of these amendments, 37 were accepted by the Sejm. The Senate tabled seven motions to reject laws made by the Sejm, three of which were accepted by the Sejm.

COMMITTEES—POWERS AND PROCEDURES—PUBLIC HEARINGS

In the Polish parliamentary terminology committees of the Sejm are called commissions (*Komisje*).

The 25 parliamentary committees are the most important organs of the Sejm. They handle the core of activities of the Sejm and enjoy a large measure of independence. Their function is to express opinions on issues submitted to them by the Sejm and analyze the activity of different branches of the economy or state administration. They send their desiderata and opinions to the executive and other state organs.

Each Sejm Deputy, except for the Speaker of the Sejm and Deputy Speakers, is obliged to serve on at least one committee of the Sejm and, if he or she so wishes, can serve on two committees, as most of the Deputies do. Special permission from the Presidium of the Chamber is needed to sit on three Sejm committees. The same rules apply to the Senate.

Status of Sejm Standing Committees as of Nov 15, 1993

Name of the Committee	Members	Chairperson (Party)
Administration and Internal Affairs	32	Z. Bujak (UP)
European Union Affairs	28	J. Borkowski (PSL)
Education, Science & Technical Adv.	40	. Zaciura (SLD)
Commerce & Services	31	A. Szarawarski (SLD)
Culture & Communication Media	32	J. Braun (UD)
Liaison with Poles Abroad	22	L. Moczulski (KPN)
Youth, Physical Culture & Sport	32	M. Wielgus (BBWR)
National & Ethnic Minorities	17	J. Kuroń (UD)
National Defense	33	J. Szmajdziński (SLD)
Environment, Minerals, Forests	33	S. Zelichowski (PSL)
Constitutional Responsibility	16	J. Wiatr (SLD)
Economic Policy, Budget, Finance	41	W. Ziółkowska (UP)
Land, Construction, Housing Policy	27	T. Biliński (SLD)
Social Policy	43	A. Bankowska (SLD)

Property Privatisation	35	B. Pek (PSL)
Sejm Rules & Deputy Affairs	29	R. Grodzicki (SLD)
Agriculture and Food Economy	40	R. Smolarek (PSL)
Local Self-government	47	P. Buczkowski (UD)
Justice	27	A. Bentkowski (PSL)
Foreign Affairs	45	B. Geremek (UD)
Foreign Commerce & Maritime Affairs	35	L. Podkański (PSL)
Economic System & Industry	33	J. Lochowski (PSL)
Legislative	26	J. Jaskiernia (SLD)
Health	30	R. Zochowski (SLD)
Constitutional (National Assembly)	47	A. Kwaśniewski (SLD)*

* Elected president in September 1995. Replaced as committee charirman .

The Senate operates through 13 standing committees. The Chairpersons of these committees and their membership are elected by the Senate at large.

Standing Committees of the Senate as of Dec. 6, 1993

Name of the Committee	Members	Chairperson (Party)
National Economy	20	E. Kienig (PSL)
Motions and Legislation	9	H. Rot (SLD)
Culture, Media, Phys. Ed.& Sport	11	J. Mulak (SLD)
Science and National Education	14	M. Łopatkowa (PSL)
National Defense	13	R. Szwonder (SLD)
Environmental Protection	14	R. Ochwat (PSL)
Social Policy & Health	16	M. Wyględowski (SLD)
Human Rights & Rule of Law	12	L. Czerwiński (SLD)
Agriculture	13	S. Gajewski (PSL)
Local Government & Public Administ.	15	A. Wos (PSL)
Emigration & Poles Abroad	17	J. Sek (PSL)
Foreign Affairs	19	H. Markiewicz (PSL)
Rules & Senate Affairs	11	G. Kruczuk (SLD)
Constitutional (National Assembly)	10	S. L. Pastuszka (SLD)

Drafts of Senate bills may be submitted by a committee or a group of any 10 senators.

Decisions of the committee are by majority vote, with at least 1/3 of its members present. If two or more committees hold a joint meeting, the decisions of the joint body require agreement of at least 2/5 of members of each committee.

BUDGET PROCEDURES

The Council of Ministers drafts a budget proposal and submits it for the first reading to the Economic Policy, Budget and Finance Committee of the Sejm. The timing of the submission of the proposal must be such that the Sejm be able to accept the proposal before the beginning of the budget year. In exceptional circumstances, this deadline can be extended to the end of the first quarter.

Following the review and modifications by the Committee, the budget proposal is submitted for a second reading to the Sejm. After the budget is passed by the Sejm, the Speaker of the Sejm sends the budget act to the Speaker of the Senate, who in turn sends it to the Senate Committees. The Senate committees may require authorized representatives of the respective ministries to appear before them to answer questions related to the budget. After having considered the appropriate parts of the budget, the various committees refer their opinions to the National Economy Committee which formulates the Senate's response to the Sejm. The Senate has no power to reject the budget proposal, but can submit amendments to the Sejm within 20 days.

The Senate amendments to the budget can be either accepted in the third reading in the Sejm, or rejected by a two thirds majority vote, cast in the presence of at least half of the deputies. If the budget is passed in the third reading, it is sent to the President of the Republic for his signature.

The time allotted to the Sejm and the Senate for all of the above steps by the Constitution is four months from the date the proposal is submitted to the Sejm by the Prime Minister. Should this time limit be missed, the President has the power to dissolve the Sejm and the Senate and call new elections.

During the budget year the Sejm receives from the Supreme Board of Supervision (NIK) analyses on the execution of the budget. These constitute the basis for the Sejm's resolutions approving, or rejecting the execution of the budget by the appropriate ministries.

RELATIONS WITH THE EXECUTIVE—MONITORING EXECUTIVE PERFORMANCE—OMBUDSMAN

On 27 November 1990, the Sejm amended the constitution of the Polish Republic in the matter of election of the President. According to this amendment the President is elected in a popular election for a five year term of office and can be reelected only once for a second term. Any Polish citizen 35 years of age and entitled to vote in the elections to the Sejm is eligible to be a candidate for the Presidency. [The same applies under the new Constitution of April 1997.]

In order to implement statutes, and on the basis of powers specified therein, the President issues ordinances and executive orders. Which, to be valid, must be countersigned by the Prime Minister, or the minister who submitted the matter to the President.

The President appoints and recalls ministers of state, authorized to carry out in his name activities with which they were entrusted. The executive organ of the President is his Chancellory.

The President ratifies and repudiates international agreements. Ratification of international agreements involving significant financial burdens to the state, or the necessity of changes in legislation require prior consent of the Sejm.

The ministers are responsible before the Sejm and report to it on their actions. The Sejm can refuse to absolve a minister even when it absolves the rest of the cabinet as a body.

The office of the Ombudsman (Rzecznik Praw Obywatelskich) was established on January 1, 1988. He, or she, is appointed by the Sejm with the consent of the Senate for a four year term of office to guard the laws and liberties of the citizens. The Ombudsman is independent of other organs of the state and is responsible only to the Sejm.

The Supreme Board of Supervision (NIK) provides help in overseeing the operations of state administration and correctness of its finances and legality. The Chairman of NIK is appointed and dismissed by the Sejm with the consent of the Senate.

EXECUTIVE VETO AND OVERRIDING VETOES

Laws passed by the Sejm and the Senate are sent to the President of the Republic for his signature and publication in the Journal of Laws (Dziennik Ustaw) to bring them into force. If the President has reservations about them, he may refuse to sign, thus exercising Executive Veto, or may request the Constitutional Court to pass on their compliance with the Constitution.

The Presidential veto may be accepted by the Sejm, thus ending the law's legislative path, or it may be overruled by the Sejm, by a two-thirds majority. The successful over-rule means in effect that the Sejm disagrees with the President's objections and obliges him to sign the law.

On authorization by the Sejm, the Council of Ministers may issue regulations with the force of law. The President can sign them into law and publish them in the Journal of Laws, or veto them, thus terminating their life. This veto cannot be overridden by the Cabinet. The only recourse is to submit the decree to the Sejm for passage in the normal legislative way. The regulations may also be sent by the President to the Constitutional Court to verify their compliance with the Constitution.

OFFICE OF THE SPEAKER—POWERS

The Speakers of the Sejm and the Senate are elected from among the membership during the first session of the Sejm and the Senate following the General Election. Assisted by deputy Speakers, they are responsible for the day-to-day conduct of debates, giving, or denying the floor to members who signed up for debate, and assuring an orderly conduct of the house. All correspondence between the legislative, the executive, and the judiciary branches of government goes out over the Speaker's signature.

The Speaker of the Sejm and the Deputy Speakers constitute the Presidium of the Sejm that stands guard of its rights, assures the realization of its plan of action, coordinates the operations of the Sejm committees, and represents the Sejm in dealings with the outside world.

The Speaker of the Sejm, Deputy Speakers and the Chairpersons of Party Caucuses constitute the Convention of Seniors (Konwent **Seniorów**) and serve as an advisory body in the selection of Deputies to the membership of Sejm committees.

In the event that the office of the President of the Republic is vacated, or the President is temporarily unable to exercise the powers of his office, the Speaker of the Sejm acts for him.

PARTY CAUCUSES AND GROUPS—WHIPS AND MAJORITY AND MINORITY LEADERS—PARTY DISCIPLINE

In 1994 no party had an absolute majority in the Sejm and the government was formed by the coalition of the Democratic Left Alliance (SLD) led in the Sejm by Aleksander Kwaśniewski and the Polish Peasant Alliance (PSL), with Waldemar Pawlak of PSL serving as Prime Minister.

The minority parties do not operate as a block with a clear leader, although the largest opposition party, the Democratic Union (UD), combined in the spring of 1994 with the Liberal-Democratic Congress (KLD), a party currently without Sejm representation, to form the Liberty Union (UW) led by Tadeusz Mazowiecki, the former first non-communist Prime Minister of Poland. For a period of time, the new party organized extraparliamentary secretariats, led by Bronisław Geremek, with specific members assigned to follow the operations of each ministry of Mr. Pawlak's cabinet. However, this mode of operating by the opposition has not turned into a regular practice.

Party caucuses are known in the Sejm and the Senate as "Parliamentary Clubs," (at least 15 members), or "Parliamentary Circles," (at least 3 members), and their leaders as "Chairmen." They include both deputies and senators of a given political persuasion. When appearing as a group in meetings with the Speakers, the chairmen of clubs are known as "Seniors' Convention (Konwent Seniorów).

Clubs and Parliamentary Circles, as of September 19, 1993.

Name of the Club	(Chairperson)	Deput	Senat.
SLD Democratic Left Alliance	A. Kwaśniewski	171	37
PSL Polish Peasant Alliance	W. Pawlak	132	34
UD Democratic Union	B. Geremek	74	6
UP Union of Labor	R. Bugaj	41	-
KPN Confed.for Independent Poland	K. Król	22	-
BBWR Nonparty Reform Block	A. Gąsienica-Makowski	16	-
MN German Minority	H. Kroll	4	-
NSZZ "Solidarity"	Z. Romaszewski	-	12
N Independent Senators	J. Madej	-	7
		460	96

Party discipline may be enforced by expulsion from parliamentary clubs or circles, a foolhardy move for small parties, because a membership drop below 15 Deputies deprives them of the right to submit legislative proposals.

DEBATES—INTERPELLATION—OFFICIAL RECORD—VOTING PROCEDURES

Debates in the Sejm and the Senate take place on topics designated by the respective Speakers in the Order of Business for the day. The Deputies and the Senators desiring to take part in the debate sign up with the secretaries of the Sejm and the Senate. Signed motions aimed at passing a bill must be filed in writing, whereas legislative motions, entailing encumbrances on the state budget, must specify the sources of financial coverage.

THE SEYM IN POST-COMMUNIST POLAND

The respective Speakers give the floor to the parliamentarians in the order in which they appear on the Speaker's list. For each bill under discussion, the first to speak is the reporter for the respective commission. His presentation may not exceed 20 minutes, whereas that of a participant in the subsequent debate, no more than 10 minutes, except when the Speaker extends these time limits due to the gravity of the matter under discussion. A parliamentarian can speak only twice on the same issue, the second time no longer than 5 minutes.

Interpellations were a declining form of control over the executive in the Polish People's Republic. From the peak of 69 in 1956 they gradually declined to as few as 1 per year in 1967, with an occasional rise in the years of social unrest (10 in 1966, 36 in 1971). With the restoration of the Polish Republic in 1989, they regained their control function and rose in number.

The official record of proceedings is the responsibility of the Shorthand Report Department of the Sejm, and of the Shorthand Editorial Department of the Senate Information Office. The Senate proceedings are written in shorthand, recorded on tape and filmed by the Polish Television. Typing of Senate speeches and the debate from the taped recording begins ten minutes after the session starts. The text is entered into a computer, edited by introduction of punctuation marks, removal of repetitions and linguistic errors, and double-checked. The rough "Shorthand Report" is printed during the night. Next day the Senators can check the text and submit their corrections, but no substantial changes, such as new proposals or justifications, are allowed. The final copy appears six weeks later as the "Shorthand Report of the Sitting of the Senate of the Polish Republic".

A "Senate Diary" is published every two weeks by the Senate Chancellery with detail of Senate activities, Senate Presidium resolutions, work of the Senate commissions, and Senate representation at state ceremonies and visits of official guests.

It is worth noting here that censorship was imposed on the published transactions of the Sejm of the Polish People's Republic and only lifted in 1983, thanks to the efforts of Deputy Edmund Osmańczyk.[*] In consequence, the picture of the operation of that Sejm emerging from the published materials is incomplete.

In voting, the majority carries the outcome. However, the following types of majority are recognized: relative majority or plurality, i.e. any excess of votes "for" the measure over votes against (i. e. 2 votes for, 300 abstaining from voting, 1 vote against - relative majority achieved). This type of majority is relatively easy to achieve and is required for passing Sejm resolutions and ordinary Acts.

---

[*] Edmund Osmańczyk was elected Senator to the first Senate of the III Republic in 1991.

Absolute majority, more difficult to achieve—motion "for" must collect at least 50% of votes cast plus one (e.g. 400 deputies vote, 201 votes are for the measure—the act is passed). This type of vote is used in selecting the Chairman of the Supreme Board of Supervision (NIK), the Chairman of the Supreme Court, the President of the National Bank or in passing the vote of non-confidence for the cabinet, in granting "special authorizations" to the Council of Ministers to issue decrees with the power of the Act of Sejm.

"Qualified Majority," for instance 3/5 or 2/3 votes for a measure is needed for the change of articles of the constitution or for overriding the vetoes of the Senate or the President of the Republic. In any type of majority the voting can only be carried out in the presence of the quorum, set at 50% of all Deputies (230), or 50 Senators.

RELATIONS BETWEEN THE SEJM AND THE SENATE

The formal relations between the Sejm and the Senate involve their constitutional roles in governing the country. Thus, both chambers meet as the National Assembly to receive from the newly elected President of the Republic his oath of office.

Members of the Presidium of the Sejm and the Senate, i.e. the Speaker and the Deputy Speakers of both chambers, may sit in during the sessions of the other body, or any of its committees, without right to vote. An exception here are the rules of the Constitutional Committee of the National Assembly where Senators (10) and Deputies (46) work together.

Formal communication between the two chambers is by letters between the two speakers, and is handled by the Chancellery of the Sejm and of the Senate. It involves the principal duty of the Senate which is to examine and approve, or reject, bills received from the Sejm, or submittal of Senate bills for legislation.

The political relations between the two chambers were of key importance during the transfer of power in the country, from Communist control to a democratic form of government. Following the agreements reached in 1989 at the "Round Table" talks between the government and the "Solidarity" workers' movement, unhindered elections to the Senate were permitted, while the Communist-led coalition reserved for itself 2/3 of the seats in the Sejm. In the event, only one independent was elected to the 100 seat Senate, and in the Sejm "Solidarity" candidates did well, whereas the Communist-led coalition had difficulty achieving the required minimum 50% of votes cast for their candidates, necessitating a second, run-off election.

The outcome of this half-free election had a shattering effect on the morale of the Communist-led coalition. It led to the disintegration of the governing coalition and the eventual dissolution of the Communist Party (PZPR). At that time the Sejm and the Senate stood at opposite ends of the political spectrum and the relations between them reflected that fact. The Sejm thus elected was counted as the last (X) Sejm of the communist-dominated Polish People's Republic, whereas the Senate elected in fully free elections was counted as the first (I) of the Polish Republic which was just being reestablished.

In the elections of 1991 remnants of the formerly ruling communist party (PZPR) reorganized along the lines of western democratic parties as the Democratic Left Alliance and with its coalition partner, the United Peasant Party (PSL), declared their support for market economy and pluralistic political society, and in 1993 regained control of both houses. Consequently, much of the controversy between the two chambers has now disappeared.

The Sejm Library of over 400,000 volumes and a Research and Analysis Office (Biuro Studiów i Ekspertyz) are available to help the legislators.

PARLIAMENTARY PRIVILEGES AND IMMUNITIES—RECALL, EXPULSION, RESIGNATION

Article 6 of the Small Constitution of October 17, 1992 states that a Sejm Deputy represents the entire Nation and not just his electoral district, is not bound in the execution of his duties in the Chamber by instructions from the electorate, and cannot be recalled. [Also stated in Article 104 of Constitution of April 1997.]

Among the parliamentary privileges of Senators and Deputies is the immunity from arrest or prosecution for their political activities. However, this does not grant immunity from prosecution in criminal cases.

Permission to detain, or arrest a Senator or a Deputy in case of a criminal prosecution must be requested from the Speaker of the respective Chamber, who then presents it to the Presidium of the Chamber which forwards it to the Rules Committee for review. The Committee's report is then presented to the full Chamber. The accused has a chance to present his or her side of the case to the full Chamber and to answer questions.

A Sejm Deputy cannot be arrested or indicted without consent of at least 2/3 of Deputies voting, with at least half of all Deputies present. The Senate has the same procedure, plus the power to terminate the mandate of the Senator in question.

PARLIAMENTARY PAY AND PERQUISITES

The pay of Deputies and Senators consists of two components: first is the tax free reimbursement (dieta) of costs connected with the execution of their office, currently 8,000,000 złoty, and increased by a fixed percent for execution of specific functions in the Sejm. The second is the salary (ryczałt) paid to deputies who take unpaid leave of absence from their regular employment, currently also 8,000,000 złoty. In addition there are the travel privileges.

In June, 1994, the following scale of monthly pay applied:

	Pay (old złoty)
President of the Republic	32,795,000
Prime Minister, Sejm & Senate Speakers	30,000,000
Ministers, Ombudsman, Constit. Tribunal Chairman	24,800,000
Sejm Deputies and Senators	16,000,000

Note: average country wide pay was 5,000,000 zl in June 1994, and the exchange rate was 22,000 zl/$. [In 1995 a conversion took place of złoty at a ratio of 10,000:1.]

In addition to the above, members of the Sejm and Senate are entitled to 25,000,000 old złoty per month allowance to cover the cost of maintaining an office in their constituency.

Deputies who are appointed Ministers are paid concurrently for both positions.

The perquisites include the use of the Sejm hotel and restaurants, and Deputies and Senators have free passes on state railways and state airline for travel to any destination in the country, as well as free passes on Warsaw streetcars.

PARLIAMENTARY ETHICS—DISCIPLINE

Parliamentary ethics are enforced by the Speaker of each chamber, jointly with the Rules Committee. That committee considers the cases of Deputies or Senators whose conduct is deemed unbecoming to the dignity of their office, or who do not fulfill their duties by absenting themselves from the sessions without prior notification of the Speaker, or from sittings of the Committees on which they serve.

Every unexcused absence from a plenary session of the Senate brings with it a 10% deduction from the per diem, whereas absence from a sitting in the Committee leads to a 5% deduction in the per diem. The rules of the Sejm in treating the absences are somewhat different. If a Sejm deputy is absent from more than 1/3 of the sessions of the Committee on which he or she serves, and does not justify the absence, his or her pay is reduced by 1/3 during the period for the next 3 months.

The Rules Committee of the respective Chamber may bring the matter of transgression to the attention of the Deputy or Senator, issue an admonition, and in more severe cases, reprimand the person concerned, who then has 14 days in which to appeal the decision.

In a recent case of abuse of voting procedures, one Deputy pressed two voting buttons, one for himself and one for his absent colleague, thus initiating a disciplinary procedure.

It is worth noting that in the communist-dominated Sejms of Polish People's Republic, although it was not spelled out in the law, the rule of unanimity in voting was strictly enforced under the guise of party discipline for over 30 years, i.e. during that period no vote was ever cast against any bill presented to the Sejm. In that period there were only three instances when a single Deputy abstained from voting. In all appearances it was a return to the rule of "Unanimitas" applied in the Sejms of the First Republic from 1655 to 1791, until it was abolished by the Constitution passed by the Sejm on May 3, 1791.

JUDICIAL FUNCTIONS OF THE SEJM

The Sejm has the power to indict members of the executive in cases of unethical or unconstitutional conduct, with actual trial conducted by the Tribunal of State.

The Tribunal of State is the body established to pronounce on the responsibility of persons in high office for transgressions against the constitution or the laws, that is, on the impeachment of such individuals. Its members are selected by the Sejm from outside the Sejm's membership for the same term as the term of the Sejm.

On September 19, 1992, the Sejm indicted three ministers: D. Jastrzębski, A. Wróblewski and A. Mackiewicz, members of M. Rakowski's cabinet, for dereliction of duty and for allowing the import of large quantities of alcohol without payment of customs duty. Deputies K. Kamiński (KPN) and S. Zając (ZChN) were designated by the Sejm to head the indictment team.

On December 12, 1992 the Sejm accepted a Senate amendment to Article 4, section 1 of the "Small Constitution" of October 17, 1992, making it possible for 1/4 of all Deputies and Senators to indict the President of the Republic for breach of Constitution and to call for his trial by the Tribunal of State.

PARLIAMENT AND MEDIA—BROADCASTING OF PROCEEDINGS

Since 1963 the Tele-Radiophonic section of the Chancellery of the Sejm records the proceedings of the Sejm on audiotape, and starting with the X Sejm the proceedings of the Sejm committees. The tapes are archived. The sessions of the Sejm and the Senate recorded on audio-phonic tape constitute part of the record of parliamentary proceedings, in addition to the stenographer's record. Both media are used in the production of the Diary of the Sejm and the Senate.

The Sejm sessions have been recorded on video tape since 1991 as an archival record for the Sejm Library and constitute the "Mediateka" of that library. The Sejm sessions are broadcast live on Channel 2 of Polish Television from 9 am till 3 pm on every day the Sejm is in session.

The Chairpersons of the committees of the Sejm and the Senate can invite live radio or television coverage of their plenary sessions, as well as sessions involving witnesses who testify for the committees of either body.

CONSTITUTIONALITY OF LAWS—EMERGENCY POWERS

In cases when the President of the Republic questions the constitutionality of laws sent to him for his signature after having been passed by both the Sejm and the Senate, he has the option to consult the Constitutional Tribunal.

Members of the Constitutional Tribunal are selected by the Sejm from among distinguished legal experts. The Constitutional Tribunal is independent and governed only by the constitution.

The rulings of the Tribunal are binding on the President if positive, i.e. when the Tribunal finds the law constitutional. In such a case, the President must sign the Act into law and order it to be published in the Journal of Laws (Dziennik Ustaw).

If the Constitutional Tribunal declares the Sejm act sent up to it by the President as unconstitutional, the President can base his refusal to sign the act into law on the opinion of the Tribunal.

The above two cases are distinct from the regular functions of the Constitutional Tribunal which consist in pronouncing on the constitutionality of laws already passed by the Sejm and the Senate, signed into law by the President and published in the Journal of Laws. Such declaration of unconstitutionality of a law is sent to the Legislative Commission of the Sejm, which studies it and sends its opinion to the Deputies of the Sejm. The Sejm may override the unconstitutionality opinion by no less than 2/3 majority vote in the presence of at least half the Deputies. If no such action is taken, the unconstitutionality of the law is accepted and the law becomes null and void.

Emergency powers are vested in the President. The President has the power to declare the state of war over part or whole of the territory of the Republic, if such a declaration is needed for the defence against external threat, or protection of order in the interior of the country. For the same reasons he can declare partial or full mobilization. He can also declare, for a period no longer than 3 months, a state of emergency in the case of threat to the internal security or of a natural disaster. Extension of the state of emergency is permitted only once for an additional period of 3 months, with the consent of the Sejm and the Senate.

STATISTICS, TABLES AND CHARTS

The word cadence (kadencja) is used to describe the term of the Sejm and the Senate. Presently, the Sejm and the Senate term numbers do not coincide. The Sejm, sworn in on Sept. 19, 1993 is formally called the II-nd Sejm of the Republic of Poland while the present Senate is already the III-rd, because the first free election of the Senate preceded that of the Sejm by one term.

	Term Numbering	
Term dates	**Sejm**	**Senate**
--------------------------------	-------	-------
18 June 1989 to 25 Nov 1991	X	I
27 Nov 1991 to 31 May 1993	I	II
19 Sept 1993 to 1997	II	III
--------------------------------	-------	-------

	Sejm		Senate	
Legislative Statistics	**X**	**I**	**I**	**II**
--------------------------------	-------		-------	
Days in session	177	136	90	69
laws passed	248	94	289	111
resolutions passed	162	135	164	
interpellations	600	773		
questions	150	508		
declarations	520	506		

| Senate legislative initiatives | 27 | 9 |
| Senate amendments to Sejm proposals | 84 | 47 |
Senate resolutions to veto laws	6	

Sex of Legislators	I Senate	II Senate	III Senate
Men	93	92	87
Women	7	8	13

	X Sejm	I Sejm	II Sejm
Men	395	416	400
Women	62	44	60

WHO'S WHO OF PARLIAMENTARY LEADERS

II Sejm (1994)

Józef Oleksy (1946 -) (SLD), Speaker of the Sejm, Deputy of X and I Sejm for the city of Siedlce, married, father of two children. Education: Doctorate in economic sciences. Chairman of Social Democracy of the Republic of Poland.

Jacek Kuroń (1934-) UD, Deputy of X and I Sejm for Warsaw. Married, one child. University degree in history; social activist. Presidium of Sejm UD club. Serves as the Chairman of the Sejm Committee for National and Ethnic Minorities.

Aleksander Kwaśniewski (1954 -) SLD, Sejm Deputy for Warsaw, I Sejm. Education: studied towards a degree in Economics, Chairman of Supreme Council of SdRP, Chairman of SLD Sejm club, Chairman of the National Assembly. Elected president in September of 1995.

Bronisław Geremek (1932 -) UD, Deputy from Warsaw to the X and I Sejm. Married, two children. University degrees, Professor of the Institute of History of Polish Academy of Sciences. Chairman of UD Sejm club. Chairman of the Sejm Foreign Relations Commission.

Olga Krzyżanowska (1929 -) UD, Deputy Speaker of Sejm, Deputy for Gdańsk to the X and I Sejm. Married, one child. Doctor of medicine. UD Chairwoman of regional Council of Gdańsk, Member of Supreme Council of UD. Chairwoman of the Presidium of UD Sejm Club.

Tadeusz Mazowiecki (1927 -) UD, Deputy for Poznań to the III, IV, V and I Sejm. Widower, 3 children. Law Degree. Chairman of UD, and member of UD Sejm club. Member of the National Defence and the National Assembly Constitutional committee.

III Senate (1994)

Adam Struzik (1957 -) PSL, Senator for Płock in the II Senate, Speaker of the III Senate. Married, two children. Graduate of the Medical Academy, Director of Płock hospital. Member of the Supreme Council and the PSL Płock Directorate.

Zofia Kuratowska (1931 -), UD, Senator for Warsaw District in the I and II Senate, Deputy Speaker in the I and III Senate. Married, one child. Doctor of Medicine, university professor. Member of Council of UD, Chairwoman of

Social-Liberal Faction of UD. Member of Social Policy and Health Sejm Committee.

August Chełkowski (1927 -), Senator for Katowice district in the II and III Senate, served as Deputy Speaker in the II Senate. Professor of Silesian University, member of Presidium of Physics Committee of Polish Academy of Sciences. Member of Foreign Relations Sejm Committee.

BIBLIOGRAPHY

1. Jacek Jędruch, *Constitutions, Elections and Legislatures of Poland, 1493-1977*, University Press of America, Washington, DC, 1982.

2. Juliusz Bardach, edit. *Dzieje Sejmu Polskiego* (History of the Polish Sejm), Wydawnictwo Sejmowe, Warszawa 1993.

3. Andrzej Burda, Andrzej Gwiżdż, Wiesław Skrzydło, Witold Zakrzewski, *Sejm Polskiej Rzeczpospolitej Ludowej* (Sejm of the Polish People's Republic), Polska Akademia Nauk, Zakład Narodowy Im. Ossolińskich, Wroclaw 1975.

4. *Volumina Legum*, (Legislation of the 251 Sejms of the pre-partition Poland), Warszawa, Kraków, Poznań, 1732-1786, 1889, 1952, 10 volumes.

5. *Dziennik Praw Księstwa Warszawskiego*, (Law Gazette of the Duchy of Warsaw) Warszawa, 1808-1812, 4 volumes.

6. *Dziennik Praw Królestwa Polskiego* (Law Gazette of the Kingdom of Poland), Warszawa, 1815-1849, 49 volumes.

7. *Tranzakcye Sejmu prowincyalnego prowincyi Poznańskiej* (Transactions of the Sejm of Poznań), Poznań, 1827-1877. 19 volumes

8. *Dziennik Praw i Rozporządzeń Krajowych Królestwa Galicji* (Law Gazette of the Kingdom of Galicia), Lwów, 1866-1918.

9. *Konstytucje i Podstawowe Akty Ustawodawcze Rzeczpospolitej Polskiej, 1918-1939* (Constitutions and more important laws of the Second Republic), Warszawa, 1967.

10. *Konstytucja i Podstawowe Akty Ustawodawcze Polskiej Rzeczpospolitej Ludowej* (Constitutions and more important laws of Polish People's Republic), Warszawa, 1971.

11. Jacek Jędruch, *Election Boycotts in the Second and Polish People's Republics of Poland, and Their Social Implications*, Parliaments, Estates and Representation, Vol 7, No. 2, December 1987.

12. Jacek Jędruch, *Revival of the Senate of Poland in the Light of Its History*, pp. 395-408, in *Bicameralisme, Tweekamerstelsel vroeger en nu*, Handelingen van de Internationale Conferentie ter gelegenheid van het 175-jarig bestaan van de Eerste Kamer der Staten Generaal in de Nederlanden, 's-Gravenhage 1992.

APPENDICES

APPENDIX A
KEY PARAGRAPHS IN THE FOUNDING CHARTERS
OF LIBERTIES

Confirmatio privilegiorum, et aliorum jurium, cum additione aliquorum articulorum, per Vladislaum Jegellonem, regem, ipsis regnicolis in loco campestri prope Czerwinsko, de anno Domini 1422 concessorum. Jus Polonicum.

(Nec bona recipiantur privilege of Czerwińsk)

Item ut gratia uberiori consolentur a nobis, etiam nos fide et sevitiis amplioribus prosequantur, promittimus: quod ex nunc et de caetero nunquam alicujus subditi regni nostri, cujuscunque dignitatis, eminentiae, status, aut gradus fuerit, bona haereditaria recipiemus, confiscabimus, recipi vel confiscari faciemus; nec se de eis per nos. vel officiales nostros, vel alios quoscunque homines, intromittemus, vel intromitti faciemus, pro quibuscunque excessibus aut culpis, nisi prius super hoc praecedat judicium nostrorum, quos ad hoc, deputaverimus, cum nostris praelatis, baronibus, matura cognitio et sententia sequatur.

Likewise, in order that we might please them by more abundant favors, and also that they might honor us with loyalty and better services, we promise that, from this day forward, we will neither possess nor confiscate, nor cause to be possessed or confiscated, the hereditary property of any royal subject, of whatever rank, position, or prominence he may be, or rank he may have been; nor, through us, our officials, or any others, will we visit the penalty of this confiscation, for any illegal or blameworthy act, unless, first, our judges, which we have assigned to the case, together with our bishops and barons, have conducted a full legal inquiry, and second, a sentence has been handed down.

Vladislai Jagello Statuta de Libertatibus, Anno 1433, Volumina Legum I.

(Neminem captivabimus privilege of Jedlna-Cracow)

Caeterum promittimus et spondemus: quod nullum terrigenam possessionatum pro aliquo excessu, seu culpa capiemus, seu capi mandabimus; nec aliquam vindictam in ipso faciemus, nisi judicio rationabiliter fuerit convictus: et: ad manus nostras, vel nostrorum Capitaneorum, per Judices ejusdem Terrae, in qua idem terrigena residet praesentatus; illo tamen homine, qui in furto, vel in publico maleficio, (utpote incendio, homicidio Voluntario, raptu virginum et mulierum, villarum depopulationibus, et spoliis) deprehenderetur; similiter illis, qui de se nollent debitam facere cautionem vel dare, juxta quantitatem excessus vel delicti, duntaxat exceptis.

Moreover, we promise and pledge that: for some impropriety, we will neither seize at once, nor order the seizure of, any propertied native individual; nor shall the same be punished, unless justly convicted through a criminal proceeding. As for jurisdiction and judges, an accused will be tried in the locale of his home, by judges of that same place. Exceptions to the foregoing: the above does not apply in the case of a man caught in the act of stealing or of public crime (viz, arson, voluntary manslaughter, rape of maidens and matrons, pillaging and despoiling of villages), nor in the case of those, who should be unwilling to honor or pay an outstanding debt, bordering on an excessive or criminal amount.

Alexandri Regis Decreta in Comitijs Radomien, Anno 1505,—Volumina Legum I. (Nihil novi Act of Radom)

De non faciendis constitutionibus sine consensu Consiliariorum et Nuntiorum Terrestrium.

Quoniam jura communia et constitutiones publicae non unum, sed communem populum afficiunt, itaque in hac Radomiensi Conventione cum universis Regni nostri Praelatis, Consiliarijs, Baronibus et Nuntijs Terrarum, aequum et rationabile con- suimus, ac etiam statuimus, ut deinceps futuris temporibus perpetuis, nihil novi constitui debeat per Nos et successores nostros sine communi Consiliariorum et Nuntiorum Terrestrium consensu, quod fieret in praejudicium gravamenque Reipub- licae, et damnum atque incommodum cujuslibet privatum, ad innovationemque juris communis et publicae libertatis.

Because common laws and public ordinances affect not one, but all people in common, therefore, at this Seym of Radom, with all the judges, councillors, barons, and territorial deputies assembled together, we have reasonably moved and, further, adopted, the following equitable resolution: that, because such might become a detriment and injury to the State, an injury and misfortune of whatever sort to the private individual, and make for change in regard to public right and liberty, henceforth, and in future times in perpetuity, no new laws shall be made by us or our successors, without the consent of the councillors and territorial deputies.

APPENDIX B
DEVELOPMENT OF SEYMIKS AS ELECTORAL DISTRICTS

Hereditary Monarchy	(1550)
First Republic	(1660 and 1791)
Congress Kingdom	(1820)
Grand Duchy of Poznań	(1840)

Note: Numbers in parenthesis denote the number of Deputies elected by the gentry assembled in each Seymik. In the Congress Kingdom and the Grand Duchy of Poznań these were supplemented by the Deputies elected by the towns and villages through the communal assemblies.

SEYMIKS OF MASOVIA

PALATINATE	1550	1660	1791	1820
Płock	(2) Raciąż	(4) Raciąż	(2) Raciąż	(1)Płock
			(2) Bielsk	(1) Pułtusk
			(2) Mława	(1) Mława
				(1) Lipnowo
				(1) Przasnycz
				(1) Ostrołęka
Rawa	(2) Rawa	(2) Bolimów	(2) Rawa	(1) Rawa
		(2) Sochaczew	(2) Sochaczew	(1) Sochaczew
		(2) Gąbin	(2) Gąbin	
Warsaw	(2) Warsaw	(2) Warsaw	(2) Warsaw	(1) Warsaw
	(2) Czersk	(2) Czersk	(2) Czersk	(1) Czersk
	(2) Wizna	(2) Wizna	(2) Wizna	(1) Stanisławów
	(2) Wyszogrod	(2) Wyszogrod	(2) Wyszogrod	(1) Gosynin
	(2) Zakroczym	(2) Zakroczym	(2) Zakroczym	(1) Kowal
	(2) Ciechanów	(2) Ciechanów	(2) Ciechanów	(1) Sienno
	(2) Rożan	(2) Rożan	(2) Rożan	(1) Błonie
	(2) Liw	(2) Liw	(2) Liw	(1) Zgierz
	(2) Nur	(2) Nur	(2) Ostrów	(1) Orłów
	(2) Łomża	(2) Łomża	(2) Łomża	
Augustów				(1) Łomża
				(1) Seyny
				(1) Kalwaria
				(1) Maryampol
				(1) Augustów
				(1) Trykocin
				(1) Dąbrowa
				(1) Biobrze

SEYMIKS OF GREATER POLAND

PALATINATE	1550	1660	1791	1820	1840
Poznań			(2) Poznań		(1) Poznań
					(1) Buk
			(2) Kościana		(1) Kościana
					(1) Szamotuły
					(1) Międzychód
			(2) Międzyrzec		(1) Międzyrzec
					(1) Czarnków
			(2) Wschowa		(1) Wschowa
	(2) Środa	(2) Środa	(2) Środa		(1) Środa
Kalisz			(2) Kalisz	(1) Kalisz	(1) Września
			(2) Konin	(1) Konin	(1) Śrem
			(2) Pyzdry	(1) Pyzdry	(1) Odolanów
Innowrocław				(1) Czestowchowa	(1) Innowrocław
Dobrzyń	(2) Radziejów	(2) Radziejów	(2) Radziejów	(1)Radziejów	(1) Pleszów
	(2) Lipno	(2) Lipno	(2) Lipno		(1) Bydgoszcz
Brześć K.		(2) Brześć K.	(2) Brześć K.	(1) Brześć K.	
Gniezno			(2) Gniezno		(1) Gniezno
			(2) Wągrowiec		
Łęczyca	(2) Łęczyca	(2) Łęczyca	(2) Łęczyca	(1) Łęczyca	
		(2) Parzeczew	(2) Brzeziny	(1) Brzeziny	
Wieluń	(2) Wieluń	(2) Wieluń	(2) Wieluń	(1) Wieluń	
	(4) Szadek	(4) Szadek	(2) Szadek	(1) Szadek	
			(2) Piotrków	(1) Piotrków	
				(1) Sieradz	
				(1) Ostrzeszów	
				(1) Radomsko	
				(1) Warta	

SEYMIKS OF LESSER POLAND

PALATINATE	1550	1660	1791	1820
Cracow	(6) Proszowice	(6) Proszowice	(2) Proszowice	(1) Kielce
	(2) Cracow	(2) Cracow	(2) Cracow	(2) Cracow
			(2) Żarnowiec	(1) Jędrzejów
			(2) Częstochowa	(1) Szkalmir
				(1) Miechów
				(1) Stopnica
				(1) Szydłów
				(1) Olkusz
				(1) Pilica
		(2) Zator		(1) Lelów
Sandomierz	(6) Opatów	(7) Opatów	(2) Opatów	(1) Opatów
			(2) Radom	(1) Radom
			(2) Stopnica	(1) Sandomierz
			(2) Opoczno	(1) Opoczno
				(1) Kozienice
				(1) Staszów
				(1) Solec
				(1) Końskie
				(1) Szydłowiec
Lublin	(3) Lublin		(2) Lublin	(1) Lublin
			(2) Łuków	(1) Lubartów
		(3) Urzędów	(2) Urzędów	(1) Kazimierz
				(1) Zamość
				(1) Tarnogród
				(1) Tomaszów
				(1) Kraśnik
Ruś	(2) Chełm	(2) Chełm	(2) Chełm	(1) Chełm
	(6) Halicz	(6) Halicz		(1) Krasnystaw
	(6) Wisznia S.	(6) Wisznia S.		(1) Hrubieszów

APPENDIX

SEYMIKS OF PODLASIA, RUTHENIA, VOLYNIA, PODOLIA

PALATINATE	1550	1660	1791	1820
Podlasie		(2) Drohiczyn	(2) Drohiczyn	(1) Węgrów
		(2) Mielnik	(2) Mielnik	(1) Łosice
		(2) Brańsk	(2) Brańsk	(1) Siedlce
				(1) Garwolin
				(1) Żelechów
				(1) Radzyń
				(1) Biała P.
				(1) Włodawa
Bełz	(4) Bełz	(4) Bełz	(2) Dubienka	(1) Łuków
Wołyń		(6) Łuck	(2) Łuck	
			(2) Krzemieniec	
			(2) Równe	
			(2) Krasiłów	
		(4) Włodzimierz	(2) Włodzimierz	
			(2) Rafałówka	
Kiev			(2) Pawłocz	
		(6) Włodzimierz	(2) Żytomierz	
			(2) Owrocz	
			(2) Bohusław	
Bracław		(6) Włodzimierz	(2) Winnica	
			(2) Bracław	
			(2) Zwinogródka	
			(2) Granów	
Podole	(3) Kamieniec	(6) Kamieniec	(2) Dunajowice	
			(2) Gródek	
			(2) Latyczów	
			(2) Bar	

SEYMIKS OF LITHUANIA

PALATINATE	1570	1630	1660	1791
Wilno	(10) Wilno	(2) Wilno	(2) Kamieniec L	(2) Wilno
		(2) Oszmiana	(2) Grodno	(2) Oszmiana
		(2) Lida	(2) Wasiliczki	(2) Lida
		(2) Wilkomierz	(2) Wilkomierz	(2) Wilkomierz
		(2) Brasław	(2) Szaty	(2) Brasław
				(2) Eyszyszki
				(2) Postawy
Troki	(8) Troki	(2) Grodno	(2) Grodno	(2) Grodno
		(2) Troki	(2) Siemno	(2) Troki
		(2) Kowno	(2) Gielenie	(2) Kowno
		(2) Upita	(2) Upita	(2) Poniewież
				(4) Merecz
				(2) Preny
Brześć,	(5) Brześć L.	(2) Brześć L.	(2) Brześć L.	(2) Brześć L.
Lithuania		(2) Pińsk	(2) Pińsk	(2) Pińsk
				(2) Kobryń
				(2) Płotnica
Nowogródek	(6) Nowogródek	(2) Nowogródek	(2) Nowogródek	(2) Nowogródek
		(2) Słonim	(2) Słonim	(2) Słonim
		(2) Wołkowysk	(2) Wołkowysk	(2) Wołkowysk
				(2) Słuck
Mińsk	(6)Mińsk	(2) Mińsk	(2) Mińsk	(2) Mińsk
		(2) Mozyr	(2) Kobryn	(2) Mozyr
		(2) Rohaczew	(2) Kiejdany	(2) Bobrujsk
Żmudź	(2) Rosienie	(2) Rosienie	(2) Rosienie	(2) Rosienie
				(2) Szawły
				(2) Telesze

APPENDIX

SEYMIKS OF INFLANTY AND SEYMIKS OF LITHUANIA IN EXILE

PALATINATE	1570	1630	1660	1791
Inflanty	(6) Wenda	(6) Wenda	(6) Pozwole	(2) Illukszta
				(2) Hasenpoth
Połock		(2) Połock	(2) Kobryń	(2) Czaszniki*
			Madzieje	
Witebsk		(2) Witebsk	(2) Bezdzierze	(2) Czereja*
		(2) Orsza	(2) Mińsk	(2) Chłopienicze*
Mścisław		(2) Mścisław	(2) Krynki	
Smoleńsk		(2) Smoleńsk	(2) Grodno*	(2) Olita
		(2) Starodubów	(2) Wierzbołów*	(2) Zyzmory

*Counties contended with Muscovy. Their Seymiks met in exile in Poland and returned Deputies to the Seym.

SEYMIKS OF ROYAL PRUSSIA (POMERANIA)*

PALATINATE	1570	1630	1660	1791
Gdańsk	( ) Stargard	( ) Stargard	( ) Stargard	(1) Gdańsk**
(Pomerania)	( ) Puck	( ) Puck	( ) Puck	
	( ) Mirachowa	( ) Mirachowa	( ) Mirachowa	
	( ) Słuchowo	( ) Słuchowo	( ) Słuchowo	
	( ) Świecie	( ) Świecie	( ) Świecie	
	( ) Tuchola	( ) Tuchola	( ) Tuchola	
Malbork	( ) Malbork	( ) Kiszpork	( ) Kiszpork	
Grudziądz	( ) Chełmno	( ) Kowalewo	( ) Kowalewo	(1) Toruń**
	( ) Grudziądz	( ) Grudziądz	( ) Grudziądz	

*Number of Deputies elected set by the General Seymik, not to exceed 40 total
**Represented by one resident each in Warsaw

APPENDIX C
CHRONOLOGY OF ELECTIONS AND SEYMS HELD IN POLAND

The columns in the table list the following information:

1) Year of the first session of the Seym. Seyms which started in December extended into the next year are so marked. The elections in the 1st Republic preceeded the first session by six weeks.

2) Place where the Seym was held

3) Type of Seym:

      Cn—Convocation, following the death of a King

      Cr—Coronation, for swearing in a new King

      Cs—Council of State

      Ct—Constitutional, held to pass a Constitution

      Dl—Delegation, committees formed, Seym adjourned

      El—Election, held to elect a King

      Ex—Extraordinary, of two weeks duration

      Gc—General Council, held without a King

      Gs—General Seymik, held in lieu of a Seym

      In—Inquest, held for impeaching a King

      Or—Ordinary, of six weeks durations in First Republic

      Pc—Pacification, held to pacify the electorate

4) Outcome of Seym:

      Ds—Disbanded, King could not attend

      Ic—Incomplete for lack of quorum

      Lg—Legislation on the books

      Nl—No legislation extant

      Vt—Legislation vetoed

5) Name of the Speaker, if known

APPENDIX

Horizontal lines are set apart sequences of the Royal Election Seyms in the First Republic and separate the provincial Seym sequences in the Period of Partitions as well as separating the Second from the Polish People's and the Third Republics.

1	2	3, 4	5	1	2	3, 4	5
1493	Piotrków	Or, Lg	--	1520	Bydgoszcz	Or, Lg	--
1494	Radom	Or, Ds	--	1521/2	Piotrków	Or, Lg	--
1496	Piotrków	Or, Lg	--	1523	Cracow	Or, Lg	--
1498	Piotrków	Or, Lg	--	1523	Piotrków	Or, Lg	--
1499	Cracow	Or, Lg	--	1524/5	Piotrków	Or, Lg	--
1500	Sandomierz	Or, Nl--		1525/6	Piotrków	Or, Lg	--
1501	Piotrków	Or, Nl--		1527	Cracow	Or, Lg	--
1501	Piotrków	El, Nl	--	1527/8	Piotrków	Or, Lg	--
1502	Cracow	Cr, Lg	--	1529	Warsaw	Or, Lg	--
1503	Piotrków	Or, Lg	--	1529/30	Piotrków	El, Lg	--
1504	Piotrków	Or, Lg	--	1530	Cracow	Cr, Lg	--
1505	Radom	Or, Lg	--	1530/1	Piotrków	Or, Lg	--
1506	Lublin	Or, Lg	--	1531/2	Cracow	Or, Lg	--
1506	Piotrków	El, Nl	--	1533	Piotrków	Or, Nl	--
1507	Cracow	Cr, Lg	--	1534	Piotrków	Or, Lg	--
1508	Cracow	Or, Lg	--	1534/5	Piotrków	Or, Lg	--
1509	Piotrków	Or, Lg	--	1535	Piotrków	Or, Lg	--
1510	Piotrków	Or, Lg	--	1536/7	Cracow	Or, Lg	--
1511	Piotrków	Or, Lg	--	1538	Piotrków	Or, Lg	--
1511	Korczyn	Gs, Lg	--	1538/9	Cracow	Or, Lg	--
1512	Cracow	Cr, Nl--		1540	Cracow	Or, Lg	--
1512	Piotrków	Or, Lg	--	1542	Piotrków	Or, Nl	--
1513	Poznań	Gs, Lg	--	1543	Cracow	Or, Lg	--
1514	Piotrków	Or, Lg	--	1544	Piotrków	Or, Nl	--
1515	Cracow	Or, Lg	--	1545	Cracow	Or, Nl	--
1517	Piotrków	Or, Lg	--	1545/6	Cracow	Or, Nl	--
1518	Cracow	Or, Lg	--	1547	Cracow	Or, Nl	--
1519	Piotrków	Or, Lg	--	1547/8	Piotrków	Or, Nl	--
1519	Sandomierz	Gs, Lg	--	1548	Piotrków	Or, Nl	J. Sierakowski
1519/20	Toruń	Or, Lg	--	1550	Piotrków	Or, Lg	M. Sienicki

1552	Piotrków	Or, Lg	R. Leszczyński	1593	Warsaw	Or, Lg	M. Daniłowicz
1553	Cracow	Or, Nl	M. Sienicki	1595	Cracow	Or, Lg	S.S. Kraśnicki
1554	Lublin	Or, Ds	--	1596	Warsaw	Or, Lg	P. Myszkowski
1555	Piotrków	Or, Nl	M. Sienicki	1597	Warsaw	Or, Nl	P. Myszkowski
1556/7	Warsaw	Or, Lg	M. Sienicki	1598	Warsaw	Or, Lg	F. Gomoliński
1558/9	Piotrków	Or, Nl	M. Sienicki	1600	Warsaw	Or, Nl	?. Świrski
1562/3	Piotrków	Or, Lg	R. Leszczyński	1601	Warsaw	Or, Lg	Z. Ossoliński
1563/4	Warsaw	Or, Lg	M. Sienicki	1603	Cracow	Or, Lg	F. Kryski
1564	Parczów	Or, Nl	M. Sienicki	1605	Warsaw	Or, Nl	S. Białozor
1565	Piotrków	Or, Lg	M. Sienicki	1606	Warsaw	Or, Nl	S. Ryszkowski
1566	Lublin	Or, Lg	--	1607	Warsaw	Or, Lg	M. VVVVMieliński
1567	Piotrków	Or, Lg	--	1609	Warsaw	Or, Lg	K. Wiesiołowski
1569	Lublin	Or, Lg	S. Czarnkowski	1611	Warsaw	Or, Lg	J. Swoszowski
1570	Warsaw	Or, Lg	S. Szafraniec	1613	Warsaw	Or, Lg	M. Przerębski
1572	Warsaw	Or, Lg	M. Grzybowski	1613	Warsaw	Ex, Lg	A.K. Gosiewski
1573	Warsaw	Cn, Lg	--	1615	Warsaw	Or, Nl	J. Swiętosławski
1573	Kamień	El, Lg	J. Firley	1616	Warsaw	Or, Lg	J. Szczawiński
1574	Cracow	Cr, Lg	W. Agrippa	1618	Warsaw	Or, Lg	K. Wiesiołowski
1574	Warsaw	Cn, Lg	S. Szafraniec	1619	Warsaw	Or, Lg	J. Swiętosławski
1574	Warsaw	El, Lg	M. Sienicki	1620	Warsaw	Or, Lg	J. Szczawiński
1576	Jędrzejów	Gc, Lg	--	1621	Warsaw	Or, Lg	J.D. Sokoliński
1576	Cracow	Cr, Lg	A. Firley	1623	Warsaw	Or, Lg	J. Sobieski
1577	Toruń	Or, Nl	--	1624	Warsaw	Ex, Lg	J. Łowicki
1577	Koło, Korczyn	Gs, Nl	--	1625	Warsaw	Or, Lg	J. Drucki-Sokoliński
1578	Warsaw	Or, Lg	--	1626	Warsaw	Or, Lg	J. Sobieski
1579/80	Warsaw	Or, Lg	--	1626	Toruń	Ex, Lg.	M. Żegocki
1581	Warsaw	Or, Lg	S. Przyjemski	1627	Warsaw	Or, Lg	A. Chalecki
1582	Warsaw	Or, Nl	L. Sapieha	1628	Warsaw	Ex, Lg	J. Sobieski
1585	Warsaw	Or, Nl	S. Pękosławski	1629	Warsaw	Or, Lg	M. Maniecki
1587	Warsaw	Cn, Lg	S. Uchański	1629	Warsaw	Ex, Lg	S. Pac
1587	Warsaw	El, Lg	K. Dębiński	1631	Warsaw	Or, Lg	J. Ossoliński
1587/8	Cracow	Cr, Lg	J. Gajewski	1632	Warsaw	Ex, Lg	M. Żegocki
1589	Warsaw	Pc, Lg	D. Chalecki	1632	Warsaw	Cn, Lg	K. Radziwiłł
1590	Warsaw	Or, Lg	H. Gostomski	1632	Warsaw	El, Lg	J. Sobieski
1590/1	Warsaw	Or, Lg	J.I. Rusiecki	1633	Cracow	Cr, Lg	M. Ostroróg
1592	Warsaw	In, Nl	J. Pac	1634	Warsaw	Ex, Lg	G.M. Tryzna

APPENDIX

1635	Warsaw	Or, Lg	J. Ossoliński	1670	Warsaw	Ex, Vt	J.K. Kierdey
1635	Warsaw	Ex, Lg	M. Łopacki	1670	Warsaw	Or, Lg	S. Lubomirski
1637	Warsaw	Or, Nl	K.L. Sapieha	1672	Warsaw	Or, Vt	M. Oborski
1637	Warsaw	Ex, Lg	J. Jabłonowski	1672	Warsaw	Ex, Vt	G.D. Sokoliński
1638	Warsaw	Or, Lg	L. Opaliński	1673	Warsaw	Pc, Lg	S. Czarniecki
1639	Warsaw	Or, Nl	W. Kierdey	1674	Warsaw	Cn, Lg	F. Bieliński
1640	Warsaw	Or, Lg	J. Jabłonowski	1674	Warsaw	El, Lg	B. Sapieha
1641	Warsaw	Or, Lg	B. Leszczyński	1676	Cracow	Cr, Lg	M. Sieniawski
1642	Warsaw	Ex, Lg	K. Zawisza	1677	Warsaw	Or, Lg	W. Skoroszewski
1643	Warsaw	Or, Lg	J. Lubomirski	1678/9	Grodno	Or, Lg	F. Sapieha
1645	Warsaw	Or, Nl	H. Radziejowski	1681	Warsaw	Or, Vt	H. Lubomirski
1646	Warsaw	In, Lg	J. Stankiewicz	1683	Warsaw	Or, Lg	R. Leszczyński
1647	Warsaw	Ex, Lg	S. Sarbiewski	1685	Warsaw	Or, Lg	A. Giełgud
1648	Warsaw	Cn, Lg	B. Leszczyński	1688	Grodno	Or, Vt	A. Giełgud
1648	Warsaw	El, Lg	F. Obuchowicz	1688	Warsaw	Ex,Vt	S. Szczuka
1649	Cracow	Cr, Lg	F. Dubrawski	1690	Warsaw	Or, Lg	T. Działyński
1649/50	Warsaw	Or, Lg	B. Leszczyński	1693	Grodno	Or, Vt	M. Kryszpin de
1650	Warsaw	Ex, Lg	W.K. Gosiewski				Kirszenstein
1652	Warsaw	Or, Vt	A.M. Fredro	1693	Grodno	Ex, Ds	M. Kryszpin de
1652	Warsaw	Ex, Lg	A. Sielski				Kirszenstein
1653	Brześć L.	Ex, Lg	K. Pac	1695	Warsaw	Or, Vt	M. Kryszpin de
1654	Warsaw	Or, Vt	F. Dubrawski				Kirszenstein
1654	Warsaw	Ex, Lg	K. Grzymułtowski	1696	Warsaw	Cn, Lg	S. Humiecki
1655	Warsaw	Ex, Lg	J. Umiastowski	1697	Warsaw	El, Lg	K.L. Bieliński
1658	Warsaw	Ex, Lg	W. Lubowiedzki	1697	Cracow	Cr, Lg	K.S. Zawisza
1659	Warsaw	Or, Lg	J.T. Gniński	1698	Warsaw	Pc, Ic	K.S. Zawisza
1661	Warsaw	Or, Lg	M.K. Radziwiłł	1699	Warsaw	Pc, Lg	S. Szczuka
1662	Warsaw	Ex, Lg	J. Wielopolski	1701	Warsaw	Or, Ic	--(a)
1664/5	Warsaw	Or, Vt	J.T. Gniński	1701/2	Warsaw	Or, Ct	J. Szembek
1665	Warsaw	Ex, Bt	J. Chrapowicki	1703	Lublin	Ex, Lg	M. Wiśniowiecki
1666	Warsaw	Or, Vt	J.O. Pieniążek	1710	Warsaw	Gc, Lg	S. Denhoff
1666	Warsaw	Or, Vt	M. Oborski	1712	Warsaw	Ex, Lg	S. Denhoff
1667	Warsaw	Or, Lg	A. Kotowicz	1712/3	Warsaw	Ex, Vt	S. Denhoff
1668	Warsaw	Ex, Vt	K. Czartoryski	1717	Warsaw	Ex, Lg	S. Ledóchowski
1668	Warsaw	Ex, Lg	S. Sarnowski	1718	Grodno	Or, Lg	K. Zawisza
1668	Warsaw	Cn, Lg	J. Chrapowicki	1719/20	Warsaw	Or, Vt	K. Zawisza
1669	Warsaw	El, Lg	F. Potocki	1720	Warsaw	Or, Vt.	K. Zawisza
1669	Cracow	Cr, Vt	A. Krzycki	1722	Warsaw	Or, Vt	F. Ossoliński

429

1724	Warsaw	Or, Lg	S. Potocki
1726	Grodno	Or, Nl	S. Potocki
1728	Warsaw	Or, Ic	-- (a)
1729	Grodno	Ex, Vt	--
1730	Grodno	Ex, Vt	--
1732	Warsaw	Ex, Vt	--
1733	Warsaw	Ex, Ic	J. Ożarowski
1733	Warsaw	Cn, Lg	M. Massalski
1733	Warsaw	El, Lg	F. Radzewski
1734	Cracow	Cr, Lg	A. Poniński
1735	Warsaw	Pc, Vt	A. Poniński
1736	Warsaw	Ex, Lg	W. Rzewuski
1738	Warsaw	Or, Nl	K. Rudzieński
1740	Warsaw	Or, Nl	K. Karwowski
1744	Grodno	Or, Nl	T. Ogiński
1746	Warsaw	Or, Nl	A. Lubomirski
1748	Warsaw	Or, Nl	W. Siemieński
1750	Warsaw	Ex, Vt	W. Siemieński
1752	Grodno	Or, Vt	J. Massalski
1754	Warsaw	Or, Vt	J. Massalski
1756	Warsaw	Or, Ds	-- (b)
1758	Warsaw	Or, Vt	A. Małachowski
1760	Warsaw	Or, Vt	A. Małachowski
1761	Warsaw	Ex, Vt	A. Małachowski
1762	Warsaw	Or, Vt	A. Małachowski
1764	Warsaw	Cn, Lg	A. Czartoryski
1764	Warsaw	El, Lg	J. Sosnowski
1764	Warsaw	Cr, Lg	J. Małachowski
1766	Warsaw	Or, Lg	C. Czaplic
1767/8	Warsaw	Ex, Lg	K. Radziwiłł
1768	Warsaw	Or, Ic	K. Radziwiłł
1773/5	Warsaw	Dl, Lg	A. Poniński
			M. Radziwiłł
1776	Warsaw	Or, Lg	A. Mokronowski
			A. Ogiński
1778	Warsaw	Or, Lg	L. Tyszkiewicz
1780	Warsaw	Or, Lg	A. Małachowski
1782	Warsaw	Or, Lg	K. Krasiński

1784	Grodno	Or, Lg	K. Chomiński
1786	Warsaw	Or, Lg	S. Gadomski
1788	Warsaw	Or, Lg	S. Małachowski
1790	Warsaw	Ct, Lg	K.N. Sapieha
1793	Grodno	Ex, Lg	S. Bieliński
1809	Warsaw	Or, Lg	T. Ostrowski
1811	Warsaw	Or, Lg	S. Sołtyk
			A. Czartoryski
1818	Warsaw	Or, Lg	W. Krasiński
1820	Warsaw	Or, Lg	R. Rembieliński
1825	Warsaw	Or, Lg	S. Piwnicki
1830	Warsaw	Ct, Lg	J. Lubowidzki
			W. Ostrowski
1827	Poznań	Or, Lg	P.A. Sułkowski
1830	Poznań	Or, Lg	P.A. Sułkowski
1834	Poznań	Or, Lg	P.A. Sułkowski
1837	Poznań	Or, Lg	S. Poniński
1841	Poznań	Or, Lg	S. Poniński
1843	Poznań	Or, Lg	E. Potworowski
1845	Poznań	Or, Lg	J. Grabowski
1861	Lwów	Or, Lg	L. Sapieha
1867	Lwów	Or, Lg	L. Sapieha
1870	Lwów	Or, Lg	L. Sapieha
			W. Dzieduszycki
1875	Lwów	Or, Lg	A. Potocki
1877	Lwów	Or, Lg	L. Wodzicki
			M. Zyblikiewicz
1883	Lwów	Or, Lg	J. Tarnowski
1889	Lwów	Or, Lg	E. Sanguszko
1895	Lwów	Or, Lg	S. Badeni
			A. Potocki
1901	Lwów	Or, Lg	S. Badeni
1908	Lwów	Or, Lg	S. Badeni
1913	Lwów	Or, Lg	A. Gołuchowski
			S. Niezabitowski
1918	Warsaw	Cs, Lg	F. Pułaski
1919	Warsaw	Ct, Lg	W. Trąmpczyński
1922	Warsaw	Or, Lg	M. Rataj

APPENDIX

1928	Warsaw	Or, Lg	I. Daszyński	1976	Warsaw	Or, Lg	S. Gucwa
1930	Warsaw	Or, Lg	K. Świtalski*	1980	Warsaw	Or, Lg	S. Gucwa
1935	Warsaw	Ct, Lg	S. Car	1985	Warsaw	Or, Lg	R. Malinowski
1938	Warsaw	Or, Lg	W. Sławek	1989	Warsaw	Or, Lg	M Kozakiewicz
			W. Makowski	1991	Warsaw	Or, Lg	W. Chrzanowski
1947	Warsaw	Ct, Lg	W. Kowalski	1993	Warsaw	Or, Lg	J. Oleksy
1952	Warsaw	Ct, Lg	J. Dembowski	1995	Warsaw	Or, Lg	J. Zych
1957	Warsaw	Or, Lg	C. Wycech	1997	Warsaw	Or, Lg	M. Płażyński
1961	Warsaw	Or, Lg	C. Wycech				
1965	Warsaw	Or, Lg	C. Wycech				
1969	Warsaw	Or, Lg	D. Gałaj				
1972	Warsaw	Or, Lg	S. Gucwa				

(a) disbanded for lack of quorum.

(b) disbanded bacause the King could not attend.

In the Senate, restored under the Third Republic, the first four speakers were:

Andrzej Stelmachowski	1989-1993
August Chełkowski	1993-1995
Adam Struzik	1995-1997
Alicja Grześkowiak	1997-

APPENDIX D
TEXT OF NAZI-SOVIET AGREEMENTS

Secret Additional Protocol to the Treaty of Non-Agression between Germany and the USSR concerning delimitation of German and Soviet spheres of interest in Eastern Europe.

Moscow, August 23, 1939
D.Germ.F.P., VII, No.229

On the occasion of the signature of the NonAggression Treaty between the German Reich and the Union of Soviet Socialist Republics, the undersigned plenipotentiaries of the two Parties discussed in strictly confidential conversations the question of the delimitation of their respective spheres of interest in Eastern Europe. These conversations led to the following result:

1. In the event of a territorial and political transformation in the territories belonging to the Baltic States (Finland, Estonia, Latvia, Lithuania), the northern frontier of Lithuania shall represent the frontier of the spheres of interest both of Germany and the USSR. In this connection the) interest of Lithuania in the Vilna territory is recognized by both Parties.

2. In the event of a territorial and political transformation of the territories belonging to the Polish State, the spheres of interest of both Germany and the USSR shall be bounded approximately by the line of the rivers Narew, Vistula, and San.

The question whether the interests of both Parties make the maintenance of an independent Polish State appear desirable and how the frontiers of this State should be drawn can be definitely determined only in the course of further political developments. In any case both Governments will resolve this question by means of a friendly understanding.

3. With regard to South-Eastern Europe, the Soviet side emphasizes its interest in Bess-arabia. The German side declares complete political desinteressement in these territories.

4. This Protocol will be treated by both parties as strictly secret.

Moscow, August 23 1939
For the Government of the German Reich v. Ribbentrop
With full power of the Government of the USSR V. Molotov

APPENDIX

Secret Additional Protocol to the German-Soviet Boundary and Friendship Treaty of September 28, 1939, containing an alteration to the Secret Additional Protocol of August 23, 1939, relating to Poland and Lithuania.

Moscow, September 28, 1939
D.Germ.F.P., VIII, No.159

The undersigned plenipotentiaries declare the agreement of the Government of the German Reich and the Government of the USSR upon the following:

1. The Secret Additional Protocol signed on August 23, 1939 shall be amended in Item 1 to the effect that the territory of the Lithuanian state falls in the sphere of influence of the USSR, while, on the other hand, the province of Lublin and parts of the province of Warsaw fall to the sphere of influence of Germany (cf. the map attached to the Boundary and Friendship Treaty signed today). As soon as the Government of the USSR shall take special measures on Lithuanian territory to protect its interests, the present German-Lithuanian border, for the purpose of a natural and simple boundary delineation, shall be rectified in such a way that the Lithuanian territory situated to the southwest of the line marked on the attached map falls to Germany.

2.Further it is declared that the economic agreements now in force between Germany and Lithuania shall not be affected by the measures of the Soviet Union referred to above.

For the Government of the German Reich v. Ribbentrop
By authority of the Government of the USSR V. Molotov

APPENDIX E—EVOLUTION OF ROLES OF SEYM AND SENATE

Constitutional Status/Date	Executive Branch Head of State/Ministers	Legislative Branch Senate/Seym
Hereditary Kingdom/1493	Hereditary King, appoints ministers for life	81 appointed Senators 54 elected Deputies
1st "Gentry" Republic/1572	Elected King, appoints ministers for life	149 appointed Senators 168 elected Deputies
1st (late) Republic/1773	Elected king & Permanent Council of 36 legislators	157 appointed Senators 181 elected Deputies
Hereditary Kingdom Constitution: 1791	Hereditary King, chooses ministers for 2 yrs.	130 appointed Senators 225 elected Deputies
1st "Restored" Republic/1793	Elected King & Permanent Council of 24 legislators	64 appointed Senators 108 elected Deputies
Duchy of Warsaw Constitution: 1807	Hereditary Duke, appoints ministers	18 appointed Senators 100 elected Deputies
Congress Kingdom Constitution: 1815	Hereditary King, chooses Viceroy, ministers	44 appointed Senators 128 elected Deputies
Grand Duchy of Poznań/1827	Hereditary king, chooses Viceroy, ministers	4 hereditary Deputies 46 elected Deputies
Kingdom of Galicia & Lodomeria/1861	Hereditary King-Emperor appoints ministers	10 Virilists 150 elected Deputies
2nd Republic "small" Constitution: 1919	Sejm elects Head of State, who appoints & dismisses ministers	432 elected Deputies
2nd Republic "March" Constitution: 1921	Sejm & Senate elect & dismiss ministers	111 elected Senators 444 elected Deputies
2nd Republic "April" Constitution: 1935	Sejm & Senate elect President who appoints & dismisses ministers	64 elected Senators 32 appointed Senators 208 elected Deputies
"People's Republic" "Small" Constitution: 1947	Sejm elects president who appoints Prime Minister & ministers	444 elected Deputies
"People's Republic" "Stalinist" Constitution: 1952	Sejm selects 15-men State Council, appoints & dismisses ministers	460 elected Deputies
3rd Republic, Small Constitution: 1992	Public elects President Sejm selects ministers	100 elected Senators 460 elected Deputies
3rd Republic Constitution: 1997	Public elects president President appoints ministers	100 elected Senators 460 elected Deputies

Judiciary Branch Judge Selection	Bill of Rights Inviolability of:	Voting Rights for, Electoral System
appointed for gentry & towns	person & property for gentry only	Seym: elected by gentry males by majority rule
elected by gentry elected by burghers	person & property for gentry only	Seym: elected by gentry males by majority rule
elected by gentry elected by burghers	person & property gentry & burghers	Seym: elected by gentry & burgher proprietors
elected by gentry elected by burghers	person & property gentry & burghers	Seym: elected by gentry elect by majority rule
elected by gentry elected by burghers	person & property restricted press	Seym: gentry males elect by majority rule
appointed for life by the Duke	person & property restricted press	Seym: gentry males burghers, officers vote
appointed for life by Emperor-King	person & property restricted press	Seym: gentry, land tenants, teachers vote
appointed & removed by the king	person & property restricted press	Seym: proprietors elect by majority rule
appointed & removed by Emperor-King	person & property free press, speech	Sejm: landowners, by weighted curia rule
appointed & removed by Justice Minister	person & property free press, speech	Sejm: popular, elected by proportional rule
appointed by the President, removed by the courts	person & property free press free speech	Sejm & Senate: popular, elected by proportional rule
appointed by the President, removed by the courts	person & property free speech, press restricted	Sejm: popular, elected by majority rule Senate: elitist voters
appointed & removed by Justice Minister	person & property press restricted speech restricted	Sejm: popular, elected by proportional rule restricted candidacy
appointed & removed by Council of State	person & property press restricted speech restricted	Sejm: popular, elected by proportional rule restricted candidacy
appointed & removed by Sejm: 2 tribunals	person & property free press & speech	Sejm: proportional Senate: majority rule
appointed by the President	person and property free press & speech	Seym: proportional Senate: majority rule

Bibliography

Constitutions

Original statements of Cardinal Laws are contained in Volumina Legum for years 1422, 1433, 1505, 1573, 1607, 1609 and 1669. They have been collected and restated under the heading of "Prawa Kardynalne" (leges cardinales) by the Seyms of 1767-8, 1772-5, 1791, and 1793. These restatements are reprinted in:

Kaczmarczyk, Zdzisław, "Prawa Kardynalne (1768-1791)," Księgarnia Akademicka, Poznań, 1947. Text of Cardinal Laws of 1768, 1775, 1791 is given.

"New Constitution of the Government of Poland, as established by the Rebolution, May 3, 1791," The Annual Register, Dodsley Publishers, London, 1791.

"Ustawa Rządowa z Dnia 3–go Maja 1791 Roku" Fiszer I Majewski, Poznań, 1926. Constitution of 1791 and the Law on the Cities.

Kaczmarczyk, Zdzisław, "Volumina Legum, Tom X" Poznańskie Tow. Przyjaciół Nauk, Poznań, 1952. Last restatement of Cardinal Laws, repealing the Constitution of 1791.

"Ustawa Konstytucyina, Charte Constitutionnelle du Royaume de Pologne," W Drukarni Rządowez, Warszawa, 1815. Text of the Constitution of 1815 of Congress Kingdom, text in Polish and French.

Handelsman, Marceli, "Trzy Konstytucje: 1791, 1807, 1815" E. Wende Publishers, Warszawa–Lwów, 1915. The text and history of three Constitutions of Poland is given.

Tyrowicz, Marian, "Galicja od Pierwszego Rozbioru do Wiosny Ludów, 1772–1849," Ossolineum, Kraków, 1956. Constitution of the Seym of the Estates of Galacia is given.

Kieniewicz, Stefan, "Galicja w Dobie Autonomicznej (1850–1914), Ossolinuem, Wrocław, 1952. Text of the Constitution of Galicia in the era of autonomy is quoted in the text.

Czarnomski, Francis Bauer, "The Polish Handbook, 1925," Eyre and Spottiswoode, London, 1925. Text of the constitution of 1921 is included in the handbook.

"Constitution of the Republic of Poland, April 23, 1935" Polish Commission for International Law Cooperation, Warsaw, 1935. Text of the Second Constitution of the Second Republic is given.

BIBLIOGRAPHY

"Konstytucje i Podstawowe Akty Ustawodawcze Rzeczpospolitej Polskiej, 1918–1939," Gwiżdż, Andrzej, edit., Wydawnictwo Prawnicze, Warszawa, 1967. Contains Constitutions and more important laws passed in the period 1918-1939.

"Constitution of Polish People's Republic," Polonia Publishing House, Warsaw, 1964. Gives the text of the Stalinist Constitution of 1952.

"Konstytucja i Podstawawe Akty Ustawodawcze Polskiej Rzeczpospolitej Ludowej," Wydawnictwo Prawnicze, Warszawa, 1971. Contains the Constitution and the more important laws of the Polish People's Republic.

Sokolewicz, Wojciech, "Konstytucja PRL po Zmianach z 1976 r," Państwowe Wydawnictwo naukowe, Warszawa, 1978. Text of the Constitution of the Polish People's Republic as amended in 1976 and a discussion of its desireability.

Diaries of Seym Debates

Dzienniki Sejmów Walnych Koronnych za Panowania Zygmunta Augusta, Króla Polskiego, W.X. Liteskiego, 1555 i 1558 w Piotrkówie Złożonych. Wyd. Braci Lubomirskich, Kraków, 1869.

Diariusz Sejmu Walnego Warszawskiego z Roku 1556-1557. Stanisław Bondniak, edit., Biblioteka Kórnicka, 1939.

Dyaryusze Sejmów Koronnych 1548, 1553 i 1570 r. J. Szujski, edit., Akademia Umiejętności, Scriptores Rerum Polonicarum, t.1 Kraków, 1872.

Dzienniki Sejmów Walnych Koronnych za Panowania Zygmunta Augusta, 1555 i 1558 w Piotrkowie Złożonych. T. Lubomirski, edit., Kraków, 1869.

Dyaryusz Sejmu Piotrkowskiego, r.p. 1565, poprzedzony Kroniką 1559-1562, Chomentowski, W., edit., Biblioteka Ordynacji Krasińskich, Warszawa, 1868.

Diariusz Lubelskiego Sejmu Unii. Rok 1569, Działyński, A.T., Edit., Biblioteka Kórnicka, Źródłopisma do Dziejów Unii, Part 3, 1856.

Dyjaryjusze Sejmowe R. 1587. Sejmy Konwokacyjny i Elekcyjny. Sokozłowski A., edit., Akademia Umiejętności, Kraków, Scriptores Rerum Polonicarum, t. 11, 1872 etc.

Dyaryusze Sejmowe r. 1585. Aleksander Czuczyński, edit., Akademia Umiejętności, Kraków, 1911.

Dyaryuszse i Akta Sejmowe r. 1591-1592. Eugeniusz Barwiński, edit., Akademia Umiejętności, Kraków, 1911.

Dyaryusze Sejmowe r. 1597, Eugeniusz Barwiński, edit., Akademia Umiejętności, Kraków. 1907.

Diariusz Seymu Warszawskiego w Styczniu roku 1672. F. Kluczycki, edit,. Akademia Umiejętności, Kraków, 1880.

Diariusz Sejmu Warszawskiego w Roku 1672 Drugiego. F. Kluczycki, edit., Akademia Umiejętności, Kraków, 1880.

Diariusz Seymu Warszawskiego w Roku 1673. F. Kluczycki, edit., Akademia Umiejętności, Kraków, 1881.

Dwa Diariusze Seymów Warszawskich w r. 1674 Odprawionych. F. Kluczycki, edit., Akademia Umiejętności, Kraków, 1881.

Diariusz Sejmu Walnego Warszawskiego 1701-1702. Przemysław Smolarek, edit., Warszawa 1962.

Dyaryusze Sejmów z r. 1746, 1748, 1750, 1754, 1758. Władysław Konopczyński, edit., Tow. Nauk. Warszawskie, Warszawa, 1911-37, 3 volumes.

Dyaryusze Sejmowe, 1572-1763. A. Pawiński, edit., Geberthner i Wolff, Kraków, 1900, 6 volumes.

Zebranie Dyaryuszów Trzech Walnych Seymów Convocationis, Electionis, y Coronationis w Roku 1764 Odprawionych. Collegium Soc. Jesu, 1765.

Dyaryusz Seymu Królestwa Polskiego 1818. N. Glucksberg, Warszawa, 1818.

Dziennik Posiedzeń Izby Poselskiej w Czasie Seymu Królestwa Polskiego w Roku 1820 Odbytego. Druk Xięży Piirów, 1820.

Dyaryusz Senatu Seymu Królestwa Polskiego, 1825. A. Gałęzowski, Warszawa, 1828.

Dyaryusz Sejmu z r. 1830-1831. M. Rostworowski, edit., Akademia Umiejętności, Kraków, 1907-12, 6 volumes.

Sejm Wileński 1992. Przebieg posiedzeń według sprawozdań stenograficznych w opracowaniu kancelarji sejmowej. Księgarnia J. Zawadzkiego, Wilno 1922. Stenographic record of the Sejm of Wilno of 1922 and its decision to merge with the Seym of Warsaw.

Diarjusz Senatu z roku 1830-1831. Pomarański, Stefan, edit., Akademia Umiejętności, Komisja Historyczna, Series 2, vol. 2 Kraków, 1930.

Seym Wielkiego Księstwa Poznańskiego, Dziennik Posiedzeń. Poznań, 1827-1919, 49 volumes. Proceedings of the Seym of the Grand Duchy of Poznań. After 1875 in German only.

Dziennik Polskiego Sejmu Dzielnicowego. Poznań, 1918. Proceedings of the Seym of Poznań held in 1918.

Repertorium Czynności Galicyjskiego Sejmu Krajowego od Roku 1861 po Rok 1883. W. Koziebrodzki, edit., Wydział Krajowy, Lwów, 1885. Activities of the Seym of Galicia, later extended to 1904.

Sejm Ustawodawczy, 1919-22. Sprawozdania Stenograficzne z Posiedzeń. Warszawa, 1919-1922. Stenographic reports from the Seym of the Second Republic.

Sejm Ustawodawczy, Sprawozdania Stenograficzne z Posiedzeń. Warszawa, 1947-1977. Stenographic reports from sessions of Seym of the Polish People's Republic.

BIBLIOGRAPHY

Directories of Deputies and Senators

Kaniewska, Irena. *Małopolska Reprezentacja Sejmowa za Czasów Zygmunta Augusta.* Zeszyty Naukowe Uniw. Jagiellońskiego, PWN, Kraków 1974 Seym representation of Lesser Poland in mid-sixteenth century is described and lists of Deputies to the Seyms between 1548 and 1572 are given.

Kolankowski, L., *Posłowie Sejmów Zygmunta Augusta*, Reformacja w Polsce, r.V, 121-138 (1928). Lists Deputies in the Seyms of the Reformation Era.

Lelewel, Joachim, *Polska i Rzeczy Jej.* T.IV, [IX], 155-218, 1854-68. Lists of senator castellans and palatines are given.

Woff, J., *Senatorowie i Dygnitarze Wielkiego Księstwa Litewskiego, (1386-1795).* Kraków, 1885. A directory of Senators and other dignitaries of the Grand Duchy of Lithuania during the 400 years of personal and later political union with Poland.

Czaplewski, P., *Senatorowi Świeccy, Podkomorzowie i Starostowie Prus Królewskich (1454-1772), Toruń 1921.* A directory of Senators and other dignitaries of Royal Prussia during its 300 years of union with Poland.

Giza, Stanisław, *Władze Naczelne Stronnictw Ludowych (1861-1965).* Roczniki Dziejów Ruchu Ludowego, 7, 387-448 (1965). Lists of Deputies of Peasant Parties in the Seyms during the last 100 years are given no pp. 425-442.

Mościcki, H., Dzwonkowski, W., *Parlament Rzeczpospolitej Polskiej.* L. Złotnicki, Publ., Warszawa, 1928. Summary of parliamentary history of Poland and an illustrated directory of Deputies.

Album Skorowidz Senatu i Sejmu Rzeczpospolitej Polskiej Oraz Sejmu Śląskiego, Kadencja 1935-40. Drukarnia Ludowa, Kraków, 1936. Directory of Senators and Deputies in the national and the Silesian Seym of the Second Republic.

Rocznik Polityczny i Gospodarczy, 1966. Państwowe Wydawnictwo Ekonomiczne, Warszawa, 1966. List of Deputies of the Seym, included in a political and economic annual.

Informacja o Działalności Sejmu Polskiej Rzeczpospolitej Ludowej, IV Kadencja, 1965-1969. Warszawa, 1969. Summary of activities and directory of Deputies of the Seym of the Polish People's Republic.

Summaries and Journals of Seym Legislation

Royal decrees and privileges issued during the hereditary monarchy, and laws made by Seyms of the First Republic appear in:

Acta Tomiciana in 8 volumes, Poznań 1858-1860

Volumina Legum. a. Załuski, S Konarski, edit., 6 volumes published 1732-39. Volumes 7 and 8 were published in 1786 by Piarist Friars. Volume 9 was published in 1889 by Cracow Academy of Learning. Last volume 10, edited by Z. Kaczmarczyk was published as late as 1952 in Poznań by the Society of Friends of Learning. The contents of the volumes are divided as follows:

Volume	Laws (constitutions) of	Years Passed
1	*Statutes of Wiślica and early Seyms	1347-1548
2	Seyms of the period:	1559-1609
3	Seyms of the period:	1611-1640
4	Seyms of the period:	1641-1668
5	Seyms of the period:	1669-1697
6	Laws of the Duchy of Kurland and Prussia	1697-1736
7	Convocation Confederation of 1764	1764-1768
8	Seyms of the period:	1773-1780
9	Seyms of the period:	1782-1792
10	Last Seym of the First Republic	1793

*Text of laws is given in Latin in Volume I. Polish is used in the remaining volumes.

Laws as made by the Seyms of the Partition Period appear in :

Dziennik Praw Księstwa Warszawskiego (Law Gazette of the Duchy of Warsaw). Warszawa, 1808-1812, 4 volumes.

Ustawodawstwo Księstwa Warszawskiego, Akty Normatywne Władzy Najwyższej. Barte. W.M., Kosim, J., Rostocki, W., edit., Warszawa 1964-69, 14 volumes. Legislation of the Duchy of Warsaw systematized.

Dziennik Praw Królewstwa Polskiego (Law Gazette of the Kingdom of Poland). Warszawa, 1815-1849, vol. 1-49.

Dziennik Praw i Rozporządzeń Krajowych Królestwa Galicji (Law Gazette of the Kingdom of Galicia). Lwów, 1866-1918.

Dziennik Ustaw Rzeczpospolitej Polskiej (Law Gazette of the Polish Republic). Warszawa, 1918-1939. Laws made by the Seym of the Second Republic.

Dziennik Ustaw Rzeczpospolitej Polskiej (Law Gazette of the Polish Republic). Warszawa, 1947-1952. Laws made by the Seym of the Polish People's Republic in the period 1947-1952.

Dziennik Ustaw Polskiej Rzeczpospolitej Ludowej (Law Gazette of the Polish People's Republic). Warszawa, 1952- . Laws made by the Seym from 1952 onwards.

Selection of Most Important Acts Published in the Journal of Laws of the Republic of Poland. Warsaw, 1949- . Legislation of the Polish People's Republic in English translation.

BIBLIOGRAPHY

Seyms of the Hereditary Monarchy

Cackowski, Stefan, *Mikołaj Kopernik jako Ekonomista*. Towarzystwo Naukowe w Toruniu, Toruń, 1970. The economic and monetary interests of Copernicus are described.

Uruszczak, Wacław, *Sejm Walny Koronny w Latach 1506-1540. Państwowe Wydawnictwo Naukowe*. Warszawa, 1780. Seym of late hereditary monarchy is discussed in detail, in the era of rise of movement for the execution of laws.

Fox, Paul. *The Reformation in Poland*. John Hopkins Press, Baltimore, 1924. Religious and parliamentary influences of Protestantism in Poland are described.

Grzybowski, Konstanty. *Teoria Reprezentacji w Polsce Epoki Odrodzenia*. Państwowe Wydawnicwo Naukowe, Warszawa, 1959. Theory of representation in Renaissance Poland is examined.

Kaniewska, Irena. *Stan Badań nad Parlamentaryzmem Polskim w Latach 1506-1572*. Zeszyty Naukowe UJ, CCXI, Prace Historyczne, 2.35, 49-58 (1971), Kraków. Review of studies of early Seyms.

Karbownik, Henryk. *Udział Przedstawicieli Kapituł w Sejmach i Sejmikach Dawnej Reczpospolitej w XV-XVIII w.* Czasopismo Prawno-Historyczne, 22, 169-178 (1971). Role of clergy in Seyms and Seymiks.

Kutrzeba, St., Wł. Semkowicz, edit. *Akta Unii Polski z Litwą 1385-1791*. Kraków, 1932. Acts of personal and later political union between Poland and Lithuania are given.

Labuda, G., Miśkiewicz, B., edit. *Wybór zródeł do Historii Polski Średniowiecznej do Połowy XV w.* Univ. of Poznań Press, 1970. Texts of selected sources to history of medieval Poland, including some early charters and grants.

Odyniec, Wacław. *Dzieje Prus Królewskich, 1454-1772*. Państwowe Wydawnictwo Naukowe, Warszawa, 1972. History of Royal Prussia, and parliamentary participation of the province is reviewed.

Piekosiński, Fr. *Sejm Walny Warszawski z r. 1572*. Rozprawy Wydz. Hist. Filoz. PAU, Kraków, 35 256-269 (1898). A discussion of the last Seym of the hereditary monarchy.

Prochaska, Antoni. *Geneza i Rozwój Parlamentaryzmu w Polsce za Jagiellonów*. Roczniki Akademii Umiejętności, Kraków, v. 37, 1898. The origins and development of Polish parliamentarism in fourteenth century are described.

Roman, Stanisław. *Zagadnienie Prawomocności Przywileju Czerwińskiego 1422r.* Czasopismo Prawno-Historyczne, Tom 11, Zesz. 1, 1959. Validity of the privilege of Czerwińsk is discussed.

Russocki, Stanisław. *Początki Zgromadzeń Stanowych w Europie Środkowej.* Przegląd Historyczny, 66, 171-188 (1975). Early representative gatherings in Central Europe are discussed.

Sobol, Bogdan. *Sejm i Sejmiki Ziemskie na Mazowszu Książęcym.* Państwowe Wydawnictwo Naukowe, Warszawa, 1968. Composition, legislation and meeting places of the Masovian Seyms and Seymiks are described.

Wagner, W.J., A.P. Coleman, C.S. Haight. *Laurentius Grimaldus Goslicius and His Age.* Polish Review, 3 37-57 (1958). W.G. Goślicki and his influence on English and American political thought are described.

Royal Elections

Porządek na Seymie Walnym Elekcyey, Między Warszawą a Wolą, Przez Opisane Artykuły, do Samego Tylko Aktu Elekcyey Należące, Uchwalony y Postanowiony Roku Pańskiego MDCXXXII, die 27 Września. Warszawa, 1632. Ordinance of the Royal Election of 1632.

Porządek na Seymie Walnym Elekcyey, Między Warszawą a Wolą, Przez Opisane Artykuły do Samego Tylko Aktu Elekcyey Należące, Uchwalony y Postanowiony Roku Pańskiego 1648, dnia 6 Października. Warszawa, 1648. Ordinance of the Royal Election of 1648.

Borucki, Marek. *Jak w Dawnej Polsce Królów Obierano.* Ludowa Spółdzielnia Wydawcza, Warszawa, 1976. Describes all the royal elections in the period 1573-1764.

Dzieduszycki, Jerzy. *Traktat o Elekcji Królów Polskich z r. 1707.* Biblioteka Zapomnianych Poetów i Prozaików Polskich XVI-XVII w, Zesz. 23, Warszawa, 1908. Treatise on the election of kings, written in 1707.

Lengenich, Gotfryd. *Prawo Pospolite Królewstwa Polskiego.* Kwartalnik Naukowy, Kraków, 1836 (reissue of the 1761 original). This description of Law of Poland contains a chapter with detailed summary of all royal elections.

Pietruski, O., *Elektorów Poczet Który Niegdyś Głosowali na Elektów: Jana Kazimierza r. 1648, Jana III r. 1674, Augusta II, r. 1697 i Stanisława Augusta, r. 1764, Królów Polski.* Lwów, 1845. Gives a list of signatories of acts of royal election from 1648 until 1764.

Seyms of the First Republic

The Lithuanian Statute of 1529. Karl von Loewe, transl., Leiden, Brill, 1976. Text of the Lithuanian Code of Law, enforced for some 300 years, is presented in English.

BIBLIOGRAPHY

Respublica sive Status Regnii Poloniae, Lituaniae, Prussiae, Livoniae, etc. Publ. Lugd: Batavorum ex officina Elzeviriana, 1642. Description of the Polish-Lithuanian state and its political institutions is given in Latin.

Borucki, M. *Sejmy i Sejmiki Szlacheckie.* Książka i Wiedza, Warsaw, 1972. Popular description of Seyms and Seymiks of the First Republic.

Byliński, J. *Sejm z Roku 1611.* Wrocławskie Towarzystwo Naukowe, Wrocław, 1970. a study of the Seym held in 1611.

Czapliński, Władysław. *Dwa Sejmy w Roku 1652.* Ossolineum, Wrocław, 1955. Personages and activities in the two Seyms held in 1652 are described.

Czapliński, Władysław. *Polish Seym in the Light of Recent Research.* Acta Poloniae Historica, 22 180-192 (1970). A summary of recent Polish studies of the pre-Partition Seym.

Częścik, Łucja. *Sejm Warszawski w 1649-1650 Roku.* Ossolineum, Wrocław, 1978. A detailed study of the first Seym in John Casimir's administration is presented.

Konopczyński, L. *Le Liberum Veto, Etude sur le Developement du Principe Majoritaire.* Librarie Ancienne Honoré Champion, Paris, 1930. A thorough study of the voting principles in the Seyms of the First Republic.

Konopczyński, W. *Prusy Królewskie w Unii z Polską 1569-1772.* Poznań, 1927. The two hundred years of history of Royal Prussia in Union with Poland are described.

Konopczyński Władysław. *Chronologia Sejmów Polskich 1493-1793.* Archiwum Komisji Historycznej PAU, Ser.2, Vol. IV, Cracow, 1948. Chronological list of all Seyms of the Hereditary Monarchy and the First Republic from 1493 onwards is given.

Kutrzeba, S. *Sejm Walny Dawnej Rzeczpospolitej.* Polska Składnica Pomocy Szkolnych, Warszawa, 1923. A basic study of the Seym of the First Republic.

Kutrzeba Stanisław. *Skład Sejmu Polskiego, 1493-1793.* Przegląd Historyczny, 2, 179-203, 1906. Composition of the Seym of the hereditary monarchy and the First Republic is described.

Leszczyński, J. *Projekty Reformy Państwa Polskiego na Sejmie Koronacyjnym Jana Kazimierza w 1649 r,* pp. 89-96 in *O naprawę Rzeczpospolitej XVII-XVIII w.* J. Gierowski, edit. Warszawa, 1965. Proposals for constitutional reform raised at the coronation Seym of 1649 are discussed in one of the articles celebrating the sixtieth birthday of W. Czapliński, the dean of Polish historians.

Matwijowski, Krystyn. *Pierwsze Sejmy z Czasów Jana III Sobieskiego.* Ossolineum, Wrocław, 1976. Coronation and ordinary Seyms of 1676 and 1677 are discussed in detail, together with the corresponding pre-Seym and debriefing Seymiks.

Ochmann, Stefania. *Sejmy z lat 1615 i 1616.* Wrocławskie Towarzystwo Naukowe, Wrocław, 1970. Two Seyms in the years 1615 and 1616 are studied in detail.

Olszewski, Henryk. *Sejm Rzeczpospolitej Epoki Oligarchii 1652-1763.* University of Poznań Press, 1966. Seyms in the Vasa and Saxon administrations are studied in detail.

Olszewski, Henryk. *Nowe Materiały do Chronologii Sejmów Polskich.* Tom IX, Zeszyt 2, 1957. Further elaboration of Seym chronology, with supporting discussion.

Płaza Stanisław. *Próby Reform Ustrojowych w Czasie Pierwszego Bezkrólewia (1572-1574).* Zeszyty Naukowe Uniwersytetu Jagiellońskiego CCXVI, Prace Prawnicze, z. 42, Kraków, 1969. Describes the efforts at political reform made during the first interregnum.

Radwański, Z. *Uzupełnienie do Chronologii Sejmów Polskich.* Czasopismo Prawno-Historyczne, Poznań, Vol. II, pp. 449-451, 1949. Supplement to the Seym chronology of W. Konopczyński.

Seredyka, J. *Sejm w Toruniu z 1626 Roku.* Ossolineum, Wrocław, 1966. A discussion of the Seym held in Toruń in 1626.

Sobieski, Wacław. *Trybun Ludu Szlacheckiego. Pamiętny Sejm.* Polish Research Center and Orbis Publishers, London, 1963. Political activities of Chancellor J. Zamoyski and the Seym of 1606 are described.

Strzelecki, A. *Sejm w 1605 r.* PAU, Geberthner, Wolff, Kraków, 1921. Political activities at the Seym of 1605 are described.

Triller, Eugenia. *Bibliografia konstytucji sejmowych XVII wieku w Polsce.* Wrocławskie Towarzystwo Naukowe, vol. VII, Wrocław 1963. a report on archival studies of Seym constitutions in the XVIIc.

Seym and the Cossack Question

Bethell, Nicholas. *The Last Secret.* Basic Books Publishers, New York, 1974. Forced repatriation of Cossacks to Russia in 1945 covered in Chapters 4 and 6.

Kot, Stanisław. *Jerzy Niemirycz, Inicjator Ugody Hadziackiej.* Instytut Literacki, Paryż, 1960. Seym agreement of Hadziacz with the Cossacks and its initiator are described.

Kukiel, Marian. *Zarys Historii Wojskowości w Polsce.* Orbis Publishers, London, 1949. History of military establishment and the Cossack troops is also covered.

Mackiewicz, Józef. *Kontra.* Instytut Literacki, Paryż, 1957. Account of events at Lienz, in 1945, when the Cossacks were being handed over to the Soviets.

BIBLIOGRAPHY

Jewish Autonomy in Poland

Oblastnoj Pinkos Waada Glawnych. Jewrejskich Obszczin Litwy. St. Pietierburg, 1909. Proceedings of the Lithuanian Vaad translated into Russian.

Dubnow, S.M. *Nowiejszaja Istoria Jewrejskawo Naroda.* Grani Publishers, Berlin, 1923 (in Russian). Modern history of the Jewish nation, including self-government in Poland.

Dubnow, S.M. *History of the Jews in Russia and Poland from the Earliest Times until the Present Day.* The Jewish Publication Society of America, Philadelphia, 1916, 2 volumes. Chapter IV in Vol. I describes the Jewish representative system.

Halperin, Israel. *Pinkas Vaad Arba Aratzot.* Jerusalem, 1945 (in Hebrew). Materials on the history of the Council of Four Lands.

Lewin, Izak. *Udział Żydów Polskich w Wyborach Sejmowych w Dawnej Polsce. Miesięcznik Żydowski.* r. 1932, t. 1, z. 1. Describes the participation of Jews in the election to the Seyms.

Weinryb, Bernard D. *The Jews of Poland.* Jewish Publication Society of America, Philadelphia, PA, 1973. A social and economic history covering the period 1100-1800.

Era of Decay and Reform

The Annual Register. Edmund Burke, edit. London, England, 1759 to the present. Issues for 1791 and 1795 give lengthy coverage of events in Poland during the sessions of the Reform Seym.

Bain, Nisbet R. *The Last King of Poland.* Methuen and Co., London, 1909. Describes the last administration of the First Republic.

Bardach, Juliusz. *Studia z Ustroju i Prawa Wielkiego Księstwa Litewskiego XIV-XVII w.* Państwowe Wydawnictwo Naukowe, Warszawa, 1970. Constitution and laws of Lithuania, including the early Seyms are examined.

Bateman, Thomas, edit. *DuPont and Allied Families.* The American Historical Company, New York, 1965. Biography of Pierre Samuel du Pont de Nemours opens the work.

Chojecki, Ryszard. *Patriotyczna Opozycja na Sejmie 1773 R.* Kwartalnik Historyczny, 79, 545-561 (1972). The group opposed to the ratification of the treaties of the First Partition is identified and the composition of that Seym is given.

Drozdowski, Marian. *Przyjęcie Traktatów Rozbiorowych przez Delegację i Sejm Polski w 1773 r.* Poznańskie Towarzystwo Przyjaciół Nauk, Roczniki Historyczne, 41, 81-123, 1975. Debate on the acceptance of the treaty of the First Partition by the Seym of 1773 are described.

CONSTITUTIONS, ELECTIONS AND LEGISLATURES OF POLAND

Drozdowski, Marian. *Początki Działalnosci Budżetowej Sejmu w Czasach Stanisława Augusta Poniatowskiego.* Zeszyty Naukowe Uniwersytetu im. Adama Mickiewicza, Historia, 12, 7-29, 1972. Start of the budgetary activity of the Seym is traced in the late 1700s.

Eversley, G.J. *The Partitions of Poland.* H. Fertig, New York, 1973. A modern study of the fall of the First Republic.

Hoensch, Jörg K. *Manipulacje Walutowe Frederyka II w Okresie Wojny Siedmioletniej i Ich Wpływ na Polską Reformę Monetarną w Roku 1765-1766.* Roczniki Historyczne, 41-104 (1973). Monetary swindles of Frederick II and their influence on the Polish monetary reform are described.

Jasienica, Paweł. *Rzeczpospolita Obojga Narodów, Dzieje Agonii.* Państwowy Instytut Wydawczy, Warszawa, 1972. Literary treatment of the agony of the *Republic of Both Nations.*

Jebert, Ambroise. *Magnats Polonais et Physiocrates français.* Les Belles Lettres, Paris, 1941. Program of national education and Dupont de Nemours visit are described.

Kalinka, Walerjan. *Sejm Czteroletni.* Lwów, 1881; 4th edition, 1895, 2 volumes. Volume 2 lists the political literature of the Reform Seym of 1788-1782.

Kaplan, Herbert H. *The First Partition of Poland.* Columbia University Press, New York 1962. Scholarly treatment of the start of collapse of the First Republic.

Kołłątay, Hugo. *O Ustanowieniu i Upadku Konstytucji Polskiej 3 maja, 1791.* Księgarnia Luxemburgska, Paryż 1868. The rise and fall of the Constitution of 1791, as seen by its coauthor.

Łaszewski, Ryszard. *Delegacja Sejmowa Jako Instrument Ratifikacji I i II Rozbioru Polski.* Czasopismo Prawno-Historyczne, Tom XXII, Zesz. 2, 1971. Use of Seym committees in ratificaiton of partition treaties is described.

Łaszewski Ryszard. *Sejm Polski w Latach 1764-1793.* Tow. Naukowe w Toruniu, Studia Iuridica, Tom XII, z.3, Warszawa, Poznań, 1973. Describes the composition of the Seym and the status of Deputies in the last three decades of the First Republic.

Leśnodorski, B. *Kuźnica Kołłątajowska, Wybór Źródeł.* Ossolineum, Wrocław, 1949. Collection of materials relating to Kołłątay's *Constitutional Forge.*

Leśnodorski, B. *Dzieło Sejmu Czteroletniego (1788-1792).* Ossolineum, Wrocław, 1951. Achievements of the 4-year Reform Seym are reviewed.

Leśnodorski, B. *Konstytucja 3-go Maja 1791 Jako Dokument Oświecenia.* Czytelnik, Warszawa, 1946. Constitution of 1791 discussed as a product of the Era of Enlightenment.

Leśnodorski, Bogusław. *Polska w Epoce Oświecenia.* Wiedza Powszechna, Warszawa, 1971. Contains a discussion of the Association of Friends of the Constitution of 1791.

BIBLIOGRAPHY

Liubavski, Matviej. *Litovsko-Ruskii Sejm.* Universtitetskaja Tipogrfia, Mockva, 1900. Development of early Lithuanian assemblies into a Seym is described in Russian.

Lord, Robert H. *The Second Partition of Poland.* Harvard University Press, 1915. Describes how the passage of the Constitution of 1791 doomed the state.

Marshall, J.P., John A. Woods, edit. *The Correspondence of Edmund Burke.* University of Chicago Press, Chicago, 1968. Correspondence between Edmund Burke and King Poniatowski is included in Vol. 7.

Michalski, J., E. Rostworowski, J. Woliński, edit. *Materiały do Dziejów Sejmu Czteroletniego.* Ossolineum, Wrocław, 1955-1964, 5 volumes. Materials to the history of the 4-year Reform Seym are collected.

Michalski, Jerzy. *Historiografia Polska Wobec Problematyki 1-go Rozbioru.* Przegląd Historyczny, <u>63</u>, 425-436 (1972). Treatment of the first Partition in Polish historiography is reviewed.

Palmer, R.R. *The Age of the Democratic Revolution.* Princeton University Press, 1959-64, 2 volumes. The rise and defense of American, French and Polish Constitutions are lucidly described.

Płaza, Stanisław, Anna Sucheni-Grabowska. *Z Badań nad Polskim Parlamentaryzmem XVI wieku.* Czasopismo Prawno-Historyczne, Tom XXVI, Zesz. 1, 1974. Describes the recent studies of the Polish parliamentarism in the sixteenth century.

Rousseau, Jean-Jacques. *The Government of Poland.* The Bobbs-Merrill Company, Inc., Indianapolis and New York 1972. a study of political institutions of Poland around 1770.

Stone, Daniel. *Polish Politics and National Reform, 1775-1788.* East European Quarterly, Boulder, 1976. Critical review of events and personalities of the reform era.

Szczątstka, Zbigniew. *Odpowiedzialność Rządu w Polsce w latach 1775-1792.* Czasopismo Prawno-Historyczne, Tom XXVII, Zesz. 1, 1975. Responsibility of Ministers to the Seym in the last two decades of the First Republic is described.

Trębicki Antoni. *Opisanie Sejmu Ekstraordynaryjnego Podziałowego Roku 1793 w Grodnie. O Rewolucji Roku 1794.* Państwowy Instytut Wydawczy, Warszawa, 1967. Contemporary account of the Seym of 1793 and the following revolution, when the country rejected its enactments.

Zieńkowska, Krystyna. *Sławetni i Urodzeni.* Państwowe Wydawnictwo Naukowe, Warszawa, 1976. Discusses the burghers and their Deputies in the Seym of the Reform Era.

Seymiks of the First Republic

Lauda Sejmików Ziemi Dobrzyńskiej. Kulczycki, F., edit., Komisja Historyczna Akademii Nauk, Kraków, 1887, Vol. X. Resolutions and instructions passed by Seymiks of Dobrzyn, 1658-1793.

Akta Sejmikowe Województw Ukrainnych. Archiv Jugozapadnoj Rosii, Part II, Vol. I-III, Kiev 1861, 1888. 1910. Acts of the Seymiks of Ukrainian palatinates of the First Republic.

Dworzaczek, W., edit. *Akta Sejmikowe Województw Poznańskiego i Kaliskiego.* Vol. 1, 1572-1632, parts 1, 2, Poznań, 1957, 1962. The acts of the Seymiks of palatinates of Poznań and Kalisz.

Górski, Karol. *Inventarz Aktów Sejmikowych Prus Królewskich, 1600-1764.* Tow. Naukowe w Toruniu, Toruń, 1950. Inventory of enactments of Seymiks of Royal Prussia is given.

Gierowski, J. *Sejmik Generalny Księstwa Mazowieckiego na Tle Ustroju Sejmikowego Mazowsza.* Wrocław, 1948. Operation of the Seymik system in the province of Masovia is described.

Jarochowski, K., edit. *Lauda Połączonych Województw Kaliskiego i Poznańskiego za Panowania Augusta II.* Ateneum 1884, Vol III. Acts of the Seymiks of palatinates of Kalisz and Poznań in 1700s.

Kutrzeba, Stanisław, edit. *Akta Sejmikowe Województwa Krakowskiego.* Kraków, 1932, 1953, 1963, Vol. 1, 2, 3. Vol. 2, 3 edited by A. Przyboś. The acts of the Seymik of the platinate of Cracow.

Lityński, Adam. *Sejmiki Dawnej Rzeczpospolitej.* Przegląd Historyczny, Vol. LVII, 1975. Review of recent literature dealing with the Seymiks.

Olszewski, Henryk. *Praktyka Limitowania Sejmików.* Czasopismo Prawno-Historyczne, Vol. XIII, issue 1, 1961. The practice of adjourning the Seymik meetings is discussed.

Pawiński, Adolf. *Sejmiki Ziemskie, Początek Ich i Rozwój aż do Ustalenia się Udziału Posłów Ziemskich w Ustawodawstwie Sejmu Walnego, 1374-1505.* Private printing, Warszawa, 1895. Early history of the Seymiks and the rise of their electoral functions is described.

Pawiński, A. *Lauda i Instrukcje 1572-1674.* Dzieje Ziemi Kujawskiej, Vol. II, Warszawa, 1888. Resolutions and instructions for Deputies from the Seymik of Kujawy.

Chodynicki, H. *Sejmiki ziem ruskich w wieku XV.* Studya nad historyą prawa polskiego, O. Balzer editor, III, 21, Universytet Jagielloński, Kraków, 1906. Seymiks of Ruthenian palatinates in the XV century are described.

BIBLIOGRAPHY

Pawiński, Adolf. *Rządy Sejmikowe w Polsce 1572-1795.* Warszawa, 1888 first edition; PIW, Warszawa, 1978, second edition. Description of the mode of operation of Seymiks in the First Republic. A basic work.

Piotrowski, S. *Uchwały Podatkowe Sejmiku Generalnego Wisznieńskiego 1572-1772.* Studia nad Historią Prawa Polskiego, Vol. XIII, Lwów, 1932. Tax resolutions of the General Seymik of Wisznia.

Prochaska, A., edit. *Lauda Sejmikowe Halickie 1575-1695.* Akta Grodzkie i Ziemskie z Czasów Rzeczpospolitej Polskiej, Vol. XXIV, Lwów, 1931. Acts and proceedings of the General Seymik of Halicz.

Prochaska, A., edit. *Lauda Wisznieńskie 1572-1648.* Akta Grodzkie i Ziemskie z Czasów Rzeczpospolitej Polskiej, Vol. XXI, Lwów, 1909. Acts and proceedings of the General Seymik of Wisznia.

Przyboś, A., edit. *Akta Sejmikowe Województwa Krakowskiego, 1621-1660.* V.I.; Kutrzeba S., Kraków, 1932, V. II, Polska Akademia Umiejętności, Wrocław, 1955. Enactments of Seymiks of palatinate of Cracow issued in 1621-60.

Śrenowski, S. *Organizacja Sejmiku Halickiego.* Studia nad Historią Prawa Polskiego, Vol. XVI, Lwów, 1938. Organization and structure of Seymik of Halicz is described.

Samsonowicz, Henryk. *Historia Polski do Roku 1795.* Wyd. Szkolne i Pedagogiczne, Warszawa, 1976. History of Poland up to the Partitions, with the discussion of the operation of the Seym and the Seymiks.

Włodarczyk, J. *Sejmiki Łęczyckie.* University of Łódź Press, 1973. A monograph on the Seymiks of the palatinate of Łęczyca.

Dygdała, Jerzy. *Kwestja Dopuszczenia Małych Miast Prus Królewskich do Sejmiku Generalnego w Latach 1764-1768.* Zapiski Historyczne, Vol. XLVI, 1881, 2.1, 47-75. Demands of 27 smaller towns of Prussia for restoration of representation, in abeyance since 1662.

Confederations of the First Republic

Confoederacya Generalna Omnium Ordinvm Regni, et Magni Ducat; Lith. na Conwokocyey główney Warszawskiey, vchwalona roku Pań. MDCXXXII, dnia 16 lipca. W Krakowie, W. Drukarni A. Piotrowczyka, 1632. Act of Confederation held at the Convocation Seym of 1632.

Confoederacya Generalna Omnium Ordinvm Regni, et Magni Ducat: Lith. na Conwokacyey główney Warszawskiey, vchwalona roku pańskiego MDCXLVIII, dnia 16 miesiąca lipca. W Krakowie, W druk. wdowy A. Piotrowczyka, 1648. Act of Confederation held at the Convocation Seym of 1648.

Manifestum Statuum Confoederatorum Republicae Poloniarum, Łańcut, Jul. 28, 1704. Manifesto of the Confederation held in defense of Augustus II.

Poparcie Generalney Sandomirskiey Confederacyey przez stany całey Rzeczypospolitey na walnym Zieżdzie Warszawskim zgromadzone, w Warszawie dia 4 Lutego roku 1710. General Council of 1710 supporting the Confederation of Sandomierz.

Dziennik Konfederacyi Tarnogrodzkiej Przeciw Wojskom Saskim Zawiązány w Polsce. (1715-1717). In E. Raczyński, *Obraz Polaków i Polski w XVIII wieku*, vol. 14, Poznań, 1840. Diary of the Confederation of Tarnogród held against the Saxon Army.

Konfederacya Generalna Omnium Ordinum Regni et Magni Ducatus Litt. na Konwokacyi Główney Warszawskiey Uchwalona. Dnia siódmego miesiąca maja roku pańskiego 1764. W Warszawie. W druk. Rzeczpospolitey w collegium XX Scho. Piarum, 1764. Act of Confederation held at the Convocation Seym of 1764.

Akt Konfederacyi Generalney Oboyga Narodów, Warszawa, 1776. Act of Confederation of 1776 held at the Seym of that year.

Łukowski, George T. *The Szlachta and the Confederacy of Radom 1764-1767/68: A Study of the Polish Nobility*. Autemuriale, Vol. 21, Rome (1977). Effect of religious issues on the political life of Poland in the latter half of the 18th century is discussed in connection with the Confederation of Radom.

Tuchim, S. *Konfederacja Dzikowska*. Drukarnia poynańska, 1921. History of Confederation of 1734 held in support of Stanisław Leszczyński's claim to the throne.

Russkoe Isoricheskoe Obshchestvo, Sbornik, Petersburg, 1901, Vol. 128. All texts in Polish and Russian. Acts, Documents and Materials to the Confederation of Warsaw of 1812.

Walczak, R., *Konfederacja Gdańska, Elbląga i Torunia, 1615-1632*. Rocznik Gdański, XV-XVI, Gdańsk 1957-57. Confederation of the three cities in Royal Prussia is described.

Rembowski, Al. *Konfederacja i Rokosz w Dawnem Prawie Polskiem*. Introduction to the study: *Rokosz Zebrzydowskiego*. Biblioteka Ordynacji Krasińskich, Vol. IX-XII, Warszawa, 1893. The legal position of confederations and the Rokosz in the old law of Poland are reviewed in the study of Rokosz of Zebrzydowski.

Grzybowski, Stanisław. *The Warsaw Confederation of 1573 and Other Acts of Religious Tolerance in Europe*. Acta Polonia Historica, 40, 75-96 (1979). This review article puts the act of the Confederation of Warsaw in the context of similar attempts to assure religious peace in other countries.

Seyms of the Partition Period

General Studies

Kościuszko, Tadeusz, Jefferson, Thomas. *Korespondencja (1798-1817)*. Państwowy Instytut Wydawczy, Warszawa, 1976. Two decades of correspondence between Kościuszko and Jefferson; text in Polish, English and French.

Chmielewski, Edward. *The Polish Question in the Russian State Duma*. University of Tennessee Press, Knoxville, 1970. A recent study describes the unsuccessful efforts of the Polish Deputies in the Russian parliament of 1906-1914 to restore legislature in central Poland.

Kukiel, Marian. *Dzieje Polski Porozbiorowe 1795-1921*. B. Świderski Publishers, London, 1963. A study of the period of partitions by the dean of Polish historians in England.

Pobóg-Malinowski, Władysław. *Najnowsza Historia Polityczna Polski*. B. Świderski Publishers, London, 1963, second edition, 2 volumes. Most recent history of Poland, Volume I covers the period 1864-1914 in all zones of partition.

Wandycz, Piotr S. *The Lands of Partitioned Poland 1795-1918*. University of Washington Press, Seattle, 1974. Partition period in the light of modern research.

Duchy of Warsaw

Rembowski, Aleksander. *Z Życia Konstytucyjnego Księstwa Warszawskiego*. Geberthner and Wolff, Kraków, 1900. A study of the constitutional movement in the Duchy of Warsaw.

Dutka, Józef. *Sejm Księstwa Warszawskiego w Świetle Konstytucji i Dekretów Królewsko-Książęcych*. Kwartalink Historyczny, <u>84</u>, 368-383 (1977). Constitutional base and the operating ordinances for the Seym of the Duchy of Warsaw are described.

Congress Kingdom

Kostanecki, Stanisław. *Ostatnie Posiedzenie Sejmu Królestwa Polskiego w 1831 r. w Płocku.* Notatki Płockie, <u>17</u>, 29-33 (1972). The story of the last session of Seym of the Congress Kingdom, before the Seym went into exile.

Leslie, R.F. *Polish Politics and the Revolution of 1830.* University of London, The Althone Press, 1957. Politics and the Seym in Congress Kingdom prior to the Uprisising of 1830 are analyzed.

Przelaskowski, Ryszard. *Sejm Warszawski Roku 1825.* Tow. Naukowe Warszawskie, Warszawa, 1929. A detailed analysis of the 1825 Seym in Warsaw.

Thackeray, F.W. *Antecedents of Revolution: Alexander I and the Polish Kingdom 1815-1825.* East European Monographs, LXVII, 1980. Political interactions of Russia and Poland in the era of the Congress Kingdom are explored.

Zajewski, W. *Koronacja i Detronizacja Mikołaja I w Zamku Królewskim.* Przegląd Humanistyczny, <u>15</u>, 15-28 (1971). Coronation of Nicholas I of Russia and his dethronement by the Seym of 1831 in Warsaw are described.

Zajewski, Władysław. *Walki Wewnętrzne Ugrupowań Politycznych w Powstaniu Listopadowym 1830-1831.* Gdańskie Tow. Naukowe, Gdańsk, 1967. Gives the background of the political controversies and dethronement of Nicholas I by the Seym.

Greater Poland

Bernhard, Ludwig. *Die Polenfrage.* Duncker and Humblot Publishers, Leipzig, 1910. "The Polish Question" in Greater Poland as seen through the German eyes.

Czubiński, Antoni. *Powstanie Wielkopolski 1918-1919.* Wydawnictwo Poznańskie, Poznań, 1978. The uprising in Greater Poland and the Seym of Poznań are discussed.

Karwowski, S. *Historia Wielkiego Księstwa Poznańskiego.* Drukarnia Uniwersytecka, 1917, Poznań, 1917, 1919, 1931, 3 volumes. History of the Grand Duchy of Poznań.

Kwilecki, Andrzej. *Poznań Jako Ośrodek Polskości na Ziemiach Zaboru Pruskiego.* Przegląd Zachodni 5/6, 17-50 (1974). Describes Poznań as the Polish center in Prussian partition.

Wasicki, Jan. *Ziemie Polskie pod Zaborem Pruskim.* Poznańskie Towarzystwo Przyjaciół Nauk, Proc. Vol. XXX, 1, 1963. Percentage of gentry in the population of North-Central Poland, 1800 is discussed in the context of the description of Prussian zone of Partition.

Wojtkowski, Andrzej. *Edward Raczyński i Jego Dzieło.* Biblioteka Raczyńskich, Poznań, 1929. Biography of one of the most prominent Deputies of the Seym of Poznań.

Lesser Poland (Galicia)

Collective. *Poczet Szlachty Galicyjskiej i Bukowińskiej.* Wyd. Wydziału Stanów, Lwów, 1857. Statistics on Galician gentry and Seym of the Estates are given.

Z Sesji Zimowej Sejmu Galicyjskiego r. 1910. Stronnictwo Pracy Narodowej, Kraków, 1910. Contains five speeches of Deputies of the Seym of Galicia on key issues in 1910.

Bartoszewicz, Kazimierz. *Dzieje Galicji, Jej Stan Przed Wojną i Wyodrębnienie.* Geberthner i Wolff, Kraków, 1917. History of Galicia and the achievement of its autonomy are covered.

Bobrzyński, M. Jaworski, W.L., Milewski, J. *Z Dziejów Odrodzenia Politycznego Galicji, 1859-1873.* Geberthner and Wolff, Warszawa, 1905. The rise of political parties in Galicia is described.

Buszko, Józef. *Sejmowa Reforma w Galicji 1905-1914.* Państwowe Wydawnictwo Naukowe, Warszawa, 1956. Discusses the reform of the electoral law of Galicia just before the First World War.

Dulczewski, Zygmunt. *Walka o Szkołę na Wsi Galicyjskiej w Świetle Stenogramów Sejmu Krajowego, 1861-1914.* Ludowa Spółdzielna Wydawcza, Warszawa, 1953. Debates on the educational budget in the Seym of Galicia are described.

Dzikowska, Irena. *Mikołaj Zyblikiewicz, 1823-1887.* Ossolineum, Wrocław, 1964. Biography of one-time Speaker of the Seym of Galicia.

Grodzicki, Stanisław. *W Królestwie Galicji i Lodomerii.* Wydawnictwo Literackie, Kraków, 1976. Describes the social, political and literary life in Galicia.

Grzybowski, Konstanty. *Galicja 1848-1914.* Ossolineum, Wrocław, 1959. Political system of Galicia in 1848-1914 within Austrian Empire is discussed.

Kieniewicz, Stefan. *Galicja w Dobie Autonomicznej, 1850-1914.* Ossolineum, Wrocław, 1952. Political autonomy of Galicia and its development are discussed.

Koronowicz, Stefan. *Galicja w Dobie Autonomizmu, 1860-1914.* Wrocław, 1962. Political and social history of autonomy of Galicia.

Knauer, Oswald. *Österreichs Männer des öffentlichen Lebens von 1848 bis heute.* Manz Publ. Wien, 1960. Political personalities of Galicia are listed among Austrian officials.

Łoziński, Bronisław. *Szkice z Historii Galicji.* Gubrynowicz Publ., Lwów, 1913. Covers the personalities and politics in Galicia.

Łoziński, Bronisław. *Galicyjski Sejm Stanowy (1817-1845)*. Lwów, 1903. The activities of the Galician Seym of the Estates, preceding the era of autonomy, are discussed.

Łoziński, Bronisław. *Agenor hr. Gołuchowski*. Altenberd Publishers, Lwów, 1901. Biography of the three-time Viceroy of Galicia.

Pannenkowa, Irena. *Walka Galicji z Centralizmem Wiedeńskim*. Wydawnictwo Polskie, Lwów, 1918. The tug-of-war between the Galician separatism and the Austrian centralism is described.

Popiel, Jan, edit. *Eustachy Sanguszko*. Kraków, 1907. Collection of documents, and Seym speeches of the one-time Speaker of the Seym of Lwów.

Schnur-Pepłowski, Stanisław. *Obrazy z Przeszłości Galicji i Krakowa*. Gubrynowicz and Schmidt Publ., Lwów, 1896. Galician past is described, including the Seym of the Estates.

Starzyński, Stanisław. *Sejm Galicyjski Roku 1885-1886*. Lwów, 1887. Insider's view of the workings of the Seym of Galicia.

Tyrowicz, Marian. *Galicja od Pierwszego Rozbioru do Wiosny Ludów, 1772-1849, Wybiór Tekstów Źródłowych*. Ossolineum, Kraków, 1956. Edition of basic texts from the history of Galicia.

Zdrada, Jerzy. *Galicyjskie Wybory Sejmowe i Parlamentarne w Latach 1861-1889*. Annals of Libr. of PAN, Cracow, R. 19:1973. Covers elections to the Seym of Galicia in the second half of XIX c.

Seyms of the Second Republic

Dziesięciolecie Polski Odrodzonej, 1918-1928. Ilustrowany Kuryer Codzienny, Warszawa, 1928. A commemorative book with summary of political highlights of the first decade of the Second Republic.

Projekty Konstytucji Rzeczpospolitej Polskiej. Komisja Konstytucyjna Sejmu Ustawodawczego, Warszawa, 1920. Describes the constitutional proposals introduced prior to the passage of the Constitution of 1921.

Ajnenkiel, Andrzej. *Sejmy i Konstytucje w Polsce, 1918-1939*. Państwowy Zakład Wydawnictw Szkolnych, Warszawa, 1968. Seym and Constitutions of the Second Republic described, for school use.

Anonymous. *Sprawa Brzeska*. Publisher and place of issue not given. Reprinted in London, 1941. Transcript of the trial of eleven former Deputies, held in Warsaw in 1931.

B. H. *Ukraińskie Wspomnienia z Berezy*. Instytut Literacki, Paryż, Kultura, 78-85, December 1955. Ukrainian nationalist describes his incarceration in the Bereza camp.

Bartel, K. *Niedomagania Parlamentaryzmu*. Kurier Wileński, 4 paźdź., 1928. A former minister describes the deficiencies of the Seym in 1920s.

BIBLIOGRAPHY

Czubiński, Antoni. *Wybory do Sejmy 16 XI 1930 R.*Zeszyty Naukowe Uniw. Poznańskiego, Historia, z. 4, 165-202 (1959). Elections to the Seym of 1930 are analyzed.

Drozdowski, Marian. *National Minorities in Poland, 1918-1939*. Acta Poloniae Historica, 22, 226-251 (1970). A useful review of problems and statistics of the national minorities in the Second Republic.

Grzybowski, K. *Parlamentaryzm Polski w Dwudziestoleciu (1918-1939)*. VII Powszechny Zjazd Historyków, Polskich: Historia Najnowsza Polski, 229-264, Kraków, 1958. Review of parliamentary life in the Second Republic.

Holzer, Jerzy. *Mozaika Polityczna Drugiej Rzeczpospolitej*. Książka i Wiedza, Warszawa, 1974. Describes the political party system of the Second Republic.

Janiszewski, Janusz. *Wyniki Wyborów Parlamentarnych w Polsce w Roku 1922 w Świetle Ordynacji Oraz Praktyki Wyborczej*. Zeszyty Nauk. Uniw. M. Kopernika w Toruniu, Zeszyt 37, Prawo IX, 1966. Analysis of results of elections to the Seym of 1922.

Jędrzejewicz, Wacław. *Kronika Życia Józefa Piłsudskiego, 1867-1935*. Polska Fundacja Kulturalna, London, 1977. Chronicle of life and quotations from documents of first head of state in the Second Republic.

Komarnicki, Tytus. *Rebirth of the Polish Republic*. Heinemann, London, 1957. Contains a discussion of the activities of the Seym Peace Delegation to the Soviet Union.

Nowak, Kazimierz. *Autonomia Śląska*. Prace Prawnicze, 107-143 (1969) Univ. of Silesia, Katowice. Autonomy of Silesia in the Second Republic and its Seym described.

Podoski, Bohdan. *Prace Nad Konstytucją Kwietniową*. Niepodległość, 12, 184-198 (1979) New York/London. One of its coauthors describes the work on the Constitution of 1935.

Polonsky, Anthony. *Politics in Independent Poland, 1921-1939*. Clarendon Press, Oxford, 1972. A recent and complete study of politics in interwar Poland.

Rechowicz, H. *Sejm Śląski 1922-1939*. Śląski Instytut Naukowy, Katowice, 1965. History and activities of the Seym of Silesia.

Roos, Hans. *A History of Modern Poland*. Alfred A. Knopf, New York, 1966. A German historian follows the rise of the Second Republic.

Rothschild, Joseph. *Piłsudski's Coup d'État*. Columbia University Press, New York, 1966. A study of the constitutional crisis of the Second Republic.

Rothschild, Joseph. *East Central Europe Between Two World Wars*. University of Washignton Press, 1974. Chapters on Poland contain much informative material on parliamentary activities.

Polish People's Republic, Note on Interpretation of Sources

A researcher into the history of Polish parliamentarism in the Polish People's Republic has two main sources of information: the material published abroad, for the most part by Seym Deputies who fled abroad to preserve their lives when the opposition to Communist Party rule was eliminated, and the official publications of the Polish Government.

The first of these generally mean what they say, and though tinged by personal feelings, are factual. The government publications, on the other hand, were produced under strict censorship, and for this reason either omitted all mention of a large list of topics or were given to tactful euphemism. To make matters worse, what was published appeared in coded language. As an example, the manner of death of a number of prominent members of Polish CP was never explicitly stated, particularly if they fell victim to Russian execution. The tipoff regarding the victims' fate in SU was usually the following two phrases, appearing with astounding regularity in the biographies of Polish CP leaders and former Seym Deputies: "fell victim to provocation" and "posthumously rehabilitated." They concealed the message that Stalin's homicidal instincts were easily provoked by any hint of disobedience, and that the CP leadership of the day needed an ancestry in good standing.

Other commonly met coded phrases were: "sought shelter in SU"—an item in the biography of people who were deported to Soviet Union for slave labor in 1940-41, but who survived the experience.

"Poland chose socialism," as in the speech of E. Gierek on the thirtieth anniversary of the communist take-over, refered to the outcome of the elections in 1947 when the Communists "disqualified" some 323 non-communist candidates for the 444 Deputy seats in the Seym.

"Period of strengthening of socialism"—euphemism for the Civil War of 1946-47 in which the combined forces of NKVD, Polish UB and the Internal Security Forces subdued the resistance of the population to the Communist takeover with the loss of life in the vicinity of 100,000.

"Period of errors and distortions"—euphemism for the period of police terror and executions without trial, 1952-56.

"Leading role of the Party"—a euphemism for CP ownership of industry, commerce, all communication media and a good part of agriculture, as well as all important positions in government.

"Excesses of anti-social elements"—description given to workers' strikes for better pay, or against massive hikes in prices of foodstuffs, as in 1956, 1968, 1970, 1976 accompnaied by the burning of regional Party headquarters, as in Szczecin, Gdańsk, Poznań, Radom.

BIBLIOGRAPHY

Seyms of the Polish People's Republic

Episkopat a Zmiany Konstytucji. Instytut Literacki, Paryż, "Kultura" Nr. 5/344, 69-76 (1976). Objections of Polish Episcopate to the 1976 constitutional amendments are spelled out.

Ordynacja Wyborcza do Sejmu PRL i Rad Narodowych. Książka i Wiedza, Warszawa, 1961. Electoral Ordinance used in the Polish People's Republic is described.

Proces Krakowski, Niepokojczycki, Mierzwa i Inni Przed Sądem Rzeczpospolitej. Państwowy Instytut Wydawczy, Warszawa, 1948. Record of a rigged trial held in Cracow against the Peasant Party leaders after that party won the election in the Cracow electoral district.

Posiedzenia Sejmu Polskiej Rzeczpospolitej Ludowej 25 i 27 Marca 1976. Książka i Wiedza, Warszawa, 1976. Seym speeches supporting the amendments of 1976 to the Constitution.

Borsuk, Otton, (pseud. of Jacek Jędruch). *Wielopoglądowość a Człowiek.* Kultura, Instytut Literacki, Paryż, No. 1/219-2/220, 131-136 (1966). Pluralistic society identified as an indispensible condition for democracy.

Burda, Andrzej, edit. *Sejm Polskiej Rzeczyspospolitej Ludowej.* Polish Academy of Sciences, Ossolineum, Wrocław, 1975. A brave effort to explain the workings of the controlled Seym.

Dziewanowski, M.K. *The Communist Party of Poland.* Harvard University Press, 1976, Second Edition. CP of Poland portrayed without touchups, "warts and all."

Frendl, Ludwik. *Kodeks Pracy w Polsce.* Kultura 1/352-2/353, Instytut Literacki, Paryż, 1977. Shortcomings of the 1975 Labor Code are shown in detail.

Gidyński, Józef. *Neostalinizm Bez Terroru.* Kultura, Instytut Literacki, Paryż, No. 11/338, 107-116 (1975). Operation of the Seym and the administrative reorganization of 1975 are discussed in detail.

Gwiżdż, Andrzej, *Zagadnienia Parlamentaryzmu w Polsce Ludowej.* Publication of Univ. of Warsaw, Waszawa, 1972. Seym of the Polish People's Republic seen through the eyes of an admirer.

Horak, Stephan. *Poland and Her National Minorities, 1919-39.* Vantage Press, New York, 1961. Ukrainian, Jewish and German minorities of Poland are discussed in relation to the State.

Kołakowski, Thomas. *Black Elflock of a Red Parliament.* Arlington Printing Co., New York, 1950. Memoirs of a Roman Catholic Priest elected Deputy to the 1947 Seym of the Polish People's Republic.

Korboński, Stefan. *W Imieniu Kremla.* Instytut Literacki, Paryż, 1956. Leader of the anti-German underground describes the Communist take-over of Poland in 1944-1947.

Lane, Arthur Bliss. *I Saw Poland Betrayed*. Bobbs-Merrill Co., Indianapolis (1948). United States Ambassador to Poland describes the elections of 1947.

Mikołajcyk, Stanisław. *The Rape of Poland*. Whittlesey House, New York, 1948. Seym Deputy and leader of Peasant Party describes its destruction.

Patrzałek, Aleksander. *Nabycie i Objęcie Mandatu Posła na Sejm PRL*. Acta Univ. Wratislaviensis, No. 292, 43-57 (1976). Procedure for becoming a Deputy to the Seym of the Polish People's Republic is described.

Sharp, Samuel. *New Constitutions in the Soviet Sphere*. Foundation for Foreign Affairs, Washington, 1950. Discusses the introduction of Stalinist constitutions in Eastern Europe.

Szlabek Henryk, *Struktura Nowo-Powstałych i Powiększonych Gospodarstw z Parcelacji i Osadnictwa na Ziemach Dawnych (1944-1949)*. Roczniki Dziejów Ruchu Ludowego, 14, 258-286 (1972). Statistics of the last land reform showing 2.8 ha as the average size of newly created farms.

Strzelecka, Jolanta. *Działalność Sejmu PRL po 13 grudnia 1981 roku*. Zeszyty Historycznen Instytut Literacki, Paryż., 70, 30-48, (1984). Accelerated mode of operation of the Seym, with breaches of its ordinance are described for the period following the imposition of the martial law. [in 1981].

Stypułkowski, Zbigniew. *Invitation to Moscow*. Thames and Hudson, London (1951). Former Deputy of Seym put on trial in Moscow for non-cooperation describes his experiences.

Wacowska, Ewa. *Ile Polskę Kosztuje PZPR?* Kultura, 10/313, Instytut Literacki, Paryż, 1973. Cost to the national treasury of supporting the Polish CP is reviewed.

Weit, Erwin. *At the Red Summit*. MacMillan Publishing Co., New York, 1973. An interpreter illuminates the politics and the legislatures under Soviet rule.

Wende, Jan K. *The Parliament of Poland*. Publishing House Interpress, Warsaw, 1969. Seym with licensed party system explained to foreigners.

Wojciechowski, Adam. *Dwa Listy do prof. H. Jabłońskiego*. Instytut Literacki, Paryż, *Kultura*. Nr. 5/344, 63-68 (1976). Letters criticizing the electoral ordinance and Front of National Unity addressed to the head of state.

Wójcik, Stanisław. *Na 30-lecie Wyborów w Polsce*. Zeszyty Historyczne, z. 43, Instytut Literacki, Paryż, 1978. A summary of the mayhem perpetrated at the elections of 1947.

Yaremko, Michael. *Galicia-Halychyna, From Separation to Unity*. Shevchenko Scientific Society, Toronto, New York, Paris, 1967. Problems of Galicia from Ukrainian point-of-view.

Selected Legislative Problems

Suffrage

Bardach, J., Leśnodorski, B., Pietrzak, M. *Historia Prawa i Państwa Polskiego.* Państwowe Wydawnictwo Naukowe, Warszawa, 1976. Size of the electorate in Congress Kingdom and Galicia is discussed in a history of Polish law.

Bergasse, Henri. *Histoire de l'Assemblée, des Elections de 1789 aux Elections de 1967.* Payot, Paris, 1967. Statistics on the size of the French electorate are given.

Kowalenko, Władysław. *Geneza Udziało Stołecznego Miasta Wilna w Sejmach Rzeczpospolitej.* Ateneum Wileńskie, r. 1925, Vol. 3, pp. 327-73, Vol. 4., pp. 79-173. The origin of the participation of Deputies from the City of Vilno in the Seyms of the Republic.

Kieniewicz, Stefan. *Historia Polski 1795-1918.* Państwowe Wydawnictwo Naukowe, Warszawa, 1975. Political and socio-economic history of Poland in the Partition period. Suffrage statistics are given by province.

Mitchell, B.R. *European Historical Statistics, 1750-1970.* Columbia University Press, New York, 1975. Suffrage statistics are given by province.

Mitchell, B.R. *European Historical Statistics, 1750-1970.* Columbia University Press, New York, 1975. Contains useful population statistics.

Mitchell, B.R., H.G. Jones. *Second Abstract of British Historical Statistics.* Cambridge University Press, 1971. Statistics of British general elections are included.

Pierce, Neal R. *The People's President.* Simon and Schuster, New York, 1968. Includes the tables of voting age population in the U.S.

Porter, Kirk H. *A History of Suffrage in the United States.* Greenwood Press Publishers, New York, 1969. Property and racial qualifications traced through U.S. history.

Płasnik, Jan. *Udział Miast Polskich w Dawnych Sejmach.* Samaorząd Miejski. Vol. 5 1925, z.8, pp. 705-30. Participation of cities in the Seyms of the First Republic is described.

Williamson, Chilton. *American Suffrage from Property to Democracy, 1760-1860.* Princeton Univ. Press, 1960. History of property qualifications in American elections.

Impeachment and Judiciary Powers of the Seym

Correspondence of French Ambassadors in Poland with Louis XIV for 1680. Acta Historica Res Gestas Poloniae Illustrantia, Akademia Umiejętności,

Kraków, 7, 37-38, 63-63, 1884. This correspondence contains information used in the impeachment proceedings against Jan Andrzej Morsztyn.

Dziennik Sądów Seymowych Zaczęty dnia 24 Sierpnia roku 1789. Tom 1, Warszawa, 1789. Diary of Seym Tribunal; contains impeachment proceedings of Adam Poniński.

Processvs ivdiciarivs in casa illvstri and magnifico Georgio Comiti in Wisnicz et Iaroslaw, Lvbomierski... ex instantia Instigatoris Regni and delatione generosi Hieronymi de Magna Skrzynno Dunin ad Comitia Regni anni 1664 institutae .... O. Elert, S.R.M. Typogr. Varsovia, 1664. Act of impeachment of Jerzy Sebastian Lubomirski by the Seym of 1664.

Sąd Sejmowy 1827-1829 na Przestępców Stanu. Bieczyński, T., edit., J.I. Kraszewski Publisher, Poznań, 1873. Proceedings of Seym Tribunal in the trial of the 1825 consipracy.

Fierich, Franciszek K. *Sąd Trzeciej Instancji i Najwyższy Sąd Sejmowy na Tle Całokształtu Organizacji Sądownictwa, Rzeczpospolitej Krakowskiej.* Akademja Umiejtności, Geberthner and Wolff, Kraków, 1917. Judicial functions of the Seym of the Republic of Cracow are described.

Landau, Z., B. Skrzeszewska, edit. *Sprawa Gabriela Czechowicza przed Trybunałem Stanu.* Państwowe Wydawnictwo naukowe, Warszawa, 1961. Proceedings of the impeachment trial of Gabriel Czechowicz, 1929.

Ostrżyński, Władysław. *Sprawa Zamachu na Stanisława Augusta z 3 Listopada 1771 r. przed Sądem Sejmowym.* Lwów, 1891. Describes the trial of abductor of King Stanisław.

Szcząstka, Zbigniew. *Sąd Sejmowy w Polsce od Końca XVI do Końca XVIII wieku.* Czasopismo Prawno-Historyczne, Tom XX, z. 1, 1968. History and area of competence of Seym Tribunal are described.

Szcząstka, Zbigniew. *Sąd Sejmowy w Okresie Rządów Rady Nieustającej.* Przegląd Historyczny, 62, 421-443 (1971). The impeachment activities of the Seym in the late eighteenth century are described.

Taxation

Drozdowski, Marian. *Budżet Państwowy Rzeczpospolitej Polskiej w Świetle Polskiej Literatury Politycznej XVIIIw.* Przegląd Historyczny, 67, 15-37 (1976). Budget of the First Republic in political literature of eighteenth century.

Ingolt, Stefan, edit. *Rejestr Poborowy Województwa Krakowskiego z r. 1629.* Państwowe Wydawnyctwo Naukowe, Wrocław, 1956. Reprint of tax tables for the palatinate of Cracow for 1629.

Ingolt, Stefan, edit. *Rejestr Poborowy Województwa Krakowskiego z r. 1680.* Państwowe Wydawnictwo Naukowe, Wrocław, 1959. Reprint of tax tables for the palatinate of Cracow for 1680.

Ingolt, Stefan, edit. *Rejestr Poborowy Województwa Lubelskiego z r. 1626.* Państwowe Wydawnictwo Naukowe, Wrocław, 1957. Reprint of tax tables for the palatinate of Lublin for 1626.

Kałkowski, Tadeusz. *Tysiąc Lat Monety Polskiej.* Wydawnictwo Literackie, Kraków, 1963. One thousand years of Polish coinage is described and illustrated. Proof, dimensions and mass of coins are listed.

Małcurzyński W. *Szkice do Dziejów Skarbowości Polskiej.*Ekonomista, 2, 1-118 (1915), 3, 1-90 (1916). Contributions to the history of treasury in Poland.

Nycz, N. *Geneza Reform Skarbowych Sejmu Niemego; Studium z Dziejów Skarbowo-Wojskowych 1697-1717.* Poźnanskie Tow. Przyjaciół Nauk, Poznań, 1938. The origin of the reform of Treasury carried out by the Seym of 1717 is investigated.

Pawiński, A. *Skarbowość w Polsce i jej Dzieje za Stefana Batorego.* Źródła Dziejowe, Vol. VIII, Warszawa, 1881. Discusses treasury and taxation in the administration of Stephen Bathory.

Sucheni-Grabowska, A. *Odbudowa Domeny Królewskiej w Polsce 1504-1548* Ossolineum, Wrocław, 1967. A study of the restitution of Crown lands in the era of the Executive Movement.

Rutkowski, J. *Skarbowość Polska za Aleksandra Jagiellończyka.* Kwartalnik Historyczny, Vol. 23, Kraków, 1909. Treasury and taxation in the hereditary kingdom is described.

Rybarski, R. *Skarb i Pieniądz za Jana Kazimierza, Michała Korybuta i Jana III.* Tow. Naukowe Warszawskie, Warszawa, 1939. Treasury and currency in three administrations 1648-1696 are described.

Rybarski, R. *Skarbowość Polska w Dobie Rozbiorów.* Polska Akademia Umiejętności, Kraków, 1937. Activities of the Treasury in the period of Partitions is described.

Seym as a Career

Dworzaczek, W. *Skład Społeczny Wielkopolskiej Reprezentacji Sejmowej w Latach 1572-1655.* Roczniki Historyczne, Poznań, pp. 281-310, 1957. Social background of Deputies from Greater Poland is discussed.

Zielińska, Teresa. *Magnateria Polska Epoki Saskiej.* Ossolineum, Wrocław, 1977. Rise of senatorial families in the Saxon Era is traced.

General History of Poland and Lithuania

Collective work, *Ukraine, A Concise Encyclopaedia*. University of Toronto Press, 1963. One chapter deals with the Seym of Galicia in Lwów from Ukrainian point-of-view.

Słownik Geograficzny Królewstwa Polskiego. Walewski Publishers, Warszawa, 1887. A multi-volume geographical dictionary; includes historical and legislative references.

The New Cambridge Modern History, 14 vols. Cambridge University Press, 1960. Each volume contains a chapter devoted to Poland.

Ajnenkiel A., Leśnodorski, B., Rostocki, W. *Historia Ustroju Polski 1764-1939*. Państw. Wydawnictwo Naukowe, Warszawa, 1974. History of the government of Poland in the last two centuries.

Bobrzyński, Michał. *Dzieje Polski w Zarysie*. Geberthner and Wolff, Warszawa, 1931, 3 volumes. Outline of Polish history written by a former Deputy and Viceroy of Galicia.

Connor, Bernard. *The History of Poland*. Dan. Brown, London, 1696. Historical and political account of Poland in the later 1600s is given in several letters to prominent persons, written by the Irish doctor of King John III Sobieski. Discusses several Seyms.

Finkel, Ludwik. *Bibliografia Historyi Polskiej*. Komisja Historyczna PAU, Lwów, 1891. Basic bibliography of Polish history, currently continued by the Polish Academy of Sciences.

Gloger, Zygmunt. *Encyklopedia Staropolska Ilustrowana*. Photo-reprint, Wiedza Powszechna, Warszawa, 1972, 4 volumes. An early reference work, with wealth of information on the Commonwealth of Poland and Lithuania.

Hoskins, Janina W. *Early and Rare Polonica of the Fifteenth through Seventeenth Centuries in American Libraries*. G.K. Hall and Co., Boston, 1973. Pages 110-122 list American holdings pertaining to legislation and the Seym.

Kaczmarek, Z., Leśnodorski, B. *Historia Państwa i Prawa Polskiego*. Państwowe Wydawnictwo Naukowe, Warszawa, 1976. History of the state and the law of Poland from Marxist view point.

Kantautas, Adam and Filomena. *A Lithuanian Bibliography*. Univ. of Alberta Press, 1975, Suppl., 1979. Lists books and articles held by major libraries of Canada and the United States. Very complete listing of material on Polish-Lithuanian Union.

Kasparek-Obst, Joseph. *The Constitutions of Poland and of the United States, Kinships and Genealogy*. The American Institute of Polish Culture, Miami, Florida, 1980. A study of the formal side of the two constitutions, and of the influence of Polish Brethren (Arians) on the rise of the Unitarian Church.

BIBLIOGRAPHY

Knoll, Paul W. *The Rise of the Polish Monarchy, Piast Poland in East Central Europe 1320-1370.* Univ. of Chicago Press, 1972. Good study of the pre-parliamentary period in Poland.

Kuśnierz, Bronisław. *Stalin and the Poles.* Hollis and Carter, London, 1949. Gives details and chronology of the Soviet invasion, deportations from Poland, and the fate of Polish prisoners of War in the Soviet Union.

Kutrzeba, Stanisław. *Historia Ustroju Polski.* Geberthner i Wolff, Warszawa, 1949. Basic study of the development of government of Poland.

Lam, Stanisław, edit. *Polska, Jej Dzieje i Kultura.* Trzaska, Evert and Michalski, Warszawa, 1927-1932. A 3-volume compendium of political and cultural history of Poland up to 1928.

Łepkowski, Tadeusz, edit. *Słownik Historii Polskiej.* Wiedza Powszechna, Warszawa, 1973, sixth edition. A recent dictionary of history, unreliable in the area of Polish-Soviet relations.

Reddaway, W.F., edit. *The Cambridge History of Poland,* 2 vols. Cambridge University Press, 1941-52. A standard work on Polish history in English.

Stupnicki, Hipolit. *Herbarz Polski.* Kornel Piffer Publ., Lwów 1855, photocopy, London, 1963. Heraldry and name list of noted personages in the First Republic.

Wagner, W.J., edit. *Polish Law Throughout the Ages.* Hoover Institution Press, Stanford, California, 1970. Various aspects of the history of jurisprudence of Poland and the influence fo Goślicki are covered.

Zaleski, Wojciech. *Tysiąc Lat Naszej Wspólnoty.* Veritas, London, 1961. socio-economic history of Poland during last millenium.

Memoirs of Legislators, A Sampling

Pasek, Jan Chryzostom. *Memoirs of the Polish Baroque.* Catherine S. Leach, trans., Univ. of California Press, 1976. Politics, military and domestic life in the late 1600s are described, including the porceedings of one Seymik of Rawa.

Radziwiłł, Albrycht S. *Pamiętnik.* Państwowy Instytut Wydawczy, Warszawa, 1980, 3 volumes. Memoirs of a Deputy, speaker of the Seym and finally a Chancellor of Lithuania, covering the period 1632-1655. More or less complete diaries of 25 Seyms are embedded in the text.

Sapieha, Leon. *Wspomnienia z lat 1803-1863.* B. Pawłowski, edit., H. Altenberg, Lwów, 1913. Memoirs of the first Speaker of the Seym of Galicia.

Witos, Wincenty. *Moje Wspomnienia.* Instytut Literacki, Paris, 3 vol., 1964. Memoirs of the future leader of the Peasant Party. His activities in the Seym of Lwów are covered in Vol. 1.

About the Author

Jacek Jędruch was born in 1927 in Warsaw, Poland, where he grew up in the latter years of the Second World War. During the war years he participated in the Polish Resistance movement. Following the war, hunted by the communist security forces, he escaped to the West and found himself in England. There he started his university education, but for family reasons decided to emigrate to the United States. In Boston he continued his university studies, earning in turn degrees from Northeastern University and Massachussetts Institute of Technology; later he obtained his doctorate from the Pennsylvania State University. In his professional life Dr. Jędruch worked in the field of nuclear energy and authored a book and numerous papers dealing with various aspects of nuclear technology.

A scientist and a humanist, he shared with his wife, Eva, a chemical engineer, not only a love of travel, but also a passion for history. His lifelong avocation was his interest in the operation of representative governments, the evolution of government policy in relation to public needs, and the political developments in Eastern Europe. It was the combination of these interests, together with the rise of the "Solidarity" movement in Poland in 1980, that prompted him to write the guide to the parliamentary history of Poland, *Constitutions, Elections and Legislatures of Poland, 1493-1977*. In 1985, as a result of the book, he became a member of the International Commission for the History of Representative and Parliamentary Institutions. In subsequent years he published a number of papers on topics of parliamentary history: "Election Boycotts in the Second and Polish People's Republics"; "Publication of the Records of the Seyms and Seymiks of Poland": "Polish Constitutional Heritage in the Light of the French Revolution"; "Revival of the Senate of Poland in the Light of Its History"; "Rise of Parliamentary Institutions in Lettland, Estland and Finland."

In March of 1995, while travelling with his wife in Greece, Dr. Jędruch suffered a fatal accident on the Acropolis in Athens.

Index

Key to Abbreviations in the Index

Abbr.	Position	Abbr.	Position
am	ambassador	ki	king
ar	architect	mi	minister
ca	candidate	pa	painter
de	deputy	pr	president
em	emperor	pu	publisher
ed	editor	se	senator
ge	general	sp	speaker
hi	historian	ty	typographer
in	interrex	vi	viceroy
ju	jurist	wr	writer

Ablegate, Deputy, 22, 23, 35, 88, 89, 346, 384
Abdication of:
    John Casimir Vasa, 123, 144, 190, 356,
    Stanisław Leszczyński, 154,
    Augustus II Wettin, 154, 190,
    Stanisław A. Poniatowski, 185, 188, 190,
    Henri Valois, 190
Abrahamowicz, Dawid, de, 300
Academy of Learning of Cracow, 245,
    263, 264
"Accomplished Senator" by W.G.
    Goślicki, 105, 106
Act of Confederation of Warsaw
    (1812), 206-207
Act of Dethronement, 221-223
Act of Union, Polish-Lithuanian, 60-61
Administrative divisions, 26
Africa, Polish Army units in, 310
Agricultural Society, 377-378
Agrippa, Wacław, sp, 430

Albrecht I Hohenzollern, 370
Alexander I of Poland, ki, 32, 65, 87, 88
Alexander I Romanov, em, 212-213, 215-216,
    217-218
Alessandrini Marco, pa, 76
Alexandrine Constitution, see
    Constitution (1815)
Allodial ownership, see dominium
    directum
Alphonso II, Duke of Ferrara, ca, 79
Amendment to
    Constitution (1825), 218, 333,
    Constitution (1926), 280, 281
American Philosophical Society, 208,
    228
American Revolutionary War, 160, 184
Ankwicz Józef, de, 18, 170, 186, 187, 192-193
"Annual Register" of London, 180
"Anonymous Letters to Stanisław
    Małachowski, " by H. Kołłatay, 167

Antitrinitarians, see Arians
Appellate Courts, 355
Apportionment of Seats
  in the Seym, 55-57
  in the Senate, 25-26, 100-103, 276-277,
    290-292
Arab-Israeli War, 332
Archangielsk, Russia, 380
Archbishop of Gniezno, 74, 85, 86, 105, 233
Arians, (Polish Brethern), 59, 60, 118-120
Aristocratic Titles
  awarded by Austria, 110
  banned by Poland, 110
Armenians, 27, 300
Army, Commanders of, 109
Articles of
  Agreement, 74, 84, 135
  American Confederation, 61
"Assembly of Friends of the Constitution," 179
Assessors, Seymik, 38, 41
Augustus II of Poland, ki, 56, 75, 80,
  81, 83, 137, 152, 155, 190
Augustus III of Poland, ki, 75, 77, 80,
  81, 82, 98, 137, 155, 157, 190
Auschwitz, concentration camp, 293
Austria, 142, 254, 392
Austrian Parliament, Polish Deputies
  in, 39, 255, 256
Authentication of Laws, 55

Bacciarelli, Marcello, pa, 204
Baczyński, Władysław, de, 387
Badeni, Kazimierz, vi, 260, 352
Badeni, Stanisław, sp, 260, 262
Badeni, Władysław, de, 243
Badinelli, Stanisław, de, 89
Bagiński, Kazimierz, de, 282, 310
Baltic Sea, 25
Baltic States, 373, 374
Bańczyk, Stanisław, de, 359
Bank of Agriculture, 379
Bar, Confederation of, see
  Confederations
Barlicki, Norbert, de, 275, 282, 372, 387
Baron, use of term in Poland defined, 23, 64
Bartel, Kazimierz, de, 387
Bathory, Andreas, 79
Bathory, Stephen, ki, see Stephen

Bathory of Poland
Battenberg, (Mountbatten), family, 221
Bazin, Ch., pa, 217
Belgium, 354
Belveder Palace, 220, 221
Bełza, A., de, 90
Benedictines, Order of, 123
Berg, Grand Duchy of, 204
Berlin, 234
Bereza Kartuska, detention camp, 282, 329
Bernoulli, Johannes, wr, 99
BBWR, Non-Party Block of Cooperation,
  281-282, 283-284, 287, 398
Białłozor, Stanisław, sp, 428
Białobłocki, Paweł, de, 118
Bicameral Seym, 51, 346
  appearance of, 29, 31
Bieliński, Franciszek, sp, 429
Bieliński, Kazimierz L., sp, 429
Bieliński, Piotr, 283
Bieliński, Stanisław, sp, 186, 430
Bień, Adam, mi, 248, 310
Bierut, Bolesław, pr, 276, 323, 337
Bilak, Stefan, de, 387
Bill of Rights, 64, 112, 145-146, 182,
  192, 210, 216, 226, 248, 260,
  277, 299, 336
Biniszkiewicz, Józef, de, 387
Bishop, (Biskup), 23, 101
Bismarck, Otto, mi, 235
Bitner, Henryk, de, 387
Black Procession in Paris, 173
Black Procession in Warsaw, 88, 90, 172, 173
Błonie, Seym of, 47
Bniński, Adolf, de, 387
Board of Judicial Review, 355
Bobrzyński, Michał, vi, 19, 261, 262-263
Bohemia, 254
Bochnia, salt mines, 367
Bohuszewicz, Stanisław, de, 162
Bojko, Jakub, de, 254, 263
Bolsheviks, Party of, 141
Bolt, Feliks, de, 387
Borucki, Marek, hi, 19
Boyars, Ruthenian gentry, 49
Bracław, palatinate of, 39, 139, 189
Brandenburg Hohenzollerns 119-120
Brandenburg-Prussia, 366

INDEX

Branicki, Ksawery F., se, 178, 184
Branicki, Jan Klemens, ca, 80
Brazda, Stefania, de, 321
"Bread riots", see "Food riots"
Brezhniev, Leonid, pr, 316
Brześć-Kujawy, palatinate of, 35
Brest-Litovsk (Brześć Litewski)
  Lithuanian Seym of 1569, 49,
  treaty of, 371,
  trial of, 282, 282, 287
Buczacz, treaty of, 370
Budgeting, state, 363, 366-367
Bulgaria, 316, 323
Burgher representation, 144, 172
Burke Edmund, wr, 179, 180
Burzyński, Stanisław, de, 387
Byczyna, battle of, 85
Bydgoszcz,
  Seym of, 95, 363-364,
  treaty of, 120, 372
Byelorussia, 371, 372, 373
Byelorussians, 27, 274-275
Byelorussian CP, 276
Byliński, Jan, hi, 19
Bzowski, M., Electoral Commissioner, 354

Cabaj, Władysław, de, 321
Call-up, military,   31, 36, 38
Calvinists, 60, 119
Canada Act, 178
"Candidature to membership" (CP), 314
Candidates in Royal Elections, 78, 79-80
Capitol, United States, 98
Car, Stanisław, sp, 21-22, 283, 284, 285, 286,
  288-289, 299, 300, 431
Cardinal Laws, 21, 39, 54, 155, 159, 370
Casimir the Great, ki, 25, 37, 72, 355
Castles, Seym quarters in,
  Cracow, 92, 93, 94,
  Grodno, 100,
  Piotrków, 91,
  Warsaw, 94-100, 141, 214, 220, 224
Castellan, (Kasztelan), 34, 100, 346
Catherine II of Russia, em, 185
Cathedral Chapter of Cracow, 165
Celewicz, Włodzimierz, de, 387
Censorship, 216
Central powers, collapse of, 269
Chalecki, Aleksander, sp, 428

Chalecki, Dymitr A., sp, 428
Chambers of
  Demolition of, by the Russians, 100, 188,
  Deputies, 21, 92, 390, 391, 394,
    Cracow, 92,
    Lwów, 252, 253,
    Warsaw, 96, 98, 99,
  Representatives, Capitol, 99,
  Senate, 98, 99, 394, 396, 397,
    Cracow, 93,
    Warsaw, 96, 97, 98, 220
Chancellor, 103, 104
Chaciński, Józef, 310
Charles Bourbon, ca, 79
Charles Ferdinand Vasa of Poland, ca, 79
Charles I, Stuart, ki, 116, 118
Charles II, Stuart, ki, 177
Charles V of Lorraine, 79
Charles XII of Sweden, ki, 81, 358
Charter of
  Czerwińsk, 31, 64,
  Jedlna-Kraków, 31, 64,
  Koszyce, 31, 64,
  Nieszawa, 31
Chełm, palatinate, 39, 58, 60
Checiński, Wojciech, de, 175
Chełmno,
  bishopric of, 45,
  palatinate of, 39, 45,
  town of, 45
Chevalier, Antoni, de, 175
Chief Justice, 104
China, 135, 148-149
Chłapowski, Desydery, ge, de, 239
Chmielnicki Rebellion, 139
Choborski, Ludwik P., vi, 261
Chomiński, Ksawery, sp, 430
Chomiński, Franciszek K., de, wr, 193
Chrapowicki, Jan A., sp, 429
Christian Democratic Party, 252, 275, 293, 295
Chief Executives, 299, 337
Chronology of Constitutional Movements,
  France, Poland, United States, 183-184
Chronology of Major Laws, 41

Chronology of Seyms, 31, 36, 48-49, 51,
  426-431
Church of Poland, 59
Church,

Greek Catholic, 257,
Greek Orthodox, 27, 159,
Protestant, 58-59,
Roman Catholic, 59, 364
Churchill, Winston, 374
Ciołkosz, Adam, de, 282
Ciechanów, Seym of, 48
Cistercian Order, 27, 31
Cities, representation of, 175-176, 346, 347, 348
Civil Code of 1825, 216
Civil War, in Poland (1945-1947), 381
Civil War, in Russia, 141
Civitatum Nuncii, 33, 34, 87
Code Napoleon, 204, 208, 209, 216
Codex of Prażmowski, 49
Codification of law, 48, 63, 355
Colard, Hermann, vi, 261
Collectivization,
    in Russia, 237, 329-330, 373, 381, 382,
    in Poland, 237, 329-330, 373, 381, 382
Commission for National Education, 154, 163, 358
Commonwealth of Poland and Lithuania, 22, 42, 57, 102-103, 139, 206
Composition of Senate, 102-103
Composition of Seym, 319
Communist International (Comintern), 276
Communist Party, (CP) of Poland, 275, 368, 374, 382, 386, 409
    annihilation by Stalin (1938), 368,
    reconstitution after World War II, 314-315,
    representation in Seym, 276, 289, 292
Communists, 354, 392
Concentration camps,
    German, 309, 386,
    Soviet, 142, 380, 386
COP, Central Industrial Region, 335
Condé, Duc de, ca, 357
Confederation for an Independent Poland, 398
Confederations,
    ban on, 132,
    defined, 22, 132, 139,
    organizational structure, 132
Confederations of
    First Republic, 132-138,
    Hereditary Monarchy, 136,
    in the Seyms, 126, 127, 134 ,
    outside the Seyms, 137-138

Confederation of
    Bar, 138, 159-160,
    Dowspuda, 138,
    Dzików (Tarnobrzeg), 135, 138,
    Gorzyce, 138,
    Grodno, 137,
    Gołąb, 138,
    Lwów, 136,
    Kobuszowa, 138,
    Korczyn, 136,
    Kwidzyn, 136,
    Opatów, 138,
    Piotrków, 136,
    Prussia, 133,
    Radom, 136, 138, 158,
    Sandomierz, 73, 138,
    Sieradz, 136
    Słuck, 138,
    Środa, 138,
    Szczebrzeszyn, 138,
    Targowica, 135, 138, 185, 358,
    Tarnogród, 138, 155,
    Toruń, 138,
    Tyszowce, 138,
    Warsaw, 1572, 63, 96, 119, 133-134, 135, 137, 138,
    Warsaw, 1812, 206-207,
    Wilno, 138,
    Wieluń, 136
Confiscations of property, 31, 326, 333, 334
Congress of the United States, 175, 176, 346
Congress of Vienna, 212, 230
Constitutional amendment, 218, 324
Constitutional charters, 390-391
Constitutional committee, 283
Constitutional principles, 33, 34
Constitutional Tribunal, 412-413
Constitutions, laws, 21, 31, 32, 54
Constitution of
    Early First Republic, 111-112,
    France, 178,
    Hereditary Monarchy, 64,
    Russian Empire, draft, 220, 221,
    United States of America, 61,
    1791, First Republic, 99, 139, 177, 178, 181, 203, 346, 348, 370, 392, 411,
    Law on the cities, 175, 177,
    Law on the government,177,

Law on the Seymiks, 173, 174, 177,
1793, First Republic, 192, 348,
1807, Duchy of Warsaw, 209-210,
210, 349, 376, 377, 434,
1815, Congress Kingdom, 213-216, 223, 350,
1817, Galicia, 247, 248,
1824, Grand Duchy of Poznań, 237-238,
1861, Galicia and Lodomeria, 259-260,
1921, Second Republic, 112, 273, 274,
277-278, 277, 434,
1935, Second Republic, 21, 112,
358-362, 378-379, 370, 434,
1952, Polish People's Republic, 336, 370, 393,
434,
1992, Third Republic, 393, 401, 411, 434
1997, Third Republic, 411, 434
Constantine, Romanov, de, 216, 219
Constant, Benjamin, wr, 217
Conti, François, ca, 81
Conventiones Terrestrae, 35
Convention of Seniors, 405
Convocation Seyms, 74, 75, 126, 127
Copernicus, Nicholas, wr, 47, 68
Coronation Seyms, 74, 75, 126, 126, 127
Corporation Act of England, 155
Cossacks,
history of, 138-141,
rebellion of, 117, 139, 189, 370,
register, 139,
service against Muscovy, 139,
settlements, origin of, 138-139, 376,
Seym dealings with, 139,
troops, 139,
wars against, 139
Council of Four Lands, Jewish, 143
Council, Privy, 29
Council of State, 268-269, 312, 392
County Council, 43
Covenanting, Scottish, 132
Cracow,
city of, 82, 91, 391,
election results from, 320,
mint of, 362,
palatinate of, 35,
representation of, 35, 87, 88, 90, 347,
republic of, 248-249,
seat of Seyms, 92
Croatia, 254
Cromwell, Oliver, ge, 118

Cromwellian revolution, 116, 125
Crown jewels, 93, 357
Crown lands, 363, 363
Crown Tribunal (Supreme Court),
election of judges for, 43, 155,
establishment of, 64, 104
Crusaders, 134
"Cuius regio, eius religio" principle, 134
Curia system, 251, 352
Currency, value of, 362
Cyboni, Krzysztof, de, 89
Cyrankiewicz, Józef, pr, 337
Czacki, Tadeusz, de, 170
Czajkowski, Grzegorz K., de, 176
Czapiński, Kazimierz, de, 387
Czaplic, Celestyn, sp, 193, 430
Czapliński, Władysław, hi, 19
Czarnkowski, Stanisław, S., sp, 65, 112,
222
Czarniecki, Stefan, sp, 429
Czartoryski, Adam, 212, 213, 248, 385
Czartoryski, Adam Kazimierz, sp, 80,
163, 164, 178, 193, 385, 430
Czartoryski, Karol, sp, 429
Czartoryski, Florian K., in, 106, 107
Czechoslovakia, 282, 316, 323,
Czechowicz, Gabriel, mi, 359
Czernichów, palatinate of, 40, 139
Czerwińsk,
privilege of, 31,
Seym of, 48
Częścik, Łucja, hi, 19
Czeszejko-Sochacki, Jerzy, de, 276, 387
Czetwertyński, Seweryn, de, 387
Czuczmaj, Maksym, de, 387

Dąbal, Tadeusz, de, 276, 387
Dąbrowski, Włodzimierz, de, 387
Dąbski, Stanisław, se, 81, 107,
Dąbski, Józef S., 310
Daniłowicz, Mikołaj, sp, 428
Daszyński, Ignacy, sp, 256, 275, 281,
299, 300-301
Debating time of parliaments, compared, 325
Debriefing Seymiks, 53, 55, 125
Dębiński, Kasper, sp, 428
Dębski, Aleksander, de, 387
Dębski, Jan, de, 301, 372
Decembrist, Conspiracy, 219, 358

Decykiewicz, Włodzimierz, de, 383
Declaration of Independence, American, 105
Dekert, Jan, Mayor of Warsaw, 172, 173, 193
"Dekulakization" in Russia, 380
Delegation Seym, 158, 162
"Deluge," the, 118, 119
Dembowski, Aleksy S., de, 175
Dembowski, Jan, sp, 317, 318, 337, 338, 431
Democratic Left Alliance, 398, 405, 406
Democratic Party (licensed), 314
Democratic Society, 244
Democratic Union, 405, 406
Denhoff, Stanisław E., sp, 193-194, 429
Deportations, 380
Deputy, (Poseł, Deputowany, Ablegat),
    10, 351, 383, 384
Deputies, 401, 406, 408, 409, 410, 411, 412
    biographies of , 18, 67-69, 112-114,
        146-149, 192-199, 210-211, 227-229,
        239-241, 262-265, 300-305, 338-341,
    chambers of, 92, 97, 99,
    election of, 44, 383, 398,
    first appearance of, 50,
    immunity of, 125, 409,
    pay for, 410,
    powers of, 128-131, 391,
    term of office, 125
Detention camps, 329, 331
Diaries of Debates, 19, 53
Diller, Erich, vi, 261
Dilliard, pa, 219
Dimitriev, Georgi, 323
Disruption of Seyms, 156
Dissidents, religious, 134, 158
Divine rights of kings, 201
Djilas, Milovan, wr , 314, 326
Dmochowski, Franciszek K., de, 170
Dmowski, Roman, de, 256, 275, 301
Dnieper River, 140
Dobrogoszcz, Gabriel, de, 89
Dolabella, Tomaso, pa, 140
Dominirski, Jerzy, de, 387
Dominium directum, 375
Dominium utile, 375, 377
Dowbór-Muśnicki, J., ge, 371
Dowspuda, Confederation of, 138
Dresden, Saxony book publishers of, 166,
    Napoleon in, 178, 203,

Seym delegation to, 178
Drucki-Lubecki, Ksawery, mi, 216, 221,
    243
Dubanowicz, Edward, de, 272, 273, 301
Dubienka, battle of, 184, 185
Dubois, Stanisław, de, 282, 387
Dubrawski, Franciszek, sp, 429
Ducal Prussia, 121
Ducat, gold, 362
Duchy of Warsaw, 188, 202-209, 233, 351,
    368, 434,
    war with Austria, 202, 241
Duke (Kniaź), Lithuanian, Ruthenian, 23
Duma, Russian Parliament, 256
Dunajewski, Julian, de, 263
Dunin, Marcin, Archbisbop, 233
Dupont, Irenée, 164
Dupont, Pierre S., 164
Durer, Hans, pa, 92
Dworakowski, Tadeusz, de, 387
Dynastic Subdivision, 35
Działyński, Tytus, de, 239
Działyński, Tomasz, sp, 429
Dzieduszycki, Alexander, de, 386
Dzieduszycki, Karol, de, 386
Dzieduszycki, Kazimierz, de, 386
Dzieduszycki, Tadeusz, de, 386
Dzieduszycki, Wojciech, de, 386
Dzieduszycki, Władysław, de, 386
Dzieduszycki, Włodzimierz, sp, 259,
    260, 386, 430
Dzików, (Tarnobrzeg), see
    Confederation of Dzików

Early Seyms, 51
East Prussia, 122
Economic matters, 366-369
Eisenhower, Dwight D., pr, 81
Elblag,
    city of, 45,
    mint of, 362,
    representation of, 89
Electability of Kings, 119
Election (royal) Seyms, 74, 75, 126,
    127
Elections, 398, 408, 409
    boycott of, 287,
    chronology of, 426-431,

turnout in, 289, 292, 293, 353-354
Elector of Brandenburg, 121
Elector of Saxony, 56, 80, 137
Electoral Ordinance, 64, 112, 145, 182,
   192, 209-210, 226, 238, 247, 260,
   278, 298, 319, 336, 398
Elective Kings, 75
Electoral law, Galician, 352
Electoral rights, 347, 348, 354
Elert, Piotr, ty, 55
Emigration to America, 246
Emmanuel of Portugal, ca, 79
Enforcement of Laws, 59
England, 118, 128, 348, 351,
   parliament of, 51,
   refuge of Arians, 121,
   shires of, 130
Ermland (Warmia),
   bishopric of, 45,
   representation in Seym of Poznań, 236
Estates General of France, 52, 183
Estates of Galicia,
   defined, 241,
   uniform of members, 303
Estates of Prussia,
   described, 46,
   legates of, 21
Estonia, 356, 380
"Execution of Laws" movement, 58-64, 85, 363
Executive Branch, 64, 111, 145, 181,
   209, 225-226, 237-238, 247, 259, 277,
   297-298, 432
Expulsion of Arians, 119, 135
Extermination camps, German, 309
Extraordinary Seyms, 124, 125, 126

Falanga group, detention of members,
   282
Falck, Jaremiasz, pa, 132
"Federalist Papers" by Publius, 166,
   183
Feodor, Tsar of Russia, ca, 79
Fergis, Józef, de, 176
Ferrari, Pompeo, ar, 233
Fiedler, A., pa, 254
Finkel, Ludwik, hi, 18
Firley, Andrzej, sp, 67, 428
Firley, Jan, sp, 67, 428
Five-adjective principle in electoral law, 278

Four-adjective principle in electoral law, 286
Food riots,
   1956, Poznań, 335, 354,
   1970, Gdańsk, 335,
   1976, Radom, 335
Fontana, Jakub, ar, 98
France, 349, 350
Francis I Habsburg, em, 241, 247
François, Louis Bourbon, ca, 80, 81
Franz Joseph Habsburg, em, 259
Franklin, Benjamin, wr, 80
Frederick Augustus Wettin, Grand Duke of
   Warsaw, 80, 81, 82, 107, 178, 204, 250, 350
Frederick Wilhelm III of Prussia, ki, 231
   232, 351
Frederick Wilhelm IV of Prussia, ki, 233
Fredro, Andrzej M., sp, 121, 146, 429
Fredro, Aleksander, de, 263
Freedom of the press, 216
Freedom of speech, 218
French Constitution, Third Republic, 273
French Revolution, see Revolution in France
Front of National Unity (FJN), 317, 332, 336

Gadomski, Stanisław, sp, 430
Gajewski, Jan, sp, 428
Gałaj, Dyzma, sp, 337, 339, 431
Galicia, and Lodomeria, Kingdom of,
   25, 250, 344, 434
Galician,
   Savings Bank, 264,
   Seym in Lwów, 50, 246
Gąsiorowski, Andrzej, de, 383
Gąsiorowski, Maciej, de, 383
Gaulle, Charles de, pr, 281, 290
Gautier, Michał, de, 89, 176
Gdańsk,
   city of, 25, 57, 366-367, 370,
   mint of, 362,
   opposition to Frederick of Prussia, 189,
   representation of, 89, 90, 347
Gdynia, port of, 335, 359
General Council, 51, 126, 390
General Seymik, 56, 125,
   first appearance of, 30,
   meeting places of, 46, 130,
   revived as provincial Seym, 49-50, 50, 201
General Seymik of
   Greater Poland, 44, 56, 125,

Lesser Poland, 44, 56, 125, 249,
Lithuania, 44, 125,
Masovia, 45, 48-49,
Prussia, 45, 45, 89,
Ruthenia, 44, 125, 249
Gentry (Szlachta) defined, 24
George of Denmark, ca, 79
Geremek, Bronisław, 406
German Order, War Against, 31, 46, 133
German settlers in towns, 27
German-Soviet invasion of Poland, 26, 268, 289, 373-374, 432-433
Germany, 121, 354
Gersztański, Damian, de, 387
Gestapo, German Secret Police, 309, 386
Giełgud, Andrzej, sp, 429
Gierek, Edward, de, 321, 392
Głabiński, Stanisław, de, 387
Glücksmann, Zygmunt, de, 387
Gliwic, Hipolit, de, 387
Gniezno, archbishop of, 74, 85, 105, 233
Gniński, Jan T., sp, 146, 429
Godlewski, Józef, de, 210
Gołąb, Confederation of, 137
Gołuchowski, Adam, sp, 261, 263-264, 430
Gołuchowski, Agenor, vi, 243, 245, 260, 263
Gomoliński, Florian, sp, 428
Gomulka, Władysław, de, 415
Gorczyn, J., pu, 121
Goryński, J., codifier, 49
Górnicki, Łukasz, wr, 68
Gosiewski, Aleksander K., sp, 428
Gosiewski, Wincenty K., sp, 429
Goślicki, Grzymała W., se, 68, 104-105, 106, 165
Gostomski, Hieromim, sp, 428
Gottwald, Klement, pr, 323
Government-controlled economy, 368-369
Government, division of powers, 21-22
Government investments, 368
"Government of Poland" by J.J. Rousseau, 166, 287
Graber, Maciej, de, 89
Grabowiecki Szymon, de, 89
Grabowski, Józef, sp, 239
Grabski, Stanisław, 276, 372
Grabski, Władysław, mi, 276
Graff, Anton, pa, 180

Grand Commissions of Seym, 163
Grand Duchy of,
Berg, 203,
Lithuania, 61-62,
Poznań, 26, 351
Grand Duke of Lithuania, 61
Grant, Ulysses S., pr, 81
Great Britain, 350, 349
Greater Poland
province of, 35, 44, 350,
provincial Seym of, 44, 391
Greek Orthodox
church, 27, 158,
political rights of, 158, 347,
representation of, 155, 163
Greek Catholic Archbishop of Lwów, 257
Grochalski, Paweł, de, 175
Grocholski, Kazimierz, de, 264
Grodno,
castle of, 186,
city of, 100, 126, 391,
representation of, 347,
seat of Seyms, 93, 99, 186,
Seym of, 49, 89, 109, 186
Gros, Jean A., pa, 208
Grudziądz,
city of, 45,
General Seymik of, 44, 45, 46
Grudzińska, Joanna, 219
Grzesik, Karol, sp, 293
Grześkowiak, Alicja, sp., 431
Grzybowski, Konstanty, hi, 19
Grzybowski, Mikołaj, sp, 65, 428
Grzymułtowski, Krzysztof, sp, 146-147, 370, 429
Guam, representation of, 175
Guardians of the Law, Senate, 100, 108, 109
Gucwa, Stanisław, sp, 332, 337, 339, 431
"Gulag Archipelago" by Alexander Solzhenitsyn, 380

Habeas Corpus Act, English, 31
Habsburg, House of, 125
Habsburg, Ernest, ca, 80, 356
Habsburg, Maximilian, ca, 75, 79
Hadziacz, Agreement of, 141
Halecki, Oskar, hi, 19

Halicz, kingdom of, 25, 241
Hamilton, Alexander, wr, 166, 167
Hamlet, play, 105
Handelsman, Marceli, hi, 18
Hauke, Julia, 221
Hauke, Maurycy, ge, 221
Hemingway, Ernest, wr, 258
"Hen's war," 59, 85
Henri Valois, ki, 75, 80, 84, 230
Henrician Articles, 34, 84, 85, 96,
   222, 315
Henry VIII of England, 51
Henzel, de, 176
Herburt, Jan, de, 63, 67, 107
Hereditary Kings, 65
Hereditary Monarchy, 72, 345, 434
Hetman, Army Commander, 109, 155
Hitler, Adolf, pr, 26
Hochberger, Juliusz, ar, 250
Hohenzollerns, 120, 125, 370, 371, 372
Holland, refuge of Arians, 121
Hołowicz, Feliks, de, 275
Hołuj, Tadeusz, de, 321
Holy Land, 134
D'Hondt, Belgian, method of voting, 353
Hoover, Herbert, pr, 272
Hoover Institute, Stanford University, 381
Horn, Krzysztof, de, 89
Horodło, Union of, 61
Hospitality Tents, 77
House of Commons, England, 348
House of Lords, England, 100
Hromada Byelorussian Party, 275
Humiecki, Stefan, sp, 429
Hungarian Invasion, 118
Hungary, 254, 316
Huyn, Karl, vi, 261

Immunity, parliamentary, 126, 294
"Immutable Laws of History," 373
Impeachment,
   of G.Czechowicz, 359,
   of J.Lubomirski, 86, 122, 356-357,
   of J.A.Morsztyn, 130,
   of A.Poniński, 358,
   of K. J. Sapieha, 153,, 357,
   of S. Sołtyk, 210-211, 359,
   Seym powers of, 343, 355-360,
   trials, 86

Incorporation of new provinces, 45, 55, 57, 61
Independence Hall, Philadelphia, 99
Independent Peasant Party, 275
Independence of Poland, declaration of, 269
industrial expansion, 392-393
Innowrocław, palatinate of, 35, 60
Inquest Seym, 125, 356
Inquisition, ban on, 71
Instructions for Deputies (kartelusze), 41
International Democratic Society, 224
Interparty Club, 269
Interrex, King-pro-tempore, 62, 74, 77,
   81, 102, 105-108
Interregna, 62
Invasion of Poland
   German-Soviet, 268, 289, 373-374,
   Hungarian, 117,
   Swedish, 117
Italy, election turnout in, 354
Ivan IV of Russia, ca, 79
Izbiński-Rusiecki, Jan, sp, 428

Jabłonowski, Jan S., sp, 429
Jabłoński, Henryk, pr, 321, 337
Jagiełło, Władysław, ki, see
   Ladislaus of Poland
Jagiellonian, Alexander, 390
Jagiellonian, dynasty, 29, 72-73
Jagielski, Józef, de, 176
James Sobieski, ca, 79
James Stuart, ca, 80
Jankowski, Jan S., de, 310, 311, 339, 387
Janowski, Jan, de, 321
Japan, 135
Jarnowski, Sebastian, de, 383
Jarosław, town of, 143
Jaruzelski, Wojciech, 401
Jaworzno, detention camp, 329
Jasiukowicz, Stanisław, mi, 310, 311, 387
Jay, John, wr, 166, 167
Jedlecki, Kajetan, de, 176
Jedlna-Cracow, Privilege of, 31
Jędruch, Jan, 378
Jefferson, Thomas, wr, pr, 18, 84, 207, 261, 221,
   222
Jesuit Order, 30, 117, 135, 163, 232, 358
Jews, 27, 110, 112, 176, 231, 309
Jewish
   charter, 141, 112, 146, 210, 351

poll tax, 143-144,
representation, 141-144, 348, 350, 351
Jezierski, Franciszek S., wr, 170
John I, Albert, ki, 65
John II Casimir of Poland, ki, 75, 80,
86, 88, 116, 117, 121, 123, 130, 190,
357
John (Jan) III of Poland, ki, 75, 80, 81, 97,
107, 108, 130, 137, 149, 190, 357, 370
John III Vasa of Sweden, ca, 79
John Paul II, Karol Wojtyła, Pope, 20
Joint Seyms, Polish-Lithuanian, 48-49, 57, 62
Joseph II Habsburg, em, 241
Journal of
debates, 216,
laws, 402, 406, 414, 440
Judiciary branch, 64, 112, 145, 182,
192, 210, 226, 238, 248, 260, 277, 298, 336
Judiciary commission, 175
Judiciary powers, 343, 355-360
Jung, Jerzy, de, 89

Kahals, Jewish, 141-144
Kalaga, Ignacy, de, 387
Kalisz,
Palatinate of, 35, 60,
representation of, 216-219, 347
Kaliszewski, Andrzej, 394
Kaługa, City of, 158
Kamieniec, Podolski, representation of, 347, 352
Kamion, election Seyms at, 75
Kaniewska, Irena, hi, 19
Kaniewski, K., pa, 173
Karnkowski, Stanisław, in, 107
Kapuściński, Stefan, de, 387
Karłowice, treaty of, 371
Karpiński, Franciszek, de, 170
Karski, Antoni, de, 186
Karwicki, Stanisław D., de, 154, 194
Karwowski, Kazimierz, sp, 30, 154, 194, 430
Kaszuby, 25
Katowice, see Silesian Seym
Kazakhstan, Central Asia, 380
Kierdey, Władysław, sp, 429
Kierdey, Jan K., sp, 429
Kiernik, Władysław, de, 282, 372
Kierzkowski, Kazimierz, de, 387
Kiev, palatinate of, 40, 189

Kievan Russia, 35, 139
King-pro-tempore, see Interrex
Kings, election of, 72-83
Kisielewski, Stefan, de, 332, 339
Knesset, Jewish parliament, 143-144
Kobylański, Kazimierz, 310
Kochelski, Walenty, de, 175
Koło, General Seymik of, 44, 46, 125
Kołakowski, Tomasz, de, 313, 359
Kołłątay, Hugo, wr, 163, 167, 169, 170,
172, 179, 194, 209
"Kołłątay's Forge," 167, 179, 184
Komander, Paweł, de, 387
Komorowski Bór, Tadeusz, ge, 310
Konarski, Stanisław, wr, 166, 169
Konieczny, Marian, de, 321
Konopczyński, Władysław, de, hi, 19, 53, 131,
301
Kopernik, Mikołaj, (Copernicus), wr, 47, 68
KOR, Committee for Defense of Workers, 329
KOP, Border Guard, 275
Korboński, Stefan, de, 314
Korczyn, General Seymik of, 44, 46, 88, 125
Korfanty, Wojciech, de, 275, 294, 301
Kornacki, Jan, de, 387
Korsak, Samuel, de, 162
Korzon, Tadeusz, hi, 18
Korytowski, Witold, vi, 261
Kościuszko, Tadeusz, ge, 178, 184, 187, 212-213
Kościuszko Insurrection, 86, 187, 206, 371
Kosmowska, Irena, de, 387
Kossakowski, Józef, se, 178
Kossakowski, Szymon, se, 109
Koszyce, Charter of, 30
Kotowicz, Andrzej, sp, 429
Kowalski, Władysław, sp, 337, 339, 431
Kozubski, Borys, de, 387
Kraiński, Maurycy, de, 244
Krasicki, Ignacy, se, 179
Krasicki, Kazimierz, de, 244
Krasiński, Kazimierz, sp, 165, 430
Krasiński, Stanisław, de, 104, 104
Krasiński, Wincenty, sp, 227, 430
Kraśnicki, Stanisław, sp, 428
Królikowski, Stefan, de, 276, 387
Kryski, Feliks, sp, 428
Kryszpin de Kirszenstein, Michał, sp, 429
Krzycki, Andrzej, sp, 429

Krzywkowski, Jan, de, 170
Kułak, defined, 380
Kukiel, Marian, hi, 19
Kuran, Kazimierz, de, 321
Kutrzeba, Stanisław, hi, 18
Kuzmowycz, Włodzimierz, de, 387
Kwaśniewski, Mikołaj, de, 387
Kwaśniewski, Aleksander, 405, 406
Kwiatkowski, K., wr, 171

Labor camps, 373, 380-381
Labor code of 1975, 328, 329
Labor Party (Christian Democratic) (SP), 312, 314
Labor Union, 398
Ladislaus (Władysław) II of Poland, ki, 41, 73, 390
Ladislaus (Władysław) IV of Poland, ki, 75, 80, 81, 85, 190, 356
Ładysz, J., pa, 234
Lampi, Giovanni, B., pa, 160
Lamprecht, Michał, de, 89
Lancucki, Stanisław, de, 387
Land Credit Society of Poznan, 235
Land ownership, 365, 377, 378
Land Reform Acts, 273, 329-330, 375, 378-382
Landsgemeinde, Swiss, 35
Landtag assemblies, 231
Land tax, 360
Łaski, Jan, wr, 58, 63
Łaski, statutes of, 33
Latin, use of, 52, 53
Latvia, 380
Laudum, Seymik resolution, 37
Lauro, Giovanni, pa, 127
Law
    Cardinal, defined, 55,
    constitutions, 53,
    on the Cities (1791), 175, 177, 179,
    on the Government (1791), 179,
    on the Seymiks (1791), 173, 174, 177
Łazarz, Andrysowic, ty, 55
"Leading role of the Party," 326, 382
League of Nations, 293
Łęczyca,
    Palatinate of, 39,
    Seym of, 32
Ledóchowski, Stanisław, sp, 155, 429

Legislation, Principal, 65-66, 112, 144, 146, 191-192, 299-300, 337-338,
Legislative branch, 64, 111, 145, 181, 192, 209, 226, 238, 247, 259-260, 278, 298, 336, 412-413
    immunity, 355-356,
    record, 129, 324
Lelewel, Joachim, de, 222, 224, 227
Lelowice, village, 378
Lèse majesté, 125, 355-356
Lesser Poland,
    province of, 24, 35,
    provincial Seym of, 44, 391
Leszczyński, Bogusław, sp, 429
Leszczyński, Rafał, sp, 65, 68, 385, 428
Leszczyński, Rafał, sp, 147, 429
Leszczyński, S., ki, see Stanisław Leszczyński of Poland
Leszek the Black, 88
Leveé en masse, 23, 24, 31, 346, 347, 363
Lewandowski, Jan, de, 387
Lewandowski, Jan, de, 176
Lewandowski, Jakub, de, 89
Lewczaniwska, Olena, de, 387
Lewicki, Dmytro, de, 387
Liberal-Democratic Congress, 405
Liberman, Herman, de, 282
Liberty Union, 405-406
Liberum veto, unitary veto, 117, 119, 121, 123, 125, 135, 166
Life Peers, Senators as, 100
Lipski, Wojciech, de, 175
Literacy, related to voting rights, 352
Lithuania, 139, 373, 380,
    early Seyms of, 49,
    joint Seyms with Poland, 48-49, 57, 62,
    representation of, 55-57,
    union with, 27, 45, 61, 391
Lithuanian
    Seyms, 126,
    Seymiks, 44, 49, 50,
    statute, 49, 209, 355
Livio Odescalchi, ca, 80
Lokkaj, Jadwiga, de, 321
Lokuciewski, Antoni, sp, 293
London,
    city of, 129,
    mint of, 362
Łopacki, Mikołaj, sp, 429

Lord, Robert H., hi, 19
Lorraine, Duchy of, 81
Louis of Hungary, ki, 30, 73
Louis XIV of France, ki, 130, 258, 357
Louis XV of France, ki, 81
Louis II of Baden, ki, ca, 80
Łowicki, Jan, sp, 428
Lubarski, Symon, de, 387
Łubieński, Konstanty, de, 332
Łubieński, Maciej, in, se, 107
Łubieński, Władysław, in, se, 107
Lublin
    representation of, 87-88, 89, 346,
        347,
    Seym of, 89, 391
    Union of, 30, 58-59, 67, 72
Lubomirski, Hieronim, sp, 147, 429
Lubomirski, Jerzy, se, 86, 356-357
Lubomirski, Jerzy, sp, 122, 429
Lubomirski, Stanisław, sp, 429
Lubowidzki, Michał E., 221
Lubowidzki, Józef G., sp, 221, 227, 430
Lubowiedzki, Władysław, sp, 429
Łucki, Ostap, de, 387
Lutherans in the Seym, 60, 119
Lutheran Deputies, 60, 121
Lutosławski, Kazimierz, 273
Luxemburg, Rosa, wr, 269
Lwów,
    representation of, 87, 346, 347,
    Seym of, 249-265, 392
    University of, 163
Łyszkiewicz, Maciej, de, 175

Mackiewicz, Stanisław, de, 283
Madison, James, wr, pr, 166, 167
Magierski, Tomasz, de, 89
Magnates, 35
Majority rule of voting, 131-132
Makowski, Wacław, sp, 289, 299, 302, 431
Małachowski, Adam, sp, 430
Małachowski, Antoni, sp, 430
Małachowski, Jacek, sp, 194-195, 430
Małachowski, Stanisław, sp, 170, 171,
    195, 203, 430
Malbork (Malborg), General Seymik of, 44, 46,
    45, 125
Malski, Władysław, de, 387

Maniecki, Maciej, sp, 428
Marchlewski, Julian, 269
Marie-Louise, queen, 357
Marx, Karl, wr, 224
Masovia,
    province of, 35, 48,
    representation of, 56-57,
    reunification with Poland, 45, 49, 391
Masovian
    general Seymik of, 48-49, 104,
    statute of 1576, 355
Massalski, Józef, sp, 157, 195, 430
Massalski, Michał, sp, 430
Mastek, Mieczysław, de, 282
Maszczyk, Daniel, de, 321
Matejko, Jan, pa, 162, 253, 256
Materie status, 370
Mątwy, battle of, 357
Max Emmanuel, ca, 80
Maximilian, II, em, 80
Maximilian III, em, 80
Maximilian Habsburg, 80, 80, 85
Mazowiecki, Tadeusz, 405, 406
Mazury, representation in Seym of
    Poznań, 237
Mędrzecki, Adam, de, 171
Meeting places of
    Seyms, 72,
    Seymiks, 72
Mękarski, Stefan, de, 283
Membership of legislatures, 58
Mensdorf-Puilly, Alexander, vi, 261
"Merkuriusz Polski Extraordynaryjny," 121
Michał Korybut of Poland, ki, 75, 80,
    81, 106, 130, 137, 138, 190, 364
Michałowski, Stanisław, de, 310
Miechów, county of, 378
Mielęcin, detention camp at, 329
Miedziński, Bogusław, sp, 291
Mielnik, Union of, 61
Mieliński, Mikolaj, sp, 428
Mielżyński, Maciej, de, 240
Mierosławski, Ludwik, ge, 234
Mierzwa, Stanisław, 310
Migsowicz, Marian, de, 321
Mikorski, Dionizy, de, 186
Mikołajczyk, Stanisław, de, 313, 340
Military duty, tied to the vote,

INDEX

36-37, 121, 347
Ministers in the Senate, 100
Minor castellans, 101, 103, 383
Mińsk,
city of, 371, 372,
Deputies from, at the Seym of 1772,
162,
Polish-Soviet negotiations in, 301
Mirski, Kazimierz, de, 387
Modrzewski, Andrzej F., wr, 58, 68-69, 165
Mokronowski, Andrzej, sp, 430
Moldavia, campaigns in, 370-371
Mołodecki, Mikołaj, de, 89
Molotov-Ribbentrop Treaty, see
Ribbentrop-Molotov Pact
Mongols, invasions of, 138
Morsztyn, Jan Andrzej, de, mi, 131, 147, 357
Mosch, Karl, vi, 261
Mościcki, Ignacy, pr, 280, 299
Moscow, trial of, 310, 311
Mostowski, Tadeusz A., se, 228
Mountbattens, see Julia Hauke
Mróz, Stanisław, de, 387
Muscovy, 140,
incursions from, 57,
wars with, 370
Museum of the History of the Seym, 394
"Mute" Seym, 155
Myszkowski, Piotr, sp, 428

Naples, Kingdom of, 249
Napoleon Bonaparte, em, 50, 82, 179, 201, 203
Napoleonic
constitutions, 204, 206, 316,
wars, 135, 203, 212, 219, 241
Narutowicz, Gabriel, pr, , 279, 299
National Council of Lwów, 246
National Councils (Soviets), 354
National debt, 363
National Democratic Party, 275
National Democratic Party in
Galicia, 252, 256
National electoral lists, 278
National Minorities Second Republic, 275
National Party, 288, 374
National Seym
appearance of, 30,
relation to General Seymiks, 44
National Treasury Commission, 376

Nec bona recipiantur (ban on confiscations),
31, 33, 333, 334, 390
Neminem captivabimus, (ban on arbitrary arrest),
31, 42, 109, 165, 175, 214, 333, 334, 390
Nemine contradicente (voting rule), 53
New England, town meeting, 36
Nicholas I Romanov, em, 78, 82, 216,
219, 233, 358, 394,
dethronement of, 221, 222, 315, 371, 394
Niedziałkowski, Mieczysław, de, 275,
302-303, 387
Niegolewski, Andrzej, de, 232, 240
Niegolewski, Władysław, de, 240
Niemcewicz, Julian U., de, se, 18, 176,
207, 208, 209, 213, 221, 228, 228
Niemojewski, Andrzej, de, 383
Niemojewski, Wacław, sp, 269
Niemojowski, Bonawentura, de, 217, 218,
223, 224, 228, 386
Niemojowski, Wincenty, de, 217, 219,
223, 224, 228-229, 229, 386
Nieszawa, Charter of, 31, 35
Niezabitowski, Stanisław, sp, 261, 430
Nihil novi (ban on arbitrary laws),
32, 33, 333, 390-391
Nikorowicz, Józef, 249
NKVD, Soviet Secret Police, 258, 309, 380, 386
Nomenclature, legislative, 21
Non praestanda oboedientia (refusal of obedience
rule),
84, 85-86, 315
Norblin, Jean Pierre, pa, 41, 42, 172,177
Norway, voter turnout in, 353-354
Novosiltsov, Nicholas N., mi, 213, 215,
216, 217
Nowomiejski, Adam, de, 123
Nowy Sącz, election results from, 321
Nuntius (Deputy),
civitatum, 33, 34, 87,
terrarum, 33, 34, 130
Nüremberg Trial of war criminals, 374
Nysa, Niesse, River, 374

Oath,
Deputy's, 323,
Speaker's, 158
Oborski, Marcin, sp, 429
Obuchowicz, Filip K., sp, 429
Ochmann, Stefania, hi, 19

Ochab, Edward, pr, 337
Oder River, 25, 374
Odrzywolski, Franciszek, de, 321
Ogiński, Andrzej, sp, 430
Ogiński, Michał K., de, 171
Ogiński, Tadeusz, sp, 430
Okulicki, Kazimierz, ge, 310
Old Senate Chamber, 141
Oldisworth, William, wr, 106
Oliva,
    abbey of, 81,
    Conti's stop off at, 81,
    peace of, 370
Olkieniki, battle of, 358
"On the Effective Conduct of Debates"
    by S. Konarski, 166
Olszewski, Henryk, hi, 19, 53
Olszowski, Jędrzej, se, 107
Omsbudsman, 406
Opaliński, Łukasz, sp, 121, 148, 429
Opatów, Seymik of, 35
Operating statistics of Seyms, 325
"Optimo Senatore" by W. G. Góslicki, 104-105
Ordinary Seyms, 125, 126, 129
Order of Holy Trinity, 246
Order of Mary, German, 35, 134
Organic Statute for Silesia, 293, 299
Oriel, Russia, 386
Osiński, Ludwik, wr, 166
Osmańczyk, Edmund, 409
Ossoliński, Franciszek M., sp, 429
Ossoliński, Hieronim, de, 59
Ossoliński, Jerzy, sp, 113, 429
Ossoliński, Józef M., 243
Ossoliński, Zbigniew, sp, 428
Ossolineum, foundation, 243, 247
Oświęcim, Duchy of, 293
Ostrowski, Antoni J., se, 229
Ostrowski, Tomasz Adam, sp, 205, 210, 213, 229, 430
Ostrowski, Władysław T., sp, 221, 224

Ostroróg, J., se, 59, 69
Ostroróg, Mikołaj, sp, 148, 428
Ożarowski, Jerzy, sp, 430
Ożarowski, Piotr, se, 187
O.Z.N., Camp of National Unity, 287, 330

Pacification Seyms, 88, 125, 153
Pac, Jan, sp, 428
Pac, Krzysztof, sp, 429
Pac, Stefan, sp, 428
Pacifists (Arians), 119,-133, 135
Pacta Conventa, Articles of Agreement,
    23, 74, 87-88, 108, 124, 127, 134, 356
Paine, Thomas, wr, 85
Pajdak, Antoni, 310, 396
Palatine (Wojewoda), 23, 45, 101, 346,
Palatinate,
    representation, 45, 39-40,
    treasury of, 42
Palestine, crusades in, 25
Palmer, Robert R., hi, 19, 282
Palmiry Forest executions, 303, 505
Paris,
    "Black Procession" in, 173,
    mint of, 362
    representative of Confederation of Bar in, 166
Parliament
    and media, 412,
    description of, 396-398,
    ethics, 410-411,
    pay, 410,
    privileges, 409
Parliamentary circle, 406
Parliamentary reform, 119,-134
Parliamentary system, adjustment to, 389,
    by Lithuania, 187-189,
    by Prussia, 187-189,
    by Ruthenia, 187-189
Partition
    First, 110, 241, 367,
    Second, 109, 203,
    Third, 187, 203,
    Treaties, Seym ratification of, 160-162,
        186-187, 370-371
Patriotic Society, 221, 224
"Patriotic Letters" by I.Wybicki, 167
Party caucuses, 405-406
Pasek, Jan C., wr, 96, 123
Paszkiewicz, Daniel, de, 176
Paumgartten, Franz, vi, 261
Pawiński, Adolf, hi, 18,
    portfolios of, 34
Pawlak, Waldemar, 405, 406

INDEX

Peace Treaty
  Seym ratification of:
    Moscow, 144, 370-371,
    Karłowice, 144, 371,
    Polanów, 144, 370-371,
    Riga, 274, 334, 372,
    Versailles, 269,
  Seym rejection of:
    Buczacz, 370
Peasant Party, 346
Peasant Party in Galicia, 246
Peasants, representation of, 351
Pękosławski, Stanisław, sp, 428
Penal Code of 1818, 216
Permanent Council, 109, 110, 121, 162
Permanent Laws, 53
Pestilence (Black Death), 118
Peter's Pence, 345
Petlura, Semion, ge, 371
Petricovius, Andrzej, de, 90
Petrycy, Sebastian, wr, 88
Philadelphia,
  mint of, 362,
  Philosophical Society of, 207-208,
  U.S. Congress meetings in, 176
Philip Wilhelm of Neuburg, ca, 80
Phrygian Cap symbol, 170
Piaskowski, M., de, 171
Piast Dynasty, 25, 34, 72, 375
Piekarski, Anzelm, de, 123
Pieniążek, Jan O., sp, 429
Pieracki, Bronisław, mi, 282
Piłsudski, Józef, pr, 256, 270, 273, 274, 279, 280-281, 299
Pinnoci, Hieronim, ed, 121
Piotrków, seat of Seyms, 90, 91, 99
Piotrków,
  Seym of, 39, 51, 89, 391,
  town of, 32, 39, 50, 391
Piotrkowczyk, Andrzej, ty, 55
Piotrowski, Zygmunt, de, 387
Piramowicz, Grzegorz, wr, 164
Pitt, Moses, pu, 127
Piwnicki, S., sp, 430
Platter, K., wr, 171
Płażyński, Maciej, sp., 431
Plebiscite
  East Prussian, 372,
  Silesian, 293

Plenipotentiary (Deputy), 22, 23, 175-176, 346, 348
Płock, Seym of, 49, 224
Płońsk, Seym of, 48
Pniewski, Bohdan, ar, 328, 394
Pochmarski, Bolesław, de, 387
Podlasia (Podlasie) province of, 270, 365
Podolia (Podole) province of, 57
Podoski, Bohdan, vice-sp, 283, 303
Poland, voter turnout in, 354
Police commission, 175
Polish Academy of Sciences, 34, 338
"Polish Corridor," 133, 372
Polish government in exile, 374
Polish Brethern (Arians), 60, 119, 136, 347
Polish Legion,
  under Napoleon, 203, 219, 229, 239,
  under Piłsudski, 270, 303, 304
Polish-Lithuanian Commonwealth, 116, 206, 343
Polish Peasant Party (PSL), 312, 313, 314, 387, 398, 405, 406
Polish Socialist Party (PPS), 275, 287, 311, 312, 314, 386
Polish-Soviet War, 274, 372-373
Polish United Workers Party, CP, (PZPR), 315, 316, 319
Politechnic Institute of Lwów, 245, 252
Political distribution
  in the Senate, 291
  in the Seym, 289
"Political Law of the Polish Nation"
  by H.Kołłątay, 167
Political police, 359
"Political thoughts on civil liberties" by
  J.Wybicki, 167
Political writers, 165-169
Połock, palatinate representation of, 37
Pomerania (Pomorze), province of, 25, 48, 134, 370,
  representation in Seym of Poznań, 236
Poniatowski, Stanisław, se, 109, 155
Poniatowski, S.A., de, ki, see
  Stanisław August of Poland
Poniński, Adam, sp, 196, 358, 385
Poniński, Antoni, sp, 430
Poniński, Stanisław, sp, 430
Population, Poland, 176,
  statistics, 345, 361

"Poor Richard's Almanack" by B. Franklin, 80
Possinger-Choborski, Ludwik, vi, 261
Postulate Seym in Galicia, 241
Potocki, Alfred, sp, vi, 244, 253, 260, 430
Potocki, Andrzej, vi, sp, 261, 430
Potocki, Feliks, sp, 429
Potocki, Ignacy, se, 163, 170, 178
Potocki, Stefan, sp, 430
Potocki, Stanisław Kostka, de, 167, 171, 180, 196-197, 204
Potocki, Stanisław Szczęsny, de, 184, 185, 196-197, 385
Potocki, Teodor, in, 82, 107
Potsdam, 231, 309, 354
Potworowski, Edward, sp, 430
Potworowski, Gustaw, de, 240
Poznań
    election results for, 321,
    general Seymik of, 46,
    Grand Duchy of, 36, 351,
    palatinate of, 35,
    Seym of, 51, 372, 392
PPS, see Polish Socialist Party
Prądzyński, Józef, de, 387
Praga, suburb of Warsaw, 80
Prager, Adam, de, 282
Prażmowski, Mikolaj, in, 107
Prażmowski, Wawrzyniec, codifier, 49
President of the Republic, 399, 400, 405, 411, 412,
    duties of, 404,
    election of, 403, 404,
    emergency powers of, 413,
    pay, 410,
    relations with Seym, 403-404,
    veto powers of, 404-405
President pro tempore, 110, 276, 279, 291, 292, 303
Printers to the Seym, 55
Pripet marshes, 274, 352
Privileges, see charters

Privy council, 29, 30
Prochaska, Antoni, hi, 19
Proper names, spelling of, 24

Property qualifications for voting, 347, 348

Property, rights of, 375-382
Proportional system of representation, 353
Proszowice
    Seymik of, 35, 36, 38, 88,
    town of, 35, 36
Protectorate status, 155
Protestant, Church, 58-59,
    demands of, 85,
    Deputies, 59, 60, 347,
    political rights of, 158, 347,
    representation of, 155, 163, 347,
    Synods, 60
Provincial Seyms
    joint meetings of, 44, 50,
    relation to General Seymiks, 44,
    Masovian, 48-49,
    Lithuanian, 49, 293,
    Silesian, 293-295
Prussia, 392,
    disestablishment of, 237,
    Ducal, 35, 372,
    early (pagan) history, 25,
    incorporation of, 38, 391,
    Royal, province of, 35, 44, 122
Prussian
    cities, Seym, representation of, 36,
    Confederation, 134-135, 370,
    General Code of Law, 178,
    General Seymik, 45, 47, 89,
    Parliament, Polish Deputies in, 39-40, 234, 235,
    Senators, 56,
    Seym representation, 38, 56,
    Statute of 1598, 355
Prystor, Aleksander, sp, 291, 303, 386, 387
Przerębski, Maksymilian, sp, 428
Przyjemski, Stanisław, sp, 428
PSL, see Polish Peasant Party
Pseudo-election, royal, 73
Pstrokoński, Spytek, de, 383
Puerto Rican nationalists, 98
Pułaski, Franciszek, sp, 269, 299, 430
Pułaski, Kazimierz, ge, 160
Putek, Jozef, de, 282
Pużak, Kazimierz, de, 18, 310, 311, 340, 386, 387
PZPR, see Polish United Workers Party(CP)

INDEX

Quadro, Giovanni, ar, 94

Rabbis in Jewish self-government, 142
Raciąż, Seym of, 48
Raczyński, Edward, de, 234, 240-241
Raczyński Library of Poznań, 234
Raczkiewicz, Władysław, se, pr, 291
Radkiewicz, Stanisław, mi, 359
Radom
  election results for, 321,
  Seym of, 32, 33, 89, 391
Radzewski, Franciszek, sp, 430
Radziejów, Seymik of, 35
Radziejowski, Michał, in, 81, 107
Radziejowski, Hieronim, sp, 148, 429
Radziwiłł, Bogusław, 189
Radziwiłł, Janusz, se, 189
Radziwiłł, Karol S., se, 197, 241, 430
Radziwiłł, Krzysztof, sp, 113, 428
Radziwiłł, Michał, sp, 430
Radziwiłł, Michał K., sp, 429
Rak-Michajlowski, Szymon, de, 275
Rakos, Hungary, 85
Rataj, Maciej, sp, 279, 299, 303, 386, 387, 430
Rawa, Seymik of, 123
Rebellion
  Cossack (1651), 117, 139, 189, 370,
  Galician (1846), 246
Red Ruthenia
  annexation of, 27,
  province, 60
Reddaway, William, hi, 19
Referendum of 1946, 296-398, 326, 329, 382
Reform Seym (four-year Seym), 169-181
Reformation, 52, 58
Regalia, 376
Regency Council, 269
"Release from obedience' rule, 84, 85-86, 315
Religious
  affiliation, 27, 60,
  dissidents, political rights of, 155, 158,
  tolerance act of 1572, 135-136
"Remarks on the Life of Jan Zamoyski"
  by S.Staszic, 167
"Remarks on the Statistics of Poland,"
  by S.Staszic, 377
Rembieliński, Rajmund, sp, 216, 229, 430
Renaissance in Poland, 51
Repnin, Nicholas, am, 158

Representation, principle of, 32
Representation of cities, 87, 90, 176
Republic, Respublica, Reipublica,
  (Rzplita) development of concept, 21, 22,
  First, rise of, (1573), 133-136, 391-392,
  of Cracow, 248, 249,
  Polish People's, rise of, (1945), 354, 374, 392
  Second, rise of, (1918), 267-305, 392, 352,
  378,
  Third, rise of, 393
Resident Senators, 107
Reunification of Poland
  Fourteenth Century, 34, 90,
  Twentieth Century, 269-272
Revolution in
  France (1789), 164,
  America (1776), 160, 184,
  Warsaw (1794), 187-188,
  Warsaw (1830), 220-222
Revolutionary tribunals (1794), 186
Rey Mikołaj, de, 59, 69, 165
Reynberg, Franciszek, de, 89
Reytan, Tadeusz, de, 162, 197
Ribbentrop-Molotov Pact
  origin of, 297, 309,
  secret annex to, 372-373, 374, 379-380,
  432-433
Riga, Peace Treaty of, 274, 301, 372-373
Rodakowski, Henryk, pa, 243
Rokosz, refusal of obedience, 84-86, 124
Rokosz of
  Lubomirski, 86,
  Zebrzydowski, 85
Roman Catholic Church, 59
Romanov dynasty, 125
Romanowski, Jan, de, 176
Roos, Hans, hi, 19
Roosevelt, Franklin, D., pr, 374
Rossowski, Jan, ty, 55
Rotten boroughs, England, 348
Round Table Talks, 394, 399, 408
Rousseau, Jean Jacques, 84, 166, 222, 287
Royal demesnes, income from, 154, 365, 366-
  367
Royal elections, 72-83, 126
Royal Society of Friends of Science
  in Warsaw, 207
Rudawski, Wawrzyniec J., wr, 19
Rudolf II, em, 85

Rudzieński, Kazimierz, sp, 430
Rudowski, Jan, de, 387
Rumania, 316
Rusiecki, Jan I., sp, 428
Russia, 213, 392
Russian
army, 144,
invasion, 118,
language, imposition of in Poland, 352,
parliament, Polish Deputies in, 17
revolution, 373,
succession, 219
Ruthenia, 40, 44, 46, 57, 60
Ruthenians, 27, 50
Ruthenian Duchy, 139, 189
Rybarski, Roman, de, 387
Ryszkowski, Stanisław, sp, 428
Rzewuski, S., de, 158, 171, 184
Rzewuski, Wacław, se, 158, 171, 197, 385, 430

Sacha, Stefan, de, 387
Sandomierz
general Seymik of, 46,
palatinate of, 35
Sanguszko, Eustachy, sp, vi, 255, 261, 264,
430
Sanguszko, Władysław, de, 244
San Francisco Conference, 310
Sanhedrin, Jewish, 143-144
Sapalski, S., de, 176
Sapieha, Benedykt, sp, 358, 429
Sapieha, Franciszek, sp, 429
Sapieha, Kazimierz J., ge, 153, 357, 358
Sapieha, Kazimierz Nestor, sp, 153, 170, 172,
197
Sapieha, Lew, sp, 113, 225
Sapieha, Leon, sp, 243, 261, 264
Sapieha, Michał, t, 358
Saracens, 134
Sarnicki, Stanisław, ju, 63
Sarnowski, Stefan, sp, 429
Sarbiewski, Stanisław, sp, 429
Savage Steppe, 138-139
Savannah, Battle of, 161
Sawicki, Adolf, de, 282
Saxon Kings, 80, 131
Saxony, 80, 166
Scotland, 134

Schlüsselburg fortress prison, 311
Schultz, Daniel, pa, 104
Scope of study, defined, 17
Scots in Poland, 27
Secret police, Russian-dominated, in
Congress Kingdom, 218, 221,
Polish People's Republic, 359
Senate, 401-404, 405, 406, 409, 412, 414, 415-
416,
appearance of, 29, 31,
abolition of, 26, 291, 392,
appointments to, 43, 64, 100, 111,
145, 209, 298, 382,
as guardians of law, 108,
as Supreme Appellate Court, 355-356,
chambers, 93, 97, 99, 394, 396, 397,
composition of, 102-103,
constitutional provisions of, 393, 434, 435
diary, 407,
evolution of, roles of, 434-435,
families prominent in, 102,
in Congress Kingdom, 226,
in First Republic, 100-109,
in Second Republic, 276-277, 290-292,
Masovian, 49,
membership of, 57-58,
mode of operation, 52, 399-401, 406, 408,
powers of, 290-291, 400, 403, 409,
Prussian, 46,
relations between, and Seym, 408-409
Senators, 391, 399, 400, 406,
appointive, 100, 111, 145, 209,
290-291,
elective, 277, 297, 298, 398
executive of (1794), 109, 110, 186-187,
pay, 410,
resident, 107-108, 346,
Serfdom, 243-246, 375, 376, 378
Seta, Antoni, de, 321
Seyda, Marian, de, 275
Seym, (Sejm)
as Provincial General, 46, 50,
budget procedures, 403,
chambers, 92, 93, 96, 97-100, 188,
251, 254, 398,
committees, 346, 401-402,
confederation, 391,
constitutional provisions, 393, 434-435,

INDEX

debate in, 406, 407,
diaries of debates, 53,
dissolution of, 399,
electoral ordinance for, see
  Electoral Ordinance
evolution of roles of, 434-435,
frequency of meetings, 51,
functions of, 399-414,
hotel, 394,
judicial functions, 411,
laws, tabulated, 41, 65-66, 110-111, 139, 146,
  191-192, 299-300, 337-338, 399-400,
meeting places of, 44, 427-431,
membership of, 57-58,
National, appearance of, 30,
operating procedures of, 52, 53,
  128-130, 399,
powers of, 355-356, 393,
relations between, and Senate, 408-409,
relations with President, 403-404,
royal election, 72-83, 126,
sessions, 399,
spelling of name, 32, 232, 390,
suppression of, 188, 225,
terms, 413-414,
tribunal, 219, 355-356, 411,
types of, 125-126,
unicameral, early, 51,
veto powers of, 404-405, 407,
voting rules in, 53, 125, 126, 157, 407-408,
  411
Seym of
  Estates in Galicia, 241-248,
  Lwów, 50, 82, 224, 237, 249-265,
  Poznań, 50, 82, 230-237, 351,
  Republic of Cracow, 248, 249,
  Silesia, 293-296,
  Wilno, 271, 293, 352,
Seym of
  post-Communist, 389-414,
  1505 in Radom, 33, 89, 390-391,
  1538 in Cracow, 89, 346,
  1569 in Lublin, 26, 49, 57, 61, 66, 89,
  1573 in Warsaw, 67, 69-70, 75, 134,
  1668 in Warsaw, 75, 123, 169,
  1717 in Warsaw, "mute," 155, 333,
  1773 in Warsaw, "delegation," 162, 333,
  1788-92 in Warsaw, "Grand," 169-181,
  1793 in Grodno, 89, 99, 109, 185-186,

  274, 348, 358, 373,
  1830 in Warsaw, 221, 222, 223, 224,
  1873 in Lwów, 252,
  1918 in Poznań, 236, 372,
  1919 in Warsaw, 270-271,
  1922 in Wilno, 271,
  1947 in Warsaw, 312-315
Seymik (Sejmik)
  appearance of, 30,
  in exile, of Smoleńsk, Witebsk and
    Połock, 46, 425,
  in Lithuania, 35,
  in the Second Republic, 295-297,
  instructions for Deputies (Kartelusze), 39, 124,
  law on, 173, 174, 352,
  laws for protection of, 38, 41,
  mode of operation, 39, 34-43,
  types of, 39, 42, 43
Seymik General (Provincial)
  meeting places of, 44, 45, 46, 51,
  mode of operation, 39, 43-57
Seym Library, 409, 412
Seymocracy, 19
Sforza, Bona, 85
Shakespeare, William, wr, 104
Sholohov, m., wr, 141
Shuyski Vasil, 140
Siberia, deportation to, 333, 386
Siciński, Władysław, de, 117
Sich Cossacks, 141
Sielski, Aleksander, sp, 429
Siemieński, Wojciech, sp, 430
Sieniawski, Mikołaj, sp, 429
Sienicki, Mikołaj, sp, 58-59, 65, 69, 88,
  385, 427, 428
Sierakowski, Jan, sp, 65, 427
Sigismund I of Poland, ki, 59, 65, 85
Sigismund II Augustus, ki, 61, 62, 65, 88,
  92, 105, 134
Sigismund Rakoczy, ca, 80
Sigismund III of Poland, ki, 75, 80,
  81, 85, 86, 108, 118, 190, 356
Silesia
  organic statute for, 293,
  province of, 293, 374,
  representation in Seym of Poznań, 236,
  Seym of, 293-295, 301
Silkiewicz, Józef, de, 89
Sióda, Zygmunt, de, 387

Sixtus IV, pope, 100
Skarzyński, Szymon, de, 186
Skórewicz, Kazimierz, ar, 282
Skoroszewski, Władysław, M., sp, 429
Skorupa, Zdzisław, de, 321
Skrzyszowski, Stanisław, ju, 63
Śląski, Jan, de, 387
Sławek, Walery, sp, 283, 288-289, 299, 303, 431
Śliwa, Gustaw, de, 321
Słonim, General Seymik of, 44, 46, 125
"Small Constitution," 311, 312, 392, 409, 411
Smogulecki, Mikołaj, de, 18, 135, 148-149
Smoleńsk, representation of, 37
Smolka, Franciszek, de, 254, 264
Snopczyński, Antoni, de, 387
Sobieski, Jakub, ap, 113, 385, 428
Sobieski, Jan, de, ki, see John III of Poland
Sobol, Bohdan, hi, 19
Society for Elementary School Books, 163
"Social Contract" by J. J. Rousseau, 166, 222
Socialist Party, 252, 281
Socyniamism, 119
Sokoliński, Jan D., sp, 428
Sokoliński, Gabriel D., sp, 429
"Solidarity" movement, 136, 393, 394, 398, 406, 408
Sołtyk, Kajetan, se, 165, 198, 222,
    abduction of, 158, 160,
    Seym commission for, 164
Sołtyk, Roman, de, 221, 229-230
Sołtyk, Stanisław, sp, 207, 210-211, 358, 432
Sołtyk, Stefan, de, 387
Solzhenitsyn, Alexander, wr, 380, 381
Sontag, J., pa, 230
Sosnowski, Józef, sp, 430
Sovhoz, 381
Soviet Union, 274, 276, 289, 303, 308,
    316, 323, 324, 333-334, 339,
    368-369, 373-374, 380, 431-432
Soviet-Polish War, 289, 301,
    371, 372-373
Spain, 365
Spanish Civil War, 258
Speaker, 23
Speaker of
    Senate, 29, 31, 399,
    Seym, 52, 65, 384, 385, 399, 405, 406-407,
        408, 409, 410,

Seymik, 31, 41
Spławski, J., de, 171
Spychalski, Marian, pr, 337
Spring of Nations, 30, 234
Środa, Seymik of, 35, 36
Stalin, Joseph, 26, 275, 276, 331, 354, 386
Stalinist Constitutions, 316-317, 392
Stankiewicz, Jan M., sp, 429
Stanisław Leszczyński of Poland, ki, 75, 80, 81,
    82, 110, 124, 130, 137, 138, 154, 165
Stanisław August of Poland, ki, 75,
    79, 157, 164, 178, 180, 185, 190, 195,
    abdication of, 100,
    administration of, 42
Stapiński, Jan, de, 254, 264
Staromiejski, Jan, de, 89
Starzyński, Stefan, de, 387
Staszic, Stanisław, wr, 167, 171, 209, 211, 377
Statutes of Wiślica and Piotrków of
    1347, 355
Stecki, Iwo, de, 176
Stephen Bathory of Poland, ki, 75, 79, 81, 107,
    137, 190, 355
Stojałowski, Stanisław, de, 254
Stolarski, Błażej, de, 387
Stone, Daniel, hi, 19
Stomma, Stanisław, de, 332, 340
Stroński, Stanisław, de, 275, 284, 304
Struzik, Adam, 416, 431
Stuart, Charles I, ki, 118
Stuart, Charles II, ki, 151
Stuart Dynasty, 125
Stuart, James II, ki, 80
Stuart Restoration, 118
Styczyński, Tadeusz, de, 387
Stypułkowski, Zbigniew, de, 310
Stypura, Konstanty, de, 387
Subsidium charitativum, 364
Suchocka, Hanna, 399
Suchorzewski, Jan, de, 171, 175, 178, 198
Suffrage
    Reform Acts, England, 351-352,
    rights, 343, 344-355,
    statistics, 344, 348, 349, 350-351
Sułkowski, Paweł A., sp, 230, 241, 430
Supreme Board of Control, 359
Supreme Board of Supervision, 404, 408

Supreme Court (Trybunal Koronny), 63
Supreme Right of Appeal, 355
Surowiecki, Wawrzyniec, mi, 209, 211
Sweden, 356
Sweden, voter turnout in, 354
Swedish Invasion, 117, 135, 189, 347, 358, 370
Święcicki, Tadeusz, de, 387
Świerszczewski, Karol, ge, 258
Świętosławski, Jan, sp, 428
Świrski, sp, 428
Switalski, Kazimierz, sp, 282, 299, 304
Swoszowski, Jan, sp, 428
Szafraniec, Stanisław, sp, 65, 428
Szaniecki, Olrych, de, 377
Szarffenberger, M., ty, 55
Szczuka, Stanisław, sp, 153, 154, 198-199, 429
Szczawiński, Jakob, sp, 428
Szczebrzeszyn, see confederations
Szczecin, election results in, 320
Szembek, Jan, sp, 429
Szturmowski, Piotr, de, 387
Szulc, Henryk, de, 89
Szulczewski, Michał, de, 387
Szumowicz, Paweł, de, 176
Szydłowski, Szymon, de, 186
Szymański, Julian, sp, 291

Tarankiewicz, Ignacy, de, 176
Taraszkiewicz, Bronisław, de, 275, 387
Tarnowski, Jan, sp, 257, 261, 430
Targowica, see confederations
Tarnogród, Confederation of, 139
Tarnów, election results for, 320
Tartar Khanate of Crimea, 139
Tartars, Raids of, 57
Tax
   Excise, 42, 362-363,
   Hearth, 362-363,
   Land (łanowe), 360,
   Poll, 344, 363, 364,
   Surcharge (domiar), 369
Tax Laws, 54, 55
Taxation, 343, 360, 365, 367, 368, 368-369
Teheran, conference of, 374
Temporary Laws, 53
Teodorowicz, Jan, de, 176
Term of office, Deputy's, 125
Terszkowec, Hrynko, de, 387

Test Act of 1673, England, 155, 347
Teutonic Order, German, 35, 134, 370
Thackaray, F.W., hi, 416
Thaler, 360, 362
Thomas, N., pa, 223
Thugutt, Stanisław, de, 275, 304
Tkaczow, Ferdynand, de, 387
Toruń
   city of, 366-367,
   confederation of, 139,
   mint of, 362,
   representation of, 89, 90, 347
Trade, 366-367
Trąmpczyński, Wojciech, sp, 271, 291, 299, 304-305, 430
Treasury
   Commission, 175, 364,
   Palatinate, 42,
   Tribunals, treasury committees, 364
Trębaczkiewicz, Kazimierz, de, 321
Trial of,
   Brześć, 282, 287, 331,
   Cracow, 331,
   Moscow, 310, 311, 339, 340
Tribunal
   of Lublin, 355,
   of Piotrkńw, 355,
   of State, see Seym Tribunal
Triller, Eugenia, hi, 19
Trojanowski, Stanisław, de, 89
Tryzna, Gideon M., sp, 428
Trzebicki, Andrzej, in, 106-107
Tsar of Russia, 80, 83
Turks, Wars with, 85, 107, 141, 356, 364, 370
Turkish raids, 57
Turski, W., de, 171
Tyszkiewicz, Ludwik S., sp, 430
Tyszowce, Confederation of, 139

Uchański, Jan, in, 57, 58, 69, 106, 107
Uchański, Stanisław, sp, 428
Ukraine, 142
Ukrainian
   national movement, 252, 256-258, 371,
   representation in the Seym of Lwów, 258, 352
Umiastowski, Jan K., sp, 429
Unemployment Insurance Act of 1924, 274
Unicameral Seym, 50-51

Unions of Poland and Lithuania
  Krewo (1386), 61,
  Horodioc (1413), 61,
  Lublin (1569), 57, 61-62, 92, 139, 254, 256,
  Mielnik (1501), 61
Union of England and Scotland, 61
Unitarian Church, 119
Unitary veto (liberum veto), 119
United Nations, 310
United Netherlands, 61, 365
United States of America, 348, 349, 350, 363, 365
University of
  Cracow, 163,
  Lwów, 163, 246, 247,
  Wilno, 163
Universal Tax Proclamation, 360
Uprising, in Poland, of
  1794, 187, 187-189,
  1830, 220-221, 232, 239, 240, 377,
  1848, 234, 239,
  1864, 141, 378,
  1944, 310, 394
Urbański, Franciszek, de, 310
Usufruct ownership, see dominium utile
Utrecht, Union of, 61

Vaad Arba Aratzoth, Jewish Assembly, 142, 143
Valois, Henri, ki, see Henri Valois
Validation of Laws, 55
Vasa, Charles Ferdinand, ca, 80
Vasa Dynasty, 75, 80
Vasa, John, ki, see John III Vasa of Sweden
Vasa, John Casimir, see John Casimir of Poland
Vasa, Ladislaus, see Ladislaus IV of Poland
Vasa, Sigismund, see Sigismund III of Poland
Versailles, Conference of, 269
Viceroy of Galicia, 252, 261
Viceroys, 102
Vienna
  congress of, 212, 230, 248,
  siege of, 370
Virgin Islands, representation of, 175
Virtuti militari, order of, 185
Vistula River, 25, 366-367,
Vivente rege election, 121, 357
"Volumina Legum," 127-129, 169
Voter turnout, 354

Voting procedures
  Seym, 52-53,
  Seymiks, 41

Wadowski, Marian, de, 387
Wagner, Wenceslas J., wr, ju, 19
Wałęsa, Lech, 399
Wandycz, Piotr S., hi, 19
Wańkowicz, Stanisław, de, 387
Warsaw (Warszawa)
  election results in, 320,
  General Seymik of, 44, 46, 125,
  provincial Seym of, 44, 391,
  representation of, 347,
  Seym of, 50, 89, 392,
  as seat of Seyms, 92-99,
  Masovian Seyms held in, 48
Warsaw Pact, 392
Warszawski, Adolf, de, 276, 387
Warszewicki, Krzysztof, wr, 105
Wasilewski, Leon, mi, 372
Wasilewski, Tadeusz, sp, 244
Wasynczuk, Antoni, de, 387
Wasynczuk, Paweł, de, 387
Wawel Castle, Cracow, 92
Węgleński, J., mi, 216
Welawa, (Wehlav) treaty of, 120, 372
Welykanowicz, Dmytro, de, 387
Westphalia, Kingdom of, 203
Wettin, Frederick Augustus I, elector
  of Saxony, see Augustus II of Poland
Wettin, Frederick Augustus II, elector
  of Saxony, see Augustus II of Poland
Wettin, Frederick Augustus I, king of
  Saxony, see Frederick Augustus,
  Grand Duke of Warsaw
Wettin, Frederick Christian, ca, 80
Wężyk, Jan, in, 107
Wieczorek, Józef, de, 387
Wielhorski, Michał, am, 166
Wieliczka salt mines, 367
Wielkopolska, Greater Poland, Province
  of, 24
Wielopolski, Jan, sp, 429
Wierzbicz, Józef, de, 89
Wiesiołowski, Krzysztof, sp, 428
Wilczewski, Franciszek, de, 156
William of Orange, ki, 79

INDEX

Wilno
  mint of, 362,
  representation of, 88, 346, 347,
  Seym of, 49
Wilson, Woodrow, pr, 269, 372
Wiśniowiecki, Michał K., see Michał
  Korybut of Poland
Wiśniowiecki, Michał, sp, 429
Wisznia, General Seymik of, 44, 46, 45,
  125
Wiszowaty, Tobiasz, de, 118-119
Witebsk, palatinate representation of, 37
Witos, Wincenty, Prime mi, 254, 275,
  282, 283, 305
Włóczkiewicz, O.L., de, 171
Włodarczyk, J., hi, 19
Wodzicki, Ludwik, sp, 261, 265, 430
Wodzicki, Stanisław, sp, 249
Wodziński, Gabriel, se, 162
Wojciechowski, Stanisław, pr, 279, 280, 299
Wójcik, Stanisław, de, 312, 359
Wojewódzki, Sylwester, de, 387
Wojtyła, Karol (Pope John Paul II), 320
Wola election field, 74, 75, 76, 80
Wolny, Konstanty, sp, 293, 294, 305
Wołkowysk, general Seymik of, 46
Wołoszyn, Paweł, de, 275
Women's suffrage, 267, 277, 349, 350
Writ of Summons, 38, 108, 127
Wrocław, election results for, 320
Wybicki, Józef, de, 167, 168, 175, 203
Wycech, Czesław, sp, 337, 341, 431

Yalta, conference of, 374
Yalta Treaty, 389, 392
Yeomanry, 35

Zabiełło, Józef, se, 109, 187
Zakroczym, Masovian Seyms in, 48
Zakrzewski, Hiacynt W., de, 176
Zaleski, Filip, vi, 261
Zaleski, Wacław, vi, 261
Załuska, Jan, de, 387
Załuski, Józef, se, 158, 169
Zamoyski, Andrzej, se, 164
Zamoyski, Jan, se, 85
Żarnowski, Eugeniusz, 310
Żarski, Tadeusz, de, 387
Zator, Duchy of, 293
Zawadzki, Aleksander, pr, 337
Zawisza Krzysztof, sp, 429
Zbierski, Dominik, de, 387
Zborowski, Samuel, se, 85, 86
Zebrzydowski, Mikołaj, se, 85
Żegocki, Marcin, sp, 428
Żeligowski, Lucjan, ge, 293
Zieleńce, Battle of, 184
Ziemiecki, Bronisław, de, 387
Złoty, value of, 360, 362
Żółkiewski, Stanisław, 140
Zwierzyński, Aleksander, vice-sp, 310
Zyblikiewicz, Mikołaj, sp, 256, 261, 265, 430
Zych, J, 431
Żmudź, Samogatia, 26
Żyliński, Józef, de, 176